A BOOK ABOUT

A THOUSAND THINGS

A BOOK ABOUT
A THOUSAND THINGS

BY

GEORGE STIMPSON

AUTHOR OF

"A BOOK ABOUT THE BIBLE"

HARPER & BROTHERS PUBLISHERS

New York and London

A BOOK ABOUT A THOUSAND THINGS

COPYRIGHT, 1946, BY HARPER & BROTHERS

PRINTED AND BOUND IN THE U. S. A. BY
KINGSPORT PRESS, INC., KINGSPORT, TENN.

To

HOUSTON HARTE

PREFACE

This book is the fruit of curiosity. I wrote *A Book about a Thousand Things* to satisfy my own curiosity, and I hope that in passing along the results of my studies I may share with others some of the pleasure and profit of my work.

Satisfying my curiosity about almost anything and everything has made my life a continual voyage of discovery, filled with surprising adventures. Curiosity may have killed a cat, but it has never hurt me, so far as I know, although it has cost me some sleep. Perhaps often when I should have been doing something more useful, I have been absorbed in the pursuit of the truth about something that doesn't matter too much. My whole life has been a series of excursions into the realms of the odd and the unusual. My persistent efforts to satisfy my curiosity have kept me from being lonesome, and I have had little time to become bored.

In gathering the material for this book I have been a perpetual pack rat of information. Everything I have read—books, magazines, newspapers, bulletins, pamphlets, reports, records, letters—have been grist for my mill. Boswell quoted Dr. Johnson as saying: "The greatest part of a writer's time is spent in reading, in order to write: a man will turn over half a library to make one book." And reading means borrowing. During the twenty-five and more years that I have been collecting material for this book I have "turned over" thousands of books and papers, and I have borrowed much. I have read the Bible through eight or ten times and the complete works of Shakespeare at least thirty. In making my final selections for this book I have discarded enough material to make several books as good as this one.

I was born and brought up on a farm and spent my youth close to nature. My mother tells me that when I was still a small boy I made a considerable nuisance of myself by asking difficult questions and demanding the answers. I have never lost my interest in the folklore of the country. My early interest in cats and dogs, horses and cattle, sheep and pigs, chickens and guinea fowl, trees and plants, stars and planets, spiders and insects, birds and wild animals, snakes and fish, wind and weather, superstitions and legends, words and sayings, songs and stories, is reflected throughout this book.

Later, as a student, as a newspaper reporter, as a magazine editor and as a Washington correspondent, I extended my interests to the larger world of politics and government, history and literature, science and art. Exotic beasts and birds, reptiles and fish in remote parts of the earth —nearly everything that walks, flies, swims or creeps—attracted my interest. I became a confirmed zoo fan and still would rather visit a zoo than eat. Although I had only a smattering of French, little Latin, less Greek and not too much English, I have always been interested in almost everything relating to our own and other languages. These interests, too, are reflected in these pages.

I have tried to make this book a treasury of fascinating information on a large variety of subjects. Both small and great things are dealt with. Some of the subjects are more entertaining than useful, while others are more useful than entertaining. Often the footnotes are the most interesting part of a book. I have not used them because in a sense this book is composed largely of interesting footnotes. People often ask me how I decide what to include in a book of this nature. That is a hard question to answer. In making my selections I have not been moved by chance or caprice alone. There has been more method in my madness than may at first appear. In each case I have been governed by motives such as I can give satisfactory account of to myself but which perhaps would be hard to explain to others. But in a general way I have chosen those questions that my experience has taught me recur most frequently and on which I have completed my researches.

The best way to write a book like this is to start thirty years ago. A continuity of interest in each subject through the years has been an important factor. A personal interest in every problem has been another. For obvious reasons I have tried to exclude information easily accessible in standard dictionaries, encyclopedias and other reference books. What I have written on each subject is about as much as I think the average reader would like to know and remember. It is about what I myself would like to have in the way of a report from a specialist on the subject. Consequently, the discussions range in length from a sentence or two to more than a page. In many cases, instead of making a separate question, I have merely added a bit of interesting information to a pertinent article.

I have not tried to make my material more interesting by any "puffing-up" process. Rather I have tried to be exact, impersonal and objective and to treat each subject, no matter how trivial, with the seriousness that it deserves. In the broad sense there is no such thing as a trivial fact. A chain is no stronger than its weakest link and all facts fit somewhere into the great scheme of things. An apparently unimportant fact may turn out to be important in the hands of a scholar or scientist. Wherever possible I have let the facts speak for themselves. Facts, when clearly stated, carry their own emphasis and need no artificial coloring. My purpose has been to give the reader a concise, authentic and understandable answer to each question. I have tried to be as brief as possible without omitting any facts necessary to a complete answer. Many questions, though frequently asked, do not admit of definite answers. My practice has been in such cases to give the nearest approach to a definite answer that I can. Often, even when no satisfactory answer is possible, it is of value to know just what, if any, information is available on a particular subject. For the most part the answers are the essence of the research and thought of the most reliable authorities available.

Old as well as new questions are included. The fact that a reader has once read or heard an explanation does not mean that he would not like to refresh his memory on the subject. The human memory is a slippery faculty and few of us actually know as much as we like to think we do. As we grow older we have a greater appreciation of the observation about this or that person who has forgotten more than somebody else knows.

The question-and-answer form of presentation needs no apology. Catechism is one of the oldest and most effective ways of presenting information and instruction. Most of us go from the cradle to the grave seeking the answers to questions. From Socrates in the groves of Athens to the modern scientist in his laboratory men have widened the horizon of knowledge by asking questions and ascertaining the answers. In these pages this method has the advantage of eliminating the necessity of an introduction to many of the articles.

Whether *A Book about a Thousand Things* contains an even thousand questions and answers is an academic point. It does not matter much, for actually the book either directly or indirectly answers many thousands of questions and might very well have been entitled *A Book about Thousands of Things*. I have counted the pieces several times, but my counts don't seem to agree. Perhaps some patient reader will take a careful census of the articles in the book and give me the benefit of his findings. This would serve the double purpose of telling me exactly how many questions I have answered in this book and of providing evidence that somebody had read this preface.

I would like to include a list of acknowledgments of assistance here, but to cite all the sources of information and to name all the persons who have helped me in preparing this book would be impracticable. Their name is legion and even a mere list of them would require as much space as the book itself. I have dedicated the volume to Houston Harte because of the faith he showed in me and my work when the going was hardest.

Many parts of this book have been previously published in books, magazines and newspapers during the last twenty-five years, but all such parts have been carefully re-examined or revised for the present purpose. In many cases these earlier versions, as in *A Book about the Bible*, have been completely rewritten and served only as a framework for the articles as they now stand.

Nobody could have traveled the road that I have in quest of will-o'-the-wisps of wisdom and knowledge without appreciating the value and importance of a thorough and complete index. Every book of information is entitled to an index, which, to paraphrase Pope, holds the eel of knowledge by the tail, and the publication of a book of this sort without one would be inexcusable. I am inclined to share Lord Campbell's opinion that a writer who publishes a book of information without an index should be denied the privilege of copyright. In this book often several related and equally important questions are answered in the discussion under a leading question—the questions being really in the nature of headings—and without an index the book would not only lose much of its reference and general reading value but would be a labyrinth without key or clue to its contents. Authors are handicapped by the fact that generally indexes cannot be made until the book approaches its last stages of printing, when final proofreading has been completed and the pages have all been made up and numbered. Sometimes an index is inadequate only because hurriedly made. I hope the index at the end of this book will serve to enable the reader to get a good hold of the eel's tail.

GEORGE STIMPSON

February 6, 1946
Washington, D. C.

[x]

A BOOK ABOUT
A THOUSAND THINGS

A BOOK ABOUT
A THOUSAND THINGS

Do any birds ever sing while on the ground?

Virtually all songbirds utter their characteristic song only while on the wing or while perched on a more or less elevated object, such as the limb of a tree, a bush or a fence post. Exceptions to this general rule among birds are found among the shore birds known as turnstones, which sing from hummocks on the ground, and certain species of American field sparrows, which have the unusual habit of regularly singing from the ground. The ground-singing habit is characteristic of the savanna sparrow, a native American bird that breeds in the eastern United States; the eastern grasshopper sparrow, and several closely related species found elsewhere in North America. The wood thrush, the ovenbird, which is a small warbler that spends most of its time on the ground, and perhaps a few other species occasionally sing while on the ground.

What does "spitting image" mean?

We often hear a person described as the spitting image of another. The phrase is believed to be an incorrect variation of spit and image, which became first sp't'n image and then spitting image. There appears to be no foundation for the belief that spitting in spitting image is a corruption of spirit.

Who originated the word "cent"?

Cent as the name of an American coin was first suggested by Gouverneur Morris. In 1782, when assistant to Superintendent of Finance Robert Morris, he prepared for Congress a report in which he suggested that the monetary unit be 1/1440 of a dollar and that the lowest silver coin consist of 100 of these units and be called a cent. These proposals were not adopted, but they became the basis of the system of coinage worked out later by Jefferson and perfected by Hamilton. Undoubtedly Congress borrowed cent from Morris' report when in 1786 it adopted a system of coins based on mills, cents, dimes and dollars and prescribed that the cent should be "the highest copper piece, of which 100 shall be equal to the dollar." Morris had studied French and he probably derived *cent* from *centime*, rather than directly from Latin *centum* ("hundred"). *Cents* occurs in Shakespeare, but in French instead of English. In *King Henry V* a captured French soldier, pleading with Ancient Pistol to spare his life, says: *Je vous donnerai deux cents écus* ("I will give you two hundred crowns").

How did "cartridge" originate?

Cartridge is an Anglicized form of French *cartouche*, which in turn is from Latin *charta* ("paper"). Originally a cartridge was simply a round of powder wrapped in paper for use in a flintlock musket. Under date of August 24, 1711, William Byrd of Westover noted in his secret diary: "I got my arms in order and made cartouches." The following day he wrote: "The Frenchman made me a great number of cartouches and cleaned my arms." Cartridges were as familiar to General Washington and his Continentals during the Revolution as they were to General Eisenhower and his doughboys during the Second World War. While besieging the British in Boston in 1775 Washington frequently used *cartridges* in connection with his ammunition. After the Battle of Germantown in 1777 the Continentals were described as looking "like Negroes" because, in biting off the ends of their cartridges before ramming them into their muskets, the powder spread around their mouths and blackened their faces. The earliest use of *cartridge* recorded by the Oxford dictionary is dated 1579. After breech-loading guns came into use *cartridge* was transferred to the metal shells containing both powder and bullet. For some unexplained reason many people mispronounce the word *cat-ridge*.

What does "Barnum was right" mean?

The common saying that "there is a sucker born every minute" is popularly attributed to Phineas Taylor Barnum (1810–1891), the famous American showman. "Barnum was right" is often resorted to when a person wishes to allude to the saying without quoting it. There is no evidence that Barnum actually said "there is a sucker born every minute," and its origin in all probability is lost beyond recovery. It does, however, succinctly express the great showman's philosophy of the credulity of the public, and it has become a sort of American proverb. He once declared that "the American people like to be humbugged," and his outlandish hoaxes are proverbial. In England he delivered a lecture entitled "The Science of Money Making, and the Philosophy of Humbug." Horace Greeley expressed a somewhat similar idea in more stately language when he asserted that "the public is one immense ass." *Sucker* as a slang term for a greenhorn, simpleton, fool, victim of sharpers or one easily duped or imposed upon was in general use in 1857 and probably earlier. At one time *jay* was a common slang word for chump, fool or gullible person, and an old song that was very popular contained the line, "There's a new jay born every day."

Why are the Balkans so called?

Balkan is derived from a Turkish word signifying "mountain." The Balkans are a range of mountains extending from the Yugoslavian frontier through central Bulgaria to the Black Sea. From the Balkan Mountains (really a pleonasm) the Balkan Peninsula received its name. It is the easternmost peninsula of southern Europe and is occupied by the Balkan States. This name was first applied in the nineteenth century to several small countries that had lately won their independence from the Ottoman Empire. At present the Balkan States are Bulgaria, Turkey in Europe, Greece, Albania, Yugoslavia and Rumania.

To what does "stealing coppers from dead man's eyes" refer?

The lowest kind of thief is said to be one that will steal the coppers from a dead man's eyes. This expression alludes to the old custom of using pennies or other copper coins to close the eyes of a corpse. The practice of closing the eyes of the dead is very ancient. In *Genesis* 46:4 the Lord tells Jacob that his son "Joseph shall put his hand upon thine eyes." The custom of putting copper coins on the eyes of the dead originated in England long before the American one cent piece popularly called a penny was coined and the copper coin of the old saying referred to the larger English copper coin called a penny. In her *Reveille in Washington* Margaret Leech says of President Lincoln's death that a "doctor laid silver half-dollars on Lincoln's eyelids."

What is paddy rice?

Paddy is derived directly from Malay *padi*, "rice in the straw." The Javanese equivalent is *pari*. On the west coast of India *batty* (or *batta*) is applied to "rice in the husk." These terms are all believed to be derived ultimately from Sanskrit *bhakta*, "cooked rice." In Anglo-Indian *paddy rice* or simply *paddy* is a commercial term used to denote rough, unmilled or unhusked rice, whether cut or still growing in the field. By extension the term is often employed as a synonym for rice in general. A rice field, particularly when flooded, is called a *paddy field*. Various birds that frequent paddy or rice fields, such as certain species of herons, egrets and Oriental sparrows, are known to the English-speaking inhabitants of the East as *paddy birds*. Many seem to feel that *paddy* signifies "field" and refer to a *rice paddy*. This erroneous usage apparently is owing to an assimilation of *paddy*, "rice," to *paddock*, "a small field or inclosure," and *patch*, "a plot of ground."

Does a giraffe have horns?

A giraffe does not have true horns. The usual pair of projections on the head of a giraffe appear to be horns, but they are merely soft tufts of skin and fat without a trace of the hard growth generally described as horn. There is record of one giraffe that had as many as five of these *horns* on its head. *Giraffe* is derived from the Arabic name of this native of Africa. Another name for it is *camelopard*, which refers to the fact that it looks somewhat like a camel and is spotted like a leopard. The first giraffe seen in Europe was sent to Rome from Egypt by Julius Caesar and was referred to by Pliny the Elder.

Who said: "A man must sometimes rise above principle"?

This saying is widely quoted in varying language as a sort of American political proverb. It appears to have been first used about 1921 by Percy Edwards Quin, a picturesque and salty Congressman who represented a Mississippi district in the United States House of Representatives from 1913 until his death in 1931. "A man must sometimes rise above principle" is a concise and cynical way of expressing the difficulty that politicians often have in steering a course between what they think is right and what they think is expedient.

What is meant by "a man on horseback"?

A military leader with dictatorial or imperialistic ambitions is called a *man on horseback*. It is believed the phrase was coined by Caleb Cushing (1800–1879), American statesman, who was attorney general in President Franklin Pierce's cabinet. In January, 1860, Cushing wrote a letter in which he predicted that the slavery agitation in the United States would result in "a man on horseback with a drawn sword in his hand, some Atlantic Caesar, or Cromwell, or Napoleon." The phrase was popularized in connection with George Ernest Boulanger (1837–1891), a French military leader who advocated revenge on Germany. He acquired the title, *Man on Horseback*, because he habitually appeared before the public mounted on a magnificent charger. In 1886, after a long and honorable career in the French Army, General Boulanger became Minister of War and made many popular reforms in the military service. He became immensely popular with the royalists, Bonapartists and other disaffected elements opposed to the French Republic. His striking personality, fine military bearing and jingoistic utterances put him at the head of *Boulangism*, a movement directed against the Germans for what they had done to France in 1870. Boulangism was to France in 1886 what Hitlerism was to Germany in 1933. General Boulanger's followers waited patiently for the hour when their brave general on horseback would seize the government by a *coup d'état*. But while waiting for an opportune time to strike, Boulanger was eliminated from the cabinet. His popularity with the mob only increased, however, and he was elected a deputy on a constitutional reform platform. Then he resigned in protest, and districts all over France vied with one another to return him to the House of Deputies. He was elected from Paris by an overwhelming vote. His immense popularity did not diminish even after he was deprived of his army command and his name erased from the army lists. Even the republicans in general believed that he could make himself dictator of France any time he wanted to. But the would-be dictator let his golden opportunity slip from his grasp. Publicly proved a liar and a coward, his courage was unequal to his ambition. To the utter amazement of his ardent admirers, when a warrant for his arrest was signed, he fled the country. Two years later, disappointed and heartbroken, the man who might have been dictator of France committed suicide on the grave of his mistress in Brussels. In the United States *Man on Horseback* was first applied to Theodore Roosevelt in a purely political sense.

Who said: "Eternal vigilance is the price of liberty"?

"Eternal vigilance is the price of liberty," one of the most widely quoted of all sayings on the subject of liberty, is variously attributed to Thomas Jefferson, Patrick Henry, Thomas Paine, Voltaire, Wendell Phillips, and John Philpot Curran. It is most generally attributed to Thomas Jefferson or Patrick Henry, but it does not occur in any of the known speeches, letters or other writings of either of these two great lovers of liberty, and there is no evidence that either of them was the author of it. The available evidence points to the conclusion that Curran, the Irish statesman and orator, was author of the general idea, and that Phillips, the American orator and reformer, was author of the exact phraseology. On July 10, 1790, Curran delivered a speech upon the right of election in which he said in part: "It is the common fate of the indolent to see their rights become a prey to the active. *The condition upon which God hath given liberty to man is eternal vigilance;* which condition if he break, servitude is at once the consequence of the crime and the punishment of his guilt." This speech, along with others by Curran, was published at Dublin in 1808, a fact that probably accounts for an oft-repeated statement that Curran said "Eternal vigilance is the price of liberty" in a speech at Dublin in 1808. The earliest known occurrence of "Eternal vigilance is the price of liberty" is in an address delivered by Phillips before the Massachusetts Anti-Slavery Society January 28, 1852. Phillips did not enclose the now famous sentiment in quotation marks, and in 1878, when the authorship was disputed, he wrote a letter in which he expressed the opinion that it was original with him.

Why does "debt" contain a "b"?

The b in debt is not the survival of an obsolete pronunciation, as commonly supposed, but is the result of a deliberate tampering with the word. Debt is derived directly from Old French dette, and in early English the word was regularly spelled det or dette and pronounced as we pronounce it now. It is spelled dette in the Vision of Piers Plowman and in Chaucer's Canterbury Tales. From the thirteenth to the sixteenth centuries it was often spelled debt by grammarians and pedantic scholars who assumed it to be derived directly from Latin debita ("owed"), and who desired to make the English word conform more nearly with its supposed Latin progenitor. By Shakespeare's time debt had become the established spelling. In Love's Labour's Lost, written about 1599, the schoolmaster Holofernes facetiously advocates a pronunciation that never existed when he says he abhors "such rackers of orthography" who say det when they should "pronounce debt—d.e.b.t, not d.e.t."

Why do railway tracks seem to meet at a distance?

A person sees an object because it reflects light rays to the eye. Light is reflected from every part of the object and any two rays form an angle at the eye of the observer. Objects close to the eye look larger because the angles between the rays are larger; the farther away the objects, the smaller the light angles. Consequently a distant object appears much smaller than a close one. In looking down a railway track a person looks at an object of uniform size but of varying distances. The two rails seem to run together in the distance because the angles of the waves grow smaller and smaller along the track.

What was the Holy Roman Empire?

This is the name given in history to a loose-jointed empire that existed in central Europe from 992 to 1806. After the death of Theodosius in 395 A.D. the old Roman Empire established by Augustus Caesar in 27 B.C.

[6]

became completely separated into the Western Roman Empire and the Eastern Roman Empire. The Western Roman Empire came to an end in 476 A.D. In 800, however, Charlemagne, King of the Franks, was crowned Emperor of the West at Rome. Westerners regarded Charlemagne's empire as the direct descendant of the old Roman Empire. In 962 Otto I, known as Otto the Great, was crowned at Rome and there came into being a political entity later known as the Holy Roman Empire, although it appears that *Holy* was not added to the title until about 1155 after the death of Frederick I. It was largely a Germanic conception and consisted of numerous petty German states and principalities in Germany, Austria and northern Italy. The chief administrative body of this empire was the Diet. The princely heads of the component parts were known as Electors because they elected the emperor from among their number. These emperors, though claiming supreme sovereignty as the successors of the Caesars, seldom had much power as such and the different nations composing the Empire considered themselves as almost independent nations under their own rulers. Voltaire said the name *Holy Roman Empire* was inappropriate for three reasons: in the first place it was not holy; in the second, it was not Roman, and in the third, it was not an empire. The Holy Roman Empire, toward the last little more than a name, lasted until Napoleon broke it up in 1806. Francis II of Hapsburg was the last Holy Roman Emperor.

Why do people say "sick'm" to a dog?

Sick'm, used to incite a dog to attack, is merely a colloquial form of *seek him*, or *seek 'em*. In this sense *sick* is used chiefly with *at* or *on*. We sick a dog at or on a person, animal or object. In Shakespeare's time the common word for this purpose was *tarre*. In *King John*, when Hubert says he can revive the hot irons with his breath, Arthur replies:

> An if you do, you will but make it blush
> And glow with shame of your proceedings, Hubert:
> Nay, it perchance will sparkle in your eyes;
> And like a dog that is compell'd to fight,
> Snatch at his master that doth *tarre him on*.

Old Nestor, in *Troilus and Cressida*, says:

> Two curs shall tame each other: pride alone
> Must *tarre* the mastiffs on, as 'twere their bone.

In *Hamlet* Rosencrantz, telling the Prince of Denmark about the children actors in England, says "the nation holds it no sin to *tarre* them to controversy." Several passages in Shakespeare indicate that a sound represented variously by *lo, loo, alo, aloo, low* and *alow* was used as a cry to incite hunting dogs to the chase. The English *harass* is believed to be derived from Old French *harer* meaning to sick or set a dog on.

Which is correct, "Hay, James, Jr." or "Hay, Jr., James"?

When the surname of a person designated *Junior* or *Senior* precedes the given name, as in a directory or an index, the proper order is *Hay, James, Jr.* or *Hay, James, Sr.,* not *Hay, Jr., James* or *Hay, Sr., James,* because the latter shifts the alphabetical order in respect to the first name. If a title is given in such a list it may be written either *Lewis, Wilmott, Sir* or *Lewis, Sir Wilmott,* but in the latter case the title should be ignored in the alphabetical sequence.

Why is a gem stone called amethyst?

Amethyst is composed of two Greek words meaning "not to be drunk." The ancients believed this stone, consisting of a violet-blue variety of crystalline quartz, would keep the wearer sober. In those days drinking cups were made of amethyst to prevent the users from getting drunk. The amethyst is also known as the *bishop's stone* from its wide use in the bishop's ring, a ring worn by bishops on the third finger of the right hand and symbolizing that the bishop is wedded to his diocese.

How did the jack rabbit get its name?

The jack rabbit, which naturalists classify as a hare, received its common name from the fact that its long, large ears were thought to resemble those of a jackass. In early references to this animal in the West it is called variously the jackass rabbit, the mule rabbit and the Texas hare. Audubon and Bachman, writing in 1851 of a species along the Mexican border, said: "This species is called the jackass rabbit in Texas, owing to the length of its ears." Since a jackass is generally called a jack, in process of time *jackass rabbit* was shortened to *jack rabbit.*

What is the national flower of Wales?

The daffodil is now considered the national flower of Wales, but historically the leek, an onion-like plant with a small slender bulb and edible leaves, is the Welsh national emblem or badge. For centuries it has been a popular custom among the Welsh to wear leek blossoms on their hats on March 1, the feast day of St. David, their patron saint. This commemorates a traditional victory of the Welsh under King Cadwallader over the Saxons in the sixth century. Upon the suggestion of St. David the Welsh troops wore leeks in their caps to distinguish one another from the foe. In Shakespeare's *King Henry* V Fluellen, referring to the battle of Poitiers in 1356, says to King Henry: "If your majesty is remembered of it, the Welshman did goot service in a garden where leeks did grow, wearing leeks in their Monmouth caps, which your majesty knows, to this hour is an honourable padge of the service; and, I do believe, your majesty takes no scorn to wear the leek upon Saint Tavy's day." From the same play we get the phrase *to eat the leek*, meaning to retract one's words or take back an affront. Pistol, seeing Fluellen wearing a leek, brought him bread and salt and asked him to eat the onion-flavored emblem of his nation. The next day the mountain squire beat Pistol until the latter himself had eaten the leek. This plant, which is widely cultivated in Great Britian, was not indigenous to those islands, probably having been introduced by the Romans. The leek now is regarded as the badge of super-Welsh patriots and is worn by the Welsh guards at the British court.

How did the Baltimore oriole get its name?

The American bird known as the Baltimore oriole was so designated in 1766 by the Swedish naturalist Linnaeus, who described it from a specimen sent to him from Maryland and who chose the name in compliment to the memory of Lord Baltimore, original proprietor of that colony, whose family colors were orange and black, the two most conspicuous hues in the plumage of the male Baltimore oriole.

Why is a weak spot called "the heel of Achilles"?

The heel of Achilles was suggested by the story that the legendary Greek hero Achilles was killed by an arrow shot into his heel. In Greek mythology Achilles (pronounced a-*kill*-eez) was noted for his fine physique, handsome figure, athletic strength, warlike prowess, personal bravery and chivalry. He is the central figure and hero in the *Iliad*, but none of the Homeric poems mention the manner of his death, although they hint that he died "before the Scaean gates" during the Trojan war. Post-Homeric writers developed the story that Thetis, the mother of Achilles, had a premonition that her unusual son would die in battle and that when he was an infant she dipped him in the river Styx to make him invulnerable. The water touched every part of the child's body except the heel that she held in her hand. During a truce between the Greeks and Trojans, Achilles saw and fell in love with King Priam's daughter Polyxena. Paris, who had started the war by eloping with Helen of Greece, took advantage of the matrimonial negotiations in the Temple of Apollo to kill the Greek hero who was about to marry his sister and to use his influence to grant the Trojans a peace. The poisoned arrow shot by Paris, guided by Apollo himself, wounded Achilles in the heel, the only vulnerable spot on his body, and caused his death. This story, which has been elaborated with the passing of the centuries, is the source of *the heel of Achilles* in the sense of a vulnerable point or weak spot in the character of an individual, in the defenses of a nation, or in the structure of a system. In physiology the strong muscle connecting the calf of the leg with the heel is known as *Tendo Achillis*, the tendon of Achilles. The corresponding tendon in horses and other large quadrupeds is called *hamstring*.

How does a martin differ from a marten?

A martin is a bird of the swallow family; a marten is a fur-bearing animal of the weasel kind. Both names are of obscure origin but are believed to be from entirely different sources. The derivation of *martin* in this connection from the name of St. Martin, after whom St. Martin's summer was named, appears to be based upon insufficient evidence. Many persons confound *martin* and *marten* and suppose the pine marten to be a bird. It is a weasel-like carnivorous animal that received its common name from the fact that it lives in pine and other evergreen trees. The New World pine marten is known in fur-trade circles as Hudson's Bay Seal. This animal, noted for its grace, beauty and valuable fur, is an expert tree-climber and is seldom seen except deep in the evergreen woods. Years ago the pine marten was common in the forests of Canada and northern United States, but it has in recent years become very rare and in many sections where it was common it has been completely extirpated.

How did "the Greeks had a word for it" originate?

The Greeks Had a Word for It is the title of a play written by the American author and playwright Zoe Akins and first produced on Broadway in 1929. The word referred to in the title is the Greek *hetaera*, signifying a courtesan, mistress or female paramour of the better class according to ancient Greek standards.

How did the rabbit's foot become a good-luck charm?

The widespread belief in the rabbit's foot as a talisman or good-luck charm is of obscure origin. It may have grown out of several primitive beliefs. Since ancient times the rabbit, proverbial for the rapidity with which it multiplies, has been the emblem of fertility and fecundity. The most sacred part of the body was that which came in contact with the earth, supposedly the source of life. Feet and footprints were mystic symbols in ancient folklore. From these ideas may have evolved the association of the feet of the most prolific common animal with the smiles of the gods. Among the Negroes of the South "Br'er Rabbit" is regarded as a sort of supernatural animal, the wisest creature of forest and field, and the stories of his cleverness in outwitting his enemies are legion. A person who carries in his pocket the left hind foot of a rabbit, particularly one that has run in a graveyard, is said to be assured of good luck. So potent are the reputed magic powers of the rabbit's foot that it has been known to be used even as a specific for diseases.

What does "obiter dictum" mean?

Obiter dictum is a Latin phrase meaning literally "a thing said by the way." In law an obiter dictum is an incidental observation, comment or digression of a judge in an opinion. It is not material to the main point at issue and therefore not binding on subsequent or inferior courts. Since it is not directed to a point involved in the case and not necessary to determine the rights of the parties to the suit, an obiter dictum is not an essential part of a decision. An obiter dictum deserves no more nor less respect than the wisdom, experience and standing of the judge entitle it to. But this does not mean that obiter dicta are always trivial. They may be very important. In the narrow legal sense of the term, many of the important pronouncements of Chief Justice John Marshall were obiter dicta, and some of the arguments in Chief Justice Roger Brooke Taney's Dred Scott decision were in the same category. Such incidental and nonmaterial observations in judicial opinions are popularly called simply dicta. Obiter dicta is also sometimes applied to any random remarks, cursory comments or rambling reflections not concerned with legal or judicial matters. In 1884 Augustine Birrell, English essayist and politician, published a volume of critical essays entitled Obiter Dicta.

How did "barbecue" originate?

Barbecue is not so modern as one might suppose. It is derived through Spanish barbacoa from berbekot, the name applied by the Carib Indians in the West Indies and northern South America to the wooden framework or grill on which they broiled, smoked or dried meat and fish. The English in Guiana began to use the term as early as 1665. Before 1700 it was introduced into the southern United States, where it was at first applied to an elevated platform used either as a gridiron for cooking or as a bedstead for sleeping. Very soon barbecue came to signify a large animal, such as a hog or an ox, roasted or broiled whole over an outdoor pit. Then an open-air social or political gathering at which such was the chief food served came to be called a barbecue. As a verb the term was well established about 1738, when Alexander Pope wrote in one of his *Satires*:

> Oldfield, with more than harpy throat subdued,
> Cries, "Send me, ye gods, a whole hog barbecued."

George Washington often attended barbecues in Virginia before the Revolution. On September 18, 1773, he recorded in his diary, "Went to a Barbicue of my own giving at Accatinck." When John Calloway Walton was inaugurated governor of Oklahoma in 1923 he gave a barbe-cue at which more than 100,000 persons were served beef, pork, mutton, buffalo, bear, reindeer, antelope, squirrel, opossum, coon, rabbit, chicken goose and duck, all cooked in a mile of trenches. In addition the people were served enormous quantities of bread, and coffee made in urns holding 10,000 gallons each.

Why is "cwt." the abbreviation of "hundredweight"?

Hundredweight originally meant, and still generally means, a weight of one hundred pounds. At first it was denoted by *C.*, the abbreviation of Latin *centum* and the Roman symbol for one hundred. Owing perhaps to confusion, *dwt.*, the symbol for *pennyweight*, came about in the same way, the *D.*, being the abbreviation of Latin *denarius* ("penny"). The symbols for units of weights and measures often are of mixed origin, that is, they are derived from two different languages. Even *lbs.*, the symbol for *pounds*, is formed by adding an English plural to *lb.*, the contraction of Latin *libra*, pound. Although in the United States a hundredweight is always one hundred pounds and in England it is usually and legally so for certain articles, the English hundredweight has varied from time to time and for different articles of commerce, ranging from one hundred to one hundred and twenty pounds. The old English hundredweight was one hundred and twelve pounds, or four quarters of twenty-eight pounds each. *Long hundredweight* is the name given to one hundred and twenty pounds.

Why do some surnames begin with "ff" instead of "F"?

In several English family names, such as ffiennes, ffolliott and ffoulkes, two small f's are used instead of the capital F. This appears to be a relic of the pre-printing period when the capital F was often written ff in manuscripts. In the earliest occurrences known the second f has no cross stroke and it is believed that the modern capital F grew out of the practice of shortening the down stroke in the second letter in ff. These names are sometimes incorrectly written *Ffiennes, Ffolliott* and *Ffoulkes,* where both the double and capital letter are retained. In Rock Creek Cemetery in Washington is a monument made by the sculptor Gutzon Borglum in memory of the ffoulke family.

Did Iceland have any aboriginal inhabitants?

Iceland had no original inhabitants so far as science can learn. It was first settled sometime before 800 A.D. by a small colony of Culdees or Celtic hermits from Scotland, Ireland and perhaps Wales. The island was discovered by the Scandinavians about 850 A.D. Some Icelandic historians maintain that the Celtic colonists were still living on the island when the Scandinavians arrived; but the question is disputed and the general belief is that these Celts had disappeared before the discovery of Iceland by the Norsemen. At any rate, books, croziers and other articles found by the early Scandinavians prove beyond doubt that Irish monks had made an attempt to colonize the island. The real history of Iceland dates from about 870 when, owing to political disturbances in Scandinavia, large numbers of Norsemen began to make settlements there. Most of the present inhabitants, some 120,000, are descendants of Norwegians.

After whom was the Prince Albert coat named?

There is a general impression that the long, double-breasted frock coat known as the Prince Albert in America received this name from Prince Albert, consort of Queen Victoria. It was, however, named after Albert, Prince of Wales, afterward King Edward VII, who was the eldest son of Queen Victoria and Prince Consort Albert and who wore this type of coat when he visited the United States in 1860.

Do gorillas drum upon their breasts?

Naturalists say there is ample evidence to sustain the common assertion that gorillas, whether in captivity or in the native state, sometimes beat their breasts with their fists. It seems to be a form of nervous activity to which these great apes resort only when enraged, frightened or otherwise excited. In 1932 C. Emerson Brown, Director of the Philadelphia Zoological Garden, wrote as follows in *My Animal Friends* about a five-year-old gorilla: "Bamboo has not yet acquired the habit of wild gorillas, who stand up and beat their chests, but at times he does attempt it rather lightly with one hand." Carl Akeley, who devoted years of study to this animal, asserted that a male gorilla when ap-

[13]

proached by man in its native haunts sits for a moment with a savage expression on its face, then straightens up to full height, starts to beat its breast with both fists and utters several sharp barks followed by a characteristic roar. "Gorillas," says the guidebook of the St. Louis Zoological Garden, "often beat their chests in fast rhythm in the hollow just below the breastbone with alternate action of their slightly cupped hands, producing a peculiar, drumlike noise."

Why are certain soldiers called grenadiers?

A grenadier was originally a soldier who carried and threw hand grenades. Hand grenades, small shells filled with powder and ignited by means of a fuse, were first used in warfare during the fifteenth century. Sometimes these early bombs, instead of being thrown by hand, were projected from the end of a musket. The earliest hand grenades weighed from two to six pounds. They were called grenades from *grenade*, the French name of the fruit known as the pomegranate, because they were fancied to resemble this fruit in shape. *Pomegranate* itself is derived from Old French *pome*, apple, and *grenate*, grained, referring to the many grains or seeds in the pomegranate. The grenadiers at first were simply four or five tall, picked men in each military company whose duty is was to throw grenades. Later each regiment had a company of grenadiers. When the use of hand grenades was discontinued during the eighteenth century *grenadiers* was retained as the name of the company in each regiment composed of the tallest and finest men. Such were the British grenadiers who marched up Bunker Hill in 1775. The French and Prussian armies of the time also had companies and battalions of grenadiers who did not carry or throw grenades. In the British Army the name survived only in the Grenadier Guards, the first regiment of foot guards, who were long noted for their height, fine physique and remarkable discipline. The American Army has never had units called grenadiers. Hand grenades were not revived in warfare to any considerable extent until the Russo-Japanese War of 1904–1905. This type of bomb, filled with high explosive, was widely used in the Great War of 1914–1918.

What does the Maltese cross represent?

The Maltese cross was originally the badge of the Knights of Malta, a religious and military order formed in the twelfth century to relieve the poor and the strangers in the Holy Land. Known as the Hospitallers of St. John of Jerusalem, one of their functions was to provide military escorts to pilgrims going to visit the Holy Sepulcher at Jerusalem. After the fall of the Holy City and Acre the order removed to the Island of

Rhodes, where it was known as the Knights of Rhodes from 1309 to 1522, when it was vanquished by Solyman II. The knights then established themselves on the island of Malta where they soon became known as the Knights of Malta. The Maltese cross as usually formed consists of four barbed arrowheads or spreading triangular arms with the points meeting in the center. In various elaborate and modified forms it is also the badge of several modern orders.

Why are bayonets so called?

The bayonet is believed to have received its name from the fact that steel blades and daggers so called were first manufactured at Bayonne in France toward the close of the fifteenth century. Some authorities, however, suggest that bayonet may have originally been the diminutive of Old French bayon or baion, meaning the shaft of a cross-bow. The earliest use of the term recorded by the Oxford Dictionary is dated 1692. The first true bayonets, as the word is now understood, were of the plug type; that is, they were knives or flat daggers with a haft shaped to be fitted into the muzzle of a musket and to be removed before the gun was discharged. Such sword-bayonets, it is recorded by a participant, were employed by the French in the Battle of Ypres in 1647. When pikes and spears were being displaced by firearms it was found that the musketeers in the infantry while loading their weapons were virtually defenseless against cavalry. This handicap in battle was partly neutralized at first by mixing pikemen and musketeers in the same unit. Later the sword-bayonet was devised to give each infantryman the advantage of both firearm and pike. The next improvement was a bayonet so attached to the muzzle of the musket that the gun could be fired without removing the bayonet. This type of bayonet was first used on the Continent about 1590.

Do Rocky Mountain sheep land on their horns?

The popular notion that the large Rocky Mountain wild sheep known as bighorns land on their curved horns in leaping from ledge to ledge is without foundation in fact. In the Old World this curious belief formerly prevailed regarding both the mountain wild goat known as the Ibex and the goat-like antelope called the chamois. The belief probably arose from the fact that these agile animals often plunge head first down sheer declivities. Behind the notion is the idea that these mountain-climbing animals land on their horns when leaping from a great height because only the elastic strength of the horns would prevent a shock sufficient to kill any animal not so safeguarded by nature. Actually the bighorn, as well as the chamois and wild goat, strikes the ledges with its front feet close together and relies solely on its surefootedness in making long leaps. Occasionally a bighorn sheep miscalculates the distance or misjudges the character of a footing and somersaults down the mountainside; but these rare accidents seldom result in serious injury to these tough, muscular and agile animals.

Do chickens and ducks circle in opposite directions while fed?

There is a popular notion that when barnyard fowls are expecting to be fed the chickens and turkeys circle to the right of the person feeding them while ducks and geese move to the left, causing the two groups to stumble over one another. Apparently this belief is not confirmed by careful observation. In a letter to the author the United States Department of Agriculture says on this subject: "It is our opinion that chickens, turkeys, ducks and geese which are being fed in a flock are as likely to move in one direction as in another and that it has never been observed that there is any difference between the movements of chickens and the movements of ducks in this respect."

What is a pea-jacket?

A pea-jacket is a double-breasted short overcoat worn chiefly by seamen and sailors. Pea in pea-jacket, which dates from 1723, is believed to be derived from an old Dutch word variously spelled py, pie and pij, which was applied as early as the thirteenth century to a coarse, thick, stout, woolen cloth or felt. Later the term was applied to a garment made of such material. In the fourteenth century the Dutch seem to have called a short coat of this stuff korte py, "short py." This in English became courtepy. Chaucer wrote of, "A gay yeman. . . . He hadde vpon a courtepy of grene." Py gradually became pee and finally pea, which in this sense survives only in pea-coat and pea-jacket.

Why is the pool in a card game called the kitty?

In certain card games the kitty is a pool of stakes into which each player puts a part of his winnings and which is generally used for some special purpose, such as paying the expenses of the game, buying refreshments or helping players who have gone broke to re-enter the game. In this sense kitty seems to be a comparatively recent word and its origin is obscure. Kit, signifying a vessel, case, basket, bag or other container dates back to about the year 1400. It also means the contents of a case, such as a soldier's kit, meaning his equipment or outfit. Kitty may be merely a little kit of money. For centuries a common jail has been called a kitty in English dialect. Some authorities suggest that there may be a connection between *kitty* as used in card games and *kist* or *kiste*, an old Scotch and North-of-England form of *chest*, which refers particularly to a chest in the sense of a money box.

How did Duluth get its name?

Duluth, the name of the city on Lake Superior in Minnesota, is an Anglicized form of the surname of Daniel Greysolon Duluth, a French explorer who in 1679 made a treaty with the Sioux and Chippewa Indians and built a trading post in that vicinity. The explorer wrote his name *Dulhut* or *du Lhut*, but in most of the early English and American accounts it was written *du Luth*, and *Duluth* is now regarded as the accepted form of his name.

Which is correct, "Hertford" or "Hereford" cattle?

Hertford and *Hereford* are the names of two different counties in England, but they are often confused in America. One frequently hears people speak of *Hertford cattle* when *Hereford cattle* are referred to. *Hereford*, pronounced *her-ee-ford*, in three syllables with the first accented, is the name of a fertile shire on the border of Wales which is noted for its good pastureland and the breed of cattle to which it gave its name. Typical Hereford cattle are marked with white faces and red bodies and are regarded in both Europe and America as among the most efficient cattle in the world for the conversion of grass into beef under climatic conditions not so dependably met by most other breeds. *Hertford*, generally pronounced *har-ferd* in England and *hert-ferd* in America—only two syllables in each case—is a shire lying only a short distance north of London. The county seat of Herefordshire is Hereford and that of Hertfordshire is Hertford. Both *Hereford* and *Hertford* are common place names in the United States.

Which is correct, "Siam" or "Thailand"?

For hundreds of years *Siam* has been regarded by foreigners as the name of the country in southeastern Asia. *Siam* (*Sayam* to the natives) was also used by the government as the name of the country in external affairs. This term as the general name of the region dates back at least a thousand years. But the natives themselves generally called their country *Muang T'ai*, which means literally "land of the free" and figuratively "land of the Thai race." In English *Muang T'ai* is rendered *Thailand*, pronounced *tie-land*. On June 24, 1939, Prince Aditya Dirabha, regent of the country, affixed the royal seal to a decree changing the official name from *Sayam* to *Muang T'ai*. Most governments, including the United States, immediately adopted *Thailand* in official usage. However, on February 18, 1942, Richard K. Law, British undersecretary for foreign affairs, told the House of Commons that instructions had been issued to British officials to use *Siam* instead of *Thailand* "so far as is practical." On September 8, 1945, shortly after the end of the Second World War, the government of the Asiatic country announced that it had abandoned all efforts to induce foreigners to call the country *Thailand* and that *Siam* would again be used in all external affairs. Accordingly *Siam* remains the correct foreigner's name of the country, while the natives continue to call their country *Muang T'ai* or *Thailand*.

Why do horses have "chestnuts" on their legs?

The hard, bare, warty patches on the inner side of the legs of horses, popularly known as *chestnuts*, are believed to be survivals of scent or recognition glands and to be homologous to similar glands on the limbs of other quadrupeds. Asses and zebras (as well as the extinct quagga) are distinguished from horses by having these chestnuts or callosities on only the forelegs. During the Middle Ages these callosities on horses were believed to possess certain medicinal virtues.

Who was the "Lady of the Haystack"?

In 1776 a beautiful and graceful girl, who appeared to be familiar with the forms of good society, was found living in a haystack at Bourton, near Bristol, England. She was demented and her origin was a complete mystery. The *Lady of the Haystack*, as she was called, made her home in the haystack for four years, when she was placed in an asylum by Mrs. Hannah More, who lived in the vicinity. Mrs. More called the girl Louisa, but she died in the asylum in 1801 without her identity ever having been learned. It was generally supposed, however, that Louisa was Mlle. La Frulen, a natural daughter of Francis I, consort of Maria Theresa, co-regent of Austria and Holy Roman Emperor.

Why are greyhounds so called?

The first syllable in *greyhound* is of uncertain origin but it is believed to have no reference to the color of the dog so named. Most authorities lean toward the opinion the *grey* in this connection is the old Icelandic *grey*, "dog," and Anglo-Saxon *hund*, another word for dog, and that the word is essentially a pleonasm equivalent to *hound dog*, a term still sometimes heard. Words of the same original meaning are often so combined when one has acquired a more specific meaning than the other. *Greyhound,* variously spelled, was used in English as early as the year 1000, when it probably referred to large, rough-haired dogs of Irish stock. The "properties of a goode Grehound" were defined by Juliana Berners in the *Boke of St. Albans.* "A greyhounde," wrote that author in 1486, "shoulde be heded like a snake, and Necked like a Drake: Foted like a Kat, Tayled like a Rat, Syded like a Teme, Chyned like a Beme." The tall, slender, graceful, swift and keen-sighted dogs now known as greyhounds were developed by crossing an Eastern breed with other varieties and through centuries of careful breeding. Dogs very similarly formed have been found portrayed on ancient Egyptian monuments and both the Greeks and the Romans held such dogs in high esteem. Charlemagne is said to have had a special officer of the greyhound kennel attached to his court. To what extent these early dogs resembled the modern greyhound cannot now be determined. The speed of the dogs certainly has been increased. Modern greyhounds can run more than sixty miles an hour and some of them can clear eighteen feet in a single bound. Recurring to the origin of the term, *grey* is also an obsolete English word for badger and some authorities have suggested that the greyhound may have been so called because it was once widely used to hunt the badger or *grey.* As early as 1400 the word was sometimes written *grewhound* or *grehound,* from *Grew,* meaning Greek. In other words, it was called the Grecian dog on the supposition that it originated in Greece. The Oxford dictionary, however, pronounces this "an etymological alteration" resulting from a false theory of the origin of the word.

Why is a kind of grass called timothy?

It seems to be well established that the perennial hay grass now almost universally known as timothy received its name from Timothy Hanson, but very little is known about him, and the accounts of his connection with it are confusing. Hanson is variously referred to as the one who "first propagated" this grass, who "carried the seed from New England to Maryland," who "took the first seed from New York to Carolina about 1720" and who "introduced its cultivation into New England." Timothy is undoubtedly indigenous to Europe and Great Britain, where it still grows wild, although a closely related variety may have been native to the northeastern part of the United States. All evidence, however, indicates that it was first cultivated as an agricultural plant in the New World in the early part of the eighteenth century. The earliest known records associate it with Pennsylvania. In 1736 Jared Eliot (1685–1763), physician, Congregational minister and writer of essays on agriculture, wrote as follows in his journal: "Herd-Grass (known in Pennsylvania as Timothy-Grass) . . . It is said that Herd-Grass was first found in a swamp in Piscataqua (Maine) by one (John) Herd who propagated the same." *Herd grass* is still used in Great Britain and New England. Benjamin Franklin, writing in 1747, said that "a bushel of clean chaff of timothy or Salem grass will yield five quarts of seed." George Washington refers to timothy several times in his diary. In 1760 he makes the remarkable observation that he had "ascertained" that there were "298,000 timothy seeds" in a pound. Writing at Mount Vernon under date of Friday, June 24, 1763, he records that he "began to cut Timothy at Ashbords," and on Tuesday, June 25, 1765, he "began to cut my Timothy Meadow on Doeg Run." As early as that year of 1765 we find it stated that timothy was so called because it was taken from New York to Carolina by one Timothy Hanson. *The Pennsylvania Gazette* listed "timothy seed" soon after the close of the Revolution. Known scientifically as *Phleum pratense*, timothy is classed as a cattail grass from the long spikes on which the seed grows.

How did "big as cuffy" originate?

Cuffy or *Cuffey* is an old familiar or humorous nickname for a Negro, particularly one who puts on airs. Such expressions as *big as cuffy* and *proud as cuffy* refer to the proverbial self-importance of a Negro togged out in his glad rags or Sunday best. The history of this odd term is obscure. Some authorities suppose it to be a corruption of the old English slang term *cove* or *cofe*, thieves' cant for "individual" or "fellow"; others fancy it to be a modification of Dutch *Koffi*, a common name for a Negro in Guiana. Since *cuffy* is a common and very old name for a Negro in the West Indies, especially Jamaica, it may have originated in those islands, or it may have been brought from Africa with the Negroes. The name was borne by several Negroes who were tried in connection with the famous Negro plot in New York in 1741. *Politicians Outwitted*, a play written in 1789 by Samuel Low, has a Negro character named Cuffy. In *Putnam's Magazine* for December, 1854, is the following: "The fine dash of Virginia *cuffyism*, it is gone, gone forever. Sambo has settled down into a simply Bourgeois." Mrs. Harriet Beecher Stowe, in *Uncle Tom's Cabin*, uses *Sambo* and *Cuffy* side by side as proper names representative of the race. One of the richest and most famous Negroes in early America was named Paul Cuffee, who was born near New Bedford, Massachusetts, in 1759, his father being a free Negro named Cuffee Slocum and his mother an Indian woman named Ruth Moses. He not only adopted his father's Christian name as his surname but induced his brothers to do likewise. After making a sizable fortune as a sea captain, Paul Cuffee became a Quaker and achieved considerable fame as a philanthropist by devoting the latter years of his life until his death in 1817 to the transportation of Negro colonists from America to Sierra Leone in Africa. It is not true, as sometimes stated, that Cuffee's surname, in a modified form, became the generic name for Negroes. *Cuffee* and *Cuffy* are merely different spellings of the same name and were commonly applied to colored men long before the time of Paul Cuffee or his father, Cuffee Slocum.

Who was Dr. Fell?

Dr. John Fell (1625–1686) was an eminent English clergyman, educator and classical author who is remembered chiefly because he was the butt of a schoolboy's joke. After serving in the Loyalist forces supporting Charles I and remaining in obscurity during the Commonwealth, he became Dean of Christ Church College at Oxford, vice-chancellor of the university and Bishop of Oxford. He wrote numerous critical, moral and theological works and developed the University Press, restored discipline, supervised an extensive building program and expelled the philosopher John Locke who had incurred the displeasure of the King. Among his pupils in 1678 while he was dean of Christ Church was Thomas Brown (1663–1704), who later became notorious as the author of *Dialogues of the Dead* and numerous poems, letters, pamphlets, satires, lampoons and jests leveled at the prominent men of his time. The undergraduate, always irregular in habits, was threatened with expulsion by the prelate for some breach of the rules. Upon receiving an apologetic letter from his pupil, Dr. Fell agreed to overlook the matter provided the offender could give a satisfactory impromptu translation of the following lines from the Roman epigrammatist Martial:

> *Non amo te, Sabidi, nec possum dicere quare:*
> *Hoc tantum possum dicere non amo te.*

Without hesitation Tom Brown gave this rendering:

> I do not love thee, Doctor Fell,
> The reason why I cannot tell:
> But this alone I know full well,
> I do not love thee, Doctor Fell.

Sometimes the third line is given, "But this I know, and know full well." About thirty years earlier Thomas Forde in *Virtue Rediviva* & had translated the thirty-third epigram of Martial as follows: "I love thee not, Nell.

[21]

But why, I can't tell," etc. It is probable that Tom Brown, "of facetious memory" as Addison referred to him, got into jail through his lampoons on the great, but he squared himself with Dr. Fell's memory by writing his epitaph.

What species of fish catches birds?

A large European catfish scientifically called *Silurus* but more commonly known as Wels or Glanis, catches and eats large birds swimming on the surface. There is authentic record of a case in which one of these voracious fish swallowed a small child whole. The common angler fish, sea devil or fishing frog, *Lophius piscatorius*, which is native to both European and American waters, is popularly called the goosefish because geese, ducks, gulls, loon and other aquatic birds are sometimes found in its stomach. This species, which generally remains close to the bottom, is proverbial for its protective coloration and for its cunning in obtaining food. It is called the angler fish because the top of its head is equipped with three upright filaments surmounted by glittering flesh appendages that the fish employs as bait and line to lure other fish within its reach. The angler fish lies quietly on the slimy bottom, protected by its muddy color, and moves the glittering natural bait back and forth with the filaments until a small fish in quest of food approaches and is quickly snapped up. In several deep-sea species of this family the bait is luminous and can be switched on or off at will. Some authorities are inclined to believe that the common angler fish does not ascend to the surface to catch and drag down live birds, but merely devours those that have died and sunk to the region of their habitat. This fish, which may attain a length of four or five feet, is also known as allmouth or mouth fish because of the great size of its mouth. Ugly and voracious, it is not at all choice in its diet, all sorts of odd things having been found in its stomach. Its stomach is extensible and frequently a deep-sea variety seizes and devours other fish larger than itself, the greediness often resulting in the death of the captor as well as the victim. The angler fish is a close relative of the smaller toadfish and batfish, which often persist in taking the bait of the fisherman. Perhaps other fish catch and eat birds. A gamekeeper in Norfolkshire, England, reported that a pike was in the habit of seizing moor hens as they swam on a pond.

Why are Chinese called "Celestials"?

Celestial, often popularly applied to the old Chinese Empire and to the Chinese people, was suggested by the initial phrase in many of the edicts issued by the Manchu emperors—*T'ien Ch'ao* ("Heavenly Dynasty"), implying that the rulers of China were divinely chosen for the task. The Chinese not only never call themselves Celestials but they resent the application of the term to them by others, and consequently careful foreign writers have abandoned it. They do not, however, object to the application of *celestial* to their nation or race. In *East Wind, West Wind* Pearl Buck frequently employs the term. For instance, she says: "Her sons will be altogether of our celestial nation, citizens of the Bright Republic, and heirs of the Middle Empire." And again: "She wishes her children to belong to our ancient and celestial race forever."

What does "range" in "Home on the Range" mean?

> Home, home on the range,
> Where the deer and the antelope play;
> Where seldom is heard a discouraging word,
> And the skies are not cloudy all day.

The original version of this popular song is believed to have been written in 1873 by Dr. Brewster Higley, a Pennsylvannia country doctor, who removed to north central Kansas about 1870 and took up a homestead on Federal land near Smith Center. "The Western Home" was the original title, but, like many other popular songs, the original title was supplanted by the most popular phrase in the song. Evidence indicates that the music was composed by Dan Kelly, a neighbor of Dr. Higley's. This song has been the basis of several later versions and the authorship of both words and music have been claimed for a number of different persons. In the public land system of the United States counties were divided into ranges for survey and land location purposes. A range was a row of townships running north and south across a county. The number of both the township and the range were given in designating the location of land within a county; as, Township No. 5, N., Range No. 7, W. It appears that it was this kind of range on which Dr. Higley lived as a homesteader in Kansas and which he had in mind when he wrote of his western home on the range. The antelope mentioned in the song was the pronghorn, a common animal on the prairies in those days.

Does any species of bird hibernate?

No species of bird, so far as known, hibernates in the sense of spending the winter in a torpid state as certain mammals do. Birds have higher body temperatures than mammals have and they are not adapted to withstand the decrease in body temperature and vital activity incident to hibernation. Many species that summer in the north migrate southward when the approach of frost and snow threatens their normal food supply. Before their breeding and nesting habits were understood it was generally supposed that the sea birds known as petrels hibernated. The belief was once almost universal that swallows, upon the approach of cold weather, dived into ponds and hibernated in the mud at the bottom during the winter months, a notion suggested, no doubt, by the fact that these birds appear early and suddenly in the spring and disappear mysteriously in the fall. Aristotle explained the autumnal disappearance of swallows, storks, doves and many other birds by their passing the winter in a torpid state in caves, hollow trees and the mud of marshes. The early literature of natural history contains thousands of references to the hibernation of swallows in this manner. One early naturalist told of flocks of swallows gathering in marshes in the fall until their accumulated weight bent the reeds on which they clung, and submerged the birds. There are accounts of fishermen who during the winter brought up their nets filled with fish and swallows that had been hibernating in the mud. The theory that bank swallows hibernate in their burrows was once prevalent even among naturalists. It is small wonder that these birds were suspected of hibernating when even to this day the winter home of their cousins the chimney swifts is not definitely known. The American marsh birds called sora rails have the habit of suddenly disappearing upon the approach of cold weather from places where they have been numerous, and many people at one time believed that these birds turned into frogs and hid in the mud from fall to spring. Downy and hairy woodpeckers often, and some other woodpeckers occasionally, excavate special holes in dead stumps and limbs in the fall and use them as bedrooms and storm shelters during the cold weather. Of interest in this connection is the peculiar wintering habit of the verdin, a tiny yellow-headed North American bush tit, which is believed to keep in repair its large retort-shaped nest of twigs and stems for use as a winter sleeping place. The Canada jay builds its feather-lined nest in the latter part of the winter and lays its eggs in March or April when the temperature is often below zero.

Do rabbits swim?

Ordinary rabbits and hares, like most other mammals, swim naturally when thrown or forced into water, but their fur and skin are not impervious to water and they gradually drown as they swim. The swamp rabbit, a native of swamps, marshes and low woodlands in the South, is a good swimmer and it often takes to the water when pursued, even swimming across rivers. Its trails frequently lead through shallow water and it has been observed to swim back and forth across creeks and bayous to elude dogs. The arctic hare is said to swim freely across the small streams common in its habitat. A common European hare readily takes to water and swims well. One was seen swimming across an arm of the sea a mile wide.

What is "Boxing Day"?

Boxing Day has no reference to things pugilistic. In England the day after Christmas is so called because on that day the Christmas boxes placed in the churches for casual contributions are opened and the contents distributed to those who render small services without pay. The night of the same day is known as Boxing Night. Boxing Day is a survival of an older custom. In medieval times the monks of certain orders used to offer mass for the safety of vessels and at the same time place a small box on each ship to receive contributions from the sailors. Carrying a box from door to door for the collection of Christmas money and presents was an early custom, and in the course of time alms boxes were placed in churches for donations to be distributed to the poor on Christmas morning.

What is "the gay science"?

The art of poetry is known as "the gay science," the phrase being a translation of old Provençal gai saber, which alludes to the fact that the minstrels and troubadours of Provence insisted on the joyfulness of their art. In 1323 a guild known as Gai Saber or "The Very Gay Company of the Seven Troubadours of Toulose" was formed to revive and perpetuate the moribund language and culture of Provence. Thomas Carlyle, writing On the Nigger Question in 1849, originated the name Dismal Science for the study of economics. "The social science—not a gay science," declared the Scotch philosopher, "but a rueful—which finds the secret of this Universe in 'supply and demand'—what we might call by way of eminence the dismal science." In 1866 the old Provençal phrase was revived by E. S. Dallas, who published a treatise on criticism entitled The Gay Science.

What is a Roman nose?

A high, convex nose with a pointed tip like the beak of an eagle is called a Roman nose because it is popularly supposed to have been characteristic of the ancient Romans. Whether the aquiline nose actually prevailed among the Romans is a disputed point. The evidence indicates, however, that at least many members of the ruling class had noses distinguished by their prominent bridges. But there is no reason for supposing that this type of nose was typical of the Roman people as a whole. Shakespeare, in II King Henry IV, has Sir John Falstaff refer to Julius Caesar as "the hook-nosed fellow of Rome," and in Cymbeline Cloten says that other Caesars besides Julius may have had "crooked noses."

To what race did Hannibal belong?

Ancient Carthage was founded and settled by Phœnicians from the famous maritime city of Tyre on the coast of what is now Syria. The Phœnicians were a branch of the Semites, the same race to which the ancient Hebrews belonged. Although there was probably a large infusion of other races, Hannibal and the native Carthaginians who fought against the Romans in the Punic Wars may be regarded as of the Semitic race. The adjective semitic or shemitic, was coined in 1781 by the German historian and scholar August von Schlozer, who deemed it particularly appropriate from a lingual standpoint because most of the peoples speaking the languages so denominated were traditionally supposed to be descended from Shem, the eldest son of Noah.

What fish can swallow fish larger than themselves?

A small, blackish deep-sea fish known scientifically as Chiasmodon niger and popularly as "black swallower," sometimes swallows another fish much larger than itself. A few specimens have been captured distended with fish inside them two or three times their own size. Widemouths, which belong to the suborder Stomiatidae, not only prey upon fish of their own kind but individuals have been found that had swallowed other fish at least three times their own bulk. A deep-sea variety of the angler fish also seizes and devours other fish larger than itself. In all these fish the stomach, mouth and throat are distensible and the teeth are depressible backwards. The throat and stomach stretch like a rubber balloon. Not infrequently when one of these fish swallows another several times its own bulk the result is the death of both.

What is the origin of "within the pale"?

Pale comes from Latin palus, "stake." Literally a pale is a place inclosed by a fence of pales. As early as the fourteenth century pale was used figuratively in the sense of a limit, boundary or restriction. In Shakespeare's Comedy of Errors Adriana compares her husband to a "too unruly deer" that "breaks the pale, and feeds from home." Within the pale, beyond the pale and outside the pale originally referred to the English pales in France and Ireland. The English pale in France, a territory under English jurisdiction around Calais, was established in 1494. From the twelfth to the seventeenth centuries the territory controlled by the English in Ireland was known as The English Pale or simply as The Pale. The actual size of The Pale varied with the rise and fall of the power of England. English authority prevailed within The Pale, but was powerless outside or beyond The Pale. In 1786 Catherine II issued a ukase compelling Jews to live in certain specified towns and territories in Poland and southwestern Russia. This was known as the Jewish Pale.

What birds eat feathers?

The grebes, aquatic birds notable for their agility in the water, not only eat feathers but also feed them to their young. As a general rule more than fifty per cent of the contents of a grebe's stomach consists of masses of feathers. Presumably the feathers are from the bird's own body. The nutritive value of feathers is not known, nor have naturalists agreed what part this type of food plays in the digestive economy of these remarkable birds. It has been suggested that the feathers in the bird's stomach act as strainers for fishbones and other hard substances.

Should a live rabbit be lifted by the ears?

Many think the proper way to handle pet rabbits and hares is to lift them by the ears. Naturalists say this is a cruel and unjustified practice, because the ears of the rabbit are very sensitive. The best way to lift a rabbit is to grasp the loose skin above the shoulders with one hand and to support the under part of its body with the other. That rabbits are not injured by being lifted in this manner is indicated by the fact that they generally do not struggle, as they do when lifted by the ears or legs. The danger of injuring rabbits by lifting them by the ears increases as they grow older and heavier.

Who first described treaties as "scraps of paper"?

One of the historic remarks of the First World War was made by Theobold von Bethmann-Hollweg, German Chancellor, when he cynically referred to the treaty guaranteeing the independence and neutrality of Belgium as "a scrap of paper." In a note to the British Foreign Office dated August 4, 1914, Sir Edward Goschen, British Ambassador to Berlin, reported that the German Chancellor had said to him: "Just for a word, neutrality, a word which in wartime has so often been disregarded —just for a scrap of paper, Great Britain is going to make war on a kindred nation who desires nothing better than to be friends with her." Bethmann-Hollweg himself afterwards gave a somewhat different version

[27]

of his statement. He explained to Colonel E. M. House that what he really said was that in comparison to the great harm that would result from war between Great Britain and Germany, the treaty with Belgium was "as a mere scrap of paper." The treaty referred to as "a scrap of paper" was signed April 19, 1839, at Berlin by Great Britain, Russia, Prussia, France, Austria, and Belgium. But the phrase was not original with Bethmann-Hollweg. Scrap of paper had been used as a sneering designation for treaties and international agreements for many years. In 1887 Kaiser Wilhelm I of Germany told the Prussian Diet: "I will do my duty as I see it, without regard to scraps of paper called constitutions." Prince Bismarck (1815–1898), the Iron Chancellor of Germany; Baron Jomini (1779–1869), Swiss-born French and Russian general and military writer, and Pere Hyacinthe (1827–1912), famous French preacher, all referred to treaties as "scraps of paper."

Why is the furlong so called?

Furlong, the name of a lineal measure now equivalent to forty rods, two hundred and twenty yards or one-eighth of an English mile, is derived from Anglo-Saxon furh ("furrow"), and lang ("long"), and literally means furrow-long or the length of a furrow. The original furlong was the length of a furrow across a square field of ten acres and was the traditional distance that a yoke of oxen were supposed to pull a plow without stopping to rest. As a measure of distance the furlong has varied from time to time with the size of the acre.

How did "bungalow" originate?

This word is an English corruption of Hindustani bangla (often pronounced bang-a-la by the natives), literally meaning "of or belonging to Bengal," one of the provinces of British India. The bungalow was originally the type of house most frequently occupied by Europeans in the interior of Malaysia and the name suggests that these first bungalows resembled houses common in Bengal. In India a bungalow is a one-story, lightly built cottage, with a pyramidal, thatched roof and an extensive veranda.

Are the tail and the train of the peacock the same?

The true tail of the male peafowl is comparatively short and seldom reaches twenty inches in length. The magnificent train for which the peacock is noted does not represent the tail, as popularly believed, but is composed of unduly elongated feathers growing on the lower part of the back above the tail and extending far beyond it. Ornithologists term the long train feathers *tail-coverts.* Twenty short, stiff and plain-colored feathers constitute the real tail in the typical peacock. When the train feathers are erected and spread into the characteristic fan-shaped disk the short tail is employed as a support. The gorgeously colored quetzal, national bird of Guatemala, also has a comparatively short tail under the long train feathers. In the quetzal, however, the train feathers are pendent rather than erectile, although the bird can cause the train to vibrate gracefully by jerking its true tail. The notion that the train and tail of a peacock are the same is a very old one. In *I King Henry VI* Shakespeare has Joan of Arc say:

> Let frantic Talbot triumph for a while,
> And like a peacock sweep along his tail;
> We'll pull his plumes and take away his train,
> If Dauphin and the rest will be but rul'd.

What birds perch lengthwise on limbs?

Virtually all species of birds ordinarily perch crosswise on the limbs of trees; but the nighthawks, whippoorwills and other members of the goat-sucker family regularly perch lengthwise instead of crosswise. Whippoorwills and nighthawks are active at night and inactive during the day and their habit of perching longitudinally on the limbs of trees affords them considerable protection from enemies. Their dull color and lengthwise perching position cause them to appear to be only knots or excrescences on the limbs.

What is nutria?

Nutria, which is Spanish for otter, is the trade name for the reddish brown fur of the large South and Central American semi-aquatic rodent known as the coypu. The coypu (pronounced *koy-poo*) has partially webbed hind feet and a long, naked, round and scaly tail. Ratlike in appearance and beaverlike in size, this animal is often referred to as the beaver-rat. In fact the coypu was sometimes exhibited as a giant rat in the days when traveling menageries were in their heyday. A coypu of average size weighs about ten pounds and measures between twenty inches and two feet from tip of tail to tip of nose. The female gives birth to several young at a time and carries them on her back when swimming. A remarkable characteristic of this animal is that the teats of the female are located far up on her side so that the young are able to nurse without diving. Actually the coypu is more closely related to the porcupine than to the beaver, although its stiffer, harsher, thinner and somewhat less durable fur makes a good imitation of beaver and has often been dyed and sold as one kind of "seal" or another. Nutria is valuable for many purposes but is now chiefly used in the making of hats. At one time nutria was sought so eagerly for coat linings that the coypu probably would have become extinct had not the style changed. As many as 500,-000 coypu pelts were exported from South America in a single year. In the last century the Argentine government prohibited the hunting and trapping of coypus, which then multiplied so fast that they left the water and swarmed over the land until checked by an epidemic among them. Before the outbreak of the Second World War several hundred thousand coypu pelts went into the fur trade every year.

What is German silver composed of?

German silver contains no silver. It is a silver-white alloy of copper, nickel and zinc in proportions that vary with the use intended. A good quality of German silver made in Great Britain, where it is often called nickel silver, consists of 19 parts nickel, 59 parts copper and 22 parts zinc. German silver is harder than silver, takes a high polish and is used as a substitute for silver in making bells, candlesticks, ornaments, utensils and many other articles. It is used as the base for expensive silver-plated ware and unplated for cheap tableware. The popular name German silver arose from the fact that this alloy was made in Europe first at Hildburghausen in Germany in the early part of the nineteenth century. It had, however, been made in China under the name white copper since ancient times. There seems to be no authority for the statement that German in the name is really german, meaning "related to," as in cousin-german, and that the metal was called German because it was "like" silver.

How did "in the limelight" originate?

In the limelight, meaning a conspicuous position in the public eye, was originally theatrical slang. The system of lighting known as the limelight was invented in 1825 by a British army officer, surveyor and administrator named Thomas Drummond. After serving in the royal engineers, Captain Drummond became assistant to the chief of the British trigonometrical survey. He learned of the brilliant luminosity of lime when incandescent while attending a series of lectures on chemistry and physics delivered before the Royal Institution of London by the great scientists William Thomas Brande and Michael Faraday. It occurred to him that a lime light might be used to make distant surveying stations visible, and he produced a steady, intense white light by directing an oxyhydrogen flame on a cylinder of lime. In 1825, while surveying in northern Ireland, he put his new "Drummond light," as it is sometimes called, to a practical test by making successful observations between two mountains sixty-seven miles apart. A few years later Captain Drummond adapted his limelight for use in lighthouses. In those days before the use of electricity there was no satisfactory or adequate system of lighting the stage in theaters. Stage lights, footlights, floodlights and spotlights as we know them were not yet developed. Naturally the new limelight was quickly adapted for theatrical use. The stage lighting instrument was equipped with a lens to concentrate on a particular point on the stage a beam of light produced by oxyhydrogen flame on a cylinder of lime. That part of the stage where the most important action was taking place came to be referred to as *the limelight*. In process of time the leading player in the piece was said to be *in the limelight*. This phrase passed into general speech and still survives, although the system of lighting to which it refers has long been supplanted by other systems. Thomas Drummond, inventor of the limelight, became undersecretary for Ireland in 1836 and proved an able and successful administrator. "Property," he told the Irish landlords, "has its duties as well as its rights." He died in Dublin in 1840 at the age of forty-three.

Who were "The Old Contemptibles"?

The original British Expeditionary Force of about 160,000 men that went to France and Belgium under General Sir John French immediately after the outbreak of the First World War in 1914 is known in history as "The Old Contemptibles." This name was adopted by the British soldiers themselves after the Battle of Mons in Belgium on August 23 and the historic retreat from that place on the following day. It was suggested by an "army order" that the German Emperor was alleged to have issued at Aix-la-Chapelle on August 19 to Alexander von Kluck and the other German generals. This alleged "army order of August 19" reads as follows:

> It is my royal and imperial command that you concentrate your strength for the immediate present upon one single purpose, and that is, that you address your skill, and all the valor of my soldiers, to exterminate, first, the treacherous English, and to walk over General French's contemptible little army.

No German army order corresponding to this in language and date has ever been verified, and the Kaiser later denied that he had ever made any such reference to the British. Some writers have surmised that the alleged order may have been invented by a clever propagandist to appeal to the pride and to fire the zeal of the British Tommies who had just arrived at their advanced positions on the western front and who a few days later were to be forced back from Mons by the overwhelming superior forces of General von Kluck. However that may be, the order was widely published and generally accepted as genuine by the Allies at the time. The British soldiers in the original B.E.F. in 1914 took the alleged slur of the Kaiser as a compliment and ever after they rejoiced in the nickname of "The Old Contemptibles." Whether or not the Kaiser's alleged order was apocryphal, it reflected the typical contemptuous attitude of the Germans toward the British Army before the First World War. "We Germans fear God but nothing else in the world," Bismarck had boasted in a speech to the Reichstag in 1888, and the Kaiser told his soldiers on August 4, 1914, that "The German people are the chosen of God." There is a story that when Bismarck, to whom Germans refer as the greatest statesman, was once asked what he would do if England landed an army on the German coast, he replied that he would call out the police and have them arrested.

How does a hare differ from a rabbit?

Popularly *rabbit* and *hare* are interchangeable in America, but naturalists apply the terms to two distinct groups of rodents with fairly well-defined characteristics. Originally in England *rabbit* was applied only to a small burrowing species of Leporidae, which is the scientific name of the family embracing all animals of the rabbit and hare kind. In that sense there are many hares but no rabbits in North America. In the United States, however, *rabbit* has been extended to include many members of this family found in different parts of the world. According to the present system of classification, typical hares have long, large ears, large feet, and long legs with the hind ones considerably longer than the front ones; they can run swiftly for considerable distances and they rear their young in shallow open depressions called nests or forms. Typical rabbits have shorter and smaller ears, small feet, and more equal legs; they are weak runners for long distances, and they rear their young in burrows of various kinds. Rabbits are born almost hairless, with eyes closed; hares are born covered with hair, with open eyes. Hares are generally but not necessarily larger than rabbits. But the names are hopelessly confused in the popular mind. So many rabbits are harelike and so many hares are rabbitlike in general appearance that often they are not easily distinguishable by casual observers. Scientifically speaking, pygmy hares, swamp hares and Belgian hares are true rabbits, as are the common cottontails, while jack rabbits and snowshoe rabbits are true hares. Early English settlers in America were more familiar with rabbits than with hares, and there is still a tendency in this country to use *rabbit* almost to the exclusion of *hare* when referring to animals of this family.

What is a pollyanna statement?

A *pollyanna statement* is one to the effect that things might have been worse. In this sense the term originated in Mrs. Eleanor Hodgman Porter's *Pollyanna*, which was first printed serially in the *Christian Herald* in 1912 and published in book form the following year. Mrs. Porter (1868–1920), who was a daughter of Francis Fletcher Hodgman and a direct descendant of Governor William Bradford of the "Mayflower" group, was born at Littleton, New Hampshire. *Pollyanna* was the first of "the glad books" and its great popularity led to the publication in 1915 of *Pollyanna Grows Up* and a dramatization under the title *Pollyanna, the Glad Girl*. The story hinges on the life of an orphan girl named Pollyanna who played a game of always finding something to be glad about, no matter how discouraging the events. Pollyanna learned the game from her missionary father in the West and put it into practice after she went to live with her austere and conventional Aunt Polly in the East. The girl ultimately succeeded in introducing a tone of friendliness and brightness into the puritanical community. Dr. Chilton, another character in the story, described the game as an overwhelming, unquenchable gladness for everything that had happened or was going to happen. We now hear not only of pollyannas and pollyannaisms, but also of pollyanna statements, pollyanna propaganda, etc. A pollyanna, according to the cynics and pessimists, is a person who is foolish enough to think that this world is a pretty satisfactory place to live in. On October 14, 1932, John Nance Garner, when Speaker of the House of Representatives and the Democratic nominee for Vice-President, delivered a radio address in New York in which he said: "It is merely a question of whether directness and adequacy and frankness is more likely to put and keep us on the road to economic recovery, than *pollyanna* statements and hiding the truth, and substituting pretense for actuality, because it may be more palatable to the electorate." *Polly* is a familiar form of *Mary* and *Pollyanna* is a compound of two Hebrew feminine names meaning "bitter grace."

What is felt composed of?

Felt consists of wool, hair, fur or other fibrous materials matted together into a compact fabric without spinning or weaving. The manufacturer of felt takes advantage of the natural tendency of certain fibers to interlace and adhere to one another. Blending of the different fibers, moistening, heating, rolling, pressing, gluing and stretching all enter into the making of the various kinds of modern felt. The produce is put to many uses, the most highly finished varieties being used in hats, and the felt hat industry involves the expenditure of millions of dollars annually. Felt, being simple in structure, is probably the oldest fabric used by man and it undoubtedly antedates spinning and weaving. Apparently it was known when the Homeric poems were written, and several ancient authors not only mention the fabric but explain the process of its manufacture. The invention of felt is generally ascribed to the ancient shepherds of Asia, and there are several popular stories as to how this or that king, saint or monk accidentally discovered the fabric by observing that wool in his shoes or sandals became matted by the moisture and pressure of the foot. St. Clement, whose feast day is observed November 23 and who was the fourth Bishop of Rome, or Pope, is popularly regarded as the patron saint of hatters and feltmakers because an apocryphal as well as anachronistic story attributed the discovery and introduction of felt to him. Persecuted by the Romans, the saint finally had to flee for his life. His feet became blistered and sore on the long journey and he lined the soles of his sandals with wool to ease the pain. At the end of the journey he found that the wool had been transformed into compact pieces of fabric by the heat, moisture and the movements of his feet. As previously stated, the fabric was known long before the time of St. Clement, and in all probability was used by man before he learned to weave and spin fabrics. The earliest known mention of felt by that name in England occurred about the year 1,000. In Shakespeare's King Lear the mad monarch says, "It were a delicate stratagem to shoe a troop of horse with felt."

Is "consensus of opinion" correct?

Consensus of opinion is good English. Some purists object to it on the ground that consensus means an agreement of opinion and that the last two words in the phrase are redundant. That position, however, is not tenable. Consensus is derived from two Latin words, con, together, and sentire, to feel. Literally consensus signifies a "feeling together." Comparatively speaking, the term is a new one in the English language. The earliest use of consensus recorded by the Oxford dictionary is dated 1854. It was first employed in physiology in the sense of harmony, co-operation or sympathy in different parts of an organism, or a general concord of different organs of the body in effecting a given purpose. Later the term came to mean a unanimity in various matters. As now used, consensus is virtually synonymous with concord or general agreement. There may be a consensus of testimony, evidence, authority, etc., as well as of opinion. At least two eminent authorities have given consensus of opinion a clean bill of health. The late Frank H. Vizetelly, managing editor of the New Standard Dictionary of the English Language, said in his *How To Use English*: "But as there may be consensus of thought, of functions, of forces, etc., it is not tautological to speak of a consensus of opinion. Besides, the phrase is an English idiom." The Second Edition of Webster's New International Dictionary, makes this observation: "The expression consensus of opinion, although objected to by some, is now generally accepted in good use." As a matter of fact, consensus of opinion is not tautological in the accepted sense of that term. Tautology is a fault in language only when it involves actual redundant or superfluous words or ideas. Many perfectly good English phrases retain traces of tautology in respect to their origin. *Sahara*, the name of the great desert in northern Africa, is believed to be derived from Arabic *sahira*, which is plural in form and which means deserts, wastes or wilds. Therefore the *Sahara Desert* is, strictly speaking, tautological. Likewise, the war in *guerrilla warfare*, a perfectly acceptable phrase, is redundant, because *guerrilla* is the diminutive of Spanish *guerra*, war, and literally means little war. Many other instances could be cited. The *sensus* in *consensus* is often confused with *census*. Accordingly *consensus* is frequently both misspelled and misused. *Census* is derived from Latin *censere*, to value or to tax, and there is no relationship between the two words in origin or meaning. To speak of "taking a concensus" is nonsense.

Do chimney swifts nest in used chimneys?

North American chimney swifts, popularly but erroneously known as chimney swallows, nest and sleep only in unused chimneys. Smoke and heat passing through a chimney drive out the birds and suffocate their broods. This species originally nested in hollow trees and perhaps occasionally on the sides of sheer cliffs. As the forests gradually disappeared swifts began to nest inside chimneys, which increased in number at the same time that hollow trees became scarcer. The birds are migratory and it so happens that they arrive from their winter home late in the spring and leave for it early in the fall when most chimneys are not in use. It has been observed that some swifts now have a tendency to abandon chimneys in favor of attics and other sheltered places in buildings. The saucerlike nest of twigs is glued together and attached to the side of the chimney or wall by means of hardened saliva. Swifts are able to cling in an upright position to a perpendicular surface by means of their toes and the support of spine-tipped feathers in the tail. A similarity in outward appearance as well as in habits suggests that swifts and swallows might be near kin; but swallows are passerine birds while swifts are not, and there is no close relationship between the two families. Strangely enough, the nearest relatives of swifts are hummingbirds and nighthawks. The old belief that swifts do not migrate but hibernate in the mud at the bottom of ponds has been exploded as a myth. They go south each fall, some of them wintering in Central America. It is estimated that they can fly at a speed of a hundred miles an hour. Their ability to fly straight up and straight down enables them to enter and leave chimneys with ease.

Why is the typical Scotsman called Sandy?

Sandy or Sawney is a familiar form of Alexander and it is used as a nickname for any Scotsman because the name is such a common one in Scotland. Now it is generally used either facetiously or derisively. The earliest use of the nickname recorded by the Oxford dictionary is dated about 1740. The name Alexander is of Greek origin and literally means "helper of men."

Why is a kind of cloth called denim?

The original English form of denim was de Nim and it was at first applied to a twilled serge cloth manufactured at de Nîmes, the capital of the department of Gard in southern France. Several centuries ago de Nîmes was already noted for its extensive textile industry, and serge de Nîmes was known throughout the western commercial world. In 1695 the Merchant's Magazine, published in London, listed "Serge Denims that cost 6£ each," and five years later the London Gazette referred to "A pair of Flower'd Serge de Nim Breeches." Nîmes, or Nismes as it is also written, is pronounced neem. Denim is now applied in America to a colored drilling or twilled cotton cloth used chiefly in making overalls, wall hangings, carpeting, cushions, etc.

Are black snakes and blue racers of the same species?

The American snake commonly known as the blue racer is a light-colored phase of the black snake or black racer, Coluber constrictor. In a general way it may be said that the black snake of the East is the blue racer and green racer of the West and Southwest, for they are all regional representatives of the same species. Black and blue racers are so called because of their color and swiftness. They readily climb trees by twisting about the smaller branches and occasionally leap from the branches of one tree to those of another. Even among bushes and undergrowth the racer can crawl faster than a man can walk. Its diet consists of insects, frogs, toads, birds, small mammals and other snakes. All varieties of this family are nonvenomous, and, contrary to a popular belief supported by the scientific name of the species, they do not constrict or wind around their prey. The larger specimens sometimes attain a length of six or seven feet, and when crawling in the grass they often elevate the head and carry it a foot or more from the surface, a habit that some authorities believe suggested the hoop-snake myth. Stories of attacks upon human beings by racers or black snakes are probably unfounded. These snakes are feared because they sometimes follow persons, but they are not dangerous and will invariably retreat if one turns upon them. The eyes of certain reptiles have a slightly luminous appearance at night and this characteristic is particularly marked in black snakes. There is a popular notion that black snakes and rattlesnakes are deadly enemies and that where there are black snakes there will be no rattlesnakes. But members of the two families are often found in the same vicinity, even basking in the sunshine close together, and the popular belief appears to be unfounded.

Do beavers eat fish?

Although beavers are aquatic in habits and spend a great deal of time in the water, they never touch fish or any other animal food. They are rodents and in the wild state they subsist entirely on a vegetable diet consisting principally of bark and tender shoots. The beavers in the park of the Zoological Society of London are fed bread, carrots and green vegetables. When beavers in captivity are given an ample supply of their favorite food-woods to gnaw they seem to care for little else to eat. *Magnolia glauca* is known as the beaver tree in the West and as the Castor tree elsewhere because beavers, which belong to the species *Castor americanus*, use the bark for food and the wood for building dams.

Why was the Black Prince so called?

Edward (1330–1376), eldest son of Edward III and the second English crown prince to bear the title Prince of Wales, was called the *Black Prince* because of his warlike qualities and martial deeds. At the Battle of Crécy in 1346 the sixteen-year-old Prince of Wales was in the front of the fight and when his life seemed in peril the Earl of Warwick sent a messenger to ask reinforcements of Edward III, who was stationed on a hill with the reserves. The King refused to send help, saying "Let the boy win his spurs." The Black Prince did not live to ascend the throne, but died a year before his father's death in 1377, his eldest son succeeding to the throne as Richard II. The earliest known mention of "the Black Prince" occurred in a parliamentary document of 1379, only three years after his death. Shakespeare, in *King Richard II* and *King Henry V*, refers to him as "the Black Prince, that young Mars of men" and "that black name, Edward black Prince of Wales." Historians are now inclined to reject the once popular theory that Edward was called the Black Prince by the French because he had on black armor at the Battle of Crécy or because he habitually wore such mail. Portraits of the time represent him in armor of burnished silver, gold or copper. The color black has often been associated in literature with persons whose fighting qualities were a terror to their enemies.

How is "gladiolus" pronounced?

Gladiolus, the name of a common member of the iris family, probably comes in for a larger share of discussion than the name of any other plant or flower. According to the general rule of pronunciation, *gladiolus* should be pronounced gla-*dye*-o-lus, with the second syllable accented, and virtually all dictionaries give that as the preferred pronunciation. Very few people, however, pronounce the word that way. Popularly it is almost invariably pronounced glad-ee-*oh*-lus, with the primary accent on the third syllable and a secondary accent on the first, and that is the pronunciation used by nearly all growers of the flower. Some authorities maintain that this is incorrect because a syllable is accented that is neither long in quantity nor stressed in the original Latin. The fact is, as H. W. Fowler points out in *A Dictionary of Modern English Usage*, that in determining the quality of a vowel sound in English words classical Latin quantity is of no value whatever and its influence on the syllable to be accented is negligible. Present-day usage is much more important. More attention, perhaps, might be paid to the classical precedent in this case if *gladiolus* were a recent borrowing from Latin; but the term, in one form or other, has been used in English as a plant name since the year 1000, and there seems to be no good reason why it should be regarded as a Latin term or why the generally accepted pronunciation should not be considered correct. The formation of the plural is also the subject of discussion. In Latin the plural is *gladioli*, in English *gladioluses*. Some writers use the singular *gladiolus* with a collective force in preference to either *gladioli* or *gladioluses*. Others have a hazy feeling that *gladiolus* itself is a plural and make the blunder of adopting *gladiola* as the singular. This word, like *gladiator*, is derived from *gladius*, "sword." *Gladiolus* is the diminutive and literally means "small sword," having reference to the sword shape of the leaves. The name was applied to a species of lily in the time of Pliny. There are many species of *gladiolus* and the listed varieties number some 7,000. The lilies of the field, referred to by Jesus in one of the most beautiful passages in the New Testament, are believed by some to have been gladioluses, although others suppose them to have been tulips or other plants of the lily kind.

How can cotton be detected in wool cloth?

People frequently ask whether there is any simple and practical test whereby they can detect the presence of cotton in cloth that is represented as being all wool. The relative amount of cotton and wool in fabrics made of both can readily be determined by boiling a piece of the cloth in a solution of water and lye for about a quarter of an hour. Under such conditions the wool will dissolve and completely disappear while the cotton will scarcely be affected at all. The solution should consist of a tablespoonful of lye (or a greater quantity of alkaline washing powder) to a pint of water.

Which is correct, "while" or "wile" away time?

In present-day English usage either while or wile is regarded as correct in this phrase, which means to cause time to pass lightly or pleasantly, especially by doing some trifling or amusing thing to relieve what would otherwise be tedious or irksome hours. While is an Anglo-Saxon word signifying "a space of time," and apparently it was used as a verb in this sense before wile was. The earliest use of while away recorded by the Oxford dictionary is dated 1635, that of wile away 1796. Because while away appears to have been the earlier form of the phrase, some authorities insist that while away is correct and wile away incorrect. Wile as a noun denotes a trick or artifice and is of unknown origin. As a verb it means to bring, draw, lead, induce or get by wile, cunning or craft. In wile away, wile was probably substituted partly through confusion with while and partly through association with such phrases as beguile the day or time. Oddly enough, some authorities insist that wile away is right and while away wrong, but their contention seems to be supported by neither usage nor the history of the phrase.

How does a turtle differ from a tortoise?

Turtle and tortoise are both applied to species of reptiles belonging to the order Chelonia, and in their broadest sense they are interchangeable, every turtle being a tortoise and every tortoise a turtle. Although these terms are not consistently restricted to different groups of reptiles, in a general way the marine and larger fresh-water species are called turtles, while the land species are called tortoises. Dr. William T. Hornaday, the celebrated naturalist, classified the Chelonians as follows: Tortoises, all

Chelonians of the land only; terrapins, all Chelonians of fresh water; and turtles, all Chelonians of the sea. In British usage the terms are employed in a somewhat more specific sense, the terrestrial species being known as tortoises and the marine species as turtles. The London Zoological Society says: "The tortoises are terrestrial, the terrapins amphibious, and the turtles marine." This confusion in names among naturalists leads many people to disregard the scientific classification and to call all of them turtles. *Turtle* was applied to a dove long before it was to a reptile. The word is believed to have acquired the latter sense through the assimilation of French *tortue* or Spanish *tortuga*, meaning a tortoise, to the English *turtle*, meaning a dove. One etymologist suggests that the French and Spanish terms for tortoise may be derived from Latin *tortus*, "crooked," referring to the reptile's peculiar feet. The Spanish apply *tortuga* to both land and marine species. Columbus named an island off the northwest coast of Hispaniola *Tortuga Island*, which name it still bears, from its fancied resemblance to the humped shell of a turtle asleep on the sea. Ponce de León, returning from his first expedition to Florida in 1513, discovered near the coast a group of islands that he named the Dry Tortugas because they contained no springs but abounded in turtles. On one tiny island the Spanish voyagers caught 170 of these reptiles in one night. The Chelonians are among the most primitive existing reptiles. In a general way a tortoise, turtle or terrapin may be described as a reptile with its skeleton on the outside of its body and with its vital organs completely encased in a bony box known as a shell. Chelonians are the only backboned animals with their vital organs inside their ribs, the shell being partly formed of ribs that are outside the shoulder and pelvic girdles.

Is any species of antelope native to America?

No species of true antelope is native to North America. The Rocky Mountain goat, which is a connecting link between the true goats and the true antelopes, is the nearest relative of the antelope in the New World. The pronghorn or prongbuck, commonly called an antelope in the United States, is not a true antelope, but the sole representative of a distinctive family of ruminants called *Antilocarpridae*, which is formed from the words meaning "antelope" and "goat." It is this animal that is referred to in the line in *Home on the Range*, "Where the deer and the antelope play." This interesting animal, which has no close relative on any other continent, combines some of the characteristics of the giraffes, the goats, the African antelopes and the deer. When Europeans first visited the West they found these beautiful, sprightly and fleet antelope-like pronghorns in abundance on the prairies and plains and supposed them to be antelopes. But when zoologists came to classify the pronghorn they found it to be so peculiar structurally that they had to create a new family for it. All ruminant animals with hollow horns except oxen, sheep, goats and pronghorns are classed as antelopes. True antelopes are near kin to the goats. They differ from the deer in several respects. The horns of deer are solid and are shed and replaced annually; those of antelopes resemble those of cattle, sheep and goats in being hollow, set on a bony core and not shed or renewed each year. The pronghorn resembles the antelope in that both sexes have horns, and the deer in that their horns are shed annually. Of the deer family the reindeer is the only member whose sexes both have horns. The pronghorn is the only living mammal having hollow horns that are planted on a bony core and that are shed annually, and it is the only animal that has pronged or bifurcated horns that are hollow. The hollow horns of all other animals are persistent. Pronghorns also differ from other ruminants in having no "dewclaws" or false hoofs and in having the horns directly above the eyes. A deer's horns come off clean at the head, but those of the pronghorn fall as the result of degeneration at the base. The horns of a female pronghorn are so imperceptible that many early authorities have stated that they had no horns at all. On a kid female pronghorn the horns cannot be detected; on a yearling they can easily be felt, while on an adult female they appear above the hair and occasionally reach a length of two or three inches. A prongbuck may have horns a foot long.

How did Acadia get its name?

Acadia, the historic and literary name of a district comprising Nova Scotia and eastern New Brunswick in Canada, is the Latinized form of *akade*, a Micmac Indian word meaning "the land," "the region" or "where a thing is abundant" and occurring as a suffix in many place names of Algonquian Indian origin. The first occurrence of this poetic name in writing was in a petition sent to the French King by Pierre de Gast Sieur de Monts, who wrote it *Acadie* and who in 1604 established a French colony in the district so designated. This colony on the Bay of Fundy in Acadia was the first permanent French settlement in North America. Most of the people popularly known as Acadians, however, were descended from a number of families established there in 1633 under the leadership of Isaac de Razilly. It is very likely that the spelling of the name of the colony was influenced by the classical *Arcadia* of Greece. In fact it is believed that the Florentine navigator Giovanni de Verrazano, who made a voyage of exploration for the French crown in 1524, actually gave the name *Arcadia* to a part of the coast in that region. The forced removal and dispersal of 3,000 Acadians among the other colonies by the British in 1755 is the theme of Longfellow's *Evangeline*. After the peace of 1763 about 800 of these former inhabitants of Acadia found their way back to their homeland and among their descendants the name *Acadien* is still current. Many of the Acadians settled in the Teche region of Louisiana, often known as the Evangeline country, and persons reputed to be of Acadian French descent are locally known as *Cajuns*, a corrupted form of *Acadians*.

Who said: "The style is the man himself"?

Georges Louis Leclerc de Buffon (1707–1788), French naturalist and writer, is believed to have originated the famous aphorism, *Le style c'est l'homme même*, "The style is the man himself." He used it in his address delivered when he was admitted into the French Academy in 1753. The saying is generally shortened to, "The style is the man."

How did rabbits almost ruin Australia?

Rabbits and hares originally did not live in Australia and New Zealand. About 1850 a man in the province of New South Wales turned loose three pairs of common English rabbits. They increased and spread so fast that within ten years they became a national pest and a menace to the agriculture of Australia. Millions of rabbits threatened to drive farmers and ranchers out of business. Seven rabbits eat about as much as one sheep, and the stock-supporting capacity of the continent was reduced by one-fifth. Enormous sums have been spent in efforts to exterminate the pest. Weasels, ferrets and mongooses introduced for that purpose failed to distinguish between rabbits and poultry. Men trapped, shot, gassed and poisoned rabbits for government bounties, but the rodents, apparently free of all diseases, continued to multiply, to eat grass, to destroy crops and to bark trees. Fences at first were ineffective because the rabbits soon learned to dig under or climb over them. Higher rabbit-proof fences, three feet high and sunk well into the ground, were next built, around whole districts as well as individual farms and gardens. One such fence a thousand miles long was built. Finally the Australians discovered how to convert the pest into cash and began to export yearly millions of dollars worth of frozen rabbit meat as well as rabbit skins for clothing and felt hats. Rabbits of the same kind got a foothold in New Zealand about 1875 and became such a pest that farmers seriously considered abandoning whole districts. A few rabbits placed on a tiny island in the Pacific multiplied so fast that they ate up all the vegetation and then starved to death. These are good examples of the danger incurred when the balance of nature is upset by transplanting animals from one part of the earth to another where their natural enemies and other checks are wanting.

Is one named "after" or "for" another person?

We may say correctly that a child is named either *after* or *for* another person. Both are recognized by good usage and both are used throughout the English-speaking world, although the former seems to be preferred in Great Britain and the latter in the United States. Some authorities, however, attempt to draw a slight distinction between the two phrases. *Named for*, they say, emphasizes the fact that the name was chosen "in recognition of," or "out of respect or honor" to somebody else bearing the name; as, George Felix Stimpson was named for Felix T. Cotten and his uncle George." On the other hand, *named after* emphasizes the fact that the name was suggested by that of another who achieved fame or significance before the one given the name was born; as, George Washington Glick was named after George Washington." Persons and places may be *named after* other persons and places. Likewise, *named from* implies that the person or thing was named because of some condition or fact that existed and bore the name before; as, "Kenesaw Mountain Landis was named from the Battle of Kenesaw Mountain." But these distinctions appear to be too fine to be generally observed.

What does "Helgoland" mean?

The tiny island lying in the North Sea 28 miles off the northwest coast of the German mainland is generally called *Heligoland* by the British and *Helgoland* by the Americans. The first element of the name is from a Teutonic word meaning "holy" and the name literally means "holy land." It is believed that the island received its name from the presence there of some kind of religious shrine in ancient times. One authority says the ancient Angles, from whom the English get their name, used to go to this island to worship in the temple of Hertha. Helgoland is only about 150 acres in area, although its sheer red sandstone sides rise 200 feet above the sea. The island was much larger in area within historic times and is still gradually reduced by sea erosion. For a thousand years sea rovers fought for this dreary island in the North Sea. During the Middle Ages Helgoland belonged to the dukes of Schleswig-Holstein who several times hocked it to the free city of Hamburg for ready cash. In 1807, during the Napoleonic Wars, Great Britain obtained possession of it from Denmark, but in 1890 Britain traded it to Germany for Zanzibar, a large island in the Indian Ocean lying 23 miles off the eastern coast of Africa and often called the Isle of Cloves because it produces the greater part of the world's supply of that spice. The trade turned out to be a bad bargain for Britain. Germany used Helgoland as a naval base against Britain in the First World War. The Treaty of Versailles provided that Germany should remain in possession of Helgoland on condition that she dismantle all fortifications and not fortify it again. But Germany refortified the island heavily later and proceeded to use it as a naval and air base against Britain in the Second World War. Helgoland really consists of two islets that were connected by a neck of land until 1720 when a violent sea eruption separated them. The larger, Rock Island, has an area of 21 acres and normally 2,000 or 3,000 inhabitants. Unterland, or Lower Town, on the shore below is connected with Uberland, or Upper Town, only by a stairway and elevator. The smaller island is little more than a sandbank. The waters between Helgoland and the mainland are known as the Bight of Helgoland, which in 1914 was the scene of a British victory over the German fleet in the first important naval engagement in the First World War.

Who said: "A man's house is his castle"?

The thought expressed by the proverbial legal maxim, "A man's house is his castle," is very ancient and of obscure origin, but the language in which it is now clothed seems to be traceable to Sir Edward Coke (1552–1634), the great oracle of the English common law. In the third volume of his *Institutes*, published in 1628, the former Chief Justice said, "A man's house is his castle," and in Semayne's Case, decided in 1605, he declared that, "The house of every one is to him his castle and fortress, as well for his defense against injury and violence as for his repose." But John Manningham had already written in his *Diary* in 1602: "His house . . . is his castle." Shakespeare may have alluded to this maxim in *The Merry Wives of Windsor* (written about 1599) when he had the host of the Garter Inn direct Simple to Sir John Falstaff's room: "There's his chamber, his house, his castle, his standing-bed, and his truckle-bed." Coke was born twelve years before Shakespeare and survived him eighteen. The legal principle embodied in "A man's house is his castle" is much more comprehensive than many people suppose. It means that a home is inviolable not only to arbitrary invasion and search but also to officers armed with legal warrants. No officer, according to this maxim, may force open the door of a home if the occupant refuses to admit him. In practice, however, the principle applied only to civil cases. "No outward doors of a man's house," wrote William Blackstone in 1765, "can in general be broken open to execute any civil process; though in criminal cases the public safety supersedes the private." In a speech in the House of Commons on the Excise Bill in 1760 the Elder Pitt graphically illustrated the importance of this legal maxim to the ordinary citizen: "The poorest man may in his cottage bid defiance to all the force of the crown. It may be frail, its roof may shake; the wind may blow through it; the storms may enter,—the rain may enter,—but the King of England cannot enter; all his forces dare not cross the threshold of the ruined tenement." An Irish lawyer trying a case before Justice John Toler (1740–1831), the first Earl of Norbury, said of his client's home that the rain might enter but not the King. "What," exclaimed the jurist, "not even the reigning King?"

How did "corduroy" originate?

Corduroy, the name of a thick, coarse and durable cotton fabric with the surface corded, ridged or ribbed like velvet, is believed to be derived from the French corde du roi ("cord of the king" or "king's cord"). What the original application or significance of the name may have been is not known. The oft-repeated assertion that the term was at first applied to a fine cloth manufactured in France and worn by the king and his suite when hunting seems to be a pure invention, unsupported by a particle of etymological evidence. It probably originated as a theory to account for the odd name of the cloth. Another theory, cousin-german to this, holds that the original form of the word was colourduroy or couleur de roi ("king's color"), that is, the royal purple. That too is no more than a guess. Apparently corduroy is of English rather than French origin, for neither corduroy nor corde du roi occurs in French as the name of a fabric. On the contrary, the Oxford dictionary points out, a list of articles manufactured at Sens in France in 1807 included kingscordes, indicating that the term was borrowed from English and was foreign to French at that time. The earliest use of the term found thus far occurred in 1795 when the Hull Advertiser referred to "old corduroy breeches." In 1722 the London Gazette mentioned "a grey duroy coat"; in 1746 a writer listed "Serges, Duroys, Druggets, Shalloons" etc., and after his marriage to Martha Custis in 1759 George Washington ordered through his London agent "a light summer suit of Duroy." But no direct relation between duroy and corduroy has been established. Corduroy is an English surname and it is not improbable that the fabric took its name from an early manufacturer; or perhaps corde du roi was adopted as a trade name of this article without any specific reference to French usage or to royalty. In the early part of the nineteenth century corduroy was applied to a kind of rough road built in America by laying logs side

[45]

by side transversely. Rough and tough corduroy is sometimes used as a substitute for mercury-coated copper plates to catch gold in placer mines and milling plants.

What is julienne soup?

Julienne is the name given by chefs and cooks to a clear meat soup containing finely cut herbs and vegetables, particularly carrots and onions. It is supposed to have been named after a French caterer named Julien who established himself in Boston about the time of the French Revolution. His restaurant was on Milk Street and was called the Restorator. In his La Physiologie du gout, a compendium of the art of dining, Anthelme Brillat-Savarin, French lawyer, economist and gastronomist, says that in 1794, while he was a refugee in America from the French Reign of Terror, he dined in Julien's restaurant in Boston and enjoyed the caterer's famous soupe julienne. It is possible, however, that the name had been applied to soup in France long before it was in America and that the Boston Julien was merely capitalizing on a name already familiar in cookery. Adolphe Hatzfeld and Arsène Darmesteter, in their French dictionary, say potage à la julienne in French dates back to at least 1722.

Do trees grow out of the ground or the air?

By far the greater part of a tree comes from the atmosphere, not from the soil as commonly supposed. Ordinary trees and plants, it is estimated, receive about 90 per cent of their nutrition from the atmosphere and only about 10 per cent from the soil. From the time of Aristotle until the eighteenth century even most naturalists supposed that the bulk of a plant comes from the ground. Plant fiber and tissue are formed by that amazing agent known as chlorophyl or green stuff, which uses the energy of sunlight to create starch, sugar and related substances by combining carbon from the air and water and other materials from the soil. Trees, shrubs and other plants eat carbon with their leaves and drink water with their roots. The leaves supply by far the greater amount of bulk, while the roots, besides anchoring the plant firmly, supply water containing other materials essential to the production of chlorophyl and the growth of the plant. Carbon, oxygen, hydrogen, nitrogen and sulphur are regarded as the elements essential to plant as well as to animal growth; but nine other elements—phosphorus, potassium, calcium, magnesium, iron, manganese, boron, copper and zinc—are important to healthy plant development. Excess water is given off by the leaves in the form of vapor. It has been estimated that an ordinary elm tree of medium size will transpire 15,000 pounds of water on a clear, dry, hot day. One authority estimated that an ordinary white oak tree may give off 150 gallons of moisture in a single day during the summer. The average tree may evaporate 80 gallons of water a day, and it has been estimated that a sizable oak tree will give off 28,000 gallons of water during one growing season. It is hard to believe, but true, that the great redwoods of California and the gums of Australia, hundreds of feet tall, receive the greater part of their bulk, not from the ground, but from the minute quantities of carbon floating in the air. Some plants grow unanchored in the water; others are parasitic on other plants and objects and derive all their nourishment from the atmosphere. Growing food plants in chemically treated water without soil is known as "tray farming." Vitalized sand has proved superior to soil in growing certain plants in greenhouses because it lasts longer, can be cleaned and sterilized more easily and does not produce weeds.

Why are the Moslems in the Philippines called Moros?

Moro is simply the Spanish form of Moor. The Moros are about half a million Filipinos living on Mindanao, second largest island in the Philippines, and on the Sulu (Jolo) archipelago, which comprises several hundred islands stretching toward Borneo. They were called Moros by the early Spaniards because they resembled the Moors of North Africa in being dark in complexion and Moslem in religion. The Spanish conquerors of the Philippines had just succeeded in expelling the Moors from Spain and they regarded the Moslem inhabitants of Mindanao and the Sulu Archipelago as natural enemies. The Moros were converted to Islam by Moslem missionaries from India in the fifteenth and sixteenth centuries. Although the Moros are not uniform in race and they speak various languages, they are chiefly of Malay stock with a sprinkling of Arab blood. The Moros in British Borneo are similar to those in the Philippines. When the Spanish arrived on the scene the Sulu Moros had engaged in piracy and regarded it as an honorable occupation for centuries. Their vintas, fishing boats hewn from single long logs, were marvels of workmanship and efficiency. The Sulus were good workers in metal and made excellent steel spears, knives and hatchets for use by their fierce warriors. They are devout Moslems and attached to their ancient feudal customs. Even the United States found it more practical to bribe the Sulu sultans with pensions than to try to subdue their ungovernable tribesmen. It was not until April, 1940, that Princess Hadji Piandao ("last Sultana of Sulu"), niece and adopted daughter of Sultan Jamalul Kiram II of Sulu, transferred legal ownership of hundreds of islands in the Sulu Archipelago to the Commonwealth of the Philippines and abandoned the ancient right of her royal family to govern the inhabitants. The present Sultan of Sulu is only spiritual and de facto ruler of the Moros.

What causes hail?

As a rule hail is formed chiefly during the summer. It generally falls over a small area in very hot weather at the beginning of violent thunderstorms. Hailstones fall occasionally during the night and morning but more often during the afternoon. There are several theories respecting the formation of true or summer hail. One theory is that the hailstones are formed by the freezing of raindrops as they fall through strata of air varying in degrees of coldness. In other words, raindrops are carried so high by the uprush of air during a thunderstorm that they freeze. After freezing the raindrops fall back to a lower level. There they pick up more water and again are caught in an upward current and carried to the freezing levels. This is repeated several times until the hailstones get so heavy they fall through the rising air down to the ground. The theory is supported by the fact that true hailstorms almost always occur in the season when the difference in temperature between the upper and lower layers of atmosphere is most decided. No doubt some of the smaller hail is formed in this way; but the theory does not adequately account for the larger hailstones, which are usually formed in concentric layers around a central nucleus of snow and ice. Some scientists suppose such hailstones are formed around snowflakes that are blown violently by a whirling wind between two cloud layers of different temperatures. Others believe the snowflake starts in an upper cloud and falls through a number of clouds of varying temperature, each cloud adding its layer of ice and snow. Years ago French farmers put up "hail rods," similar to lightning rods, to "de-energize" the atmosphere and to prevent hail. Perhaps they were not so far wrong. Some authorities suspect that electrical attraction and repulsion have something to do with the formation of hail, since hailstones are closely related to thunderstorms. Sleet, or winter hail, consists of raindrops that have been frozen while falling through a surface layer of cold air.

Does rain clear the air?

The widespread popular belief that rain purifies the atmosphere appears to be unfounded. In 1936 the United States Public Health Service reported that automatic air filters in fourteen large cities in America showed no decrease of atmospheric pollution either during or after rainfall. Air free of dust and other impurities exists nowhere in nature. Of course, rain, snow and hail do remove some of the impurities from the air, but the investigation referred to indicates that the percentage is not large enough to *purify* the atmosphere in the popular sense.

What is birdlime?

Birdlime is a sticky substance used to entangle small birds by smearing it on twigs and other places where they are likely to alight. *Lime* in *birdlime* is derived from Latin *limus*, mud, slime, mire, dirt and filth. The word for glue is *Leim* in German, *lym* in Dutch and *lim* in the Scandinavian languages. In Old English any adhesive viscid substance was called lime. It used to be a common practice to catch birds with lime made from the middle bark of the European holly tree. Shakespeare refers to birdlime several times. In *Macbeth* Lady MacDuff says of her small son: "Poor bird! thou'dst never fear the net, nor lime, the pit-fall, nor the gin." Iago in *Othello* says: "I am about it, but, indeed, my invention comes from my pate, as birdlime does from frieze, it plucks out brains and all," which alludes to the fact that birdlime was often spread on the frieze or ornamental strip nailed to the outside wall of a building. The traditional method of making birdlime in England and northern Europe was to strip the middle bark of the holly from the tree in June or July, boil it in water for seven or eight hours and then let it ferment for several weeks, adding water if necessary. When the product assumed a mucilaginous form it was pounded in a mortar and worked under water with the hands until it was a viscid substance, greenish in color and tenacious enough to entangle mice and small birds. Birdlime of inferior quality can be made from the berries of the European mistletoe, from the breadfruit tree and from linseed oil. The use of birdlime is now prohibited by law in many parts of the world.

What is Kendal green?

Kendal green was a famous green woolen cloth widely worn by English foresters, hunters and outlaws in the fourteenth, fifteenth and sixteenth centuries. It received its name from the fact that it was first woven by Flemish weavers at Kendal in Westmoreland County. Cloth weaving was established at Kendal in the early part of the fourteenth century, during the reign of Edward III, by John Kempe of Flanders. Robin Hood and his followers, according to legend, habitually wore Kendal green. In Shakespeare's *I King Henry IV* Sir John Falstaff says to Prince Henry: "But, as the devil would have it, three misbegotten knaves, in Kendal green, came at my back, and let drive at me; for it was so dark, Hal, that thou couldst not see thy hand." The wild Prince then wants to know:

"Why, how couldst thou know these men in Kendal green, when it was so dark thou couldst not see thy hand?" Kendal, a town of some 14,000 inhabitants, still manufactures woolen cloth, but Kendal green is no longer made. It is supposed that the original green cloth made at Kendal by the Flemish weavers was colored with a dye obtained from the plant known as woadwaxen. Another famous green cloth widely worn by hunters, outlaws and foresters was manufactured at Lincoln and was known as Lincoln green. It was dyed to resemble light green leaves.

Why are cockroaches called Croton bugs?

Certain small cockroaches, introduced into America from Europe, are called *Croton bugs* because they first became common around indoor water pipes in New York City about 1842, when the aqueduct carrying water from the Croton River was completed. It is supposed that the Croton River, a tributary of the Hudson, is a corruption of an Algonquian Indian word signifying "he struggles." *Croton* as applied to a genus of plants, one species of which is the source of a famous vegetable oil, is from a Greek word meaning "tick" and refers to the fact that the seeds of these plants were thought to resemble ticks.

How did Lloyd's get its name?

The Lloyd's association of underwriters received its name from the fact that it was loosely formed by a group of marine underwriters who were in the habit of meeting in a London coffee shop established in 1688 by Edward Lloyd. In 1774 "Lloyd's Rooms" were moved to their present quarters in the Royal Exchange. It was not until 1871 that Lloyd's was incorporated by act of Parliament. Lloyd's now has more than eighteen hundred members and five thousand employees and is the largest body of individual underwriters in the world. The association is governed by a committee of twelve members and has strict membership requirements. One of the most widespread misconceptions is that Lloyd's is "an insurance company." As an association Lloyd's does not write insurance. It is merely an insurance and business exchange and each member does business on his own account or in partnership with other members. The members, working in groups or "syndicates," write virtually every conceivable kind of insurance except life insurance. We often hear or read of Lloyd's underwriting this, that or the other kind of unusual risk or freak insurance. The fact is that all risks are accepted or rejected by individual or group underwriters who are members of Lloyd's and who must observe the regulations of the association. All policies are written on a yearly basis and gambling and betting by the members is forbidden.

Lloyd's, like a stock exchange, guarantees nothing that its members do. Besides providing a meeting place and facilities for its members, Lloyd's collects, classifies and disseminates important shipping information. Shipping news received at "Lloyd's Rooms" has been published daily in Lloyd's List since 1800. In normal times, unusual events, such as a lost or overdue ship, are announced by ringing the "Lutine bell." This bell, which hangs in a clock-topped tower in "Lloyd's Rooms," was salvaged from the frigate Lutine, a British bullion ship that was wrecked off the Netherlands coast in 1799 with some 1,000,000 pounds sterling in gold on board.

Why do Chinese say "Melican" for "American"?

Chinese say Melican or Amelican for American because their language contains no r sound and they substitute the l sound in pronouncing English and other words in which the r sound occurs. Even some Chinese brought up and educated among English-speaking people have considerable difficulty in mastering this sound. The Japanese language, on the other hand, contains no l sound and Japanese commonly substitute r for l in pronouncing foreign words. Thus the Japanese is apt to say red for led, while the Chinese say led for red. The American defenders of Bataan Peninsula under General Douglas MacArthur are said to have taken advantage of the inability of the Japanese to pronounce the l sound. One of the tricks adopted by the Japanese was to attempt to pass the lines of the defenders of Bataan by passing the sentries at night dressed in American and Filipino uniforms. In an Associated Press dispatch from the Bataan front dated January 21, 1942, Clark Lee said: "The Americans discovered an infallible way to detect them, due to the inability of the Japanese to pronounce the letter l, which they say as r. They simply pick a password with numerous l's, such as lollapalooza. Sentries challenge approaching figures and if the first two syllables of lollapalooza, for instance, should come back as rorra, they open fire without waiting to hear the remainder." As a rule Chinese and Japanese do not overcome these difficulties in pronouncing r and l even with years of practice. The liquid consonant l and r tend to run into each other and they are supposed to be not only closely related in formation but also the last and most difficult consonants added to human speech. Demosthenes, the Greek orator who corrected his speech by speaking within sound of the sea with pebbles in his mouth, was unable to pronounce the sound expressed by the letter r. Imperfect enunciation of the r sound, in which it is made to sound like l, is called lallation, from Greek lalia, meaning talking or chat. R, which was probably added to human speech even later than *m*, requires the greatest flexibility of the vocal organs in utterance and consequently is the most likely to be dropped by slovenly speakers. Children frequently find it difficult to utter the r sound and resort to the Chinese practice of substituting *l*. John Wallis, English mathematician, logician and grammarian, wrote in 1658 that some of the New England Indians said *nobstan* for *lobster* because they were unable to utter either the *l* or r sounds. In his life of Cortes, Salvador de Madariaga says of the Indian woman Dona Marina: "The Aztects gave her the name *Malintzin*, made up of Marina (the sound r being unknown to the Mexicans, who imitated it, like the Chinese, with *l*) and the suffix *tzin*, conveying rank or nobility." Many educated Englishmen and Americans at the present time suppress the r sound at the end of a syllable or before a consonant and say *daw* for *door*, *laud* for *lord*, and so forth.

Why is a loud voice called "stentorian"?

Stentorian as applied to a very loud voice refers to the voice of Stentor, a Greek herald in the Trojan War, who, according to Homer, had a voice equal in volume to that of fifty ordinary men combined. In the *Iliad*, Book V, is the following reference to Stentor's voice: "And when they were now come where the most valiant stood, thronging about mighty Diomedes tamer of horses, in the semblance of ravening lions or wild boars whose strength is nowise feeble, then stood the white-armed goddess Hera and shouted in the likeness of great-hearted Stentor with voice of bronze, whose cry was loud as the cry of fifty other men: 'Fie upon you, Argives, base things of shame, so brave in semblance! While yet noble Achilles entered continually into battle, then issued not the Trojans even from the Dardanian gate; for they had dread of his terrible spear. But now fight they far from the city at the hollow ships.' " That was the original Stentorian shout.

What was the oath taken by the young men of Athens?

In ancient Greece, and in Attica particularly, a free-born youth upon reaching the age of eighteen and completing his secondary education was required to take an examination. If he passed he was enrolled on the list of his tribe as a citizen of the commonwealth. Such a youth in Athens was called an *ephebus*. He was provided with a uniform and for two years was maintained at public expense while he was put through a severe course in military and gymnastic training by being compelled to perform regular garrison duty. Two centuries before the Christian Era it became optional with a youth of Athens whether he would be an ephebus, and he was permitted to substitute two years of literary and philosophical studies

[52]

for the two years of military service. Before entering upon his training as an ephebus the young man of Athens was required to take the ephebic oath, which read substantially as follows: "We will never bring disgrace to our city by any act of dishonesty or cowardice, nor ever desert our suffering comrades in the ranks; we will fight for the ideals and sacred things of the city, both alone and with many; we will revere and obey the city's laws and do our best to incite a like respect and reverence in those about us; we will strive unceasingly to quicken the public's sense of civic duty; and thus, in all these ways, we will strive to transmit this city not only not less but greater, better and more beautiful than it was transmitted to us."

What is pewter?

Pewter, as originally made and used in making various vessels, consisted of a gray alloy of four parts of tin and one part of lead by weight. A more modern pewter of superior hardness and color is made by mixing tin and lead and certain other metals, such as zinc, bismuth, antimony and copper. Like the names of many other early alloys and metals, the origin of pewter, though widely discussed, is obscure. Articles of pewter were highly prized by the early American colonists. The fragment of a pewter spoon "by Joseph Copeland" and dated "Chuckatuck 1675" was found some years ago while excavations were being made on Jamestown Island in Virginia. During the Revolution many patriots melted down their pewter ware to obtain the lead for bullets.

What is a catchpole?

A catchpole, or catchpoll, is a constable, bailiff, or other petty law officer who serves warrants and makes arrests. The term comes through old French and English from medieval Latin *cacepollis*, one who chases fowls, and literally means a chicken catcher. *Pullet, poultry* and *polecat* are all derived from this old word *pullus*, meaning fowl, hen, cock or chicken.

How fast can a jack rabbit run?

The average jack rabbit can keep up a top speed of thirty-five or forty miles an hour for considerable distances. In a straight run a jack rabbit is quickly overtaken by greyhounds, but not by ordinary dogs, which are soon left behind. The jack rabbit, which is really a western American hare, makes bounds from ten to fifteen feet in length when running fast. An African species, the Cape jumping hare, when in full flight makes remarkable bounds of twenty to thirty feet. Ordinary rabbits get off to a quicker start than hares, and frequently they can outrun hares for the first twenty-five or thirty yards, but their top speed seldom exceeds thirty miles an hour. Individual jack rabbits may exceed forty miles an hour, but reports that these animals sometimes run ahead of automobiles at a speed of sixty miles an hour should not be accepted at face value.

What is the source of tortoise shell?

The original and true tortoise shell of commerce, used in making spectacle frames, combs and many other articles, is obtained from the shell of the hawksbill turtle, *Caretta imbricata*, the smallest but most beautiful of the sea turtles. This species is peculiar in having thin, curved, horny plates on the back that overlap like shingles on a roof or scales on a fish, each plate terminating in a saw-tooth point. These plates are transparent yellowish in color, mottled with black and brown. The substance when heated in oil can be fashioned into any required shape. Formerly tortoise shell was obtained for the market in some parts of the world in a barbarous manner. Living hawksbill turtles were held over a fire until the plates separated from the hard shell and were then turned loose under the mistaken impression that the reptiles would live and grow new plates on their shells. A substitute tortoise shell is now made synthetically. Whole turtle shells have been used for many purposes. It is said that Henry IV of France was cradled in the shell of a large turtle.

Why is a cow called "Bossy"?

Bossy is a general name for a cow, just as *Dobbin* refers to a horse and *Tabby* to a cat. The Latin word for ox or cow is *bos*, and it is probable that the first person to call a cow Bossy was equipped with both a knowledge of Latin and a sense of humor. Some authorities, however, suppose the term to be related in origin to the dialectic English word *boss calf*, a young calf. In the Teutonic languages there is a root word variously spelled *bos*, *boose* and *buss*, which means barn, stall or crib. The thought is that originally a *boss calf* was a calf kept in a barn or stall as distinguished from one grazing at large and that *bossy* as applied to a cow is derived from the same source. On the western plains before the Civil War a buffalo was called a boss and a buffalo calf a bossy.

How did the phrase "to curry favor" originate?

The phrase to *curry favor*, meaning to ingratiate oneself with another for ulterior purposes, is believed to be a corruption of the older phrase to *curry favel*. Centuries ago *Favel* was the general name for any horse that was roan, sorrel, chestnut or yellow in color. Some authorities derive the term from French *faveau*, the color of fallow land. Apparently in its original sense to *curry favel* meant merely to rub, comb and dress a chestnut horse. In the fourteenth century French satire entitled *Roman de Fauvel*, a sort of counterpart to *Reynard the Fox*, Fauvel is a fallow-colored horse symbolizing duplicity and cunning. Perhaps this satire influenced the significance of the phrase to *curry favel*, which came to mean obtaining the good will of another by means of flattery and officiousness. Some writers suppose the phrase to refer to a case in which the favor of a master was won by a groom through attentions to a favorite horse Favel. The theory that to *curry favor* is a corruption of to *curry favel* is borne out by the fact that in German a phrase literally meaning to "rub down the chestnut" signifies to flatter or cajole.

How many front toes does a parrot have?

Most birds have four toes on each foot, three in front and one behind. Members of the parrot and woodpecker families are yoke-toed; that is, two of the toes point forward and two backward. This yoke-toed characteristic is found among even such members of the parrot family as the road runners, cuckoos and kingfishers.

What is a rain crow?

The American cuckoo is known to country people as the rain or storm crow because its plaintive note—interpreted as *koo, koo, koo*, and generally heard when the bird is concealed in a wood or thicket—is regarded as a sign of rain or storm. These birds, unlike their European cousins, are not parasitic and do not lay their eggs in the nests of other birds.

Do male and female songbirds migrate together?

In a general way it may be said that among migratory songbirds the old males start north first in the spring toward the summer nesting region and are followed later by the young males and the females. There are, however, many exceptions to this rule, even among birds of the same species. Frequently large flocks of male red-winged blackbirds reach a given locality in the spring before any of the females arrive. In the United States the first robins, song sparrows, rose-breasted grosbeaks, scarlet tanagers and many other species of songbirds are almost invariably males. It appears that among these species the male arrives early, selects the nesting area, takes "territorial possession," attempts to protect his domain from other males and is on hand to invite the females to inspect the home he has chosen. It is said that the male long-billed marsh wren not only arrives in the nesting area before the female but builds dummy nests while he is waiting for a mate. The males and females of other species migrate together and start nest building soon after their arrival at the breeding grounds. Wild ducks and geese are said to do their courting while migrating and are mated and ready to raise families the moment they reach their destination. We do not have sufficient information to say whether, in the case of the majority of songbirds, the males and females return South in the fall together or separately.

How do compound and simple fractures differ?

It is surprising how many people think that a simple fracture is one in which the bone is broken in only one place and a compound fracture one in which the bone is broken in more than one place. These terms do not refer to the number of times the bone is broken. A simple fracture is one in which the bone is broken in one or more places but in which the skin is not broken and there is no communication between the injury and the external air that might result in infection. A compound fracture is one in which the bone is broken in one or more places but in which the skin and integuments are lacerated and there is communication between the external air and the injury. In other words, a bone broken in only one place may constitute a compound fracture, while a bone broken in many places may constitute only a simple fracture. Generally in the case of a simple fracture the doctor can readjust the fractured parts of the bone and let nature do the rest; but in the case of a compound fracture, where a broken bone protrudes through the skin and produces an open wound, he must also provide protection against infection from without.

How does a shire differ from a county?

Shire, the name of an administrative district in Great Britain, is now generally synonymous with *county*. Americans often erroneously use both terms in connection with counties in England and speak of *the county of Derbyshire*, forgetful of the fact that *shire* and *county* mean the same. We should say, of course, either *Derbyshire* or *the county of Derby*. When used alone *shire* is pronounced to rhyme with *wire* and *sire*; when used at the end of a county name it is pronounced *shirr* or *sherr*. The division of England into shires resulted from the partition of the country among local chieftains in early times. There are two theories as to the origin of *shire*. One derives it from the root of *shear*, "to cut off." According to this theory, *Berkshire* is a corruption of *Baroc's share*, "the share of Baroc," an important chieftain. The other theory derives *shire* from Anglo-Saxon *scir* (probably cognate with *scirian*, "to distribute" or "to appoint"), meaning official charge, office or administration. In either case the term seems to be derived from a root signifying "to divide" or "to partition." *Sheriff* is from the roots of *shire* and *reeve*. The sheriff was originally the reeve of the shire or the king's representative in the county. The Arabic *sherif* or *shereef* (*shrf* in vowel-less Arabic) literally means "honor," "noble" or "great one" and is not etymologically related to English *sheriff*. Under Norman rule the Anglo-French *counté* (from Latin *comitatus*, the domain of a count) was introduced as a substitute for *shire*. In England *shire* is not restricted to counties. The term survives in *Richmondshire* and *Hallamshire*, in Yorkshire, and *Norhamshire* and *Hexamshire* in Northumberland. These districts were once regarded as distinct entities. Many people in England restrict *shire* to these districts and those counties having names ending in *shire*, such as Berkshire, Derbyshire and Wiltshire. The inhabitants of East Anglia, Kent, Sussex and Surrey do not generally apply either *shire* or *county* to their own counties, but refer to the rest of England as *the shires*, which is also a general designation of Leichester, Rutland and Northampton as "hunting country." The English regularly shorten several of the names of their shires. For instance, *Berkshire* becomes *Berks; Wiltshire, Wilts, Buckinghamshire, Bucks* and *Hampshire, Hants.*

Do fish swim backwards?

Fish can and occasionally do back up in the water, and many species regularly face the current and drift downstream tail first, but no known species is equipped to swim backwards at full speed for any considerable distance.

How did "companion" originate?

The ultimate sources of the English word *companion*, as well as of *company*, are the Latin *com*, with or together, and *panis*, bread; and the underlying idea embraced in the term is that of messmate or one who eats with another. *Comrade* had a similar origin. Indirectly it is from the Latin *camera*, chamber, and the essential thought behind it is roommate or one who shares the same chamber.

Why is a stale joke or worn-out story called a chestnut?

Chestnut in the sense of a stale joke or worn-out story is believed by some to be derived from the old fable about the monkey that used the paws of a cat to rake roasted chestnuts from the fire. But no satisfactory explanation has ever been offered for this slang or colloquial term. The generally accepted story is that *chestnut* in this sense originated in a play entitled "The Broken Sword," in which the chief characters are Captain Zavier, a Baron Munchausen type of storyteller, and Pablo, a comic person. This play contains the following colloquy:

> CAPTAIN ZAVIER: I entered the woods of Collaway, when suddenly from the thick boughs of a cork tree—
> PABLO: A chestnut, Captain; a chestnut.
> CAPTAIN ZAVIER: Bah, I tell you it was a cork tree.
> PABLO: A chestnut; I guess I ought to know, for haven't I heard you tell this story twenty-seven times?

An English-born Philadelphia actor named William Warren (1767–1832), who had played the part of Pablo, was at a stage dinner when one of those present told a story that he had often heard. Warren, taking his cue from the play, remarked: "A chestnut; for haven't I heard that story twenty-seven times?" From this incident, it is said, *chestnut* acquired its meaning of an old joke or stale story. But the association of the chestnut with weariness and satiety may be ancient. In his *Art of Love* Ovid says: "Let your boy take to your mistress grapes, or what Amaryllis so delighted in; but at the present time she is fond of chestnuts no longer." This appears to be an allusion to Virgil's *Second Eclogue* in which the Latin poet tells how chestnuts pleased Amaryllis, the shepherdess who became the symbol of sweethearts.

Do funeral processions create public rights of way?

There is an old English belief, which has been transplanted in America, that the carrying of a corpse over private ground creates a general right of way and makes it a public or open road. This notion, which still occasionally crops up in England in connection with the legal determination of the status of by-roads, is without basis either in statutory or common law, and its origin is not known for certain. In *English Folklore* A. R. Wright says: "The dead . . . were carried to burial, as a mark of honor, by the old and well known ways and never by a new road or short-cut, even if this involved a roundabout journey. It is possible, though I do not offer it as a satisfactory belief that, if the corpse did chance to travel another path, that became *ipso facto* a high road." No doubt another circumstance entered into the genesis of the belief. When courts undertook to decide whether a certain road was public or private it would, in the absence of formal evidence, hear testimony as to the uninterrupted use of the road by the public. Deaths and burials are more likely to impress themselves upon the memory than are ordinary events and the witnesses would recall funeral processions that had passed over the route long years before. More than a century ago funeral processions were exempted by law in England from paying tolls. Perhaps the same explanation applies to a similar belief, namely, that any ground over which the king passes in royal procession thereby becomes a public road forever.

What monkeys use their tails in grasping?

Many of the New World monkeys, notably the spider monkeys of Central and South America, have strong prehensile tails, with which they grasp, climb and swing in a remarkable manner. No Old World monkeys, not even the long-tailed ones, employ their tails as a "fifth hand." All the large manlike apes are tailless. The tails of some of the New World monkeys are amazing organs. The underpart of the tails of these monkeys is hairless and is scored with lines similar to those of the human finger joint. But not all the monkeys of the New World are equipped with "fifth hands." For instance, the tails of the Douroucolis monkeys of Brazil and Guiana and those of the Marmosets are not prehensile.

How did the dandelion get its name?

The common plant known as the dandelion received its name from the fact that the jagged edges of its leaves are popularly fancied to resemble the teeth of the lion. *Dandelion* is a sixteenth century English corruption of the French *dent de lion*, literally "lion's tooth," the name the plant bears in several European languages. The dandelion was introduced into the United States from Europe. Its roots, like those of chicory, are sometimes used as a substitute for coffee.

Is a sardine a particular species of fish?

In the strict sense of the term, *sardine* is not the name of a species of fish and there is no such thing as a living sardine. The original and true sardine is the cured and preserved young of a species of pilchard common in western European waters. It is supposed, though not established beyond question, that the sardine received its name from Sardinia, second largest island in the Mediterranean, either because this fish was abundant in neighboring waters or because it was first caught and packed there. The species from which true sardines are made is known scientifically as *Clupea pilchardus*. Later the English applied *sardine* to the young of the Cornish pilchard. Nowadays, both popularly and com-

[59]

mercially, the term is applied to several small food fish, found in both Atlantic and Pacific waters, whether fry or adults, which resemble the original sardines in having rich flesh and delicate bones that make them suitable for preserving in vegetable oil and packing in airtight cans. The New England sardine is a young herring, while the California sardine is a young pilchard of a species common to Pacific waters.

How much is a sou?

A sou, figuratively speaking, is the current coin of smallest value. We say of a poor person that he hasn't a sou, cent or penny. The term was borrowed from the French, who have applied it to a coin since about the fourth century. The French government has not for many years struck off a coin specifically and officially called a sou, but before the Second World War the term was popularly applied in France to the bronze five-centime piece, which was worth one-twentieth of a franc. In Roman times the sou was a gold coin; during the reign of Philip Augustus in the twelfth and thirteenth centuries the name was transferred to a silver piece; and in the eighteenth century the sou became a copper coin representing the twentieth part of a livre.

Who was "the inspired idiot"?

That was the name applied by Horace Walpole, the English politician, wit and man of letters, to Oliver Goldsmith (1728–1774), Anglo-Irish poet, novelist and playwright. Among his friends Goldsmith was known as Noll, a familiar form of Oliver. Though an unquestioned literary genius, he was possessed of few advantages in personality and physique, was supersensitive and self-conscious, and was notorious for his confused thought, silly remarks, foolish blunders and idle chatter in private conversation, which contrasted sharply with his inimitable writings. "Noll," said the active David Garrick, "wrote like an angel, and talked like a poor Poll." Goldsmith's old friend and mentor Samuel Johnson pronounced the final verdict: "Let not his frailties be remembered; he was a very great man."

How is "gums" pronounced?

Gums, referring to the dense, fleshy tissues in which the necks of the teeth are embedded, is now correctly pronounced gumz, with the u sounded as in chewing gum. The pronunciation goomz, rhyming with looms, is rejected by all authorities, but there is historical reason for it and it still survives in dialects. Gums, which is the plural of gum, is from Anglo-Saxon goma, meaning "palate." The o is believed to be a substitution for *ou* and the plural was sometimes written *goomys* by the Anglo-Saxons. In Robert Burns's *Holy Willie's Prayer* it is spelled *gooms*. Occasionally the singular form *gum* is applied to the fleshy tissues attached to a single tooth. It is not related to the same word in the sense of a tree or resinous substance.

Is there such a word as "heighth"?

Heighth, or *highth* as it was spelled by John Milton, is an obsolete form of *height*. It is a carry-over from the English of the Stuart period and survives in Ireland as well as in the United States. Many people erroneously pronounce *height* as if it were spelled *highth*. *Hite*, rhyming with *kite*, is the only recognized pronunciation.

What was Lafayette's first name?

The full name of Marquis de Lafayette, the French general who served in the American Revolution, was Marie Joseph Yves Gilbert Du Motier Lafayette. Oddly, the first name of his wife was Marie also. Before her marriage she was Marie Adrienne Françoise de Noailles. Lafayette was not known by his first name because at the age of two he succeeded to his father's title and was referred to during the rest of his life as Marquis de Lafayette. George Washington often referred to Lafayette simply as *Fayette*.

Where was Julius Caesar killed?

There is a popular notion that Julius Caesar was killed in the Capitol at Rome; actually he met his death at the foot of Pompey's statue in the senate house in a different part of the city. *Capitol*, or *Capitolium* as it was written in Latin, was not applied by the Romans to the building in which the senate or legislative branch of the government held its sessions; the word in that sense is an American adaptation. The Capitolium in Rome was the ancient citadel and the national temple of Jupiter Optimus Maximus, both of which were on Mons Capitolinus or Capitoline Hill, the smallest but most famous of the seven hills on which the city was built. The Curia or senate house was in the forum, which was not on Capitoline Hill at all, but between that elevation and Palentine Hill. It was called Curia Hostilia, owing to a tradition that the first senate house was built by an ancient king named Hostilius. Shakespeare and other Elizabethan writers were largely responsible for the prevalent impression that Caesar was murdered in the Capitol or that the Capitol and the senate house were one and the same building. In *Antony and Cleopatra* Sextus Pompey alludes to the subject when he refers to Brutus drenching "the Capitol," and in *Hamlet* Polonius says that he once played the part of Julius Caesar and was killed "in the Capitol" by Brutus. The "foremost man of all the world" is represented in *Julius Caesar* as being assassinated in the Capitol, but reference to the senate house indicates that Shakespeare employed the terms interchangeably.

What is the Tyler grippe?

Some time between 1841 and 1845, when John Tyler was President of the United States, a Bostonian called at the White House and was presented to the Chief Executive. A few hours later the Hub man contracted influenza, or grippe, and he facetiously told his friends that apparently he had caught cold from shaking hands with the President, who had the reputation of being formally cordial, but courtly and cold rather than warm in his manner. After that influenza was popularly called the Tyler grippe, the term being suggested by a pun on the word *grip*, the grasp in shaking hands. Newspapers took up the term and it was common for several decades, although it is now seldom heard. The epidemic catarrh known as grippe or *la grippe* has been recognized as a specific disease since the early part of the fourteenth century. During the seventeenth century the Italians named it influenza because their astrologers attributed it to the *influence* of the planets or stars. Persons in Ohio who were carried away by a similar disease in 1816 died of the "cold plague."

How do elephants bend their legs in lying down?

When an elephant lies down it extends the hind legs backward and the front ones forward. All other large quadrupeds, including horses, bring the hind legs forward in lying down. Formerly it was believed that elephants had no joints at all, and in his *Vulgar Errors*, published in 1646, Sir Thomas Browne advanced proof to correct the popular impression. "The elephant," wrote Shakespeare in *Troilus and Cressida*, "has joints, but none for courtesy; his legs are legs for necessity, not for flexure." Elephants are peculiar among quadrupeds in that the knee joints of the hind legs as well as those of the front ones are in front and the angle formed by the bent knee of both hind and front legs is toward the head. When an elephant lies down it kneels like a man, with the knees actually touching the ground. The stout, perpendicularly set, pillarlike legs of the elephant enable it to support its enormous weight, to sleep while standing and to climb and descend steep declivities with remarkable ease. In spite of their great bulk and their postlike legs, elephants can lie down and rise with ease when they want to, but apparently they seldom want to. The Asiatic elephant often lies down to rest and sleep, but the African species seldom lies down except occasionally to roll. Frederick C. Selous, English author and African game hunter, said he had seen several thousand wild elephants in Africa sleeping while standing, but had never seen one of them lying down nor found any impress on the ground, or any other evidence to indicate that they ever did so.

Does a rising fog indicate fair weather?

Weather experts say fog is not a dependable weather sign. A fog is merely condensed water vapor and differs from a cloud only in being closer to the ground. The popular notion that a rising fog is a sign of fair weather and a settling fog a sign of foul weather has only a slight basis in fact. On this subject the United States Weather Bureau says: "The familiar saying that a rising fog signifies clearing weather and a settling one foul weather applies to mountainous or at least hilly regions, and the fog in question is more of the nature of a low stratus cloud on the mountains or hills. With increasing humidity the clouds often settle lower and lower until rain actually begins, and with the oncoming of drier air the clouds lift higher until finally cleared away. Hence, in part, the source and more or less justification of the familiar saying." Oddly enough, many people believe that a rising fog indicates foul weather, because the moisture rises and must fall again, and a settling fog indicates fair weather, because the moisture comes down and clears the air.

Is "bad success" good English?

Many people maintain that *success* is not susceptible of qualification by such words as *good*, *bad* and *complete* and that a thing is either a success or a failure. They argue that *bad success* is a contradiction in terms. Degrees of success, however, have been recognized in literary usage for several centuries and the qualification of the term by *good* and *bad* is justified by its historical development. Originally *success* meant "issue," "outcome," "result" or that which comes after. Every time the word is employed in the King James Version of the Bible— four in all—it is qualified by *good*. For instance, in *Joshua* 1:8 it is written: "This book of the law shall not depart out of thy mouth; but thou shalt meditate therein day and night, that thou mayest observe to do according to all that is written therein: for then thou shalt make thy way prosperous, and then thou shalt have *good success*." In *King*

[63]

Lear Shakespeare says "not sure, but hoping, of this *good success*," and in the third part of *King Henry VI* he says "things ill got had ever *bad success*." In the latter play *best success* also occurs. The Egyptian queen, in *Antony and Cleopatra*, prays that *smooth success* may be strewed before Antony's feet, and elsewhere in the same play Mecaenas and Agrippa wish Lepidus *good success*. In *Othello* Iago fears that his speech to the Moor may "fall into such *vile success*, as my thoughts aim not at." When Shakespeare wrote and when the authorized version of the Bible was translated *success* still retained some of its original meaning of "result," "issue" or "ending," and accordingly it was almost always qualified. *Bad cess to*, an Anglo-Irish phrase meaning *bad luck to*, is a corruption of *bad success to*.

Why are bananas picked green?

All bananas, even those eaten locally in the tropics, are picked green. They are not fit to eat if permitted to ripen on the plants. People naturally presume that bunches of bananas are cut from the plants green to preserve the fruit during shipment and storage. Many fruits are picked green for that reason, but not bananas, which will not ripen satisfactorily on the plants. If allowed to turn yellow on the plant bananas lose their characteristic good flavor, the skin breaks open, bacteria and insects enter the inside, the fruit rots rather than ripens and becomes so unpalatable that it is worthless for human consumption. Only when bananas are picked while the fruit still has a green color will the starch in them turn to sugar and become desirable for food. Sometimes the sun turns bananas dark brown on the plant before they ripen. Such sunburned bananas are edible.

What city is known as the Bride of the Sea?

Venice is called the Bride of the Sea from the medieval ceremony known as the "marriage of the Adriatic," in which the Doge of Venice threw a ring into the sea, saying, "We wed thee with this ring, O sea, in token of our true and perpetual sovereignty." The ceremony symbolized the fact that the sea was subject to the republic of Venice as a wife is subject to her husband. A procession of gondolas, led by the Doge and his grandees in his state galley, the *Bucentaur*, was the chief feature in the ceremony, which was held on Ascension Day each year. In those days Venice was mistress of the Adriatic and her ships visited nearly every important port in the civilized world. The ceremony of the marriage of the Adriatic, it is supposed, was at first only supplicatory in character and originated during the dogeship of Pietro Orseolo I about the year 1000 A.D. Under this Doge the prestige of the republic was revived after a lapse. In 1177, when the peace between Pope Alexander III and Emperor Frederick Barbarossa was solemnized at Venice, the Pope gave the ceremony a nuptial character by bidding the Doge cast a ring into the sea each year in commemoration of the victory of the Venetian fleet at Istria over the Holy Roman Emperor's anti-papal forces. The first gold ring, according to tradition, was from the Pope's own finger. This ceremony was discontinued after Napoleon's armies overthrew the thousand-year-old republican government of Venice and the last doge, Lodovico Manin, abdicated in 1798.

What is the origin of "mob"?

Mob is a good example of a word that originated as slang and ultimately became sound English. It is derived from Latin mobile vulgus, "excited crowd." During the sixteenth and the early part of the seventeenth centuries the phrase was gradually shortened to mobile, which was a scornful term for the rabble, the masses, a tumultuous crowd bent on lawlessness, the disorderly and riotous part of the population, or the lowest order of common people. During the latter part of the seventeenth and the early part of the eighteenth centuries the term was further shortened to mob. At that time it was vigorously and violently attacked by purists as slang that had no proper place in respectable writing and speech. Richard Steele wrote in his Tatler: "I have done my utmost for some years past to stop the progress of mob and banter, but have been plainly borne down by numbers, and betrayed by those who promised to assist me."

What makes popcorn pop?

Popcorn was so called because when it is roasted or parched the kernel bursts open with a pop. Formerly it was supposed that the popping of corn was caused by the volatilization of air or oil in the grain. But experts now believe that popping in corn is an explosion due to the expansion under pressure of moisture in the starch grains when the kernel is dry heated. Popping seems to be an inherent characteristic of some varieties of corn. Popcorn, Zea mays everta, is a variety of corn that produces small stalks, ears and kernels. The wall of the kernel is harder than that of ordinary field corn, a fact that causes the entire kernel to explode when heated and to throw out the pure white pulp of the interior. When the moisture within the grain is heated it is converted into steam, and until the instant of the explosion the expansion is prevented by the hard exterior and the material in which the starch

[65]

grains are embedded. The explosion is due simply to the formation of steam within the grain when it is heated. Neither air nor volatile oil, experts say, is concerned in the process.

What are blue-sky laws?

Blue-sky laws are acts regulating the sale of stocks and bonds issued by corporations and investment companies. Their purpose is to prevent the public from being defrauded. The first blue-sky law was passed by the Kansas legislature in 1911 during a period of speculation. This act required investment companies to file with the state secretary of state a full description of their business and forbade them to sell securities until authorized to do so by the state bank commissioner. The majority of states soon passed similar laws. It is supposed that the popular name of these laws originated in the legislative committee that drew up the first law of this kind in Kansas. A member of the committee declared that many of the *wildcat* promoters, if they got a chance, would "capitalize the blue skies." Then, replied another advocate of the measure, restriction on investment concerns should be "as far-reaching as the blue sky." From this circumstance such acts became known as blue-sky laws.

Do flatirons get so they will not hold heat?

Housewives often complain that their flatirons get so they will not hold heat, particularly if they are left on the stove continually. A flatiron with a highly polished upper surface will lose considerably less heat by radiation than one having a blackened surface. If an iron, originally bright, were heated so as to tarnish this surface badly, it would lose its heat more rapidly than it did before. The difference, according to the United States Bureau of Standards, is large enough to be easily measured and might possibly be noticeable in ordinary use. Old-fashioned flatirons used to be known as *sad irons. Sad* in that connection is derived from Anglo-Saxon *saed*, "full" or "sated," and means "weighty," "ponderous" or "massive."

How did "news" originate?

Popular etymology derives *news* from the initial letters of the names of the four cardinal points of the compass—North, East, West and *South*. It is said that before the time of newspapers it was customary to post recent events and occurrences of general interest in public places under four columns headed N.E.W.S., the happenings from the north being recorded under N., those from the east under E., and so on.

Hence the word *news*. The theory is without foundation. *News* is merely the plural of *new*, and originally meant "new things." If any proof were needed to show the absurdity of the popular derivation, it is supplied in the fact that in the fourteenth and fifteenth centuries the word was variously written *newes*, *newis* and *newys*, when it was pronounced in two syllables. The medieval Latin form was *nova*, plural of *novum*, while the Anglo-Saxon form was *niwi*. Both signified "new things." The root of the term meant "recent" or "fresh." At one time *news* was construed as either singular or plural, and Shakespeare uses "this news" and "these news" interchangeably.

What is Canada's national anthem?

"God Save the King" is the only anthem that has official sanction in Canada. It is always played and sung as the official national anthem. But "The Maple Leaf Forever," with both words and music by Alexander Muir, is sometimes called the national anthem of Canada and in practice it is popularly treated as a second national anthem, being known by virtually every school child in Ontario and being widely sung throughout the Dominion. "O Canada," with music by Calixte Levallée and the French words by Judge A. B. Routhier, is probably the most distinctive patriotic song among the Canadians of French extraction. There are several English versions of this song. Neither "The Maple Leaf Forever" nor "O Canada" has any official recognition. Since 1926 the Dominion of Canada has been a self-governing member of the British Commonwealth of Nations and its status has been that of an independent nation with the same sovereign as that of Great Britain and other self-governing units in the British Empire.

Do rattlesnakes intentionally give warning?

The rattlesnake is the one species of venomous snake that gives warning before it strikes, and because of this characteristic it is sometimes referred to as "the gentleman among snakes." But it is doubtful that this reptile, the deadliest and most hated North American snake, is the gentleman and good sport it is sometimes represented to be. The rattles of a rattlesnake's tail are merely rings of dried and hardened skin that do not come off when the snake sloughs its skin, because of the button on the end of the tail. When the reptile is excited and poises to strike it nervously moves its tail and causes the rings of old skin to rattle. Naturalists do not subscribe to the popular belief that the rattlesnake's rattle is a deliberate warning. They believe rather that it is a nervous, protective action over which the snake has no control. Rattlesnakes are the only species that have rattles, but other species, such as the bull snake and the fox snake, vibrate the tail violently when they are excited, and when they are in contact with leaves or sand they make a sound similar to that of the rattlesnake. Charles Darwin observed that it is no more likely that a rattlesnake would give deliberate warning of its stroke than that a cat would warn a doomed mouse. He believed that the rattlesnake wiggles its tail for the same reason that the cobra expands its hood, the puff-adder spreads its head, the cat arches its back and the hen with a brood of chicks ruffles its feathers when frightened or threatened with danger. Most snakes are timid and avoid human beings. They generally try to escape when encountered and fight only when cornered. The deadly fer-de-lance (French for "iron of a lance," that is, "lancehead") is said to be one of the few venomous snakes that attack man without being molested. This aggressive native of Latin America is closely related to the rattlesnakes but has no rattles.

Who said that Hell hath no fury like a woman scorned?

"Hell hath no fury like a woman scorned" is the popular and improved version of a line in William Congreve's The Mourning Bride, a play produced in 1697. The exact words of Congreve's couplet are as follows:

> Heav'n has no rage like love to hatred turn'd,
> Nor hell a fury like a woman scorn'd.

Congreve borrowed the idea from Love's Last Shift, produced by Colley Cibber (sibb-ur) in 1696, a year earlier than The Mourning Bride. Cibber wrote: "We shall find no fiend in hell can match the fury of a disappointed woman,—scorned, slighted, dismissed without a parting pang." The famous line, "Music hath charms to soothe a savage breast," is also from Congreve's The Mourning Bride.

Who said he was a bold man who first ate an oyster?

In The History of the Worthies of England (1662) Thomas Fuller ascribed to King James I of England the saying, "He was a very valiant man that first adventured on eating oysters." No earlier reference to the saying has been found. "He was a bold man that first eat an oyster" occurs in Jonathan Swift's Polite Conversation, written in 1731 but not published until 1738. This work is a satire on worn-out and overworked phrases and expressions used in polite society, a fact indicating that "He was a bold man that first ate an oyster" was a proverbial saying even in Swift's time. The first person to eat an oyster probably lived many, many thousands of years ago, and it is not likely that he was imbued with any particular valor, boldness, bravery or spirit of adventure. In all probability oysters were among the primitive and natural foods of mankind. They are found along the seacoasts in many parts of the world and most peoples, even primitive ones, eat these bivalves as a matter of course when they are available. Oysters were first eaten because they taste good and because they are a nourishing and wholesome food when fresh or properly preserved.

Why is driving dog teams called "mushing"?

Mushing in the sense of traveling over the snow with sledge dogs has a curious origin. The early French Canadian *voyageurs* and *coureurs de bois* were in the habit of shouting *Marchons!* (literally "Let us march!") to their sledge dogs when they wanted them to start moving. It corresponded to the horse and ox driver's "Giddap" ("Get up"). English-speaking dog drivers in the Northwest corrupted *Marchons!* into *mush-on* and *mush on*. Dog drivers in Alaska and Canada still train their dogs to heed the commands, "Gee," "Haw," "Whoa" and "Mushon." In process of time *mushon* was shortened to *mush* and used as a verb to signify marching on foot over the snow with sledge dogs.

What is the motto of the United States Postal Service?

The traditional and unofficial motto of the United States Postal Service is: "Neither snow, nor rain, nor heat, nor gloom of night stays these couriers from the swift completion of their appointed rounds." These words are carved over the entrance of the central post office building in New York City. This motto is really a paraphrase of a reference to the ancient postriders of Persia in Herodotus, the Father of History, who wrote about 430 B.C. In 480 B.C., when Herodotus was three or four years old, King Xerxes of Persia, with a vast army and fleet, attacked Greece and captured and pillaged Athens. Later in the same year, however, the Greek allies destroyed the Persian fleet off Salamis, and Xerxes decided to withdraw his land forces into Asia. The King "sent off a messenger to carry intelligence of his misfortunes to Persia. Nothing mortal travels so fast as these Persian messengers," wrote Herodotus, according to George Rawlinson's translation. "The entire plan is a Persian invention; and this is the method of it. Along the whole line of road there are men, they say, stationed with horses, in number equal to the number of days which the journey takes, allowing a man and a horse to each day; and these men will not be hindered from accomplishing at their best speed the distance which they have to go, either by snow, or rain, or heat, or by the darkness of night. The first rider delivers his despatch to the second, and the second passes it to the third; and so it is borne from hand to hand along the whole line, like the light in the torch-race, which the Greeks celebrate to Vulcan. The Persians give the riding post in this manner the name of *Angarum*." In Esther 8:10 we are told that Mordecai the Jew wrote in the name of King Ahasuerus of the Medes and Persians and "sent letters by posts on horseback, and riders on mules, camels, and young dromedaries."

Which is correct, "Porto" or "Puerto" Rico?

On May 17, 1932, President Herbert Hoover approved the following joint resolution of Congress: "That from and after the passage of this resolution the island designated *Porto Rico* in the Act entitled 'An Act to provide a civil government for Porto Rico, and for other purposes,' approved March 2, 1917, as amended, shall be known and designated as *Puerto Rico*. All laws, regulations, and public documents and records of the United States in which such island is designated or referred to under the name of *Porto Rico* shall be held to refer to such island under and by the name of *Puerto Rico*." This resolution was introduced in the Senate by Hiram Bingham, of Connecticut, at the request of the Porto Rico legislature, and when it came up for consideration on the consent calendar February 17, 1932, Senator Clarence C. Dill, of Washington, objected. "Instead of making geography more difficult," he declared, "we ought to simplify it, and I think it is a ridiculous proposition to go back to an ancient spelling of the name." Previously the United States Geographic Board ruled that *Porto Rico*, not *Puerto Rico*, was the correct English spelling of the name of the West Indian island that was seized by force by General Nelson A. Miles in 1898 during the Spanish-American War and later annexed outright as a "possession" of the United States. *Puerto Rico* (pronounced pwer-toe ree-koe) is the Spanish spelling of the name, which literally means "Port Rich" or "Port of Riches" and which was given to the island by Columbus when he discovered it on his second voyage in 1493. The inhabitants themselves generally preferred the original spelling and before Congress finally acted they more than once petitioned the United States government to make *Puerto Rico* the official name of the island.

What birds fly under water?

The family of birds known as dippers and water ouzels exhibit remarkable agility under water and while submerged use their wings much as they do in flying. These birds, which are thrushlike in build, walk or run along the bottom of swift streams in search of insect larvae and small mollusks and crustacea. While thus submerged the birds continually move their wings like flippers to keep themselves down, for their bodies are only three-fourths as heavy as water and would rise like corks except for the wing motions. They are able to remain under water for short periods without getting wet because nature protects them from the chilly water by a coat of thick down underneath the feathers, which are kept oily by a gland under the tail. When a dipper or water ouzel moves from one place to another under water it uses its wings in a manner that all observers describe as "flying under water." From all appearances the bird manipulates its wings under water in exactly the same fashion that it does when flying in the air. Although not webfooted, birds of this family swim with ease on the surface. Some species build their nests behind waterfalls. "Subaqueous flight" is also characteristic of some other birds. Some of the little sea birds known variously as murres, guillemots and auklets dive into the water with half-opened wings and "fly under water." Cormorants make flying motions with their wings while diving in pursuit of fish, and penguins, which cannot fly, use their featherless wings like paddles to propel themselves beneath the surface of the water.

What are edible birds' nests?

Edible birds' nests are the natural nests of various species of small swifts that inhabit the mainland of eastern Asia, the Philippines and numerous Indian and Pacific ocean islands. Although swifts look much like small, dull-colored swallows, actually they are more closely akin to the New World hummingbirds. Ordinary swifts make their nests of twigs glued together with a mucous secretion from special glands in the mouth. They are found attached to the walls of cliffs, caves, chimneys and similar surfaces. But the little oriental swifts make their nests almost entirely of the secretion from the special glands in their mouths. The nest is about the size and shape of half a teacup. This dried glutinous substance, resembling fibrous isinglass or gelatin, is eagerly sought by Chinese epicures as the chief ingredient of a kind of soup, often flavored with the gravy of a boned fowl. These swifts nest in large numbers in caves and build thousands of nests together. Throughout the Orient there are Chinese engaged in buying, preparing and selling edible birds' nests. Frequently the birds' nests are mixed with feathers and other foreign substances and their original value depends on their color and purity. The nests are collected after the young swifts are fledged, and cleansing the dried mucus is a long and tedious process. So eager are Chinese gourmands for this delicacy that they have been known to pay the equivalent of twenty-five dollars or more for a pound of it. At one time the business ran into millions of dollars a year. In 1939 the Siamese government broke up the Chinese monopoly in edible birds' nests by adopting a "Birds' Nest Concession Act."

What is broadcloth?

Broadcloth formerly referred to cloth of double width, but as now popularly used, especially in the United States, the term denotes little more than cloth of good quality. In earlier days of weaving the width of cloth was much more important than at present. As early as 1482 we find "broad cloths," two yards wide, distinguished from "streits," one yard wide "within the lists." The English chronicler and antiquarian John Stow (1525?–1605), himself a tailor by trade, wrote that "King Henry the Eighth did weare onely cloath hose, or hose cut out of ell-broade taffety." As a measure of length the English ell was 45 inches. The term is derived indirectly from Latin ulna, "arm," and ellbow (elbow) was equivalent to "arm-bow," that is, the bow or bend of the arm. For centuries English weavers made a fine, plain-woven, dressed, black woolen cloth for special use by tailors in making men's garments. Originally this cloth was two yards wide and it is said that two weavers standing side by side were required to "fling the shuttle across it." Later the width was reduced to 54 inches. The best black cloth for men's clothes came to be known as broadcloth. In Epistle to Joseph Hill William Cowper wrote:

> An honest man, close-button'd to the chin,
> Broadcloth without, and a warm heart within.

Such broadcloth was generally fulled or felted; that is, the wool hairs of the weft and the warp were entangled to prevent unraveling when the cloth was cut. In course of time broadcloth was extended to any finely woven, firm, smooth-surfaced dark fabric whether of wool, cotton, silk or other material and whether used in men's or women's wearing apparel. In the United States the original meaning of the term has been completely lost sight of and now we even see "English broadcloth shirts" advertised.

How much of the moon's surface is visible?

The moon has three definitely understood motions. It rotates on its own axis, it revolves around the earth, and, along with the earth, it revolves around the sun. As it moves around the earth it rotates just enough to keep the same side toward the earth at all times. Accordingly part of the surface of the moon is never visible from the earth. The visible part does not consist of an even half of the total surface, as one might suppose, but about three-fifths. To be exact, fifty-nine per cent of the moon's surface is seen at one time or other, while forty-one per cent is not visible from the earth at any time. This is due to the fact that the rotation of the moon on its axis is not uniform; that is, it wobbles slightly, disclosing both of its poles at different times and making more than a hemisphere visible from the earth. The moon, the only heavenly body that revolves around the earth, makes one rotation on its axis and one revolution around the earth about every twenty-seven and one-half days; that is, it makes about thirteen trips around the earth each year.

How is the surname of Anne Boleyn pronounced?

Boleyn, the maiden name of the second wife of Henry VIII and mother of Queen Elizabeth, is correctly pronounced *bool-in*, the first syllable rhyming with *wool*. Anne Boleyn was the daughter of Sir Thomas Bullen, and in her time the name was spelled either *Boleyn* or *Bullen*. In Shakespeare's *Henry VIII* it occurs as *Bullen*, not *Boleyn*. It is also spelled *Bullen* on tapestries presented to her by Henry VIII and still preserved at Hampton Court. The pronunciation is the same for both spellings. Anne Bullen was about thirty-nine years old when Bluff King Hal had her beheaded in 1536.

Where is Flanders?

Flanders is the historical and popular name of a more or less indefinite district in Europe stretching along the North Sea from the Scheldt River to the entrance of the Strait of Dover and now lying in the Netherlands, Belgium and France. This region has been the scene of so many military campaigns since the days of Julius Caesar that it is known as "the cockpit of Europe." The bulk of old Flanders still retains the ancient name and includes the Belgian provinces of East and West Flanders. One of the royal princes of Belgium generally bears the title Count of Flanders. The remainder of Flanders lies mainly in the southern part of the Dutch province of Zeeland and the French departments of Le Nord and Ardennes. Sometimes in historical writing *Flanders* is loosely applied to an even more extensive part of the low countries. As the name of this district, *Flanders* occurs for the first time in the seventh century. Two centuries later most of this territory became a fief of France, and in 1384 it was united with Burgundy by the marriage of the daughter of the Count of Flanders to the Duke of Burgundy. During the

Middle Ages Flanders played a prominent role in the political and military affairs of the Continent and the counts of Flanders were richer and more powerful than many neighboring kings. At the time of the Reformation the region was one of the leading seats of manufacture, commerce and art. Shakespeare mentions Flanders twice. In *III Henry VI* when King Edward asks where they are to go, Hastings replies, "To Lynn, my lord; and ship from thence to Flanders." Cardinal Wolsey, in *King Henry VIII*, was charged by Suffolk with making bold "To carry into Flanders the great seal." The inhabitants of Flanders are called Flemings and their language Flemish. In the sixteenth century Flemish was the language of the court of Flanders and Brabant and it is still spoken by about half of the inhabitants of Belgium. It belongs to the Low German branch of the Teutonic tongues and is closely allied to Dutch.

How often does the year contain 53 Sundays?

According to the Gregorian calendar, every year has 53 of the day it begins on. Generally speaking, the year contains 53 Sundays every five or six years. "In any continuous series of 28 years," says the United States Naval Observatory, "five have 53 Sundays, unless the series includes a year whose number ends in two ciphers without its being a leap year, as 1700, 1800 and 1900." When leap year begins on Saturday two of the six-year periods fall consecutively.

What causes white specks on fingernails?

White spots and lines appearing on the fingernails are popularly known as "good luck spots" and they are said to be a sign of coming good fortune. These spots are merely imperfections in the nail. Nails are formed by the gradual fossilization of living cells into the nonliving tissue called "keratin." The specks result when some of the cells near the root of the nail fail to be converted completely into nail substance. As the nail grows these blemishes are pushed outward. They may be natural imperfections or they may be produced by any slight cut, bruise or injury near the line where the fresh nail is being formed. Not infrequently they are caused by careless manicuring or the nervous habit of "biting one's nails."

How does a dove differ from a pigeon?

Dove and *pigeon* are virtually synonymous. Both terms are applied almost interchangeably to members of the family *Columbidae*, which includes the domestic pigeons. There is no scientific distinction between pigeons and doves and even in general literature the two words are used interchangeably. When used without modification the words are coextensive in application. Every dove is a pigeon and every pigeon is a dove. Dove is derived from a Teutonic root of unknown origin and meaning, while *pigeon* is derived through French from a root signifying "little bird." *Pigeon* is now the more ordinary of the two terms. It is a somewhat broader term than *dove* and is applied in a general way to all members of the family in question. In plain prose *dove* is often applied to the smaller and wilder species to distinguish them from the larger and tamer ones more commonly called pigeons. Thus we speak of mourning doves, stock doves, ground doves, scaled doves, turtledoves, rock doves and wild doves. But even this distinction is not always made. In Great Britain the largest native species is called the ring or turtledove. Likewise we speak of wood pigeons, homing pigeons, pouter pigeons, passenger pigeons, ground pigeons, tumbler pigeons and wild pigeons. In the Bible and in Shakespeare *dove* and *pigeon* are used interchangeably for the same birds. *Dove*, however, is generally preferred to *pigeon* in poetry and in a sacred or "elevated style." Likewise *dove* is generally preferred when referring to this bird as the emblem of peace and the symbol of domestic bliss.

What was the longest reign in history?

The reign of Pepi II of the sixth Egyptian dynasty is believed to be the longest on record. James Henry Breasted, the Egyptologist, says Pepi II ascended the throne about 2566 B.C. at the age of six and reigned ninety-one years. The reign of Louis XIV of France is the longest on record since ancient times. He ascended the throne in 1643 at the age of five and reigned until his death in 1715—a period of seventy-two years. He outlived sons and grandsons in the direct line and was succeeded by his five-year-old great-grandson, Louis XV, who reigned fifty-nine years and who outlived his sons and was succeeded by a grandson, Louis XVI. Louis XIV and Louis XV occupied the throne 131 successive years. Prince John II of Liechtenstein ruled over his little principality from 1858 to 1929—seventy-one years. Francis Joseph of Austria-Hungary reigned nearly sixty-eight years—from 1848 to 1916. The longest reign in English history was that of Queen Victoria, who reigned longer than any other woman on record. She ascended the throne in 1837 and reigned until her death in 1901—sixty-four years. Her nearest rival in respect to length of service as sovereign of England was George III, who reigned sixty years—from 1760 to 1820. Henry III reigned fifty-six years—from 1216 to 1272. Pedro II was Emperor of Brazil from 1831 to 1889—fifty-eight years. Alphonso XIII of Spain, the posthumous son of Alphonso

XII, was proclaimed King when he was born May 17, 1886. When he was deposed in 1931 he had been on the throne fifty-five years. Queen Wilhelmina of the Netherlands, although not "inaugurated" until 1898, succeeded her father on the throne in 1890 and up to the present (1946) has reigned fifty-five years.

Why is a dead soldier's horse led at his funeral?

The practice of having the charger of a deceased military officer led in the funeral procession is a survival of the ancient custom of sacrificing a horse at the burial of a warrior. The Mongols and Tartars in the days of Genghis Khan and Tamerlane believed that the spirit of a sacrificed horse went through "the gate of the sky" to serve its master in the after-world. According to a European folk belief, the spirit of a dead horse would find its dead master if permitted to follow him into the hereafter. Otherwise the dead master's spirit would have to walk. When General Kasimer was buried at Treves as late as 1781 his horse was killed and placed in the grave with the dead general. Some of the Plains Indians in America adopted this custom after they came into possession of horses. In about 1800 Blackbird, an Omaha chief, was buried sitting on his favorite horse. Horses are no longer sacrificed in such cases, but sometimes a riderless horse is still led in a funeral procession as the symbol of a fallen warrior. When Abraham Lincoln's body was taken from the White House to lie in state in the rotunda of the capitol in 1865, the casket was followed by the dead President's horse with its master's boots in the stirrups. Likewise, when Franklin D. Roosevelt was buried at Hyde Park April 15, 1945, the caisson bearing the body of the dead President was followed by a colored trooper leading a riderless horse. The horse was hooded, sheathed in black and bore a saddle with the stirrups inverted and a sword through them. This symbolized the fact that the President as Commander-in-Chief of the armed forces of the nation in wartime had fallen as a warrior.

How do cement and concrete differ?

Many people speak of cement and concrete as if they were the same. Cement and concrete are not synonymous. Cement is merely one of the several ingredients of concrete, which is a mixture of sand or gravel and water that has been hardened by cement as the active agent. The purpose of cement is to bind the other solid materials, just as that of mortar is to bind bricks or stones. Just what causes cement to harden or "to set" is not completely understood. In a general way it is due to the decomposition of the components of lime when moistened. Calcium hydrate

[76]

is formed and this, upon crystallization, binds together the solid ingredients and produces concrete. It is supposed that the initial hardening is caused by the action of the aluminates and the final hardening by that of the silicates. The purpose of air spaces in concrete blocks is to lighten them and to facilitate their handling. Air spaces also make the blocks somewhat better insulators of heat. Ocean and canal barges of reinforced concrete were first made during the First World War. In recent years there has been developed a type of concrete so much lighter than ordinary concrete that it floats in water.

Why is tuberculosis called the white plague?

White plague as a common name for tuberculosis of the lungs is believed to have been coined by Dr. Oliver Wendell Holmes. At least the earliest known application of the term in that sense occurs in his *Elsie Venner*, which was first published in 1861 under the title *The Professor's Story*. The narrative deals with a country doctor who drove a Morgan mare hitched to an old-fashioned sulky. One clause reads, "—In the dead winter, when the *white plague* of the north has caged its wasted victims, shuddering as they think of the frozen soil which must be quarried like rock to receive them, if their perpetual convalescence should happen to be interfered with by any untoward accident—." *White plague* was probably suggested in contrast to *black plague* by the pallor associated with tuberculosis in advanced stages, by the great toll of life the disease takes, and by the insidious manner in which it claims its victims. At that time tuberculosis was much more prevalent in New England than at present and it was regarded as an incurable disease. Tuberculosis, formerly known as consumption, is one of the most widespread diseases. It occurs in all parts of the world, affects all races as well as lower animals, and it attacks every organ and part of the body. Tuberculosis of the lungs was described in ancient times by Hippocrates among the Greeks and by Galen among the Romans.

How do cantaloupes differ from muskmelons?

In popular American usage *cantaloupe* and *muskmelon* are virtually synonymous. Since the sixteenth century *muskmelon* has been applied to a group of musk-scented melons native to the Old World. They were cultivated by the ancient Egyptians and Romans and were introduced into the New World by the Spaniards. Scientifically they belong to *Cucumis melo*, which includes the true muskmelons, cantaloupes, rock melons, Persian melons and casabas. *Cantaloupe* is derived from *Cantalupo* Castle in d'Ancona, a former country seat of the popes near Rome,

[77]

where a variety of small, round, ribbed muskmelons were first grown in Europe from seed imported from Armenia. The earliest use of *cantaloupe* recorded by the Oxford dictionary is dated 1839. For many years true cantaloupes were supposed to be small, round, hard-shelled melons with little of the characteristic musky odor of the true muskmelons, a name applied specifically to the larger, nutmeg-shaped varieties with soft rind and netted surface markings. For instance, in Liberty Hyde Bailey's *Standard Cyclopedia of Horticulture* the musk-scented melons are classified in one group, which includes the nutmeg or netted melons and the cantaloupes or hard-rind melons. In other words, according to botanical authorities, the cantaloupe is merely one kind of muskmelon. But the question is confused by the fact that in the United States *cantaloupe* is used as a generic trade name for muskmelons in general. Botanically speaking, virtually all of the melons sold in the markets under the name *cantaloupes* are really muskmelons.

How did "let George do it" originate?

Let George do it is believed to have originated in France in the fifteenth century, the French being *laissez faire à Georges*. Apparently it originally had a satirical reference to the many activities of Cardinal Georges d'Amboise (1460–1510), Archbishop of Rouen and Prime Minister of Louis XII. Later it became a common saying and was translated into English without any comprehension of its original meaning. According to some authorities, it was Louis XII himself who first made this satirical allusion to his Prime Minister. Now the slang expression generally means, "Let the other fellow, or somebody who is willing, do it." The saying was popularized by the American cartoonist George McManus in his early comic supplement feature entitled *Let George Do It*.

Do all salmon die after spawning?

There are at least ten different known species of salmon. Only the members of a species common along the Pacific coast of the United States are known to die immediately after spawning. The odd thing is that all members of the species, the males as well as the females, die after the females get through laying their eggs. As the spawning season approaches these fish work their way as far as possible up streams. Some of them, before depositing their eggs, work their way up into brooks so shallow that their backs stick out. During this season the salmon get very thin, their eyes become sunken, their appetites grow smaller and smaller, their throats begin to narrow and their stomachs shrink until they become incapacitated for receiving food. When they have spawned they turn over and die, leaving windrows of rotting carcasses on the banks of the rivers and creeks. The members of other species of salmon do not all die after spawning, but large numbers of them, especially the males, do not survive the spawning season.

How do "thoroughbred" and "purebred" animals differ?

In popular usage *purebred* and *thoroughbred* are virtually synonymous. They both refer to animals that have been bred from the best blood through a long line and whose pedigrees have been recorded for a number of generations. *Pureblooded, registered* and *pedigreed* are used in a similar sense. All of these words, when used in the popular and general sense, apply to domestic animals of all kinds. It is equally correct to speak of purebred and thoroughbred sheep, cattle, hogs, and even chickens. Farmers often refer to such animals as *blooded stock*. Sometimes *thoroughbred* is extended to the vegetable world, and we hear of thoroughbred strawberries and other plants. However, when *thoroughbred* is applied to horses it has a specific meaning. Horse breeders like to restrict the term to breeds of running horses eligible to registration in the American Stud Book, the General Stud Book of England and affiliated stud books for thoroughbred horses in other countries. A thoroughbred horse must have a pedigree, but every pedigreed horse is not necessarily a thoroughbred. Likewise an animal may be registered without being either purebred or thoroughbred. A purebred or thoroughbred animal must be of one breed and of unmixed strains. To be a thoroughbred a horse's ancestors must be recorded in the studbook for several generations—five in America and seven in England. Some authorities, including the United States Department of Agriculture, favor restricting *thoroughbred* to thoroughbred horses exclusively and using *purebred* and *pureblooded* when referring to other animals.

What is caviar?

Caviar is a piquant table delicacy consisting of the prepared roe or eggs of various species of fish, particularly the sturgeons. It is generally used as a flavoring for other foods or spread on toast, flavored with a few drops of lemon juice and eaten as an appetizer or *canapé* with cocktails. Like olives, caviar is an acquired taste and seldom appeals to the uninitiated. Accordingly it has become the symbol of something choice and exclusive, a titbit beyond vulgar taste and popular appreciation. This sense was borrowed from Shakespeare's *Hamlet*, in which the Prince of Denmark refers to a play that was never acted "above once" because it "pleased not the million" and was "caviar to the general." Caviar, or caviare as it is also spelled, is believed to be of Tartar or perhaps Turkish origin and is generally pronounced kav-i-ahr or ka-vyahr with the last syllable accented. Oddly enough, the term occurs in one form or other in all the major European languages except Russian. Its earliest known occurrence in English was in 1591, about ten years before Shakespeare used it. The author of Hamlet spelled it caviarie and at that time it was probably pronounced in four syllables. Although the word itself does not occur in the Russian language, the product so styled has been a staple in Russia since ancient times. Archeologists have unearthed vats and stone platforms on which caviar was prepared for shipment to Rome two thousand years ago. Caviar is prepared particularly in Astra-khan and the other regions around the Caspian Sea, where sturgeon are caught in large numbers. It is expensive because the best grade can be prepared only in winter and because it is difficult to preserve. Great care must be exercised in cleaning and drying the roe. The eggs are loosened in the sturgeon ovaries by beating, strained through a sieve to remove muscular matter, freed of excess liquid, dried in the sun, salted and then packed in kegs or hermetically sealed cans. Several different grades and types of caviar are prepared in Russia. In 1935 the United States Department of Commerce issued a bulletin containing the following sentence: "Virtually all the red caviar being sold in Germany, it is pointed out, is displayed as of Russian origin, the terms Russian and caviar being so closely associated in the public mind as to prejudice the sale of goods labeled as from another source of supply." The sturgeon from which caviar is made is a bottom feeder and eats small fish and crustacea. A similar product is made from the roe of various other fish.

Why is a Master Mason's lodge called a blue lodge?

In Freemasonry a blue lodge is a symbolic lodge in which the first three degrees of Masonry are conferred. It was originally so called from the blue color of its decorations. One Masonic authority believes the blue in this connection symbolizes the heavens and alludes to ancient times when the members of the order held their meetings in the open under the blue sky. A Master Mason is a Freemason who has taken the third degree.

How is the compass boxed?

When a person adopts successively all possible opinions on a question he is said "to box the compass." This is merely a figurative use of a nautical expression of unknown origin. In the language of seamen "to box the compass" means to recite the names of the thirty-two points of the compass forward and then backward in consecutive order. A wind is said to box the compass when, within a short time, it blows from every quarter in succession. Boxing the compass is to go completely around and return to the starting point. A point of the compass is one of the thirty-two divisions or "rhumbs" or the angle between two adjacent divisions equal to 11¼ degrees.

Why are Italians called "dagos"?

Dago is believed to be a corruption of Diego, a common Spanish first or Christian name equivalent to James in English. So many Spaniards bear the name that Diego was at one time a generic name in England for any Spaniard. Thomas Dekker, the English dramatist, wrote as early as 1613: "The Diego [the Spaniard] was a dapper fellow." For more than a century English and American seamen have applied dago to Spanish, Portuguese, Italian and other dark-complexioned people from southern Europe. In the same manner they apply Dutchman indiscriminately to Germans, Norwegians, Swedes and Danes as well as to the natives of the Netherlands. In Two Years and a Half in the Navy (1832) an American named Enoch Cobb Wines, referring to the Spanish inhabitants of Minorca, wrote: "These Degos, as they are pleasantly called by our people, were always a great pest when we were in the harbor of Mahon." John Russell Bartlett did not include the term in the first edition of his Dictionary of Americanisms, published in 1848, but in the fourth edition of that work, published in 1877, he noted: "Dagos, originally people of Spanish parentage, born in Louisiana, now applied there to all Italians, Sicilians, Spanish, and Portuguese." Later dago came to be applied specifically in the United States to the lower class of Italian laborers and immigrants. As such it acquired a stinging, contemptuous connotation that is keenly resented by those to whom it is applied, and consequently it is now seldom used except carelessly or when an insult is intended.

How is dew a sign of fair weather?

Many people believe it never rains when the dew falls. They regard the presence of dew in the morning as a sign that it will be a fair day. There appears to be some scientific basis for the belief. The United States Weather Bureau explains the relation between rain and dew as follows: Dew is formed when objects near the ground cool to temperatures below the dew point. During the day the ground gets warm. After nightfall the moisture in the warm air rising from the ground comes in contact with the cooler air above the surface and condenses as dew on grass, plants and other objects. Dew forms when the air is still and the sky clear. These are the conditions near the center of a well-marked anti-cyclone, where rain does not occur. On the other hand, dew forms but slightly, if at all, on windy and cloudy nights. Hence, in general, heavy dew is a sign that the day will be fair.

Why are postal officials called "Nasbys"?

Postal officials, particularly postmasters, acquired the generic nick-name *Nasby* from the fact that David Ross Locke (1833–1888), American newspaperman and whimsical humorist, wrote a series of satirical letters and signed them "The Rev. Petroleum Vesuvius Nasby, Post-master at Confedrit X Roads, which is in the State of Kentucky." The first of these letters, which are credited with having aided the Union cause, began to appear in the Findlay (Ohio) *Jeffersonian* in 1861. The writer pretended to be an old-fashioned, ignorant, whisky-drinking, Negro-hating politician who was determined to be postmaster of the "post orifice" at "Confedrit X Roads, Ky.," a position then held by a "niggur." His sly satire, comical spelling and experiences as an office seeker furnished the entire nation with much fun. The particular slant of his humor was no doubt inspired by that of Charles Farrar Browne (1834–1867), who wrote under the name "Artemus Ward." After the Civil War, Locke continued the *Nasby Letters* in the Toledo *Blade*, a paper of which he became editor and part owner. His comic articles saddled *Nasby* on postmasters and other postal officials. The famous humorist himself is known as Petroleum V. Nasby rather than as David R. Locke. He delivered a lecture entitled "Cursed Be Canaan" 225 times. It began with the sentence: "We are all descended from grand-fathers."

Why is "ounce" abbreviated "oz."?

Ounce is derived from French *once*, which in turn comes from Latin *uncia*, "twelfth part." There is no z in the word and therefore *oz.* is a symbol rather than a true abbreviation or contraction. Two theories have been advanced to account for the use of z in *oz.* The Oxford dictionary regards it as a fifteenth century abbreviation of *onza*, Italian for *ounce*, and adds that "in manuscript forms of abbreviation the z had the length-ened form, its tail being usually carried in a circle under, round, and over the o, so as to form the line of contraction over the word." The Italian abbreviation was retained in English, according to this theory, because it had become a sort of symbol like the dollar and per cent signs. Some authorities, however, are of the opinion that z got in oz. in the same manner that it got in *viz.*, the abbreviation of *videlicet*, a Latin word literally meaning "it is easy to see" or "one may see." *Videlicet*, pronounced vee-*dell*-i-set, now signifies "to wit" or "namely" and is generally so read. Although the third letter in *viz.* is now identified with the letter z, it was originally the character used by early printers for the arbitrary mark of terminal contraction. During the Middle Ages a character similar to z was used at the ends of abbreviated words as the abbreviation of *et*. The symbol was equivalent to modern &. Medieval writers, for instance, abbreviated *habet* by writing *hab* plus the symbol of terminal contraction. The early printers had no type for the symbol and therefore used z, the nearest thing to it in the printer's case. Thus *viz.* at first represented the first two letters of *videlicet* with the sign of contraction at the end. William Byrd of Westover, writing in 1729, employed *vizt* as the abbreviation of *videlicet*. It is possible that oz. originally represented the first letter of *ounce* plus the sign of terminal contraction.

How much is a "point" in market reports?

Point as employed in market reports means a recognized unit of variation in price and is used in quoting the prices of stocks as well as various commodities. In the United States stock market one point ordinarily means one dollar a share. The value of a point, however, varies according to the commodity in question. Therefore to understand the market reports one must be acquainted with the value of a point in reference to any given commodity. In the coffee and cotton markets, for instance, a point is the hundredth part of a cent; in oil, grain, sugar and pork it is one cent. When cotton goes up two hundred points it goes up two cents; when grain goes up five points it goes up five cents.

What English king was nicknamed Lackland?

John, who was King of England from 1199 to 1216, was known as "Lackland" because, unlike his elder brothers, he had no considerable possessions in land while he was a prince. His father, Henry II, parceled out his continental territories to his three eldest sons—Henry, Richard the Lion-Hearted and Geoffrey—and John was given no domain worthy the name. He is reputed to have been the favorite son of Henry II despite this unequal distribution of territories, and his father made him "King of Ireland," where John's reign was brief and unfortunate. No other English king has borne the name John. The only English king to bear that name has such an unsavory reputation in history that none of his successors have cared to assume it upon their succession to the throne.

In his *King John* Shakespeare portrays Lackland as cruel and ruthless but able and likeable. He is remembered chiefly because of his connection with Magna Charta, an event in his life that, oddly, Shakespeare does not so much as allude to.

How do worms get in cigars?

The so-called cigar worm is the larva or young of the tobacco beetle. It is likely to be found wherever large quantities of leaf or manufactured tobacco are handled or stored. Contrary to a common notion, the adult beetle does not lay its eggs in the green tobacco leaves, but in the dry or manufactured product, and in no stage of its life cycle does the insect attack the growing plants. The eggs are small, white, oval objects about one-fiftieth of an inch long, and when first hatched the wormlike larva is very small and active, becoming more sluggish as it increases in size. Before it develops into a beetle, the larva passes through a pupa or quiescent stage. The adult beetle varies considerably in size and is reddish yellow or brownish red in color. *Tobacco worm* and *tobacco hornworm* are names given to the larvae of two species of hawk moth. The larvae, which feed on the tobacco plant, are large, green, obliquely white-striped caterpillars with a hornlike projection near the posterior end. The tobacco bug is a small insect that sucks the juice from the tobacco plant and causes it to wilt and turn yellow.

Will certain plants keep snakes away?

It is commonly believed that certain ornamental plants have remarkable attributes as snake repellents. The mountain ash is said to be especially obnoxious to snakes because of its odor or certain emanations from its dead leaves on the ground. For generations many Indians and Negroes in the southern states planted the snake calabash and the snake gourd and trained the vines to grow over their houses and along their garden fences in the belief that the odor of these gourd vines would drive away snakes. According to some, the pungent, fishy odor given off by the full-grown leaves of the horseshoe geranium will accomplish the same result. In 1729 Colonel William Byrd of Westover in Virginia wrote in *The History of the Dividing Line*: "I found near our Camp some Plants of that kind of Rattle-Snake Root, called Star-grass. The Leaves shoot out circularly, and grow Horizontally and near the Ground. The root is in Shape not unlike the Rattle of that Serpent, and is a Strong Antidote against the bite of it. . . . The Rattle-snake has an utter Antipathy to this Plant, insomuch that if you Smear your hands with the Juice of it, you may handle the Viper Safely. This much I can say on my own Experience, that once in July, when these Snakes are in their greatest Vigour, I besmear'd a Dog's Nose with the Powder of this Root, and made him trample on a large Snake Several times, which, however, was so far from biting him, that it perfectly Sicken'd at the Dog's Approach, and turn'd its Head from him with the Utmost Aversion." In *Astoria* (1836) Washington Irving wrote: "One of the greatest dangers that beset the travellers in this part of their expedition, was the vast number of rattlesnakes which infested the rocks about the rapids and portages, and on which the men were in danger of treading. They were often found, too, in quantities about the encampments. . . . To prevent any unwelcome visits from them in the night, tobacco was occasionally strewed around the tents, a weed for which they have a very proper abhorrence." According to Pliny the Elder, no serpent would touch the trefoil known as the shamrock. Scientific investigation of this subject has failed thus far to corroborate any potency of this sort on the part of plants. So far as known, no plant, including tobacco, will drive away snakes or cause them to avoid places where it is growing. Snakes of various species are often found in and around tobacco barns. This does not mean, however, that some drug, chemical compound or other concoction might not be developed that would act effectively as a snake repellent.

Is the backbone of a camel curved upward in the middle?

The backbone of the single-humped camel is not curved upward in the middle, as many people suppose. It is as straight as the backbone of a horse of an elephant. Humps on camels are composed chiefly of fat, and they vary in size according to the physical condition of the individuals. When camels are worked hard and poorly fed their humps shrivel up and become flaccid. Much of their ability to travel long distances over the desert without food and water is owing to the reabsorption of the extra fat carried in the humps. Thus the hump serves as a sort of commissary department from which the camel receives sustenance in time of famine. Similarly in certain breeds of sheep extra fat is stored in the tail.

What are the horse latitudes?

Horse latitudes is applied by seamen to a region in the North Atlantic between 30 and 35 degrees latitude, which is notorious for its alternate calms and baffling winds. In the days of sailing craft many difficulties were encountered in the horse latitudes. Of this ocean belt one writer says: "Gales and dead calms, terrible thunderstorms and breezes, fair one hour and foul the next, are the characteristics of these parallels." According to one theory, which is accepted by some authorities and rejected by others, the region received its name from the fact that in colonial times vessels carrying horses from Europe and New England to the West Indies were sometimes obliged, when detained in those latitudes, to throw part of the livestock overboard for lack of feed. Another theory attributes the name to the fact that horses on sailing ships were killed by the unfavorable weather conditions in these latitudes. It is possible that the name originally compared the boisterous and unruly winds of this region to the actions of restive horses. The horse latitudes, as well as the *roaring forties*, are contrasted to the *calm latitudes*. In connection with Columbus' third voyage in 1498, Washington Irving in his *Life of Columbus* wrote: "He had entered that region which extends eight or ten degrees on each side of the line, and is known among seamen by the name of the calm latitudes. The tradewinds from the south-east and north-east, meeting in the neighborhood of the equator, neutralize each other, and a steady calmness of the elements is produced. The whole sea is like a mirror, and vessels remain almost motionless, with flapping sails, the crews panting under the heat of a vertical sun, unmitigated by any refreshing breeze."

When is the longest day in the year?

About ninety-nine persons out of a hundred will answer this question by saying June 21. That, however, is only the approximate date of the longest day. Under our present calendar the longest day in the year may be either June 21 or June 22 in places using standard time. In each year preceding a leap year the longest day is June 22, while in all other years it is June 21. Likewise the shortest day in the year may be either December 21 or December 22. The longest and shortest days in the year are determined by the summer and winter solstices, the exact time of which is determined by mathematical calculation. *Solstice* is derived from Latin *sol* ("sun") and *sistere* ("to cause to stand"), and is so called because the sun then apparently stands still in its course. The solstices are the times of the year when the sun is at its greatest declination, either north or south. The winter solstice in northern latitudes is the time at which the sun reaches its farthest point in its swing southward from the equator and accordingly marks the shortest day in the year, while the summer solstice is the time at which the sun reaches its farthest point in its swing northward from the equator and accordingly marks the longest day in the year. The year consists of approximately 365¼ days, and the solstices fluctuate because of the fractional day of each year, which is adjusted by leap years. The longest and shortest days differ in length from the days immediately preceding and following them only by a fraction of a minute.

[86]

According to the calendar, summer begins on the longest day of the year and winter on the shortest, while spring and fall begin halfway between these dates; that is about March 20 and September 23 respectively.

What flag has endured longest without change?

The Danish flag, consisting of a large white cross on a red field, is the oldest unchanged national flag in existence. About 1218 A.D. King Valdemar II of Denmark led a crusade against the pagans who were continually attacking his colonies on the Baltic. The Danes were surprised in their camp at Lindanissa, near what is now Revel in Estonia, and only the personal exertions of the King himself saved them from disaster. According to a legend, a red banner bearing a white cross appeared in the sky at the most critical moment of the battle. This was taken by Valdemar as an answer to his prayers and a promise of aid from heaven. After routing the enemy the King adopted the banner as the standard of the Danes and called it *Dannebrog*, literally meaning "Danes' cloth." Apart from this legend, however, there is unquestioned evidence that this flag has been in continual existence as the national emblem of Denmark since the thirteenth century.

Why are naval cadets called "midshipmen"?

This term originated in the British Navy more then two centuries ago. It arose from the fact that young men who were going through a course of training to become officers were assigned quarters *amidships* on the lower deck. Thus *midshipman* came to be applied in the British Navy to cadets or line and executive officers of the lowest grade. When the American colonies first organized their navy the British practice was followed in respect to this as well as other ranks. The cadets in the United States Naval Academy at Annapolis are still called midshipmen.

What is the origin of "johnnycake"?

Johnnycake is an Americanism of uncertain origin. In the Southern States this food is usually made of corn-meal toasted or baked before a fire, often in the ashes; elsewhere the meal is generally baked in an oven. The Australians make a cake of wheat-meal which they bake in ashes or fry in a pan and which they also call johnnycake. It is generally believed that *johnnycake* is a corruption of *journey-cake*. In 1775 a writer said that "notwithstanding it (rice) is . . . only fit for puddings . . . or to make the wafer-like bread called journey-cakes in Carolina." The theory is that the name was suggested by the fact that in pioneer days this food was ideally adapted to being carried in a saddlebag and eaten on a journey. *Johnnycake*, however, may be the corruption of an Indian or some old English word now lost. This article of food may be referred to in the following lines in Benjamin Thomson's *New England Crisis*, written in 1675:

> Then times were good; merchants cared not a rush
> For other fare than *jonakin* and mush.

Another interesting theory is advanced by Will H. Lowermilk in his *History of Cumberland*, Maryland. A favorite article of diet among the Shawnee Indians, who lived in Maryland, Pennsylvania, Virginia and Ohio, he says, was a cake made of corn beaten as fine as the means at command would permit. This was mixed with water and baked on a flat stone that had been previously heated in the fire. The early hunters and trappers in that region followed the example of the Indians in making these cakes, which they called *Shawnee cakes* after the tribe. In the course of time *Shawnee cake* was corrupted into *johnnycake* by those who did not know its origin or real meaning.

What is the Riviera?

The Riviera, invariably written with the definite article, is a stretch of beautiful Mediterranean shore lying in France and Italy and famous for its almost tropical climate and many health and pleasure resorts. In the narrow sense of the term the Riviera extends only from Nice in France to Spezzia in Italy, but in the broad sense it comprises the entire coast of the French department of Alpes Maritimes and the Italian coast as far as Leghorn. The region is divided into two sections, the part between Nice and Genoa being known as *Riviera di Ponente* ("The western Riviera") or the "Coast of the Setting Sun," and the part between Genoa and Spezzia as *Riviera di Levante* ("The eastern Riviera") or the "Coast of the Rising Sun." *Riviera* is derived from Italian *riva* (Latin *ripa*), signifying bank, and literally the name means simply "the shore."

How was the Kaiser's left arm injured?

The late William II of Germany was born with a withered left arm, which surgery and medicine were powerless to remedy. For that reason in most studio photographs of the last German Emperor his left arm is more or less concealed and the hand on that arm is either gloved or partly covered. The imperial German royal family carefully suppressed all evidence pertaining to the deformity and consequently information on the subject is meager. Examination of the literature bearing on the point indicates that the birth of William was difficult and that he suffered what physicians call an obstetrical paralysis. It seems that he hovered between life and death for several days and when he finally took a turn for the better it was discovered that the left arm was paralyzed, the shoulder socket slightly torn away and the surrounding tissues seriously injured. Knowledge of surgery was comparatively limited in those days and none of the court surgeons would undertake to readjust the arm of the royal child by means of a surgical operation. The result was that William went through life in delicate health and with his left arm deformed and somewhat shorter than the other. There is no evidence to support the story that the Kaiser's arm was injured by a fall from a horse when his mother, then Crown Princess Frederick, took him on horseback and dropped him when he was two years old. Another story, even less probable, is to the effect that one of the German physicians attending the Kaiser's birth, angered because Crown Prince Frederick had called in the royal physician of England without the consent of the physicians attached to the royal Prussian household, dropped the newly born baby on the floor and caused its left arm to be paralyzed. Because of his almost useless left hand, William, it is said, ate in private with a utensil that combined the features of both knife and fork, and never ate in public at all, but sat out banquets before an empty plate. To what extent this physical deformity may have affected the German Emperor's character has been the subject of considerable discussion. The Kaiser was a grandson of Queen Victoria of England and is said to have referred to his withered arm as "the taint of my English blood."

Why were the Germans called Huns?

The Huns were a barbarous Asiatic people who invaded Europe in the fourth century. Later, under Attila, they conquered large parts of central Europe and even made the Romans pay tribute. They became notorious in history for acts of vandalism and the wanton destruction of property. The application of Hun to the modern Germans originated in a speech made July 27, 1900, by the Kaiser to the German Expeditionary Forces just before they sailed to China to co-operate in suppressing the Boxer uprising. On that occasion Emperor Wilhelm II said: "No mercy must be shown. No prisoners must be taken. As the Huns under King Attila made a name for themselves which is still mighty in tradition and legend today, may the name of German be so fixed in China by your deeds, that no Chinese shall ever again dare to look a German askance." Rudyard Kipling, so far as known, was the first English writer to apply Hun to the Germans. In 1902 Germany proposed to Great Britain that the two countries co-operate in a naval demonstration against Venezuela to effect the collection of certain debts. It was generally believed in England at the time that Germany desired to embroil Great Britain and the United States. The occasion prompted Kipling to write his poem entitled "The Rowers," which was published in the London *Times* in 1902. The last stanza of the poem reads:

> In sight of peace—from the Narrow Seas
> O'er half the world to run—
> With a cheated crew, to league anew
> With the Goth and the shameless Hun!

Upon the outbreak of the First World War, when reports of German cruelty and vandalism were common, it was natural for the newspapers and political leaders to hurl this epithet at their enemies. Americans, who seldom use a long word when a short one will answer, followed suit. The Germans deeply resent being called Huns. After the First World War the term fell into disuse and was not revived to any considerable extent after the outbreak of the Second World War.

What famous man was buried in a sitting position?

Tradition says that Ben Jonson, the English poet and playwright, was buried in a sitting posture because the plot provided for him on the north side of the nave in Westminster Abbey was not large enough for the corpse to be placed in the grave in a horizontal position. According to a legend, King Charles I personally promised Jonson that he should be interred in the Abbey in any spot that he might choose. After his death August 6, 1637, it was found that the space he had selected for burial was already occupied except about "eighteen inches of square ground." Charles kept his promise and the coffin was placed in an upright position with the head of the corpse toward the sky, the only occupant of the Abbey to be so honored. Jonson died in extreme poverty and it is possible that he was buried in this position to economize not only on space but on expenses as well. The famous inscription by Sir John Young—"O Rare Ben Jonson"—was cut in the slab over the grave. Many years later a portrait bust to his memory was placed in the Poet's Corner.

Why is the face called the phiz?

Phiz as a colloquial name for the face is a corrupted abbreviation of *phiznomy,* an old humorous form of *physiognomy,* a term applied to the face or countenance, particularly in reference to its features as indicative of character, disposition and temper of mind. Sometimes the word is spelled *phyz*. Strictly speaking, *phiz* is the correct name of the face only with reference to the cast of features. In *The Great Stone Face* Nathaniel Hawthorne refers to a famous orator and politician who was known as "Old Stony Phiz" because he was reputed to resemble the great natural profile in the White Mountains of New Hampshire. Some etymologists have erroneously supposed *phiz* to be a corruption of French *vis* ("face") from which *visage* is derived. *Vis-à-vis* means face to face.

What is the Quai d'Orsay?

Quai d'Orsay, pronounced kay-dor-say, is the name of a famous street in Paris. In French *quai* is applied to a street along the waterfront and the Quai d'Orsay was so named because it extends along the left bank of the Seine River. Since the French Foreign Office and other public buildings were located on this street, *Quai d'Orsay* came to be applied to the Foreign Office, which contained the Foreign Minister's official residence as well as the offices of the Ministry, and, by extension, the French government, particularly in relation to foreign affairs.

How did Johns Hopkins University get its name?

Johns Hopkins University in Baltimore was named after Johns Hopkins (1794–1873), a Maryland merchant and philanthropist, who bequeathed the money for its establishment. Early in his career Johns Hopkins dealt in farm products, groceries and Maryland whisky. The original board of trustees of the university was chosen by Hopkins himself and incorporated in 1867, but nothing was actually done in the way of establishing the institution until after his death in 1873, when his estate of seven million dollars was divided equally between Johns Hopkins University and Johns Hopkins Hospital, the latter being intended as a sort of auxiliary to the medical school of the university. In 1874 the university was formally opened with an address delivered by Thomas Henry Huxley, the English biologist. Hopkins' first name was *Johns*, not *John*, it being a family name.

How did T. B. in Maryland get its name?

One of the oddest and shortest names on the map of the United States is *T. B.*, a small village in the southern part of Prince Georges County, Maryland. Because *t.b.* is the slang abbreviation of *tuberculosis*, many people mistakenly suppose that the Maryland village received its name from a sanatorium for the treatment of tuberculosis patients. The letters composing the name are the initials of Thomas Brooke, whose father, Robert Brooke, acquired a vast estate in that vicinity in 1648. The stones used by the early surveyors to mark the limits of the plantation bore the initials of Thomas Brooke. There is a tradition that one of the original Brooke boundary stones was found within the village limits and that from this circumstance the inhabitants fell into the habit of calling their village T. B.

Which is correct, "Hudson" or "Hudson's" Bay?

The vast inland sea in Canada is correctly called either "*Hudson's* Bay" or "*Hudson* Bay." "*Hudson's* Bay" is the older name, but in modern usage "*Hudson* Bay" is preferred. Although the famous fur company is still officially styled "*Hudson's* Bay Company," it is popularly referred to as "The *Hudson* Bay Company." This company was founded in 1670 under a charter granted by King Charles II and was originally styled "The Governor and Company of Adventurers of England Trading into Hudson's Bay."

Does a fish weigh less in water?

It is said that the Roman senate once spent an entire day debating the question: "Why does a pail of water, with a fish swimming in it, weigh no more than the same pail of water without the fish?" The senators gravely offered various explanations for the singular phenomenon. Finally a senator, more scientifically minded than his colleagues, weighed a pail of water with and without a live fish in it and demonstrated that the question was based on a false premise. This ancient question owes its persistent popularity to a misunderstanding of the meaning of *weighing in water*. Suppose a vessel weighing five pounds is placed on a set of scales, and five pounds of water is poured into it, and then a live fish also weighing five pounds is put in the water. The scales will register fifteen pounds; that is, five pounds more than before the fish was added. The total weight will be the sum of the weights of the vessel, the water and the fish. If the fish were weighed *in water*—the fish and the scales both being under water—it would weigh less than five pounds, or possibly nothing at all, owing to the buoyance of the water, but that would not affect the weight of the vessel, water and fish weighed as a whole.

Why are the dead buried above the ground in New Orleans?

In New Orleans many of the dead are interred above the ground in tombs or vaults of stuccoed brick, granite or marble. The old cemeteries, with their long rows of tombs shaded by trees, are one of the unique features of the city. Formerly the poor were about the only persons in New Orleans who buried their dead in shallow graves in the ground.

There were two reasons for this burial practice. New Orleans is French and Spanish in its origin and the mausoleum form of burial is a favorite among both peoples. The chief reason, however, was the undrained condition of the subsoil, which made burials in the ground impractical because of dampness. New Orleans is built on low land that was gradually formed by silt carried in the waters of the Mississippi. Although a modern drainage system has lowered the water in the ground considerably, many bodies are still buried according to the old method. In fact there are compartively few interments below the surface even at the present time. Canal Street, the most famous thoroughfare in the city, begins at the Mississippi River and ends at a cemetery.

Why is a holiday called a red letter day?

In early prayerbooks and church almanacs the saints' days and religious festivals were printed in red ink, a practice that probably originated in the calendar of days in the Book of Common Prayer. Some prayerbooks are still printed in this style and many secular calendars have the Sundays and holidays indicated by red letters or figures. From this custom *red letter day* acquired its present meaning—any day or holiday that we look forward to with pleasure or back to because of some important event or benefit. The ancient Romans marked auspicious days on the calendar with chalk and unauspicious days with charcoal. From this custom *black-letter day* became associated with bad luck. A date remembered with regret is still sometimes referred to as a *black-letter day*. In *King John* Shakespeare says:

> What hath this day deserved? What hath it done,
> That it in golden letters should be set
> Among the high tides in the calendar?

Who originated, "Down, but not out"?

"Down, but not out" is a shortened version of, "A man may be down, but he's never out," which is the slogan of the Salvation Army. For that purpose it is said to have been suggested by Elmore Cornell Leffingwell (1878–1942), a noted newspaperman who served for several years as the Salvation Army's publicity director. The saying is supposed to have originated during the Boer War. *Down and out* is an old prize-fighting phrase. A *down-and-outer* is a person who has been knocked out and who has no hope of staging a comeback. On one occasion, while food and clothing were being distributed to people who had been made homeless and penniless by the South African war, somebody referred to the unfortunate victims as down-and-outers. A salvation Army worker snapped back: "A man may be down, but he's never out." The expression contained so much optimism and hope in plain and simple words that it survived and was adopted as a slogan by the Salvation Army.

Do mice ever sing?

The singing mouse is not a myth. Dozens of competent authorities have investigated the subject and there are many well authenicated cases of mice that make musical sounds suggesting the twittering, chirping, whistling or warbling of small birds. Such noises are made by individuals of various species, including the common house mouse. The song of singing mice is commonly described as like the faint twittering of a canary. Some authorities suppose that the noise made by so-called singing mice is always owing to some obstruction or unusual development in their bronchial tubes; in other words, the singing is merely a whistling sound made by mice that have caught cold and are having trouble with their breathing. But Roy Chapman Andrews, director of the American Museum of Natural History, reported that a singing mouse observed by him in China uttered musical chirps and twitters that were birdlike in quality and that varied in notes and tones. The sound, he declared, was just as definitely a song as that of a bird and did not appear to be a whistle caused by an inflammation of the respiratory tract. Some years ago the American public was privileged to hear a mouse sing over the radio. From Lincoln, Illinois, came a report of a mouse that had "a grand opera complex and an affinity for canaries." This mouse, according to the report, was captured by Richard P. Steiner "after it had squeezed into his canary's cage and joined the bird in a duet."

Why are newspapers called the fourth estate?

The press is called the fourth estate because of its great influence upon public affairs. The first application of the term to newspapers is variously attributed to Edmund Burke, Thomas Carlyle and Thomas Babington Macaulay. But fourth estate was applied to several elements of society before it was to the press. Formerly in England and France the church, the nobility and the common people were known as the three estates of the realm. In England the three estates were specifically the lords spiritual, the lords temporal and the Commons. It is a common mistake to call the sovereign, the lords and the Commons the three estates. In a speech in Parliament in 1638 Lord Falkland applied fourth estate to the Army. The term was applied to the mob in 1752 in a newspaper article written by Henry Fielding. In 1789 an unidentified writer applied it to a proposed board of commissioners as well as to the Queen and her council. Later the term was applied to the working class. In *Heroes and Hero Worship*, published in 1840, Carlyle said: "Burke said there were Three Estates in Parliament; but, in the Reporters' Gallery yonder, there sat a Fourth Estate more important far than they all. It is not a figure of speech, or a witty saying; it is a literal fact,—very momentous to us in these times." Carlyle's style is such that it is not clear whether he intended to give Burke's exact phraseology. *Fourth estate* occurs nowhere in Burke's published writings and it is not known where Carlyle obtained his information. Some authorities think he may have coined the term himself. Three years earlier he had published *The French Revolution*. One chapter is entitled *The Fourth Estate* and contains the sentence: "A Fourth Estate, of Able Editors, springs up." But in 1828 Macaulay had written in the *Edinburgh Review*: "The gallery in which the reporters sit has become a fourth estate of the realm." A correspondent to London *Notes and Queries* said he heard Lord Brougham use the term in the House of Commons about 1823.

What is a free lance?

A free lance is a person not permanently affiliated with an organization. Free-lance writers are persons who write on their own account and not as members of the staff of any publication. A free lance is often only a newspaperman who is out of work and looking for a job. *Free lance* dates back only to about 1820. About that time Sir Walter Scott and other writers began to apply the term to professional soldiers of the Middle Ages whose services were purchasable by any feudal lord willing to pay the required price. Sometimes the free lance was a roving knight who had a handful of armed horsemen under his command and who plundered on his own or as a mercenary of a belligerent state.

How did the barber pole originate?

The barber pole with spiral stripes is a relic of the days when barbers were also surgeons. As early as the fifth century A.D. the barbers in Rome extracted teeth, treated wounds and bled patients as part of their professional work. When the London barbers were incorporated in 1461 they were the only persons practicing surgery in the city. In the reign of Henry VIII Parliament passed a law providing that barbers should confine themselves to minor operations such as bloodletting and drawing teeth, while surgeons were prohibited from "barbery and shaving." It was not until 1745, only thirty years before the American Revolution, that the barbers and surgeons of London were separated into distinct corporations, and the practice of surgery by barbers was not abolished in France, Germany and other European countries until much later. The barber-surgeons generally bled their patients in the arm, and, in the days when few people could read and pictures and emblems were used as shop signs, the emblem of the profession was a spirally painted white and red pole from which was suspended a brass basin with a semicircular opening in the rim. The white ground represented the bandage used in bloodletting, the red stripe represented blood, and the basin represented the vessel used to receive the blood. Strangely it has been the barbers and not the surgeons who have retained, in a modified form, this ancient symbol of their profession. In the United States the brass basin is generally omitted from the barber pole, but it is still common in Britain. American barbers also added a blue stripe, perhaps to make the colors conform with those of the national flag.

What are tidal waves?

Tidal wave is a popular rather than a scientific term and accordingly is not susceptible of exact definition. Waves in the ocean are produced by the action of wind. An ordinary wave is not a forward movement of water, except when it "breaks," but the advance of a mere form. Objects floating on the surface of the sea are not carried along by the waves except when they are struck by the loose masses of water from breaking crests. A "whitecap" is the crest of a wave breaking into foam. A ship may be in the hollow of a large wave one minute and on the crest the next, and wave after wave may rush under her, but she is not driven from her course unless the waves break and the water beats against her. Ordinary waves may travel at the rate of fifty miles an hour without increasing or decreasing the speed of a ship. Only the heaping up and breaking of waves is perilous to vessels. But waves may break against a shore with terrific force. The most powerful "breakers" occur on the coast of Guinea in Africa, where there is a continual westerly swell from the Atlantic. Tidal waves are not so called because they are influenced by the tides, which they seldom are, but because they rush from the sea toward the land like tides. Popularly the term is sometimes applied to a great rise in water along a shore due to exceptionally high winds. The flood that destroyed Galveston, Texas, in September, 1900, was such a tidal wave. More often, however, the term is popularly applied to great sea waves that follow an earthquake. Meteorologists call this type of tidal wave a "seismic sea wave." It is a gravitational water wave propagated outward in all directions from the surface center of a submarine earthquake. As they sweep into shoal water such waves may pile up a wall of water 80 or 90 feet high. Tidal waves of this type may travel at a rate of 1,000 miles an hour and when they strike the shore they wreck virtually everything in their path.

Why is "IIII" used for "IV" on clock dials?

It has been a more or less general custom from time immemorial to use *IIII* instead of *IV* on clock dials when Roman numerals are employed. Several theories have been advanced to account for this practice. Some authorities believe that the original purpose was to harmonize the appearance of the dial by making the *IIII* balance with the *VIII* on the opposite side. Others maintain that *IIII* was the original way of writing four in Roman numerals, and that since clocks were manufactured long before the change to *IV* was made, the older form was retained, just as many other old forms are retained purely for conservative reasons. Among clockmakers there is a tradition as to the origin of the custom. It is said that about 1370 a clockmaker named Henry de Vick made a clock for Charles V of France, who was popularly known as Charles the Wise. This monarch, although he was reputed to be very wise, often pretended to understand things that he did not. When Vick submitted his clock to His Majesty for approval, Charles the Wise examined it very carefully, but was unable to find any flaw in the workmanship. Finally, anxious to find some fault, he complained that the clockmaker had made an error in the numbers on the dial and that the *IV* should be *IIII*. "Your Majesty is wrong," replied Vick. "I am never wrong," thundered back Charles. "Take the clock and return it when you have corrected this error." So Vick changed the *IV* to *IIII* on the dial, and ever since it has been customary to use that form on clocks.

Do elephants resent being fed tobacco?

There is a widespread belief that elephants resent being fed tobacco and that they will for years nurse a grudge against a person who so treats them. Those in a position to judge correctly of the habits and characteristics of elephants testify that many of these animals like chewing tobacco because of the licorice and sugar that it contains. Dr. William M. Mann, director of the National Zoological Park, says on this subject: "I do not think elephants resent being fed tobacco. Some of them are fond of it in small portions. Elephants do have good memories and sometimes form strong dislikes toward certain people, but in regard to their remembering people who feed them tobacco and afterward attacking them, I have heard only stories of it. It seems to be a very general belief." The late Raymond L. Ditmars, curator of mammals at the New

York Zoological Park, wrote to the author in the following vein: "I have never noted that elephants have any aversion to tobacco, but I do think that if an elephant were given a lighted cigarette and had his trunk burnt, by some malicious individual, the animal would remember the incident and have a decided aversion to tobacco and to the individual who fed it to him." How much truth there is in the notion that elephants have good memories is hard to ascertain. The common saying that "elephants never forget" is an exaggeration to say the least. C. Emerson Brown, for many years director of the Philadelphia Zoological Garden, says: "All elephants are intelligent and possess remarkable memories." In *My Animal Friends* he writes: "Typical of their long memory is the story printed in school books many years ago about the circus elephant who, while passing through a town in a parade, playfully put his trunk out toward a tailor sewing in front of his shop. The tailor mischievously pricked the trunk with his needle. Several years later the circus returned to the town. As the parade reached the street on which the tailor lived, the elephant filled his trunk with dirty water from a puddle and blew the entire contents over the tailor and his stock in revenge for the needle thrust. This tale always seemed a bit exaggerated to me, but as I became more familiar with elephants, I began to suspect that it might have some foundation in truth."

What English queen had six fingers on one hand?

One of the hands of Anne Boleyn, second wife of Henry VIII of England, was deformed by the presence of an extra finger. The sixth finger, however, was little more than a stump covered by a nail turned up at the sides. Anne wore gloves whenever possible, but Queen Catherine used to get revenge on her rival by compelling her to play cards without gloves, thus exposing the deformity and disgusting the King. Many cases of hexadactylism, that is, persons having six fingers on each hand or six toes on each foot, have been reported by science and apparently in some instances it is hereditary in certain families.

Was there ever a real "wild man of Borneo"?

The famous wild man claimed by showmen of past generations to have been captured in the jungles of Borneo was a fake. The notion of such a wild man probably originated in the fertile brain of some master showman like P. T. Barnum of white elephant fame. For many years nearly every circus and Wild West show in the United States pretended to have on exhibition the original "wild man of Borneo." That island was probably selected as the native haunt of the wild man because it has long been notorious as the land of head-hunters. It seems, however, that the ferocity of the Borneo head-hunters has been greatly exaggerated, although the natives still occasionally take the heads of their enemies in time of war. But head-hunting is no longer a favorite sport with the Dyaks, who resort to the practice only when times are dull and other amusements wanting.

How long is the gestation period in apes?

The period of gestation for orangutans, like human beings, is about nine months, while for chimpanzees it is slightly shorter. Gorillas have seldom been bred in captivity and accordingly their period of gestation has not been definitely determined. As a matter of fact, compartively few species of monkeys and apes have been bred in captivity. The Old World monkeys known as macaques carry their young about five months.

What is a chauvinist?

Chauvinist is applied to a jingo, rampant patriot or one exhibiting excessive and unreasoning loyalty to a person or cause. It is derived from the surname of Nicolas Chauvin, a native of Rochefort, France, and a soldier of the first republic and the empire, whose demonstrative loyalty to Napoleon became notorious. The battle-scarred veteran adored the Man of Destiny and never wearied of telling of his exploits at Austerlitz, Jena and other fields of battle. Early in the nineteenth century Chauvin was impersonated on the vaudeville stage in Paris and was represented as a character in numerous plays as the typical jingo or blind enthusiast for military glory. Hence Chauvinism (pronounced show-vin-iz'm in English) became the French equivalent of the English jingoism.

What is a dead man's hand in cards?

In poker a hand consisting of a pair of aces (some say jacks) and a pair of eights is known as a dead man's hand from the report that James Butler Hickok ("Wild Bill") held such a hand at the time he was shot by Jack McCall during a card game in Deadwood, South Dakota, August 2, 1876. Hickok was a pioneer law-enforcement officer and was noted for the many men he killed in self-defense and in the discharge of his duty. Some poker players maintain that a dead man's hand is very lucky and seldom beaten. In certain wild games it wins over everything, even a royal flush.

Who said: "Thou hast conquered, O Galilean"?

These, according to a legend, were the dying words of the Roman Emperor Julian, who was the son of the half brother of Constantine the Great and who succeeded Constantine as Emperor in 361 A.D. Julian was brought up a Christian, but his early teaching was soon modified by a keen interest in Neoplatonism and other philosophy and he became known as "Julian the Apostate" because after his assumption of the purple he ordered a return to pagan worship and issued many decrees injurious to the Christian religion. His, however, was not the old paganism as it had been practiced by his ancestors; it was rather an idealized mixture of paganism and philosophy which he acquired from the rhetoricians who taught him and which was the result of the preference that he had for the ancient Hellenic culture. Julian the Apostate resolved to conquer Persia and in 363 he invaded that country with a powerful army. The Emperor was always in the thickest of the combat, and many times he repulsed the Persian host, but after many desperate hand-to-hand encounters he fell mortally wounded, treacherously stabbed by a Christian, according to an unauthenticated story. Just before Julian breathed his last, the legend says, he threw some of his blood toward heaven and exclaimed, *Vicisti Galilaee*, "Thou hast conquered, O Galilean!" This legend was mentioned in the fifth century by Theodoret, Bishop of Cyrrhus, but most authorities regard it either as a pure fabrication or merely as an elaboration of the account of the Emperor's death given in a poem by Ephraem Syrus, who died in 373. Nevertheless, the story symbolizes the fact that the work of Julian the Apostate perished with him and that his death left the religion founded by Jesus of Galilee supreme in the Roman world.

Who said that "corporations have no souls"?

It is supposed that Sir Edward Coke (1552–1634), the celebrated English jurist, was the first to express this idea. In the *Case of Sutton's Hospital* Coke declared that corporations "cannot commit treason, nor be outlawed nor excommunicated, for they have no souls." Lord Thurlow (1732–1806), another great English jurist, paraphrased Coke's statement in the following words: "A corporation has neither a soul to lose nor a body to be kicked."

How did "brand-new" originate?

Brand-new literally means "fresh from the fire" and is equivalent to *fire-new*, the form used by Shakespeare. The following examples illustrate his use of the term: "Your fire-new stamp of honour is scarce current."— *Richard III*: "A man of fire-new words."—*Love's Labour's Lost*: "Some excellent jests, fire-new from the mint."—*Twelfth Night*: "Despite thy victor sword and fire-new fortune."—*Lear*, and, "Love's brand new-fired." —*Sonnet 153*. In the last Shakespearean example *brand* and *new-fired* are associated. *Brand* is derived from an old Anglo-Saxon root signifying "burn." Hence an article fresh from the forge or furnace was said to be brand-new. The notion that *brand-new* originated from the practice of putting brands or trade marks on manufactured articles is incorrect. This word is commonly but erroneously written and pronounced *bran-new*. *Span-new*, which also means quite or perfectly new, had a somewhat similar origin. It is derived from Old Norse *spann*, "chip," and *nyr*, "new," and originally signified as bright and new as a freshly cut chip.

What is the origin of "the ghost walks"?

The ghost walks, meaning that salaries are being paid, was originally theatrical slang. According to a common story, the phrase originated among a troupe of English actors while rehearsing Shakespeare's *Hamlet*. The members of the troupe had not been paid for several weeks and some of them were getting rebellious. When the actor playing the part of Hamlet said of the ghost, "Perchance 'twill walk again," the one taking the ghost's part replied, "No, I'm damned if the ghost walks until our salaries are paid!" The phrase is no longer restricted to the theatrical world but is used by the employees of any firm in connection with the periodical visits of the person who distributes the pay envelopes.

Does a baby elephant suck with its trunk?

The baby elephant sucks with its mouth, not its trunk. Two teats situated between the forelegs of the female supply the young elephant with nourishment. When the calf sucks it curls back its trunk. In *Bring 'Em Back Alive*, Frank Buck says a baby elephant at first doesn't know what to do with its trunk and has a hard time keeping it out of the way when it sucks the mother. It is a common mistake to suppose that elephants drink through their trunks. The use of the trunk in drinking is confined to taking up water and squirting it into the mouth. Trunks of newly born elephants are short compared to those of adults. A baby elephant weighing 200 pounds has a trunk only 10 or 15 inches long.

What is the size of the smallest fish in the world?

The smallest known species of fish in the world reaches an average length of $\frac{3}{8}$ of an inch and a maximum length of $\frac{7}{16}$ of an inch. It is about the size of an ant and is probably the tiniest backboned creature that has ever been called to the attention of science. The species is found in certain creeks in the Philippines and is known scientifically as *Pandaka pygmea*. Specimens are not numerous. The bodies of these fish are slender and almost transparent, the comparatively large eyes being the only features clearly visible. The next fish in respect to size is *Mistichthys luzonensis* and is also found in the Philippines. Its average length is about $\frac{1}{12}$ of an inch greater than that of *Pandaka pygmea*. Fish of this species are so numerous in Lake Buhi, Luzon, that the natives catch them for food. *Sinarapan* is the local name for the species. Many thousands of these dwarf fish are mixed with batter, seasoned with herbs and spices and baked into little cakes that are said to be tasty.

What causes the designs in "bird's-eye maple"?

Bird's-eye is the name given to a certain type of wood from the tree variously known as hard, rock and sugar maple. It is called *bird's-eye maple* because frequently the grain of the wood exhibits a spotted appearance supposed to resemble the eyes of birds. Sometimes, instead of being spotted, the grain has a wavy appearance. Similar bird's-eye and wavy or curly markings are found in ash, birch, walnut, cherry, redwood and some pines. Such wood is widely used for veneer and finishing purposes. These odd designs are believed to be largely, if not wholly, due to an accidental arrangement in the wood fibers. The exact cause is not known positively. According to one theory, these peculiar markings are due to numerous drillings made in the living trees by the small birds called sapsuckers. As a rule, the bird's-eye markings appear through the tree, even in the smaller branches, which indicates that the designs are not due to woodpeckers, since it is not likely that the sapsuckers work to any considerable extent on the small twigs. Another theory holds that the bird's-eye and curly effects are due to the presence of fungi or other parasitic growths, or to buds under the bark that are too weak to force themselves out. In Japan a somewhat similar effect has been produced in certain maples by introducing substances under the bark that act as irritants. These theories do not conform with the popular belief that trees with bird's-eye wood can be propagated from seed. Experiments in growing bird's-eye maple from the seed of such trees have shown conclusively that this cannot be done with certainty. Such forms are just as likely to result from the seed of any straight-grained tree. Bird's-eye maple occurs throughout the natural range of the species.

What is the antipodes of America?

Antipodes (pronounced an-*tipp*-o-deez) is the plural form of a word derived through Latin from Greek *anti* ("against") and *podos* ("foot") and literally means "with feet opposite." Any two places or peoples on opposite sides of the globe, so situated that a straight line drawn from one to the other passes through the center of the earth, are called the antipodes of each other. Every point on the earth is the antipodes of some other point. Antipodes are separated by 180 degrees of longitude, that is, half of the circumference of the earth, and one must be as far south as the other is north of the equator unless both are on that line. When it is noonday at one it is midnight at the other. China is popularly supposed to be the antipodes of the United States and there is an old saying that if one were to dig a hole deep enough he would fall into China. This, however, is a misconception, for China and the United States are both in the Northern Hemisphere. The true antipodes of the United States is a region in the Indian Ocean west of Australia and east of southern Africa, where there are few islands. Very little of the North American continent has its antipodes in any land surface. New Amsterdam and St. Paul, small islands nearly midway between Australia and South Africa, are more nearly the antipodes of Washington, D. C., than any other land. The antipodes of South America falls in the region of China, the Philippines and Borneo. The approximate antipodes of London is the Antipodes Islands, a group of rocky, uninhabited islands 460 miles southeast of New Zealand. Antipodes, while originally plural, is now often construed as singular.

Did Nathaniel Hawthorne change the spelling of his name?

On this subject Julian Hawthorne, son of Nathaniel Hawthorne, wrote to the author as follows: "The name, before the first emigrant from England, was Hawthorne, with the w. The first emigrant, William, spelled it in the same way himself, but in prints current in his time, it was occasionally misspelled Hathorne. Later, the family itself adopted the abbreviation. Nathaniel Hawthorne's father wrote the name Hathorne. But Nathaniel (my father), on the basis of old documents, and because the name in England was (and still is, in the remnant of the family surviving there) spelled Hawthorne, restored the exiled w. But friends of his boyhood, in college and elsewhere, generally pronounced it Hathorne, and in letters to him often addressed him as Hath."

Why do lodges use white and black balls in voting?

The use of white and black balls in voting upon the admission of new members is a survival of the method used by the ancient Greeks. In many of their elections the Greeks had an urn to represent each candidate. The voter would toss a white pebble into the urn if he favored the candidate, and a black one if he wished to vote against him. Many lodges and fraternal organizations have revived this system, a white ball being in favor of a candidate for membership and a black one for rejection. In some organizations a single black ball is sufficient to defeat the candidate; in other words, the person cannot become a member of the organization without the approval of the entire membership. Thus we have the phrase *to blackball*, meaning to reject. It is interesting to note in this connection that *ballot* is derived from French *ballotte*, "little ball."

How did the Morris chair get its name?

The Morris chair, an easy chair with a movable back, took its name from William Morris (1834–1896), English poet, artist, decorator and socialist, who designed the first chair of this type and put it on the market. In 1859 Morris was married to Jane Burden, a beautiful Oxford girl who had sat to him as a model, and they set about to build at Upton, England, a "house beautiful," which was to embody all the principles of the artist's decorative art. The Morris chair was one of the creations of this period. It was composed of mahogany, finished in black to resemble ebony and carved distinctively. This chair was put on the market after Morris and his friends organized the firm of Morris, Marshall, Faulkner and Company in 1862. The famous Red House at Upton proved to be situated in an unhealthful location and serious illness obliged the family to abandon it.

What is a harelip?

Harelip is a congenital deformity in the human lip, usually the upper one, and is the result of an imperfect union of the nasal and maxillary developments of the fetus. This malformation consists of a cleft or fissure on or near the middle line and derives its name from its resemblance to the division in the lip of the hare. In human beings the lip normally divides on one or both sides of the median line, while in hares it divides at or near that line. Harelip is frequently associated with cleft palate, another congenital fault, consisting of a cleavage in the roof of the mouth. Both imperfections may be hereditary and both are likely to interfere with the normal processes of speech. As a rule they can be corrected by a surgical operation performed while the child is still in its infancy. Just why the development of the fetus should occasionally miss the mark in forming the lips and palate has never been adequately explained. Many people believe that the malformation is due to maternal impressions during gestation, such as fright, but an examination of numerous cases indicates that most of the instances of supposed fright preceding the birth of a harelipped child occur considerably after the ninth week of fetal life, when the lips are already developed. In olden times the superstitious supposed harelip to be caused at birth by an evil spirit or malicious fairy. Shakespeare alludes to this belief when in *King Lear* he has Edgar point out "the foul fiend Flibbertigibbet" who "squints the eye, and makes the harelip."

What highwayman became Chief Justice of England?

Sir John Popham (c. 1531–1607), who served as Chief Justice of England from 1592 until his death and who presided at the trials of Sir Walter Raleigh and Guy Fawkes, is reputed to have been a highwayman in his youth. Lord Campbell in his *Lives of the Chief Justices* says that Popham, when he was a law student in the Middle Temple, used to go out after nightfall with his pistols and take purses on Hounslow Heath, partly to show that he was a young man of spirit and partly to replenish his meager finances impaired by riotous living.

Is Alaska part of continental United States?

Continental United States is a somewhat ambiguous term. Strictly speaking, *continental* means pertaining to a continent and *continental United States* should include all of the United States on the continent of North America, but as commonly used the term is synonymous with *United States* proper and excludes Alaska as well as all other noncontiguous territories, dependencies and possessions.

How did "cynosure" originate?

Cynosure, pronounced *sigh*-no-shoor, is derived from two Greek words and literally means "dog's tail." The term is the ancient name of the constellation known as the Little Bear, and also of the North Star (Polaris), which is the end of the tail of the Little Bear. Since mariners have for thousands of years guided their ships by the North Star, *cynosure* has come to signify anything that attracts attention or the object toward which all eyes are turned. Hence the popular phrase *the cynosure of all eyes* means simply the center of attraction.

Why is "V" used for "U" in inscriptions?

The use of V for U in inscriptions is a survival of a custom that began when V and U were merely different forms of the same letter. There is no U in the Latin alphabet. The earlier of the two forms was V. At first U was a cursive or rounded form of V and was in no way distinguished from it. Gradually, however, U became differentiated from V and acquired a distinct sound of its own, although for centuries thereafter V was preferred to U as the capital initial form. The fact that we still call W, which is composed of two V's, *double-U* harks back to the time when these letters were identical. English dictionaries did not give V and U separate alphabetical positions until about 1800. The United States Fine Arts Commission says V is regarded as more artistic than U and lends itself more readily to the chisel of the sculptor, and for that reason is still widely used in inscriptions on monuments and buildings as well as on coins. It is not, however, generally used where the U sound predominates. For instance, it would be regarded as bad taste to use the V form in UNITED STATES, while it is frequently used in PVBLIC LIBRARY and IN GOD WE TRVST. When V is used for U it is technically known as the *Manuscript U*. In 1940, under the caption of *OVR CVRIOVS CVSTOM*, the Des Moines (Iowa) *Register* printed the following satire on the practice of using V for U in inscriptions:

Pvblic bvildings are bvilt for the pvblic, not jvst for the limited nvmber of vnvsval persons, who are not confvsed by the cvstom of svbstitvting the letter V for the rovnd-based letter in the inscriptions scvlptvred above entrances.

Most of vs, if we wovld bvt admit the trvth, are pvzzled, at ovr first casval glance, to vnderstand them. We mvst scrvtinize them carefvlly to be svre whether a strvctvre is a mvsevm or whether we have vnwittingly started throvgh the door of a cvstoms hovse.

Perhaps it's easier to cvt the straight lines of a V than to carve the cvrves of the less cvltvred letter, bvt we covld endvre it if, on fvtvre constrvction of chvrches, vniversity stadivms, covrt hovses and other pvblic bvildings, the Vnited States avthorities and those of States, covnties, and mvnicipalities wovld retvrn to the vse of the letter pronovnced "yov."

What are anti-kink hair preparations composed of?

The preparations widely used by colored people to remove the kinks from their hair are generally composed of various gums, such as gum tragacanth, which is a reddish gum obtained from several different species of spiny shrubs and small trees native to southwestern Asia. Ordinarily the preparation is applied to kinky hair while it is held out straight with a comb and the gum is permitted to dry while the hair is still held straight, thus preventing it from curling. Since hair grows from the roots the gum preparation has to be applied at frequent intervals, just as dyed hair must be redyed to color the new hair as it grows.

Why is a certain kind of lock called a "Yale lock"?

The name comes from Linus Yale, a lockmaker, who was born at Middletown, Connecticut, in 1797, and reared in Herkimer County, New York. In 1847 Linus Yale put up a stone building at Newport,

New York, which is still standing and known as the "Yale Lock Shop." He had a son, Linus Yale, Jr., who also became a lockmaker. In 1868 Linus Yale, Jr., and Henry Towne organized a corporation to manufacture locks at Stamford, Connecticut. Yale, however, died a few months later, before the enterprise really got under way. The company was at first known as "The Yale Lock Manufacturing Company," but in 1883 the name of the firm was changed to "The Yale & Towne Manufacturing Company." *Yale lock* was first applied to certain cylinder or bank locks patented and manufactured by Linus Yale, Jr. These were decided improvements on all earlier locks. The Tremont Hotel in Boston, opened in 1828, introduced the novelty of having a lock on the door of every guest room, no two of which could be opened with the same key, but these locks were large and clumsy compared with the later Yale locks.

Does washing eggs cause them to spoil quicker?

The shells of eggs are covered with a natural mucilaginous coating that delays the entrance of harmful germs into the interior. Washing eggs softens or removes this viscid coating, thus diminishing their keeping quality and hastening their deterioration. Clean unwashed eggs bring the highest prices, and the United States Department of Agriculture advises poultrymen against washing eggs before sending them to market.

What state is called the Flickertail State?

One of the nicknames of North Dakota is "Flickertail State." The nickname was suggested by the abundance in that region of the flickertail, which is the popular name of the Richardson ground squirrel or gopher. These animals are called flickertails from their habit of flipping or *flicking* their tails. *Flickertail* in this connection does not refer to the prairie dog, as is sometimes supposed.

What would happen if an irresistible force met an immovable object?

This question presupposes impossible conditions, according to all known laws of matter and energy. The terms *irresistible force* and *immovable object* are mutually exclusive. If a force is irresistible it will move any object in its path; or, in other words, there can be no immovable object in respect to an irresistible force. On the other hand, if an object is immovable no force can move it; which is another way of saying that there is no irresistible force in respect to an immovable object. Since the existence of the two conditions cannot take place at the same time, it is impossible to say what would happen if they did exist. The question is reduced to an absurdity by a careful definition of terms. You cannot conceive of an irresistible force meeting an immovable object any more than you can conceive of two men, each one taller than the other.

How is "Roosevelt" pronounced?

The surname of Theodore Roosevelt and Franklin D. Roosevelt is probably mispronounced more frequently than that of any other American Presidents. It is correctly pronounced ro-ze-velt, with the o long as in so. The second syllable is somewhat suppressed, making the name sound almost, but not quite, like roze-velt. In a letter to the author of this book Franklin D. Roosevelt said: "Every member of the Roosevelt family that I have ever known or heard of has pronounced the name as if there were only one o, and with the accent on the first syllable, i.e., ro-ze-velt." In names of Dutch origin oo is generally pronounced like o. For instance, the last element in Hendrik Van Loon is pronounced loan. Roosevelt is often mispronounced roo-ze-velt, the first syllable rhyming with too.

What are dungarees?

Sailors call overalls or fatigue clothes dungarees. A dungaree suit in the Navy generally consists of a jumper and trousers made of blue denim or drill. The name is of Anglo-Indian origin and was borrowed from the British sailors. Dungri, the native word, is derived from the name of a suburb of Bombay where a coarse kind of blue cotton cloth was first manufactured. Such cloth is much used for tents and sails as well as clothing among the poor classes in India.

Why are certain ships called schooners?

Schooner is believed to be derived from scoon, an old Scottish dialectical word meaning to skip or skim over the surface of the water. According to a popular story, the first vessel of this type was built at Gloucester, Massachusetts, in 1713 by Captain Andrew Robinson, a Scotsman. When the ship was being launched a bystander exclaimed, "Oh, how she scoons!" Captain Robinson replied, "A scooner let her be!" The word soon came into general use as the name of vessels of this type. Although the story was first recorded in 1790 on the authority of tradition, the derivation that it suggests is not improbable. There is good reason for believing that schooner originated in Massachusetts, and probably in Gloucester, about 1713, and early examples show that it was originally sometimes spelled *scooner* and *skooner*. In 1721 a man named Moses Prince wrote: "Went to see Capt. Robinson's lady. This gentleman was the first contriver of schooners, and built the first of the sort about eight years ago." In point of fact similar vessels had been built in England during the previous century. From this nautical use of *schooner* the typical covered wagons in which the early pioneers migrated westward in the nineteenth century were called "prairie schooners."

Was Benedict Arnold a Mason?

Benedict Arnold was made a member of Hiram Lodge No. 1, New Haven, Connecticut, on April 10, 1765. According to the secretary of Hiram Lodge No. 1, that is the only authentic information known concerning the Masonic record of Benedict Arnold. The old records of the New Haven lodge, says the secretary, are very incomplete compared with those kept at present. The *New Age Magazine*, official organ of the Supreme Council of the Thirty-Third and Last Degree, Scottish Rite, asserted that after his treason Arnold's name was erased from the membership roll and he was dropped as a Mason. Arnold never applied for reinstatement, as has often been claimed.

What does "Rubaiyat" mean?

Rubaiyat, pronounced roo-bye-ya*ht*, is the plural form of *rubai*, a word of Arabic origin meaning something made up of four parts. In poetry *rubai* signifies simply a quatrain or stanza of four lines. The plural form of the word has become famous in connection with the *Rubaiyat* of Omar Khayyam, a Persian mathematician, astronomer, freethinker and epigrammatist, who was born in or near Naishapur in the early part of the eleventh century. *Khayyam*, pronounced kye-yam, is a Persian word signifying tent maker and probably refers to the occupation of Omar's father. Although Omar is known in the Western world chiefly as a poet and freethinker, he was a man of profound learning and by profession a mathematician and astronomer. His treatise on algebra is considered the greatest contribution of his country and age to the subject of mathematics and it led Sultan Malik-Shah to appoint him one of the eight distinguished scientists to make astronomical researches with a view of reforming the Mohammedan calendar. When offered preferment at court Omar requested that instead he be given an independent income and be permitted to live in retirement and devote his entire time to scientific pursuits. Nominally he was a Moslem, but his verses clearly reveal a freethinker protesting against the narrow austerity, bigotry and hypocrisy of the various Moslem sects of his time. It is doubtful whether Omar wrote all of the more than 500 epigrammatic verses ascribed to him. Omar bears about the same relation to the *Rubaiyat* that Aesop does to the writings known as *Aesop's Fables*. The earliest known manuscripts containing *rubaiyat* ascribed to Omar date back only to the fifteenth century. Edward Fitzgerald (1809–1883), an English man of letters, made Omar Khayyam famous in the Western world by his classic translation of the *Rubaiyat*, which is now among the most widely read verse in the world.

Is it legal to make a profit on postage stamps?

The law provides that United States postage stamps shall not be sold by postmasters and postal employees for more or less than the face value of the stamps. This restriction, however, does not apply to persons not connected with the postal service. Private individuals and business firms have the legal right to sell postage stamps at a profit or a loss if they desire to do so. A stamp collector may pay a large sum for an uncanceled postage stamp of small face value, and the owner of a stamp vending machine is permitted to make a profit on the stamps sold.

How did "khaki" originate?

Khaki as applied to military uniforms is derived from the Hindu and Persian *khak*, meaning "earth" or "dust." Literally the term signifies dusty or dust-colored and is applicable to a color rather than a fabric. In parts of India the fields and roads are very dusty during the dry season. The wind raises the dust to such an extent that all the foliage of the trees and shrubs presents a dust or ash colored hue. This is the shade of color originally described by *khaki*. In the early days of the British occupation of India the regulars and the royal troops wore regulation red uniforms or white cotton and duck. These uniforms stood out so distinctly against the prevailing color of the landscape that their wearers presented excellent targets for snipers and sharpshooters. Bitter experience taught the British to make themselves less conspicuous by dipping their white cotton uniforms in muddy pools and streams to give them the same hue as the landscape. This crude application of the principle of camouflage is said to have been first resorted to by the British during the wars with the Sikhs in the years from 1845 to 1849. The knowledge was quickly put to more practical use. Sir Harry Burnett Lumsden's English regiment was issued khaki uniforms as early as 1848. During the siege of Delhi in 1857, some of the Indian soldiers in the British service wore uniforms made of a brownish-colored twilled cotton cloth. For many years *khaki* was applied to such cloth rather than to the color. In 1882 the British government adopted khaki uniforms for all field service. Other nations soon followed suit. Khaki uniforms were first worn by American soldiers during the Spanish-American War. A uniform of khaki was introduced because the regulation dark blue uniforms were too warm for service in the tropics. The new uniforms, however, were not introduced throughout the Army at once, but were issued from time to time as they became available to replace the blue uniforms previously worn. *Khaki* is now generally applied to drab shades of gray, brown and green rather than to any particular type of cloth.

Is a spider an insect?

Spiders are not insects and are no nearer to insects than reptiles are to birds. They belong to the class Arachnida, which also includes scorpions, mites and ticks. Spiders differ from insects in several respects. They have no feelers nor antennae, such as all insects have, and they have four pairs of legs and two pairs of jaws, while insects have three pairs of legs and three pairs of jaws. In Greek mythology Arachne was a Lydian maiden skilled in weaving. She challenged Athena (Minerva) to a contest in her art, but the jealous goddess changed the girl into a spider as a punishment for mocking the gods.

How did "when Greek meets Greek" originate?

Although generally given as, "When Greek meets Greek, then comes the tug of war," the exact quotation is, "When Greeks joined Greeks, then was the tug of war." It is from the fourth act of a tragedy in blank verse entitled *The Rival Queens, or the Death of Alexander the Great* and written in 1677 by Nathaniel Lee (1653?–1692), an English dramatist. This play made the author's reputation and remained a favorite on the British stage until the time of Edmund Kean. The line in question refers to the stubborn resistance made by the Greek cities to the Macedonian armies of Philip and his son Alexander the Great. *When Greek meets Greek* is now employed to suggest the severity of the conflict that is likely to result when two men or armies of equal courage and strength are opposed to each other.

Why are soldiers called doughboys?

Doughboy was first applied to United States infantry soldiers shortly after the Civil War. The earliest recorded use of the term in this sense is dated 1867. In that year General George A. Custer, a cavalry officer, wrote that he was "not a doughboy." There are several theories as to the origin of the term, but all of them lack positive confirmation. A doughboy is a dumpling of raised dough. In this sense the word is a corruption of *doughbah* and was used in England as early as 1685. According to one theory, *doughboy* was first applied humorously to the Federal infantry by the cavalry during the Civil War because the large globular buttons on the uniforms of the foot soldiers bore some resemblance to doughboys or gobs of dough. Another theory holds that the name originated during the Mexican War and was suggested by the *adobe* huts in which the infantry were frequently quartered. *Adobe*, a Spanish word meaning "sun-dried clay," is often pronounced *doe-by*. Variations of this theory suppose that *adobe* or *dobe* was used in the army to mean mud and that the infantrymen were so called because they are the soldiers who have to march in the mud, or because their uniforms often became smeared with adobe or mud. This theory is partly confirmed by the fact that during the late sixties infantrymen were variously called *dobe crushers, dobe makers* and *mud crushers*. Another theory is that American infantrymen were first called doughboys in the days when they used to clean their white trimmings with pipe clay. If the infantryman, after cleaning his trimmings, was caught in the rain the whiting would run and form a kind of dough. Still another theory traces the term to General Albert Sidney Johnston's expedition against the Mormons. It is said that the artillerymen, who disliked the infantry, called them doughboys because a certain bugle call seemed to say, "dirty, dirty doughboys!" *Doughboy* was not applied promiscuously to men in all branches of the service until World War I. When the first American troops arrived in France they were greeted by the Allies with such names as "Sammies" and "Teddies." These nicknames were resented so keenly by some of the troops that Major General William Sibert, commander of the first American division in France, asked publicly for suggestions for a name corresponding to the British *Tommy Atkins*. Most of the men preferred *doughboy*, although *Yank, Johnny Yank* and *Sammy* were also suggested.

What is a kangaroo court?

A kangaroo court is a sham court or mock trial. The term, which is of unknown origin, is applied especially to a sham trial conducted by the inmates of a jail or penitentiary. Some authorities think that it is a relic of the trials on board pirate ships in the days of the Spanish Main. The kangaroo, however, probably became associated with mock trials in prisons in the days when Australia was a penal colony. In many prisons the convicts organize permanent kangaroo courts for punishing minor offenses among themselves, such, for instance, as failure to wash the neck, keeping an untidy cell or petty theft. The punishment generally consists of a fine of a few cents, which is given to some charitable or recreational fund. This form of self-discipline among inmates is approved and encouraged by some jailers and wardens who regard it as helpful in running the institution. Kangaroo courts sometimes get out of bounds and impose severe and cruel sentences upon the victims and have to be broken up by the authorities. In recent years *kangaroo court* has come to be applied also to petty local courts presided over by mayors and justices of the peace who receive fees only in case the defendant is convicted and fined.

How did "kick the bucket" originate?

The origin of this popular phrase, which means "to die," is not known for certain. In one of its senses *bucket* means a beam or yoke on which anything is hung or carried. It is said that in parts of England, especially in Norfolkshire, *bucket* is the common word applied to a beam. Pigs are hung from such a beam by their hind legs with their heads down and when they are killed they kick the beam or bucket, and thus *bucket* may have become associated with dying. But this is little more than conjecture. Another theory accepts the word in its more usual meaning, namely, a "pail." The phrase, according to this theory, refers to the method of committing suicide by standing on a pail or bucket, tying one end of a rope around one's neck and the other to a beam, and then kicking over the bucket. In this connection a passage in Shakespeare's *II Henry IV* is interesting. This passage, supposedly written about 1597, is: "Swifter then hee that gibbets on the Brewers Bucket."

Why does a red schoolhouse symbolize education?

Although most wooden schoolhouses in the United States are now painted white, a few generations ago it was customary, especially in New England and other northeastern sections of the country, to paint frame schoolhouses red, not because that color was preferred, but because red paint was cheaper than any other kind obtainable. Thus the little red schoolhouse became a symbol of popular education in general.

How did applause by hand clapping originate?

Applause in one form or another is probably almost as old as civilization. Clapping the hands is among the most natural ways of applauding. In fact *applaud* itself comes from two Latin words meaning to "strike together." Nobody can say when such customs began. An untutored child instinctively expresses delight by clapping its hands. The ancient Greeks and Romans applauded by hand clapping as well as by snapping their fingers and waving the flaps of their garments. About 1820, Paris theaters began to pay persons to applaud the actors, to insure the success of plays. The hired applauders were called a claque, from French claquer, to applaud. Some of the claquers laughed at the proper time, some wept, while others merely applauded. Women in the claque held their handkerchiefs to their eyes during the sad scenes.

How did "mumblety-peg" originate?

The original form of the name of this popular children's game was mumble-the-peg, which is descriptive of one of the penalties imposed on the loser. There are several local names of the game, such as mumble-peg, mumbled-peg and mumbly-peg, all being corruptions of the earlier name. It is called knifie in Scotland. In mumblety-peg, now the most common of the names, each player in turn throws a pocket knife from a specified series of positions and continues until he fails to make the blade stick in the ground or on a piece of wood as the case may be. Sometimes the loser is compelled to draw out of the ground with his teeth a wooden peg that the other players have driven with the handle of the knife. In parts of Ireland a game resembling mumblety-peg is played with a fork.

How did Smithfield ham get its name?

This product was developed in the South and reached its greatest fame in and around Smithfield, Virginia, from which it received its name. It is a common mistake to suppose that Smithfield ham got its name from the famous Smithfield market in London. Although there are several recipes for producing Smithfield hams, they are all based on a strong, dry, salt cure. After being cured the hams are given a long cool smoke, often lasting ten or fifteen days, which is in contrast to the twenty or thirty-hour smoke at a high temperature given to ordinary commerical hams. The hams are then covered with pepper, generally bagged and hung in unrefrigerated storage for about a year. During this storage or ripening period the hams develop a peculiarly characteristic flavor that is sometimes described as "cheesy." It is this pungent flavor that constitutes the chief difference between them and other hams. Smithfield hams of the best quality are traditionally from hogs fattened on peanuts, although this is not always true. In 1939 William Denissen, a representative of Swift and Company, made the following observation at a restaurant men's banquet in Washington: "All Smithfield ham is

Virginia ham, but not all Virginia ham is Smithfield ham. I am in favor of prohibiting restaurateurs from designating Smithfield ham on their menus when what they are serving is ham that is not from the fragrant curing sheds of Smithfield, Virginia." A ham generally weighs seven per cent of the weight of the live hog. Occasionally hams weigh as much as one hundred pounds.

How were the Plains of Abraham named?

The heights near Quebec known as the Plains of Abraham took their name from Abraham Martin, a Canadian pioneer said to have been of Scotch descent, who was a pilot on the St. Lawrence River in the time of Samuel de Champlain, founder of the city. Champlain himself authorized a deed granting the pilot a homestead on the heights of Quebec. Martin was affectionately known among the French inhabitants as *Maître Abraham* and his herds of cattle and sheep were a common sight on the tableland along the St. Lawrence. On September 15, 1759, on the Plains of Abraham was fought a historic battle that determined whether the French or the British were to dominate Canada. General James Wolfe, the victorious British commander, and the Marquis de Montcalm, the defeated French commander, were both killed in the battle. A forty foot monument marks the spot where Wolfe fell.

Why were women formerly excluded from mines?

Among the more ignorant class of miners in Great Britain, the United States, Canada, Mexico, and perhaps other countries, there used to be a superstition that the presence of a woman in a mine was an evil omen. If a woman entered a mine many of the miners would walk out. For this reason women were forbidden to enter many mines while the men were at work. In northern England it was a sign of ill luck merely to meet a woman on the way to work in the mines. That this old sex taboo survives to a limited extent is evidenced by the fact that it was commented upon as late as 1940 when Secretary of Labor Frances Perkins, the first woman cabinet member in the United States, visited lead and zinc mines in Missouri on a tour of investigation of health and working conditions.

What is a slush fund?

In the political sense a slush fund is a campaign fund collected to influence public opinion by improper means. This application of the term, however, is of comparatively recent origin. *Slush fund* originated in the British Navy. It was formerly customary on war vessels to sell slush and other refuse to raise a fund for the benefit of the enlisted men. Originally the slush consisted of fat, grease and other refuse from the cook's galley that was not needed for slushing the masts and spars. There is an old verb *to slush*, meaning to grease or lubricate with slush. Later the slush fund was raised by selling worn-out equipment, personal effects left on board by deserters, etc. Army camps and garrisons imitated the custom and also raised slush funds. The modern slush fund consists of money contributed by the enlisted men themselves and used to support athletics and other activities. Slush funds have been largely done away with in the United States Navy.

Does the hippopotamus sweat blood?

The hippopotamus, which ranks second to the elephant in size among land mammals, has been famous since ancient times for its *bloody sweat*. Itinerant menageries used to advertise the hippopotamus as "the blood-sweating behemoth of the Nile." The skin of the hippopotamus is very thick, as much as two inches in some places. Spread over the hairless hide of the body and head are numerous large pores that exude a thick, reddish, oily fluid, particularly when the animal is out of the water. This carmine perspiration seems to be nature's way of protecting the skin from drying and cracking. It may be compared to the water-proofing oil secreted by glands near the tail of a duck. There is this difference, however: the oil protects the duck from water while the *bloody sweat* protects the hippopotamus from the air while out of the water. When the hippopotamus emerges from the water the pores in its skin begin to secrete the oily fluid, which often trickles from the body in streamlets. When the animal is hot, excited or in pain the fluid flows more freely and is redder in color than usual. But the reddish color of the sweat is not produced by blood, which forms no part of the fluid, but by a peculiar carmine pigment.

When does a cow manufacture her milk?

Many farmers, teachers and professional people engaged in dairy cattle work believe that the udder of a cow will hold only about half a pint of milk to the quarter and that the liquid is manufactured just as the cow gives it down at milking time. In 1926 the United States Department of Agriculture proved that most of the milk is not manufactured during the few minutes required for the milking process. This proof was obtained by a novel experiment in post-mortem milking. A cow was killed, her udder immediately removed and mounted on a framework and then milked. She had been giving an average of about 12 pounds

[116]

at each milking. A total of 10 and 27/100ths pounds of milk was drawn from her udder after it had been severed from the body, proving that more than 85 per cent of her milk had been stored in her udder before she was slaughtered.

How did "bootlegger" originate?

Bootlegging, as applied to the illegal selling of liquor, originated many years ago on the Indian reservations in the West. The original bootlegger peddled booze unlawfully among the Indians. He was so called from the practice of carrying the flasks of *fire water* in the legs of his boots to conceal them from government officials. Later, when prohibition laws were adopted in different part of the country, violators of these laws were called bootleggers. Even at the present time it is unlawful to sell liquor on Indian reservations or to give it to Indians.

Which is correct, "maddening" or "madding" crowd?

The correct title of Thomas Hardy's novel is *Far from the Madding Crowd*. It is taken from Thomas Gray's *Elegy Written in a Country Churchyard*, in which occurs the line: "Far from the *madding* crowd's ignoble strife." This line is often misquoted by substituting *maddening* for *madding*, which not only mars the meter but also alters the meaning. *Madding* here is a poetic survival of *to mad*, an old intransitive verb meaning to act madly. In the line quoted *madding* signifies wild, furious, raving, mad. *Maddening*, on the other hand, means distracting or annoying.

What is a cow's cud?

The stomach of a cow, like that of other ruminants, is divided into four separate compartments. As a cow eats, the food is not at first thoroughly chewed. It passes immediately into a large compartment of the stomach known as the paunch. Later while the cow is resting, either standing up or lying down, this undigested food is regurgitated from the paunch, masticated, mixed with saliva and swallowed again. The quid or returned bolus of food in the cow's mouth is called the cud. Sometimes a cow *loses her cud*; that is, rumination stops because the food ceases to come up from the paunch into the mouth. This is frequently one of the first indications of sickness in ruminant animals. Rumination is resumed when the animal returns to a normal state of health. In such cases some farmers give a cow an artificial cud, such as a dried herring or a strip of salted pork to aid the animal to recover her natural cud. The United States Department of Agriculture frowns on this method and says it is impractical. Besides animals of the bovine kind, sheep, goats, antelopes, giraffes, deer and camels are true ruminants, have four-chambered stomachs and chew the cud.

How did "according to Hoyle" originate?

The Hoyle in *according to Hoyle* was Edmond Hoyle (1672–1769), English writer on games. Little is known about his personal life. Tradition says he was educated for the bar. At any rate he settled in London and seems to have made his living, partly at least, by teaching various games, particularly the card game known as whist. In 1742, for the use of his pupils, Hoyle published *A Short Treatise on the Game of Whist,* which contained the first systematic code of laws and rules for the game. Later he published a general book on games, which included his earlier treatise on whist. Hoyle was considered an authority on whist until 1864 and his name became proverbial as an authority on games in general. Playing a game *according to Hoyle* means playing it according to the recognized rules.

Which is correct, "nerve-racking" or "nerve-wracking"?

Owing perhaps to a false theory of its origin, *nerve-racking* is often incorrectly written *nerve-wracking. Racking* here is the participial form of *to rack,* from Anglo-Saxon *raxan* ("to stretch"). It means to distress or cause prolonged suffering and alludes to the pain inflicted by torture on the instrument of punishment known as the rack. *Wrack* is derived from Anglo-Saxon *wrecan* ("to drive out"), and is employed in several senses, including that of a wreck.

Should "double" be used in oral spelling?

It is a disputed question whether in oral spelling one should repeat double letters or use the word "double"; as, *s, p, o, o, n,* or *s, p, double-o, n.* There is no accepted rule covering the practice and both methods are used by teachers, depending on individual preference. In 1928 the United States Bureau of Education expressed the following opinion on the subject: "The best authorities contend that *double-l* for *ll,* or *double-e* for *ee,* is not permissible on the ground that there are no double letters in the alphabet, and that the current practice should be to spell *l-l* or *e-e,* as the case may be. Practice varies, however, in different schools, as no standard has ever been set for this particular type of spelling." Joy Elmer Morgan, editor of the *Journal of the National Education Association,* said about the same time: "So far as I know neither the Association nor any of its committees has ever passed judgment on the

[118]

question as to whether pupils should be taught to say *double-e*, or *e-e*. My personal preference would be for *double-e*, which is perfectly clear and simple." The double letter method of oral spelling is used in some foreign languages also. Some teachers restrict the double method to words in which the double letters are in the same syllable. For instance, they would spell *pull* orally *p, u, double-l*, but *pulley* would be spelled *p, u, l, l, e, y*. Obviously the double-letter method would not be practical in *vacuum, residuum, continuum, perpetuum* and other words containing *uu*. *Vacuum* would sound queer if spelled *v, a, c, double-u, m*, where *double-u* might be taken for the letter *w*.

What is meant by the white man's burden?

"The White Man's Burden" is the title of a poem written by Rudyard Kipling and first published in 1899. Each stanza begins with the line, "Take up the white man's burden." The poem was addressed to the United States and contained what purported to be John Bull's gloomy advice to Uncle Sam after the latter had won the Spanish-American War and had entered the field of colonial administration. The first stanza reads:

> Take up the White Man's burden—
> Send forth the best ye breed—
> Go bind your sons to exile
> To serve your captives' need;
> To wait, in heavy harness,
> On fluttered folk and wild—
> Your new-caught, sullen peoples,
> Half-devil and half-child.

The *white man's burden* was later used in referring to the supposed responsibility of the white race for the moral and physical welfare of the dark races of the world.

How did "praise from Sir Hubert" originate?

This expression was suggested by a quotation from "A Cure for the Heartache," written by Thomas Morton (1764?–1838) and first produced in London in 1797. Sir Hubert Stanley appears in the play as a kindly, but unthrifty and impoverished baronet whose family pride compels him to live beyond his means. In the last scene of the last act Sir Hubert says to Young Rapid, son of Old Rapid the tailor: "Mr. Rapid, by asserting your character as a man of honor, in rewarding the affection of this amiable woman, you command my praise; for bestowing happiness on my dear Charles, receive an old man's blessing." To which Young Rapid replies: "Approbation from Sir Hubert Stanley is praise indeed." In popular usage this has become, "Praise from Sir Hubert is praise indeed."

How did Hell Gate get its name?

Hell Gate is a formerly dangerous passage in the East River between Manhattan and Long Island. The name is a rough translation of Dutch *Helle Gat*. In Dutch *helle* may mean "hell" or "bright, clear, beautiful," and *gat* "hole" or "passageway." In 1614 Adrian Block, an early Dutch settler at New Amsterdam, passed through the East River in the "Restless," first vessel built on Manhattan Island, and called the entire river *Helle Gat* after *Die Helle Gat* ("bright passage"), a tributary of the Scheldt in his native Zeeland. The name, first applied to the entire East River, was narrowed down by the English until it referred only to the rocky and dangerous point where the waters of the river merge into those of Long Island Sound. So far as the form of the name goes, it may mean either entrance to hell or a clear passageway. Early in the nineteenth century delicate New Yorkers changed this picturesque and suggestive name to *Hurlgate* on the theory that it was first applied to the whirlpool and that it was a corruption of old Dutch *Hoellgut* or *Horligat*, literally meaning "whirling strait." Washington Irving denounced this change in the following language: "Certain mealy-mouthed men of squeamish consciences, who are loth to give the Devil his due, have softened the above characteristic into *Hurlgate*, forsooth!" But commonsense prevailed and *Hell Gate* was revived. Between 1870 and 1885 many of the natural obstructions in the channel were removed by the Federal Government and Hell Gate became navigable by vessels of limited draft.

Why is a ship referred to as "she"?

It has always been customary to personify certain inanimate objects and attribute to them characteristics peculiar to living creatures. Thus things without life are often spoken of as having sex. Some objects are regarded as masculine. *He, him* and *his* are applied to the sun, to winter, to death, etc. Others are regarded as feminine, especially those things that are so dear to us. The earth as Mother Earth is regarded as the common maternal parent of all life. Likewise seamen invariably speak of their ship in the feminine gender. To a sailor a vessel is always *she* or *her*. This is because the seafaring man depends upon the ship and it is dear to him. It is natural that he should compare it with woman,

man's dearest and most cherished friend, from whom he is often long separated by the nature of his employment. In most of the older languages inanimate objects are regarded as having either masculine or feminine gender. Almost invariably the feminine gender is attributed to boats and ships as well as vehicles of all kinds. But the English language is devoid of true gender and pronouns denoting sex are used in personifying objects.

Does the female turtledove coo?

Many people erroneously suppose that the plaintive note known as cooing is uttered exclusively by the male of the American turtledove, or mourning dove as it is more properly called. Both sexes of this species make the cooing sound. However, the male mourning dove does much more cooing than the female and begins cooing earlier in the morning. The female's call or note is not particularly different from that of the male.

Does Uncle Sam lose or profit by special stamps?

The government generally makes a profit on special stamps issued to commemorate historical and other important events. The income from new stamps sold to collectors alone more than reimburses the Post Office Department for all expenses incurred in manufacturing and distributing the special issues.

What animals get up hind legs first?

Cattle, camels, sheep, goats, antelopes, deer, giraffes and all other members of the ruminant or cud-chewing family invariably rise hind part first. Other large four-footed animals get up front legs first.

What is a Frankenstein?

A Frankenstein is a person destroyed by his own works. The term is often erroneously applied to a monster. In Mary W. Shelley's *Frankenstein, or the Modern Prometheus*, published in 1818, Victor Frankenstein is a young Swiss student who, while attending a German university, constructs a monster of materials obtained from cemeteries and dissecting rooms and endues it with life by means of galvanism. The soulless monster, shunned by every living thing, is made frantic by unsatisfied human cravings and commits atrocious crimes, finally inflicting a horrible retribution upon the man who usurped the prerogative of the Creator. The author of the book, who was the second wife of the poet, Percy Bysshe Shelley, gave the monster no name in her narrative, a fact

[121]

that leads many into the error of referring to it as Frankenstein. Frankenstein was the creator and the victim; the creature was Frankenstein's monster.

Is water a food?

Water, although essential to life, is not generally classed as a food. Two-thirds of the human body is composed of water and most of the chemical changes that take place in the body occur in solution in that liquid, but the water itself is never decomposed in the digestive processes. Health authorities generally define food as anything that nourishes the body, a definition that excludes pure water. Sometimes, however, water is regarded as a food in the broad sense that food is anything normally taken into the body, either solid or liquid, or any element necessary to maintain life. Most ordinary drinking water has food value also in the sense that it is generally rich in mineral salts necessary to the well-being of the body. It is not true, as often supposed, that water will make a person fat. Retention of water in the tissues of the body will add to one's weight, but it will not produce fat in the strict sense of the term.

Why is a packing material called "excelsior"?

How excelsior came to be applied to long, fine wood shavings used as a stuffing or packing material for eggs and other breakable objects is not known for certain. It is a purely American term and apparently originated as a trade name. Undoubtedly it is the same word as the comparative degree of Latin excelsus, meaning elevated. Thus "Excelsior," the title of a well known poem by Henry Wadsworth Longfellow, signifies "still higher," "more lofty" or "ever upward." The term is the motto of New York State. In normal times hundreds of thousands of tons of excelsior are manufactured in the United States. Aspen, cottonwood, basswood, willow, red gum, spruce and certain pines are the favorite woods used in making excelsior, or wool wood as it is also called. The logs are first cut into blocks about eighteen inches long and the fibers are separated from the blocks by knife points. A cord of wood produces about two thousand pounds of excelsior. The grade depends on the fineness of the shavings.

How is "slough" pronounced in "Slough of Despond"?

The pronunciation of slough varies with the meaning. When the word signifies a hole full of mud or a deep, miry place it is correctly pronounced slou, rhyming with now and plough. This is the proper pronunciation of the word as employed in John Bunyan's *Pilgrim's Progress*, where the Slough of Despond is a deep bog into which Christian falls at the beginning of his journey and from which Help extricates him. When *slough* refers to a marshy place or a piece of low, wet land—the usual sense in the United States—it is pronounced *sloo*, rhyming with *too*. Frequently the word in this sense is locally spelled *slew*, *sloo* or *slue*. When *slough* refers to the skin of an animal or reptile it has still a different pronunciation—*sluff*. *Slew* or *slue* as slang is used in the sense of a great quantity, an abundance or a crowd; as, a slew of people.

What does "drawing a red herring across the trail" mean?

A red herring is a herring of special grade that has been heavily salted and slowly smoked to give it a rich brown or reddish color. The red color of the red herring is due to the peculiar process of curing. Red herring has been a famous product in England for hundreds of years. John Strange, a Member of Parliament in the time of Edward II (1307–1327), agreed with the burgesses of his district to take his wages in red herrings. "To draw a red herring across one's path, track or trail" means to attempt to divert one's attention from the real question by raising a side issue. The saying originated among sportsmen and was suggested by an old practice described as follows in *Gentlemen's Recreation* in 1686: "The trailing or dragging of a dead Cat, or Fox, (and in case of necessity a Red-Herring) three or four miles . . . and then laying the Dogs on the scent." Dogs have a keen scent for red herring, and if one is drawn across the trail of a fox it will mislead the hounds. In England *track* is generally substituted for *trail* in the saying. As a matter of fact, *drawing a red herring across the trail*, in that exact form, is an American phrase and dates back only to the nineteenth century.

Why is China called the Land of Han?

China is called the Land of Han and its inhabitants the Sons of Han from the famous Han or Twenty-sixth Dynasty which began to reign over that country in 206 B.C., the date when modern Chinese history commences. The old empire disintegrated under the later rulers of the Chou Dynasty and the last ruler of that line was deposed in 249 B.C. Three years afterward a prince of the state or province of Ch'in and one of the greatest political geniuses of China, ascended the throne and began to weld the vast domain inhabited by Chinese into a unified empire. He styled himself Shih Huang Ti, meaning "the first emperor." His empire, however, collapsed after his death in 210 B.C., and his feeble successor, known as the second emperor of the Ch'in Dynasty, was murdered three years later. Out of the civil strife that ensued Liu Pang, chief of the village of Han, emerged victorious in 202 B.C. and founded the Han Dynasty, which he regarded as having begun four years earlier and which lasted until 220 A.D. This period of more than four centuries was marked by the revival of letters, the introduction of Buddhism into China and the extension of Chinese rule over Mongolia.

How did the Nickel Plate Railroad get its name?

The New York, Chicago and St. Louis Railroad was nicknamed the "Nickel Plate" as the result of a pun printed in a small Ohio newspaper. Construction work on the first stretch of the railroad was begun in 1881 between Arcadia and McComb, Ohio, and the first trains were operated on the line in the following year. In glancing over the editorial comments on the new enterprise in the exchanges on his desk, Edward L. Young, associate editor of the *Norwalk Chronicle*, noticed that the initials of the name of the new railroad were N.Y.C.L. The process of finishing known as nickel-plating was just becoming popular at that time and the young editor could not resist making a pun. He said in his comment that it was a "N.Y.C.L.-plated railroad." The pun caught the public fancy and was reprinted in other papers. Ever after the New York, Chicago and St. Louis Railroad was known as the "Nickel Plate." The proprietors of the railroad saw Young's editorial and they granted a life pass over the Nickel Plate line to F. R. Loomis, editor in chief of the *Chronicle*, as an expression of their appreciation for the publicity that the complimentary pun had brought the new enterprise. A short time later the Vanderbilt interests purchased the road and William H. Vanderbilt became its president. The railroad magnate, according to a popular story, said that "for the price we paid for it, it ought to be nickel-plated." The Hampden Railroad in Massachusetts, the northern terminus of which was Belchertown, was known as "the gold-plated line" because no train ever ran on its tracks.

How did bloomers get their name?

Bloomers received their name from Mrs. Amelia Jenks Bloomer, who was born at Homer, New York, in 1818. In 1840, after a short career as schoolteacher and governess, she was married to Dexter C. Bloomer, of Seneca Falls, New York, where for several years she and her husband were engaged in publishing the *Seneca County Courier*, a semi-monthly magazine. In 1849 she founded the *Lily*, a periodical devoted to temperance and women's rights. The February issue of 1851 contained a description of a "sanitary attire" for women designed and worn by Mrs. Elizabeth

Smith Miller, a daughter of Gerrit Smith, who was later a Representative in Congress from New York. The costume consisted of skirts reaching to the knees and loose trousers gathered round the ankles like Turkish trousers. Dressed in such attire Mrs. Miller visited her cousin, Elizabeth Cady Stanton, at Seneca Falls. In her *Eighty Years and More* Mrs. Stanton wrote of this demonstration of the new costume for women: "To see my cousin, with a lamp in one hand and a baby in the other, walk up stairs with ease and grace, while, with flowing robes, I pulled myself up with difficulty, lamp and baby out of the question, really convinced me that there was sore need of reform in woman's dress." Mrs. Bloomer, who had for several years advocated reform in women's dress, adopted the new costume and wrote many articles in favor of it. After eight years she abandoned the new costume because she thought her influence would be greater in more conventional women's dress. Although in her magazine, as well as in lectures, she continually said that Mrs. Miller was the real originator of the style, the public insisted on giving her the credit, and *Bloomer costume* or *Bloomers* soon became the accepted name of the attire. Mrs. Bloomer died at Council Bluffs, Iowa, in 1894.

Why do sea shells roar?

When certain sea shells are held close to the ear a noise resembling the distant roar or rumble of the sea can be heard. Many people believe this rumbling sound is an actual echo of the waves of the ocean. Such is not the case. The noise is merely a composite of the echoes of a great number of ordinary sounds occurring in the vicinity of the shell. Because of the peculiar shape of the shell and the smoothness of its interior, the least vibration produces an echo, and numerous such echoes are blended into the rumble of roar. The effect is heightened by the fact that the shell magnifies the pulses in the head as well as the sounds produced in the vicinity.

Does lightning ever strike water?

It used to be commonly believed that lightning never strikes water. There is considerable evidence, however, that lightning does often strike water and accordingly persons are advised to keep out of the water during electrical storms. In this connection it is interesting to note that one of the laws of Genghis Khan forbade the Mongols to bathe or wash garments in running water during a thunderstorm. The Mongols were very much afraid of thunder and the provision in the *Yassa* may have been designed to prevent them from throwing themselves into lakes and rivers during a storm. Whether lightning ever strikes the surface of the open ocean is a disputed question. The United States Weather Bureau believes that it does. According to that authority, this meteorological phenomenon is well known, though not very common. Some years ago a scientist attempted to demonstrate indirectly by a laboratory experiment that lightning does not strike in the open ocean. He used long and powerful electric sparks, resembling lightning as nearly as possible. The sparks persistently refused to strike the surface of water; instead they invariably struck the edge of the container. Experiments like this, however, cannot be regarded as conclusive. It would be difficult, in a laboratory experiment, even to approximate the conditions that exist in the open sea hundreds of miles from land. There is a common belief that often fish are killed in large bodies of water by lightning striking the surface. In August, 1932, it was reported that fishermen picked up more than 100 stunned fish after lightning struck Upper Saranac near Doctors Island in New York.

What is a gadget?

Gadget is synonymous with thingumbob, thingumabob, thingumajig and doodad. It is virtually equivalent to thing and is so broad in meaning that it can be applied to almost anything. It is employed as a convenient slang name for anything novel or as a substitute word when the speaker is unable to recall the right name. Gadget originated in the Navy and is applied by sailors to all sorts of small tools and mechanical devices. When a sailor says "Hand me that gadget," he may mean anything from a nail to a monkey wrench. He usually employs the word only when the correct name of the article does not readily occur to him, just as a landsman might say, "Hand me that doodad." Two theories have been advanced to account for the origin of the term, neither being supported by evidence. According to one, gadget is derived from French gachette, diminutive of gache, a "catch" or "staple." The other derives it from gadge, an obsolete Scottish word meaning "gauge."

What is a moonless month?

Moonless month is the name popularly given to a month in which no full moon occurs. Under our present calendar February is the only month that is shorter than the lunar cycle and consequently the only one that can have fewer than four moon phases. The absent phase, however, need not necessarily be the full moon, but may be any one of the four. Likewise five phases of the moon occasionally fall in the other months. The average time from one full moon to another is twenty-nine and one-half days, and the time from one phase to the next varies from less than seven days to more than eight. About every six years February has only three phases; it is, of course, without a full moon much less frequently. In 1866 February had no full moon while the preceding January and the following March had two full moons each. This remarkable sequence, astronomers estimate, will not occur again for some 2,500,000 years. February was without a full moon in 1885, 1915 and 1934, and from approximate computations made by the United States Naval Observatory that month will be without a full moon in 1961. Februaries without new moons or either of the other two phases occur at about the same intervals, but, of course, in different years.

How did Pershing get the nickname "Black Jack"?

The nickname "Black Jack" was given to John J. Pershing by the cadets while he was tactical instructor at West Point in 1897. Since 1892 Pershing had been an officer in the Tenth United States Cavalry, the famous colored regiment that later distinguished itself in the Spanish-American War by coming to the support of Colonel Theodore Roosevelt and the Rough Riders. It was only natural that Jack Pershing's long service with this unit of Negro troops should give birth to a nickname. At first he was called "Nigger Jack," which was gradually supplanted by the more acceptable "Black Jack." This nickname, however, was not new in the American Army. Major General John A. Logan of Civil War fame was known as "Black Jack" because of his swarthy complexion and black hair and mustache. He had a strain of Indian blood.

Why is lighting three cigarettes with one match unlucky?

Two theories have been advanced to explain the origin of the superstition that it is unlucky to light three cigarettes with the same match. According to one, the superstition originated during the First World War and arose from the real danger incident to keeping a match lighted in the trenches long enough to light three cigarettes. If a match were made to do triple duty it might not only attract the enemy's attention but give him time enough to aim. But a match extinguished quickly after lighting one or two cigarettes would not give the enemy sufficient time to direct his fire. The continual caution on this point, it is said, gave rise to the odd superstition that was so common for twenty years after the First World War. According to the other theory, the superstition originated in eastern Europe in connection with the funeral service in the Russian church in which three altar candles are lighted with one taper. The Russians, this story has it, regarded it as sacrilegious and impious to make any other lights in groups of three and hence the superstition that ill luck will befall anybody who lights three cigarettes with the same match, or anybody who even accepts such a light. One writer expresses the opinion that the superstition originated among the British troops in South Africa during the Boer War. The acute match shortage during the Second World War did much to eliminate this superstition, which had become almost universal. Everybody then was urged to ignore the superstition and to conserve matches by "borrowing lights" and getting as many lights as possible from each match.

Can bees sting a person while he holds his breath?

Many people believe that bees, wasps and other stinging insects cannot sting a person while he holds his breath, clenches his fists tightly or grasps one wrist firmly with the opposite hand. According to the popular notion, the insect is physically unable to penetrate the human skin under such conditions, no matter how hard it may ply its stinger, because the pores are then closed. The United States Bureau of Entomology investigated this question and reported that the belief has no foundation in fact. The stinger of a bee does enter the skin through the pores, and these tiny openings may be slightly affected by breathing, but the difference is not sufficient to interfere with the operation of a bee's stinger. If bees do not sting a person while he holds his breath or clenches his fists it is not because they cannot sting under such conditions, but because the person is then likely to be more quiet. Bees seem to be able to detect the slightest sign of fear in a human being and are stimulated to sting by any quick, nervous movements. A person who remains quiet and who shows no fear is not in great danger of being stung. Bees, however, are repelled by certain body odors, and some persons do not excite and anger bees as others do. It is absurd to suppose that a person tampering with bees would be immune from their stings merely because he held his breath or clenched his fists. Some have tested the popular belief to their sorrow.

How do maggots get on meat?

It was once universally believed that maggots are produced on dead flesh by abiogenesis or spontaneous generation; that is, the production of living from nonliving matter. Aristotle taught spontaneous generation and stated as an observed fact that some animals spring from putrid meat. This belief persisted through the Middle Ages and was not finally disproved scientifically until 1668, when an Italian named Francesco Redi (1626?–1697) advanced the theory that every living thing comes from a pre-existing living thing. Redi, a Florentine doctor, was not only court physician to the Grand Duke of Tuscany but also one of the most brilliant poets of his time. His *Baccho in Toscana*, translated into English by Leigh Hunt, is regarded as one of the finest pieces of genuine dithyrambic poetry in existence. As the first step in the scientific refutation of the theory of spontaneous generation, Redi exposed meat to the air during hot weather. It soon began to putrify and within a few days was covered with maggots. He then put similar meat in a jar covered with fine gauze and exposed it in the same manner. The meat began to putrify as before, but no maggots appeared on it. Blowflies, however, swarmed over the wire screen covering the jar and within a few days the gauze was covered with maggots. This proved that the maggots were not generated by the corruption of the meat, but were hatched from eggs laid by the flies. Although this may have been the first scientific demonstration of the fact, it had long been known that maggots were somehow produced by flies. Shakespeare knew it, and he died twenty years before Redi was born. In *I Henry VI* Joan of Arc says of Talbot: "Him that thou magnifiest with all these titles, stinking and fly-blown, lies here at our feet." Trinculo, in *The Tempest*, says: "I have been in such a pickle since I saw you last that, I fear me, will never out of my bones; I shall not fear fly-blowing." And in *Love's Labour's Lost* Biron says: "These summer flies have blown me full of maggot ostentation." In recent years it has been discovered that blowflies secrete drugs with remarkable healing properties and that sterile blowflies are effective in healing certain types of stubborn wounds in human beings.

Why are small places called "jerkwater" towns?

Jerkwater is applied as a term of depreciation to a small, out of the way and insignificant town or station. It is supposed that the original jerkwater town was a place where trains stopped to take on water. In the early days of railroads the engine was often stopped at wayside streams to replenish the water supply. This was called *jerking* water because the water was carried to the locomotives in leather buckets carried for the purpose. In time *jerkwater* came to be applied to small towns noted for nothing in particular except that trains stopped there to take on water.

Where are the highest tides in the world?

According to the United States Hydrographic Office, the tides in the Bay of Fundy are the highest known. The greatest difference between high and low water is in Minas Basin at Burntcoat Head. Under normal conditions it is 54.5 feet. It is said that owing to local conditions of wind and weather the tide of the Bay of Fundy has been known to reach 60 feet. These high tides are due largely to the confirguration of the bay. As a general rule bays that open directly into the sea and which have narrow heads exhibit this phenomenon. The highest tides in waters adjoining the United States proper occur near Calais, Maine. There the mean range in the height of the tide is 20 feet and the spring range is 22.8 feet. In the harbor of Granville on the Normandy coast of France the tide rises and falls 46 feet. Cook Inlet on the coast of Alaska is also noted for its exceptionally high tides. In the open ocean the greatest difference between high tide and low tide is normally only a foot or two.

What laws were "written in blood"?

Draco, an Athenian lawmaker in the seventh century B.C. is reputed to have been the author of the first written code of laws in Athens. These laws became proverbial for their severity, and the orator Demandes, who lived three centuries later, said they were "written, not in ink, but in blood." According to the Draconian code, slight offenses, such as vagrancy, laziness and petty stealing, were punished as severely as murder, sacrilege and treason. In fact it was said that Draco made the violation of every law a capital offense. Once, according to tradition, Draco was asked why he punished such petty crimes with death. He replied: "The smallest of them deserve death, and there is no greater punishment I can find for the greater crimes." This code was largely superseded by the milder laws of Solon, one of the seven sages of Greece. Later Draco is said to have removed to Aegina, where he introduced a similar code of laws. The story is that he was accidentally killed in a theater, smothered to death by the garments thrown upon him as a gesture of admiration by the people. Severe and sanguinary laws are still referred to as Draconic.

Where is Podunk?

Podunk is a humorous name for any small, out of the way country village or jerkwater town. Webster's New International dictionary defines the term as "an imaginary town, taken as typical of placid dullness and lack of contact with the progress of the world." Letters from Podunk was the title of a series of magazine articles as early as 1846. In Abraham Lincoln: The War Years, Carl Sandburg wrote: "In 1861 Vanity Fair said: 'Lincoln is a brick, but no man can be happy till he is dead.' It pictured a little fat man who routed Lincoln out at midnight, embraced his knees, and said: 'Old Hoss, how are you anyhow? I voted for you, I worked for you, and now I'm here; and by the living jingo, stir I'll not, until you've promised me the Podunk Post Office.' " Just how Podunk acquired this meaning is not known. No such post office is listed in the

United States Postal Guide, although the name is applied to a village in Massachusetts and a neighborhood in Connecticut. The name is apparently of Indian origin. The Podunk Indians were a small tribe who lived in South Windsor, Hartford County, Connecticut, and Podunk, their chief village, was at the mouth of the small stream that still bears the name Podunk. At the close of King Philip's War in 1676 the Podunks, or Windsor Indians as they were also called, disappeared with the hostile tribes and never returned. There is a Podunk Pond in North Brookfield, Worcester County, Massachusetts, and a local historian gives the Indian meaning of the name as "place of burning," which is said to refer to the fact that Indians brought captives there to burn them at the stake. It seems more probable, however, that *Podunk* is related to *Potunk*, a place name on Long Island, which is supposed to be derived from *P'tuk-ohke*, an Algonquian word signifying "a neck or corner of land." *Squeedunk* as a synonym of *Podunk* was a deliberate coinage of more recent date.

How does a frog breathe?

The frog has no ribs and therefore breathing is not accomplished by the expansion and contraction of the chest, as in most air-breathing animals. The air must be swallowed in order to be conveyed to the lungs. For this reason it is not necessary for the frog to hold his breath when he jumps into the water. All he has to do is to quit swallowing air. The anatomy of a frog is such that it must close its eyes to swallow, and if its mouth is held open too long it will suffocate. A frog can go for a considerable time without breathing because it gets part of its oxygen supply through the skin. In cold weather frogs frequently sink to the bottom of a body of water and remain there for an extended period. The breathing movements then cease, the blood circulating in the skin being able to absorb enough oxygen to support life while the animal is in this inactive state.

What caused the jog in South Dakota's boundary?

It was intended that the twenty-seventh meridian west from Washington should be the western boundary of both the Dakotas and the northern part of Nebraska, but a glance at a good map shows a slight jog or offset in the western boundary of South Dakota where it intersects the Montana-Wyoming line. This jog was due to errors made in determining the twenty-seventh meridian from two widely separated points. The western boundary of South Dakota between latitude 43 degrees and 45 minutes was first surveyed in 1877, beginning at a post set in 1869 to mark the northwest corner of Nebraska, and the part of the line north of 45 degrees was surveyed eight years later. When the work was completed the line brought down from the north was 41.6 seconds too far east and that brought up from the south was 23.3 seconds too far west, with the result that the line runs east a distance of nearly a mile from the northeast corner of Wyoming to the southeast corner of Montana.

What is living stone?

Living stone is applied in sculpture to stone in its natural or original position as contrasted with marble or granite that has been quarried. The Lion of Lucerne in Switzerland, the Confederate Memorial on Stone Mountain in Georgia and the Rushmore Memorial in South Dakota are among the famous pieces of sculpture carved in living rock.

How did "knock into a cocked hat" originate?

To knock into a cocked hat means to knock out of shape with a single blow, to alter beyond recognition, or to put an antagonist completely out of a contest, either physically or figuratively. Despite its English sound, the phrase appears to be of American origin. It is generally supposed to have originally referred to striking a thing such a blow that it becomes limp and can be doubled up and carried flat under the arm like the old-fashioned cocked hats worn in the latter part of the eighteenth century and the first part of the nineteenth. Cocked hats became fashionable among court fops and gallants in the time of Louis XV of France. Their heads sufficiently protected from the elements by their perukes and wigs, the courtiers carried their hats doubled up or cocked under the arm. Party badges worn on these hats were called cockades, from French coq, "cock." Later this type of useless headgear was abandoned in favor of the somewhat more practical hat worn by military and naval officers. These hats were three-cornered and had the brim permanently turned up. Like their foppish forerunners they also were called cocked hats. To cock is an old verb meaning to turn, and to cock one's hat still means to turn it up on one side or to set it on the head at a peculiar angle. The British military hat worn by officers with the full dress uniform is still called a cocked hat, although it differs widely from the cocked hats formerly worn by British naval and military officers, as well as those once worn by church dignitaries. The island of Saba in the Dutch West Indies, because of its peculiar shape, is known as "Napoleon's Cocked Hat." James Monroe, last President of the United States to wear such headgear, was called "The Last Cocked Hat." Some authorities believe that knock into a cocked hat is only indirectly derived from the headgear so called and that the expression originated in the game of tenpins or bowls. Occasionally a player, with a single ball will roll down all the pins of a frame except the two corner pins and the head pin, leaving a triangular figure. This is called knocking the pins into a cocked hat, which the three-cornered figure is supposed to resemble. On April 29, 1907, Woodrow Wilson, then president of Princeton University, wrote as follows to Adrian H. Joline: "Would that we could do something at once dignified and effective to knock Mr. Bryan once for all into a cocked hat." This letter was published in January, 1912, when Wilson was seeking the Democratic nomination for the presidency, in an attempt to injure him with William Jennings Bryan and the latter's political following. But Bryan chose to ignore the letter and was largely instrumental in Wilson's nomination at the Baltimore convention later in the same year.

Where in the New World does the sun rise in the Pacific?

To observers on parts of the Isthmus of Panama the sun rises in the Pacific and sets in the Atlantic. The Isthmus turns and twists in such a manner that the end of the Panama Canal farthest east touches the Pacific and the end farthest west touches the Atlantic. This is contrary to what one unfamiliar with the Isthmus would suppose, because the majority of people imagine that the Canal runs east and west when as a matter of fact it runs in a northwesterly-southeasterly direction. Balboa, at the Pacific entrance, is farther east than Cristobal, at the Atlantic entrance.

Have human beings ever been crossed with animals?

There is no authentic record of a cross between the human race and lower animals of any species whatever. According to the Smithsonian Institution, numerous reports of crosses between human beings on the one hand and apes, bears, dogs and other animals on the other have invariably proved groundless when investigated by competent scientists.

What produces cobwebs?

Cobweb means spiderweb. Cob is an old English word signifying spider. A poisonous spider used to be called attercob, from attor, poison, and coppa, head. Cobweb is the common name given to the more or less formless webs spun in buildings by certain species of spiders and the larvae of some insects. Most of the tangled webs that annoy thrifty housewives are produced by the little house spider, Theridion tepidariorum. Cobwebs on the ceilings and in the corners of rooms are usually not noticed until they become covered with dust, a circumstance that

[133]

probably gave rise to the popular belief that cobwebs consist merely of dust. The impression was strengthened by the fact that the house spider is seldom observed at work.

Where is the southernmost point in Europe?

A point near Gibraltar, Spain, is farther south than any other point on the mainland of Europe. It is farther south by many miles than any point in Italy or Greece. It is even farther south than many points on the coast of northern Africa.

When is the best time to girdle trees?

There is no particular time of the year when girdling or ringing trees is most effective. If a girdle is made deep enough into the sapwood a tree will die no matter what time of year it is done. Generally speaking, the best time to cut trees in order to kill the stumps is in the spring after the sprouts have started and the tree is in full leaf. Many people believe that there is a certain period in midsummer—a particular day during dog days according to some—when a tree can be killed by merely wounding it, such as cutting a limb or making a gash in the trunk with an ax. A popular almanac asserted a few years ago that "scotching or chipping a tree on the twenty-ninth of August has never been known to fail to kill a tree provided a little of the sap seeped out on the bark." This, of course, is a myth. Some trees have a remarkable capacity for reproducing themselves from shoots and consequently they are hard to exterminate. Among these are the persimmon, sassafras, cottonwood, soft maple, willow, sycamore and yellow poplar or tulip. Owing to their peculiar root systems the stumps of these and certain other species persistently send out shoots and sprouts after the upper trunks have been removed. As a general rule cuts made in trees during the dormant period in winter are not so injurious as cuts made during the spring, summer and early fall. Certain trees, particularly the sugar maple, bleed seriously when wounded in the spring just before the appearance of the foliage, and a large cut at that season might prove fatal, but generally cuts that do not approach girdling of the trunk will not kill trees. "It is a common belief," says the United States Department of Agriculture, "that brush cut in the summer or early fall is not apt to sprout again, but investigations have demonstrated that there will always be some second and even third growth, regardless of when the brush is cut." Trees are often cut during the winter because the wood is then less liable to deteriorate, farmers have more time for such work at that season and the temperature is more favorable for chopping wood. But that is the poorest time of the year to chop down trees with a view of exterminating them. During the growing season trees store up nutritive elements in their roots, and when injured they draw on this reserve to re-establish themselves. This reserve is at its lowest ebb when the sprouts are starting and the tree is getting into full leaf. Hence that is the best time to cut a tree to kill it. The death and decay of some species can be hastened by introducing poison into the circulatory sap system of the living tree.

Why is a sailor called "Jack"?

Jack as the common designation for a sailor is a shortened form of the older *Jack Tar*. This nickname came about in an indirect way. A waterproof canvas impregnated with tar is called a tarpaulin. By extension the wide-brimmed storm hat formerly worn by sailors was called a tarpaulin also. Generally these hats were made of oiled or tarred cloth. As time went on the sailors themselves came to be called *tarpaulins*. The word was applied to sailors by Charles Dickens and other writers of his period. Finally it was shortened into *tar* and the *Jack* supplied to make the name picturesque. *Jack* was probably selected because *John* and its various familiar derivatives is one of the most common names. The popular belief that a sailor is called a tar because of the practice of using tar to seal the seams of the ship apparently is disapproved by the fact that sailors were called tarpaulins before they were called tars. Sailors call one another Jack, but they often resent the civilian Jackie.

Why is a ruffian or cutthroat called a thug?

Thug in the sense of a ruffian, cutthroat, gangster or robber is derived from the name of a caste or confederacy of professional murderers and robbers who terrorized India for seven hundred years. The Thugs worshiped Kali Ma, Hindu goddess of destruction, and with them assassination for gain was regarded as a religious duty. Usually wealthy persons were selected as victims, because plunder was one of the chief purposes of the killing. Part of the plunder was sacrificed to Kali and part of it kept by the Thugs to live on. Sometimes the Thugs would follow a victim hundreds of miles before a good opportunity presented itself to carry out their design of murder. Again they would worm themselves into the confidence of an unsuspecting traveler and go with him as companions until they got a chance to assassinate him and seize his belongings. The killing was generally done by throwing a handkerchief or noose around the neck of the victim and strangling him. Hence they were also called *Phansigars* ("stranglers"). Religious rites were then performed and the body buried. The Thugs had a religious rule against killing and robbing women, members of certain castes and classes and persons possessing a cow, which was sacred to them. The Thugs were exceedingly well organized; they even had a jargon and sign language by which members of the caste or sect were known to one another all over India. The order was unmasked by the British between 1830 and 1840 and was later finally stamped out entirely. Several hundred of the Thugs and their descendants were kept in prison at Jubbulpore. Captain W. N. Sleeman of the British East India Company, who distinguished himself as a Thug hunter, estimated that a man named Buhram had strangled 931 persons to death during the forty years he was a leader of the Thugs.

Which is correct, "coldslaw" or "coleslaw"?

The correct name for the salad made of sliced or chopped cabbage is *coleslaw*, not *coldslaw*. *Cole* is an old English name for cabbage and plants belonging to the same genus. *Kale, cole, cauli* in *cauliflower* and *kohl* in *kohlrabi* all stem from Latin *caulis*, "cabbage." The early Dutch settlers in New York made a salad consisting of finely cut cabbage leaves dressed with vinegar, oil, pepper and salt which they called *kool-slaa*, literally "cabbage salad." By the operation of the law of hobson-jobson *kool-slaa* became *coleslaw* in English. Further, by operation of the law of folk etymology, *coleslaw* became *coldslaw*. The erroneous form, suggested no doubt by the fact that coleslaw is usually cold, has been used so frequently that it has found its way into the dictionaries as a variation of *coleslaw*, which is still regarded as the preferred form.

How did "sandwich" originate?

Sandwich, meaning two slices of bread with meat, cheese or other food between them, is derived from the name of the fourth Earl of Sandwich, who lived in the time of George III. He was the same nobleman after whom Captain James Cook named the Sandwich Islands, now the Hawaiian Islands. The sandwich was a great favorite with the Earl. He was a notorious gambler and often became so engrossed in his cards that he would not stop to eat his meals. Instead he would have an attendant put meat between two pieces of bread, which he ate without leaving the gaming table. Although the Earl thus gave his name to the sandwich, he was not the first to eat bread or biscuits and meat so combined. Under different names the sandwich has been popular in several countries since ancient times. The Romans knew the sandwich under the name *offula*, diminutive of *offa*, signifying bit or morsel. The sandwich may very well have been introduced into England by the Romans nearly 1800 years before the birth of the Earl of Sandwich. Charles

Dickens, in his *Sketches by Boz*, appears to have been the first to use *sandwich man* in the sense of a man who walks about carrying advertising placards on his breast and back.

Can a naturalized citizen be deported?

A naturalized citizen of the United States cannot be legally deported to the country of his birth, or to any other country. American citizens, whether natural-born or naturalized, are not subject to the immigration laws. However, the naturalization of an alien who has acquired citizenship fraudulently may be declared null and void, in which event he may be subject to deportation like any other alien.

How long is a "coon's age"?

A coon's age, meaning a very long time, is a misnomer of unknown origin. Apparently it was formerly believed in the South that the raccoon lives to a great age. Raccoons in captivity have been known to live more than ten years, but it is probable these animals do not live to a greater age than foxes, martens, minks, opossums and many other animals of similar size. A *dog's age* was formerly used in England in the same sense and a *coon's age* may have been suggested by the earlier phrase.

What does the "O" in "A.W.O.L." stand for?

In the military service these letters are the official abbreviation of *absent without leave*. There has been considerable popular speculation as to why o is included in the abbreviation since *without* is one word. The common explanation is that the letter stands for *official* and that the complete phrase is *absent without official leave*. This is incorrect. The United States War Department explains that A.W.O.L. was adopted instead of A.W.L. to eliminate possible confusion with *absent with leave*.

What causes "ink balls" on oaks?

Certain species of four-winged insects of the family *Cynipidae*, variously known as gall-flies and gall-wasps, deposit their eggs under the cuticle of plants and trees and cause the formation of an excrescence called nut-galls, oak apples and ink balls. The last name arises from the fact that in the Old World the dark fluid in many kinds of these galls is used commercially in the ink and dyeing industries. These galls also contain tannic acid, which is used in tanning. The best ink balls or oak apples are found in Asia Minor, the Persian Gulf region and India. They are produced by the oak tree in response to some enzymic agent inserted when the female insect punctures the bark or leaves and deposits an egg in the hole. The enzymic agent produces a different type of plant tissue and an abnormal growth results around the spot punctured. After the egg hatches the larva lives in the gall until it reaches a mature state, when it bores its way out. The common oak gall-wasp or fly is glistening black in color.

Do fish live in Great Salt Lake?

The average salinity of Great Salt Lake, Utah, is almost six times greater than that of the oceans and no fish can live in such water. With the exception of the larvae of certain flies, the only animal life found in the lake consists of tiny brine shrimps, and recent investigations indicate that even they are disappearing. The earliest recorded mention of Great Salt Lake was made in 1776 in a report made to the Franciscan order by Father Escalante, who, with a number of companions, appears to have traveled from Mexico to that region. John C. Fremont explored the area in 1843 and his report of 1845 is the earliest actual description of Great Salt Lake. In 1849–1850 Captain Howard Stansbury of the United States Army made a survey of it. So far as known Great Salt Lake has never frozen over, although occasionally pieces of ice formed in the outlets of incoming streams float into the lake.

Do snakes suck cows?

It is popularly believed that certain snakes sometimes suck the teats of cows. Blacksnakes and milk or house snakes are most commonly accused of this practice. Thousands of country people throughout the United States are willing to swear upon oath that cases of snakes sucking cows have come under their personal observation. Herpetologists, however, frown upon the notion and put it in the same class as the hoop snake myth. Scientific proof or disproof is difficult to obtain, but no reputable naturalist believes that any snake ever sucked a cow. The United States Department of Agriculture, after giving considerable study to snake myths, said on this subject: "Anyone who has ever milked a cow knows that the suction required to obtain a flow of milk is much greater than could be exerted by any snake. Furthermore, a snake has two rows of sharp recurved teeth in the upper jaw. If the mouth of the milk snake were closed to permit suction, the teeth would sink into the teat and the snake would find itself fully occupied in efforts to avoid injury by the cow." It should be remembered that the mouth of a snake is without cheeks or closable lips. The only way a snake could suck **a** cow would be to get the teat at least part way down the throat. It is not likely any cow would stand for the tooth pricks incident to such a performance. The milk snake was so called because it was popularly supposed to frequent milkhouses and dairy barns to drink milk. Actually its presence is accounted for by its habit of preying upon mice that infest such places. Another version of the cow-sucking belief is that blacksnakes coil themselves around the udders of cows when lying down and squeeze the milk out. This notion is based on the erroneous belief that the blacksnake is a constrictor, which it is not. That turtles also sometimes milk cows is another common belief that is, in all probability, equally unfounded.

Can there be sound without an ear to hear it?

The question is often asked: "If a tree should fall in a forest thousands of miles from any living creature, would any sound be produced?" The question owes its continued popularity to a confusion of two distinct definitions of sound. Ordinarily sound is defined as the sensation stimulated by waves set in motion by a vibrating object. Consequently there is no such sound unless there is some kind of ear to receive the sensation. In this sense, then, if a tree should fall thousands of miles from any living creature, there would be no sound. This is the psychological sense of the term. But in physical science sound is defined as the cause of the sensation; that is, the waves which are set in motion by a vibrating object and which produce the sensation popularly called sound. So the answer to the question is, in the psychological sense of the term, no sound is produced unless there is an ear to hear. But in the physical sense sound is produced irrespective of the presence of a living creature with auditory organs. In the one case sound is a sensation; in the other, the waves that stimulate the sensation.

What does "carrying coals to Newcastle" mean?

Newcastle is a city in England in the center of a great coal-producing region. In fact there are two cities by that name in England, both in sections producing much coal. But carrying coals to Newcastle refers to the more populous Newcastle upon Tyne, which began to export coal as early as the thirteenth century. The historian David Hume says Henry III (1216–1272) "granted a charter to the town of Newcastle, in which he gave the inhabitants a license to dig coal. This is the first mention of coal in England." Coal was brought down from Newcastle to London by sea and for centuries it was known as sea-coal. Just when the popular expression, "carrying coals to Newcastle," originated is unknown. As early as 1583, when Shakespeare was twenty years old, the Scottish reformer James Melville wrote in his diary, "Salt to Dysart, or coals to Newcastle." In those days Dysart, a town in Fifeshire, Scotland, was a leading seat of the salt industry. Since Newcastle is in the coal country it would be quite superfluous to carry coals there. Hence *carrying coals to Newcastle* signifies to do what is superfluous; to take goods to a place where they already abound—and, by extension, to throw away one's labor. The French have a similar saying—*to carry water to the river*, and the Romans expressed the same idea in *carrying wood to the forest*. In America *coal* is generally substituted for *coals* in the popular saying.

What is the population of the world?

On the basis of 1939 figures the League of Nations estimated the total population of the world at that time at about 2,170,000,000. In 1927 the World Peace Foundation, using figures prepared by the Secretariat of the League of Nations, estimated the world's population at 1,906,000,-000. Such figures are naturally little more than good guesses. In some countries no census has ever been taken; in others the censuses have been very inaccurate and incomplete, and in still others the census has been taken at such irregular intervals that the figures provide no accurate basis of comparison. It has been roughly estimated that the population of the world at the present time is increasing at the rate of about thirty million a year. One economist estimated that under present economic conditions the earth would support about six billion persons, or about three times the present population. It is impossible, however, to anticipate the economic conditions of the future. In 1939 more than one half of the some two billion inhabitants of the earth lived on less than six per cent of its land area. A few years ago the eugenics department of the Carnegie Institution estimated that some thirty billion people have lived on the earth since the beginning of recorded history about six thousand or seven thousand years ago.

How tall do elephants grow?

Elephants do not grow so tall as is generally supposed. They are so great in bulk that there is a tendency to overestimate their size, and in consequence many extravagant estimates of their height have been reported. The largest elephants are the adult males of the African species. A specimen more than ten feet tall at the shoulders would be regarded as an extremely tall animal. Herbert Lang and Carl E. Akeley measured two elephants in East Africa that were eleven feet four inches in height.

They were probably the tallest elephants of which there is authentic record. Such a specimen in good physical condition would weigh four or five tons. Of course there is no reason why there may not be elephants in the jungles larger than any that have ever been measured, but it is not probable that any specimen belonging to a living species has grown much taller than twelve feet. It is very difficult to measure a wild elephant on the hoof. "When a big elephant is dead," declared Dr. William Hornaday, "probably no man on earth could measure its shoulder height as it lies and hit upon the figure representing its standing height while alive. Nor is it likely that any two men could measure a dead elephant and find their figures for height in agreement. The position of the dead fore leg is a puzzle. As that member lies prone and relaxed in death, it would be almost impossible to know how much to push it up into the shoulder in order to place it just as in life." Jumbo, the famous African elephant exhibited first in the London Zoological Park and later by the Barnum and Bailey Circus, weighed six tons and was ten feet nine inches tall. Indian elephants seldom exceed ten feet in height, and the average for adult males is about eight feet. It has been determined that the circumference of an elephant's forefoot is roughly equal to one half of the animal's height. In the British Museum there is the fossil of a prehistoric elephant that was fourteen feet tall.

What was the Sublime Porte?

The Ottoman Court or the Turkish government under the sultans was officially known as "The Lofty Gate of the Royal Tent." The Italians rendered this phrase *La Porte Sublima*, and the French *Sublime Porte*, both literally signifying "lofty gate." This picturesque name was a relic of the Eastern custom of proclaiming decrees and administering justice from the chief gate of the monarch's pavilion. The Turks found the equivalent of the phrase in common use by the Byzantines when they captured Constantinople in 1453 and adopted it when they established their empire. The French form of the phrase, used by foreigners, is accounted for by the fact that French was the language of diplomacy. The Sublime Porte was the principal gate of the Seraglio in the old Turkish capital and was originally the place from which imperial edicts of the sultan were issued. *Sublime Porte* was also applied to a large government building in Constantinople that housed four Turkish departments of state—the Grand Vizarat, the State Council, the Foreign Office and the Department of Home Affairs. It was never applied by the Turks to the person of the sultan. *Sublime* literally means "up to the lintel," being derived from Latin *sub*, "up to," and *limen*, "lintel," meaning a horizontal piece of timber, stone or other material over a door, window or other opening in a building. The origin of *Mikado*, a popular title used by foreigners to designate the Japanese Emperor, is analogous to that of *Sublime Porte*. It is derived from Japanese *mi*, a term of honor or respect, and *kado* ("door" or "gate"). Literally *Mikado* is equivalent to the English "honorable gate." The official Japanese title of the Emperor is *Tenno* ("Heavenly Sovereign").

What is the source of tapioca?

Tapioca, a word of South American Indian origin, is the name applied to a vegetable food obtained from the starch in the roots of the poisonous plant known as bitter cassava, which is indigenous to tropical America but now widely cultivated in other parts of the world. According to Latin American tradition, the food value of the cassava root was accidentally discovered by a Spanish explorer lost in the jungles of Brazil. He had heard from the Indians that the sap of the cassava plant was highly poisonous, and, preferring a quick death by poison to a slow one by starvation and fever, he ate a bowl of soup prepared by boiling cassava roots in water. Instead of dying he lived to tell the world how this pleasant and digestible food saved him from death. As a matter of fact the milky juice of the bitter cassava is highly poisonous and cannot be eaten in its natural condition without considerable danger, but the application of heat, as the explorer discovered, destroys the poisonous property. Not infrequently the tubers of the cassava plant, which may attain a height of ten feet or more, weigh as much as twenty-five or thirty pounds. The juice is squeezed from them and placed in vessels where the starch deposits on the bottom. After being thus separated from the fibrous constituents of the root the moist starch is spread on iron plates and exposed to heat sufficient, with the aid of constant stirring, to partly rupture the granules and cause them to agglomerate into the irregular pellets which, when cooked, become the hard, translucent tapioca used in puddings and soups. Pearly tapioca, a substitute product, consists of small, smooth grains prepared from potato starch. In Latin America the cassava plant is widely known as yuca and manioc.

What are "quaker guns"?

Quaker guns, or *quakers*, is the name given dummy cannon placed in the portholes of ships or the embrasures of forts to deceive the enemy. The term originated in America and refers to the doctrines of nonresistance taught by orthodox Quakers or members of the Society of Friends. Washington Irving, writing in 1809, spoke of a "formidable battery of quaker guns." Perhaps the most famous quaker guns in history were those used by the Confederate army at Centreville, Virginia, in the fall of 1861. General Joseph E. Johnston describes the incident in his *Narrative of Military Operations Directed During the Late War Between the States*. The Confederate commander wrote: "As we had not artillery enough for their works and for the army fighting elsewhere, at the same time, rough wooden imitations of guns were made, and kept near the embrasures, in readiness for exhibition in them. To conceal the absence of carriages, the embrasures were covered with sheds made of bushes. These were the quaker guns afterward noticed in Northern papers." John Beauchamp Jones, in *A Rebel War Clerk's Diary*, also refers to these dummy guns: "They found they had been awed by a few quaker guns—logs of wood in position, and so painted as to resemble cannon." Quaker guns are still used to deceive the enemy and to train troops when real weapons are not available. Although genuine implements of war are regarded by military men as more desirable for training purposes, it is sometimes necessary to employ imitation weapons for tactical training, such as broomsticks, sticks of wood, steel pipes and simulated wooden rifles, cardboard tanks, and other dummy guns and improvised weapons. In 1941 news dispatches from Moscow reported that the Germans had removed so much of their artillery to the Russian front that they had to leave dummy wooden cannon to face the British on the French and Belgian coast. An Associated Press dispatch from North Africa under date of July 13, 1943, reported that "A fully authenticated statement said yesterday that some Italian coastal defense guns on Sicily were found to be made of wood." Earlier in the same year quite a howl went up when a North Carolina Congressman discovered that the antiaircraft guns on the House Office Building on Capitol Hill were merely imitation guns served by dummy soldiers used as decoys.

Is there a flying snake?

No known species of snake actually flies. However, *Chrysopela ornata*, a species of arboreal constrictor found in Burma, India, southeastern Asia and the Malay Archipelago, is known as the "flying snake." Although this species cannot fly in the ordinary sense of the term as birds and bats do, it can glide through the air from some distance from an elevation to a lower altitude, as the flying squirrel does. The so-called flying snake, the usual length of which is two or three feet, accomplishes this feat by flattering out its body to check its fall. A weblike membrane runs along both sides of the body from near the head to a few inches from the tail. It holds itself rigid and straight, with ribs pushed outward and belly drawn in to form a concave surface about six or eight inches wide, which enables it to descend with safety from a considerable height. Ordinarily the flying snake resorts to this mode of travel only in volplaning from tree to tree after the manner of the flying squirrel. Major Stanley Fowler of the London Zoological Society reported he saw one of these snakes "fly" eight feet, and another parachuted or glided to the ground from a height of twenty feet. It is doubtful whether the snake ever resorts to this method of travel except in emergencies. *Chrysopela* feeds chiefly on lizards and is reputed to be very fierce, resisting capture by striking and biting furiously. The species is variable in color. The body may be black or green, ornamented with yellow, red or orange; the head is black with yellow markings. Reports that a species of "flying snake" is native to southern Mexico and Central America have not been confirmed.

Is it improper to wash a United States flag?

Many people seem to have a notion that there is some provision of law or flag etiquette that forbids the washing of the United States flag. Such is not the case. No disrespect for the national emblem is shown simply by cleaning it, and it is perfectly in keeping with flag etiquette to wash or dry clean an American flag. In fact that is the proper thing to do with it when it has become soiled. "There is no objection, so far as this Department has knowledge," wrote the United States War Department to the author, "to the cleaning of United States flags by washing them, this practice being generally resorted to by the United States Army." Likewise it is proper to mend a flag when torn unless it is in such bad condition that it would be a discredit to the owner if displayed.

Why is profanity called "billingsgate"?

Profanity and vulgar language in general are known as *billingsgate* from the famous Billingsgate fish market in London. For centuries the Billingsgate fishmongers, particularly the women venders, known as "fishwives," have been notorious for their coarse, vulgar, profane, abusive, scurrilous and foul-mouthed language. It is said that Jonathan Swift used to visit the Billingsgate fish market to improve his vocabulary and sharpen his wits by verbal exchanges with the fishwives. On one occasion a fishwife temporarily silenced the Dean by her torrent of unprintable epithets and vituperation. The Dean, in a desperate attempt to match the verbal abuse of his antagonist, called her "an isosceles triangle," whereupon the poor creature broke down and wept, charging that the Dean had exceeded all the bounds of decency in the contest.

This fish market is below London Bridge on the left bank of the Thames on the site of a water gate in the ancient wall that protected London on the river side. Geoffrey of Monmouth, twelfth century English chronicler, wrote that *Billingsgate* took its name from *Belin*, the name of a king of the Britons about 400 B.C., who built a watergate and wharf near the site. Another tradition traces the name to Billings, the English name of the royal race of the Varini, an ancient tribe of Britons mentioned by the Roman historian Tacitus. The oldest wharf on the Thames was called Billingsgate as early as 949 A.D. Records show there was a market on the site of the old Billings water gate as early as the time of the Norman conquest. For hundreds of years it was a general market for all sorts of produce and foodstuffs, but since the reign of William and Mary it has been used exclusively for the sale of fish. Even now Billingsgate market is one of the impressive sights of London, particularly in the early hours of the morning, when most of the wholesale business is done. Striking examples of Billingsgate rhetoric may still occasionally be heard in the famous fish market. Such language already was called billingsgate in the seventeenth century. "Most bitter Billingsgate rhetoric" occurs in Edmund Gayton's *Festivous Notes on Don Quixote* (1654). Some writers have taken up the cudgels in behalf of the Billingsgate fishmongers and say that the use of the name as a synonym for coarse and abusive language is an unjust aspersion on them.

What country was moved on the map from South to North America?

Before Panama seceded from Colombia in 1903 and became an independent republic it was generally indicated on maps as part of South America. Since then geographers have regarded the boundary between Panama and Colombia as the boundary between South and Central America. Thus it happened that Panama has had the distinction of being moved from one continent to another, for Central America is merely the extreme southern part of North America.

Does lightning follow drafts?

There is little foundation for the popular notion that lightning has a tendency to follow drafts. Such would be the case only when the air stream is filled with smoke or vapor, thus creating a better conductor of electricity than the surrounding atmosphere. Electricity generated in the clouds follows the line of least resistance to the earth and would not turn from its normal course to run horizontally merely because a door or window was open. There is no scientific knowledge to support the general belief that lightning that strikes buildings generally comes in through open doors and windows. Standing near a chimney during an electrical storm is hazardous for two reasons. An elevated object like a chimney is a natural target for lightning. Hot air conducts electricity better than cold air and a column of hot air rising from a chimney, whether or not it contains smoke, may be more likely to carry the lightning than the surrounding air.

Why do oaks shed their leaves last?

Oaks are usually the last trees in the forest to shed their leaves in the fall. Frequently the leaves of this species remain on the trees all winter. This is supposed to be due to the fact that in oaks, as well as in a few other species of trees, growth has not entirely ceased when frost arrives. A sudden drop in temperature stops growth when the fibrovascular bundles or woody fiber connecting the leaves with the twigs are still in a vegetative condition. In other words, the natural partition usually preceding the falling of leaves has not taken place. The connecting fibers that have been suddenly killed by frost become hard and tough and consequently the leaves sometimes cling to the twigs until the next spring when they are shed largely through the action of wind and rain.

Why are dummy clocks set at 8:18?

The hands on dummy clocks and watches used by jewelers for advertising purposes almost invariably point to about eighteen minutes past eight. There is a popular belief in the United States that the man who painted the first of these wooden clocks and watches had just heard of the death of Abraham Lincoln and that he painted the hands to perpetuate the fatal hour. According to one version of the story, the hands commemorate the exact time of Lincoln's death, and according to another, the exact time of his assassination. As a matter of fact Lincoln was shot at 10:10 in the evening and died about 7:30 the next morning. But the belief is more conclusively disproved by the fact that these wooden clocks and watches, with the hands pointing to about eighteen minutes past eight, were hanging as signs in front of jewelry shops long before the assassination of Lincoln. In England there is a popular notion that these clocks commemorate the time of day on November 5, 1605, when Guy Fawkes and his fellow conspirators planned to blow up the British houses of Parliament and King James I, or the time when the Gunpowder Plot was discovered. The real reason for so placing the hands is obvious. It is the most symmetrical arrangement possible for the hands, being pleasing to the eye, and at the same time leaving the greatest possible amount of space for advertising matter, such as the name of the

[146]

jeweler. At 8:18 the hands are about the same distance from the twelve and the six and two-thirds of the space on the dial is above the hands. In 1942 the United Horological Association of America at its annual convention in Chicago seriously considered a proposal to recommend to its members that all painted signboard clocks and watches be set at 7:55 to commemorate the exact time of day that the Japanese attacked Pearl Harbor on the morning of December 7, 1941.

What was Ben Jonson's religion?

Ben Jonson (1573–1637), the English poet and playwright, who was a contemporary of Shakespeare, was brought up a member of the Anglican Church and he adhered to that faith throughout most of his life. In 1598, however, when he was 25 years old, he killed an actor named Gabriel Spenser in a duel and was confined for a time in prison. While thus incarcerated he was visited by a Catholic priest who converted him to the Roman faith, to which he adhered for twelve years. The dramatist, who was also an actor, pleaded guilty to the charge of manslaughter and was released by benefit of clergy upon his forfeiting his "goods and chattels" and being branded on the left thumb. Jonson's religion involved him in the history of the famous Gunpowder Plot, which was a conspiracy to blow up King James I and the Parliament when they met November 5, 1605. It seems that a day or two after the plot was discovered the King's Council sent for Jonson and requested him, as a loyal member of the Roman Catholic church, to use his influence in an effort to induce the priests to supply the government with certain information desired. The playwright, however, failed in his misson. In a letter to Lord Salisbury he wrote that the priests "are all so enweaved in it that it will make five hundred gentlemen less of the religion with this week, if they carry their understanding about them." Though it would have been to Jonson's personal advantage to return to the Anglican communion at that time, he did not do so until five years later.

Can a fire started by lightning be put out with water?

That a fire caused by lightning cannot be extinguished with water is an old popular belief that still survives in many localities. Fire is fire no matter how started, whether by a match, spontaneous combustion or a flash of lightning. A fire produced by lightning has the same physical properties that other fire has and can be extinguished in the same manner. Another belief is that there are two kinds of lightning, hot and cold, and that a flash of hot lightning will start a fire while a streak of cold lightning will not. Although all lightning is composed of electricity and will start a fire under proper conditions, there is a grain of truth in the latter notion. Scientists do employ the terms *hot* and *cold* in reference to types of lightning. Hot lightning is a type that lasts longer than average strokes, while cold lightning is a short stroke that does not last long enough to produce great heat in the substances through which it passes. Most bolts of ordinary lightning are *cold* and last only a few millionths of a second; hot lightning lasts a hundredth of a second or more. Lightning is also described as *red* and *white*. Electric discharges through dry air owe their light only to two gases, oxygen and nitrogen, and accordingly are white or bluish white in color. Electric discharges through moist air sometimes break up some of the water vapor along their path and thus produce the brilliant red light of hydrogen in addition to the bluish white light of oxygen and nitrogen. Red lightning differs in no way from white lightning, but it is less a fire hazard because it passes through rain and strikes only wet objects, while white lightning passes through dry air and may strike substances that are easily set on fire.

Why is it easier to swim in salt water?

One can swim more easily in salt water than in fresh water because the former is naturally heavier and consequently has greater buoyancy. Owing to the great quantities of salt in solution, the specific gravity of the water in Great Salt Lake, Utah, and the Dead Sea in Palestine is so great that one cannot sink or completely submerge oneself in it. Contrary to general belief, however, an inexperienced swimmer can easily drown in such water. If he goes beyond his depth he is likely to lose his balance and be suffocated in the brine, although his body will float on the surface.

What is a bucket shop?

Bucket shop is the popular name of the office of a broker who is not a member of the official stock exchange. It is nominally maintained as an exchange dealing in stocks, grains or other commodities, but really to register bets on the rise and fall of prices. No actual buying or selling, no transfer of goods or securities takes place. Gambling, not legitimate investment, is the sole purpose of the typical bucket shop. Customers who buy merely bet that certain stocks or commodities will go up in price. The proprietor of the bucket shop charges a commission and the customer makes a deposit, just as if the goods or stocks were actually bought and sold. A regular brokerage house actually buys or sells as ordered and supports the transaction with its own or with borrowed money. In the case of the bucket shop, if the market goes against the customer his deposit is sacrificed and the proprietor appropriates it; if

[148]

the customer wins he is supposed to receive his profit. Private wires run from the bucket shop to prominent exchanges and the fluctuations are generally chalked on a blackboard as they are received. The proprietor has a good opportunity to cheat and he frequently takes advantage of it. Nowadays the operation of bucket shops is widely forbidden by security and exchange statutes. *Bucket shop* is an Americanism of uncertain origin. It may have been suggested by the obsolete verb *to bucket*, meaning to cheat. Apparently it was first used with reference to small gambling transactions in grain. One writer believes the term originated in Chicago a few years after the Civil War. The official Board of Trade would not permit *options* of less than 5,000 bushels of grain. For the benefit of men of small means what was called the Open Board of Trade began business in an alley under the regular Board of Trade rooms. The members of the Board of Trade jokingly spoke of the unauthorized exchange below as the *bucket shop* because they said it dealt only in *bucketfuls* of grain.

Why did Samuel Clemens adopt the name Mark Twain?

This name was first used by an old Mississippi River pilot named Isaiah Sellers, who used to write items for the New Orleans *Picayune*, in which he told of his adventures in a quaintly egotistical tone. The paragraphs usually began, "My opinion for the benefit of the citizens of New Orleans." They were signed "Mark Twain," which, in the parlance of pilots, is a leadsman call, meaning "two fathoms"—twelve feet. Samuel Clemens, then a cub pilot, wrote a burlesque on Captain Sellers' articles and published it in a rival paper under the signature *Sergeant Fathom*. Sellers was so hurt by the burlesque that he never wrote another article. In 1863 Clemens was working for the *Enterprise*, published in Virginia City, Nevada. He wanted a good pen name. While he was trying to think of one he received news of the death of Isaiah Sellers. This suggested to him Mark Twain, the name once used by Sellers. Clemens signed it first to a letter from Carson City to the *Enterprise* under date of February 2, 1863.

What is the harvest moon?

Harvest moon is the popular name given in northern temperate latitudes to the full moon that occurs about harvest time. Astronomers usually regard as the harvest moon the full moon nearest in date to the autumnal equinox, which is September 23. Country people, however, are more likely to regard the next full moon as the harvest moon; namely, the full moon that occurs about the middle of October. At this season the path of the moon, especially in high latitudes, passes quite closely above and below the horizon at the time of the full moon, causing it to rise nearly at sunset for several nights in succession. Thus the harvest moon prolongs the natural twilight and permits tardy farmers, so it is said, to complete their belated harvesting before the coming of frost and winter. In south temperate latitudes the phenomenon occurs in late March or early April. The moon that follows the harvest moon and that has similar characteristics is called the hunter's moon, alluding to the fact that the hunting season generally does not begin until after the harvest.

Do snakes lay all their eggs at one time?

Egg-laying snakes, unlike birds, do not lay an egg each day until the laying is completed. As a general rule all the eggs laid by an oviparous snake are laid at one time, or in one day, although occasionally a female snake will lay part of her eggs one day and the remainder the next. A twenty-eight-foot python laid a hundred eggs in one day. Little ring-necked snakes under observation deposited all their eggs within one day except in two instances.

Why are the inhabitants of the Philippines called Filipinos?

The Spanish called these islands *las Islas Filipinas* in honor of Felipe II of Spain, and they called the inhabitants Filipinos. In Spanish *ph* is not used to represent the *f* sound as in English. Translated into English *las Islas Filipinas* became the "Philippine Islands," *Philippine* being an old adjective formed from the proper name Philip. Since there was no English noun corresponding to Spanish *Filipino*, English writers naturally adopted the Spanish name for the inhabitants.

Who was the first circumnavigator of the globe?

It is often said that Ferdinand Magellan, the first European discoverer of the Philippines, did not actually circumnavigate the earth because he was killed in the Philippines before his famous voyage was completed, and that accordingly the honor of having been the first circumnavigator of the globe belongs to Juan Sebastián del Cano, who returned to Seville in the "Vittorio" with thirty-one of the survivors of the ill-fated expedition. When Magellan was killed in a battle with the natives of Mactan Island on April 27, 1521, he had sailed west to a point 124 degrees longitude east of Greenwich. In 1512, however, when he was still a subject of Portugal, Magellan sailed as far east as Banda Island, which is about 130 degrees longitude east. Therefore he, and not his subordinate del Cano, deserves the honor of having been the first person to circumnavigate the globe, although he was not the first to perform the feat in a single voyage. Sir Francis Drake was the first Englishman to circumnavigate the earth. In the "Pelican" (afterwards called the "Golden Hind") he sailed from Plymouth, England, December 13, 1577, and returned to the same port September 26, 1580, by way of the Cape of Good Hope.

What is logrolling in politics?

The early settlers in America helped one another clear the land by combining to roll the logs from their fields. This exchange in work came to be known as logrolling. Later the term entered the political vocabulary in the sense of combinations of different interests, based on the principle, "I'll scratch your back if you'll scratch mine." For instance, two members of a legislature have bills they want to get passed. One wants to prevent interference with a railroad in his section; the other wants a protective tariff on a product produced in his district. As a result of this "community of interest" they agree to support each other's bill. In effect, one says to the other: "If you will help me roll my log, which is too heavy for me alone, I will help you roll yours." *Logrolling*, like *pork barrel*, is associated in the public mind particularly with authorizations and appropriations for rivers and harbors and other public works. In England the term has been adopted in reference to literary criticism rather than legislation.

Why is a horse called "dobbin"?

Dobbin is a general or familiar name for any horse, especially an ordinary draft or farm horse. It is a diminutive of the proper name *Dob*, which is a variation of *Robin* and *Rob*, which in turn are variations of the proper name *Robert*. *Dobbin* was so widely used in England as a pet name for horses that it became a general nickname for the entire equine species. It was a familiar name for a horse as early as Shakespeare's time. In *The Merchant of Venice*, first printed in 1596, Old Gobbo says to Launcelot: "Thou hast got more hairs on thy chin, than Dobbin my fillhorse has on his taile."

What is meant by second wind?

Second wind is the name given to the return of normal breathing after a temporary loss of breath during sustained physical exertion, especially running. It is an adjustment of the heart rate of breathing. When a person begins to run he generally uses more energy than is necessary, which results in rapid breathing and so-called loss of breath; but after running some distance he may become adjusted to the gait and regain normal respiration. Horses and other animals are affected in the same manner. Physiologists say that when a person begins to run the sudden action produces large quantities of lactic acid in the muscles, and the heart is speeded up by the automatic impulses of the nervous system. Some time, however, is required for the entire system to adjust itself to the higher speed of operation. When the runner's heart and lung action is approximately fast enough to take care of the extra energy expended by the body he is said to have his "second wind."

Is the polestar visible from all points on the earth?

The North Star is never visible to persons in the Southern Hemisphere. It is, however, always visible on clear nights from points north of the equator. This is because the axis of the earth points almost directly toward the polestar. From any given point in the Northern Hemisphere the North Star occupies about the same apparent position throughout every night of the year. As a rule, it can be located readily by means of the "pointers" in the constellation variously known as *Charles's Wain* or *Wagon, Ursa Major* (Great Bear), and the *Great Dipper*. The Great Dipper consists of seven visible stars, three composing the handle and four the cup or bowl. The pointers—the two stars farthest from the handle—are approximately in line with the polestar.

What does "on the lap of the gods" mean?

This phrase comes to us from the ancient Greeks and means that everything possible has been done and the result depends on a power beyond human control. According to the translation by Andrew Lang and S. H. Butcher, Homer says in the seventeenth book of the *Iliad*: "Yet verily these issues lie on the lap of the gods." A similar expression occurs in the first book of the *Odyssey*. Some translators render the phrase "on the knees of the gods." It is believed that the phrase originally referred to the ancient pagan practice of placing wax tablets containing invocations or prayers on the knees of the statues of gods.

How did "reading the riot act" originate?

Reading the riot act literally means to give warning to a crowd to disperse under penalty of law. By extension it means to give warning, call up for reprimand or rebuke severely. Originally the phrase referred to the Riot Act, which was enacted by the British Parliament in 1714, during the first year of the reign of George I. Although riot laws had been previously passed, the Riot Act of 1714 was the first comprehensive law enacted to prevent or suppress tumultuous and riotous meetings.

It provided that if twelve or more persons were unlawfully assembled and disturbing the peace, the sheriff, justice of the peace, or mayor should read the following proclamation in their presence: "Our Sovereign Lord the King chargeth and commandeth all persons being assembled immediately to disperse themselves, and peacefully to depart to their habitations or to their lawful business, upon the pains contained in the act made in the first year of King George for preventing tumultuous and riotous assemblies. God save the King." Many of the states of the Union have passed laws of similar import.

What is the boundary between Europe and Asia?

Popularly Europe and Asia are regarded as being separate continents, but they are merely vast geographical divisions of the greater land mass known as Eurasia. There is not now and never has been a geographical boundary between them. The Caucasus Mountains are on the general boundary between Europe and Asia and between the Caspian and Black seas; they are partly in Asia and partly in Europe. Where no bodies of water separate Europe and Asia the boundary is merely imaginary. The conception that the grand land mass of Eurasia consists of two separate divisions probably originated among the Assyrians, who dwelt east of the Mediterranean. They naturally considered Europe and Asia as two continents because civilization in both first developed in those parts where they were separated by large bodies of water—the Strait of Gibraltar, the Mediterranean Sea, the Aegean Sea, the Sea of Marmara, the Bosporus and the Black Sea. In those remote times the vast regions north of the Black Sea were an unknown wilderness and the Assyrians did not know that the two land masses were not separated by seas in what is now Russia. The Assyrians, whose language was closely related to Hebrew and Arabic, called the Greek peninsula *Irib* or *Ireb*, "west" or "sunset," to distinguish it from Asia Minor, which they called *Assu*, "east" or "sunrise." Hebrew *ereb* signifies "west," "land of the setting sun" or "evening." *Irib* was corrupted by Westerners into *Europe* and *Assu* into *Asia*. In time these names were extended, the one from Greece to all Europe, and the other from Asia Minor to all Asia. It should be mentioned, however, that some early etymologists derived *Europe* from two Greek words signifying "broad" and "face." The idea was that Europe was so called from the *broad line* or *face* of coast that the western part of Eurasia presented to the Asiatic Greeks. In the days of the czars the Russian government had a stone placed on the Ural River to denote the arbitrary boundary between European Russia and Asiatic Russia, and this river, which discharges into the Caspian Sea, is now, for the sake of convenience, regarded as the boundary between the two so-called continents. There was a few years ago, and probably is now, near a junction of the trans-Siberian railway in the Urals a stone obelisk bearing the Russian word for Europe on one side and the Russian word for Asia on the other. Continent, from Latin continere ("to hold together"), has no very clearly defined meaning when applied to a land mass. Geographers, however, apply it in a general way to a very large continuous body of land, differing from an island or peninsula not merely in size but also in structure. Seven grand land divisions are now regarded as continents—Europe, Asia, Africa, South America, North America, Australia and Antarctica. Of these Australia is by far the smallest. Greenland, being entirely separated by water from North America and being much smaller than any of the continents named, is often referred to as an island continent, although a few geographers classify it as a separate continent.

What causes the London fogs?

The famous London fogs, like most inland fogs, are caused by the cooling of humid surface air to a relatively low temperature. This occurs on clear nights and when there is practically no wind. Ordinary fog consists of tiny drops of water like fine spray and is precisely the same thing as cloud except it is near the ground instead of high in the air. Town fogs, such as those over London, are denser because they consist of a mixture of moisture, dust, smoke, soot and chimney gases. Clear nights and the absence of wind are atmospheric conditions that have the double effect of producing fog and causing smoke to hover over the city. The millions of particles in the air serve as centers upon which droplets of moisture condense, just as invisible moisture in the atmosphere condenses on the sides of a pitcher of cold water in hot weather. A typical heavy London fog contains 820,000 dust particles to the cubic inch. Some of the tiny drops may condense on invisible electrified atoms of the gases of the air. That the formation of all fog is some kind of electrical phenomenon has long been suspected by many scientists, and it may be that all the nuclei and particles are somewhat electrified. Many investigators believe that the fog particles are prevented from evaporating by an oily film produced by smoke; but, according to the United States Weather Bureau, the existence of this film has not been definitely established. The London fogs have been decreasing in number in recent years, owing undoubtedly to the introduction of electricity and gas for heating and power purposes. Now the dense fogs that enshroud London a day or two in late November or early December may not be repeated during the remainder of the winter. These fogs, however, are still a serious problem in the regions bordering on the English Channel. A dense fog that descended over the Meuse valley in Belgium early in December, 1930, resulted in the death of seventy-five persons and much livestock. In London the fogs are often so dense that objects are indistinguishable only a few feet away. Automobiles and bus drivers are compelled to proceed slowly behind men carrying lanterns. Such a fog is known as a *pea-souper*. *Smog* is a recent telescopic term for a fog blackened and thickened by city smoke.

Why is land at the mouth of a river called a delta?

The triangular tract of land that often forms at the mouth of a river is called a delta because in outline it resembles *Delta*, the fourth letter of the Greek alphabet, which is shaped like a small triangle and corresponds to *D*. *Delta* in this sense was originally applied by the Greeks to the three-cornered tract of land formed by the diverging mouths of the Nile and the seacoast. This area was compared to the Greek letter Delta as early as the time of Herodotus, the father of history, who lived in the fifth century B.C. Centuries later Strabo used the term in reference to the alluvial deposit at the mouth of the Indus. The Mississippi, Danube and Rhine are other great rivers of the world that have clearly defined deltas.

What insects give birth to living young?

Many species of flies deposit larvae or maggots instead of eggs. The eggs are hatched inside the female's body. Most viviparous flies belong to the family *Sarcophagidae* and are popularly known as flesh flies because the larvae feed on flesh. As a rule the female flesh fly lays her young on fresh meat or on the wounds of living animals. Sometimes she deposits maggots in the nostrils of man, where they may cause death.

Do toads cause warts?

That toads and frogs cause warts is still one of the most widely believed superstitions in America. No reputable scientist or medical authority believes that the handling of toads or frogs produces warts on the hands, notwithstanding the time-honored popular belief to the contrary. Most of the warts that occur on adults are supposed to be produced by irritation and are infections that are more or less contagious. Medical men admit that the cause of warts that occur on the hands of children is not very well understood. Such warts often come suddenly, sometimes in groups, and also often disappear suddenly. This fact, coupled with the resemblance of the warty skin of toads to the wart-covered hands of children, probably gave rise to the belief that handling toads caused the warts. Although no warts ever result from handling toads, the skin of these reptiles secretes poison that acts as a violent irritant to the eyes and mouth and produces a burning pain, and even inflammation lasting for hours, when it comes in contact with cuts or open sores, but the poisonous substance has no ill effects on the unbruised skin of man. Medical scientists have observed that susceptibility to warts in childhood seems to run in certain families. Our forefathers had all sorts of preposterous remedies for curing warts. One way to get rid of them was to steal a dishrag and hide it in the stump of a tree. Another was to tie as many knots in a string as you had warts and bury the string under a stone. Still another was to rub the warts with stones, peas, beans or seeds and throw the latter in a roadway. All of these cures are just as effective as that suggested by Pliny in his Natural History nearly two thousand years ago: "Lie on your back along a boundary line on the twentieth day of the moon, extend the hands over the head, and with whatever thing you grasp when so doing rub the warts, and they will soon disappear." Physicians can remove warts without trouble with strong acids and electric currents.

How did "drawing room" originate?

Drawing room is merely a contraction of withdrawing room. The original drawing room was a room to withdraw to. Withdrawing room is still sometimes used and it occurs frequently in the literature of the seventeenth century. For instance, in 1611 Lodowick Barry wrote in Ram Alley: "Ile waite in the with-drawing-room, Vntil you call."

What is the Trench of Bayonets?

On June 10, 1916, two battalions of the 137th French Infantry commanded by Lieutenant Polimann went into position in trenches on the slopes of a ravine near the Thiaumont farm several miles north of Verdun. These troops were subjected to heavy fire by the Germans during the next day and they lost more than half their number in killed and wounded. Throughout the night of June 11 and 12 they were under convergent fire and their losses continued to be heavy. Their rifles being choked with earth, the French troops fixed bayonets and determined to resist the enemy to the last man. When the Germans assaulted in the morning many of the French had been buried alive by the explosion of shells. Only their bayonets could be seen protruding from the soft earth. This is the now famous Trench of Bayonets. It is estimated that out of the 1000 men composing the two battalions not more than 250 survived. The Trench of Bayonets was preserved just as it was found after the battle and the bayonets may still be seen projecting from the ground. A monument was erected over the site by the French government to commemorate the heroism of the men who permitted themselves to be buried alive rather than abandon their post.

What is the meaning of "SS." in legal documents?

When used in legal documents the letters SS. are the abbreviation of Latin *scilicet*, meaning "to wit, "that is to say," "namely." In English *scilicet* is pronounced *sil-i-set*. It is derived from two Latin words, *scire* ("to know"), and *licet* ("it is permitted"). Hence *scilicet* literally means "it is permitted to know." SS. has various uses in legal documents. Sometimes it means "summons"; when used at the beginning of documents it may indicate the court in which the action or pleading is taking place. Generally, however, it is used in the simple sense of "to wit" and calls attention to what is to follow or introduces explanatory matter pertaining to what has preceded. Like many other Latin abbreviations, it is a relic of the days when all legal documents were written in Latin.

Why don't ducks get wet?

Ducks and certain other waterfowl don't get wet because their feathers are kept in an oily condition by small oil glands. Oil is a repellent of water. During a rain, or while paddling about in a pond, ducks frequently bend back and rub oil on their heads from the glands at the base of the tail. They then oil their feathers with their heads. Ducks are proverbial for their ability to shed water and "it runs off like water from a duck's back" is an ancient simile. In addition to being supplied with oil, the feathers of a duck are exceedingly close together, a fact that aids considerably in keeping out water.

What are deeds of derring do?

Deeds of derring do are feats of daring and acts of bravery. In this sense *derring do* is largely the result of an error made by Edmund Spenser and copied by Sir Walter Scott and other writers of the romantic school. Literally *derring do* means *daring to do*. In *Troilus and Criseyde*, written about 1385, Chaucer describes Troilus as second to none "in doryng don that longeth to a knyght." In other words, Troilus was second to none "in daring to do what belonged to a knight." In the manuscript edition of *The Hystory, Sege and Destruccyon of Troye*, probably written between 1412 and 1420, John Lydgate spelled the phrase *dorryng do*, but in the printed edition of 1513, as well as in the edition of 1555, it was spelled *derrynge do*. This apparently misled Edmund Spenser, who was fond of archaic language, into construing it as a noun phrase. At any rate, he picked up the curious phrase and made it part of his vocabulary. A note in the glossary of his *Shepherd's Calendar*, published in 1579, explained that *derring do* meant "manhood and chevalrie." Later Spenser employed it in the *Faerie Queene*. In Book II, Canto IV, section 42, the poet wrote:

> So from immortall race he does proceede,
> That mortall hands may not withstand his might,
> Drad for his derring doe and bloody deed;
> For all in blood and spoile is his delight.

Sir Walter Scott revived and accentuated this erroneous usage in *Ivanhoe*, published in 1820. In Chapter 29 is this passage: " 'Singular,' he, Ivanhoe muttered to himself, 'if there be two who can do a deed of such derring-do.' " Scott, in a footnote, gave the meaning of *derring-do* as "desperate courage." Thus, says the Oxford dictionary, by a chain of misunderstandings and errors *derring do* has come to be regarded as a kind of substantive combination meaning daring feats.

Are any two things exactly alike?

So far as science has been able to discover, there are no two objects in the world exactly alike, no matter whether they are natural or artificial. No two leaves or snowflakes, no two objects manufactured by man, are exactly alike. Scientists believe that even each infinitesimal atom composing the elements differs from all the rest.

Does the hunter walk "around" the squirrel?

Suppose a squirrel on the trunk of a tree keeps the tree between it and a hunter walking around the tree, does the hunter walk around the squirrel? The answer to this question depends on the definition of the preposition *around*. One definition of *around* given by all standard dictionaries is "on all sides of." Since the squirrel always keeps its back away from the hunter it is clear that, if this definition of *around* is intended, the hunter does not go around the squirrel. The most usual definition of *around*, however, is "encircling, entirely about, or about the place or position of." This definition ignores any rotary motion of the object being gone around. Under this definition the Standard dictionary gives the following example: "The hunter goes around the squirrel as the squirrel goes around the tree to escape him." In this sense, then, the hunter does go around the squirrel. This is one of those questions that can be answered "yes" or "no," depending on the definition of a term that has more than one meaning. The same principle applies to the following questions: Does the valve of an automobile tire go around the hub of the wheel? If two horses running side by side around a race track make the complete circuit, does the outside horse go around the horse on the inside?

Where are the Bad Lands?

An extensive region lying between the White River and the South Fork of the Cheyenne in southwestern South Dakota has long been popularly called the Bad Lands. Among the Dakota Indians the area was known as *Maka Sicha*, and the early Canadian French hunters, trappers and traders called it *Terres Mauvaises*. Both terms literally mean "bad lands" and refer to the roughness and barrenness of the region and its general inhospitableness to man. *Bad lands* has been extended to include other sterile, arid regions with similar topographical characteristics. There are notable bad lands in Texas, Nebraska, New Mexico and other western states as well as other parts of the world. The bad lands southeast of the Black Hills, sometimes known more specifically as the "Big Bad Lands" or the "White River Bad Lands," constitute one of the most picturesque, weird and desolate areas in North America. They consist geologically of an uplifted plain covered with loose soil and easily eroded soft rock. Rainfall is so light or irregular that little vegetation other than sagebrush can exist. In the course of thousands of years the waters and winds have eroded and carved the clays, shale, sandstone and other surface materials into many fantastic and scenic shapes. Often these forms suggest abandoned cities, cathedrals, towers, pinnacles, pyramids, obelisks and monuments. The Bad Lands are rich in the fossils of all sorts of queer beasts that inhabited that region millions of years ago.

Why do people knock on wood?

Knocking or rapping on wood to ward off punishment for boasting is one of the most prevalent of all superstitions. It is not uncommon to meet intelligent and educated persons who invariably knock on wood after bragging about their success or good health. In February, 1940, Winston Churchill, then First Lord of the Admiralty, told the House of Commons that up to that date, aside from the battleship "Royal Oak" and the aircraft carrier "Courageous," no large British warships had been sunk during the war. Ellen Wilkinson, a Labor member, shouted, "Touch wood!" "I sympathize with that feeling," replied Churchill. "I rarely like to be any considerable distance from a piece of wood." Whereupon the First Lord of the Admiralty touched his dispatch box. Many persons carry wooden charms to have wood convenient for this purpose. How wood acquired this supposed protective power against misfortune and ill luck is not definitely known. Numerous theories have been offered to account for the superstition. Some attribute it to the old game known as "touching wood" or "wood tag," in which a player who succeeds in touching wood is safe from capture. Others hold that this game and "knocking on wood" had a common origin in primitive tree worship, when trees were believed to harbor protective spirits. To rap on a tree—the dwelling place of a friendly spirit—was to call up the spirit of the tree to protect one against impending misfortune. Later, people would place the hand on a wooden statue of a deity for the same purpose. It is said that among certain European peasants it is still common to knock loudly on wood to keep away evil spirits. Still others believe the superstition is of Christian origin and that it is in some way associated with the wooden cross upon which Jesus was crucified. Perhaps, they think, it is a survival of the religious rite of touching a crucifix when taking an oath or the beads of the rosary when praying.

What is a nine-day wonder?

A nine-day wonder is something that causes a great sensation for a few days and then passes into the limbo of things forgotten. The phrase dates back at least to the fourteenth century and probably much earlier. In *Troilus* Chaucer wrote: "A wonder last but nine night never in town." "The wonder (as wonders last) lasted nine days," is recorded in John Heywood's *Proverbs*, published in 1546. In an old handbook of proverbs we find it stated that a "wonder lasts nine days and then the puppy's eyes are open." This, of course, refers to the fact that dogs are born blind and their eyes do not open for about nine days. The proverb suggests that the eyes of the public are blind with astonishment for nine days, but then their eyes are opened and they cease to wonder any longer. In Shakespeare's *III Henry VI* is the following allusion to the proverb that a wonder lasts but nine days: "You'd think it strange if I should marry her," says King Edward. Gloster replies: "That would be ten days' wonder, at the least." Clarence then interposes: "That's a day longer than a wonder lasts."

What was the sword of Damocles?

Damocles (pronounced *dam-o-cleez*) was a courtier at the court of Dionysius of Syracuse in the fourth century B.C. One day the sycophant was extolling the happy condition in which princes live, whereupon Dionysius invited Damocles to a sumptuous banquet and seated him with an unsheathed sword suspended over his head by a single hair. The sycophant was afraid to stir and the banquet was a tantalizing torment to him. This was supposed to contradict what Damocles had said about the happiness of princes and to symbolize the constant dread in which they live. "Uneasy lies the head that wears a crown," as Shakespeare expressed it in *II Henry IV*. A person who is in constant danger is said to have a sword of Damocles hanging over his head.

How did "Jiminy" originate?

Two theories have been advanced to account for *Jiminy* or *Jimminy* when used as an expletive, exclamation or mild oath. One, which is the less probable, regards it as a corruption of the Latin *Jesu domine* ("Lord Jesus"). The other regards it as a corrupt form of *gemini*, plural of Latin *geminus*, signifying "twin." It is still frequently spelled *Geminy*, *Gemony* and *Gemini*. In Roman mythology *Gemini* is applied to Castor and Pollux, the twin sons of Jupiter and Leda. It is also the name of a constellation, as well as the third sign of the zodiac, which is represented by the twin gods sitting side by side. To swear by Castor and Pollux, or by Gemini, was to use a powerful oath in ancient Rome. It is possible, however, that the quaint and homely *Jiminy* is of Teutonic origin. German, Dutch and the Scandinavian languages all have it in one form or other, and *by Jiminy* is used more widely by persons speaking those languages than by persons speaking any others.

Which is the right bank of a river?

Many people find it hard to distinguish between the right and the left bank of a stream. The right bank of a river is the bank to the right of a person looking down stream, that is, in the direction of the current. St. Louis, Missouri, is on the right bank of the Mississippi. The left bank, of course, is the bank to the left of a person looking in the same direction. Memphis, Tennessee, is situated on the left bank of the Mississippi.

Why is it considered unlucky to walk under a ladder?

There is an old superstition, still quite common, that it is unlucky to walk under a ladder leaning against a building, tree or other object. It is generally assumed that this superstition was originally merely the natural outgrowth of the danger incident to walking under ladders; that is, a taboo was placed on walking under ladders for the simple reason that it was a dangerous practice. But it is also considered unlucky to walk on a ladder lying on the ground and it is probable that the association of ladders with ill luck goes back to ancient wood magic. One writer suggests that the superstition may have arisen from the fact that in early times culprits were often hanged from ladders propped against buildings. Those who believe in the superstition say that ill luck will follow a person who walks either under or over a ladder, unless he stops to make a wish, in which event his wish will come true and no ill luck will befall him. In England the superstition has a special provision, namely, if an unmarried woman walks under a ladder she will not be married within a year.

What fabric was first used for clothing?

Man, it may be assumed, first dressed himself either with skins or crude garments made of twigs, grasses or bark, in the fashion of certain primitive peoples of the present time. That is also the Hebrew tradition. According to Genesis 3:7, Adam and Eve "sewed fig leaves together, and made themselves aprons." Later, Genesis 3:21 tells us, "Unto Adam also and to his wife did the Lord God make coats of skins, and clothed them." It is impossible to say definitely which of the common clothing fabrics— cotton, wool, linen and silk—was first developed, although most authorities are inclined to believe that wool antedates the others as a clothing material. The use of wool in fabrics, as distinguished from its use on the original pelt, undoubtedly suggested itself to primitive man before the dawn of history. Perhaps wool separated from the skin was first used as a clothing material in the form of a crude felt. Cotton, which was widely used by the ancient Egyptians as well as the Hindus, probably came second in chronological order. Silk, which the Chinese say dates from 2650 B.C., was the third textile to be developed. Linen, a fabric woven from the fibers of flax, came much later.

Who were the devil dogs?

Teufelhunde, the German equivalent of "devil dogs," is the name that the Germans are supposed to have given the American Marines after the fighting around Château-Thierry in June and July, 1918. The original *Teufelhunde* were fierce and fiendish dogs mentioned in a Bavarian legend. Henry L. Mencken, in *The American Language*, says: "Teufel-hunde (devil dogs), was invented by an American correspondent; the Germans never used it." The Office of Naval Intelligence, however, states that Marine officers at the front at the time vouched for the fact that German prisoners captured during the battle at Belleau Wood as early as June 8, 1918, said that the American Marines "fought like devil dogs." Unmailed letters found on the bodies of slain German soldiers also referred to the Marines as *devil dogs* and said that they fought like fiends. It was stated by officers who were present in the field that stories of the Marines being called devil dogs or *Teufelhunde* were prevalent in the trenches at the front two or three days after the first attack on June 6, 1918, or very shortly after the first prisoners were taken.

How should a baseball bat be held?

Manufacturers of baseball bats place the trade-mark running with the grain of the wood. When a player uses the bat the trade-mark should be held up and the ball struck with the grain of the bat. This protects the bat against splitting. The likelihood of a bat breaking is much greater if it is struck on the trade-mark or on the opposite side. Standard baseball bats are generally made of second-growth white ash, although a few are made of hickory. Experiments with bats of aluminum and various other materials have been made, but so far they have not been acceptable to baseball players. During the infancy of American baseball cricket-shaped bats were used. There was so much complaint by players against the great size of the bats that about 1860 the present standard bat was adopted. According to the rule then adopted the bat must be of wood, round and not exceeding two and one-fourth inches in its thickest part.

Who first said: "You can't eat your cake and have it"?

The origin of this oft-quoted saying is unknown. "Would ye both eat your cake and have your cake?" is quoted in John Heywood's *Proverbs*, compiled in 1546, which indicates the saying was proverbial in England in the sixteenth century. At that time *cake* signified simply any bread baked in small, regularly shaped pieces or *cakes*. George Herbert, an English poet and churchman who died in 1633 at the age of thirty-nine, followed *Heywood's* question form of the saying when he quoted it in "The Size," one of a collection of his poems published soon after his death under the title *The Temple: Sacred Poems and Private Ejaculations*. The third stanza of the poem reads:

> To be in both worlds full
> Is more than God was, who was hungry here.
> Wouldst thou his laws of fasting disannul?
> Enact good cheer?
> Lay out thy joy, yet hope to save it?
> Wouldst thou both eat thy cake, and have it?

In *The Haunted Bookshop* Christopher Morley refers to this proverb as one of "the most familiar quotations in our language." Of course the idea expressed by it dates back much further than the time of Heywood and

Herbert. More than two thousand years ago Titus Plautus, the great comic dramatist of Rome, said in his *Trinummus*: "If you spend a thing you cannot have it."

What causes gossamers?

Gossamers are filmy cobwebs floating in the air or clinging to plants and other objects. Spiders eject them, like other webs, in the form of viscid fluid. Sometimes several threads are produced simultaneously. It is supposed that the gossamers are spun when the spider is on an elevated point and that some of the webs are wafted away by the wind as they are ejected. Not infrequently the spider itself is carried away with a tangle of webs. Often the single strands of the web are so fine that they cannot be seen readily except when the sun is shining on them. Gossamer is supposed to be derived from *gos* ("goose") and *somer* ("summer"). It is generally assumed that *goose* in this connection refers to the *downy* appearance of the gossamer; but the theory has been advanced that the word may have alluded originally to the clear warm weather that frequently occurs in the fall when geese were supposed to be in season and to have been extended to the chief characteristic of this period in some sections, that is, the appearance of these webs. Far-fetched as the theory may seem, the fact that *summer-goose* is a localism in England for *gossamer* is cited in confirmation. Gossamers are in fact seen chiefly during warm weather in the fall, and this has led some naturalists to the conclusion that these cobwebs are produced only by young spiders. Chaucer referred to the gossamer as an unsolved riddle, and it was once widely believed that this phenomenon was somehow produced by dew.

Why are nails measured by pennies?

Until about the fifteenth century nails were sold in England by the hundred. The price was determined by the size of the nails. For instance, nails that sold for tenpence a hundred were called tenpenny nails, those that sold for sixpence a hundred were called sixpenny nails, etc. When the prices changed the old names survived as the designation of size only. Thus the size of nails is now indicated as 3d, 4d, 6d, 10d, etc. The d is the penny sign and is the abbreviation of *denarius*, the Latin word corresponding to the English *penny*. Etymologists regard as erroneous the explanation that *penny* in connection with nails is a corruption of *pound*. Nails may vary in diameter, style of head and point and have other differences, but they are standardized as to length. A standard sixpenny nail is two inches long regardless of whether it is a finishing nail, flooring nail, shingle nail, tobacco nail or any other type of nail. The length of standard nails by pennies is as follows: a 2d nail is 1 inch long; 3d, 1¼ inches; 4d, 1½; 5d, 1¾; 6d, 2 inches; 7d, 2¼; 8d, 2½; 9d, 2¾; 10d, 3 inches; 12d, 3¼; 16d, 3½; 20d, 4 inches; 30d, 4½; 40d, 5 inches; 50d, 5½; and 60d, 6 inches. Some manufacturers do not conform exactly to this standard and consequently nails of a specified penny may vary in length as much as ¼ of an inch. Nails four inches or more in length are popularly called spikes. A tack is a very small, short, sharp-pointed nail with a broad, flat head. Thin, flat nails with slight projections on one side instead of heads are called brads.

How did to "walk Spanish" originate?

To *walk Spanish* refers to an old sport among boys in which one boy seizes another by the collar or the scruff of his neck and the seat of the trousers and forces him along on tiptoe. To *walk turkey* is used in the same sense. Apparently the former expression originated in New England. At any rate, the earliest known uses of *walk Spanish* occur in writings from that section. The application of *Spanish* in the phrase is obscure. It may, as some suppose, allude to the manner in which the old Spanish pirates are reputed to have handled their prisoners when starting them out on the plank. The term has acquired a large variety of meanings in popular parlance. We make another *walk Spanish* when we discharge him from his job, when we make him step along gingerly, or when we compel him to do something against his will. Likewise a person is said to *walk Spanish* when he struts, and also when he walks with an unsteady gait. More often the term is equivalent to "toe the line" or "come up to the mark."

What is a whip snake?

Whip, or *coachwhip snake*, is the popular name of a slender, swift-moving, brownish-black snake found in the southern and southwestern part of the United States. It has a long tapering tail and the scales are so arranged and colored as to give it a braided appearance. Hence the name "coachwhip," which is also sometimes applied to related species. The black whip snake, *Coluber flagellum*, is one of the few American snakes that can outrun a man on a poor surface and can run at least as fast as the average man on a good surface. The coachwhip snake is the subject of a curious superstition, especially prevalent among the Indians and Negroes. It is said that this snake attacks human beings whom it whips or lashes to death with its long tail. Many are the stories of Negroes found dead in the road from having been whipped to death by coachwhip snakes. According to the generally accepted version of the superstition, the snake wraps itself around the leg or body of the person attacked and whips him with its tail. These stories may have originated in warnings given years ago to restrain the slaves from straying from the plantations at night. The stories were confirmed, so far as the slaves were concerned, by the snake's habit of raising the fore part of the body when traveling. As a matter of fact the snake is quite harmless to man and always attempts to escape when encountered.

Where are the South Seas?

The Pacific Ocean was formerly known as the South Sea, owing to the fact that Vasco Núñez de Balboa, Spanish governor of Darien, first saw it in 1513 when looking southward. Catching his first glimpse of the Pacific from a peak on the Isthmus of Panama, Balboa first called it the Golden Sea, because he was searching for gold and that metal was uppermost in his mind, but the next day when he waded into its waters and claimed it and all the land touched by it for Spain, he christened it *el Mer del Sur*, or the "Sea of the South." Almost from the beginning, however, the English used the term in the plural form and applied it to all the waters of the Southern Hemisphere. In 1528, only fifteen years after Balboa first beheld the Pacific, a man named Thorne wrote to Henry VIII as follows: "Vntill they come to thee . . . South Seas of the Indies Occidentall." In English literature *South Seas* refers especially to that part of the Pacific south of the equator. *The South Sea Islands* is generally applied to the more remote and less civilized islands in that region.

Why is the Lorraine cross the anti-tuberculosis emblem?

The double-barred cross used as the emblem of the fight against the white plague is the old patriarchal cross, which during the Middle Ages was known as the cross of Lorraine. In this type of cross the lower horizontal arm is longer than the upper, thus combining the Greek and Roman types. The patriarchal cross is frequently met with in Byzantine art and dates back at least to the ninth century, when it became the emblem of the Eastern branch of the Christian church. It is still regarded as the emblem of the Greek or Orthodox Catholic church and forms part of the heraldic arms of a patriarch, being carried before him during processions. The same type of cross is also known as the archiepiscopal cross because it figures in the heraldic arms of an archbishop of the Roman Catholic church and is carried before him in processions in his own ecclesiastical province. Joan of Arc, who was born in old Lorraine, carried a cross of Lorraine when she raised the siege of Orleans in 1429. Like the Latin cross, the cross of Lorraine symbolizes hope and humanity.

It is the emblem of the fight against the white plague, but its adoption for that purpose by anti-tuberculosis workers was purely accidental and had no specific reference to its previous history. When the International Conference on Tuberculosis met in Berlin in 1902 a Parisian doctor named Sersiron suggested that the ancient cross of Lorraine be made the distinctive badge of the war against the white plague. The suggestion was adopted and four years later the National Tuberculosis Association of the United States formally adopted the double-barred cross as its emblem. It was not until 1912, however, that it was standardized as the emblem of anti-tuberculosis work in America. In 1940 the Free French (later Fighting French) committee directed by General Charles de Gaulle adopted as its emblem a blue banner bearing the Cross of Lorraine in red, flown on the same staff with the tricolor.

Why are buttons put on men's coat sleeves?

Buttons are now put on the sleeves of men's coats as a matter of style and custom. How the style originated is not known. It is probable that buttons were originally put on coat sleeves to button back the sleeves to leave the hands free in the days when coat sleeves were much longer and looser than they are today. There is a legend that the custom originated in the Prussian Army in the time of Frederick the Great. The Prussian King was very particular about the appearance of the uniforms of his soldiers. He discovered that many of the soldiers were in the habit of wiping their faces with their coat sleeves. Naturally the sleeves soon became soiled and gave the uniforms an untidy appearance. Therefore Frederick, to stop the practice, issued an order requiring a row of buttons to be put on the upper side of the coat sleeves. When a soldier attempted to wipe perspiration from his face with his sleeve he would scratch himself. By this method the soldier monarch succeeded in breaking his men of the slovenly habit. But the custom of putting buttons on the sleeves of coats, whatever its original purpose, survived its usefulness. The buttons became part of the accepted style of coats and as styles varied with different periods the position of the buttons shifted until they were finally placed on the lower side of the sleeves.

What are "rice Christians"?

This is a name of reproach applied to natives who become Christians for what they can get out of it in a material way, such as clothes, food, books, education and medical care, which are supplied by the Christian missions. In *Following the Equator* Mark Twain says: "Protestant missionary work is coldly regarded by the commercial white colonists all over the heathen world, as a rule, and its product is nicknamed *rice Christians* (Occupationless incapables who join the church for revenue only)."

How can one tell by the tracks which way a rabbit has run?

The triangle formed by the tracks of a rabbit in the snow points in the direction opposite that in which the animal was running. When a rabbit runs it touches the ground with both small front feet close together and then strikes with the two large hind feet apart and ahead of the front feet, forming the base of the triangle with the hind feet and the apex with the front ones. In other words, the hind feet strike the ground last and leave it last with each leap, but they strike far ahead of the front feet, and consequently the two foremost and most widely separated tracks are made by the hind feet, not by the front ones as so often supposed. Unless one understands the relative position of the rabbit's feet while in motion it is sometimes hard to tell by its tracks which way it has run, because the feet are covered with hair to such an extent that the toes do not always show in the tracks. It is a general rule in bounding animals, including hares and rabbits, that the hind feet track ahead of the front ones. Strictly speaking, the gait of a running rabbit is not correctly described as a hop. Although *hop* is to some extent synonymous with jump, leap and bound, it is more applicable to the motions of birds, toads and grasshoppers than to rabbits and hares.

Why is China called the "Flowery Kingdom"?

Flowery Kingdom is a translation of Chinese *Chung hua* and is the most ancient name of China. Whether it originally referred to flowers in the literal sense is not known for certain. It probably did not. *Hua* means flowery, elegant, glorious, distinguished. The ancient Chinese so designated their country, it is supposed, because they regarded their people as the most polished and civilized nation in the world. The term, however, may have been once employed in the sense of "country full of flowers." According to one theory, the Chinese originally lived in central Asia, which is a very barren region, and they called their new country flowery in contrast to their old home in the desert.

Does any species of fish give birth to living young?

Many fish give birth to living young. There are three general types of reproduction among fish—oviparous, viviparous and ovoviviparous. Each of these types has many minor characteristics in the fertilization, deposition and development of the eggs. The great majority of fish are oviparous

[168]

and lay their eggs in the water, where they are fertilized externally by the males. But some species, in fact entire families, are viviparous and produce living young from within the body. However, most so-called viviparous fish are really ovoviviparous, that is, living young are produced from eggs fertilized by copulation and retained within the body during their development, but they do not form an attachment to the oviduct or derive nourishment from the mother. In this class are most of the rays, as well as numerous members of several other families. The true viviparous fish, such as the moonfish, Mexican swordtails, surf fish, guppies and the common top minnows, not only give birth to living young hatched from eggs fertilized by copulation, but the young are nourished in the body through placental connection with the mother. Female swordtails have been known to produce as many as one hundred young at a birth. The young are capable of taking care of themselves immediately and in most cases they are compelled to seek shelter from their cannibalistic mothers who try to devour them.

What is the function of air spaces in eggs?

It is supposed that the air sac at the large end of an egg performs an important function in the development of the embryo chick. The chick makes use of the air in this pocket during the brief period between the time when it begins to breathe and the time when it is strong enough to break through the shell with its beak. The air sac enlarges materially during incubation, and in a normal egg the chick at hatching time always has its head pointing toward the large end of the egg and the air space. It is the opinion of scientists in the United States Bureau of Animal Industry that the air sac is formed by the contraction of the contents of the egg immediately after it is laid. The temperature of an ordinary hen's body is about 107 degrees Fahrenheit, and it is reasonable to suppose that as soon as an egg is laid the yolk and white contract somewhat. Because of the peculiar shape of the egg the air space is nearly always formed at the large end. Now and then it occurs on the side, but never at the small end.

How long after mating do elephants produce their young?

Exact knowledge on this subject is not available. Estimates of the period of gestation in elephants range all the way from eighteen to twenty-two months. Dr. William M. Mann, director of the National Zoological Park, says the gestation period in elephants is "about nineteen months, although there are more or less authentic records of twenty-one months." According to the late Raymond L. Ditmars, curator of mammals at the New York Zoological Park, the period of gestation in the Indian elephant is 641 days, which is considerably more than twenty-one months. There is no positive evidence to support the belief held by the natives of India and Burma that the gestation period is longer for a male calf than for a female. Frank Buck may have been merely reflecting this native belief when he wrote in *Fang and Claw*: "Of all the animals I know, the elephant is the only one in which the period of gestation varies between male and female. A healthy girl elephant is born in nineteen months, while a male doesn't see the light of jungle day for twenty to twenty-one months." The scarcity of records on this subject is accounted for by two facts. Elephants are very secretive in their breeding habits, and in no country is this species of animal domesticated in the strict sense of the term. The elephants used as beasts of burden in southeastern Asia are maintained under conditions as similar as possible to those of wild animals, and the supply is recruited either by captures from wild herds or by animals born in a semi-wild state. As a rule Indian elephants are tractable, especially if captured young, and they are easily trained for service or show. African elephants are very rarely born in captivity and are seldom tractable. Indian elephants are not bred in confinement because the process of rearing them from birth to the adult age is slow and expensive and because wild adults captured in the jungle usually soon become gentle and cheerful workers.

When were English sparrows brought to America?

The birds known as house sparrows in England and English sparrows in the United States were first brought to America in 1850, when eight pairs were imported under the auspices of Nicholas Pike and other directors of the Brooklyn Institute. These birds were released in Brooklyn the following spring, but they did not survive. In 1852, while on his way to assume the consul generalship of Portugal, Pike made arrangements for a second shipment of English sparrows to America. Some of these birds were released as the ship entered New York Harbor, while the remainder were kept in captivity until the spring of 1853, when they were liberated in Brooklyn. These two shipments involved a total of about one hundred sparrows. The purpose in bringing them to the United States was to protect shade trees from foliage-eating caterpillars, particularly the span worm, which is the larva of the Geometrid moth. From the beginning a few persons protested against the introduction of these foreign birds on the ground that they habitually feed on seeds and buds rather than insects and might become a pest, but their counsel was unheeded. The United States Biological Survey has records of fifteen direct importations of English sparrows between the years 1852 and 1881. They were released at Cincinnati, St. Louis, San Francisco and other places. In 1869 the city of Philadelphia released a thousand pairs of sparrows. All of these importations were not made by persons interested in insect control. Some persons brought the birds to America simply because they wanted to see in their country the birds that they had been used to seeing in Europe; others did it for the mere novelty of the enterprise. It was soon learned, however, that the birds were of little value as insect destroyers and that they were a nuisance to the community. They multiplied rapidly and in the course of years spread to all sections of the country. In many places the sparrows drove out more desirable native birds, such as the martins. These birds, however, are now said to be decreasing in number in America, both in urban and rural districts. Nature, it seems, has taken them in hand and is giving them their proper place in her system of economy. As the automobile replaced the horse their food supply in cities became less certain. English or house sparrows, which are native to many parts of Europe and Asia, are really not true sparrows, but members of the family of weaver finches. Their chief economic value is in destroying weeds by eating vast amounts of the seeds.

Is there such a word as "ornery"?

Ornery and onery are corrupted forms of ordinary. They are dialectical or colloquial terms meaning insignificant, low, mean, contemptible, and they denote a higher degree of contempt and disapprobation than ordinary does. Ornary as a contraction of ordinary was a common provincialism in England in the time of the Stuarts, although it is virtually obsolete now. The phrase uppon ornarie time occurs in the Easthampton records for 1679. In Ireland and the United States ornary persists in the further corrupted form ornery and onery, which were brought to the American colonies and perpetuated largely by the Scottish-Irish immigrants, who settled chiefly in the South and West. This explains the fact that ornery and onery are generally regarded as southernisms or westernisms. In 1830 the New York Constellation published the following as a Southern expression: "You ornery fellow! do you pretend to call me to account for my language?"

How did "fight like Trojans" originate?

In Homer's Iliad and Vergil's Aeneid the inhabitants of Troy are described as truthful, brave and patriotic. The Greeks besieged Troy for ten years before they were finally able to take the city and raze it to the ground. In allusion to this famous siege, and the many battles in connection with it, a person who fights courageously and stubbornly is said to *fight like a Trojan*. Likewise a person who works with energy and perseverance is said to *work like a Trojan*. *Work like a Turk* is probably a variation of the older expression, for the Turks have never been proverbial for their activity and industry. Ancient Troy was located in what is now Turkish territory.

Do canaries live in the wild state?

Domestic canaries have been altered to such an extent by hundreds of years of selective breeding that their wild progenitors cannot be positively identified. Their early history as cage birds is obscure. It is generally supposed, however, that they sprang from a species of finch still found in the wild state in the Canary Islands and Madeira, off the northwestern coast of Africa. The wild birds in the Canary Islands are grayish brown, olive green or greenish yellow, sometimes varied with other hues, but they never have the beautifully colored plumage so common in domestic varieties. According to the accepted story, specimens of these birds were captured in the Canaries during the sixteenth century and domesticated in Italy, whence they were carried to other parts of the world. Canaries breed freely with European finches and certain other birds, a fact that leads some authorities to believe that the domestic canary is the product of interbreeding as well as selective breeding and consequently not the descendant of any one species. The color of the plumage of canaries, like that of parrots, can be altered to some extent by feeding them particular diets. *Canary* is derived from Latin *canis* ("dog"), and according to the Elder Pliny, these islands were called Canaria "from the multitude of dogs of great size" found there by King Juba of Mauretania when he visited the islands about 40 B.C. In the United States common American goldfinches or thistle birds are sometimes called "wild canaries." These birds, of course, are not canaries at all.

Why does a star precede the number on some bills?

On certain currency notes or bills issued by the United States Bureau of Engraving and Printing an asterisk precedes the serial number instead of the customary letter of the alphabet. The Treasurer of the United States says these small stars are put on only substitute bills used to replace those that are defective or spoiled in the process of printing. Paper money is printed and finished in sheets and the finishing process includes printing the serial numbers. Although all currency is subjected to several examinations before the numbering and sealing is done, it sometimes happens that after a serial number is printed the bill must be discarded because of some imperfection in it. A special bill is prepared to take the place of the discarded one and its number is not in the regular series. The asterisk before the number identifies it as a substitute bill. Naturally the percentage of spoiled bills is very small and only a few are so numbered.

Does corn grow faster at night?

Other things being equal, corn probably grows most rapidly on warm nights. Many plants, including corn or maize, continue to grow after dark, notwithstanding the fact that photosynthesis takes place only while the plants are receiving sunlight. The rate of growth in plants is influenced by many factors other than the formation of food materials through photosynthesis, and the photosynthetic products themselves may require further change before being utilized in growth. Thus it happens that some plants not only continue to grow after nightfall but actually grow more rapidly at night under ordinary conditions than they do during the day. Apparently, however, this is not true of all plants. There is no particular period in the course of the twenty-four hours of the day during which all plants grow most rapidly. Even among those that reach their maximum rate of growth in the night the period of most rapid growth in some species seems to begin in the early part of the night, while in other species it does not begin until after midnight. Certain plants will continue to elongate rapidly even in prolonged darkness, but in such cases the type of growth differs materially from that which takes place when the plants are exposed to sunlight. In Shakespeare's *Henry V* the Bishop of Ely says that Prince Hal "no doubt, grew like the summer grass, fastest by night."

Why are certain soft drinks called pop?

Certain sweet, nonintoxicating drinks containing carbon dioxide were named *pop* because when the bottles were opened the corks were expelled with a pop or quick, explosive noise. The original name was *soda pop*, which was soon shortened to *pop*. Both the name and product originated in America. It is said that the first soda pop was made in 1807 when an eminent Philadelphia physician named Philip Syng Physick asked a chemist named Townsend Speakman to prepare carbonated water for some of his patients. The chemist flavored the carbonated water with fruit juice to make it more palatable. Whether or not this was the actual beginning of the soft drink industry, Dr. Philip Syng Physick was a real person. He was born in Philadelphia in 1768 and died in the same city in 1837. He became so eminent in his profession that he is known as the

"Father of American Surgery." In 1831 he removed nearly a thousand stones from the bladder of Chief Justice John Marshall in a single operation. Soda pop came into popular use after 1832, when John Matthews, of New York City, invented an apparatus for preparing water charged with carbon dioxide gas. In New England soda pop is popularly known as *tonic*, which may be a survival of the medical origin of the drink.

Can nonvenomous snakes bite?

Nonvenomous snakes, such as bull snakes, blue racers and garter snakes, can and often do bite. Their fangs are not provided with venom glands and their bite is not more dangerous than that of most animals. In a general way it may be said that there is considerable danger of getting blood poisoning from the bite of any animal, reptile or insect, whether or not it has venom glands. For that reason any person who is bitten by a reptile, even though it is not venomous, is advised to wash and to sterilize the wound promptly.

Where are the eyes of the horsefly located?

The large compound eyes of the horsefly are located conspicuously on the head. Many people believe that the eyes of this insect consist of small yellowish specks or scales on tiny stems under the wings. This, it is said, is proved by the fact that when these clublike appendages are removed the horsefly loses its equilibrium and flies abnormally. As a matter of fact, these specks or scales represent aborted underwings. Entomologists call them *calypters* or *squamae*. Naturally the removal of the calypters affects the flight of the horsefly because they are intimately related to the wings proper. Similar phenomena occur in other insects. The common housefly has five eyes located on the upper front part of the head. Two of them are compound, being composed of some four thousand eye units, while three are single, being in the form of a triangle located in the space above and between the two compound eyes.

How do American and European plan hotels differ?

When a hotel is operated on the European plan the guest pays a stipulated amount for his lodging only. If he eats at the hotel he pays for his meals separately, just as if he were eating at an independent grill or restaurant. Under the American plan the guest pays for both lodging and meals at a regular daily, weekly or monthly rate. This plan goes back to colonial days when the guests at the inns, taverns, *ordinaries* and hotels sat at the family table and ate whatever the landlord happened to have. Until the middle of the nineteenth century most of the hotels in the United States were on the American plan, but now there are very few hotels operated exclusively on this plan except in the smaller cities and at seaside and mountain resorts. The European plan, which originated in France and which began to be introduced into America about 1830, prevails in most foreign countries. In the United States many hotels combine both plans, leaving it to the wish of the guest to pay a regular rate for lodging only or for both lodging and meals.

How is the caliber of a rifle measured?

The caliber of a rifle is the interior diameter of the barrel measured between the *lands*, which are the raised parts in the bore between the grooves. Caliber is usually expressed in inches or hundredths of an inch. A .44-caliber gun has a bore 44/100ths of an inch in diameter. A .22-caliber rifle has a 22/100ths of an inch bore. Sometimes the caliber of rifles is referred to in such figures as .30–30 and .38–30. In that case the figure in front of the hyphen denotes the caliber and the figure following the hyphen denotes the ballistic equivalent to the black powder charge. Again a rifle may be referred to as .250–3,000. In that case the figure before the hyphen denotes the caliber and that after the hyphen denotes the muzzle velocity. Strictly speaking, it is not correct to speak of "high" and "low" caliber. Caliber is "large" or "small."

Why are pirates called buccaneers?

The original *buccaneers* were Dutch, French and English freebooters who hovered around the West Indies in the seventeenth century and preyed upon the commerce of Spain. At first the buccaneers maintained themselves by systematic attacks upon Spanish cargo ships, but later they indulged in indiscriminate piracy. They were bound together by a loose and crude code that required all members of the association to share with one another the necessities of life. For a time the chief headquarters of the buccaneers was the island of Tortuga near Santo Domingo. Many of these pirates settled on Santo Domingo, Tortuga, St. Christopher and neighboring islands and devoted themselves to selling salted and smoked beef and pork to other freebooters in exchange for smuggled goods from Europe. Cattle and pigs introduced on the islands earlier by the Spanish had multiplied rapidly. From the Carib Indians the freebooters learned how to preserve meat without salt, then a costly article. They cut the meat into strips, cured it in the sun and then smoked it over green wood fires. The Indians called this process of curing meat *boucanning*. The sheds in which the freebooters lived and cured their meat were known as *boucans*. One writer of the time related that the Caribs ate their prisoners well *boucanned*. From these circumstances the pirates or free-booters themselves, and by extension all pirates, came to be called "buc-caneers." The Spanish called them "demons of the sea," while among themselves they were known as "the brethren of the coast." The bucca-neers ceased to be the terror of the Spanish Main toward the close of the seventeenth century. Their last concerted raid was the capture and looting of Carthagena on the Colombian coast in 1697.

What is the function of lucky stones in fish?

This is the popular name given to the ear stones (*otoliths*) found in a small sac near the internal ear of nearly all species of fish. The sacs are located under the gill cover and behind the eyes. In each sac there are two loose, white, irregular, stonelike objects. The Chesapeake Bay hardhead or "croaker" is noted for its exceptionally large otoliths. These otoliths are composed almost entirely of calcium carbonate and calcium phosphate and are soluble in weak acetic acid. Their popular name comes from the fact that superstitious people in many parts of the world often have used them for charms like rabbits' feet and fairy crosses. In former times the ear stones of fish were used as a preventive or a cure of colic and as a talisman to avert the evil eye. Ear stones show periodic rings of growth, somewhat analogous to the annular rings of trees, and they are frequently used to determine the age of fish. The function of otoliths is not definitely known, there being a difference of opinion among investigators. One theory regards them as auditory organs that play a role in the perception of sound waves. According to another theory, they are connected in some way with the so-called "static sense," the complex process by means of which fish maintain their equilibrium in water.

How did Mussolini acquire the title "Il Duce"?

In Italian *Il Duce* (pronounced eel *doo*-chay) literally means simply "The Leader." *Duce* is derived from Latin *dux* ("leader"), which is also the source of *duke* as well as of *doge*, the title of the Duke of Venice from 697 A.D. to 1798. *Il Duce* was originally bestowed upon Benito Mussolini by his followers, not as an official title, but merely as a nickname for the leader of the Fascist movement. Later the dictator adopted it as his title. In 1939 a government official in Rome publicly reprimanded Italians who referred to the dictator as *Il Capo* ("the Chief"), instead of *Il Duce* ("the Leader"). A year later the Italian government issued an order saying that nobody should address Musso-lini either orally or in writing as "Your Excellency." The required form, declared the order, was simply *Duce* when addressing the dictator orally, and *Duce of Fascism, Head of the Government* when addressing him in writing. Mussolini was named after a full-blooded American Indian. He was christened Benito after Benito Juarez, the "Lincoln of Mexico," who was President of Mexico in 1867 when the Emperor Maximillian was executed and whom Alessandro Mussolini, the dictator's father, admired greatly. *Mussolini* is derived from the same source as *muslin*. In his book of travels Marco Polo wrote: "All those cloths of gold and of silk which we call muslins are of the manufacture of Mosul, and all the great merchants termed Mossulini, who convey spices and drugs, in large quantities from one country to another are from this province." The Italian *ini* as a suffix to surnames signifies "of the tribe or clan of."

How did "pay through the nose" originate?

To pay through the nose, meaning "to pay a fancy price for a thing," "to pay more than it is worth" or "to get stung," is of uncertain origin. The earliest known use of the phrase in English is dated 1672. There is a legend that in the ninth century the Danes imposed a head tax in Ireland resembling the modern poll tax. It was called the "nose tax" because those who neglected to pay it were punished by having the nose slit. *Paying through the nose* may have been suggested by this penalty. Some authorities suppose the phrase was originally a facetious allusion to "nose-bleeding" and "being bled for money." Others trace the origin of the phrase to the similarity of *rhino,* an old slang term for money, to Greek *rhinos* ("nose").

Why are overshoes called "arctics"?

Arctic is derived from Greek *arktos* ("bear"), and was applied to the constellation known as the Great Bear, which revolves around the North Star. Hence the region around the North Pole came to be referred to as the Arctic and that around the South Pole as the Antarctic. Warm, waterproof overshoes were originally called arctics because they were regarded as especially suitable for cold climates. It was at first merely a trade name. *Arctic,* correctly pronounced *ark-tick,* is frequently incorrectly pronounced as if it were spelled *artic,* with the first hard *c* or *k* sound omitted.

What is the origin of "up to snuff"?

A person who is worldly wise, well informed and not easily deceived is said to be *up to snuff.* The phrase, usually classed as slang or a colloquialism, does not refer to snuff in the sense of powdered tobacco, as one might suppose. It is a figure comparing mental alertness with a keen sense of smell. *Snuff* is of Anglo-Saxon origin and is closely related to English *sniff* and Dutch *snuffen*, meaning literally to draw air up the nose to smell better and figuratively to smell or scent. The old phrase *to snuff* or *sniff danger* signifies about the same thing as the phrase *to smell a rat*. Accordingly *up to snuff* denotes up to a high standard of alertness, discernment or ability to follow a scent or clue. Powdered tobacco, of course, was called snuff because it is snuffed or sniffed.

Why does one's reflection in a spoon appear upside down?

When a person looks into the bowl of a brightly polished spoon he always sees his reflection upside down. This is because the concave part of the spoon acts like a lens. If the spoon were flat it would reflect like an ordinary mirror. To illustrate: In focusing a plate, camera images are thrown on the ground glass upside down. When rays of light are passed through a lens they converge on each other until they all meet at a single point. At this point the rays cross and when they continue their journey toward the eye their positions are reversed. That is why stereopticon slides and motion picture films must be put in the projecting machine upside down to make the pictures appear right side up on the screen. Any hollow reflecting object, like the polished bowl of a metal spoon, acts in the same manner. The rays that strike in its exact center are reflected straight back, while those that fall on the curved sides are turned inward. Hence all the rays cross at a point and the reflection appears upside down. A flat reflecting surface, like a mirror, does not reflect the light rays toward a converging point and the rays do not meet. Accordingly the reflection is right side up.

Why is the Pope's palace called the Vatican?

The Vatican received its name from an older name of the site on which it stands. In ancient times a low, level region on the right or western bank of the Tiber was known as *Ager Vaticanus* ("Vatican Field"). This name is believed to be derived from *Vaticum*, the name of an Etruscan settlement there that had vanished centuries before the earliest authentic history of Rome began. The origin and meaning of *Vaticum* is not known for certain. In Latin *vates* means "prophet," and *vaticinatio*, "prophecy." Some authorities suppose that Vaticum, which was outside the limits of ancient Rome, was so called because a legendary priestly king revealed oracles to his people there. In process of time Vatican came to be attached specifically to a near-by eminence rather than to the low, level land near the river. The popes acquired possession of large parts of Vatican Hill by purchase during the Middle Ages. A papal residence was built on the site near the ancient Basilica of St. Peter in the time of Symmachus, who was Pope from 498 to 514 A.D. The residence of the pontiff is the largest palace in the world. It is not the work of any one architect, but a great collection of a thousand rooms that took centuries to build. The state of Vatican City (*Stato della Citta del Vaticano*), which was created in 1929, has an area of about 109 acres, and comprises not only the Vatican proper but also St. Peter's, the largest church in the world, and many other buildings.

How do ruffed grouse "drum"?

The American ruffed grouse, popularly known as the pheasant in the central states and as the partridge in New England, makes a characteristic sound known as "drumming." This drumming sound is made only by the cock, chiefly in the spring, which is the mating season. The drumming is undoubtedly a "courtship song," calculated to impress the females. How ruffed grouse drum is a question that has puzzled naturalists for two hundred years or more. The ruffed grouse is a rather shy ground bird and not given to making a public exhibition of its love affairs. Few persons have actually seen a male grouse drumming and those who have often disagree as to just how it is done. Henry Thoreau, a good naturalist, thought the sound was produced by the bird striking its wings together behind its back. Others supposed that the sound was produced by beating the wings against a log. Still others were equally certain that the bird beat its own sides with its wings. All were wrong. Motion pictures of ruffed grouse caught in the very act of drumming show clearly that the cock grouse produces the drumming effect merely by beating its wings rapidly on the air close to its body. He usually perches on a log, grips the log firmly with his feet, begins to beat his wings slowly and increases the tempo until the thumping, booming or drumming sound is produced. Some members of the same family of game birds, such as the prairie chicken, make a booming "courtship song" by deflating the air sacs in the neck. The ruffed grouse is the official state bird of Pennsylvania.

Why are storks said to bring babies?

The legend that babies are brought into the home by the stork is believed to have originated in northwestern Europe where that bird is regarded with a feeling bordering on reverence. In Roman mythology the stork was sacred to Venus, the goddess of love, and whenever a pair of storks built their nest on a housetop the ancients regarded it as a sign of Venus' blessing on the family. A Norse legend says this bird received its name from a story that a stork flew around the cross when Jesus was crucified and cried *Styrka* ("Strengthen"). Probably because of these legends and because it was looked upon as a useful scavenger, the stork became the good luck bird in Germany and the Netherlands. *Ooyevaar*, the common Dutch name for the stork, signifies "bringer of good luck." The stork is a welcome guest at German and Dutch homes and wheels are provided on many houses as nesting places. A family with a stork's nest on its roof regards itself as fortunate. It is a beautiful sight to see this tall bird, with white plumage, set off by the black wing quills and red beak and legs, as it stalks about in meadows and marshes in search of fish or small water creatures, or as it stands on one leg upon some high place such as a steeple or chimney top. The stork figures prominently in European folklore, fairy tales and fables. Centuries ago there was already a superstition that a stork flies over a house where a birth is about to take place. The legend of the stork as the bringer of babies probably grew out of this superstition and the sheer inability of the fathers and mothers to explain satisfactorily to the other children where the baby came from. It would be natural to tell the children that their little brother or sister was brought to them by the tall white bird on the house, the herald of a new birth, the guardian of the home and the symbol of good luck.

How did "Hello" originate?

Hello as a conventional form of greeting and salutation is believed to have evolved from various early words or sounds used to attract the attention of persons at a distance. All such call words were probably of echoic or onomatopoeic origin. Perhaps the ancestor of *hello* was *hallow*, pronounced with the stress on the second syllable. In his English-Latin dictionary, compiled about 1440, Geoffrey the Grammarian defined *hallow* as a "sailor's hail." *Hail* itself no doubt was used as a call word before it was as a salutation or greeting. During the sixteenth century the common form was *halloo* or *hallo*. In Shakespeare's works we find *halloo*, *hillo*, *hilloa*, *holla*, *holloa* and *hollo*. These calls were widely used in Elizabethan times by huntsmen. By the middle of the nineteenth century *hullo* was the popular form of the salutation. The spelling *hello* does not occur in literature until after 1880, when the word became the common salutation over the telephone in the United States. When the first experimental telephone switchboard and exchange was installed in 1878 at New Haven, Connecticut, the signal and salutation used was *Ahoy! Ahoy!* This nautical hail is said to have been originally the war cry of the Vikings. For a year or two persons answered the telephone by saying "Are you ready to talk?" or "Are you there?" In British usage "Are you there?" persisted much longer as the customary telephone salutation. Thomas A. Edison is believed to have been the first person to use *Hello* on the telephone. One day, his biographers tell us, the famous inventor picked up the receiver of a telephone and said *Hello*. The word at once became popular and has been used ever since. In 1941 the United States War Department ordered all its employees when answering interdepartmental calls to give their names instead of saying *Hello* in order to save time.

Is there a country named San Salvador?

El Salvador, or simply *Salvador*, is the correct name of the Central American republic, which is the smallest and most densely populated country on the mainland of the New World. It is a common mistake to call the country *San Salvador*, owing to confusion with the name of its capital. *Republica De El Salvador* is the official name of the republic in Spanish. *El Salvador* means "The Saviour" and was the name given to the region by its conqueror, Pedro de Alvarado, who was sent to Salvador from Mexico by Hernando Cortez in 1524 and who overcame the natives of Cuscutlan on the Eve of the Holy Saviour. The name of the capital, San Salvador, means "Holy Saviour." Don Jorge de Alvarado founded the city in 1528 near its present site. Many reference works erroneously state that El Salvador was discovered by Christopher Columbus. As a matter of fact he never visited that country. The mistake is probably due to confusion with the name of the West Indian island in the Bahamas on which Columbus made his first landing in the New World in 1492. This island was known to the natives as Guanahane, but Columbus called it San Salvador. It is now generally identified with the island known to the British as Cat Island, although some authorities suppose it to be Watling Island, which lies a few miles to the east.

Why do we have a best man at weddings?

The custom of having a best man at weddings is believed to be a survival of primitive marriage by capture, when a man seized a woman and carried her away by force. He would naturally, under such circumstances, choose a faithful friend or follower to go with him and ward off the attacks of the girl's kinsmen while he stole away with her. Thus, if this notion is correct, the appearance of the bridegroom with his chief groomsman or best man at the bride's home really represents a prehistoric marauding expedition. *Best man* is of Scotch origin and probably does not date back further than the eighteenth century. The earliest use of the term recorded by the Oxford dictionary is dated 1814. Groom is derived from an old root signifying "male child," "man," "servant" or "attendant." Groomsmen originally were the attendants who went along to assist the best man or chief lieutenant of the bridegroom. Bridesmaids symbolize the female attendants or "girl friends" who used to help, or pretend to help, defend the bride against her abductors.

How are cannon spiked?

In former times when the old type of cannon was used the guns were disabled by driving iron spikes into the opening at the breech through which fire was communicated to the powder. This was called *spiking the cannon*. It was usually done to prevent their immediate use by the enemy when it was necessary to leave the guns behind. Such disablement was generally only temporary. The phrase is retained in modern military usage. Spiking a cannon now means breaking or carrying away essential parts of the breech mechanism, making it impossible to use the gun without considerable repairing.

Is fish a brain food?

The widespread popular notion that fish is an especially good food for developing the brain is not supported by any scientific information available. Science does not recognize any one food as more beneficial to the brain than any other. What is good for the well-being of the whole body is also good for the brain. Louis Agassiz, the famous naturalist, was largely responsible for the belief that fish is a brain food. During the nineteenth century Jacob Moleschott, Ludwig Buchner and other German scientists who sought to explain all energy in terms of material things popularized the saying, "No phosphorus, no thought." All mental processes, they claimed, were motivated by this one vital element. The French chemist Jean Dumas had previously established the fact that fish are particularly rich in phosphorus. Agassiz, an authority on fish, put these two ideas together and suggested that eating fish might be good food for developing the brain. But the inference is faulty because of the weakness of the first premise. Phosphorus is no more essential to thinking than any one of a dozen other elements in the human body. The German scientists might have stated with an equal degree of truth that there is no thought without calcium, sulphur, iron or nitrogen. As a matter of fact the human brain attains almost its full adult size during the first six years of a child's life and during the time when its chief

[182]

article of diet is milk. The association of fish with intellectual development was probably strengthened by another process of reasoning. The flesh of fish is lighter and more easily digested than most of the flesh meats. It is therefore a suitable and desirable food for so-called brain workers or persons engaged in occupations involving little physical exertion and much mental labor. In other words, fish contains no elements especially adapted to the building or renovating of the brain, but it does contain in a lesser degree than meat those food elements requiring considerable physical exercise for their assimilation.

How did "o'clock" originate?

The original form of this term was *of the clock*, of which *o'clock* is a contraction. It means by or according to the clock. The form *o'clock* began to appear first in the eighteenth century. In Chaucer's time *of the clock* was used. Later *the* in the phrase was elided and *of* was frequently slurred into *a*. Chaucer said *ten of the clokke*, while many writers of the sixteenth and seventeenth centuries said *ten of clock* or *ten a clock*. *Clock* originally signified bell, and the modern meaning is a survival of the period when all mechanical timepieces sounded the hours by bells.

What is small beer?

Small beer is beer with a small alcoholic content. As applied to alcoholic beverages *small* signifies "thin," "diluted," "weak," or "mildly alcoholic"; as, small beer, small ale, and small wine. In 1568, when Shakespeare was three years old, Richard Grafton wrote in his chronicles of England: "For drinke, they had none but small beer." Small beer was the drink of the common people and consequently the badge of the lower classes. To refer to a person as "small beer" is to disparage him. In Shakespeare's *II King Henry VI* the rebel Jack Cade promises the populace that when he is king "I will make it felony to drink small beer." Prince Hal, in *II King Henry IV*, says to Poins, "Doth it not show vilely in me to desire small beer?" Poins replies that "a prince should not be so loosely studied as to remember so weak a composition," whereupon the Prince observes: "Belike then my appetite was not princely got; for, by my troth, I do now remember the poor creature, small beer." In *Othello* Iago tells Desdemona she was a wight "to suckle fools and chronicle small beer." Shakespeare also refers to "a pot of double beer," which was strong beer. Strong beer contained about seven or more per cent of alcohol, while small beer contained four per cent or less. Under date of July 11, 1712, William Byrd of Westover wrote in his secret diary: "My wife longed for small beer and I sent to Mrs. Harrison's for some but she had none, so that she drank a bottle of strong almost herself." *Small beer* survives in popular usage only in the figurative sense or in the sense of a "small portion" of the beverage. George Washington operated a brew house for making small beer at Mount Vernon. A notebook written in his own hand in 1757 contains the following quaint recipe "To Make Small Beer":

> Take a large Siffer full of Bran. Hops to your Taste. Boil these 3 hours, then strain out 30 Gallns into a Cooler. Put in 3 Gallns Molasses while the Beer is Scalding hot or rather draw the Molasses into the Cooler & Strain the Beer on it while boiling Hot. Let this stand until it is little more than Blood warm then put in a quart of Yeast. If the weather is very Cold cover it over with a Blanket & let it Work in the Cooler 24 hours then put it into the Cask—leave the Bung open until it is almost done Working. Bottle it that day Week it was Brewed.

Is the earth's water supply increasing or decreasing?

Scientists are of the opinion that no appreciable change in the quantity of water on the earth has taken place within historic times. At any given time most of the earth's supply of water is in the oceans, seas, lakes and streams, in the interstices of the soil and rocks, in the atmosphere and in the ice floes of the arctic and antarctic. The distribution of water is constantly changing, but the actual amount of water has probably changed little since life began on the earth. Much of water on the earth is the same water that existed thousands of years ago. The water we drink today may contain some of the same molecules that composed the bath water of a Pharaoh. No water is lost in the natural process of evaporation and the consequent falling of rain, snow and hail. Water is composed of two elements—oxygen and hydrogen. A chemist in his laboratory can readily decompose water into these elements. Likewise he can combine them and produce water. But there are very few known natural agencies that produce water by combining oxygen and hydrogen, or that decompose it into these elements. Consequently there is believed to be about the same quantity of water on the earth today as there was ten thousand years ago. A limited amount of water is formed in the combustion of organic matter containing hydrogen, such as gasoline, natural gas, coal, wood, fats and oils. It is probable that a certain quantity of water is formed from the oxidation of organic matter containing hydrogen, even in cases where the oxidation is too slow to be termed combustion. But on the other hand, water is used by plants to form organic compounds. This water, however, moves in an endless cycle. It is first used to build up compounds such as cellulose and sugar. Then when these compounds are broken

[184]

down by slow decomposition or by combustion, the hydrogen unites with oxygen either from the air or from the plant material and water is again formed.

Why do the sun and moon appear larger near the horizon?

The apparent increase in the size of the sun, moon and stars when they are near the horizon is chiefly psychological. They look larger in that position because the human eye, more accustomed to estimate sizes of objects near the ground than at altitudes, compares them with objects on the earth. This can be demonstrated by holding a cardboard near the eyes to shut out the view of near objects. For the same reason the full moon appears larger when it emerges from behind clouds. As a matter of fact, the angular size of the full moon is larger when seen directly overhead than when seen near the horizon, because it is then about four thousand miles closer to the observer, which should make it seem one-sixtieth larger. This difference, however, would be too small for the casual observer to note unless he could see the two objects side by side. It is often said that refraction of light by the atmosphere magnifies heavenly bodies when near the horizon and is responsible for the apparent increase in size. This is not the case. On the contrary, refraction causes the sun and full moon when close to the horizon to appear vertically flattened. In other words, refraction decreases the apparent vertical diameter. It is probable, however, that the atmosphere, as well as the dust and moisture suspended in it, enters into this problem. Brightness seems to decrease the apparent size of an object by destroying its outline. When heavenly bodies are close to the horizon we see them through a thicker blanket of atmosphere than when they are higher up. Consequently their brightness is greatly decreased while their apparent size is increased.

How did "giving the cold shoulder" originate?

To give a person the cold shoulder means to receive him coldly, to discourage his friendly advances, or to assume a distant manner toward him, indicating that one wishes to cut his acquaintance. The origin of the expression is not known for certain. According to one theory, which has no concrete evidence to support it, the phrase arose from a social usage in medieval France. In those times it was customary to serve hot roasts when entertaining guests. However, if the guests outstayed their welcome, or made themselves obnoxious to the host, a cold shoulder of mutton or beef was served instead of the customary hot meat. In other words, the guest was given the cold shoulder, indicating

[185]

that he was no longer welcome. It is more probable that cold in the phrase is used in the sense of unfriendly, as in a cold handshake, and that the phrase merely refers to the peculiar but very effective method employed by some people to cut acquaintances, that is, keeping the back or at least one shoulder between them and a person whom they dislike.

Does the exact center of a wheel turn?

Many people believe that the exact center of a solid wheel does not move when the wheel rotates on a stationary axis. This notion, which would apply to any other object rotating under the same conditions, is based on the following reasoning: Since both time and distance enter into motion the speed of any part of a moving wheel decreases as the center is approached. Theoretically the element of distance is totally lacking at the exact center and the motion at that point should be zero. To move at all the exact center would have to move in two directions at the same time, which is clearly impossible. This, however, is true only in theory. A wheel is a rigid object and when it turns every conceivable part of it moves, for the human mind cannot conceive of an ultimate particle. If you can conceive of any particle of matter whatever, be it ever so small, you can always conceive of that particle divided in half, and this process of division can be continued indefinitely. "The particle lying in the axis of rotation of a solid wheel must turn with the wheel," says the United States Bureau of Standards. "Otherwise these particles would have to slip with respect to adjacent particles of the axis. Of course no such slipping occurs."

Does the sap of trees freeze in the winter?

Sap in trees frequently freezes in the winter. The freezing point of water is lowered by the addition of substances in solution. Since sap contains various solutes its freezing point is considerably below 32 degrees Fahrenheit and accordingly it does not freeze in moderate freezing temperatures. Trees are further protected from freezing by the fact that the moisture content near the surface is not so great in winter as in summer. But the sap freezes during extremely cold spells and sometimes much damage is done to the trees. The United States Forest Service says that in the north woods when the temperature is 40 or 50 degrees below zero the ruptures of tissue in trees caused by freezing can often be heard as a sort of sharp report. As a rule freezing that produces sufficient pressure to rupture the tissue results in vertical cracks running up and down the trunk of the tree. In succeeding seasons of growth the tree attempts to heal over these cracks, but ridges of protruding scar tissue remain as evidence of the injury. Although the wood of trees is frequently frozen hard, generally no serious ruptures result because the moisture is evenly distributed through the tissue. The temperature of the heart of a large tree remains approximately the same in winter and summer.

How did "moonshine" as applied to liquor originate?

It was formerly supposed that *moonshine* as applied to distilled liquor made in violation of the law originated in the mountain districts of Virginia, North Carolina, Kentucky and Tennessee, which are proverbial for illicit stills. Liquor made in this manner was manufactured at night by moonlight to escape detection by the revenue officers—hence *moonshine*. But it is quite probable that the term did not originate in America at all. A dictionary published in London in 1785 defines *moonshine* as white or illicit brandy smuggled by night into England from France and Holland.

Who said: "They shall not pass"?

They shall not pass became famous during the First World War. The saying cannot be definitely attributed to any particular person. It probably originated in the following order issued by General Robert Georges Nivelle on June 23, 1916: "The hour is decisive. Feeling themselves checked in every direction the Germans are launching furious and desperate attacks against our front in the hope of arriving at the gates of Verdun before being attacked by the united forces of the Allies. You will not let them pass, my comrades. The country still asks of you this supreme effort; the army of Verdun will not let itself be intimidated by the shells of the German infantry whose efforts it has defied for four months." Apparently the natural reaction or answer to these words was "They shall not pass," a saying that became famous in the trenches on the western front. Among the French the words are popularly attributed to General Henri Pétain, and also to General Joseph Joffre. According to a popular story, early in 1916 General Joffre sent General de Castelnau to Verdun to determine which would be the wiser course, to defend or to abandon that fortress. After consulting with General Pétain, who was in command at Verdun, De Castelnau gave it as his opinion that the Germans should not be permitted to take the fort. He said to the commander, "They must not pass." Pétain replied quickly: "They shall not pass." The determined and successful defense of Verdun that followed made the words famous throughout the world. In French the expression is, *Ils ne passeront pas*. The auxilliary verb *shall* is used in the accepted

English translation. In Italy similar words are attributed to General Armando Diaz at the Battle of Piave in June, 1918. Long before the First World War this saying was a watchword among the Alpine troops of Italy. When Moses sent messengers to ask the King of Edom for permission to pass through his country, the King, according to *Numbers 20:18*, replied: "Thou shalt not pass by me, lest I come out against thee with the sword."

Do fur-bearing animals inhabit Antarctica?

There are no fur-bearing animals of any kind on the land within the Antarctic Circle, and there are no aboriginal people. The Eskimo, the polar bear and the musk ox, all of which add to the fascination of the Far North, are unknown to Antarctica. The picturesque penguin and other sea birds along the coast constitute virtually the only wild life on the land around the South Pole. A few species of minute wingless insects of a degenerate type are occasionally met with. The only important mammalian life in the Antarctic is marine in form, there being numerous whales, and a few species of seals, which survive the winters by keeping open blowholes in the sea ice. The absence of animals in the south-polar regions is one of the most striking features of the Antarctic continent, which has an area greater than Australia. When Sir Ernest Shackleton, the British explorer, told William II of Germany that there were no polar bears in the Antarctic the Kaiser expressed incredulity. Vilhjalmur Stefansson, the Arctic explorer, declared that the French, who claimed a sector of the Antarctic, went so far as to issue a proclamation against shooting polar bears in those regions, notwithstanding nobody has ever seen the trace of a bear in that part of the world.

Does cutting a crow's tongue improve its ability to talk?

The popular belief that slitting the membrane that supports the underside of the tongues of certain birds will improve their ability "to talk" is without foundation. It is a cruel practice that is not justified by results. The tongue of a bird plays little if any part in the utterance of sounds. Crows, magpies, blue jays, mynahs, brown thrashers and some other species often learn to articulate words and even sentences almost as well as parrots. Crows and magpies in particular can often be taught to talk, but their ability in this respect is not favorably affected by any operation performed on the tongue. Nor is the ability of a parrot to talk improved by such an operation. Stories of pet crows which have been taught to talk and which can "speak fluently" are frequently reported by the newspapers. Experts say the most practical way to encourage a bird to talk is to confine it to a quiet room and upon entering the room to speak a single word distinctly. By this means a vocabulary of a talking bird can be increased until it will speak a number of words and phrases.

What state has the highest altitude?

The average altitude of the 48 states of the Union is about 2,500 feet above sea level. Delaware, with an average altitude of only about 60 feet, is the lowest state; Colorado, nicknamed the Mountain State, with an average altitude of 6,800 feet, is the highest. There are 41 mountain peaks in Colorado more than 14,000 feet in altitude, and the lowest point in the entire state, on the Arkansas River, has an elevation of 3,500 feet. The highest and lowest points in the United States proper are both within 100 miles of each other in Inyo County, California. They are Mount Whitney, 14,495 feet above sea level, and a point in Death Valley, 276 feet below sea level.

When is the moon "wet"?

According to a very old popular belief, if both horns of the new crescent moon point up it is a wet moon and a sign of "falling weather." It is said that the bowl then holds plenty of water and therefore will bring rain. On the other hand, when the new moon stands on end, or nearly so, it is a dry moon and is a sign of dry weather. Such a moon can hold little water. There is a legend that the Indians used to hang a bow or powder horn on the moon when they wished to go on the warpath or on a long hunting trip; if the horns of the moon both pointed up so the bow or powder horn would stay on, the warriors left it hanging and remained in their wigwams, but if the moon was tilted so the bow or powder horn slipped off, they took it and were off on their expedition sure of fine weather. Curiously enough, some weather prophets take just the opposite view of what constitutes wet and dry moons. They say if the new moon is tilted to one side it is a wet moon; the water will run out and produce rain. George Washington made several references to this phenomenon in his diary. Under date of February 26, 1767, he wrote: "Brisk wind from the Southward. Clear, warm and pleasant. According to Colo. West ye greatest part of the next Moon should be as this day i.e, the same kind of weather that happens upon thursday before the change will continue through ye course of the next Moon, at least the first and 2d quarter of it. quere—is not this an old woman's story." On March 23, 1768, Washington noted: "This Moon, wch. changed the 18th appeared with the points directly upwards exactly of a height."

Under date of April 18, 1798, referring to a severe frost, he wrote: "Peaches not killed and hoped other fruit not hurt. Points of the New Moon upwards." And just a month later: "Horns, or points of the Moon upwards." The United States Weather Bureau says wet and dry moons exist only in the imagination. It does not believe that the moon exercises a controlling influence over the weather. The position of the lunar crescent depends on the angle the moon's path makes with the horizon, and on any given date it is always the same in places having the same latitude. If the popular weather signs were reliable, the same kind of weather would prevail on any given date throughout a belt of latitude extending entirely around the globe. Of course there is no such uniformity of weather in respect to latitude. The direction of the horns of the moon can be determined many years in advance for any latitude on the earth.

How did Westminster Abbey get its name?

Minster (Anglo-Saxon mynster) is an old name for a monastery or Christian religious house. Strictly speaking, abbey is superfluous in Westminster Abbey because minster means an abbey church and is still used in that sense in York Minster, Beverly Minster and similar names. Many people habitually misspell and mispronounce Westminster under the mistaken impression that the second part of the compound name is minister. It is minster, with only one i. It is often stated that Westminster was so called to distinguish it from Eastminster, the Abbey of Grace on Tower Hill in London. This is disproved by the fact that a charter of sanctuary was granted to Westminster by Edward the Confessor, who died in 1066, while Eastminster was not founded until the fourteenth century. Westminster was probably so called because it was west of the Cathedral of St. Paul's, or because it originally referred to a monastery on the west side of London. In later years a church connected with a monastery or one which had its origin in a monastic establishment was called a minster. When the Abbey of St. Peter was built on the north bank of the Thames, on the site of old west minster, it became popularly known as Westminster Abbey, and under that name it is now the most famous church in Great Britain, although its official name is now The Collegiate Church of St. Peter's. Westminster Abbey is best known as the burial place of British sovereigns and notables. The first king of England interred there was Edward the Confessor. Since the death of Henry III in 1272 Westminster Abbey has been the usual burial place for sovereigns. The original building known as Westminster Abbey was under construction from 1050 to 1760, the great nave alone taking two

[190]

hundred years to complete. Every sovereign of England since William the Conqueror, except Edward V, who was murdered in the Tower of London at the age of thirteen, and Edward VIII, who abdicated without ever being crowned, has been crowned in Westminster Abbey.

How can male and female guinea fowls be distinguished?

The male and female guinea fowl are so nearly alike in appearance that most people are unable to distinguish one from the other. It frequently happens that persons inexperienced in raising these fowls will unknowingly keep all males or all females as breeding stock. Charles Darwin came to the conclusion that the sexes of guinea fowls are undistinguishable by the plumage or the color markings. Usually, however, the gills or wattles of the males are much larger than those of the females. The spike or helmet of the male is also larger. According to the United States Department of Agriculture, the only positive method of telling the males from the females is by the songs. The female sings the familiar two-syllable *buckwheat, buckwheat,* or as some interpret it, *come back, come back,* or *pot rack, pot rack.* The male never makes this two-syllable call. His one-syllable shriek is decidedly different. He makes a chattering sound and frequently says, *quit, quit, quit.* When excited both sexes emit the one-syllable cries.

What great poet was killed by a falling tortoise?

Aeschylus (525–456 B.C.), Athenian tragic poet and "father of Greek drama," is said to have been struck on the head and killed by a tortoise that fell from the claws of an eagle soaring in the sky above. Eagles, according to an ancient myth, drop tortoises on stones to break the shell and make the meat accessible. Aeschylus, early writers relate, had been warned that he would meet his death by something falling on him, whereupon he sought safety in the open fields, only to be killed by an eagle that mistook his bald head for a rock and dropped a turtle on it. The story possesses all the earmarks of a fable and was probably pure fabrication. It first appears in the works of Claudius Aelianus, better known simply as Aelian, who told many anecdotes about animals and who flourished under Septimius Severus and probably outlived Emperor Heliogabalus, whose death occurred in 222 A.D. In his *Vulgar Errors* Sir Thomas Browne wrote: "It much disadvantageth the panegyrick of Synesius, and is no small disparagement unto baldness, if it be true what is related by Aelian concerning Aeschylus, whose bald pate was mistaken for a rock, and so was brained by a tortoise which an eagle let fall upon it. Certainly it was a very great mistake in the perspicacity of that animal.

Some men critically disposed, would from hence confute the opinion of Copernicus, never conceiving how the motion of the earth below, should not wave him from a knock perpendicularly directed from a body in the air above." The story also appears in the eleventh century *Life of Aeschylus* appended to the Medicean manuscripts at Florence. The Greek poet died in Sicily and was buried at Gela. His admirers in that region inscribed on his tomb the following epitaph, supposedly composed by himself because it praises his soldiership and contains no reference to poetry:

> Beneath this stone lies Aeschylus, son of Euphorion, the Athenian,
> Who perished in the wheat-bearing land of Gela;
> Of his noble prowess the grove of Marathon can speak,
> Or the long-haired Persian who knows it well.

Does "patent pending" protect an inventor?

The phrases *patent pending* and *patent applied for* stamped on manufactured articles are intended merely as notices to the public that application for a patent has been filed but has not yet been granted. The law makes no provision for the use of these terms and they have no legal significance. In the eyes of the law they afford no protection to the inventor, except so far as they may be a means of establishing a claim of priority in case of litigation in respect to the patent. The right to exclude others from making, using and selling a device does not exist until a patent has been granted.

Is any species of parrot native to the United States?

Almost all parrots are native to tropical or subtropical regions. The only member of this family of birds whose natural range extended far into the United States within historic times was the Carolina parrot or parakeet, commonly found until the eighteenth century from Florida to the Great Lakes, individuals having been seen as far north as Albany, New York. Carolina parakeets, ranging about in large, noisy flocks, were a common sight in the southern states when Europeans first settled in America. Speaking of Virginia Captain John Smith recorded that "in winter there are great plenty of Parrats." As early as 1832 Audubon noted that the number of these birds was decreasing. Carolina parakeets were destructive to garden and field crops and they were hunted for food, trapped for cage birds and shot for sport until they are now extinct or nearly so. It is doubtful whether one of them has been seen since about 1906, although a few were reported near Lake Okeechobee in Florida as late as 1920. This handsome bird had a long tail, green body plumage, yellow head, red face and blue and yellow blotches on the wings. The only other member of the parrot family (called *Psittacus* from the Greek and Latin for "parrot") that is ever seen in the United States is the thick-billed parrot whose home is in northern Mexico but which occasionally crosses the international boundary and visits the Chiricahua Mountains and neighboring sections of Arizona.

Why are the Irish called "Milesians"?

Milesian as applied to the Irish is derived from *Milesius* (*Miledh*), the name of a mythical conqueror from the East who established a kingdom in Spain. In the legendary history of Ireland, the two sons of King Milesius crossed over from Spain about 1300 B.C., conquered the Emerald Isle, exterminated the Firbolgs or aborigines, repeopled the country with Celts, introduced Gaelic culture and established a new order of nobility from which many of the later inhabitants claimed descent. This story of the Milesian conquest of Ireland may be a fable. In *Myths and Myth-Makers* John Fiske wrote: "By a . . . misunderstanding of the epithet *miledh*, or warrior, applied to Fion by the Gaelic bards, there was generated a mythical hero, Milesius, and the sobriquet *Milesian*, colloquially employed in speaking of the Irish." *Milesian* is now seldom applied to the Irish except by the "elegant variationists" as a bit of pedantic or polysyllabic humor. A class of short, salacious stories that were current two thousand years ago are known as *Milesian tales*. For instance, *The Golden Ass* of Apuleius begins with these words: "In this Milesian tale I shall string together divers stories . . ." *Milesian* originally meant pertaining to Miletus, an ancient city in Asia Minor, or its inhabitants. The first Milesian tales were a collection of witty but obscene short stories composed by Antonius Diogenes and compiled by Aristides of Miletus in the second century B.C. These stories, no longer extant, were translated into Latin by Sisenna and were greedily devoured by sophisticated Romans about the time of the civil wars of Marius and Sylla.

Why was Boston called the Hub of the Universe?

Hub of the Universe, as a nickname for Boston, was suggested by a humorous quotation in the sixth paper of Oliver Wendell Holmes's *Autocrat of the Breakfast Table*, which was first published serially in *The Atlantic Monthly* in 1856 and 1857. Holmes wrote: "Boston State-house is the hub of the solar system. You couldn't pry that out of a Boston man, if you had the tire of all creation straightened out for a crowbar." The satirical observation referred to Boston as a self-satisfied community, composed of people who regarded their city as the only place in the world and themselves as superior in wisdom and culture. Downtown Boston is often referred to as The Hub, because the streets of this district form a sort of wheel, radiating from several squares lying between the statehouse on Beacon Hill and the old statehouse on State Street. When Holmes wrote Boston was still noted for the social and cultural snobbery of its upper-class inhabitants. Typical Boston children were said to wear spectacles in their cradles and their elders to go about with a nearsighted *Boston look*, affecting a studied interest in all intellectual things. The Autocrat of the Breakfast Table was merely poking good-natured fun at the alleged smugness of his fellow townsmen.

Are house mice native to the United States?

The common house mouse, *Mus musculus*, is a native of Europe or central Asia and is readily distinguishable from the native white-bellied mice of North America by its nearly uniform brownish color. It is now found in nearly every country of the world and apparently its distribution is limited only by the Arctic and Antarctic Circles. Native American mice seldom live in buildings. They are generally referred to as "field mice."

Why do bright lights attract birds?

Large numbers of birds migrating by night come to grief by being attracted to the bright lights of cities, lighthouses, lightships, flood-lighted monuments, tall bridge piers and other beacons and structures. Occasionally individual birds dash out their brains by flying against the windows of lighted buildings. Hundreds of birds of many different species are killed every year by flying at full speed against the floodlighted Washington Monument in the national capital. Wild geese, blinded by the floodlights on the near-by power plant, fly into one another and fall from great heights into Boulder Dam Lake. Literally bushels of dead passerine birds are sometimes picked up below the beacons of some of the larger lighthouses on the coasts. In one case a loon struck the lens of a lighthouse beacon with such force that it crashed through. Naturalists have thus far been unable to offer any satisfactory explanation of this phenomenon. Steady white lights have seemingly irresistible fascination for certain birds, while red lights or moving white ones repel them. Apparently a fixed dazzling light not only bewilders migrating birds but actually lures them toward it. The fact that such casualties are heaviest on dark, cloudy, windy nights when there has been a decided drop in temperature after nightfall, indicates that birds fly higher on clear, moonlight nights. One observer reports that the birds killed during the migrating seasons at the Washington Monument generally strike the lee or sheltered side of the shaft. Many animals also are fascinated or bewildered by bright lights. Pioneers used to take advantage of this in "fire hunting." Hunters would move silently through the woods or float down a stream in a canoe and flash torches until they attracted a curious deer. The light reflected in the deer's eyes provided the target.

What points in the United States are farthest apart?

The two points in the United States proper that are farthest apart, according to the United States Geological Survey, are Cape Flattery, Washington, and a point on the Florida coast south of Miami. These two points lie about 2,835 miles apart as the crow flies. The distance between West Quoddy, Maine, and Cape Alva, Washington, is 2,607 miles.

Is any species of monkey native to the United States?

There is no native species of monkey in the New World north of the Rio Grande, although many members of the monkey family inhabit Mexico, Central America and South America. The Mexican spider monkey occurs in its natural state as far north as Latitude 25 degrees and is the most northern monkey in North America. The petrified remains of small monkeylike animals that supposedly lived in prehistoric times have been found in caves in the United States.

Why are the ridges in bark vertical?

Trees grow in circumference in the cambium layer between the bark and the firmer fiber of the trunk. The diameter growth of the tree continually splits the bark into vertical lines and produces the familiar ridges. If a tree grew in height by the gradual lengthening of the entire trunk and limbs there would be horizontal ridges in the bark also; but a tree puts on height growth only from the top, that is, through the annual extension of the terminal buds, and therefore there are no ridges in the bark running horizontally around the trunk. Some trees, such as certain kinds of fruit trees, do not have ridged bark.

What is Mayfair?

Mayfair, often heard in connection with English society people, is a synonym for wealth and fashion. It is the name of what formerly was the most fashionable residential quarter of London. The district so known lies in the West End, east of Hyde Park, and is bounded by Piccadilly Street, Park Lane, Oxford Street and Bond Street. Mayfair received its name from a famous annual fair that was held there in May from the time of Charles II or earlier down to 1708, when it was abolished. The modern Mayfair is noted for the great men and women who have lived there rather than for its present residents. Years ago hotels, apartment houses and office buildings began to take the places of the stately mansions and spacious gardens once so familiar in Mayfair. In the latter part of the eighteenth century the famous "May fair" in that neighborhood was revived in a modified form. A writer described this second fair, as he knew it half a century earlier, in an article in the *Gentleman's Magazine* for April, 1816. Duck-shooting, prize fighting, donkey racing, bull-baiting and other rough amusements were the chief attractions.

Do bananas grow pointing up or down?

The stem or spike bearing a bunch of bananas projects from the main stalk of the plant. When the fruit is small the individual bananas point outward and somewhat downward from the spike, but as they grow larger the spike bends over from its own weight and the bananas then point upward. Thus bunches of bananas seen hanging in stores are usually upside down in reference to their position on the plant when picked, but right side up in reference to their position on the plant at an earlier stage of their growth. In other words, when bananas are hung up in markets to ripen the string is attached to what was the free end of the spike on the plant, and not to the end that was cut, as one unacquainted with the growing plants would naturally suppose. Each banana stalk bears only one bunch of bananas in a season. A bunch or stem may contain from 100 to 200 bananas. It varies in weight from 30 to 65 pounds, the average weight being about 35 pounds. Each bunch or stem is composed of a number of clusters, known to the fruit trade as *hands*, which contain from 10 to 20 individual bananas or *fingers*. Bunches with fewer than six hands are regarded as too small for export purposes.

What active volcanoes lie in the United States proper?

It is customary to say that Mount Lassen, a 10,465 foot peak on the border of Shasta and Plumas counties in California, is the only active volcano in the United States proper. As a matter of fact often it is very difficult to distinguish between a live volcano and one that is considered dead, and perhaps it would be more nearly correct to refer to Mount Lassen as the only volcano in the United States proper that has been witnessed in eruption. This snowcapped peak in the Sierra Nevada mountains was named after Peter Lassen, one of John C. Fremont's guides. It belches smoke and steam from time to time and a series of eruptions occurred in May, 1915. Mount Baker and several other volcanic peaks in the Cascade Range in Washington are known to have erupted in 1841, 1842 and 1843 and they still show signs of slight activity. Mount Saint Helens in that range is not entirely dead, and both Mount Hood in Oregon and Mount Rainier in Washington exhale vapor. A considerable eruption of Tres Virgines in southern California occurred in 1857, although the volcano is now regarded as dead.

What does "O.N.T." on thread mean?

The letters *O.N.T.*, which are used as the trade-mark on spools of thread, are the initials of *Our New Thread*. Sewing machines began to come into general use about the time of the Civil War. Their introduction made it desirable for manufacturers to produce a thread that would be suitable for machine as well as for hand sewing. In 1862 the Clark Thread Company developed such a thread and marketed it as *Our New Thread*. Two years later George A. Clark decided to abbreviate the phrase to *O.N.T.* with a view to arousing curiosity as to its meaning. The thread was then advertised as Clark's O.N.T. Spool Cotton, and *O.N.T.* became one of the most popular trade-marks in use.

Why is the face called "the mug"?

The face, according to the most generally accepted theory, came to be called *the mug* from the fact that in the eighteenth century drinking mugs were commonly made to represent grotesque human faces. Even at the present time *mug* survives in the sense of a grimace. The term has been applied to cylindrical vessels with a handle since the sixteenth century and is of unknown origin in that sense. Sheep belonging to a breed characterized by having the face completely covered with wool were known as mugs. Some glossaries defined the term as a hornless sheep, and that may have been its original application. A few etymologists trace *mug* in the sense of face to a similar gypsy word, which in turn is supposed to be derived from Sanskrit *mukha* ("face").

What is a gay Lothario?

A gay Lothario is a gallant rake, libertine, debauchee and deceiver of women. Lothario is the leading character in *The Fair Penitent*, a tragedy written in 1703 by Nicholas Rowe (1674–1718), who succeeded Nahum Tate as poet laureate of England in 1715. In the play the rakish hero, who seduces Calista, is described as haughty, gallant, gay and unscrupulous in his deceptions of the fair sex. *The Fair Penitent* is really an adaptation of Massinger's *The Fatal Dowery*, published in 1632. A similar character with the same name occurs in *The Cruel Brother*, a play written in 1630 by Sir William Davenant (1606–1668), who was reputed to have been a natural son of Shakespeare and who succeeded Ben Jonson as poet laureate. It is probable that Rowe borrowed Davenant's Lothario and popularized him as the typical gay libertine.

Who wore the seven league boots?

The famous seven league boots were worn by Hop-o'-My-Thumb, a character in several old nursery tales. He figures as the diminutive hero in one of Charles Perrault's fairy stories. There, through cleverness and ingenuity, Hop-o'-My-Thumb saves his brothers and himself from an ogre by means of his seven league boots, which enable him to cover seven leagues at each step. *Hop-o'-My-Thumb* is sometimes used as a generic name for pygmies, midgets and dwarfs. From these fairy stories and nursery tales *seven league boots* has come to mean anything that aids speed or achievement.

Does the moon shine at the poles during the winter?

At the North and South Poles the sun rises and sets only once annually and the year is divided into one day six months long and one night of the same length. There is no point on the earth where the moon never shines and even the long arctic and antarctic nights are brightened half of the time by the light of the moon. Around the poles the moon is above the horizon continuously during half of each lunar month and below it continuously the other half. During the dark or winter period, according to the United States Naval Observatory, full moon occurs when the moon is above the horizon and new moon when it is below the horizon. The conditions are reversed during the light or summer period. Then the new moon occurs when the lunar orb is above the horizon and the full moon when it is out of sight.

What causes cloudbursts?

Cloudburst is a popular rather than a scientific term and accordingly is not susceptible of exact definition. Cloudbursts were named before their cause was well understood. Everybody knows that a cloud is composed of minute drops of water and is not the kind of formation that can undergo a process properly described as bursting. As the term is usually understood, a cloudburst is a torrential local downpour of rain of short duration. Frequently it is merely an exceedingly heavy shower and does not differ from ordinary rains except in intensity. When a warm current of air surcharged with moisture meets a cold current the condensation sometimes takes place so rapidly that a torrential shower results. In concentration and intensity a cloudburst may be said to bear the same relation to a general rainstorm that a tornado does to a general cyclonic windstorm. Meteorologists sometimes apply *cloudburst* technically to a rain in which six or more inches of water falls at the rate of ten or more inches an hour. Occasionally, according to some meteorologists, the downpour of rain known as a cloudburst is produced at the beginning of a thunderstorm by a strong upward current that carries the condensing moisture up instead of permitting it to fall as rain immediately. When the air current is weakened at some point, or the load becomes too heavy for the air to support, a great accumulation of rain comes down at once. Formerly it was believed that all cloudbursts were caused by large volumes of water being held in the clouds in the liquid state by ascending air currents, but this theory has been abandoned as a universal explanation of downpours of unusual intensity. It may, however, explain the reports of numerous persons who state that they have seen rain come down in masses, streams or sheets instead of drops. Undoubtedly rainfall attending tornadoes also reaches cloudburst intensity at times. In June, 1903, a so-called cloudburst at Clifton, South Carolina, caused the death of fifty persons and destroyed millions of dollars worth of property.

Why are wagon wheels dished?

Wagon and carriage wheels are *dished* because wheels so made are better able to withstand forces acting perpendicularly to the direction in which the vehicle is traveling. Crushing of the spokes in shrinking tires is avoided if the wheels are properly dished. Although some automobile wheels have a dish of an inch or two, usually the wheels of motorcars are not dished because they are smaller and much stronger than ordinary carriage and wagon wheels. Pneumatic tires also protect automobile wheels against excessive lateral thrust.

What city was named by flipping a coin?

The name of Portland, Oregon, was decided by flipping a coin. Although a cabin or two had been previously built on the site, the founding of the present city of Portland dates from 1843, when William Overton and Amos L. Lovejoy, ascending the Willamette River in a canoe on their way from Fort Vancouver on the Columbia to Oregon City, selected the site as an ideal location for a town. Soon after they acquired a tract, Overton sold his interest to Francis W. Pettygrove (or Pettigrove). In 1844 the land was surveyed, boundaries determined and the first log house built, and the following year a part of the tract was laid off into streets, blocks and lots. When the problem of naming the embryo city came up Pettygrove, a native of New Brunswick, Canada, who had lived in Maine, wanted to call it Portland, while Lovejoy, who was a native of Massachusetts, favored Boston. The two New Englanders finally agreed to decide the question by tossing a penny—heads, Portland, and tails, Boston. Heads won and the city was named Portland.

Who said: "There, but for the grace of God, goes myself"?

This saying is generally attributed to John Bradford (1510–1555), English religious martyr. There is a tradition that on one occasion when Bradford saw a condemned criminal passing by on his way from prison to the gallows, he observed: "There, but for the grace of God, goes John Bradford." Soon after the accession of Queen Mary, Bradford was arrested on a charge of sedition, imprisoned, tried in a court presided over by Bishop Gardiner, condemned as a heretic and burned at the stake at Smithfield on July 1, 1555. The quotation is credited to Bradford in Frederic W. Farrar's volume of sermons entitled *Eternal Hope*, published in 1877 and the anecdote connected with it is told in a biographical preface in the second volume of the *Writings of John Bradford*, published in 1852. But in 1851, two years before the publication of the latter work, George Borrow published his *Lavengro*, in which he wrote: "It was old John Newton I think, who, when he saw a man going to be hanged, said: "There goes John Newton, but for the grace of God." John Newton (1725–1807) was a sailor, midshipman, slave trader and tide surveyor before he turned divine and was ordained a clergyman in the Church of England at thirty-nine. Probably as the result of error the same sentiment has been attributed also to Richard Baxter (1615–1691), John Bunyan (1628–1688), and John Wesley (1703–1791), all of whom lived much later than Bradford. Baxter, Newton, Bunyan and Wesley were all pious and zealous men, and it may very well be that the famous quotation and anecdote became associated with their names through their referring to it.

How did "see the elephant" originate?

To see the elephant means to take in all the notable sights. A person who has seen the elephant is presumed to have seen everything worth seeing and to know his way around. The phrase seems to have originated in America in the days when elephants were seldom seen and referred to the itinerant menageries of pioneer times when one of these animals was exhibited in a special tent as the main attraction of the show. The first live elephant was exhibited in the United States toward the close of Washington's second administration. It was brought from India to New York in April, 1796, in the famous armed ship "America" by Captain

Jacob Crowninshield, later Congressman from Massachusetts and for four days Secretary of the Navy under Jefferson. This elephant, a female six feet four inches tall, was sold for $10,000. An advertisement in the *Philadelphia Aurora* of July 28, 1796, announced that an elephant had just arrived "from New York in this city, on his way to Charleston." In Valentine's manual of old New York, published in 1926, is the following reference to Coney Island in its early days: "The outstanding features were the new and old Iron Piers, the Observatory, a tall iron tower near the piers, and the great wooden elephant hotel, a caravansary built to resemble that eccentric beast. This was the most noted feature of the place, and *seeing the elephant* passed into popular slang." The Elephant Hotel, which was destroyed by fire in 1896, was built in the form of a gigantic elephant 122 feet high. The structure contained thirty-two bedrooms besides salons and recreation rooms. A "howdah" on the back of the beastlike structure served as a dining and observation room. But this hotel at Coney Island did not suggest the phrase *seeing the elephant*, which occurs in Kendal's *Narrative of the Texan Santa Fe Expedition*, printed in 1841, and which was a common everyday expression along the California, Oregon and Santa Fe trails in the decade following.

What is a civet cat?

Strictly speaking, the name *civet cat* refers only to an Old World carnivorous animal closely related to the mongoose. This species, which is two or three feet long, is the source of the commercial civet used as a perfume. In the United States, however, *civet cat* is popularly applied to the little spotted skunk, which belongs to the genus *Spilogale*. In the Southwest *civet cat* is a local name for the cacomistle or ring-tailed cat, a carnivorous animal related to and resembling the raccoon.

When was Black Friday?

Black Friday does not refer to a particular date, as often supposed, but is the name given to several Fridays on which financial panics have occurred. Apparently the term was first applied to the Friday in December, 1745, when the news was received in London that Charles Edward Stuart, the Young Pretender, had reached Derby, only ten days' march from the British capital. A panic immediately ensued. The term was again applied in England to Friday, May 11, 1866, when a panic started as the result of the failure of Overend, Guerney and Company. *Black Friday* was probably suggested by *Black Monday* and *Blue Monday*, old names in Europe for Easter Monday, the Monday preceding the beginning of Lent. In a London chronicle written about 1435 we read: "In the same

yere [1360] the xiii day off April and the morning after Ester, Kyng
Edward with his host lay before the Citee of Parys: the which was a
ffoule Derke day . . . so bytter colde, that syttyng on horse bak men
dyed. Wherefore, vnto this day yt ys called blak monday." It was reported that a hailstorm killed one thousand of the men of King Edward
III and six thousand of his horses. According to another account, Black
Monday received its name from the fact that the Black Prince's army
sustained heavy losses from a storm on Easter Monday in 1357. In
Shakespeare's The Merchant of Venice Launcelot Gobbo is quoted as
saying, "then it was not for nothing that my nose fell a-bleeding on
Black-Monday." Easter Monday was also formerly called Blue Monday
because the churches were decorated with blue on that day. At any rate,
analogy with Black Monday was undoubtedly responsible for Black
Friday as used in 1745. In the United States Black Friday generally
refers to September 24, 1869, when a panic resulted from the efforts of
Jay Gould and James Fisk to corner the gold market by buying all the
gold in the New York banks. On that day the financial district was a
veritable bedlam and men went insane from the excitement. Business
firms feared they would have to close because of the fluctations in prices.
The panic ceased when it was announced that the government was placing part of its gold reserve on the market. Black Friday was later also applied to September 19, 1873, the worst day of the panic following failure
of Jay Cook and Company.

Is perpetual motion possible?

Perpetual motion is a very old term. In II King Henry IV, written
about 1598, Shakespeare has Sir John Falstaff say: "It were better to be
eaten to death with a rust than to be scoured to nothing with perpetual
motion." But as the term is now generally understood, perpetual motion
refers to a mechanical device or arrangement which, once set in motion,
would continue to run indefinitely without drawing on any external
source of energy. For instance, a clock or other machine that would run
by weights and would wind itself up and thus run indefinitely until worn
out would be a perpetual motion machine. But nobody has ever constructed a machine that in each complete cycle of its operation will supply
more energy than it has absorbed. Mechanical perpetual motion is impossible according to all known laws of nature. No machine will do more
work than the equivalent of the energy put into it, minus that lost by
friction, whether the original energy is in the form of heat, chemical reaction, electricity or human labor. In the transmission of energy some
of it is always lost as the result of friction. A self-generating, self-perpetu-

ating motive power that overcomes friction would be contrary to the best-established of all physical laws, that is, the principle of the conservation of energy, which is that energy is uncreatable and indestructible in the regular course of nature. Theoretically, one might suppose, the nearest approach to perpetual motion would be a tuning fork set in vibration in a vacuum or near vacuum. Since there would be no outside friction to stop the vibration, the original energy that set it in motion should continue indefinitely. Although a tuning fork in a near vacuum will continue to vibrate for a long time, the energy of the initial impulse that started the vibration is finally dissipated by internal friction. A frictionless machine would be one hundred per cent efficient; that is, as much energy could be got out of it as is put into it, but even such a machine would be far short of mechanical perpetual motion. Therefore, in the light of modern scientific knowledge, it is absurd to suppose that energy can be created or multiplied by a mere arrangement of wheels, levers, cranks, weights or other devices. One of the most common of all proposals for the mechanical creation of energy is an overbalancing wheel turned by the pull of gravity on attached mallets or on quicksilver. A perpetual motion device of this type was suggested as early as the thirteenth century. The quest for mechanical perpetual motion, in the sense of a machine doing work and operating without the aid of any power other than that which is generated by the machine itself, is now regarded as an unpromising enterprise. As early as 1775 the French Academy of Sciences concluded that perpetual motion is impossible and refused to receive any more perpetual motion schemes. The United States Patent Office, convinced that perpetual motion is a physical impossibility, stipulates that no application for a patent on such a device will be even considered unless the inventor submits a working model that demonstrates beyond question that the machine, after being started, will run indefinitely without receiving energy from any outside source whatever. This requirement was adopted to protect inventors against wasting their money in application fees. Needless to say, no working model of a perpetual motion machine has ever been submitted. Perpetual motion should not be confused with machinery that merely converts energy from one form into another.

Did Ingersoll recant on his deathbed?

Robert G. Ingersoll, the famous orator and agnostic, died suddenly and did not talk about religion and the afterlife just before his death, as is popularly supposed. On the day he died he suffered an acute attack of indigestion and lay down to rest. About an hour later he arose and sat up in a chair to put on his shoes. Noticing that he looked pale, his wife offered to have his dinner brought to him. But he refused, saying, "Oh, no, I don't want to trouble you." Then Mrs. Ingersoll offered to give him some medicine, but this he also refused with a smile, saying, "I'm better now." Those were his last words. He sank down in his chair dead. This was July 21, 1899, at Dobbs Ferry, New York. After his death his enemies circulated the report that he had recanted on his deathbed. Several members of his family later signed a sworn statement to the contrary. On July 13, 1899, eight days before his death, Ingersoll wrote a letter to C. J. Robbins in which he restated his beliefs on the subject of religion. He wrote: "You are right in thinking that I have not changed. I still believe that all religions are based on falsehoods and mistakes. I still deny the existence of the supernatural, and I still say that real religion is usefulness."

How are oars muffled?

Oars are muffled by wrapping something around them where they come in contact with the oarlocks. This, of course, is to deaden the noise. When Paul Revere started on his famous midnight ride to Lexington a petticoat was used to muffle the oars of the boat in which he crossed the Charles River. It is referred to in the following unique sentence in *The Battle of April 19, 1775*, by Frank Coburn: "Fearing that the noise of the oars in the oarlocks might alarm the sentry, Revere dispatched one of his companions for something to muffle them with, who soon returned with a petticoat, yet warm from the body of a fair daughter of liberty, who was glad to contribute to the cause." The wheels of carriages used to be muffled in a similar manner. Referring to Washington's march against Princeton early in 1777, James Ripley Jacobs says in *Tarnished Warrior*: "Meanwhile, the Americans were wrapping the wheels of the gun carriages with cast-off clothing to deaden the rumble of artillery over the frost-bitten ground." In those days it was a common practice to muffle oars with sheepskins.

Must one employ a lawyer to get a patent?

Almost all applications for patents are made through patent attorneys. The law in the United States does not require that the inventor must obtain the services of a lawyer to get a patent, but the preparation of an application for a patent is a highly complex proceeding and generally cannot be conducted properly except by an attorney familiar with this specialized practice. For that reason inventors are advised by the United States Government to employ competent attorneys to file their application for patents. A register of attorneys is kept in the United States Patent Office and no attorney who is not registered there will be permitted to prosecute such applications. After the inventor has appointed an attorney the Patent Office will hold correspondence with the attorney only. All the business can be transacted by correspondence and the personal attendance of the applicant at the Patent Office is unnecessary. Most of the inventors who originally make their own applications for patents later turn them over to attorneys to complete the highly technical phases of the procedure. Except in the case of alleged perpetual motion machines, the Patent Office does not accept models unless they are considered absolutely necessary to an understanding of the inventions. In the event they are required the Patent Office notifies the applicant or his attorney.

Which is correct, "Mount Rainier" or "Mount Tacoma"?

The United States Geographic Board decided that the correct name of the mountain peak in the Cascade Range, Pierce County, Washington, is Mount Rainier, not Mount Tacoma. It was named after Admiral Rainier of the British Navy by George Vancouver, the navigator and explorer, who discovered it in 1793. There is a dispute of long standing between the inhabitants of Seattle and Tacoma respecting the name of this mountain. Locally, particularly in Tacoma, the peak is generally called Mount Tacoma, which is derived from the Puget Sound Indian word Ta-ko-bed, meaning "snowy mountain." Early settlers in that region mistook the Indian word to be a specific name for Mount Rainier. Outside Tacoma the peak is generally known as Mount Rainier. The inhabitants of Seattle in particular objected to having this famous mountain bear the name of a rival city. In view of the dispute the mayors of the two cities once agreed to refer to the peak as "Our Mountain." This peak is the only one outside Colorado and California in the United States proper that is more than 14,000 feet above sea level. Its altitude is 14,408 feet.

Does the lunula occur on the nails of all races?

The lunula (Latin for "little moon") is the whitish, half-moon shaped area at the base of the fingernails of human beings. There is a popular belief that this crescent-shaped mark is peculiar to the white race and does not occur on the nails of members of colored races, particularly Negroes. The lunula is not a racial characteristic, but occurs in all races, although it is somewhat obscured by the pigmented skin of the darker peoples. Under the larger part of the nail the matrix is thick and the nail is firmly attached to it. There the series of ridges containing the blood vessels can be seen through the transparent tissue. But under the part of the nail near the root the matrix is thinner, the ridges are smaller, the blood vessels are fewer and the adhesion between the tissue and the nail is slighter. The different reflection of light from this part of the nail produces the lunula.

Why does corn have an even number of rows of kernels?

The number of rows of kernels on a normal ear of corn or maize ranges from eight to twenty-six, depending to some extent on the variety of corn. There is always an even number of rows of kernels if the ear is normal. This peculiarity is due to a botanical characteristic, which is explained by the United States Department of Agriculture as follows: "An ear of corn is made up of two or more connate two-rowed spikes which have grown together or failed to separate during their early development. Each spike bears at the end two two-flowered spikelets, but the lower floret of each spikelet is abortive, leaving only one pair of carpels to develop at each end. This accounts for the uniformity in the development of rows of grain in pairs. As each spike is two-rowed, the entire ear must have an even number of rows, unless, as sometimes happens, an entire row of one spike aborts, in which case the ear will be abnormal and have an odd number of rows of kernels." Good ears of corn with an odd number of rows of kernels are scarcer than four-leaved clovers. When one was found in an Iowa cornfield in 1930 it was the subject of a newspaper report. There is a story to the effect that in slavery days a southern planter once offered a slave his freedom if he would bring the master a perfect ear of corn with an odd number of rows of kernels. The Negro vainly searched for such an ear for an entire season. Early the next season he selected a growing ear and with a knife carefully cut out one row of kernels. When the ear was ripe it looked like a normal ear with an odd number of rows of grain. True to his word, the master freed the slave.

Why doesn't Louisiana have counties?

Soon after the United States purchased Louisiana from France in 1803 the legislative council of Governor William Claiborne divided that part of the territory now comprising the state of Louisiana into twelve settlements called counties. These districts, which were arbitrary and not clearly defined, proved unsatisfactory for the purposes of civil government. Therefore, in 1807, the legislature of the Territory of Orleans divided the Territory into nineteen districts that were called parishes instead of counties because the old French and Spanish ecclesiastical districts or parishes were used as a basis for the new divisions. The name was applied to additional civil districts created after the Territory was admitted into the Union as a state. In Colonial days South Carolina and several other colonies called their civil subdivisions parishes instead of counties. The United States Postal Guide lists the parishes of Louisiana as counties.

Will a spoon keep hot water from breaking a glass?

It is commonly believed that a metal spoon placed in a glass will prevent boiling liquid from cracking the glass when poured into it. A silver spoon is said to be preferable because that metal is a good conductor of heat. According to the popular theory, the metal spoon absorbs part of the heat and prevents the boiling liquid from expanding the glass as much as it otherwise would. The United States Bureau of Standards, however, doubts the efficacy of silver spoons in preventing glasses from cracking. "From theoretical considerations," that authority has asserted, "it would seem that the custom of putting a silver spoon in a glass to prevent its breaking is not well founded, because the quantity of heat that would be absorbed by a spoon is almost negligible when compared with the total quantity of heat in a glass full of water."

How did the Romans add and subtract with Roman numerals?

Many people are puzzled as to how the Romans added, subtracted and multiplied with the clumsy signs or symbols that we call Roman numerals. The Romans, like the Greeks and other ancients, had few convenient symbols to indicate mathematical processes and operations. Originally every process and operation was expressed in words of full length. Later the Romans adopted such symbols as I, II, III, V and X, and they abbreviated centum (100) to C; mille (1000) to M, and so on. Also a dash over a numeral multiplied its value by 1000. It is supposed that V (5) originated as a sort of hieroglyphic and represented the open hand with the fingers, except the thumb, held together, and that X (10) represented double V. Figuring was awkward business in the time of Julius Caesar. Virtually all calculations were performed on the abacus, an apparatus resembling the Chinese suan pan or the bead-and-frame affairs now used in kindergarten work. Abacus is derived from abax, the Greek name for a writing or ciphering tablet, which originally consisted of a slab covered with sand. The Roman abacus contained seven long and seven short rods or bars. There were four beads on each of the long bars and one on the short ones. The beads on the short bars denoted five. The first long bar was marked I, the second X, the third C, and so on up to millions. Suppose a Roman wished to write the number 25. He would push up two X-beads and pull down the V-bead on the corresponding bar. If he wished to subtract 3 from 25 he would push up the V-bead and two I-beads, leaving the two X-beads where they were. There were additional bars for making calculations involving fractions. The Romans were not reputed to be good mathematicians and they contributed little to the science. In fact all mathematical calculations were clumsy until after the development of Arabic numerals and other symbols.

Who said: "The mills of the gods grind slow"?

"The mills of the gods grind slow but sure" is an ancient Greek saying of unknown authorship. "The mills of the gods grind slowly, but they grind small" is a literal translation of the Greek aphorism as it appears in the *Oracula Sibyllina*. Friedrich von Logau (1604–1655), the German epigrammatist, appropriated the idea in his *Deutscher dichte drei Tausend* and changed "the gods" of the Greeks to "God" of the Christians. As translated in Henry Wadsworth Longfellow's *Poetic Aphorisms* Logau said:

> Though the mills of God grind slowly,
> yet they grind exceeding small;
> Though with patience He stands waiting, with
> exactness grinds He all.

George Herbert (1593–1633), English divine and poet, used the Greek aphorism in the form, "God's mill grinds slow, but sure."

What is the Domesday Book?

Domesday Book is a digest of a survey of England ordered by William the Conqueror in 1085 to ascertain and record the fiscal rights of the king. This survey, it is supposed, was modeled after a similar one made by Alfred the Great. Domesday Book is in Latin and consists of two volumes, one considerably larger than the other. The smaller deals with the three eastern counties and the other with the rest of England minus the more northern counties. Commissioners visited each county and used the hundred as a unit in gathering information. Each entry in the register was made upon the verdict of a jury of twelve men, six Normans and six English. When digested and written down in Domesday Book the data were arranged according to the names of the landowners. Most of the work deals with the valuation of rural estates, the chief source of national wealth at the time. The acreage of pasture, timber and arable land is generally indicated. In some counties the number of tenants, cottagers and serfs is included, and often water mills, tollgates, salt pans and fisheries are enumerated. A total of 60,251 fiefs were catalogued.

Livestock is listed only in the smaller volume. It was in the nature of an industrial census taken with a view of extending the central power of the government to the entire people and requiring allegiance to the king from the peer down to his subtenants and serfs. Although the reckoning is rather crude and confused, the volumes incidentally contain a great store of personal, political, ecclesiastical and social history of that period. They supply the basis for many land deeds, and in tracing genealogies Domesday Book is to England what the "Mayflower" log is to America. Originally the book was called the "Book of Winchester," after the cathedral city where it was kept, but in the twelfth century, during the reign of Henry II, it was already referred to as Domesday or Doomsday Book, supposedly because, like the day of doom or judgment, there was no appeal from the arbitrament of its record. Although the name is generally spelled *Domesday* rather than *Doomsday*, it is pronounced doomz-day regardless of spelling.

What kind of fruit is used in making prunes?

Prunes are made from certain varieties of plums. Popularly *prune* is applied to a dried plum of a certain type, or to a fresh plum capable of being dried in the sun without fermenting or souring when the pit is not removed. Hence the fruit is sometimes referred to as "fresh prune" to distinguish it from ordinary plums, and plum trees producing such plums are often called "prune trees." Only a few varieties of plums are capable of being converted into prunes; most plums, if dried with the pits in them, will ferment and sour in the process. Many people believe that prunes and plums belong to different species; they are merely varieties of *Prunus domestica*, the species to which all common plums belong. Luther Burbank, "The Plant Wizard," originated about twenty new varieties of plums and prunes, some of which are among the best and most successful kinds now grown. Japanese plums played an important part in the multiple crossings that result in these new varieties. Hundreds of thousands of seedlings produced by these crossings were grown and worked over during the forty years that Burbank spent in intensive and persistent plum experimentation. On this subject the plant wizard wrote to the author as follows: "All prunes are plums. Very few plums are prunes in the common acceptation of the term. The difference in plums and prunes is: Any plum which has sufficient sugar in its substance to dry without souring is called a prune. In France all plums are called prunes. So in the language of France all plums are prunes, while here only those that will dry in the sun without souring are prunes." English *plum* and Later Latin *pruna* may be derived from the same root word.

In making prunes, thoroughly ripe, smooth-faced plums of certain sweet and solid varieties are dipped, rinsed, graded, sun-dried and packed. Ordinary plums would spoil instead of cure and dry under this process. The prune industry of the Pacific coast started about 1854 when a Frenchman named Louis Pellier, who had gone to California in search of gold, sent to his homeland for seeds and cuttings of a popular plum called *Prune d'Argens*. By grafting these with the wild plum native to the California hills he succeeded in producing a variety of plum suitable for making prunes. In recent years processes have been developed for curing plums for prunes in artificial driers.

When was "the year without a summer"?

The year 1816 is popularly known as *the year without a summer* because in the northern states there were frosts and snow in every month of the year. Similar unseasonable weather prevailed in the British Isles, France, Spain, Italy and other parts of Europe. The term *year without a summer* apparently originated with English writers and was copied in American newspapers. Of course it is a misnomer and is not to be taken literally. The United States Weather Bureau, which has collected considerable data on the subject, believes that the worst features of the summer of 1816 have been greatly exaggerated by popular writers. Crops, according to that authority, seem to have been fairly good in most parts of the United States. Only a few of the less hardy crops and plants suffered materially from the cold during the summer. The so-called year without a summer used to be referred to as "eighteen hundred and froze to death" instead of 1816. One theory is that the unseasonably cold weather of that year was somehow produced by the eruption of Tomboro on Sumbawa, an island near Java. In 1815 this volcano exploded and produced a flow of about six cubic miles of lava, perhaps the largest flow of lava from a single volcanic eruption known to science. Powdered dust from Tomboro filled the upper atmosphere over large parts of the earth for more than a year. This dust in the air, according to this theory, lowered the temperature by reducing the intensity of the sunshine.

Do house flies breed in Alaska?

The common house fly, *Musca domestica*, does not breed in Alaska. Occasionally, however, boats, airplanes and vehicles from points farther south carry a few house flies into the Territory, but it is believed that all these perish without reproducing. This insect is tropical in origin and cannot endure extremely cold climates; even in the northern part of the United States proper only a few house flies are found in early spring and the species would not become a serious pest were it not for the great rapidity with which it reproduces. House flies occur in southern Canada but gradually disappear to the northward. Persons who insist that the house fly breeds in Alaska, and there are many such, confuse this species with certain other flies, notably the stable fly and the blue and green bottle flies, all of which seem to breed without difficulty in Alaska and other regions in the far north. The stable fly in particular is commonly mistaken for the house fly and it frequently visits human dwellings. Mosquitoes thrive in cold regions and are a common pest in Alaska. Explorers and prospectors in the far north often wear netting over their faces to protect them from mosquitoes. On the Sverdrup Islands, only four hundred miles from the North Pole, large blue flies are one of the chief summertime annoyances to explorers.

Which is larger in area, Canada or the United States?

The Dominion of Canada has a greater area than continental United States; and British North America, including Canada, Newfoundland and Labrador, has a greater area than the United States proper and all its noncontiguous territory, including Alaska, Hawaii, Puerto Rico, the Philippines, etc. The area of the United States proper is about 3,026,790 square miles; that of the Dominion of Canada is about 3,729,665. Thus the Dominion of Canada has a greater area than the combined area of the United States proper and Alaska, which is about 3,617,675 square miles. Newfoundland and that part of Labrador attached to it have an area of 162,435 square miles, making the total area of British North America 3,892,100 square miles. The gross land and water area of the United States and all of its territories and possessions is 3,738,370 square miles.

Why is a hen called a biddy?

Biddy, a popular and familiar name for any hen, particularly in newspaper and magazine articles on poultry, is of unknown origin. One authority suggests that it may be derived from *chickabiddy*, which is still used, and that it is the instinctive sound adopted in calling chickens. But in his *Americanisms: the English of the New World*, M. Schele de Vere wrote in 1871; "There is little harm, perhaps, in calling a hen a *biddy*, a term already mentioned by Halliwell, and frequently used abroad and with us in calling chickens to feed; but to make from it a *he-biddy* for the cock, and *chickabiddy* for the little ones, is a somewhat violent proceeding." Another writer attempts to connect *biddy* with Gaelic *bideah*, meaning "very small." Still another believes the term is related to *Biddy*, which in the United States was formerly applied to a female domestic, especially to an Irish serving girl. The name in this connection is a corruption of *Bridget*. *Biddy* was used by Shakespeare. In *Twelfth Night*, Act III, Scene 4, Sir Toby says to Molvolio: "Why, how now, my bawcock! how dost thou, chuck? . . . Ay, Biddy, come with me." *Bawcock* is a corruption of French *beau coq*, meaning "fine cock." *Chuck*, like *cluck*, is probably of onomtapoeic origin, having been suggested by the noise made by a hen when calling her chicks, although it may be a modification of *chick*. In Shakespeare's time it was used as a term of endearment. The association of *bawcock*, *chuck* and *Biddy* in *Twelfth Night* indicates clearly that the last alluded to a fowl.

Will gasoline freeze?

Gasoline, according to the United States Bureau of Standards, has no definite freezing point. It slowly stiffens up like wax at temperatures much lower than those commonly encountered in the Arctic, and as the temperature is lowered it gradually becomes more and more viscous until it is a solid mass. The temperature at which ordinary gasoline solidifies ranges from 180 to 240 degrees Fahrenheit below zero. Gasoline containing benzol will solidify at higher temperatures in proportion to the percentage of benzol. Kerosene freezes at temperatures of 70 degrees or more below zero Fahrenheit. Admiral Richard E. Byrd reported that kerosene stored at Little America in the Antarctic froze solid in July when the temperature was 71 degrees below zero. Gasoline and kerosene are both derived from crude petroleum. The chief difference in the two liquids is in the temperature at which they boil and freeze. Gasoline boils off first and is the more explosive. The temperature must then be raised considerably before the kerosene boils off.

How did Jimson weed get its name?

Jimson in this connection is a corruption of Jamestown and *Jamestown weed* received its name from the fact that it was found growing in abundance around Jamestown in Virginia. In Colonial Virginia the usual pronunciation of *James* was *jeems*, a usage that the settlers brought with them from England. Early in the spring this weed sprang up in the rich ground under the very shadows of the buildings that the colonists had erected on the tiny island in James River. Jimson weed is known botanically as *Datura stramonium* and popularly as thorn apple, devil's trumpet, stinwort and stinkweed. It belongs to the nightshade family, is highly poisonous and its leaves yield the official drug stramonium. Botanists believe that the plant was originally native to tropical Asia. How it was transplanted to America so early is unknown. Jimson weed is now cultivated as a source of stramonium for use in certain medicines, tonics and compounds for heart ailments. The narcotic properties of this plant were known to the Algonquin Indians as well as to the Aztecs of Mexico, both of whom used it as a ceremonial intoxicant. In his *History of Present State of Virginia*, published in 1705, Robert Beverly tells an interesting story of the effect that eating Jamestown weed had on some of the British soldiers sent over to suppress Bacon's rebellion in 1676:

> The James-Town Weed . . . is supposed to be one of the greatest Coolers in the World. This being an early Plant, was gather'd very young for a boil'd salad, by some of the Soldiers sent thither, to pacifie the troubles of Bacon; and some of them eat plentifully of it, the Effect of which was very pleasant Comedy; for they turn'd natural Fools upon it for several Days: One would blow up a Feather in the Air; another wou'd dart Straws at it with much Fury; and another stark naked was sitting up in a Corner, like a Monkey, grinning and making Mows at them; a Fourth would fondly kiss, and paw his Companions, and snear in their Faces, with a Countenance more antick, than any in a Dutch Droll. In this frantick Condition they were confined, lest they should in their Folly destroy themselves; though it was observed, that all their Actions were full of Innocence and good Nature. Indeed, they were not very cleanly; for they would have wallow'd in their own Excrements, if they had not been prevented. A Thousand such simple Tricks they play'd, and after Eleven Days, return'd themselves again, not remembring anything that had pass'd.

In his *Notes on Virginia* Thomas Jefferson referred to the "singular quality" of the Jamestown weed. "The late Dr. Bond informed me," wrote the Sage of Monticello, "that he had under his care a patient, a young girl, who had put the seeds of this plant into her eye, which dilated the pupil to such a degree, that she could see in the dark, but in the light was almost blind."

Why is "controller" sometimes spelled "comptroller"?

The spelling *comptroller* was introduced about 1500 and arose from a mistaken derivation of the word from *compte*, an obsolete form of *count* suggested by the French *compte*. *Count* was derived indirectly from Late Latin *computum*, from *computare*, "to calculate." The Shorter Oxford Dictionary says of *count* that it was "refashioned in fourteenth century, after Latin, as compte." Since a controller's business was to examine and verify accounts it was supposed that the word should be spelled *comptroller*, and this spelling was affected particularly by official scribes. The erroneous form now survives only in certain official usage; as, Comptroller General of the United States, Comptroller of the Currency, and Comptroller of the Post Office Department. *Controller* is the correct spelling for ordinary purposes. In both cases the word is pronounced the same—kon-*trole*-er. Literally a controller is one who controls. *Control* comes from French *controler*, which in turn is derived from Latin *contra*, against or counter, and *rotulus*, roll. The present French form of *controller* is *controleur*, not *comptroleur*, as often supposed.

Does lightning ever strike twice in the same place?

There is a popular notion that lightning never strikes in the same place more than once. When lightning does strike more than once in the same place the event is generally reported as remarkable because of the proverbial saying. As a matter of fact lightning has been known to strike the same building several times during a single electrical storm. Trees, steeples, chimneys and other tall objects and structures in elevated and exposed locations are likely to be struck by lightning regardless of the number of times they have been struck in the past. Of course, according to the law of probability it is not likely that lightning will strike again in exactly the same place under ordinary circumstances.

How many millions are there in a billion?

The number of millions in a billion differs with the method of numeration. According to the method used in the United States and most European countries a billion is a thousand millions—1,000,000,000—and a trillion is a thousand billions—1,000,000,000,000. Each higher denomination after a thousand is a thousand times the preceding. But according to the British and German system a billion is a million millions—1,000,000,000,000—and a trillion is a million billions—1,000,000,000,-000,000,000. Each higher denomination after a million is a million times the preceding one. The two systems of numeration are the same up to a million. The American billion—a thousand millions—is equivalent to the French milliard. During the fifteenth century *billion, trillion* and *quadrillion* were coined to designate the second, third and fourth powers of a million respectively. These terms are still retained in British usage. During the seventeenth century French and Dutch arithmeticians began to divide figures into groups of threes instead of sixes. Under this system *billion* was used to designate only a thousand millions rather than the second power of a million, that is, a million million. In the American colonies the usage was the same as in England, but later the United States gradually adopted the French usage. The result is that when Britishers and Americans talk about billions and trillions they are not referring to the same figures. Counting at the rate of one each second, it would take nearly thirty-two years to count an American billion, but it would take a thousand times longer to count a British billion.

Where is a snake's heart located?

The heart of a snake is located well forward in the body. As a general rule, it lies about one-fifth the distance from the head to the end of the tail. The reptile's stomach is also located in the fore part of the body. It is long, narrow and distensible. Owing to the heavy flow of saliva, digestion begins immediately and takes place rapidly.

How long do turtles live?

Giant tortoises are among the few creatures that are known to have an extreme life span greater than that of man. They probably attain the greatest age in the entire animal world. There is unquestionable proof that giant Galapagos tortoises have lived 150 years, and there is reason for believing they sometimes attain an age of 200 years or more. Scientists have estimated the age of some specimens at 400 years, but these estimates are little more than speculations, aided to a limited extent by the scale marks or "rings of growth" on the plates. The London Zoological Gardens contain an elephantine tortoise from the Seychelles that is supposed to be from 150 to 200 years old. Tortoises in the South Seas have been known to have a weight of more than 1000 pounds. The marine reptile variously known as the harp, lyre and leather-backed turtle may exceed even the giant Galapagos tortoise in size and weight. Specimens of this species weighing from 1000 to 1500 pounds and measuring eight feet in length have been reported. Reports of ordinary land turtles bearing dates on their shells cannot be admitted as evidence in determining the extreme life span of these reptiles. There is too much room for mistake and fraud in such cases. Mischievous boys with jackknives are fond of carving 1776, 1812 and other historic dates on the shells of turtles. A case in point is the famous tortoise of Captain James Cook. According to a story that has never been authenticated, Captain Cook captured a tortoise on the Galapagos Islands in 1773 and, after carving that date on its back, released the reptile on one of the islands of the Tonga group. Newspapers periodically publish reports from persons who claim they have seen this tortoise on different islands in the South Seas. Assuming the reports to be correct in stating a tortoise bearing the date 1773 is seen occasionally, there is no accurate method by which one could determine how, when or in what region the carving was done. A tortoise on St. Helena is pointed out as the only living thing that ever saw Napoleon. Turtles have the distinction of being proverbial both for slowness of pace and great length of life.

What is "mob psychology"?

Mob psychology refers to the mental processes of a mob. It is the unthinking infection of a crowd with an idea advanced by a leader. Persons will do things collectively, especially in a large and disorderly gathering, that they would never think of doing individually. *Mass psychology* is used in a closely related sense. Both terms are of comparatively recent origin.

Are brothers nearer kin to each other than to their parents?

From the standpoint of eugenics and biology, brothers and sisters bear a closer relationship to one another than they do to either of their parents. A parent and child have one-half common blood, while a brother and sister have all common blood. Thus half-brothers have the same percentage of common blood that a parent and child have. Theoretically a child bears no closer blood relation to one parent that it does to the other.

How is the gauge of a shotgun determined?

The gauge of a shotgun barrel is determined as follows: A lead ball that fits snugly in the muzzle of a cylinder bore is taken as the standard of measurement. The number of these lead balls in a pound determines the gauge. For instance, suppose the maximum diameter of a lead ball that will fit the bore of a shotgun barrel is 0.730 inches, and further suppose it requires twelve such lead balls to make a pound. It is a twelve-gauge shotgun. Of course, the diameter of the bore proper and not the "choke" determines the gauge.

Why were the German soldiers called Fritzies?

The German soldiers were called *Fritzies* during the First World War because *Fritzie*, like *Fritz*, is a familiar form of *Frederick*, and the latter name is so common in Germany that it is often used by foreigners as a nickname for Germans in general, just as *Paddy*, a familiar form of *Patrick*, is a generic name for Irishmen. *Frederick* (the usual German spelling is *Friedrich*) in one form or other was a favorite name for centuries in the royal families of Prussia, Saxony and other German states. Frederick the Great of Prussia (1712–1786), who was the idol of his army and the most famous of all German soldiers, was referred to affectionately as *Alter Fritz*, "Old Fritz," and Emperor Frederick III, who reigned over the German Empire only ninety-nine days and who had previously distinguished himself as a soldier, was affectionately known in Prussia as *Unser Fritz*, "Our Fritz." *Heinie* as the generic nickname for German soldiers came from the fact that it is a familiar form of *Heinrich*, German form of *Henry* and a frequent name in Germany since the Middle Ages. *Jerry*, on the other hand, is, when applied to a German soldier, merely a slang word formed from *German*. *Cousin Michael* is a colloquial nickname for the German people collectively, corresponding to *John Bull* and *Uncle Sam*.

Who lost the dollar?

A man who had only a two-dollar bill wanted to buy a railway ticket that would cost three dollars. He took the two-dollar bill to a pawnshop where he pawned it for $1.50. On the way to the railway station he met a friend to whom he sold the pawn ticket for $1.50. He then had the three dollars with which to buy his railway ticket. Who was out the extra dollar? This old problem, which is still very popular, is based on a fallacy, or rather on a mistaken notion as to the functions of a pawnbroker. To redeem the original two-dollar bill the second man would have to give the pawnbroker not only the pawn ticket, for which he had paid $1.50, but also the sum that the broker advanced on the bill, which was $1.50—making a total of three dollars. He would be out one dollar because he would be paying three dollars for a two-dollar bill.

What is the Southwick jog?

The boundary between Massachusetts and Connecticut is a straight line with the exception of one jog or notch. This deviation from the straight line is known as the Southwick jog. When the boundary between these two states was readjusted it was necessary for Massachusetts to cede to her southern neighbor a long, narrow strip of land to make the line straight. In turn Connecticut ceded Massachusetts the Southwick jog, an equivalent area.

How did "anty-over" originate?

Anty-over is a corruption of *antony-over* or *anthony-over*. It is the popular name of a boys' game in which one boy throws a ball over a building to another boy on the other side. The word is merely a compound of the proper name *Antony* or *Anthony* and the preposition *over*. Many authorities state that it originated in Pennsylvania. It is more probable that it originated in Scotland. At any rate, Alexander Warrack included it in *A Scots Dialect Dictionary*, published in 1911. In 1871 M. Schele de Vere, in *Americanisms: the English of the New World*, made the following comment relative to *Antony-over* and gave Professor Samuel S. Haldeman as his authority: "A game of ball played by two parties of boys, on opposite sides of a schoolhouse, over which the ball is thrown. Used in Pennsylvania. *Antony* is merely a proper name, pressed into the service here, as Reynard, Robin and others are for the same purpose, and *over* requires no explanation."

What creature is said to have two hearts?

It is a common notion, especially among fishermen, that the eel has two hearts. Eels, in common with other fish, possess a closed vascular system, consisting of heart, arteries, veins and capillaries, and no secondary heart is known to exist. The popular belief about eels having two hearts probably arose from the fact that there is a "pulsatile sac" in the end of the eel's tail. Sir Richard Owen, an eminent British biologist, regarded this yellowish, spindle-shaped sac as a "venous heart." Blood from one vein flows into the sac in a continuous stream and is forced out at each contraction in an interrupted current. One writer states that if an eel is pierced in the region of this so-called secondary heart the creature will die almost as quickly as if struck in the heart proper.

Why do goats like tin cans?

Goats are not particular what they eat or try to eat and it is often said that they eat tin cans and thrive on them. Of course this is only a joke, prompted no doubt by the fact that goats are frequently seen nibbling at tin cans. Generally what the goats are really doing is licking the paper labels on the cans. This paper contains salt, which is very essential to the comfort of goats as well as other ruminant animals. The common notion that goats eat discarded shoes, newspapers and clothing is not true, although they will nibble at almost anything.

What is suction?

The principle of what is popularly called *suction* is best explained by illustration. Suppose an upright pipe is inserted in a vessel of water. Then further suppose that the air is removed from the pipe, thus creating at least a partial vacuum. The water will rush up in the pipe. Although this phenomenon is called suction, the fact is that the water is pushed into the vacuum instead of being pulled up as commonly supposed. It is the pressure of the atmosphere bearing down on the water surface of the entire vessel that forces the water into the vacuum in the pipe. Sucking with the mouth is based on the same principle. By muscular action a partial vacuum is created in the forepart of the mouth. Atmospheric pressure then forces the liquid into the vacuum. In the same manner a whirling wind creates an area of low pressure and produces suction. Fires also create suction. The suction created in a forest fire has been known to be so strong that it has uprooted large trees before the flames even reach them.

What are the Roaring Forties?

Roaring Forties is a popular nautical term that was originally applied by sailors to an ocean zone in the Southern Hemisphere between the fortieth and fiftieth degrees of latitude. This region is notorious among seamen for heavy winds, stormy weather and rough seas. By extension the corresponding regions in the Northern Hemisphere are also called the Roaring Forties. The term is facetiously applied to a district in New York City lying between Fortieth and Fiftieth streets, where conditions are said to be as hectic as they were in the proverbial stormy belt of the southern oceans.

How did "foolscap" originate?

There are several theories as to how a certain kind of paper came to be called *foolscap*. The most probable theory is that the paper was so called from the watermark consisting of a fool's cap and bells that was used by early paper makers. According to an oft-repeated story, Oliver Cromwell substituted this watermark in place of the royal arms granted by Charles I to manufacturers of certain kinds of paper. When the Rump Parliament reconvened the fool's cap and bells as a watermark was abolished, but paper the size of the *Parliamentary Journal*—fourteen by seventeen inches—has been called foolscap ever since. Still another story accounts for the name as follows: Cromwell used the stamp of liberty on his stationery and after the Restoration some of the paper was brought to Charles II. The King examined the paper very carefully and observed: "Take it away; I have nothing to do with a fool's cap." But it is known definitely that paper with the fool's cap and bells as a watermark was made as early as 1540, because letters written on such paper during that year are still extant. Some authorities believe that this watermark goes back as early as the thirteenth century, long before the invention of printing. The dunce's cap, a paper cap used as a penalty in schools for poor lessons or bad behavior, was probably suggested by the name already given to foolscap, rather than this practice having suggested the name. It may be that *foolscap* is a corruption of the Italian *foglio capo*, meaning a chief or full-sized sheet of paper. That such paper was once associated in the English mind with Italy is shown by the fact that a statute of Queen Anne refers to it as *Genoa foolscap*. The standard size of foolscap printing paper is 13½ by 17 inches, and of foolscap writing paper, 13¼ by 16½ inches.

Is the flesh of the beaver good to eat?

The beaver is an aquatic rodent and its flesh, though edible, is not very palatable. Early hunters, trappers and frontiersmen, as well as the Indians, generally ate beaver meat only in the summertime when they could not get other flesh. But William Byrd of Westover, writing at Williamsburg, colonial capital of Virginia, noted in his secret diary under date of February 20, 1712: "I ate some beaver for dinner at the Governor's." The tail of the beaver, when properly cooked, has been considered a delicacy since the first settlement of America. Many early writers refer to the fact that beaver tail was regarded a great dainty at the trading posts in the Northwest. J. S. C. Abbott, in his life of Kit Carson, says: "The captured animals were skinned on the spot, and the skins only with the tails, which hunters deemed a great luxury as an article of food, were taken to the camp." The Earl of Southesk, who had beaver tail for supper at Edmonton in Canada, reported that it "tasted like fat pork sandwiched between layers of finnan haddock."

How are watermarks in paper made?

Watermarks, the partially transparent designs visible in certain writing paper when it is held up to the light, are put in the paper during the process of manufacture. These designs were first made in Italy in the thirteenth century and originally consisted of simple devices such as circles, triangles and crosses. Some authorities suppose that the design consisting of a fool's cap and bells was among the early Italian watermarks on handmade paper. Metal wires were bent to the shape of the desired design and fastened to the mould in which the pulp was formed into paper. When the paper was still somewhat soft and moist the mould left impressions in the sheets by causing the fiber to be thinner where it came in contact with the wires. The watermarks survived the processes of rolling, sizing and drying and remained as semitransparent characters, usually representing the trade-mark of the manufacturer. That is essentially the method of watermarking hand-made paper at the present time, although more complicated and artistic processes have been devised. Modern watermarks are often very elaborate, even consisting of portraits in colors. Watermarks are imprinted in the soft sheets of machine-made paper by a roller of wire gauze, in which patterns have been woven, or by a rubber cylinder equipped with projections containing designs. What are styled "artificial watermarks" are impressed in paper after the process of manufacture is complete. From 1895 to 1916 all United States postage stamps were printed on paper watermarked *U.S.P.S.*

Does the common house fly ever bite?

The common house fly could not bite no matter how hard it might try. This species, *Musca domestica*, eats all sorts of food, but neither sex has a proboscis adapted for biting or sucking blood. The rather common supposition that the house fly bites arises from the fact that this insect is frequently confused with the stable fly, *Stomoxys calcitrans*, which is very similar and which also visits human dwellings, especially in the fall. The mouth parts of the stable fly are rigid and formed for piercing and sucking blood and the insect is a severe biter.

How did Hampton Roads get its name?

Hampton Roads received its name from the town of Hampton on the near-by shore of Virginia. *Road*, in either its singular or plural form, is used in nautical affairs for a ship roadstead, that is, a sheltered place outside a harbor, where ships may ride at anchor. Hampton Roads is the channel through which the waters of the James, Nansemond and Elizabeth rivers pass into Chesapeake Bay. On March 9, 1862, it was the scene of the first battle between iron-clad vessels, the historic conflict between the "Merrimac" and the "Monitor."

Why are small airships called blimps?

Blimp is a popular name that is generally applied to small, nonrigid, lighter-than-air, dirigible airships and balloons. Sometimes it is applied to any small dirigible, whether it is rigid or nonrigid. A rigid airship is one whose form is maintained by a metallic frame within the gas bag. A nonrigid airship is kept taut merely by the pressure of the gas within the bag. How *blimp* originated is not definitely known. The late Dr. Frank H. Vizetelly suggested that it may be a combination of *b* in *balloon* and *limp*, meaning flexible, flaccid, lacking in stiffness. Webster's International dictionary says *blimp* in the sense of "a small non-rigid airship" was "probably suggested by limp." It is said that when the British were experimenting with lighter-than-air craft during the First World War the first model, designated *A-limp*, proved unsatisfactory.

The second model, which proved more satisfactory, was designated B-limp. Hence blimp. According to another story, the word was first used as a term of derision and ridicule by an airplane pilot who was making fun of certain small airships then being developed by the British government. One writer says blimp was previously employed as an English colloquialism in the sense of a small blister, such as might arise from being burned by hot water or grease.

Can the wind be seen?

Wind is air naturally and horizontally in motion with a certain degree of velocity. Thus the old question, "Where is the wind when it is not blowing?" is pointless, because there is no wind that is not blowing. Pure air is composed of absolutely colorless gases and is perfectly transparent. Therefore the wind could not be seen if the air were pure, but the atmosphere always contains minute particles of substances other than the constituent gases and one can see the wind readily enough with the aid of a bright sheet of metal a couple of feet in length with one edge straight, such as a polished handsaw of large size. A windy day when the air is dry should be selected for the experiment to get the best results. The sheet of metal or saw should be held at right angles to the wind; that is, if the wind is blowing from the south the blade should point east and west with the straight edge up and tilted away from the direction of the wind at an angle of about 35 or 40 degrees, permitting the air current to strike the smooth surface and glance upward. If one then sights carefully along the blade at some sharply defined object in the vicinity he will see the air flowing over the edge in graceful curves like water going over a dam. The speed, but not the volume, of the overflow increases with the strength of the wind. Of course the phenomenon is due to the irregular density of the air, which causes irregular refraction of the light waves. It is similar to the waves of air seen near a hot stove or over the ground, roofs and other surfaces on hot, clear summer days. Pigs, according to an old English belief, can see the wind, and among the colored people of the South there is an old saying that one can see the wind if he sucks a sow.

Is Los Angeles a seaport?

Los Angeles is a seaport, having its harbor in San Pedro Bay, which is connected with the main part of the city by a narrow strip of territory about twenty-four miles long. Santa Monica Bay is closer to Los Angeles than any other part of the Pacific Ocean, but it has no harbor. San Pedro Bay is exposed and originally provided an uncertain roadstead for vessels, but it was chosen as a harbor for Los Angeles by the Spanish because it was accessible from the city by a level land route. The Americans established a stage between the harbor and the city in 1852 and a railway in 1869. A long fight for a Los Angeles harbor within the city limits ended in 1909 by the annexation of the towns of San Pedro and Wilmington and the establishment of the harbor corridor. These towns were originally on a narrow inlet that has been widened and deepened. The harbor was greatly improved in 1910 when the Federal Government built a breakwater, forming what is known as the "outer harbor," where warships and other vessels at anchor must remain. Between 1909 and 1912 the city completed the inner harbor.

What queen of England was never in England?

Queen Berengaria, wife of Richard the Lionhearted, was never in England. Richard left England in 1190 to take part in the third crusade. Berengaria, the beautiful daughter of Sancho VI of Navarre, was brought to him by his mother Eleanor while he and his troops were wintering in southern Italy, and the marriage took place in Cyprus, May 12, 1191. Later in the same year the English Queen joined the King at Acre on the coast of Palestine. During Richard's imprisonment on the Continent Berengaria lived in Italy and France. Upon his release early in 1194 he proceeded immediately to England, where he remained less than two months, after which he left for his foreign dominions never to return. It is said that he met his wife only once again, sometime in 1195. However that may be, they became estranged, and the Queen's later years were spent chiefly at Le Mans in France, where she died about 1230 without ever having set foot on English soil. Richard died in France in 1199 of an arrow wound received while besieging the castle of Chalus. Sophia Dorothea, wife of George I, is also sometimes referred to as "the English Queen who never lived in England." But Sophia was divorced by George in 1694, twenty years before he became King of England, and accordingly she was never Queen of England at all.

What is a guinea-keet?

In some parts of the United States, particularly in the South, *guinea-keet*, or simply *keet*, is the name applied to the common guinea fowl. The word is of imitative origin and was suggested by the peculiar and unpleasant note of this bird. When excited both the guinea cock and the guinea hen emit a one-syllable cry that sounds like *quit* or *keet*. Sometimes the word is spelled *keat*. All domestic guinea fowls are descended from *Numida meleagris*, a wild species native to Africa, where it is still prized by hunters as a game bird. They derive their common name from Guinea on the west coast of that continent and have been domesticated since ancient times, both the Greeks and Romans having raised them as table fowls. Under date of June 20, 1866, David Livingstone, African explorer and missionary, wrote in his diary that a native chief "gave me an ample meal of porridge and guinea-fowl before starting." Theodore Roosevelt and his son Kermit shot wild guinea fowls in East Africa in 1909 and 1910. The birds were shy and ran rapidly through the tall grass. In *African Game Trails* the former President said that while hunting in the Gauso Nyero he "knocked off the heads of two guinea fowls" with his rifle. Domestic guinea fowls are often kept with other poultry as "sentinels." These alert, sensitive and watchful fowls are the first to sound the danger alarm when predatory animals or birds approach the flock. Turkey raisers often include guinea eggs with each incubator lot of turkey eggs. Guinea chicks, which are brighter and more alert, teach the young turkeys how to find the feed hopper and the warm spots under the brooder.

How did "reckoning without one's host" originate?

To *reckon* or *count without one's host* means to reckon from one's own standpoint alone and to neglect important facts in arriving at a conclusion. The phrase dates back several centuries and refers to counting the cost of entertainment or the expenses at a hotel before consulting the host or landlord. Almost always the landlord calls attention to some items that the guest has failed to take into consideration. In its earliest form the expression was *to reckon before one's host*.

Do dogs sweat?

Dogs sweat very little. The physiological purpose of perspiration seems to be the regulation of the body temperature. But in the case of dogs as well as many other animals body temperature is regulated largely by respiration instead of perspiration, although some heat is lost by radiation from the skin. After running, a dog breathes more rapidly, or "pants." This has the same cooling effect that sweating would have. Since the surplus body heat must be dissipated largely through the lungs, the more rapid the breathing the greater the loss of heat. In dogs the limited amount of sweating occurs almost wholly on the soles of the feet, where the largest sweat glands are located. This explains the wet tracks that a dog often leaves on a floor or other hard surface during hot weather. There are also some sweat glands in the skin of the perineum and the perineal pouches, but the skin is not elsewhere supplied with these glands. The popular notion that dogs perspire through the muzzle is incorrect. There are no sweat glands in that region. The secretion appearing on the muzzle comes from the lateral nasal gland. When hot a dog instinctively sticks out its tongue in an effort to increase the evaporating surface of the body.

What is a Garrison finish?

A Garrison finish is a close contest or a "victory by an eyelash." The phrase refers to the racing tactics of Edward H. Garrison, nicknamed "Snapper," an American jockey who retired as a rider in 1897. He was the most famous jockey of his day and his favorite trick was to keep his mount well back in the huddle during the early stages of the race and then thrill the spectators by a sudden burst of speed on the homestretch. By this means he reserved the best efforts of his mount for the last leg of the race. It is said that most of Snapper Garrison's turf victories were won in the last furlong and his ability to lift a jaded horse across the finish line only a nose ahead of the others became proverbial. Garrison died in Brooklyn, New York, in 1931.

How did plus fours originate?

Plus fours is the name of short, loose-fitting trousers widely worn by golfers and sportsmen. This style of trousers originated in the British Army and was later adopted for civilian wear. The trousers were called plus fours because four inches was added to the inside seam of each leg of the ordinary knickerbockers. Plus fours are merely knickerbockers with several inches hangover at the knees. It is often erroneously stated that English golfers found ordinary knickerbockers slightly too short for comfort and that designers of men's apparel therefore devised plus fours especially for golfers. But the Brigade of Guards and other units in the British Army were wearing plus fours long before the style was adopted by golf players and sportsmen.

Why are sailors called gobs?

Gob as a popular nickname for an American sailor is somewhat of an etymological mystery. It is often said that the word originated along the Chinese coast about 1912 when the American fleet was in the Far East. One writer says it is derived from a Chinese word having a similar sound and signifying sailor. That it originated before 1912 is well established. Many old-timers in the Navy confirm its use previous to 1900. Some hold that the word was first brought to this country by Perry after opening the ports of Japan to foreign commerce. "Undoubtedly," declared the Office of Naval Intelligence in 1928, "it was brought back from the Asiatic Station and is derived from the Japanese word meaning a fighting farmer." Another theory derives it from French *garde de l'eau*, which means "water guard" and which Americans are said to have first pronounced and written *gobbyloo*, which was later shortened to *gob*. But there is another interesting angle to the question. Long before its application to American sailors *gob* was applied in Great Britain to those in the revenue service engaged in suppressing smuggling. The English also call any coast guard a gob. There is an old English verb *to gob*, which means to stop, and also "to spit" or "to expectorate." There is a noun *gob* meaning the point of an anchor. The more usual meaning of *gob* is a large, irregular mass. It has been suggested that the members of the British coast guard and revenue service were first called gobs or gobbies because they were notorious for their gobbing—spitting, or that they were compared in derision to *gobs* of *spit*. Another suggestion is that they were called gobs because of their voracious and noisy eating habits. Perhaps originally there was some connection between *gob* and *gab* in the sense of mouth or noisy prattle. Navy officers, as a rule, frown upon the term and don't like to hear sailors called gobs. In 1928 Admiral Henry A. Wiley, Commander in Chief of the United States Fleet, sent all units under his command a letter in which he directed that the use of *gob* be discontinued in Navy publications. The word, said the admiral, is undignified, unworthy, and un-naval. But it is one of those odd nicknames that people go on using irrespective of official efforts to suppress it.

What is the Staked Plain?

Staked Plain is a translation of Spanish *Llano Estacado*, literally "palisaded or staked plain." It is the name of an extensive plateau in northwestern Texas and eastern New Mexico about 180 square miles in area. There are several theories as to how the region acquired its unusual name. According to one, the early Spanish explorers in that region called it the "staked plain" because they set stakes in the ground to mark their routes over the large stretch of woodless plain where watering places were few and far between. According to another, the Spaniards so named the plateau because the tall, naked, stakelike boles of the yucca plants, known as "Spanish bayonets" or "daggers," grow there in abundance. According to a third theory, the name was suggested by the slopes leading up to the plain, which from a distance had the appearance of stakes or palisades. Thomas Falconer, who accompanied the Santa Fe Expedition of 1841, wrote in his diary: "We commenced the ascent to the grand prairie—the Llano Estacado of the New Mexicans. This was the great plain spoken of at San Antonio as too extensive to travel over, where we should be without timber, without water, and where many of our horses would perish. At all the points where our exploring parties had previously touched it, its sides were rugged, looking, as the name denotes, as if staked from the lower ground, as if bodily lifted up, or as if the ground about it had at some former time sunk around it." The area known as Llano Estacado is bounded in a general way on the north by the Canadian River, on the west, southwest and south by the valley of the Pecos, and on the east by the headwaters of the Red, Brazos and Colorado rivers. It is a high, isolated plateau or island-like mass. The slope or escarpment of the Staked Plain is composed of limestone, which is more resistant to erosion than the underlying beds. It is remarkable in that it forms an abrupt, precipitous and nearly horizontal rim. This region, which has rather light rainfall, was in its virgin condition practically devoid of trees and contained a sparse but uniform covering of grasses. Contrary to a popular notion, the Staked Plain is not level, but undulating.

How did "tabloid" originate?

Tabloid was arbitrarily coined by the firm of Burroughs, Wellcome and Company, of London, England, and is a registered and protected trade-mark of that firm. Contrary to a popular notion, the trade-mark term is applied to various drugs and preparations and not merely to products in concentrated and condensed form. But in the United States tabloid came to be used to designate anything concise, compressed or condensed. In The Conqueror, published in 1902, Gertrude Atherton wrote: "To condense Hamilton is much like attempting to increase the density of a stone, or to reduce the alphabet to a tabloid." The term is applied in the United States particularly to a newspaper considerably smaller than the standard size and generally sensational in contents. The Illustrated News, established in New York City in June, 1919, by the Chicago Tribune was the first tabloid newspaper in the present sense of the term.

How should 12:00 o'clock noon be designated?

According to the United States Naval Observatory, 12:00 M. is almost universally used to designate 12:00 noon. M. in this connection is the abbreviation of meridiem, which is the accusative of Latin meridies ("midday"). Midnight is properly designated 12:00 P.M. P.M. is the correct abbreviation of post meridiem ("after midday"), while A.M. is the correct abbreviation of *ante meridiem* ("before midday"). They are now written either in capitals or lower case, although originally they were always capitalized. Frequently one sees 12:00 N. (noon), and 12:00 M. (midnight), but these abbreviations are confusing and should be avoided. Because of the difference in usage and the consequent confusion some writers dispense with the abbreviations and write 12:00 Noon and 12:00 Midnight, respectively. Noon is derived from Latin *nonus* ("ninth"). Originally it was applied to the ninth hour (about 3:00 P.M.) reckoned from sunrise according to the Roman method. High noon signifies exactly midday by sun time. In this phrase, as well as in *high day* and *high time*, *high* is an old English adjective meaning "far advanced" or "fully come." The underlying thought in *high noon* is that the sun is then at the highest point it reaches in the heavens.

Do snakes ever bite under water?

It is believed that ordinary land snakes seldom, if ever, bite under water. Although many of them are good swimmers, they seem to be insufficiently adapted to aquatic life to bite when submerged. Some non-venomous snakes, such as the common American water snake, spend much of their time in streams, ponds and lakes. They capture fish for food and hence are capable of biting when submerged. The only species of venomous water snake in the United States is the cottonmouth moccasin. Fish comprise a considerable part of its diet and it bites under water as well as on land. The fangs work more or less like a hypodermic syringe and poison can be readily injected into a victim under water. Snakes, however, are less likely to be annoyed while in water and consequently persons are not often bitten under such circumstances. There are many reports of sailors being bitten by sea snakes while they were swimming in tropical seas. These snakes are highly poisonous and also feed upon fish that they kill with their poison fangs. Most of these snakes live in the tropical seas between the Persian Gulf and Central America, but one species is found in Lake Taal, a landlocked body of fresh water on the island of Luzon in the Philippines. The published accounts do not mention the exact position of these snakes while striking their victims, whether under the water or on the surface.

Why is "Jno." used as the abbreviation of "John"?

Jno. as the abbreviation of *John* originated when this proper name was still in the process of formation. The English form of the name is derived from *Johannes*, which was first contracted to *Johan*; in time the *a* was either dropped or an *o* was substituted for it and the name was written *John* or *Johon*. Sometimes, however, it was spelled *Jhon*, due either to the omission of the first instead of the second o in *John*, or to the transposition of h and o in *John*. In early times the name was probably pronounced in two syllables. Centuries ago it was a common practice to use n for h and *John* was abbreviated either *Jho.* or *Jno.* The latter form prevailed and is still the favorite abbreviation. *John* is derived indirectly from Hebrew *Yohanan*, meaning "Jehovah hath been gracious." Its evolution was as follows: *Yohanan* in Hebrew, *Ioannes* in Greek, *Johannes* in Latin, *Jean* in French, and *John* in English.

Does a horse pull or push a wagon?

The answer to this question depends upon a definition of the terms. *Pull*, according to Webster's International dictionary, means "to exert force upon so as to cause, or tend to cause, motion toward the force." The same authority defines *push* as pressing "against with force in order to drive or impel." These definitions imply that a pulling force is applied in advance of the object moved, while pushing force is applied behind the thing moved. Both of these actions are involved when a horse draws a load. If the animal is hitched to a vehicle in the usual manner it presses or pushes against the collar or breast strap of the harness for the purpose of pulling the vehicle. But the collar is not the load; it is merely the mechanical equipment by which the horse draws the load. Part of the animal is even in front of the collar. Therefore it is more logical to say that the vehicle is pulled and not pushed by the horse. This is also supported by accepted usage, although some people insist on saying that a horse pushes the wagon because it pushes against the collar or harness. Perhaps *draw* expresses the idea better. According to the authority just quoted, *draw* means "to cause to move continuously by force applied in advance of the thing moved." Likewise some people insist that a locomotive pushes instead of pulls a train because the steam pushes the pistons that push the rods that turn the wheels. But the locomotive as a whole pulls or draws the train.

Why do the eyes of some portraits follow the observer?

If an artist represents the eyes of a portrait as gazing directly forward they will appear to look directly at an observer standing at any point in front of the picture where a view is possible. The same effect is obtained in photography when the subject looks straight into the camera. On the other hand, if the eyes of a picture are not painted or photographed to look directly at the observer they will not do so even if he stands at the point toward which the eyes seem to be directed. This is because the picture is on a flat surface and has only two dimensions. Suppose, by way of illustration, a portrait represents a person with his face turned somewhat to the observer's right and his eyes fixed directly at the observer. If the observer moves to the left he does not get a different view of the picture; that is, he does not obtain a profile view as he would in real life. He merely sees the same picture narrowed somewhat in perspective. The picture of the face, though elongated in proportion to the angle at which it is viewed, possesses all the same lines that it did when seen in front, and the eyes still look directly forward and consequently at the observer. In other words, if the eyes of a portrait on a flat surface are represented as looking directly forward they will appear to follow the observer no matter what the angle may be at which the picture is viewed; and if the eyes are represented as looking in some other direction the observer cannot place himself in a position so they will appear to look at him. The same thing occurs in two-dimension motion pictures. An observer at the extreme left side of a theater sees the same scenes, though slightly distorted, that are seen by a person on the extreme right side.

Do snakes dig their own holes in the ground?

Most snakes that go underground do not dig their own holes but make use of natural crevices and holes and burrows made by various animals and other creatures. There are at least four families of snakes in the United States that live a wholly or partially subterranean life. Those that excavate their own burrows are the "blind snakes" (*Typhlopidae*), the "ground snakes" (*Glauconidae*), the "coral snakes" (*Ilysiidae*), and the "shield tails" (*Uropeltidae*). In these burrowing snakes the head, body and tail are somewhat cylindrical, a modification that adapts them to their peculiar mode of life.

Why do monkeys search through their hair?

It is generally supposed that monkeys continually search through their own hair and that of other monkeys for fleas, lice and other body parasites. An expert associated with the London Zoological Park says that such is not the case. Monkeys, he says, are quite free from such parasites unless they are neglected or kept in dirty cages. Salt exudes from the pores of the skin of monkeys and remains on loose bits of skin, and it is for these that the animals are continually searching and picking. Dr. William M. Mann, director of the National Zoological Park at Washington, substantially confirms this statement. He says: "As to why monkeys search their own hair and that of other monkeys, it is usually for loose bits of skin and salty exhalations. Of course, when there are fleas and lice on the monkeys they try to get them too, but I believe that more often they are searching for these salty particles." The late Raymond L. Ditmars, for many years curator of animals and reptiles at the New York Zoological Park, made the following observation on the subject in a letter to the author: "With newly arrived specimens of monkeys, the search through the hair is for a definite purpose, and that is the capture of body parasites, which are fairly abundant on specimens from the jungle. These, however, seem quickly to disappear in captivity, and many monkeys examined have been found to be absolutely free from vermin. The search goes on, however, with every manifestation of success, but we are inclined to believe that this is actuated by a certain stimulus on the part of the monkeys—that the search is imaginary or conducted by the monkeys as a friendly token, one to the other."

Is the hide of the rhinoceros bulletproof?

It is not true, as generally supposed, that a bullet will not penetrate the thick skin of a rhinoceros except between the deep folds. In his book entitled In the Zoo Dr. W. Reid Blair, for many years director of the New York Zoological Park, wrote: "From the immense thickness and apparent toughness of its great folds, it was long considered that the hide of the Indian rhinoceros was bulletproof, except at the joints of the armor-like shield plates. As a matter of fact, the skin of the animal is quite soft and can readily be penetrated in any place by a bullet or pierced by a hunting knife. When dried, however, it becomes exceedingly hard and it was formerly employed by the Indian princes in the manufacture of shields for their soldiers." Big game hunters generally use large-caliber rifles when hunting the rhinoceros—.45 being a popular size in East Africa. Sometimes the animals are hunted and killed with guns of small caliber. "The two favorite shots," according to Dr. William M. Mann, director of the National Zoological Park, "are the heart shot, back of the right foreleg and into the heart, and the neck shot, about eight inches back of the ear and somewhat below so as to break the neck bone." Shields of tanned rhinoceros hide are still used by Ethiopian warriors and hunters.

Why are three golden balls the pawnbroker's sign?

Three golden balls as the sign of the pawnbroker are supposed to be derived from the device of the famous Medici family of Florence. A pawnbroker lends money on personal pledges left in his possession as security. This trade first flourished in Italy, and during the Middle Ages pawnshops were operated almost exclusively by the Jews and the Lombards. The first moneylenders of London were Lombards from Florence who established themselves on Lombard Street, which became proverbial as the "money market." Among the principal Lombard bankers and pawnbrokers were the members of the Medici family. Formerly, as their name indicates, the Medicis were engaged in the medical profession. Averardo de Medici was an officer under Charlemagne, and, according to a legend, he slew a giant named Mugello, on whose mace were three gilded balls. Averardo, to perpetuate his exploit, adopted the three golden balls as the device of his family. The family was so prominent that the device became the symbol of the whole profession of medicine, and a legend grew up that the three golden balls represented three gilded pills. Later, however, the Medicis became bankers and pawnbrokers and gradually the device was transferred from the medical profession to the pawnbroker's trade.

What was the Black Hole of Calcutta?

The Black Hole of Calcutta is the popular name of a small cell or dungeon that formerly constituted the guardroom in Fort William at Calcutta, India. In 1756 Siraj-ud-daula, then only nineteen years old, became nabob of Bengal. Soon afterward he broke with the British authorities. In pursuit of a relative he marched upon Calcutta with a considerable force. Many of the British officials escaped by flight. The Europeans who remained in the city took refuge in the citadel but were forced to submit after a brief resistance. One hundred and forty-six employees of the British India Company, including one woman, were forced into the Black Hole, which was only 18 feet long and 14 feet 10 inches wide and had but two small windows covered with iron bars and obstructed by a veranda. It is said that when Siraj-ud-daula stormed the citadel on June 19, 1756, he believed it contained enormous treasures and confined the occupants in the dungeon because they refused to divulge its whereabouts. At any rate, it was the season when the tropical heat of Calcutta was most oppressive and when the cell was opened early the next morning only twenty-three prisoners were taken out alive. The site of the dungeon was covered with a black marble slab and the event commemorated by a monumental shaft erected in 1902.

Why is the Black Sea called black?

Black Sea is a literal translation of Turkish *Kara Deniz*. This body of water was supposedly so named by the Turks because of its dense fogs and violent storms, *black* being used in the sense of bleak, gloomy and forbidding. In winter the waters are often covered with heavy fogs that obscure the sun and lend a dark aspect to the entire sea. The early Greeks called it *Pontos Axemos*, meaning inhospitable sea or sea unfriendly to strangers, because of its barren shores and its want of islands where navigators could find shelter from the frequent storms. Later, however, after Greek colonists had settled on its shores, the name was changed to *Pontos Euxinos*, meaning hospitable sea or sea friendly to strangers. At one time the Black Sea was referred to in English as the *Pontic*. In Shakespeare's *Othello* the Moor says:

> Like to the Pontic sea,
> Whose icy current and compulsive course
> Ne'er feels retiring ebb, but keeps due on
> To the Propontic and the Hellespont . . .

Why are some battleships called dreadnoughts?

Dreadnought, also sometimes spelled *dreadnaught*, is an old English adjective meaning fearless, dreading nothing. The term was applied to British naval vessels as early as the time of Queen Elizabeth. Edward Boscawen (1711–1761), famous British admiral who distinguished himself at Porto Bello in 1739, at Cartagena in 1741, at Louisburg in 1758 and at Toulon in 1759, was familiarly called "Old Dreadnought." The Seaman's Hospital, founded in 1821, at Greenwich, England, used to be called "Dreadnought Hospital" because it was at first housed on the Thames in a man-of-war of that name. The term is now used to designate a type of battleship which, to quote the United States Navy Department, "is characterized by simplicity and concentration of its fighting power." This type as the ideal battleship was proposed in 1903 by Vittorio Cumberti, chief inspector of the Italian Navy. The H.M.S. "Dreadnought," launched by the British Navy in 1906, was the first dreadnought actually constructed and it gave its name to the entire class. This vessel combined large tonnage, heavy armament and relatively high speed. She had a tonnage of 17,900, was covered with armor 11 inches thick, carried ten 12-inch guns, 27 12-pounders and five submerged torpedo tubes and was the first battleship fitted with steam turbines and a tripod mast. The United States Navy also built two battleships of this type in 1906—the U.S.S. "South Carolina" and the U.S.S. "Michigan." Previously battleships had carried what was known as a "mixed" battery of heavy, semi-heavy and light guns. Modern battleships—dreadnoughts—have a main battery of heavy guns, a secondary battery of light guns for defense against torpedo craft and a battery of antiaircraft guns of small caliber. Of course, great strides have been made and are being made in the construction of battleships since 1906. Battleships exceeding the original dreadnoughts in size, speed and armament are often called super-dreadnoughts. *Dreadnought* and *super-dreadnought*, however, are not used officially by the United States Navy Department in designating classes of battleships.

What is the most northern town in Europe?

Hammerfest, on the island of Kvalö off the coast of Norway, is regarded as the most northern town in Europe. Its latitude is 70 degrees 40 minutes north, or about 10 minutes farther north than Point Barrow, Alaska. In spite of its north latitude Hammerfest, which has a normal population of several thousand, has a comparatively warm climate, owing to the mild westerly winds and the Gulf Stream or the North Atlantic drift current. The average January temperature is little below freezing and the harbor is ice free.

Why are marines called leathernecks?

Leatherneck as applied to a Marine seems to have originated in the United States Navy. Apparently it was given to the Marines by their "friendly enemies" the sailors, and was suggested by the leather-lined collar or stock formerly worn as part of the regulation uniform of members of the Marine Corps. This collar, made stiff by a thin leather band on the inside, was designed to give a more military appearance to the uniform. It was about the same height as the collars on the dress uniforms of the present time. When this collar became wet with perspiration, however, it often caused discomfort as well as throat trouble. Consequently, according to the United States Marine Corps, it was abolished as part of the blouse shortly after 1875. In the second revision (1923) of *The American Language* H. L. Mencken said: "*Leatherneck* needs no explanation. It obviously refers to the sunburn suffered by marines in the tropics." This theory, however, is not so probable as it appears at first blush. If sunburned necks had suggested the term it would be applied to the sailor rather than the marine, for the sailor's collar is cut low in the back and fully exposes the neck to the sun, while the marine's neck is protected by a high, close-fitting collar, making sunburn of the neck impossible. Many sailors maintain that *leatherneck* originally referred to the dark and leathery appearance of a dirty and long-unwashed neck. It may be a myth, but according to Navy tradition marines in the early days were dirty of person. In sailor slang, washing without removing the undershirt and jumper is called a "leatherneck" or "marine wash." When a sailor washes, according to the sailors, he usually strips to the waist and washes his face, neck and arms; but when a marine washes he does so after the fashion of civilians, that is, he merely takes off his coat and rolls up the sleeves of his shirt to the elbows and washes his hands to the wrists and his face to the neck. That, at any rate, was the version formerly given by sailors.

What country is known as the Storehouse of the World?

Mexico is known as the Storehouse of the World because of the fertility of its soil and its almost inexhaustible mineral and other natural resources. This popular designation was probably suggested by a phrase used by Alexander Humboldt (1769–1859), German naturalist and traveler, who referred to Mexico as "the treasure-house of the world." The same writer compared that country to "a beggar sitting on a bag of gold." Bernal Diaz, one of the men with Cortez in 1519, reporting his impressions of the valley of Mexico, wrote: "I stood looking at it and thought that never in the world would there be discovered other lands such as these."

How did "sowing wild oats" originate?

To sow wild oats means to commit youthful excesses, to spend one's youth in dissipation. Subsequent reform is generally implied in the phrase. "He has sown his wild oats" is said of a person who has settled down to a steady and sober life. The saying, it is supposed, originated among the country people of England. The wild oat—a tall grass resembling the cultivated oat and by some regarded as its original progenitor—is a common weed in the British Isles. It was but natural that a weed so common and noxious should become the subject of a moral comparison among the English farmers. At first sowing wild oats meant sowing worthless seed, or seed that would produce a worthless crop. The transition to the figurative meaning would be easy. He who wastes the precious days of his youthful prime in dissipation is sowing seeds that will grow up into noxious weeds. The phrase may involve three original ideas. Oats are a stimulating horse feed. A spirited horse is said to "feel its oats." The phrase may contain an allusion to the parable of the sower told by Jesus. Perhaps there is also an implied comparison between a spirited youth and an unbroken colt.

What is a "limited" train?

Limited is now merely a stylish name for a fast train. This term was first applied to railway trains about the time of the Civil War. Originally the special feature of limited trains consisted of a limited number of cars and consequently a limited amount of seating space. Just so many and no more passengers were carried. Those who failed to get accommodations took another train or waited over. The limited train of today is not limited in accommodations, because extra cars, and even extra sections, are added in case of an overflow of passengers. It is merely a fast train that stops for passengers only at a limited number of important stations, as contrasted with a *local* train, which is usually slow and stops at the smaller stations. The first train to contain *Limited* in its name was the New York and Chicago Limited, which began in 1881. Ten years later it was rechristened the Pennsylvania Limited. One writer defines a limited train as an express train that is restricted to carrying passengers who pay an extra fare.

Does lightning fertilize the soil?

The popular belief that lightning fertilizes the soil where it strikes the ground has some scientific basis. Such electrical disturbances may increase the fertility of the soil by rendering the minerals in it more soluble and making the elements of fertility more readily available to plants. Possibly the common notion that lightning fertilizes soil arose from the fact that dead trees and other dry objects are sometimes struck and burned down, leaving ashes that fertilize the soil and cause vegetation to grow more luxuriantly on such spots. But electrical storms contribute to the fertility of the soil in a more substantial way. Lightning causes a chemical reaction between the oxygen and nitrogen in the air and forms a soluble substance known as nitric acid, which is brought down by rain, snow and hail. By this process lightning creates millions of tons of the finest fertilizer every year.

Why is a refuge for criminals called an Alsatia?

Alsatia is an old Latin name for the French frontier province of Alsace. Because this region was a debatable ground and long a refuge for political outcasts from both France and Germany its name was applied during the seventeenth century to Whitefriars, a district in London that provided sanctuary to debtors and lawbreakers. A Carmelite monastery, founded in 1241 and dissolved in 1538, was located in Whitefriars, and, like other religious establishments, afforded sanctuary to criminals and refugees. Sanctuary in cases where actual crime was involved was abolished throughout England in 1623 by act of Parliament during the reign of James I. The privilege, however, lingered on for civil offenses in certain districts that had once been the sites of sanctuaries and that became the haunts for debtors and lawbreakers resisting arrest. Among these alleged sanctuaries Alsatia, lying between Fleet Street and the

Thames east of the Temple, was the most notorious. Any peace officer who invaded Alsatia in pursuit of gamblers, cheats, forgers and highwaymen took his life in his hands. The abuses in connection with its alleged privileges became so flagrant that the Escape from Prison Act was passed in 1697 to abolish all such privileges, Whitefriars and about a dozen other districts being specifically mentioned in the statute. Alsatia as a name for Whitefriars first occurred in Thomas Shadwell's play entitled *The Squire of Alsatia*, written in 1688. The same neighborhood as a lawless place was immortalized by Sir Walter Scott in his *Fortunes of Nigel*, in which he borrowed freely from Shadwell.

What does "hoi polloi" mean?

Hoi polloi, pronounced hoi po-*loi* in English, is a Greek phrase in Latin letters and literally means "the many." It is applied to the masses, the multitude, the populace or the great majority, particularly in the deprecatory sense of the ordinary people or "the common herd." It is often incorrectly written *the hoi polloi*, which is equivalent to *the the many*. Since the Greek phrase contains the definite article an additional one is superfluous. Even the scholarly John Dryden fell into this error in his "Essay on Dramatic Poesy": "If by the people you understand the multitude, the *hoi polloi*, 'tis no matter what they think; they are sometimes in the right, sometimes in the wrong; their judgment is a mere lottery." But perhaps usage has made the incorrect form correct.

How long is a light year?

A light year is the distance traversed by light in one year, which is more than sixty-three thousand times the distance between the earth and sun. It is a linear unit used especially in measuring the vast distances between fixed stars and the earth. All astronomers, however, do not use the same year as a basis for such computations, although the Julian year is generally taken as the basis of the light year, since it is somewhat simpler than the others, being exactly 365 days and six hours in length. "Round numbers only," says the United States Naval Observatory, "are used in dealing with the light year. The Julian year of 365.25 days is in common use among astronomers and may be very safely employed in computing stellar distances." A light year is roughly computed by multiplying the number of seconds in a year, about 32,000,000, by the speed of light, about 186,000 miles a second. The United States Bureau of Standards says: "The term *light year* is used in astronomy to designate an approximate order of distance, and not as an exact unit of length. The year used in reckoning is the tropical or calendar year, and were the velocity of light accurately known, it would be possible to calculate the light year exactly in miles, kilometers, or other familiar units of length." On November 13, 1928, Edwin B. Frost, director of the Yerkes Observatory, wrote to the author on this subject as follows: "The light year is a perfectly definite unit of distance. It may be determined by multiplying the number of seconds in a year by the velocity of light, for which the latest value (by Professor Albert A. Michelson of the University of Chicago) is 186,227 miles per second. This equals 5,876,746,000,000. Speaking roughly, the light year is therefore a little less than six million million miles." Another unit used in measuring interstellar distances is known as the parsec, a coined word composed of the first elements in parallax and second. It is equal to 3.26 light years or about 20,000,000,000,000 miles. A million parsecs is called a megaparsec.

What land lies nearest 0° latitude and 0° longitude?

The no-latitude, no-longitude point on the earth is the point where the prime meridian of Greenwich crosses the equator. This happens to be in the Gulf of Guinea off the western coast of Africa and many miles from any land. The closest land to this point, sometimes called "the land nearest nowhere," is on Dixcove in the British Gold Coast Colony, and the capital of the Gold Coast Colony, Accra, at 5° 31' North and 0° 12' West, is the nearest town. Since the no-latitude, no-longitude point is at sea level it has been aptly described as the only point on the earth without latitude, longitude or altitude.

What was the original name of Joan of Arc?

Joan of Arc is a literal translation of French Jeanne d'Arc. Although the French heroine was known as Jeannette in the countryside around Domremy on the Meuse, where she was born in 1412, she is referred to in contemporary documents as Jeanne. Apparently she was called Jeanne d'Arc by the French and English because they were under the impression that she derived her surname from a village named Arc in the vicinity of her birthplace. The only village or town in France named Arc is many miles south of Domremy, and evidence produced by several antiquaries indicates that the name of Jeanne's father was Jacques Darc, and not Jacques d'Arc, as generally supposed. Therefore it is probable that the heroine's original name was Jeanne or Jeannette Darc, or, translated into English, Joan Darc. In the French Army she was first called simply La Pucelle, the "Maid," but after she raised the siege of Orleans she became known as La Pucelle d'Orleans, the "Maid of Orleans." In 1431, when she was nineteen years old, Joan of Arc was captured by the Burgundians, sold to the English, tried at Rouen for heresy and sorcery, condemned to death and burned at the stake. Twenty-five years later Charles VII of France, whom Joan of Arc had been instrumental in crowning, made a tardy recognition of her services by disannulling the death sentence and giving her a post-mortem trial. Although popularly referred to as a saint for centuries, it was not until 1909 that the church beatified her, and not until 1920 that she was canonized. The bronze equestrian statue of Joan of Arc on Riverside Drive in New York City, the work of Anna Vaughn Hyatt, stands on a pedestal composed in part of eighteen tons of stone from the Rouen dungeon in which she was imprisoned pending her trials by the inquisitorial and secular courts.

May one make a patented article for his own use?

There is a popular but erroneous notion that it is not infringement of a patent for an unauthorized person to make a duplicate of a patented article for his own use, particularly if it is a tool, implement or device employed in gaining a livelihood. On this subject the United States Patent Office says: "The grant of a patent by this office gives to the patentee, his heirs or assigns the right to exclude from making, using and selling the invention covered by the claims of the patent throughout the United States and its territories for a seventeen-year period. An individual would have no right to make for his own use an article covered by the claim of an unexpired patent without the consent of the owner of the patent." Infringement is the unauthorized manufacture, use or sale of a patented article. It may involve any one or all of the acts of making, using or selling, and legally it constitutes a tort in the nature of a trespass on the case. Therefore, in the language of one commentator, it is "an infringement for an unauthorized person to make a patented machine for use or sale, though in fact it is neither used nor sold." The jurisdiction of the United States Patent Office ceases with the issuance of a patent. Questions of infringement come under the jurisdiction of the Federal courts. By statute the Federal Government reserves the authority to use patented articles, devices and processes vital to national defense, although the owners are assured just compensation.

Do mice grow into rats?

That mice are merely young rats is a common belief among many people who should know better. All true rats belong to the genus *Rattus*, while true mice belong to the genus *Mus*, and they represent entirely different branches of the great order of animals known as rodents. The family *Muridae*, to which both mice and rats belong, is the largest of all families of mammals. Nearly one-fourth of all four-footed animals in North America belong to this family. Rat and mouse refer to the same general type of animals, which are distinguished from each other chiefly by size. As the species approach one another in size there is some difficulty in determining when they should be called rats and when mice. The confusion is heightened by an indiscriminate use of rat and mouse in the popular names of some of the smaller species. But there is no difficulty about common house mice and common barn rats. The fact that young rats somewhat resemble grown-up mice undoubtedly gave rise to the curious belief that mice are young rats. In 1929 Dr. A. S. Parkes of London succeeded in getting mother rats to nurse young mice, and the mice thus suckled grew not only much more rapidly but also much larger than normally suckled ones.

How did the British acquire Gibraltar?

Spain took Gibraltar from the Moors in 1492, the year Columbus discovered America, and held it until it was taken July 24, 1704, during the War of the Spanish Succession, by a combined British and Dutch fleet under Admiral George Rooke. The Spanish formally ceded Gibraltar to the English by the Treaty of Utrecht, signed April 11, 1713. Several attempts were made by Spain and France to wrest the stronghold from the English, the last great siege being from 1779 to 1782, during the American Revolution, when Gibraltar was successfully defended by Sir George Eliott. Since the Peace of Versailles in 1783, when the independence of the United States was formally recognized, Great Britain's claim to Gibraltar has not been seriously challenged. It gradually became the symbol of any impregnable stronghold or institution of unquestioned strength. Since the construction of the Suez Canal this fortress has been regarded by the British as one of the chief guardians of the shortest sea route to India. The name is a corruption of Arabic Gebel-al-Tariq, literally meaning "Mount of Tariq." In 711 A.D. a one-eyed Saracen general named Tariq with an army of Arabs and Berbers invaded Spain, defeated the Goths and built a castle on the limestone rock to which he gave his own name. The Rock of Gibraltar, which is honeycombed with natural caverns and artificial tunnels, is 1439 feet high, comprises about two square miles of area and is connected with the Spanish mainland only by a low, narrow and sandy isthmus. In ancient times Gibraltar was known as one of the two Pillars of Hercules, the other being the promontory of Abila (Gebel Musa) on the African side of the Strait of Gibraltar. According to one fable, Hercules, the strong man of Greek mythology, set up these two pillars during his travels to find the oxen of Geryon, and according to another, the two promontories were united as a single mountain range until Hercules tore it asunder to make a passage from the Mediterranean to the Atlantic. Contrary to a common impression, Gibraltar is not located at the narrowest stretch of the Strait, which is some thirteen miles to the west.

What is the average size of the states?

The average area of the forty-eight states of the Union is 63,057 square miles. Georgia, with an area of 59,265, most nearly approaches the average. Texas, with an area of 265,896 square miles, is the largest, while Rhode Island, with an area of only 3,824, is the smallest.

What is a statutory offense?

Statutory offense is a euphemism frequently used in referring to violations of the statutes against various sex offenses. The phrase is employed especially by newspapers when it would not be good taste to mention the offense specifically. Statutory charge is used in a related sense.

What does "of that ilk" mean?

Probably the majority of people who use this phrase do not know the real meaning of ilk. It does not properly mean kind, set, class, family, race or name. Ilk is from Anglo-Saxon ilca and signifies identical or same. In Scotch of that ilk denotes that a person's surname is the same as the name of his estate. Knockwinnock of that ilk means simply Knockwinnock of Knockwinnock, the name of the proprietor and his property being identical. The improper usage in which ilk is employed to mean kind or sort probably originated in carelessness or facetiousness and has been perpetuated through ignorance of the true meaning.

Which is correct, "Esthonia" or "Estonia"?

The name of the Baltic country on the Gulf of Finland opposite Finland is variously spelled Esthonia and Estonia. After the country proclaimed its independence from Russia in 1918, Estonia, without the h, was adopted as the official and correct spelling of the name, and that form was officially adopted by the Department of State at Washington. Literally the name signifies the country of the Esths. Previously to the First World War the Estonians had been ruled successively by the Danes, Germans, Swedes, Poles and Russians. In race and language they are akin to the Finns and Hungarians. Their prevailing short stature, sparse beard, oblique eyes, broad face, low forehead, small mouth and Ural-Altaic speech are said to indicate a Mongolic origin. During the nearly two hundred years of Russian rule from 1721 to 1917, part of the region comprised the Russian province of *Esthonia*. In the thirteenth century a Danish king known as Valdemar the Victorious built a stronghold on the coast of Estonia and named it Revel after a local tribe called Revele. The people, however, called the place *Taani-linn* ("Danish Castle"), and the city there is known to the Estonians as Tallinn rather than Revel to this day.

What is white gold?

Originally *white gold* was the name given to certain alloys of gold and silver. The white gold consisted of about five parts of silver to one of gold. Such metal had a brown tinge and articles of jewelry made of it tarnished rapidly, due to the silver content. As a result of this objectionable feature the old process of making white gold was largely abandoned. At the present time the white gold used in jewelry is made by an entirely different process into which no silver enters. The white gold contains the same percentage of fine or pure gold and base metals as any other ten, fourteen or twenty carat gold. The only difference is that the alloys give the metal a white appearance instead of the yellow appearance of the regulation gold. Modern white gold is white in color and remains so indefinitely. The fact that jewelry is made of white gold no longer stamps it as cheap or inferior. A white gold article may be of more value than one made of regulation gold, depending on the alloy used and the labor involved. White gold jewelry nowadays differs from regulation gold, not in the quality or the quantity of gold used, but in the kind of alloy.

How did "tip" originate?

A curious story is often told to account for the origin of *tip* in the sense of a small sum of money given for personal service rendered or expected. According to this story, *tip* was derived from the initial letters of the phrase *to insure promptness* in the following manner: It was formerly customary to have boxes in English inns and coffeehouses for the receipt of coins for the benefit of the waiters. To Insure Promptness or To Insure Prompt Service was printed on the boxes to remind guests that a coin deposited inside would bring excellent results in the way of special service. Sometimes the phrases on the boxes were abbreviated to *T.I.P.* and *T.I.P.S.*, and from this circumstance, according to the story, *tip* and *tips* came into use. The quotations given in the Oxford dictionary show the absurdity of this derivation. *Tip* in the sense of a small gratuity or present to an inferior is probably derived from an old English verb *to tip*, meaning "to give." "Tip me that cheate (booty), giue me that thing," wrote Samuel Rowlands in *Martin Mark-all, the Beadle of Bridewell,* published in 1610. In *The Beaux' Stratagem,* a play produced in 1706, George Farquhar wrote: "Then, Sir, tips me the Verger with half a crown." In 1733 Colonel William Byrd of Westover wrote in *A Journey to the Land of Eden:* "I tippt our Landlady with what I imagined a full Reward for the Trouble we had given her." "I assure you," said a writer in 1755, "I have laid out every farthing . . . in tips to his servants." One authority suggests that *tip* in the sense of a present and *dibbs* in the sense of money may both owe their origin to *diodol,* a Greek coin of small value.

Does the United States Government coin mills?

On August 8, 1786, the American Congress passed a law prescribing certain coins. This law contained the following clause: "Mills: the lowest money of accompt, of which 1000 shall be equal to the federal dollar, or money unit." Although the tenth part of a cent—the one-thousandth part of a dollar—has been called a mill ever since, the mill has no existence as a coin in the American monetary system and no coins of that denomination have ever been minted. In many state, county and local political subdivisions taxes are levied in terms of mills. The word is derived from Latin *mille* ("thousand"). The coin of lowest denomination ever issued by the Federal government was the half cent piece, worth five mills. In 1935 Secretary of the Treasury Henry Morgenthau asked Congress to authorize the coinage of one-mill pieces to take the place of one-mill tokens used by states in collecting sales taxes, and a "midget-coin bill" was introduced and considered, but no action was taken on it.

Why does a hen cackle after laying an egg?

This characteristic is supposed to have been inherited from the wild jungle fowls of India and the Malay Peninsula, which scientists believe were the progenitors of our domestic chickens. These birds cross readily with common barnyard chickens and the crow of the cocks resembles that of a young Leghorn rooster. Many eggs sold in parts of India are laid by tamed or domesticated jungle fowls. In their wild state they usually run in small flocks of six or eight—one cock and several hens. When a hen is ready to lay she steals away from the flock, lays her egg in a concealed nest and then cackles to attract the attention of her mates that have wandered away in the meantime. In response the cocks in the neighborhood begin to cackle and the lost hen recognizes her flock by the voice of its leader. This cackling characteristic has never been bred out of our domesticated fowls. Even in their present state of domestication it is not uncommon for the roosters in the barnyard to set up a clamor when a hen begins to cackle. This seems to be the most satisfactory explanation as to why a hen violates a fundamental principle of safety by advertising the fact that she has just laid an egg.

What is a Jim Crow law?

That is the name given to any law requiring the segregation of white people and Negroes in public conveyances, schools, theaters, hotels, restaurants, etc. Such separation of persons of "color" or "African descent" from the whites is required by law in most southern states. Railway or streetcars divided into sections for whites and Negroes are known as Jim Crow cars. *Jim Crow* was formerly used as a general nickname for any colored man. It was popularized in that sense by Thomas Dartmouth Rice (1808–1861), a comedian known as "the father of American minstrelsy." He employed it in a song that he introduced in *The Rifle*, a play written by Solon Robinson. This skit, produced in Washington in 1835 and in London the following year, is sometimes referred to as the first "Negro minstrel." Rice, it is said, picked up the essential part of the song, along with a peculiar limping dance, by accident in 1828 from an old Negro in Louisville, Kentucky, whom he heard singing, *Wheel about, turn about, do jist so, an' ebery time I wheel about I jump Jim Crow.* As sung by Rice the chorus ran:

> *First on de heel tap, den on de toe,*
> *Ebery time I wheel about I jump Jim Crow.*
> *Wheel about and turn and do jis so,*
> *And ebery time I wheel about I jump Jim Crow.*

It was perfectly natural that the black man should have been compared to the common and picturesque black bird known as the crow and the comparison was probably made originally in fun by the colored people themselves. In 1839 an antislavery book entitled *The History of Jim Crow* was published in London. The *Negro Year Book* for 1925–1926 published the following comment on this subject: "The origin of the expression *Jim Crow* appears to have arisen thus: In Charleston, South Carolina, in the early part of the nineteenth century there was a hotel keeper who had two slaves, both of whom were named James. In order not to have both respond when he called, he instructed one to answer only to Jim; as a further designation the boarders, because he was very black, added Crow. Jim Crow appears to have led an eventful life. He was born in Richmond about 1800, and was sold first to Charleston, then to New Orleans, and later was emancipated. He lived some time in

[244]

London, where he acquired quite a fortune." *Jim Crow* was applied specifically to "segregation railway coaches" already before the Civil War.

What does "dining with Duke Humphrey" mean?

To dine with Duke Humphrey means to go without one's dinner. Some authorities say the expression had its origin in the false report that Humphrey Plantagenet (1391–1447), Duke of Gloucester and the youngest son of Henry IV (Bolingbroke of Shakespeare's plays), was starved to death in prison. Although there was a rumor at the time that the "good Duke" met his death by foul play, it is not likely that there was any report that he was starved to death, inasmuch as he died only four days after his arrest and incarceration. The following is the more probable derivation of the phrase: Duke Humphrey was buried in St. Albans Abbey in a tomb that still exists. But it was popularly believed that he was buried in St. Paul's Cathedral. A near-by aisle, which was much frequented by tramps and beggars, was called "Duke Humphrey's Walk." Hence *to dine with Duke Humphrey* was originally applied to those who loitered dinnerless in that vicinity. There is a curious allusion to Duke Humphrey in Shakespeare's *Richard III*. When the Duchess of York, the mother of King Richard asks,

> What comfortable hour canst thou name
> That ever grac'd me in thy company?

the king replies,

> Faith, none, but Humphrey Hour, that called your Grace
> To breakfast once forth of my company.

Humphrey Hour is an obscure allusion that has never been satisfactorily explained, but the phrase is supposed to have the same source as *dine with Duke Humphrey*.

Which is correct, "harebrained" or "hairbrained"?

The original and correct form of this compound word is *harebrained*. It means "flighty," "skittish" or "reckless" and refers to the characteristics of a hare. A wild, rash, heedless, foolish, volatile or giddy person is said to be harebrained because he has or shows no more brains or sense than a hare or rabbit. The word is sometimes incorrectly written *hairbrained*, even by reputable writers, and that spelling, which began to occur before 1600, has misled many into seeking a different origin of the term: namely, that it compares the brain of the person so described to a hair, just as *pinheaded* compares the head of the person so described to the head of a pin. In Shakespeare's *I Henry IV* young Henry Percy is referred to as "A hare-brain'd Hotspur, govern'd by a spleen"; and in *I Henry VI* the English in France are described as "hare-brain'd slaves." *Hare-hearts* occurs in *Troilus and Cressida* in the sense of timidity and cowardice.

How did "not worth a rap" originate?

Often when we wish to say a thing is useless or valueless we say it is *not worth a rap*. One would naturally suppose that *rap* in the phrase refers simply to a sharp, quick blow on something with the knuckles. Etymologists, however, are of the opinion that *rap* in this connection originally referred to a small copper coin first widely used in Ireland during the reign of George I (1714–1727). Its intrinsic value was only about half a farthing, but it passed for a halfpenny. In 1755 Jonathan Swift wrote: "Copper halfpence or farthings have been for some time very scarce, and many counterfeits passed about under the name of raps." It has been suggested that possibly *rap* as applied to this coin was derived from the German *rappe*, which was originally the name of a counterfeit copper coin used on the Continent in the fourteenth century, and that it was brought to the British Isles by Irish soldiers of fortune; but there is no evidence to establish a connection between the two words. There is an interesting theory that *rap* as applied to money originated from the letters forming the initials of the names of Indian money units in English account books. In Indian accounts in London the letters r.a.p., meaning "rupees," "annas" and "pice," were used in the same manner as *l.s.d.* for "pounds," "shillings" and "pence."

Why does speed affect the mileage from gasoline?

Americans did not become generally conscious of the effect of speed upon the mileage obtained from gasoline until after the introduction of rationing during the Second World War. Other things being equal, more mileage is obtained from a gallon of gasoline when the automobile is driven at a moderate speed than when it is driven at high speed. Accordingly the motorist who speeds up to reach a filling station before his gasoline supply gives out is generally fooling himself. Experts have determined that in a general way the most efficient and economical speed of a car is about twenty-five miles an hour. The following statement concerning the relation between fuel economy and automobiles was prepared for the author by the United States Bureau of Standards: "More force is required to propel a car at high speed than at low speed, chiefly because wind resistance increases approximately as the square of the speed. The mileage from a gallon of gasoline will be better at low speeds, therefore, if the fuel-air ratio furnished at both speeds is the same. If, as frequently happens, the mixture furnished by the carburetor is different for different speeds, the actual mileage obtained in service may increase or decrease with speed, depending upon the carburetor characteristics." But in determining the most economical speed for a car the wear and tear on a car traveling at high speeds is also taken into consideration. Other types of gasoline-driven vehicles, as well as airplanes, also have their fuel-saving gait.

What is an "act of God"?

In legal phraseology an *act of God* is an overwhelming natural event, such as a storm or an earthquake, which no human being could be reasonably expected to foresee or prevent. Such events are attributed to God as the author of the laws of nature and therefore are considered beyond the control of man. According to the English common law, no person is responsible for a loss or injury when it is caused by "the act of God or the enemies of the state." In civil law if a person is sued for a breach of contract and can prove his nonperformance was owing to an *act of God*, he has a good defense. "Let each man think himself an act of God," wrote the English poet Philip J. Bailey in *Festus* (1839).

Why is a good fellow called "a brick"?

Brick is frequently applied to a likable, dependable person, a "regular sport," or one who is "all right." To call another a *brick* is one of the highest compliments that can be paid him. In 1861 *Vanity Fair* said "Lincoln is a brick." Apparently *brick* in this slang or colloquial sense is of comparatively modern origin. The earliest use of it recorded by the Oxford dictionary is dated 1840, where it occurs in the phrase "regular brick." Richard Harris Barham (1788–1845) wrote in the *Ingoldsby Legends* (1840):

> In brief, I don't stick to declare Father Dick—
> So they call'd him, "for short"—was a "Regular Brick,"
> A metaphor taken—I have not the page aright—
> Out of an ethical work by the Stagirite.

The reference is to Aristotle's *Nicomachean Ethics*, where the Stagirite (native of Stagira in Macedon) defines a happy man as "a faultless cube." *Regular brick* was suggested by the fact that a brick is plain, solid and foursquare. Popular etymologists are fond of deriving *brick* in this sense from the following classical incident: Lycurgus, the Spartan king and lawgiver, who lived about 800 B.C., believed that a wall around a city was unnecessary if the soldiers were properly trained and commanded. An ambassador from another state once asked Lycurgus why he had no walls around Sparta. "But we have walls," replied the Spartan monarch, "and if you will come with me I will show them to you." He led his guest to the field where the army was marshalled in battle array, and pointing to the ranks of men, he said: "There are the walls of Sparta, and every man is a brick." A similar story is told of Egesilaus II, who was king of Sparta from about 398 to 360 B.C. This story seems to be merely an elaboration of an incident related by Plutarch in his life of Lycurgus. Plutarch says there was a tradition that the Spartan lawgiver was once asked whether it was wise to inclose a city with walls. Lycurgus wrote a letter in reply, saying: "The city is well fortified which hath a wall of men instead of brick." It is very improbable that our slang word *brick* was suggested by or had any connection with the classical incident.

Does a snake's tail wiggle until sunset?

There is an old and persistent belief that the tail of a recently killed snake continues to live until sundown. In reptiles the spinal cord is more important than it is in higher animals; it influences the motions of the body more than the brain does. Even in higher animals all vital functions do not cease immediately when the heart stops or the brain is suddenly removed. The muscular system does not instantly lose its power of reacting to stimuli. Experiments have shown that the hind legs of a frog will "show signs of life" after they have been separated from the body. The heart of a snake has been known to continue to beat twenty-four hours after the head was severed from the body and the snake was "dead" according to the ordinary definition of the term. Owing to the reflex action of the snake's nervous system its tail often continues to wiggle long after the snake is otherwise apparently dead. But there is nothing to the notion that the tail continues to wiggle until sunset and then stops. The belief probably arose from the fact that the movements of the tail of a recently killed snake could no longer be observed after the fall of darkness. Contrary to a popular notion, snakes are not particularly hard to kill. A single sharp blow behind the head with a stick will generally dispatch even large snakes.

What state is nearest the North Pole?

The northern part of Lake of the Woods County in Minnesota is farther north than any place in any other state in the Union. This part of the United States proper cannot be reached by land without passing

[248]

over Canadian territory. This projection of United States territory into the Lake of the Woods, often referred to as "Northern Peninsula," contains an area of nearly 124 square miles. Formerly the Northern Peninsula was part of Beltrami County, Minnesota, but in 1922 it was formed into Lake of the Woods County. The treaty of 1783 between Great Britain and the United States, which terminated the American Revolution, left the boundary between the two countries west of the Lake of the Woods unsettled. In the Treaty of Ghent (1815), which terminated the War of 1812, it was agreed that the Canadian-American boundary from the Lake of the Woods westward should follow the 49th parallel and should be a straight line as that term is used in surveying. But when the actual surveys were made under these and later treaties the surveyors used inaccurate maps, with the odd result that the United States claimed the Northern Peninsula, all of which lies considerably north of the 49th parallel. It was not until 1877 that the question was finally settled in favor of the United States. This territory, which includes several small mountains, has been described as "a politico-geographical curiosity of a boundary that a glance at the map will show, that no one could have foreseen, and that would be inexplicable without some knowledge of the steps in the process by which it was brought about." Penasse, the seat of Lake of the Woods County, is the northernmost town in the United States proper. Point Pelee (near Leamington, Ontario), which projects ten miles into Lake Erie, is the southernmost point in the Dominion of Canada.

What is a jingo?

A jingo is a rabid patriot who favors a spirited and aggressive foreign policy for his country. Jingoism is to Britain what chauvinism is to France and spread-eagleism is to the United States. Originally by jingo was employed merely as a mild oath. When Motteux translated the works of Rabelais in 1694 he rendered the French phrase par dieu ("by God") with by jingo. In The Vicar of Wakefield (1766) Oliver Goldsmith writes: "By the living jingo, she was all of a muck and sweat." The Oxford dictionary supposes by jingo to have been originally "a piece of conjurer's gibberish." Richard Harris Barham, author of the Ingoldsby Legends (1840), suggested, facetiously perhaps, that the mild oath is a corruption of St. Gengulphus. Some derive jingo from Basque Jainko ("god"), and suppose it to have been introduced into England by Basque sailors. Perhaps as a common oath jingo, like golly and gosh, was no more than an euphemism for God, Jove or Jupiter. Jingo was not applied to superpatriots itching for war upon the slightest provocation until the time of the Russo-Turkish War of 1877–1878. There was much excitement in

England just before the British Mediterranean squadron was sent to Gallipoli to frustrate Russia's designs on Constantinople. It was at this time that a popular London music hall singer known as "the great Mac-Dermott" produced a war song written by a song writer named G. W. Hunt. The first lines and the chorus were:

> We don't want to fight, but by jingo if we do,
> We've got the ships, we've got the men,
>   we've got the money too.
> We've fought the Bear before and while we're Britons
> The Russians shall not have Constantinople.

This refrain instantly caught the fancy of London. The war party, the Russophobes, who urged Prime Minister Disraeli to side with the Turks against the Russians, became known as jingoes. Since then the term has been extended to rabid patriots in general.

What does "Hobson's choice" mean?

Hobson's choice means a choice without an alternative, "this or nothing," no choice at all. When we are driven to a single course of action we say we are reduced to Hobson's choice. The phrase is believed to have originated with the practice of Thomas (or Tobias) Hobson (1544–1631), a carrier and innkeeper at Cambridge, England, in the time of James I and Charles I. In No. 509 of the Spectator (1712) Richard Steele (some suppose Joseph Addison) wrote: "Tobias Hobson . . . was the first man in England that let out hackney horses. When a man came for a horse he was led into the stable, where there was a great choice, but he obliged him to take the horse which stood next to the stable-door; so that every customer was alike well served according to his chance,—from whence it became a proverb when what ought to be your election was forced upon you, to say Hobson's choice." Apparently the saying was proverbial before Hobson's death. In Thomas Ward's England's Reformation (1630?) occurs this couplet:

> Where to elect there is but one,
> 'Tis Hobson's Choice; take that or none.

It is said that Hobson kept a stable of forty horses for service between Cambridge and London. One old writer says of him that he "raised himself to considerable estate, and did much good in the town, relieving the poor, building a public conduit in the market-place, etc." The Cambridge liveryman and stage-coach operator was very popular with the professors and students at the university. John Milton, then an undergraduate at Christ's College, wrote two humorous epitaphs in verse on Thomas Hobson. These verses are unique in being the only extant specimens of Milton's humor.

When is the rope more likely to break?

This question is often asked: "If ten men of equal strength pull at each end of a rope, is the rope more likely to break than it would if one end were tied to a tree and ten men were to pull at the other?" The answer is in the negative. The tension of a rope is no greater than the pull at one of its ends. Thus if twenty men take hold of a rope, ten at each end, and pull with all their might, the stress on the rope will be no greater than if ten men pulled from one end and the other end were tied to a tree. The ten men on one end of the rope merely take the place of the tree and no part of the rope is subject to a greater tension than that exerted by the ten men pulling at one end of it. This question frequently arises in many different forms and the principle involved is of considerable importance in mechanics. Manufacturers of ropes and cables sometimes demonstrate the strength of their product by having a tractor hitched to each end of a piece of rope or cable and setting the machines in motion in opposite directions. This looks very impressive to the uninitiated. The fact is, however, owing to the principle referred to, the rope or cable would be no more likely to break—the tension would be no greater—than if one end were tied to a tree or some other solid object and only one tractor used. It is said that sixteen horses—eight back to back—were unable to pull apart the famous Magdeburg hemispheres that Otto von Guericke demonstrated at the Regensburg Diet in 1654 before the King of Prussia. Exactly the same force would have been exerted to separate the hemispheres with eight horses of like strength pulling in the same direction on one hemisphere if the other had been attached to some solid support. Very likely Otto von Guericke knew this, but was showman enough to use sixteen horses—eight pulling back to back—to make the demonstration more striking.

What were the ninety-day ships?

Certain merchant vessels constructed during the First World War were known as *ninety-day ships*. Records show that 220 merchant ships were launched during that war within ninety days after the keels were laid. A ship is generally launched when it is from 60 to 80 per cent completed. In the years 1917, 1918 and 1919 the United States built a total of 1,299 ships of all categories. Two hundred and forty-four days were required to construct the first "Liberty ship." Later, however, 23 were constructed and delivered within 90 days from the laying of the keels; two within 27 days, and one within 37 days. The keel of the 12,000-ton S.S. "Invincible" was laid in Alameda, California, on July 4, 1918, and the ship was launched August 4 of the same year. The S.S. "Tuckahoe," a 5,500-ton, 320-foot collier built by the New York Shipbuilding Corporation at Camden, New Jersey, was sent to sea in 1918 with a full cargo on the fortieth day after the laying of the keel. Owing to prefabrication and improved methods of mass production, these First World War records were broken early during the Second World War. In 1942 one of Henry J. Kaiser's shipyards constructed a 10,500-ton Liberty ship in four days and fifteen and one-half hours and delivered it for service four days later, and in the same year another of Kaiser's shipyards launched a tank landing craft within three days after the keel laying. By October, 1942, the average time from keel laying to delivery of Liberty ships had been reduced to sixty-six days. In the days of simple wooden ships both merchant and war vessels were often built in a month or two. During the Civil War, James Buchanan Eads launched eight armor-plated gunboats on the Mississippi within one hundred days after the keels were laid.

How did "Jugoslavia" originate?

Jugoslavia literally means "South Slavia" or "the country of the southern Slavs." This term was not used much previously to the First World War, but Jugo-Slav—"Southern Slav"—was. The term distinguished the Slavic peoples in the Austrian-Hungarian empire and neighboring parts of southern Europe from the Poles, Czechs, Slovaks, Russians and other Slavs to the north and the west. For generations before that time there had been agitation for a "Greater Serbia" and autonomy of the southern Slavs. On November 13, 1918, representatives of the people of Serbia, Montenegro, Bosnia, Herzegovina, Dalmatia, Croatia and Slovenia proclaimed the Triune Kingdom of the Serbs, Croats and Slovenes. The formation of the new triple kingdom of southern Slavs became effective December 29 of the same year. However, it was popularly and officially called simply Jugoslavia until a constitution was adopted in 1921, when The Kingdom of the Serbs, Croats and Slovenes was declared to be the official name. In 1929, as part of his program to destroy the identities of the different peoples and to forge the country into a unified nation, King Alexander by royal decree changed the name to The Kingdom of Jugoslavia. Jugoslavia is the Jugoslavian form; in English it is spelled either Jugoslavia or Yugoslavia. You are in good company no matter which way you spell it. But regardless of spelling, it

[252]

is pronounced yoo-go-slaw-vee-a. On November 2, 1921, the United States Geographic Board, whose rulings are observed by the Federal government as the standard authority, ruled that Yugoslavia, not Jugoslavia, should be used as the proper name of the country, while on December 5, 1925, the same agency ruled that the adjectival spelling should be Yugoslav, not Yugoslavic. These rulings are still observed by the various departments of the United States Government when referring to the country in official documents.

What is "petrified lightning"?

Petrified lightning is a popular name for fulgurite (Latin fulgur, lightning), which consists of siliceous tubes formed vertically in loose sand by the passage of lightning. When lightning strikes sand a temperature of several thousand degrees Fahrenheit is created and the particles along the central part of the path are volatilized, driven out and fused into a tube with the interior surface glossy and smooth as glass. Such tubes extending to a depth of thirty feet or more have been found, and occasionally they are three or four inches in circumference, although generally they are smaller. As a rule the thickness of the walls is not more than one-thirtieth or one-twentieth of an inch. Sand hills unprotected by vegetation are constantly shifting and not infrequently petrified lightning tubes are left projecting several feet above the surface. Sometimes the tubes are branched and a large number of them together creates the weird effect of a glass forest. Fulgurites are also occasionally produced by lightning running through a wire or cable buried in sand. Tubes resembling natural fulgurites have been produced in the laboratory by discharging electricity of high voltage through powdered glass or sand of the proper composition.

Why is winter colder than summer?

It is a common fallacy to suppose that it is colder in winter because the sun is then farther from the earth. Distance of the sun from the earth has no bearing upon winter and summer. As a matter of fact the sun is more than three million miles closer to the earth in January than it is in July. It is very difficult for many people to appreciate the fact that the sun is farthest from the earth in summer and closest in winter. In astronomy the point of nearest approach of a body to the sun is called "perihelion," and the earth is at perihelion about January 3. Likewise the earth is farthest from the sun about July 4. The seasons—spring, summer, fall and winter—occur because of the inclination of the earth's axis while the earth moves around the sun; that is, the seasons are produced mainly by the relative position of the earth's axis in respect to the sun. The chief reason for the difference in temperature between summer and winter is the angle at which the rays of the sun strike the earth, coupled with the longer duration of daylight in summer. The imaginary line from pole to pole that is known as the axis and around which the earth rotates is slightly "tilted." As the earth moves in its annual orbit the Northern Hemisphere is tilted toward the sun half the year and away from it the other half. It is summer in the Northern Hemisphere when that part of the earth is tilted toward the sun. The sun, while actually farther away then, is more directly overhead. It is winter in the Northern Hemisphere when that part of the earth is tilted away from the sun. Then the sun, while actually closer to the earth, is lower in the sky and its rays strike the earth at a much greater slant than they do in summer. This means that the rays of the sun must pass through a greater distance of atmosphere in the winter. In the Southern Hemisphere the seasons are reversed. It is winter there while it is summer in the Northern Hemisphere, because the Southern Hemisphere is inclined away from the sun while the Northern Hemisphere is inclined toward it. There would be no seasons if the earth's axis were perpendicular to the plane of its orbit. Perpetual summer would exist on a belt near the Equator, while perpetual winter would exist on the parts nearer the poles. In the Northern Hemisphere the maximum heat is radiated from the sun when that body's declination is 12 degrees north, or about August 20, while the minimum heat is radiated when the sun is 12 degrees south, or about February 10. Generally speaking, the warmest part of the day is about 2:00 P.M., and the coldest part of the night shortly before sunrise. The actual temperature at any given place, however, is modified by bodies of water, clouds, mountains and other local factors.

How do fish swim up waterfalls?

Most fish do not readily ascend waterfalls and other obstructions in streams, although such fish as salmon, alewives and a few species of trout will ascend waterfalls of considerable height. The distance that a salmon can leap straight upward has often been exaggerated by popular writers. In Astoria (1836) Washington Irving wrote that a Mr. Miller "declared that he had seen a salmon leap a distance of about thirty feet, from the commencement of the foam at the foot of the fall (Salmon Falls in Idaho), completely to the top." Salmon have been known to make vertical leaps of five or six feet in going up falls. They usually ascend only waterfalls that have pockets or back eddies and leap from one to another, or force their way through the swift current. In attempting to ascend an absolutely perpendicular fall a salmon will leap at the fall at a decided angle. If the fall is not too high the fish can often hit the falling water part way up and reach the top by swimming energetically. Experts doubt whether any salmon is able to ascend a fifteen-foot fall all the way from the bottom. If the water at the bottom of such a fall is deep enough to give the salmon a good start it may succeed in reaching the top. *Salmon* is derived from Latin *salmo*, which in turn is supposed to be derived from *salire* ("to leap"). Alewives, trout and a few other fish will pass up waterfalls or low obstructions if an efficient ladder or fishway is provided. Shad and many other species will not pass up any form of fishway so far devised. A fall of any size, therefore, is a barrier to their farther progress up a stream. No species of fish is known to be able to swim up a high, steep waterfall. The popular notion that fish swim up the falls at Niagara is erroneous.

What are "shooting stars"?

Shooting or *falling* stars are not stars at all, but meteorites, which are comparatively small masses of rock or iron flying about in space. The popular names of this phenomenon date back to times when people thought they were actually "little stars" that "shot from their fixed places," as Shakespeare expressed it in *The Rape of Lucrece*. In *Richard II* Salisbury muses,

> Ah, Richard, with the eyes of heavy mind
> I see thy glory like a shooting star
> Fall to the base earth from the firmament.

Some authorities regard so-called shooting stars as tiny fragments of disintegrating comets; others think they are "cosmic junk" left over when the great planets were formed. According to the most usual scientific explanation, meteorites are visible only when they come into contact with the upper atmosphere of the earth. The streak of light, it is supposed, is due to the enormous heat generated by friction. Usually the meteorite is heated red-hot, bursts into flame and is reduced to dust before it reaches the ground. Some scientists, however, think this explanation is inadequate. They believe that at least part of the light is due to electricity developed by the friction between the meteorite and the highly electrified upper atmosphere. What the observer really sees is only the air atoms that have been heated to the intensity of light along the path traveled by the meteorite. The light produced by one of these molten masses is also sometimes called a *fireball*. Apparently when seen they are traveling at the rate of about thirty miles a second at a distance of from forty to eighty miles from the earth. The heat generated by friction with the upper atmosphere generally completely vaporizes them, although it has not been proved that all meteorites are actually hot when they reach the ground. So-called falling stars are seldom larger than grains of sand. Sizes as large as a rifle bullet are uncommon, although meteorites weighing from forty to fifty tons have been found, and there are evidences that meteorites of enormous size have fallen on the earth. Scientifically they are known as *meteoroids* before they fall, as *meteors* while they are falling, and as *meteorites* after landing. Volume for volume meteorites are much heavier than rock. Many of them consist of iron and nickel, in some cases more than 90 per cent of iron. Although meteorites contain peculiar mineral combinations not duplicated in rocks normally found on the earth, no element has been found in a meteorite that has not already been known. It is estimated that 6,000,-000,000,000 tons of meteorites have fallen on the earth in the last sixty million years and that the weight of the earth is increased about 100,000 tons every year as the result of meteoric material, chiefly dust, that falls from the sky. For centuries even scientists refused to believe that meteorites actually came from outer space. In 1807, when Dr. Benjamin Silliman of Yale University stated that he had proved that meteorites fall from the sky, President Thomas Jefferson is reputed to have said: "Gentlemen, I would rather believe that a Yankee professor would lie than to believe that stones fall from heaven."

Do bananas ever produce seeds?

Originally all varieties of the banana produced seeds. Owing to thousands of years of cultivation, however, the seeds have almost completely disappeared from those varieties grown especially for the fruit. Occasionally edible bananas contain a few rudimentary seeds, but they will not grow. The banana and plantain family contains more than sixty species and some of them produce seeds and are propagated by planting the seeds. Varieties that are grown especially for the fiber or for ornamental purposes usually produce seeds and they are reproduced by planting the seeds because that is more economical than other methods of propagation. Such bananas, however, have no commercial importance because of their fruit. Edible bananas are propagated by means of sprouts, suckers or bits of the rootstalk containing buds or "eyes." The banana plant, which is a perennial, dies at the end of each season and is regenerated by sprouts or shoots from the old rootstalk. Suckers may be cut from the parent plant and transplanted. The current method of propagating banana plants is to cut the old rootstalk into wedge-shaped pieces that contain one or more eyes and planting them. These seed bits, according to banana growers, are preferable to suckers unless care is taken to use only the extra vigorous sword suckers.

How high are the highest waves?

Ocean waves are very deceptive in respect to both height and width and seafaring people generally have an exaggerated idea of the size of the towering waves that break over their vessels during storms. Frequently waves having heights of several hundred feet are reported. It is unusual for a wave to attain a height of more than 60 or 70 feet from trough to crest. Waves estimated to have heights of 110 and 112 feet were observed from the U.S.S. "Ramapo" in the North Pacific in February, 1933. The highest wave of which the United States Navy Department had any reliable previous report was encountered in the North Atlantic on December 22, 1922, by the British S.S. "Majestic." Its height was estimated at 80 feet. So far attempts to measure ocean waves during violent storms have been unsatisfactory owing to the difficulty of making the measurements. The width of a wave—the distance from the bottom of one trough to the bottom of the next, is estimated roughly to be fifteen times its height. Thus a wave 50 feet high would have a base 750 feet wide, and one 100 feet high would have a base 1,500 feet wide. Most of the ocean waves described as being "mountain-high" are really only 30 or 40 feet in height.

Which is heavier, milk or cream?

Milk is heavier than cream. Cream in milk rises to the surface because it is composed of infinitesimal drops of oil and fat that are lighter than water and the rest of the components of milk. It is the same principle that makes oil float on the surface of water. The rising of cream is not at first apparent because the droplets are very small and they come to the surface slowly.

How big was the largest whale ever caught?

So far as known, the largest animals that inhabit the earth or ever have inhabited it are whales. They are mammals and bring forth perfectly formed living young, which are nursed by the mother like land mammals. Some authorities believe that whales are descended from land mammals that took to the sea countless ages ago. Whales, however, are not so large as they are popularly supposed to be, nor as they appear to be on first sight. The blue, or sulphur-bottom, whale is the largest species. The adults of this species have an estimated average length of 75 feet.

A report of the American Museum of Natural History states that the blue whale reaches a length of 103 feet. One of these whales taken off South Georgia in the Pacific was reported to have been 107 feet long, while one killed off Discovery Inlet near the Bay of Whales was reported to have had a length of 125 feet. In 1926 Sir James Clark Ross reported catching blue whales measuring from 90 to 99 feet in length. A whale reputed to have been 87 feet long was stranded some years ago on the New Zealand coast. These reports, however, are not entirely dependable. There is what appears to be an authentic record of a blue whale having a length of 95 feet and an estimated weight of 147 tons—294,000 pounds. This specimen, which was captured off the west coast of North America, is regarded as the largest whale—and probably the largest animal—of which there is authentic record. Experts say that as a general rule ordinary adult whales weigh about one ton to each foot of length. About 30 per cent of the body weight consists of blubber—fat and oil— which is the "overcoat" that keeps the huge warm-blooded creature warm in its cold element. Blue whale calves are sometimes 20 feet in length at birth and weigh 5,000 pounds. Whales are among the fastest growing of all mammals and the large whales probably do not have a natural life span of more than thirty or forty years. They generally reach nearly their maximum length and weight by the end of the second or third year. A young blue whale puts on weight at the rate of 200 or 300 pounds a day.

How is the number of thread determined?

Sewing thread is numbered according to the size of the single strands or cords that compose the thread. A single strand 840 yards in length is taken as the unit. The number is computed from the number of such hanks in one pound of the thread. For instance, suppose a pound of thread contains one hank of 840 yards. It is No. 1 thread. If it contains 60 hanks, it is No. 60, and so on. Thus the number increases as the size decreases. Early cotton sewing thread was composed of three strands of No. 30 single yarn; No. 40 was composed of three strands of No. 40 single yarn, and so on. The introduction of domestic sewing machines made it necessary to develop a smoother and stronger thread than was possible with three strands. Therefore, in 1862, a six-cord thread was produced. This was the original O. N. T. sewing thread. Since the size and number of thread was well established it was found advisable to make the new six-cord thread the same size in diameter as the prevailing size of the three-cord thread. For that reason No. 30 six-strand was composed of six strands of No. 60 single thread, which makes the diam-

eter of No. 30 the same as the original No. 30 thread of three strands.
O. N. T. was first used in connection with six-cord thread and was not
applied to three-cord threads until many years afterwards, and then to
threads produced only for manufacturing purposes.

Does thunder kill chicks in the shell?

Many people are of the opinion that thunder frequently affects the
hatchability of eggs. Poultry experts assert that there are many instances
on record that apparently support the common belief that thunder
sometimes kills chicks in the shell. If such a phenomenon exists it has
not been adequately explained by either physical or biological science.
The United States Bureau of Standards stated a few years ago that
there is no apparent reason why thunder should prevent fertile and
properly incubated eggs from hatching. Although the shock resulting
from a peal of thunder is sufficient to produce a perceptible jar in buildings, the Bureau of Standards expressed the opinion that such a shock
would not be capable of affecting the hatchability of incubating eggs.
The same applies to loud blasting. The jar produced by thunder is
similar in character to the shock produced by blasting, except in the
latter case it is transmitted through both the air and the ground. Of
course a different problem is presented in cases where lightning actually
strikes in the vicinity of eggs that are being incubated. Both the terrific
shock and the lightning itself would probably have an unfavorable effect
upon the eggs.

How many kinds of meat does the turtle contain?

According to an old saying, the turtle is composed of seven different
kinds of meat. It is merely another way of saying that the flesh of the
turtle is tender, palatable and wholesome, or that it has the good
qualities of chicken, venison, beef, pork, mutton and other meats.
Probably no two epicures would agree on just what seven varieties of
meat the turtle is supposed to resemble. The number seven has no
special significance in this connection. The green fat of the turtle is
particularly celebrated for its deliciousness. Among Chinese there is a
common belief that a person can acquire the longevity of the turtle by
eating its flesh. It was reported in 1939 that Chinese bought 80 per
cent of all the turtles sold at the Fulton Fish Market in New York City.
Turtle soup has been deemed a dainty dish by epicures for centuries.
A French officer named Blanchard described in his journal a "turtle
party" given at Newport in 1780 during the American Revolution. He
related that this form of entertainment—"a sort of picnic given by a score

of men to a company of ladies"—had "great vogue" in America. "The purpose of this party," he explained, "was to eat a turtle, weighing three or four hundred pounds, which an American vessel had just brought home from one of our islands in the West Indies. This meat did not seem to me very palatable; it is true that it was badly cooked."

Why is a pawnbroker referred to as "my uncle's"?

Authorities differ as to the origin of *uncle's* as applied to pawnbrokers. One theory is that *uncle* in this slang sense is a pun on the Latin *uncus*, "hook." Before spouts or shoots were adopted, pawnbrokers used hooks to lift articles pawned. *Gone to the uncus*, according to this theory, was corrupted into *gone to my uncle's*, the pronoun *my* being supplied for the sake of euphony. This theory is slightly confirmed by the fact that a pawnbroker's shop is also sometimes called a *spout*. But there seems to be a more plausible theory. Many people are sensitive about their financial shortages and try to conceal the fact they have pawned their possessions to obtain funds. It was only natural for such persons to pretend the money thus obtained was from a rich uncle. Joaquin Miller wrote: "My money is out, my watch at my Uncle Rothschild's, and I have nothing to pay with."

What is the rule of thumb?

Originally *by rule of thumb* literally meant measuring with the thumb. Centuries ago clothiers and carpenters regarded a thumb or a thumb's breadth as equal to one inch. Brewers determined the heat of liquor in brewing, to regulate the fermentation, by dipping the thumb into the vat and ale and beer brewed in this manner was called "thumb-brewed." By extension *rule of thumb* is used figuratively for any simple and roughly practical method of measurement based on practice and experience rather than scientific knowledge or exact formula. The term was so used already in the seventeenth century. In 1692 a man named Hope, writing on fencing, said: "What he doth, he doth by rule of Thumb, and not by Art." There is a Scottish proverb: "No rule so good as rule of thumb, if it hit."

What does the Lion of Lucerne commemorate?

The Lion of Lucerne is a sculptured lion hewn from living sandstone in a niche on a sequestered hillside near Lucerne, Switzerland. It was cut by a Swiss artist named Ahorn from a model made by the Danish sculptor Albert Bertel Thorwaldsen (1770–1844). The statue was dedicated in 1821 and is a memorial commemorating the tragic fate of the twenty-six officers and seven hundred and sixty privates of the Swiss Guard who sacrificed their lives in defense of Louis XVI and Marie Antoinette after the French guards had deserted during the attack of a mob on the Tuileries in Paris August 19, 1792. The colossal stone lion, twenty-one feet long and eighteen feet high, is represented as being transfixed with a broken spear; and, although dying, it is still trying to protect with its paw a shield bearing the lilies of France. The base of the statue contains the following Latin inscription: *Helvetiorum fidei ac virtuti* ("To the faithfulness and virtue of the Swiss"). In the rock below are carved the names of the Swiss officers.

Which is sweeter, cane or beet sugar?

Contrary to a popular belief, pure cane sugar and pure beet sugar do not differ in sweetness. Completely refined sugar made from sugar beets and completely refined sugar made from sugar cane are chemically identical and there is no evidence that one is sweeter than the other. The ordinary granulated sugar of commerce, regardless whether it is made from beets or cane, consists essentially of sucrose, the better grades running as high as 99.8 per cent, and contains such extremely small amounts of other substances that it is practically impossible to distinguish beet sugar from cane sugar either chemically or by physical appearance. All raw sugar before it is whitened by refining is yellowish brown in color. Commercial brown sugar is partially refined cane sugar. Because of certain undesirable impurities, beet sugar as presently made is palatable and marketable only after being completely refined. Accordingly there is no brown beet sugar on the market. There are hundreds of different kinds of sugar known to science. Most of them are sweet, but some are bitter. In addition to sucrose, dextrose (grape) and lactose (milk) sugar are widely used as food. Levulose, found in honey, is the sweetest of all common sugars. Corn sugar is the same chemically as cane and beet sugar.

When were the Dark Ages?

Dark Ages as applied to a period of European history is a popular term without specific meaning. Roughly speaking, the Dark Ages were the period from the fall of Romulus Augustulus (476 A.D.), last western Roman emperor, to the revival of learning on the discovery of the Pandects at Amalfi, Italy, in 1150 A.D.—altogether about seven centuries. The Pandects are a vast code of laws collected from Roman writings on jurisprudence, systematically arranged by a commission and enacted into law under Emperor Justinian in 533 A.D. These laws had been virtually lost after Justinian's time and their discovery at Amalfi in Calabria by the Pisans stimulated general study of Roman and Greek literature, which led to what is known as the Classic Age. The period in European history between ancient and modern times is known as the Middle Ages. Different dates for the beginning and end of the period are adopted by different writers. In a general way the Middle Ages extended from the fall of the Western Roman Empire in 476 A.D. to the fall of the eastern Roman Empire in 1453, the year Constantinople was captured by the Turks. The Dark Ages were the first seven centuries of the Middle Ages. *Dark Ages* was suggested by the fact that during this period learning was at its lowest ebb in Europe and civilization seemed to retrograde, owing to the masses of barbarians who emerged from northern Europe and overran the former seats of learning. The term, however, is somewhat misleading. Although a period of general anarchy, many lights of learning continued to burn, much progress was made in many fields of endeavor and Christianity spread and became universal on the Continent.

What are sun dogs?

Sun dogs, technically known as *parhelia*, are mock suns or bright spots near the sun that appear when sunlight shines through a thin cloud composed of ice crystals floating in the atmosphere. They, like numerous other halos, are due to the refraction of the solar rays by these crystals. Sun dogs may appear at all times of the year, because even in the warmest weather the temperature of the upper atmosphere is below freezing.

Why are colleges for teachers called normal schools?

Normal school is a literal translation of French *école normale*. Both the French and English forms of *normal* are derived from Latin *norma*, signifying carpenter's rule, pattern or model. The French called colleges for training teachers normal schools because they were intended to be model schools whose methods of instruction were for imitation in other institutions. The first *école normale* was founded in 1685 at Rheims, France, by Abbe de la Salle, founder of "The Brothers of the Christian Schools," who desired to train teachers for the schools of the order, which were designed to offer free religious primary education to the children of the working classes. Although the name is of French origin, normal schools as they are known today first flourished in Germany, whence they spread to England and the United States. In America the first regular teachers' school was established privately in 1823 at Concord, Vermont, by the Reverend Samuel Reed Hall, who had been a teacher and who accepted the pastorate of the Congressional Church at Concord on condition that he might be permitted to conduct a seminary for training teachers. James G. Carter is sometimes called "the father of normal schools" because he was influential in the passage of the Massachusetts normal school bill in 1838. The first state normal was established at Lexington the following year. The oldest normal in the Mississippi Valley is the State Normal University, founded at Normal, Illinois, in 1857.

What is a human body worth?

It has been estimated that if the chemical elements composing an average human body were isolated and sold at commercial prices they would be worth only about a dollar. Two thirds or more of the body is composed of oxygen and hydrogen in the form of water. The various elements composing the human body occur in the following percentages: Oxygen, 65; carbon, 18; hydrogen, 10; nitrogen, 3; calcium, 1.5; phosphorus, 1; potassium, 0.35; sulphur, 0.25; sodium, 0.15; chlorine, 0.15; magnesium, 0.05; iron, 0.004, and iodine, 0.00004. Besides these thirteen essential elements, the normal body also contains minute quantities of fluorine and silicon, and perhaps manganese, zinc, copper, aluminum and cobalt. Some authorities suppose that arsenic is also an essential constituent of a normal human body. Those who have attempted to evaluate the elements composing an average human body have met with many difficulties and their figures are nothing more than rough estimates.

Will snakes crawl over a hair rope?

There is a popular notion that snakes will not crawl over a rope made of hair. Because of this belief it was formerly a rather common custom for cowboys, shepherds, ranchers, prospectors and explorers in the west, when they slept on the ground in the open, to surround their beds with horsehair or cowhair ropes, confident that no snake would cross the rope to molest them. Experiments with rattlesnakes, as well as harmless snakes, show that no protection whatever against snakes is afforded by encircling camps with hair ropes as such. Repeated tests proved that snakes would crawl over such ropes without hesitation. Rattlesnakes crawled over a hair rope when by going only a few inches farther they could have gone around it. Although the usual explanation of the belief is erroneous, the belief itself may be based upon fact to some extent. There is evidence that most snakes are inclined to give human beings a wide berth and avoid their odor. It is possible that a rattlesnake would be inclined not to crawl over a rope which had been handled and which consequently carried the odor of human beings. If this is the true explanation, a person sleeping in the open could protect himself from the intrusions of snakes by encircling his bed with old clothes just as well as with a hair rope. It would be the human odor rather than the particular material that acted as a snake repellent. Another popular notion is that snakes will not crawl over anything prickly or thorny, such as a Manila hemp rope. This belief has also been disproved by tests. Snakes do not hesitate to crawl over prickly substances and their skins are not injured even by the sharp spines of the cactus.

Which floats easier, a fat or lean person?

A fat person floats more readily in water than a lean person. This is because fat is lighter than muscle and bone, and in proportion to size a fat person is lighter than a lean one.

How did "Simon-pure" originate?

Simon-pure, meaning authentic, genuine or the real McCoy, originated in A Bold Stroke for a Wife, written by Mrs. Susanna Centlivre in 1718. In the play Simon Pure is a "Quaking preacher" from Philadelphia who visits the home of Obadiah Prim, a London hosier, who is a "rigid Quaker" and one of the four guardians of pretty Anne Lovely, heiress of thirty thousand pounds. Colonel Fainwell gains entrance into the Prim home by impersonating Simon Pure, and while thus disguised obtains the guardian's written consent to marry Anne. The Philadelphian then appears on the scene with witnesses to prove that he is the real Simon Pure.

Can blackbirds be white?

Blackbird is the name of a species of bird, just as crow and robin are. Therefore if one of this species happens to be white, and such albinistic freaks do occasionally occur, it is correctly called a white blackbird. Likewise, there may be white redbirds and white bluebirds.

Do elephants shed their tusks?

The projections on an elephant known as tusks are merely elongated incisor teeth in the upper jaw. They are peculiar in that they keep on growing as long as the animal lives. That is why the tusks of an old elephant appear to be about the same length no matter how much they use them. But these teeth are not shed. If they are broken off or extracted they are never replaced. They are preceded, however, by milk teeth, which come out at an early age like those of most other mammals. Good-sized tusks are produced on both sexes of the African species, but they seldom occur on the females of the Asiatic or Indian species. In Ceylon only about one per cent of either sex have any tusks at all. Elephant tusks, which may be white, brown, black or even rose-colored, supply most of the ivory that is so highly esteemed the world over for ornamental purposes.

What creature swallows its own skin?

The common toad molts or sheds its outer skin several times a year. After the skin is sloughed the toad swallows it. This swallowing of the sloughed skin is merely incidental to shedding. Toads are rather clumsy in their actions and movements and apparently they swallow the loose skin in their efforts to free themselves from the encumbrance.

Why do some shoes squeak?

Squeaking in shoes is usually caused by the rubbing together of the different layers of leather composing the soles. Shoes do not squeak if the proper kind of filler is used between the outer and inner sole layers. The squeaking can be removed temporarily by soaking the shoes in water to a depth of about three-quarters of the thickness of the soles. Cobblers take the squeak out of shoes permanently by driving pegs into the soles, or by removing the outer sole and inserting either some kind of powder or a piece of felt between the layers. During the Second World War noisy shoes became fashionable in England. In 1942 the Associated Press quoted Esther Van Wagoner Tufty, Washington correspondent: "The war has made squeaky shoes fashionable in London. A poor grade of leather used is responsible—but it's patriotic."

What is the highest point of land in the New World?

Mount Aconcagua (pronounced aw-kon-kaw-gwa) on the Chile-Argentine border in South America is the highest point of land in the New World. It has an altitude of 22,834 feet above sea level. Mount McKinley in Alaska, with an altitude of 20,300 feet, is not only the highest point of land in North America but is also the highest point in territory under the jurisdiction of the United States. There are at least fifteen mountain peaks in Alaska higher than any in the United States proper, where the highest peak and the lowest point of dry land lie within eighty-six miles of each other in California. Mount Whitney has an altitude of 14,496 feet, while part of Death Valley is 276 feet below sea level. One can see the highest point in the United States proper while standing on the lowest. The second highest mountain in the United States proper is Mount Elbert in Colorado, which has an altitude of 14,420 feet, being only 76 feet lower than Mount Whitney. There are fifty other peaks in Colorado that are 14,000 or more feet high. Mount Everest in Asia, with an altitude of 29,141 feet, is the highest point on earth. The highest peaks on the other continents are as follows: Kibo Peak in British East Africa, 19,710; Mount Elbruz in the Caucasus Mountains of Europe, 18,465; Mount Markham in Antarctica, 15,000, and Mount Kosciusko in Australia, 7,328. Mauna Kea in the Hawaiian Islands, with an altitude of 13,825 feet, is the highest mountain on any island.

Do all whirling winds turn counterclockwise?

All cyclones, tornadoes or twisters, and those waterspouts that originate at cloud level and after the manner of tornadoes, turn counterclockwise in the Northern Hemisphere and clockwise in the Southern. Cyclone is here used in the technical sense of an extensive system of winds blowing around a center of relatively low atmospheric pressure. Waterspouts that originate at the surface, as well as small whirlwinds and dust whirls, which also originate at the surface, turn in either direction, some turning clockwise and some counterclockwise in both hemispheres. We do not have sufficient space here to give an intelligible explanation as to why these air whirls turn as they do. The rotation of the earth, of course, is an important factor, but how it acts, and why it is a determining factor in some cases and only a minor one in others, present highly intricate problems. It has often been stated that when water is released through a small hole, such as the outlet of a bathtub or wash basin, the whirlpool thus formed always turns clockwise south of the equator and counterclockwise north of the equator. That is not true. Such whirlpools may turn in either direction in both hemispheres. The United States Weather Bureau says the phenomenon of whirling water running through a hole is due entirely to conditions that have nothing to do with location in reference to the equator.

What is a diamond "of the first water"?

A diamond of the highest degree of purity and fineness is said to be "of the first water." Color is the most important thing in judging a diamond for gem purposes. Those of the finest quality are perfectly clear. Some varieties of diamonds are green, orange, red, yellow or blue. Of these the most valuable are the ones in which the tint is decided and equal throughout. Even the least tint of a different color in a diamond affects its commercial value unfavorably. The finest gems, of course, can be spoiled by poor cutting. The origin of *water* to denote the degree of limpidity and luster of diamonds and other precious stones is unknown. It may have originally referred merely to the resemblance of the gem to the sparkling of clear water, or to the fact that a clear diamond is invisible in pure water. One authority suggests the term may have originated in a mistake made by the Normans. The Anglo-Saxons, he thinks, may have spoken of a diamond of the finest or purest *hue*, the Anglo-Saxon word for "color" or "hue" being *hiw*. The Normans supposed this word to be their own *ewe*, "water," and used it in that sense. But this is mere speculation. At one time the three highest grades of quality in diamonds were known as the "first" "second" and "third" *water*. But these classifications are no longer used in the diamond trade. Only *diamond of the first water* survives as a designation of "the finest quality." *River* and *extra river* are now used to denote diamonds of the finer qualities. A diamond of the very highest grade is said to be *extra river*. The classification of gems by *waters* is alluded to in Shakespeare. In the opening scene of *Timon of Athens* the Jeweller, looking at a jewel in his hand, says, "Here is a water, look ye."

What was the good news?

The question is often asked, What was the good news referred to in Robert Browning's poem entitled "How They Brought the Good News from Ghent to Aix"? The poet had no particular news or incident in mind when he wrote the poem. On January 23, 1882, Browning published the following letter on the subject in an English newspaper called the *Oracle*: "There is no sort of historical foundation for the poem about "Good News from Ghent to Aix"; I wrote it under the bulwark of a vessel off the African coast, after I had been at sea long enough to appreciate even the fancy of a gallop on the back of a certain good horse York, then in my stable at home. It was written in pencil on the flyleaf of Bartolio's *Simbolid*, I remember."

What is free verse?

Free verse is a literal translation of French *vers libre* and is the name given to a form of poetry written without regular meter or rhyme and generally without regular stanzas. Sir Robert Bridges, poet laureate of England from 1913 to 1930, defined free verse as "cadenced prose arranged in sections resembling stanzas or verses." In *A Dictionary of Modern English Usage* H. W. Fowler defines free verse as, "Versification or verses in which different metres are mingled, or prosodical restrictions disregarded, or variable rhythm substituted for definite metre." It is based on the assumption that true poetry depends on the substance rather than the form, and the free verse writer deliberately discards customary meter and rhyme, attempting to isolate his essential thought and convey it to the reader unhampered by form. Although free verse did not become common in any country until about the time of the First World War, and is popularly associated with Amy Lawrence Lowell, it was not an entirely new form of poetry at that time. Walt Whitman in America and Matthew Arnold in England had written such poetry, and *The Song of Solomon*, whether intentionally or accidentally, meets the essential requirements of free verse. The writer of free verse is an imagist; he claims absolute liberty in choosing his subject matter and attempts to express his ideas and emotions through a unified series of precise images.

Is Great Britain a part of Europe?

Great Britain, although an island, is so close to the continent of Europe that it is generally regarded as being a part of it. Scientists are of the opinion that the British Isles, which are on what is known as the continental shelf, were formerly joined to the mainland and were not separated from it until comparatively recent times, geologically speaking. The rest of the world regards Great Britain as a European nation, although the British people themselves refer to continental Europe as "the Continent" to distinguish it from the British Isles. Europe itself, strictly speaking, is not a continent, but merely part of the continent of Eurasia.

Do monkeys make bridges?

It is often said that monkeys sometimes cross streams by means of monkey *bridges*. According to the popular notion, the monkeys take hold of one another's tails and suspend themselves in a living rope from the limb of a tree on the bank of a river that they wish to cross. They begin to sway back and forth until they gain enough momentum to swing the lower end of the column to a tree on the opposite bank. The other end of the *bridge* is then released and swung across the stream. Naturalists are inclined to doubt these stories. Dr. William T. Hornaday, the noted zoologist, who for thirty years was director of the New York Zoological Park, expressed the opinion that the living monkey bridge is a myth. Still, he said, one should be very cautious in stating what animals never *did* and what they *cannot* do. Monkeys do hang on to one another from time to time and frequently one will climb up the tail of another. One monkey will sometimes even draw another up. Dr. William M. Mann, superintendent of the National Zoological Park, thinks the stories of monkeys making bridges by taking hold of one another may have been suggested by the habits of the spider monkeys of South America. At any rate, these natural acrobats of the forest and jungle are the animals that usually figure in the monkey bridge stories. They are very fond of taking hold of each other and performing all kinds of gymnastics. Their remarkable prehensile tails serve as a "fifth hand." More than one writer has reported cases of the red howling monkeys of Central and South America spanning tree tops by linking hands and tails and forming a living chain.

What do mosquitoes eat where there are no people?

This question is interesting because mosquitoes seem to be always ready to bite human beings and animals and to suck blood from them notwithstanding the fact that in many cases the insects could not possibly have ever tasted such food before. There are at least 1500 known varieties of mosquitoes and there is hardly a place on the earth where they are not found. Entomologists are not yet familiar with the feeding habits of all species. Mosquitoes are common not only in the vast deserts, where they breed and develop rapidly in temporary pools of water, but also in the Arctic regions, where they breed in icy waters from melting snow. In no known species is the male equipped with the piercing mandibles necessary for bloodsucking and it never bites human beings and animals. So far as known the male is a vegetarian and feeds largely on the sweet juices of plants. Apparently the female also subsists on a similar diet in the absence of blood. Experts say some mosquitoes reproduce without partaking of blood meals. In certain cases the insects while still in the larval stages seem to store up a sufficient food supply to develop eggs. In other cases adult mosquitoes may partake of the sap of plants. "It is assumed, however, that most of the true pest mosquitoes must have blood in order to reproduce successfully," says the United States Bureau of Entomology. "It is certainly difficult to see how the hordes of mosquitoes in the Arctic region can be maintained on the animal life available. . . . Of course, there are many wild animals in the Arctic region from which mosquitoes may obtain blood, and no doubt there is a very high mortality without reproduction among the mosquitoes. In general, mosquitoes are not averse to feeding upon any warm-blooded animal at hand, and some of them feed freely upon cold-blooded animals." Tests show that ordinary mosquitoes, when they have a choice, prefer to bite horses, cattle, pigs and dogs rather than human beings. Some individuals attract mosquitoes more than others. Mosquitoes prefer children to adults and blonds to brunets. Although mosquitoes generally do not fly far from their breeding grounds, they have been known to fly twenty-five or thirty miles. The females fly farther and faster and live longer than the males.

Can the entire nation be placed under martial law?

Martial law is arbitrary government in cases where the safety of the state or nation is menaced. It may be necessary in the presence of actual war, rebellion or rioting and is justified only when the courts are closed and justice cannot be administered according to civil law. Thus so-called martial law is really not law at all, but military control. The Duke of Wellington defined martial law as, "The will of the commander-in-chief for the time being." It has no relation to military law, which is a code of rules and regulations prescribed for the government of a military establishment. But formerly *martial law* and *military law* were synonymous. In Shakespeare's *King Henry V* Fluellen tells the King: "And please your majesty, let his neck answer for it, if there is any martial law in the world." Martial law is not specifically mentioned in the Constitution of the United States. The United States Supreme Court, however, has held that the executive of state may proclaim martial law over the whole state or any part of it when the safety of the state demands it. It is presumed that the Federal Constitution by implication also permits the declaring of martial law in the United States as a whole. The implication is contained in the clause providing that the privileges of the writ of habeas corpus shall not be suspended except in cases of rebellion or invasion, when such suspension might be essential to the public welfare. A modified form of martial law in some countries is called a *state of siege*. In such countries a state of siege may be declared in a single city or part of the country and martial law in the rest at the same time. Ordinarily martial law does not abrogate all civil law, but extends only so far as is necessary to meet the existing emergency, to restore public order and to permit the civil authorities to resume their normal functions. Complete martial law applies to all civilian and military persons in the district, suspends important civil safeguards such as the habeas corpus, liberty of speech, press and assembly, and provides military courts in which to try offenders. English-speaking people are generally more opposed to martial law and the use of militia to govern civilians than any other people. General Andrew Jackson, while commander of the American troops defending New Orleans against a British invasion, was compelled to pay a fine by a civil court in New Orleans after he had declared martial law in the city. Martial is derived from Latin martialis, which means "pertaining to Mars," the god of war, while military comes to us through French from Latin miles ("soldier").

Do thunderstorms cause buds to grow more rapidly?

There is a common belief that a loud thunderstorm will cause the young buds on trees to grow so rapidly that the difference in the rate of growth is noticeable even to the casual observer. Scientists do not believe that the noise of loud thunder has any particular influence on the rate of growth in either the trees themselves or the buds. Thunderstorms are usually accompanied by rain and if the buds come out more rapidly after a thunderstorm the increased growth is due to the shower that accompanies the storm rather than the thunder.

What is a past master?

In Freemasonry a person who has been master of his lodge is called a past master. Hence past master has come to mean anyone versed in a subject, an adept, or one experienced in a particular line.

How is "Boer" pronounced?

Boer, as applied to the descendants of the Dutch settlers in South Africa, is frequently mispronounced. It is the Dutch word for farmer and is correctly pronounced like English boor, rhyming with moor, not door. Dutch boer, German Bauer and English boor had a common origin, and at one time they all had the same meaning—a farmer, peasant or countryman. The English called the Dutch in South Africa Boers because most of them were engaged in farming and cattle raising. The Afrikanders never called themselves boers unless they were actually farmers. At first English writers, when referring to the South Africans, spelled the word Boer and Boor interchangeably, but gradually the Dutch spelling was appropriated to this sense, due no doubt to the fact that the English word boor was largely restricted to an unfavorable sense; namely, a clownish or unrefined rustic or countryman.

Who invented punctuation?

The present system of punctuation, which divides written language into sections by means of various signs and points, grew out of a system developed by Aldus Manutius, Italian scholar and printer, who printed Greek classics on his press at Venice in the latter part of the fifteenth century and the beginning of the sixteenth. Manutius was born in 1450,

[271]

about the time Johann Gutenberg is supposed to have first experimented with movable type; he died in 1515. It should not be supposed, however, that Manutius was the sole inventor of punctuation, no one man being entitled to that honor, although the main features of our modern system are due chiefly to his ingenuity and that of the Greek scholars employed by him at Venice. Among the later ancient Greeks, particularly at Alexandria in Egypt, various dots had been used for oratorical and rhetorical purposes. Aristophanes, a Greek grammarian of Alexandria who died about 185 or 180 B.C., is said to have devised a system of punctuation by means of dots. A crude system of prose punctuation was probably employed even before the time of Aristophanes. St. Jerome, who died in 420 A.D., knew nothing whatever about punctuation. In the early part of the ninth century the Greek systems had been so completely forgotten that Charlemagne requested scholars to revive them. During the Middle Ages and up to the time of Manutius it was customary to write letters together in lines without breaks or pause marks for either words or sentences. It was only by degrees that words were divided from one another by spacing in the lines. Then came a haphazard division of words into sentences by means of signs and points, borrowed chiefly from the dots of the Greek grammarians. The invention of printing made it very desirable to have a conventional system of punctuation. This Manutius supplied, and his system, with numerous variations, is still in general use.

How did "printer's devil" originate?

The newest apprentice in a printing shop is called the *printer's devil*. He helps the printers, runs errands and does chores around the shop. It is supposed that the name arose from the fact that he frequently became blackened with ink in the days of hand presses. "The Press-man," wrote Joseph Moxon in 1683 in *Mechancial Exercises*, "sometimes has a Week-Boy to Take Sheets, as they are Printed off the Tympan: These Boys do in a Printing-House, commonly black and Dawb themselves; whence the workmen do jocosely call them Devils; and sometimes Spirits, and sometimes Flies." Some authorities, however, believe the name was suggested by a traditional incident at Venice. According to a legend, Aldus Manutius, who became celebrated as a printer in the latter part of the fifteenth and the first part of the sixteenth century, employed a Negro boy as a helper in his shop. The Venetians were not familiar with the colored race and in those days belief in witchcraft was common. Many devout people in the city suspected the Negro boy was an imp or evil genius and began to clamor for an investigation.

When the matter came to the attention of Manutius he not only let many citizens examine the boy, but issued a statement to the following effect: "I, Aldus Manutius, printer to the Doge and the Holy Church, have this day made public exposure of the printer's devil. All who think he is not flesh and blood are invited to come and pinch him." There is no evidence that the incident, if it actually happened at all, was responsible for *printer's devil* as the name for a printer's helper.

What softens the bones in canned fish?

The bones in canned fish are softened by heat, not by oil, as popularly supposed. Canned foods are processed after the containers are sealed. Processing is heating for a certain period at temperatures sufficiently high to kill all organisms that may cause spoilage. It is this heating that softens the bones in canned salmon, sardines, kippered herring and similar fish products.

Was "Voltaire" a real name or a pen name?

The original name of the great French poet, dramatist, wit and philosopher who is known to the world as Voltaire was François Marie Arouet. He was born in 1694 and was the son of François and Marie Marguerite Daumart Arouet. When he was about twenty-four years old he was imprisoned in the Bastille for writing verses and epigrams that displeased the regent of France. During this sojourn in the Bastille he changed his name to Arouet de Voltaire. The new name seems to have been suggested by the name of one of his mother's ancestors. It was very common for French writers in those days to adopt pseudonyms. Voltaire himself said he made the change because he had made such a miserable failure under his old name. As time passed the *Arouet* was dropped and the celebrated Frenchman became known simply as Voltaire.

Is Brooklyn part of New York City?

Brooklyn, New York, was formerly a separately chartered city, but in 1898 it was incorporated with New York City and since then has been a borough of Greater New York. In that year New York City annexed Kings (Brooklyn), Richmond (Staten Island) and parts of Queens counties and obtained a new charter for the enlarged city. As now organized New York City consists of five boroughs—Manhattan, Bronx, Brooklyn, Queens and Richmond—and is governed by a mayor elected at large and a city council elected by districts. Each of the five boroughs, including Brooklyn, has a president. Although Brooklyn is part of New York City it has an independent post office. There are also independent post offices at Jamaica, Flushing and Long Island City, all of which are now in New York City. This does not mean that these four post offices are *branches* of the main New York post office. They are entirely separate. "It is not deemed practical, for service reasons," wrote the United States Post Office Department to the author, "to consolidate these large independent post offices under one general office."

Why are Irishmen called Paddies?

Paddy is an affectionate nickname for Patrick and Irishmen in general are so designated because so many of them are named for St. Patrick, the tutelar saint of the Emerald Isle. The nickname, however, was not formed directly from *Patrick*; if it had been so formed it would probably have been spelled *Patty* instead of *Paddy*. It was derived from the Old Irish form of *Patrick*, which is *Padraig*.

What does Nova Scotia mean?

Nova Scotia, the name of the province on the southeast coast of Canada, is Latin for "New Scotland." The French, who made the first permanent settlements in what is now Nova Scotia, called the region Acadia. Quarrels among the original inhabitants resulted in an invasion of the province in 1613 by English colonists from Virginia who expelled most of the French settlers. The territory was first called Nova Scotia in a patent granted in 1621 by King James I, when the province was transferred to his favorite courtier, Sir William Alexander. Both the King and Sir William were Scottish, which accounts for the name chosen.

Does the body weigh the same immediately after death?

There is no appreciable decrease or increase in the weight of the human body at the instant death occurs. If a body is weighed immediately before and immediately after death the scales will register the same in each case. Charles II of England, who was an amateur anatomist, attempted to determine whether the human soul had weight by having the body of a condemned man weighed before and after execution. Those in charge of the experiment reported that the body actually weighed less after the departure of the spirit. The experiment, of course, is merely a curiosity without scientific value. Strangely enough, there is a popular belief that the body *increases* in weight immediately after death. "One reason that a dead body is thought to be heavier than a living one," wrote Dr. J. B. Harrison, a British surgeon, "is probably this, that in carrying a living person we have the center of gravity adapted by the person carried to suit the convenience of the carrier and maintained in a position as far as possible to fall within the base of his body. Again, the elasticity of the structures of the body, especially the cartilages, though not in reality diminishing in weight, gives an appearance of lightness, as we see in the beautiful movements of the stag, and this would seem to corroborate the notion of living creatures being lighter than dead ones." *Dead weight*, meaning the unrelieved weight of an inert object, may have been suggested by this belief.

Why are submarines called U-boats?

U-boat is merely the Anglicized spelling of German *U-Boot*, which is an abbreviation of *Untersee-Boot*, literally "undersea boat." The difference in capitalization of the words in German and English is owing to the fact that in German all nouns are capitalized. During the First World War, German and Austro-Hungarian submarines were designated by *U* followed by a number: as, *U-12*, *U-28*, *U-398*, etc. From this circumstance German submarines in general came to be popularly called *U-boats*. The term is seldom applied to the submarines of other nations, whether friend or foe.

What becomes of the heart of a hollow tree?

What becomes of the part of a tree that decays and makes a tree hollow is somewhat of a mystery to many people. Still there is nothing very mysterious about the disappearance of the dead wood from the interior of hollow tree trunks. In a hollow trunk with no opening to the outside the rotted wood gradually falls to the bottom of the trunk where still further decay takes place. The accumulated mass becomes more and more decayed and condensed until finally it represents in bulk only a very small percentage of the original volume of living wood. When the hollow trunk has an opening in it swarms of ants and other insects often carry out quantities of the decayed wood. Frequently they clean out hollow trunks completely.

Where does honeydew come from?

Honeydew is a sticky, sugary liquid that appears on the leaves of certain trees and plants during hot weather. There are two kinds of honeydew. One kind is excreted by aphids or plant lice. Entomologists say certain species of ant carefully protect and tend colonies of plant lice for the sake of the honeydew they produce. The other kind is an exudation from the leaves themselves. It may be caused by punctures made by aphids, leaf hoppers or other insects, or by the ordinary processes of over-turgescence. In some cases fungi may act as agents in the process. It is a form of *bleeding* that results from sap pressure. Hot weather and high atmospheric humidity are the conditions most conducive to the production of this type of honeydew. Both kinds of honeydew attract wasps, ants, bees and numerous other insects. Honey made by bees from honeydew is generally of poor quality. It is dark, disagreeable to the palate and does not candy like good honey. Frequently a whole crop of honey is spoiled by an infusion of honey from this source. It is an interesting fact that *mildew* is derived from two Teutonic roots signifying "honey" and "dew" and originally signified "honeydew."

Can an object be wider than it is long?

The answer to this question depends on the meaning of the terms. Strictly speaking, the length of an object is greater than its width. Whenever the width is increased to such an extent that it is greater than the length, the width becomes the length and the length becomes the width. On the other hand, *width* and *length* often imply more than mere dimensions. For instance, the length of a fish is generally taken to be the distance from the tip of its nose to the tip of its tail, regardless of its width. It is conceivable that a blowfish might be wider than it is long. Often height is equivalent to length irrespective of actual dimensions. For instance, in measuring window sashes the height is referred to as the length even when it is less than the width. Likewise the ribbonlike form of sea creature known as Venus's-girdle, which developes laterally, may be said to grow four or five feet wide and only an inch or two long, because the mouth is located at about the middle of one of the borders.

Do puffing adders blow poisonous spray?

It is widely believed that the small American snake known as the puffing adder blows poisonous powder or spray from its mouth. Occasionally reports are published to the effect that persons have been seriously injured by venomous spray spat into their faces by these serpents. The breath of the puffing adder, it is said, will kill a person at a distance of twenty-five feet. All this is fancy, pure and simple. These stories probably originated because the puffing adder was confused with an entirely different snake: the puff adder of Africa, a heavily built and exceedingly venomous viper that attains a length of four or five feet and that has the power of greatly distending its body when excited. The little American puffing adder is perfectly harmless and resembles its large African namesake only in its power to distend parts of its body and to look ferocious. The American species is not a poisonous snake and does not eject a spray or powder from its mouth. Its teeth are too short to inflict a wound even if it did strike a person. This species has many local names: as, spreading viper or adder, blowing adder or viper, blow snake, hissing viper, sand snake or viper, flat-headed adder, hognose snake, and puff or puffing adder. Most of these names refer to its habit of spreading its head and neck when angry or excited and hissing in a threatening manner. As a matter of fact it is one of the biggest bluffers among snakes.

Is the banana plant a tree?

Banana stalks are popularly referred to as "trees" because frequently they attain heights of thirty feet or more. But they are not trees in the correct sense of the term, but large perennial herbs that reach their full growth in one season. The banana is one of the largest known plants without a woody stem or trunk. It is really a giant "shoot." What appears to be the solid stalk or trunk of the plant is actually only a hollow sheath of leaves. Through this tubular stalk a stem or spike shoots up, bears the flowers and fruit and then dies in the same season. The next season new stalks grow up from the old root. The quality of the fruit is determined largely by the number of leaves on the plant.

Do Moslems have music with their religious services?

Music plays no part in the typical religious service of orthodox Mohammedans. Every man professing Mohammedanism, or Islam as it is known to its adherents, is required under ordinary circumstances to perform divine worship five times every day. Only on the Sabbath is it required that the daily religious ceremonies be performed in a mosque. The mosque service, like private prayers, is not performed under the direction of a priest and it consists of various recitals, ejaculations, ablutions and physical exercises on the part of the worshipper. Women take little part in the formal religious services in Islam, but they do visit the mosques for devotional purposes when the men are not present. The architecture and decorations of Moslem mosques contain no portrayals of human or animal forms.

Where is the Calumet District?

This is the popular name given to a district in northern Indiana and Illinois lying between the Calumet River and Lake Michigan. Originally the region was covered almost entirely with sand ridges and marshes. It is now a great industrial district, comprising such cities as Hammond,

Gary, East Chicago, Whiting and Indiana Harbor. Sometimes the entire region around the southern shore of Lake Michigan is spoken of as the Calumet District. The Calumet River, from which the district takes its name, was so called from the Indian peace pipe known as the calumet. This name is not of Indian origin. When the French first saw the Indians use this reedlike emblem they called it *chalumet*, an old French literary term signifying "little read" and ultimately derived from Latin *calamus*, "reed" or "tube."

Is Denmark in Scandinavia?

Scandinavia has two distinct geographical meanings. In one sense it refers to the Scandinavian Peninsula in northern Europe and comprises Norway and Sweden but not Denmark and Finland. In another sense the term refers to all the countries where the Scandinavian languages prevail; that is, Sweden, Norway and Denmark, together with the neighboring islands, including Iceland. Finland, which forms the base of the Scandinavian peninsula in the far north, is sometimes grouped with the Scandinavian countries for convenience, because Scandinavia has exercised a marked cultural influence on the Finns for eight centuries. Although there are many Scandinavians in Finland, Finnish itself is not a Scandinavian language and differs greatly from that group of tongues. In fact, Finnish and Estonian belong to the Ural-Altaic languages and are more closely related to the Magyar of Hungary than to Swedish, Norwegian and Danish, which are Teutonic languages. Estonia, Latvia and Lithuania are known as "the Baltic countries." In ancient times little was known of the great land mass of the peninsula in northern Europe and *Scandia*, from which *Scandinavia* is derived, was the apellation used by the Romans to designate what was supposed to be a large island either in or north of the Baltic Sea. The most southern part of Sweden is known as *Scania* at the present time.

Which is correct, "A.B." or "B.A."?

The degree of Bachelor of Arts is indicated either by *A.B.* or *B.A.* This variation in the order of the letters in the abbreviation arose from the fact that the degree was originally written in Latin and in that language the order of the words is not so essential to the sense as it is in English. In Latin *Artium Baccalaureus* and *Baccalaureus Artium*, both meaning Bachelor of Arts, are equally correct. The difference in the order of *A.M.* and *M.A.* is explained in the same way. In Latin it is correct to write either *Artium Magister* or *Magister Artium*. Both mean Master of Arts. Many people prefer *M.A.* and *B.A.* because these letters are the correct abbreviations for both the original Latin phrases and their English translations. Such abbreviations as *M.S.* or *M.Sc.* (Master of Science) and *B.S.* or *B.Sc.* (Bachelor of Science) are of modern origin and the letters usually occur in the regular English order.

Can monkeys swim?

One often hears it said that men and monkeys are the only members of the animal kingdom unable to swim without being taught. Although most monkeys and apes shun water, there are some species that are known to swim and even to dive in their wild state. Many of the African monkeys, particularly the velvet monkey, are fond of playing in water and some species not only swim well but are in the habit of swimming across streams of considerable width. Monkeys do not differ much from many other animals in this respect.

How is the surname "Cabell" pronounced?

All branches of the American Cabell family pronounce their name *kabb-'l*. The name is frequently mispronounced ka-*bell* and kay-b'l. "*Cabell*," wrote James Branch Cabell, the novelist, to the author in 1926, "is pronounced as an exact rhyme to *rabble*." In 1931 the celebrated author dropped his first name and began to write under the name Branch Cabell.

How does a "sanitarium" differ from a "sanatorium"?

Many people apply *sanitarium* and *sanatorium* interchangeably to any hospital or institution in which sick and injured persons are given medical and surgical treatment. In this sense *sanitarium* is the more common. In *A Dictionary of Modern English Usage* H. W. Fowler says: "*Sanitarium* is a possible but now undesirable equivalent of *sanatorium*." Some American authorities, however, attempt to distinguish between the two terms in present-day usage. *Sanitarium* is derived directly from Latin *sanitas* ("health"), and indirectly from *sanus* ("whole" or "sound"). *Sanatorium* is derived from Latin *sanatorius* ("curing" or "health-giving"). Accordingly, it is maintained, the function of a sanitarium is to preserve health, while that of a sanatorium is to restore health; that is, a sanitarium is a health resort where people go to keep well and a sanatorium is a hospital where sick people go to get well. A sanitarium might be a retreat in the mountains or on the seashore where people in a run-down condition go to recuperate and to build up their health by means of natural therapeutic agents such as rest, sunlight, diet and beneficial climate. If treatment is given in such a sanitarium it is chiefly prophylactic or preventive. A sanatorium, on the other hand, is an establishment where healing is performed by active and artificial means, such as medicine and surgery. A person with indigestion or a broken leg would go to a sanatorium for treatment. Often the term is restricted to mean a hospital in which persons with a particular disease are treated by the application of a specific remedy. For instance, institutions for the treatment of tuberculosis patients are almost invariably called sanatoriums in America. Usage does not always bear out these distinctions and not infrequently the definitions in dictionaries are unsatisfactory. Sometimes sanatorium is erroneously spelled sanitorium, due to confusion with sanitarium, and sanitarium is incorrectly spelled sanatarium, due to a similar confusion with sanatorium.

What was the big wind of Ireland?

The Irish people of a former generation were in the habit of dividing history into two periods—before and after the big wind. This refers to a storm that began January 6, 1839, and raged for two days and nights along the coasts of England and Ireland. It was the most severe and devastating storm that had ever occurred in Ireland within the memory of people then living. Many lives were lost in Dublin and Liverpool, the Irish Sea was strewn with the wrecks of ships and hundreds of houses were blown down in Galway, Limerick, Athlone and other places. Much additional damage was done by fires started and fanned by the gale.

Were Noah Webster and Daniel Webster related?

There was no known relationship between Noah and Daniel Webster. Noah Webster, of dictionary and spelling book fame, who was born in Hartford, Connecticut, October 16, 1758, was descended from John Webster, one of the first settlers at Hartford in 1636. Daniel Webster, the statesman and orator, who was born at Salisbury, New Hampshire, January 18, 1782, was descended from Thomas Webster, who first appeared in Watertown, Massachusetts, in 1638. The relationship, if any, between Thomas and John Webster has never been established.

What are weasel words?

The expression weasel words in the sense of words of convenient ambiguity was popularized by Theodore Roosevelt in a speech at St. Louis, May 31, 1916, in which he criticized President Wilson in the following language: "In connection with the word training the words universal voluntary have exactly the same effect an acid has on an alkali—a neutralizing effect. One of our defects as a nation is a tendency to use what have been called *weasel words*. When a weasel sucks eggs, the meat is sucked out of the egg. If you use a weasel word after another there is nothing left of the other. Now, you can have universal training, or you can have voluntary training, but when you use the word *voluntary* to qualify the word *universal* you are using a weasel word; it has sucked all the meaning out of *universal*. The two words flatly contradict one another." It is quite certain that Theodore Roosevelt got the idea of weasel words from Stewart Chaplin's story entitled "Stained-Glass Political Platform," which appeared in the *Century Magazine* in June, 1900. In that story this passage occurs:

> Why *weasel words* are words that suck the life out of the words next to them, just as a weasel sucks an egg and leaves the shell. If you heft the egg afterwards it's as light as a feather, and not very filling when you are hungry, but a basketful of them would make quite a show, and would bamboozle the unwary. I know them well, and mighty useful they are, too. Although the gentleman couldn't write much of a platform, he's an expert on *weaseling*. I've seen him take his pen and go through a proposed plank or resolution and *weasel* every flatfooted word in it. Then the *weasel word* pleases one man, and the word that's been weaseled pleases another.

The egg-sucking propensity of the weasel is proverbial. In Shakespeare's *King Henry V* Westmoreland says:

> For once the eagle England being in prey,
> To her unguarded nest the weasel Scot
> Comes sneaking and so sucks her princely eggs,
> Playing the mouse in absence of the cat,
> To tear and havoc more than she can eat.

And in *As You Like It* Jacques says, "I can suck melancholy out of a song, as a weasel sucks eggs." A person who indulges in weasel words— a political fence straddler, is sometimes known as a *weasler*.

What is a picture bride?

A picture bride is a bride whom the bridegroom has not seen before marriage. She is a woman who has been selected as a wife "sight unseen" by her picture alone. The term is particularly associated with a practice formerly prevalent among the Japanese in the United States. Because of the comparative scarcity of oriental women from whom the Japanese could choose wives, those who desired to marry sent to their native land for a collection of photographs of marriageable women who were willing to migrate to America. From these pictures a man made a selection and the woman of his choice, after being married at a "picture marriage ceremony," was sent to America as his wife. Formerly long lines of Japanese men could be seen waiting at the wharves for the arrival of their picture brides from the Orient. The United States Government always protested vigorously against the entrance of picture brides, and granting such women passports was discontinued by the Tokio government in 1920. Later immigration laws largely put a stop to the practice among the Japanese as well as among other nationalities. The United States Department of Labor refused to issue immigration visas to Japanese in behalf of picture brides even if the Japanese were native-born American citizens. But Japan continued to issue passports and to provide for the transportation of picture brides emigrating to Manchuria and other Japanese possessions and territories. As late as 1939 the Japanese government was reported to be seriously considering a proposal to train thirty thousand women in special schools and to send them as picture brides to Japanese farmers in the Amazon Valley in Brazil.

What does "Ibid" mean?

Ibid is a contraction of the Latin adverb *ibidem* and literally means "in the same place." It is employed chiefly to avoid repeating a reference, particularly after a quotation to indicate that it is taken from the same book, chapter, passage or other source as the preceding one. In this sense the term came into general use during the seventeenth century when it was still fashionable to borrow freely from the classical languages upon the slightest provocation. It is not uncommon to meet with persons who suppose *Ibid* to be a noted author whose writings are frequently quoted.

How many ribs do monkeys have?

In monkeys and apes the number of pairs of ribs varies from eleven in some species to fifteen in others. The orangutan, like man, has twelve pairs, while gorillas and chimpanzees have thirteen. Only the New World night apes have as many as fifteen pairs of ribs.

What English queen had seventeen children?

Queen Anne, who reigned over England from 1702 to 1714, gave birth to seventeen children, not one of whom survived her. Several of them were stillborn. The queen's life has been described as a mournful series of childbirths, miscarriages and infant funerals. She, her husband and the seventeen children are buried in a single tomb in Westminster Abbey. Anne was the second daughter of James II and Anne Hyde. In 1683 she was married to Prince George of Denmark. Only one of the seventeen children born to this union survived infancy. This was William, the Duke of Gloucester, who died in 1700 at the age of eleven.

What birds can fly immediately after being hatched?

The mound builders, a family of birds inhabiting Australia and certain South Sea islands, are unique in that the young are hatched fully fledged and are able to fly and live an independent life from the moment they emerge from the shell. These birds are called *megapodes* because of their large feet. Most species lay their eggs in large mounds constructed of loose soil, leaves, grass, twigs, etc. Not infrequently the mounds are ten or twelve feet high and contain several wagonloads of material. After the eggs are deposited they are left to hatch out by the heat of the decaying vegetable matter. The brush turkeys are the most common of the mound builders. One species of megapodes lays its eggs in the sand on the seashore and leaves them to be hatched by the heat of the sun.

How does a polecat differ from a skunk?

Polecat as used in the United States is merely a popular name for the common skunk. The early settlers in America were acquainted with the European fitchet weasel and they applied its common name, *polecat,* to the skunk because of the similarity in the latter's objectionable odor. *Pole* in *polecat* is derived from the French *poule,* meaning "pullet" or "chicken," and the fitchet weasel was so called from its preference for a chicken diet.

What is a "cold" moon?

When the moon is far to the north it is popularly called a *cold* moon because many people suppose it then to be a sign of cold weather. There is probably no relation whatever between the weather and the apparent position of the moon. The moon's motions are uniform and its position can be accurately computed for years and even centuries ahead. No such uniformity exists in regard to the weather.

Why does John Bull represent England?

As the personification of the English nation, John Bull originated in a pamphlet entitled *The History of John Bull* and published anonymously in 1712 by John Arbuthnot, Scottish satirist and court physician to Queen Anne. It was intended as a satire on the Duke of Marlborough and the War of the Spanish Succession. At first the pamphlet was attributed to Jonathan Swift, but Arbuthnot's authorship was later established beyond doubt. John Bull was portrayed as a good-natured, bluff, portly and bull-headed Englishman of the country gentleman type. Lewis Baboon, a Frenchman, Nicholas Frog, a Dutchman, as well as others, figure in the satire. Although the pamphlet itself was quickly forgotten and is now seldom read, it fastened the nickname *John Bull* on the English people.

How did "bring home the bacon" originate?

Bring home the bacon, in the American sense of "to be successful in a venture" or "to bring home the spoils," is of disputed origin. Some authorities suppose it to be derived from the old practice of greasing a pig and letting it loose among blindfolded persons at a country fair. The one who caught the pig "brought home the bacon." This derivation, however, seems improbable, since *bacon* is generally applied to hogs and pigs, not on the hoof, but after they have been butchered. A more probable theory is that *bring home the bacon* originated as a mere alliterative figure of speech in reference to the chief supporter of the family, *bacon* being a term for food in general. In a similar manner we speak of the chief supporter of the family as the "bread-winner." Attempts have been made to find a connection between *bring home the bacon* and the old saying, "He may fetch a flitch of bacon from Dunmow," meaning that he is so good-natured and easy to get along with that he never quarrels with his wife. The allusion is to a custom alleged to have been started in England during the twelfth or thirteenth century. It was then decreed, according to legend, that "any person from any part of England going to Dunmow, in Essex, and humbly kneeling on the stones at the church door, may claim a gammon or flitch of bacon, if he can swear that for twelve months and a day he has never had a household brawl or wished himself unmarried." The offer is variously said to have been first made by a noble lady named Juga, by the monks of the Dunmow priory, by Sir Philip de Somerville, and by Lord Robert de Fitzwalter. It may have been started by the monks and continued by the secular proprietors of the manor after the priory was dissolved under Henry VIII. It is said that a flitch of bacon was delivered to only twelve couples during the first five hundred years the custom was observed. Whatever the truth of the story, the custom was revived or perhaps established under an old name in 1855 as a sort of local festival. At any rate, because of the legend, a person who lives in conjugal harmony, without desiring the marriage bands to be loosened, is said "to eat Dunmow bacon." The saying that one has just *saved his bacon* may possibly allude to this same old story. If it does, its original meaning would be that a couple barely prevented losing a chance to get a flitch of bacon by averting a quarrel that was impending. The Dunmow legend was popularized by William Harrison Ainsworth's novel entitled *The Flitch of Bacon*, published in 1855. But no connection between the story and *bring home the bacon* has been established. An improbable theory is that the phrase somehow was suggested by a practice of the ancient pagan Prussians, who sacrificed a flitch of bacon to appease Percunnos, the god of thunder and fertility.

Is it unlawful to write a check for less than a dollar?

It is not unlawful in the United States, as many suppose, to write a check for less than a dollar. The belief that it is arose from a misinterpretation of Section 178 of the Federal Criminal Code. This section, approved March 4, 1909, reads: "No person shall make, issue, circulate, or pay out any note, check, memorandum, token, or other obligation for a less sum than one dollar, intended to circulate as money or to be received or used in lieu of lawful money of the United States; and every person so offending shall be fined not more than $500, or imprisoned not more than six months, or both." A bank check is not intended to circulate as money or to be received and used in lieu of lawful money. It is merely an order to pay money. In a statement prepared for the author the Department of Justice said: "The statute is aimed against such checks as are 'intended to circulate as lawful money or to be received or used in lieu of lawful money of the United States' and does not apparently have any reference to an ordinary individual bank check, and it has always been the view of the Department that the statute does not apply to such a check." In some countries tokens and checks issued by private firms and associations are used for money. For instance, in France tokens issued by chambers of commerce are generally employed for small change. The section of the criminal code in question was designed to forbid the circulation of such private money. Certain banks are permitted to issue currency in the form of bank notes, but under this section such notes cannot be issued for sums less than one dollar.

Why is cement called Portland?

Portland was first applied to a cement made in 1824 by Joseph Aspdin, a bricklayer of Leeds, England. Aspdin, seeking a better masonry binder than the ordinary lime mortar and cement then known, mixed clay and lime in definite proportions, burned the mixture in a kiln and pulverized the resulting mass. He called his product "Portland cement" because concrete made from it somewhat resembled "Portland stone," a famous building limestone obtained from the peninsula of Portland on the Dorsetshire coast. Aspdin, however, was not the first to make the comparison. More than fifty years earlier John Smeaton had stated that cement made of such materials would "equal the best merchantable Portland stone in solidity and durability." Neither was Aspdin the "inventor of cement." Inferior cements were made in ancient times by the Egyptians, Babylonians and Romans, who used lime, gypsum and volcanic ashes. Cements of various kinds had been used to some extent ever since. A cement made of "hydraulic lime" found underground in New York State was used in the stone work of the Erie Canal, which was begun in 1817 and completed in 1825. Benjamin Wright, chief engineer of the Canal, reported that the peculiar lime "is pulverized (as it will not slack) and then used by mixing two parts of lime and one part sand. It hardens best under water." Canvass White patented the hydraulic use of this cement in 1820 and his patent marks the real beginning of concrete in the United States. Aspdin's cement was not clinkered but merely calcined. He was granted a patent on his "Portland cement" in 1824. His invention was revolutionary in its ultimate effects and made possible the modern cement age. In 1828 his product, manufactured at Wakefield, ten miles from Leeds, was used in the Thames tunnel. The first concrete road pavement made with Portland cement was built at Inverness, Scotland, in 1865. As early as 1872 a Portland cement mill was established in Pennsylvania, but a stretch of pavement at Bellefontaine, Ohio, built in 1893–1894 was the first concrete road in America. Modern Portland cement, made by greatly improved methods, sets more rapidly and produces harder concrete than did Aspdin's original product. It is made by burning a natural or artificial mixture of clay and lime to a clinking temperature and then grinding the clinker. Like the Erie Canal cement, it sets under water, something Aspdin's product would not do.

What is a paper blockade?

When a nation declares a blockade against another nation and does not have sufficient military and naval strength to enforce it, it is called a paper blockade, because the blockade is said to exist only in the proclamation. Such a condition is also sometimes called a cabinet blockade, referring to the fact that the blockade exists merely as the result of a cabinet decree. The abuse of paper blockades is notorious in international law. Perhaps the most famous paper blockade in history was proclaimed at Berlin by Napoleon in 1806. Great Britain was declared to be in a state of blockade, her subjects and property were made liable to capture and seizure, and all countries under French dominion or allied with

France were forbidden to have communication with the British Isles, notwithstanding the fact Napoleon had hardly a single vessel of war that he could send to support the blockade. It was the beginning of Napoleon's so-called Continental system, which was intended to bar England from trade with continental Europe. Naturally the inconvenience that resulted to neutral nations was great. The blockade, however, continued in effect on paper until 1812, when it was abolished by international agreement. In 1856, to prevent such abuses, the leading powers of Europe, including Britain, France, Austria, Prussia, Russia, Turkey and Sardinia, signed what is known as the Declaration of Paris. The fourth article of that compact provided: "Blockades, in order to be binding, must be effective—that is to say, maintained by a force sufficient really to prevent access to the coast of the enemy." In other words, a blockade should not be respected unless it is effective enough to make its evasion a dangerous act. Modern air warfare, however, has greatly altered the former concept of blockades.

How did "monkey" get in "monkey wrench"?

It is supposed that monkey in monkey wrench is a corruption of the proper name Moncke (pronounced mun-ke). There is a tradition that wrenches with moving jaws adjustable by a screw were first made by a London blacksmith named Charles Moncke and that the implements were originally called "Moncke wrenches." Owing to a popular ignorance as to the origin of the word, it was naturally corrupted into monkey, which was pronounced nearly the same.

What is the White Horse in England?

The White Horse is the gigantic but sketchy outline of a galloping horse cut on the northern slope of a hill in Berkshire, England, about sixty miles west of London. It gives its name not only to this particular hill, which is about 856 feet high, but also to the entire range, as well as the "Vale of the White Horse," which is the common name of the valley of the Ock, a small river uniting with the Thames from the west at Abingdon. The White Horse is 374 feet in length and was formed by removing the turf to show the white chalky subsoil. It is rude in outline, there being little difference in the width of the neck, body and tail, but the figure is clearly visible and may be seen from a distance of ten or twelve miles on a fair day. Nobody knows the origin of the White Horse. It is variously ascribed to the Druids, Danes and Saxons. Tradition says that Alfred the Great, who was born at near-by Wantage, made it to commemorate his victory over the Danes at Ashdown in 871 A.D. This battle, however, probably took place near Compton Beauchamp at the east end of the Berkshire downs in the vicinity of Reading. There is reason for believing the White Horse is of great antiquity and antedates the Roman occupation. The earliest record of the figure occurs in the Abingdon Abbey register under date of 1171 A.D. Naturally the trench forming the outline gradually fills up and the figure is obscured. Accordingly from time to time the side of White Horse hill is cleared of vegetation and the trench is cleaned to make the outline more easily distinguishable, and "scouring the White Horse" used to be the annual occasion of a popular festival by the people living in the neighborhood. There are other ancient outlines of the same character in southern England. On a chalk hill just outside the village of Cerne Abbas in Dorsetshire there is the outline of a giant with a club in his right hand. Local tradition says a giant was buried in the hill in ancient times. As late as 1857 a schoolmaster named John Hodgson cut the figure of a horse—314 by 228 feet—on a hillside near Kilburn in Yorkshire. A white horse was the symbol of the Saxons.

How did "get one's goat" originate?

Get one's goat, meaning to annoy, irritate or make angry, is of obscure origin. One lexicographer suggested that goat in the expression may be a contraction of goatee, a chin tuft or pointed beard, which is supposed to resemble the beard of a goat. If this theory is correct, to get one's goat would literally mean to pull one's beard, which, like tweaking the nose, is considered a very humiliating insult. Horse breeders have a curious theory on the subject that deserves mention. It is a well known fact that thoroughbred horses often form close attachments to goats. In fact, goats are often deliberately put in the stall of a nervous and high-strung race horse to keep it company. Sometimes a horse and a goat become so inseparable that the horse will become nervous and restive when the goat is taken away. Hence the phrase, got his goat.

Does the queen honeybee have a sting?

The queen honeybee has a sting but it differs from that of the worker in being longer, curved and having fewer and shorter barbs on the lancet. It is also more firmly attached in the sting chamber than is the sting of the worker, which is easily torn from its body when the sting penetrates an object beyond the barbs that extend backward as does the barb on a fishhook. The queen honeybee seldom uses her sting except to kill rival queens, although there are a few cases on record where queens have stung the beekeeper when they were handled. This instinct to sting other queens is so strong that they will often sting queens that have been dead for a considerable length of time when brought into contact with them. Stinging is generally fatal to a worker bee. If it stings deeply the stinger is left in the wound of the victim and the bee dies. But a queen can sting repeatedly without injury to herself.

How should worn-out flags be disposed of?

In 1923 the National Flag Conference, composed of representatives of 71 patriotic organizations, met in Washington, D. C., and framed *The Flag Code*. Paragraph 6 of this code describes the proper method of destroying United States flags no longer fit for display. It reads: "When the Flag is in such a condition that it is no longer a fitting emblem for display, it should not be cast aside or used in any way that might be viewed as disrespectful to the National colors, but should be destroyed as a whole privately, preferably by burning or by some other method in harmony with the reverence and respect we owe to the emblem representing our country." The United States Government disposes of its worn-out flags by burning them.

What phase of the moon is "light"?

The terms *light moon* or *light of the moon*, and *dark moon* or *dark of the moon* are purely popular and have no scientific significance. Light moon, according to the more popular conception, is the period between the new moon and the full moon, while dark moon is the period between the full moon and the new moon. In other words, light of the moon immediately follows the new moon, while dark of the moon precedes it. The United States Weather Bureau defines the terms differently. According to that authority, *light moon* means all that time during which the moon is above the horizon through the fore part of the night, say from dusk to midnight, while *dark moon* means all the rest of the time —all the time it is not light of the moon.

How often does one born on February 29 have a birthday?

A person born on February 29 in leap year has a birthday only once every four years so far as the calendar is concerned. It is, however, purely a calendar problem. In reality there is no problem at all, because none of us observe our birthdays on exactly the proper twenty-four hours, owing to imperfections in the calendar. Every four years the calendar is about twenty-four hours behind the astronomical or true solar year. This difference is made up by adding an extra day to February every four years, making leap year. According to our present calendar, every year represented by a number divisible by four is a leap year, except those represented by numbers divisible by one hundred but not by four hundred. This arises from the fact that the addition of a whole day every fourth year is a few minutes too much to make the calendar come out even. A person born on February 29 in leap year would be one year old exactly a year later, and his true birthday would begin then and would last for twenty-four hours, regardless of the calendar. The same holds true of a person born on any other date. But it is customary to adopt as one's birthday the entire calendar day nearest the astronomical date. These born on February 29 have a choice of observing their birthdays on February 28 or March 1, except in leap years, when they can observe the actual calendar date. Most persons born on February 29 observe their birthday anniversaries on February 28 in non-leap-year years. Gioacchino Antonio Rossini, the Italian operatic composer, was born February 29, 1792. On February 29, 1864, when he was seventy-two, he celebrated what he facetiously called his eighteenth birthday. He announced to his friends his intention to "turn over a new leaf and disregard the frivolities of youth, and the indiscretions of his teens." But the great musical composer overlooked the fact that 1800 was not a leap year and that even according to his own facetious reckoning he was seventeen instead of eighteen on February 29, 1864. A few years ago an English lawyer, whose son was born February 29, made an investigation to determine the status of his son's birthday under English law. He found, he reported, that an act of Parliament passed in the time of Henry VIII provided that persons born February 29 were entitled to regard February 28 as their birthday anniversary in all years other than leap years.

What is a bread and butter letter?

Bread and butter letter is the popular name given to a brief note of thanks written by a departed guest to his host or hostess. The term is applicable particularly to the letter of appreciation that a person is expected to write to a friend after having spent a few days under his roof. It received its name from the fact that the writer of such a letter has enjoyed his friend's "bread and butter," that is, his hospitality. According to the etiquette authorities, a bread and butter letter should be posted within two days after the guest's departure.

What animals have no gall bladders?

The gall bladder is absent from all common members of the deer family. Deer have livers but no organ that takes the place of the gall bladder in other animals. This anatomical peculiarity, however, is not found in the Asiatic musk deer, which for that reason are sometimes classed in a separate family closer to cattle. Likewise antelopes, which are not true deer, have gall bladders.

How is the size of stockings determined?

The size of hose is based on the distance in inches between a point on the toe and a point on the heel measured in a straight line. Size 8 is eight inches more or less from the tip of the toe to the end of the heel. Both men's and women's stockings are measured in this manner. According to the United States Bureau of Standards, the standard method of measuring hosiery is as follows: After the hose has been pressed and is flat and unwrinkled, a ruler is placed along a line in which the tip of the toe and the bottom of the heel gore are connected. The hosiery size is the distance in inches along this line from tip of toe to the intersection of the ruler with the back of the heel. Only inches and half inches are represented in commercial size numbers. Preference is given to the lower number. For instance, if the exact measurement is 10¼ inches the stocking is called size 10 rather than 10½.

How did "fit to a T" originate?

It is supposed that the T in to fit to a T alludes to the T square used by carpenters and mechanics. To fit to a T originally meant "to fit exactly," as the T square does to the surface of a board or block. The phrase dates back at least to the seventeenth century and probably much earlier. In 1699 George Farquhar wrote in Love and a Bottle: "He answered the description the page gave to a T, sir."

How did "dun" originate?

Dun in the sense of requesting payment of a bill is believed to have been derived from the surname of Joseph Dun, an English petty official, who was noted for his success in collecting debts. Many stories have been published about Joe Dun's unusual and picturesque methods of making debtors pay. In 1708 the following explanation of the term was printed in the British Apollo: "The word Dun owes its birth to one Joe Dun, a famous Bailiff of the Town of Lincoln. It became a Proverb . . . when a man refused to pay his debts, why don't you Dun him? That is, why don't you send Dun to arrest him? . . . It is now as old as since the days of King Henry the Seventh." The monarch mentioned reigned from 1485 to 1509. Whether this was the true origin of the term cannot be stated positively, because there is no contemporary evidence. The earliest known use of the word occurs in Microcosmographie, or a Peece *of the World Discovered in Essayes and Characters,* published in 1628 by John Earle (1601–1665), afterwards bishop of Salisbury. Earle wrote: "An Vniversitie Dunne . . . Hee is an inferiour Creditor of some ten shillings or downwards. He is a sore beleaguer of Chambers." This quotation definitely disposes of the theory, advanced by Maitland in his *American Slang Dictionary,* that *dun* is an Americanism derived from *din,* meaning "noise." Dr. Samuel Johnson derived the word from Saxon *donon,* signifying "to clamor." It is possible that *dun* is from French *donne,* a familiar imperative form of *donner* ("to give").

Which is the mother of the chick, the hen that lays the egg or the one that hatches it?

This old question has the habit of bobbing up at frequent intervals. The fact that a hen incubates an egg that she did not lay gives her no blood relationship to the chick. The hen that lays the egg is the blood mother of the chick regardless of how it is incubated. A hen that incubates an egg laid by another hen, although she contributes materially to the hatching process, is merely a foster mother to the chick. Her relationship to the chick would be the same physiologically as that of a goose, duck or even a mechanical incubator that happened to incubate the egg. The term *mother* usually indicates actual parentage, and in that sense, which certainly is the most general, the hen that lays the egg is the chick's mother. But most people are not particularly interested in the actual maternity of their chicks, and therefore the hen that incubates the egg and *mothers* the chick is popularly regarded as the mother of the chick irrespective of the source of the egg.

How do bees hum?

Honeybees make the characteristic monotonous noise known as *humming* as well as the louder *buzzing* sound entirely by vibrating the wings rapidly. It is now believed that they do not produce any appreciable sound with their mouths or within their breathing systems, as often supposed. It was formerly believed that the loud *droning* sound made by bumblebees was produced mainly within the tracheae, but it is probable that the only appreciable sound made by these large social bees is produced solely by the motion of the wings. In other words, it is now believed that honeybees and bumblebees do not have true "voices." Nor are they known to make any rubbing noises. The characteristic sounds made by bees are made with the wings while the insects are flying, crawling or at rest. The shrillness of the sound of honeybees increases with the number of vibrations of the wings. The slow flapping of a

[292]

butterfly, for instance, produces no audible sound, but the rapid vibration of the wings of a bee produces a very distinctive one. Scientists say an ordinary honeybee may vibrate its wings at the rate of 440 times a second or 26,400 times a minute. Honeybees were among the original air conditioners. Certain workers, known as "fanner bees," perform the function of ventilating the hive by crawling about beating their wings at the rate of 11,400 strokes a minute.

Do monkeys have two sets of teeth?

Monkeys like human beings have two sets of teeth. Their first or milk teeth are replaced by a second and more permanent set. This, however, is not peculiar to monkeys and apes in the animal world. "All mammals," says the American Museum of Natural History in a letter to the author, "have two sets of teeth, the first or milk dentition being followed by the permanent set. In the case of most mammals the milk set functions as in human beings and serves the young mammal for an appreciable interval of time. In exceptional cases the milk teeth are almost nonfunctional and are replaced by the second set so early in life that the milk teeth serve only a very slight useful function. The primates show a condition very similar to that in human beings, the milk dentition persisting for some time and the permanent teeth appearing at a considerable interval after birth, especially the last molars." Generally speaking, Old World monkeys, like man, have thirty-two teeth, while New World monkeys have thirty-six; but the New World marmosets have thirty-two like the Old World monkeys, while the Old World lemurs have thirty-six like the New World monkeys. The teeth of monkeys and apes are much less regular than those of man.

Does fright cause the guinea fowl's flesh to turn blue?

Fright or excitement, according to a common belief, causes the flesh of the guinea fowl to turn blue, and accordingly many poultrymen shoot off the heads of these fowls while they are feeding instead of catching them and chopping off their heads as they do in the case of other fowls, such as ducks, geese and chickens. The meat of the guinea fowl, especially the pearl variety, is naturally darker than that of other common fowls, and this fact probably gave rise to the notion that the darkness is caused by fright at the time of killing. Those experienced in preparing guinea fowl for the market on a large scale report that there is no more difference in the color of the flesh of different individuals of this species than there is in the different individuals of other fowls. There is, however, a slight basis for the popular belief that fright or excitement affects the color of flesh, and it is not improbable that the effect of fright on the flesh is more noticeable in some fowls than in others. No animal or bird bleeds well if it is killed in an excited or overheated condition. It has been observed that beef from cattle not properly bled does not keep as well as beef from animals properly bled. Guinea fowls, like other birds, should be bled by removing the head or severing the vein in the roof of the mouth and allowing the bird to hang head downward. Their flesh is tender, fine in texture, gamy in flavor, and said by many to be similar in quality to prairie chicken, grouse, quail, pheasant, partridge and other similar game birds. As a rule the flesh of the pearl guinea is considerably darker than that of the white and lavender varieties.

What is a curtain lecture?

A curtain lecture is a private scolding received by a husband from his wife. By extension, any faultfinding, nagging or caviling talk is figuratively called a curtain lecture. The term originated in the days of canopied beds surrounded by curtains. A curtain lecture was originally a scolding administered by a wife after she and her husband had gone to bed and had drawn the curtains. Dr. Samuel Johnson defined the phrase as "a reproof given by a wife to her husband in bed." In Rip Van Winkle Washington Irving wrote: "A curtain lecture is worth all the sermons in the world for teaching the virtues of patience and long-suffering." Curtain lecture was a common phrase already early in the seventeenth century. A Curtain Lecture; as it is Read by a Country Farmer's Wife to Her Good Man was the title of an English book published in 1638. Sometimes Caudle lecture is used as a synonym for the term. This usage dates from 1846 when Douglas Jerrold (1803–1857), English author, humorist and playwright published his Curtain Lectures in London Punch. In these papers Jerrold represented Job Caudle as the patient and long-suffering victim of the lectures of his querulous and nagging wife, Margaret Caudle, after they had gone to bed and drawn the curtains.

Why is Delaware called the Blue Hen State?

This nickname of Delaware originated in 1776. Captain Jonathan Caldwell of Haslet's Delaware regiment in the Continental Army was very fond of gamecocks and his company carried a number of the fighting fowl as mascots. These birds were celebrated in Kent County for their fighting qualities, and they were said to be the offspring of a certain renowned hen. The captain and his men were in the habit of amusing themselves with cockfights. When the fame of these battles spread among the soldiers of the Continental Army the Delaware troops became known as the Blue Hen's Chickens, and in time Delaware was nicknamed the Blue Hen State. It was the opinion of Captain Caldwell himself that no cock could be truly game unless his mother was a blue hen. In 1939 both houses of the Delaware legislature unanimously passed a bill to make the blue hen the official bird of the state.

Is La Paz or Sucre the capital of Bolivia?

Bolivia has two capitals—a legal capital and a de facto capital. Sucre, formerly called Charcas, is the legal capital of the Republic of Bolivia, and it was there that General Antonio Jose de Sucre, the victor of the battle of Ayachucho, exercised his functions as the first president of the republic. For many years, however, Sucre took its turn with La Paz, Cochabamba and Oruro as the seat of government. In December, 1898, an attempt was made to pass a law making Sucre the perpetual legal capital of the republic. La Paz revolted and there was some bloodshed. Chiefly because of its greater accessibility and growing commercial importance La Paz gradually became the actual seat of government, and since 1899 it has been regarded as the de facto capital of the country. This situation accounts for the confusion in the popular mind as to which city is the capital of Bolivia. In La Paz the president and his official advisers reside, the national congress meets there, and it is the residence of the foreign diplomats accredited to the Bolivian government. On the other hand, the supreme court of Bolivia still holds its sessions at Sucre, which has the honor of being called the legal capital. Of course the situation as it exists at present (1946) may be altered by law at any time. Bolivia has one of the most strangely located capitals of any country. It lies in a natural basin 1,500 feet deep, is nearly 12,000 feet above sea level, and, despite the fact it is in a deep canyon, it is the highest capital in the world. Sucre, Bolivia's other capital, is 9,300 feet above sea level, which is 43 feet lower than Quito, capital of Ecuador. Lhasa, capital of quasi-independent Tibet, is 11,830 feet above sea level.

What is guerrilla warfare?

Guerrilla is the diminutive of Spanish guerra ("war" or "fighting"), and therefore literally means "little war." Strictly speaking, guerrilla warfare signifies "little-war warfare" and is tautological, but the phrase is firmly fixed in good usage. The true meaning of guerrilla is not a person but a type of fighting. During the Peninsular War of 1808–1814 bands of Spanish peasants who harassed Napoleon's armies were called guerrilleros and the style of partisan fighting adopted by them was known as *guerrilla*. The Duke of Wellington used these Spanish terms in his reports at the time. Guerrilla warfare is fighting between petty bands or companies of irregular troops who conduct their operations independently of one another and without orders from their own or any other government, or it is systematic fighting by "partisan rangers" duly commissioned by a government and operating under its direction. *Guerrilla* is often spelled *guerilla*, with one *r*, which is recognized as good usage.

What is the Levant?

Levant is a generic name for the eastern Mediterranean coastlands from Egypt to Greece, but particularly those of Asia Minor and Syria. The term is derived from the participial form of Latin *levare*, through French *lever*, meaning literally "rising" and figuratively "sunrising" or "the Orient." From France across the Mediterranean the eastern shore of that sea was the land of the rising sun. Strictly speaking, the Levant is the eastern shores of the Mediterranean or those countries washed by the eastern part of that sea and its contiguous waters; but occasionally the term is applied in Europe to the entire East. In the sixteenth and seventeenth centuries the Far East was known as the *High Levant*. More recently Syria, Latakia, Lebanon and Jebel Druze have become known specifically as the Levant states. Throughout the Mediterranean region the east wind frequently is called the *levant wind* and the west wind the *ponent wind*, the latter being derived from Latin *ponere* ("to set"), and alluding to the setting sun or the Occident. The Levantines, the inhabitants of the Levant, were noted as traders already in the time of ancient Greece and still have the reputation of being shrewd dealers.

How did "peeping Tom" originate?

A peeping Tom is a prying or inquisitive person, especially in respect to prurient matters, such as one who peeps at night through the windows of a house. The term originated with the legend of Lady Godiva of Coventry, according to which Leofric, Saxon Earl of Mercia and Lord of Coventry, imposed burdensome tolls upon his subjects. His wife, Lady Godiva, a sympathetic woman who had the welfare of the town at heart, appealed to him again and again to remit the obnoxious taxes. Finally, to get rid of her importunities, Leofric agreed to grant her request if she would ride naked through the town. Lady Godiva took her lord at his word and issued a proclamation requesting all persons to remain indoors and close the shutters while she rode through the town clothed only in her long hair and her chastity. Everybody complied except Tom the tailor, who bored a hole through his shutter that he might see Lady Godiva pass. It is said that he was stricken blind for his impudence. At any rate, he has been known as Peeping Tom ever since. Leofric kept his promise and the oppressive tolls were abolished. The legendary incident was commemorated by a stained glass window in St. Michael's Church at Coventry, mentioned as early as 1690, and for centuries there was an effigy of "Peeping Tom of Coventry" in a niche of one of the public buildings in the town. At one time the ride of Lady Godiva was the theme of an annual pageant in Coventry. Some local historians insist that the modern version of the legend is a distortion and that Lady Godiva did not ride naked but merely barebacked. In other words, it was the horse and not the lady who was naked. On this subject Isaac Disraeli wrote in his *Curiosities of English Literature*: "This anecdote some have suspected to be fictitious, from its extreme barbarity; but the character of the Middle Ages will admit of any kind of wanton barbarism."

How did "dead as a dodo" originate?

The dodo was a bird that once inhabited Mauritius, a British island in the Indian Ocean east of Madagascar. Its name is a corruption of Portuguese *duodo* ("silly" or "foolish"). This bird, although larger than a turkey, was closely related to the pigeons. It was very clumsy and had only rudimentary wings. These huge ground pigeons were very numerous in Mauritius when the Portuguese discovered the island in 1507. Several years later a crew of Portuguese sailors touched at the island for provisions and killed a number of dodoes with clubs, but they found the flesh unpalatable. The bird was first described in detail by a Dutchman named van Neck in 1598, when a specimen was shipped to Holland. This bird, which died on the voyage, was long preserved at Leyden and one of its feet is still preserved in the British Museum. In 1638 a living dodo was taken to England by Sir Hamon l'Estrange, who wrote that the back of the bird had a "dunn or deare colour." This specimen was exhibited in London for a small admission fee in a house bearing a figure of the strange bird on canvas. When hogs were introduced on Mauritius the dodoes fared ill, for they were slow on their feet and could not fly. Besides, they laid only one egg for a setting in a nest of grass on the ground. Thus this queer bird became totally extinct. There is no record of a live dodo having been seen since 1681. Three skeletons or parts of skeletons of dodoes are still preserved in museums, but no eggs. Most people know nothing of the dodo except that it is extinct, a fact they are continually reminded of by the frequent use of the phrase *dead as a dodo*, which, like *dead as a doornail*, survives chiefly because of the alliteration rather than the importance of the bird it refers to. The solitaire, a bird closely related to the dodo and native to Rodiguez, became extinct about 1761.

How did "French leave" originate?

French leave is a secret 'departure, especially without paying one's debts. To take French leave, in the modern sense, is to go away or do something without notice or permission. The phrase, it is believed, originated with an eighteenth century social custom in France. According to accepted practice, a person withdrawing from a reception or other social gathering takes formal leave of the host or hostess. The ceremony was dispensed with according to a fad introduced in France. A person who wished to leave early would merely withdraw quietly without disturbing the remainder of the company. The practice had some vogue in England, where it was frowned upon by conservative society people. They called it taking *French leave*. The earliest use of the phrase recorded by the Oxford dictionary is one from Smollett written in 1771. To *desert* in French is *S'en aller* (or *filer*) a *l'anglaise*; that is, to leave English fashion. This has led some etymologists to suppose that *French leave* originally meant desertion from the Army and originated during the early wars between France and England, when it was customary for each people to accuse the other of cowardice. But evidence to support the theory is lacking. Another theory, equally unsupported by evidence, is that *French* in the phrase is merely a corruption of *frank*, meaning free.

What does "sabotage" mean?

Sabotage is the secret and systematic interference with the normal processes of industry by employees to reduce production in order to reduce the profits of the employers or to impair their capital and thus compel them to grant the demands of labor, such as higher wages, shorter hours, better working conditions, etc. Sabotage is also resorted to by foreign secret agents within a country to cripple its war efficiency. A sabot is a wooden shoe made of a single piece of wood and shaped and hollowed out to fit the foot. Such shoes are worn by many French, Flemish and Dutch peasants because they are inexpensive and adapted to keeping the feet dry in damp regions. In France persons who wear sabots are called *sabotiers*, a name formerly applied in contempt to the Waldenses. It is said that *sabotage*, pronounced sab-o-*tazh*, acquired its present meaning from the fact that in the early days of the introduction of industrial machinery in France workmen who wanted to rest or desired to spite the employer would kick their sabots or wooden shoes into the machines and pretend that it was an accident. *Sabotage*, however, is also applied to the act of cutting shoes or sockets for rails in railroad ties, and its application to the tying up of a railroad by malicious damage may have antedated its use in the more general sense. As now understood sabotage was first defined and recognized as a weapon of organized labor in 1887 by the General Confederation of Labor of France. The French syndicalists and revolutionary labor groups in other countries, including the Industrial Workers of the World (I. W. W.) in the United States, accepted sabotage as an instrument of industrial warfare no less effective than the strike. Sabotage as now practiced consists of an elaborate system of disabling machinery, misplacing tools, wasting materials, betraying trade secrets, telling customers the literal truth, and tying up enterprises like railroads by observing orders too exactly. As a rule the advocates of sabotage do not favor the complete destruction of machinery, the wrecking of trains or placing of human life in peril; they want the machinery of production to remain practically intact so work can be resumed when the employers yield to their demands. But in recent years the term has been extended to cover more violent and destructive actions, such as blowing up bridges, derailing trains, starting fires and explosions, etc. One who commits sabotage is not called a *sabotier*, but a *saboteur*, pronounced sab-o-ter.

Are honeybees native to America?

Honey or hive bees, which belong to the genus *Apis*, are not native to the New World. Wild honeybees in America all sprang from bees imported from abroad. It is supposed that colonies of these insects were first introduced into New England from Europe at some time between 1638 and 1640. Reports that honeybees were introduced into Mexico, Central America, the West Indies and South America earlier than these dates cannot be verified and probably are untrue. From the beginning the Indians associated the honeybee with the European colonists and called it "the white man's fly." The prevalent idea that honeybees are indigenous to the American continents is undoubtedly due to the fact that swarms escaped at an early date and established themselves in hollow trees in the wilderness. By 1800 honeybees had crossed the Mississippi in their westward migration. Stephen F. Austin, while on his first trip to Texas in 1821, recorded in his diary that his party discovered a bee tree and got a gallon and a half of honey. Honeybees, however, should not be confused with the native wild bees of America. Many species of social bees belonging to the families *Melipona* and *Trigona* are indigenous to the New World, especially its tropical and semitropical regions. These insects, which make their nests in trees or in the ground, are called stingless bees because their stings are only vestigial, and they are often known as "mosquito bees" because of their small size. They are not hive bees and produce honey and wax in small quantities only. Honey and wax referred to in the records of the conquest of Mexico by Cortez may have been produced by these insects. Fossilized bees dating back to prehistoric periods of America probably belonged to the same families. Out of the ten or twelve thousand varieties of bees that have been identified only four or five store honey.

Which is correct, "Serbia" or "Servia"?

Serbia is now the accepted English form of the name of the Balkan country that became part of Jugoslavia after the First World War. Before the outbreak of that war Servia was the favored spelling of the name in America. In 1897 the United States Geographic Board adopted that spelling and it was followed by the Department of State. But Servia was objectionable to the inhabitants of that country because of its analogy with Latin servus, "slave," and because the Slavic spelling of the name in Latin characters is Srba or Srbija. Accordingly in 1915 the Geographic Board reversed its early decision in favor of Serbia.

What king tried to make several clocks tick together?

It is said that during his retirement at the monastery of Yuste in Spain the Emperor Charles V (1500–1558) indulged his mechanical tastes by trying to make several clocks tick in absolute unison. He finally gave up in despair, observing, according to tradition, that if he could not make two clocks run together how foolish it had been for him to try to make a number of men conform to the same sentiments. That Charles had a passion for timepieces is a well-known fact. His chief companion at Yuste was Torriano, who was skilled in the manufacture of timepieces and who had made many elaborate clocks to adorn the apartments of the monastery. William Hickling Prescott, however, does not accept the story of the Emperor's alleged philosophical comment upon his experiments. In The Life of Charles the Fifth After His Abdication, the American historian says: "The difficulty which he found in adjusting his clocks and watches is said to have drawn from the monarch a philosophical reflection on the absurdity of his having attempted to bring men to anything like uniformity of belief in matters of faith, when he could not make any two of his time-pieces agree with each other. But that he never reached the degree of philosophy required for such reflection is abundantly shown by more than one sentiment that fell from his pen, as well as his lips, during his residence at Yuste." As Holy Roman Emperor Charles V ruled over more territory than any other European monarch who has ever lived.

What do "8vo." and "12mo." mean?

These book symbols are relics of a time when all paper was made by hand and all sheets were virtually the same size. The number of times a sheet had to be folded in making a book was a fair indication of the page dimensions of the book. If the sheet were folded only once, each sheet making two leaves and four pages, the book was called a *folio* irrespective of the actual size. If the sheets were folded twice, each sheet making four leaves and eight pages, the book was called a *quarto*, from Latin *quartus* ("fourth"). This was abbreviated *4to.*, the last two letters of *quarto* combined with the figure *4. Folio*, from Latin *folium* ("leaf"), was not generally abbreviated. If the sheets were folded three times, each making eight leaves and sixteen pages, the book was called an *octavo*, which was abbreviated to *8vo.*, the figure 8 being combined with the last two letters of *octavo* ("eight"). If the sheets were folded so as to make twelve leaves and twenty-four pages the book was called a *duodecimo* (from Latin *duodecimus*, "twelfth"), which was abbreviated to *12mo.* Although these symbols have lost their original significance they are still used by publishers to represent arbitrary sizes. For instance, an 8vo. book is about six by nine and a half inches and a 12mo. book is about five by seven and one half inches. Nowadays books are generally printed thirty-two or sixty-four pages at a time.

In what country is Mont Blanc?

Mont Blanc, the highest peak in the Alps, is in the French province of Haute Savoie near the Italian border. Owing to the fact that many travelers and tourists see the peak from Geneva, which is forty miles away, Mont Blanc is often erroneously supposed to be in Switzerland. It is the highest mountain in Europe west of the Caucasus.

Do the legs of a colt grow longer?

Nature provides the young of many species of animals with legs long in proportion to their height so they can follow their mothers. The legs of a newly born colt are disproportionately long and it is commonly believed that they are as long at birth as they will ever be. Such, strictly speaking, is not the case, although the relative length of the legs to the height of the body is greater at birth than at maturity. Measurements made at the Iowa State College of Agriculture and Mechanic Arts indicate that the legs of colts increase materially in length. During the first year alone the increase in the length of a horse's legs may be from seven to ten inches. According to the United States Department of Agriculture, the legs of horses continue to increase in length after the animals are four years old. Measurements taken between the ages of four and eight years showed that during that time the legs increased in length a quarter of an inch. In all probability similar results would be obtained if the legs of other grazing animals were measured at various ages. The legs of a colt are so long in proportion to the body that it has to spread its front feet apart to reach the ground to graze.

Why was paper money called shinplasters?

The original shinplaster was a curative plaster made of brown paper covered with tar and vinegar. It was applied to a sore shin. How *shinplaster* came to mean paper money is unknown for certain. Apparently it was first used as a nickname for the worthless paper currency that flooded the country during and immediately after the American Revolution. Quite probably the name originally had a humorous application, the Continental paper money being regarded as worthless except as *plasters for broken shins*. One authority thinks the name may be a corruption of French *cinque piastres*, a five-dollar bill issued by the government of Santo Domingo. The value of these bills was so ridiculously small as compared to gold that it became a common joke in the West Indies, so it is said, to say that a worthless thing was worth no more than a *cinque piastre*. It is easy to see how American sailors and traders might corrupt this into *shinplaster*. This, however, is merely a conjecture. *Shinplaster* was again widely used as the name of the small notes issued by private banks during the panic of 1837. The fractional currency issued during the Civil War period was also called *shinplaster* money. Because of the metal shortage and the disappearance of coin from circulation the Federal government first issued fractional paper currency August 1, 1862. The fifth and last issue of such currency was made from February 26, 1874, to February 15, 1876.

How long is the longest elephant tusk on record?

The longest elephant tusk of which there is authentic record is eleven feet five and one-half inches in length, and eighteen inches in circumference at its girth. This tusk and its mate, which is somewhat shorter, weigh together 292 pounds. They were taken from an elephant of the Sudan species—*Loxodonta africanus*—which was shot by an American a short distance from the border of Ethiopia at the beginning of the nineteenth century. King Menelik of Ethiopia obtained possession of the pair, which finally, by way of the London ivory market, found their way to the National Collection of Heads and Horns in New York City, where they are now on exhibition. Single elephant tusks weighing 255 pounds and measuring 26 inches in circumference have been reported, but these figures cannot now be verified. The longest Indian elephant tusk on record is 8 feet 9 inches in length. Its maximum circumference is 17¼ inches and it weighs 81 pounds. David Livingstone, the African missionary and explorer, reported that African elephants sometimes lift their young from the ground on their great tusks and carry them for a considerable distance. The average newly born calf of this species weighs 200 pounds and stands about 3 feet high.

How did Nome, Alaska, get its name?

Nome, Alaska, was originally called Anvil City. The present name was suggested by Cape Nome, near which the town is situated. The cape itself was named in the following manner: When a chart of the Alaskan coast was being prepared on board the British ship "Herald," it was observed that this point had no name. It was indicated by *? Name*, meaning that the name was unknown. A draftsman carelessly copied it as *Cape Name*, but the *a* in *Name* was so indistinct that in London the word was interpreted as *Nome*, and the name of the point was written *Cape Nome*. The earliest known use of the name *Cape Nome* appears on a chart dated 1849. This information was given to the British Admiralty by a British officer who was on board the "Herald" when the original chart was made. There appears to be no foundation to the legend that *Nome* is a corruption of Eskimo *Ka-no-me* ("I do not know"), the reply of the natives when asked by Europeans what the name of the place was. There are post offices named Nome in Texas and North Dakota.

Why are so many companies incorporated in Delaware?

A large number of firms doing business on a national or international scale are incorporated under the laws of Delaware because the corporation laws of that state are more liberal than similar laws in other states, with the possible exception of Maryland and Maine. Under American law a corporation chartered in one state may not enter another state without its consent, but once admitted into another state it may enjoy all privileges written into its charter under the laws of the parent state and even function in other states in a manner not permitted to corporations created in those states. Consequently many firms incorporate in those states having the most lenient incorporation laws. New Jersey, the first state to make a bid for the profitable business of incorporating firms, used to be known as the "mother of trusts." But since 1913, Delaware, Maryland and Maine have been more liberal in granting legal privileges to corporations. Delaware requires a smaller percentage of subscribed stock, and grants many privileges to corporations not granted by most of the other states. By incorporating in Delaware a firm can obtain advantages peculiar to that state, which derives considerable revenue from the several thousand charters issued annually. The present charter law of Delaware was passed in 1898, but it was not until after it was found that the courts in that state were more favorable to corporations in interpreting the law that large numbers of firms were incorporated there. *Incorporated in Delaware* and *This is a Delaware Corporation* have become bywords throughout the business world.

Did Harvard men found Yale?

The first movement leading to the establishment of what is now Yale University was a meeting of ten ministers at Brandford, Connecticut in 1700. Nine of these ministers were graduates of Harvard and therefore it may be said with some truth that Yale was founded by Harvard men. These ministers contributed forty volumes for the library of the proposed college. An act of incorporation creating a body of trustees was passed by the Connecticut legislature in 1701. The college was originally located at Saybrook, but in 1716 it was removed to New Haven. It was not at first called Yale, but the Collegiate College of America. In 1711 a donation for the college was requested from Elihu Yale, a childless London merchant, whose father had been an early settler in New England. Three years later Yale contributed some books. Cotton Mather, a Harvard man and one of the most famous of all the Puritans, may be said to have named Yale. A letter that he wrote to Yale in 1716, the year the college was moved to New Haven, said in part: "If what is forming at New Haven might bear the name of Yale College it would be better than a name of sons and daughters. And your munificence might easily obtain for you such commemoration." Yale responded to this suggestion and in 1718 he sent three boxes of merchandise to Boston to be sold for the benefit of the school. These goods brought more than 562 pounds and later gifts brought Yale's contribution to the school to a total of about 800 pounds, which was the largest single donation to the college until 1837. Little is known about Elihu Yale. He was born in New England but educated in London. About 1670 he went to India in the service of the British

East India Company, and from 1687 to 1692 he was governor of Fort George at Madras, but was removed because of scandals concerning his administration. Apparently he amassed a considerable fortune. The inscription on his tombstone at Wrexham, Wales, reads: "Born in America, in Europe bred, In Africa travell'd, and in Asia wed, Where long he liv'd and thriv'd, In London dead, Much Good, Some ill he did, So Hope all's even and that His Soul, Through Mercy's Gone to Heaven."

What is condign punishment?

Condign in condign punishment originally meant "deserved," "appropriate or merited," "not severe." It is derived from Latin cum ("with"), and dignus ("worthy"). Strictly speaking, condign punishment may be either severe or mild; it is what the person punished deserves. At one time condign was employed in many different contexts, such for instance with praise as well as with words denoting punishment. In Shakespeare's Love's Labor's Lost Moth asks, "Speak you this in my praise, master?" and Armado replies, "In thy condign praise." But even in Shakespeare's time the word was equivalent to deservedly severe. In II King Henry VI Cardinal Beaufort and the Duke of York accuse Gloucester of devising "strange deaths for small offenses done" and "strange tortures for offenders never heard of" contrary to form of law while he was protector. To which Gloucester replies:

> Unless it were a bloody murderer,
> Or foul felonious thief that fleeced poor passengers,
> I never gave them condign punishment;
> Murder indeed, that bloody sin, I tortured
> Above the felon or what trespass else.

Nowadays condign is used only with punishment or words equivalent in meaning and signifies justly severe. The severity is the point emphasized and desert is only a condition of its appropriateness. A person put to death for a trivial offense would not receive condign punishment.

What is dry ice?

Dry ice is carbon dioxide, common soda fountain gas, that has been solidified under pressure. In appearance solid carbon dioxide is a dense, snowlike substance that can be cut or sawed like ordinary water ice. The same kind of gas as that used in carbonated drinks is used in making dry ice and a piece of the substance placed in a glass of water causes the water to foam and give off bubbles of gas. Dry ice does not melt in the ordinary sense of the term, but goes directly from a solid to a vapor. It evaporates or sublimates to a dry, noncorrosive gas without leaving a drop of liquid. At atmosphere pressure dry ice has a temperature of nearly 110 degrees below zero, or 140 degrees lower than natural or artificial ice. It weighs much less than water ice and is fifteen or twenty times as effective, pound for pound. One cubic foot of dry ice is equivalent to 450 cubic feet of carbon dioxide gas. Its commercial popularity as a refrigerant is owing largely to the fact that when properly stored it loses only about ten per cent of its weight a day and makes possible the preservation of perishable foods for more than a week without elaborate refrigerators. Solidified carbon dioxide was first produced incidentally by a Swiss engineer named P. Picted while experimenting with mechanical refrigeration. Under the name *carbon dioxide snow* it was for a long time regarded merely as a laboratory curiosity. The American physicist Percy W. Bridgman, noted for his researches in high pressure, demonstrated that dry ice could be used as a practical refrigerant. Although dry ice looks harmless, it is capable of causing severe "burns" and therefore should be handled with care, but the popular notion that dry ice gives off poisonous fumes while evaporating is not true. Carbon dioxide gas, at first produced only artificially in plants, is now also obtained from "dry ice wells." Dry ice has been used to propel bullets in guns, to operate motors, to condition rivets and to distinguish genuine diamonds and pearls from imitations. Sometimes *dry ice is* applied to water ice when its temperature is below 32 degrees Fahrenheit to distinguish it from *wet* or melting ice at higher temperatures.

Why is Cupid called Dan Cupid?

Dan is an old title of honor equivalent to lord, master or sir. It is related to the Spanish *don* and like that title is probably derived from Latin *dominus*, lord. It is the masculine form of *dame*. Except in a few special connections *dan* is now obsolete, but formerly it was applied to all sorts of distinguished men, nobles, scholars, poets and even deities. Edmund Spenser applied the title to Geoffrey Chaucer, the greatest English poet before Shakespeare, and since then it has been frequently applied to poets. In Book IV of the *Faerie Queene* Spenser wrote:

> Dan Chaucer, well of English undefyled,
> On Fame's eternal beadroll worthie to be filed.

In Roman mythology Cupid, the son of Mercury and Venus, is the god of love and is identified with the Greek Eros. The name is derived from Latin *cupido*, meaning desire, passion or love, and Cupid was the personification of the amatory passions. He is generally represented as a beautiful naked boy with wings, carrying a bow and arrow and sometimes blindfolded. As a rule the early English writers, like modern writers, seldom referred to Cupid except in a light vein, and they gave him many different titles. We find him playfully spoken of as "dan Cupido" as early as 1384. *Dan Cupid* was already part of everyday speech in Shakespeare's time. In *Love's Labor's Lost*, Act III, the poet puts the following words in the mouth of Biron, one of the lords attending King Ferdinand of Navarre:

> This whimpled, whining, purblind, wayward boy;
> This senior-junior, giant-dwarf, Dan Cupid.

As early as the fourth century B.C. Praxiteles and Lysippus, two great Greek sculptors, made statues of the god of love and represented him as holding a bow and arrow. With the bow Cupid is supposed to send the love dart through the heart of the one desired.

Which is correct, "Pittsburgh" or "Pittsburg"?

The name of the Pennsylvania city is correctly spelled *Pittsburgh*, not *Pittsburg*. It is one of the most frequently misspelled place names in the United States. In 1891 the United States Geographic Board, the highest Federal authority on such matters, was asked by the Post Office Department to rule on the correct spelling of the name, and it decided in favor of *Pittsburg*. This decision met with considerable local opposition. Accordingly, in response to petitions from local officials and numerous citizens, the United States Geographic Board reconsidered the case and in 1911 decided in favor of *Pittsburgh*. The French had called the site "Fort Duquesne." In November, 1758, during the French and Indian War, it was taken by the British under General John Forbes. A stockade was built around a cluster of traders' and soldiers' huts and the embryo village was named after William Pitt, then Prime Minister of England. On November 26, 1758, General Forbes reported to Lieutenant Governor William Denny of Pennsylvania, dating his letter from "Fort Duquesne, or now *Pitts-bourg*." The next day he wrote to Pitt as follows: I have used the freedom of giving your name to Fort du Quesne, as I hope it was in some measure the being actuated by your spirit that now makes me master of the place." In the fall of 1759 General John Stanwix rebuilt the fortifications and named the place "Fort Pitt." The Penns set aside 5,700 acres at this point in 1769 and called it *Manor of Pittsburgh*. They began to sell building lots in 1784. George Washington, who visited the area in 1770, referred to it in his diary as both *Pittsburg* and *Fort Pitt*. On April 22, 1794, it was incorporated as the *Borough of Pittsburgh*, and the name was so spelled in the seal then adopted. It was incorporated as a city March 16, 1816, and in the law it is called *Pittsburg*, but in the seal, which is still used, it is called *City of Pittsburgh*. There are, however, places with post offices named *Pittsburg* in at least nine states.

How does a Commonwealth differ from a State?

Officially speaking, the American Union consists of forty-four *states* and four *commonwealths*. The four members of the Union that are officially styled commonwealths instead of states are Massachusetts, Pennsylvania, Virginia and Kentucky. But the four commonwealths are states in the eyes of the Federal Constitution and their status is no different from that of the forty-four members of the Union officially styled states. The two words have about the same meaning, but *commonwealth* originally connoted more of self-government than *state*.

What is meant by, "Possession is nine points of the law"?

"Possession is nine points of the law" was a familiar proverb already early in the seventeenth century. It is merely an old popular saying and does not refer to any actual principle of law or set of legal points. The proverb signifies simply that, in a dispute over property, possession is a decided advantage, or, "that possession is the strongest tenure of the law," as it was expressed in *The Fables of Bidpai*, a collection of ancient Sanskrit fables. The number nine is not particularly significant in this connection. In fact, the original saying appears to have been, "Possession is *eleven* points of the law." Thomas Adams, in 1630, wrote: "The devil hath eleven points of the law against you, that is, possession." In his *Collection of English Proverbs*, published in 1670, John Ray gave it: "Possession is but eleven points of the law and there are but twelve." Nine, like seven and eleven, is a favorite number in folklore and popular phrases. An English lawyer once facetiously enumerated the nine points of the law as follows: (1) a good case; (2) a good deal of money; (3) a good deal of patience; (4) a good lawyer; (5) a good counsel; (6) good witnesses; (7) a good jury; (8) a good judge; and (9) good luck.

Where could a house be built with each corner in a different state?

There is only one spot in the United States where a house could be built with each of its four corners in a different state. That spot is at the common meeting point of Utah, Colorado, Arizona and New Mexico. If such a house were built the occupant could sleep in his bedroom in New Mexico, shave himself in his bathroom in Arizona, eat his breakfast in his dining room in Colorado, and read his morning paper on his porch in Utah. The *four-states boundary* is at the intersection of the 37th parallel of north latitude and the 109th meridian of west longitude. This position was determined in 1868 by a surveyor named E. N. Darling, who marked the spot by burying a sandstone three feet underground and erecting over it a sandstone on which he chiseled inscriptions. The spot is on a plateau 3,500 feet above sea level. No vegetation except cactus and greasewood grows in the sandy soil of the region. There are no human habitations for many miles around the boundary point, it being in the heart of the Indian country, quite inaccessible to the ordinary traveler, and used only as winter grazing land for sheep and cattle.

Who said: "Trust in God and keep your powder dry"?

This famous saying is attributed to Oliver Cromwell. It is supposed to have originated during one of his campaigns in Ireland in 1649 or 1650. According to a tradition, Cromwell made an impassioned address to his Ironsides when they were about to attack the enemy who had taken position on the opposite side of a river. He concluded his speech with the admonition: "Put your trust in God, but mind to keep your powder dry." This tradition is vouched for by Edward Hayes in his *Ballads of Ireland*, published in 1855. The compiler comments on the subject in a note under "Oliver's Advice," an "Orange ballad" composed in 1834 by Colonel Valentine Blacker, a British officer. Each stanza of Blacker's ballad ends with the sentiment, *Put your trust in God, my boys, and keep your powder dry.*

Why is the card game called bridge?

Bridge as applied to a card game has given philologists endless difficulty and many fantastic explanations of the term have been offered. The game itself is believed to be merely a modification of old Russian whist. We first meet with it in Constantinople and Egypt about 1865, where it was the favorite card game in social clubs. Before the end of the century it had reached the Riviera and Paris. It made its appearance in London about 1894 and quickly superseded ordinary whist as the society game of cards. Auction bridge, a modification in the method of bidding, came later. At first the game was known in England as bridge whist. This was not the first time *bridge* had been used in connection with card games. *To bridge* is an old verb meaning to bend a card so that a confederate can cut the pack wherever the bent card is placed. Webster's International dictionary defines *bender* as, "A card bent lengthwise and placed beneath that part of the pack which a confederate is to lift in cutting;—also called *bridge*." This trick is referred to in an issue of the *Sporting Examiner* printed in 1879: "By slightly bending a card—termed *bridging*—he could force, as it were, his opponent in the game to cut the cards wherever he wished." In the game of euchre *bridge* is applied to a position where one side has scored four points and the other only one. But there is no reason to suppose that *bridge* as the name of a game is related to the word in these senses. It is often said that the name is derived from Russian *britch*, but investigation reveals that *britch* itself was borrowed by the Russians from English *bridge*. Another theory is that bridge whist was originally so called because the dealer could name the trumps or could *bridge* this prerogative over to a partner. *To bridge* in the sense of to pass over by or as by a bridge is an old verb. Webster's International dictionary says of *bridge* as the name of a card game: "Formerly *biritch* (of unknown origin; not Russian, as often stated), apparently changed to *bridge* from the dealer's *bridging*, or passing, the declaration of trumps to his partner." The fact is, the origin of bridge in this sense is unknown. The most probable theory is that it is a corruption of *biritch*, a word of unknown origin. Among the fantastic theories is one contained in a popular story to the effect that *bridge* originated in the latter part of the nineteenth century in a village in Leicestershire, England, in the following manner: Two families in the village were devoted to this form of whist and paid each other visits on alternate nights in order to play. Their way, however, lay over an old rickety bridge that was dangerous to cross in the dark. The families fell into the habit of saying to each other, "Thank goodness, it's your bridge tomorrow night." In time, according to the story, they referred to the game itself as simply *bridge*, which finally found its way to London. Bridge whist was probably played under that name in London before it was heard of in Leicestershire. Some authorities think auction bridge originated among British officers in India. The *London Times* of January 16, 1903, referred to it as "the new game of auction bridge for three players." In 1907 the Bath Club made it a four-handed game.

How did "horselaugh" originate?

A horselaugh is a loud, coarse, boisterous laugh. The term dates back to the early part of the eighteenth century, if not much further. In 1713 Richard Steele wrote in No. 29 of the *Guardian*: "The Horse-Laugh is a distinguishing characteristick of the rural hoyden." Thomas Carlyle, in his life of Frederick the Great, says of Prince Leopold of Anhalt-Dessau: "He plays rough pranks, too, on occasion; and has a big horse-laugh in him, where there is a fop to be roasted, or the like." A few authorities are of the opinion that *horselaugh* was suggested by the loud, laughter-like noise frequently made by horses. According to the King James Version of the Bible, the patriarch, in *Job* 39:25, says the horse "saith among the trumpets, Ha, ha." One etymologist believes that *horse* in this connection is merely a corruption of *coarse*. In *Vanity Fair* William Makepeace Thackeray wrote: "And the old gentleman gave his knowing grin and coarse laugh." Be that as it may, *horse* is widely used attributively to denote anything large, inferior, coarse or unrefined. That was probably its original application in *horselaugh*, just as it probably was in many plant names, such as horse chestnut, horse-radish, horsebeans, horse balm, horsebane, horse cassia, etc. Likewise, rude, boisterous play is called horseplay, and a person with a long, coarse face is said to be horse-faced. In view of this common usage it is not probable, as sometimes stated, that *horse chestnut* was suggested by the horseshoe-shaped scars left on the twigs of this tree when the leaves fall.

What is white coal?

White coal is a figurative name for falling water that is capable of being used for power purposes. The term originated in France and is a literal translation of French *houille blanche*. It was probably suggested either by the fact that much of the falling water in France originated in snow-covered mountains or by the fact that falling water when filled with air bubbles appears clear and white compared with coal, which is black. Tide water capable of being used for power purposes is sometimes called "blue coal." *Tasmanite*, a compound of carbon, hydrogen, oxygen and sulphur, also is known as "white coal." This substance is found in the form of minute reddish-brown scales in certain shales in Tasmania.

What is the Bronx?

Formerly the Bronx was a district comprising several towns in Westchester County, New York. It received its name from an early settler named Jonas (or Jacob) Bronck. Whether he was Dutch, Swedish or Danish by birth is not known for certain. He arrived in America in 1639 and is described as having been a "pious Lutheran." At any rate, in 1642 Jonas Bronck bought about five hundred acres of land in the vicinity of the district that still bears his name. The old Dutch pronunciation of the name survives to this day in some quarters and one often hears it pronounced as if it were spelled Bronk. The land originally owned by Jonas Bronck was acquired by the Morris family and it was the birthplace of Gouverneur Morris of Revolutionary fame. In 1898 the district known as "The Bronx" became one of the five boroughs of New York City. Since 1914, when a county named Bronx was formed, the borough of Bronx and the county of Bronx have been coterminous. The New York Zoological Park is in the Bronx and for that reason is popularly referred to as the Bronx Zoo. Some authorities suppose the Bronx River, a small stream emptying into the East River and nearly bisecting the Bronx borough, bore the name before the district did.

How is Leigh Hunt's first name pronounced?

Leigh Hunt (1784–1859), English critic, poet and essayist, pronounced his first name *lee*. It is frequently mispronounced *lay*. His full name was James Henry Leigh Hunt, but he is known simply as Leigh Hunt. His father was the son of a West Indian merchant and lived for a time in Philadelphia, where he married the daughter of a local merchant and the sister of the wife of Benjamin West, the famous artist. The elder Hunt was a loyalist and during the Revolution was attacked by a patriot mob, after which he fled to England, where he "took orders." Leigh Hunt and his brother John established a weekly newspaper called the *Examiner* in which they published many harsh criticisms of the higher-ups. In 1813 the two brothers were prosecuted and sentenced to two years imprisonment for referring to George IV, then Prince Regent, as "a corpulent Adonis of forty." Leigh Hunt is best known for two short poems, "Abou ben Adhem" and "Jenny Kissed Me."

What countries comprise the Near East?

Near East is merely a popular term that is generally applied rather loosely to a large geographical region in southeastern Europe, southwestern Asia and northeastern Africa. As usually understood, the Near East comprises Turkey in Europe, Asia Minor, Armenia, Georgia, Azerbaijan, the south Russian republics, Persia, Syria, Palestine, Mesopotamia, some of the Mediterranean islands, and perhaps Arabia and Egypt. Greece, Bulgaria and Albania were included in the term as it was understood by the Near East Relief after the First World War. The Division of the Near East in the United States Department of State embraces most of North Africa, and even Liberia, as well as the countries at the eastern end of the Mediterranean. In official British usage *Middle East* is applied to a vast region in southern and southwestern Asia lying between Constantinople and the borders of China. The

Middle East includes most of what is commonly known as the Near East and much more. For some purposes even Egypt is included. *Far East* comprises China, Japan, the Philippines and other lands on or near the eastern coast of Asia. *Near East, Middle East* and *Far East* have never been defined for official purposes and the boundaries of the areas they describe are rather vague. *Mediterranean* is derived from two Latin words meaning "middle land" and the name dates back to the time when western civilization was largely restricted to the lands bordering on that sea. Likewise *Mesopotamia* is from two Greek words meaning "land between two rivers" and alludes to the territory lying between the Euphrates and Tigris rivers when that region was the center of the ancient Babylonian and Assyrian empires.

How do birds locate earthworms in the ground?

Many people believe that birds, such as robins, locate earthworms in the ground by hearing them. The fact is birds find their food chiefly by the sense of sight. Their behavior in cocking their heads while searching for worms and other food on the ground leads to the belief that the sense of hearing is involved, but this gesture on the part of birds is merely to aid in seeing. They do not have bifocal vision and they can see best when a single eye is pointed directly at the spot or object to be examined. Birds have a poor sense of smell. The only sound made by earthworms is very slight and resembles that made by a person when he moistens his lips and then opens and closes them without moving his jaws. It is estimated that the average robin requires about seventy earthworms or the equivalent of insect food a day. Incidentally, the eyesight of birds is superior to that of human beings.

Why do wild geese fly in a V-shaped formation?

Wild geese and ducks when migrating often fly in a V-shaped formation with the leader of the flock at the apex of the triangle. Many people suppose that the birds fly in this order because the wedge formation reduces the wind resistance. According to the popular notion, when geese and ducks advance in the form of a triangle the front bird acts as a sort of pioneer in breaking the wind for the entire flock. Such, however, is not the case. In fact naturalists believe that the opposite is true. A certain amount of wind is advantageous to the sustained flight of birds. In advancing against the wind in the form of a wedge each bird avoids the wake of the bird preceding. At the same time, the V-shaped formation is the most convenient from the standpoint of following the leader. The wedge formation enables the birds in the flock to see the leader more clearly when flying at angles rather than one directly behind the other. Observers of wild geese and ducks have noted that when the wind blows on the side of the V formation one limb of the V is generally much longer than the other, or the birds forming one limb occupy positions that coincide with the spaces between the birds on the windward side. This arrangement exposes each bird to the full wind current. Sometimes a strong side wind causes the birds to abandon the V formation and to fly in single file. In any event the regular distances between the birds are always accurately maintained. "A goose," wrote Oliver Wendell Holmes, "flies by a chart which the Royal Geographical Society could not improve."

How did "greenhorn" originate?

Greenhorn was originally applied to a deer or other animal with green or fresh horns, and the term was so employed as early as 1460. Later newly enlisted soldiers or raw recruits were called greenhorns. A chronicle written in 1650 about a fight near Leith in Scotland says: "The Scotch king being upon the castle-hill to see his men, which he called Green Horns, beaten." In 1682 the word was used as a synonym of "fresh-water Soldiers, or new levyed." As time passed greenhorn acquired the meaning of an inexperienced person or a novice, particularly a raw countryman easily imposed upon. Caleb Carman first met Abraham Lincoln in 1831 while he had a cabin near where Lincoln and John Hanks were building a flatboat in which to go to New Orleans. At first, wrote Carman to William H. Herndon in 1866, he thought Lincoln "a Green horn tho after half hours Conversation with him I found Him no Green Horn." In England at the present time an inexperienced domestic or a green workman, particularly a newly arrived foreigner, is called a greener. There seems to be no foundation for the common story that greenhorn originally referred to pointed, horn-shaped caps of green cloth that insolvent persons were compelled to wear in France during the reign of Louis XV in order to receive the protection of the bankruptcy law.

Is the art of hardening copper lost?

A popular belief exists that the Egyptians and other ancient peoples, including the Mexicans and Peruvians, knew a process of hardening copper that is unknown to modern metallurgists. About the turn of the last century the New York *Herald* published an article in which a South American explorer was quoted as follows: "I found a copper chisel in a mound near Callao which proved to be tempered to the hardness of steel. It was tested on a railroad rail of iron and could have cut it in two.

The tempering of copper is a lost art, however, and was known to the Incas only. Humboldt analyzed one of these chisels and found it to contain 94 per cent copper and 6 per cent silica. Despite the discovery of these component parts all experiments have failed to reproduce a similar hardness." There is also a notion that the United States Government has a standing offer of a large reward for the rediscovery of this so-called *lost art* of tempering copper. Neither belief has any foundation in fact. The reputed hardened product is always an alloy. No specimen of pure copper has been found that had a greater degree of hardness than can be produced by hammering. Any expert metallurgist of today knows how to produce edged tools of hardened copper as good as any made in prehistoric times, but the knowledge does him no good because of the vast superiority of the steel tools now available. Hardening is produced either by hammering and cold rolling, or by the addition of alloying elements, in which case the material cannot truly be called copper. Amateur inventors seeking the lost art of hardening copper and the government prize for its rediscovery are wasting their time, for neither ever existed.

What is fool's gold?

Fool's gold is the popular name of various iron, copper and nickel pyrites. They are called fool's gold because inexperienced prospectors frequently mistake them for gold ore. The early colonists at Jamestown made this mistake. Somebody discovered a bank of bright yellow dirt and its color was thought to be due to particles of gold. Captain John Smith wrote: "There was no thought, no discourse, no hope, and no work but to dig gold, wash gold, refine gold, and load gold." Captain Christopher Newport carried a shipload of the worthless mineral to the London Company in England and soon learned to his chagrin and the disappointment of the gold-hungry colonists that all is not gold that glisters. *Pyrites* is derived from Greek *pyr*, meaning "fire." It was originally applied to disulphide of iron because it strikes fire with steel and was used for igniting powder in musket pans before gunflints were introduced. Iron pyrites is a source of both sulphur and sulphuric acid.

What is eminent domain?

Eminent domain is the sovereign right of a government to take private property for public uses without asking permission of the owner, provided just compensation is given. In British usage *eminent domain* is seldom used except in connection with international law; but in the United States it is commonly applied to the right of the Federal government and the states to take private property for public use within their borders. *Eminent* in the phrase refers to the fact that the right of the public is superior or pre-eminent to that of individuals. By eminent domain the Federal government obtains land for parks, post offices, forts, military and naval camps and stations and sites for other public purposes. Governments often confer a limited right of eminent domain on railroad, telephone and other private companies that render services generally regarded as essential to the public welfare. Eminent domain is based on the principle that an individual's private interest should not be permitted to stand in the way of the interest of the entire community in which he lives. Amendment V of the Federal Constitution provides that private property shall not "be taken for public use, without just compensation."

Why is fashionable society called "the four hundred"?

In 1889 Ward McAllister, a New York society leader who was regarded by the smart set as an authority on fashionable matters, declared that there were only about four hundred persons who could claim admission into the best social circles in New York City. He also said there were not more than four hundred persons in the city who could walk gracefully across a ballroom floor. In 1892 he boasted in the Union League Club that he had cut down the list of guests for Mrs. William Astor's ball to a mere 400. *Four hundred* in the sense of the "cream of society" or the smart set of any place caught the public fancy, was taken up by the press and entered the idiom of the language. Previously the fashionables were known as *the upper ten*, which was a shortened form of *the upper ten thousand*. In 1850 James Fenimore Cooper, in *Ways of the Hour*, wrote: "These families, you know, are our upper crust, not upper ten thousand." Ten years later N. P. Willis, in *Necessity for a Promenade Drive*, said: "At present there is no distinction among the upper ten thousand of the city." At that time the theory was that the fashionables of New York City did not exceed ten thousand in number. In 1878 James Payn, in *By Proxy*, wrote: "Warren . . . is a *novus homo*, and only a Conservative on that account; it being the quickest method to gain admission among the Upper Ten."

Who painted grapes that birds pecked at?

Zeuxis (pronounced *zewk- sis*), a famous Greek painter who lived in the latter part of the fifth century B.C., is said to have painted a bunch of grapes that looked so natural that birds pecked at them. This is supposed to have occurred during a competition between Zeuxis and a young rival named Parrhasius. Pliny gives a somewhat different version of the grape story. He says that Zeuxis painted a boy holding grapes toward which birds flew. Zeuxis, commenting upon the incident, remarked that if Parrhasius had painted the boy as well as the grapes the birds would have been afraid to approach. According to a legend, Zeuxis died from laughing at a hag he had just painted. Parrhasius, one of the greatest of the Greek painters, was known as the "legislator of painting" because of his realistic portraits. He was the first, wrote Pliny, to give true expression to the features, elegance to the hair and gracefulness to the mouth. There is not a single piece of ancient Greek painting on canvas in existence today. Our knowledge of Greek painting is based on ancient writings and faded remnants on sculpture. It is said that when Thomas Gainsborough, the eighteenth century English portrait and landscape painter, was a boy he once made a rapid sketch of a man whom he saw leaning over the fence of an orchard. His picture was so realistic that the man was identified and arrested as a poacher.

What does "limited" after firm names mean?

Limited (abbreviated Ltd.) as used after the names of British firms is short for limited liability. It implies not that the number of members of the firm is limited but that their financial liability is limited. In a British limited bank or trading company the liability of each partner or stockholder is limited to the amount of his stock or shares, or to an amount fixed by a guarantee. The law requires that limited follow the name of the firm, except in cases of certain companies not organized and operated for profit. In the United States the nearest approach to the British limited company is the corporation. An American writes Inc. after the name of a firm or corporation much as the Englishman writes Ltd.

What state has the greatest coast line?

Florida has a longer coast line than any other state in the Union. California is second in the extent of its seacoast. It should be borne in mind that unless the scale of the maps employed and the method of measurement are given, a numerical statement of the length of the coast line of a body of land conveys no definite information, because the results will vary so widely that there will be no common basis of comparison. The smaller the unit of measure the greater will be the number of indentations included. No matter what method is adopted the scale of the maps will be an important factor. According to the method employed by the United States Coast and Geodetic Survey, the general coast line of Florida, exclusive of islands, is 1,197 statute miles—399 on the Atlantic and 798 on the Gulf of Mexico—while that of California is 913 miles. But these figures really mean very little. The two ends of Maine are only 225 miles apart as the crow flies and the general coast line of that state is 339 miles. Yet its coast is so indentured that if a small unit of measurement were employed it would have a coast line of about 3,000 miles, the distance a person would have to walk if he traveled it on foot. The total general coast line of the United States proper is 7,314: 1,888 on the Atlantic, 1,629 on the Gulf and 1,366 on the Pacific. Alaska's general coast line is 6,640 miles and is greater than the total coast line of the United States proper. Lake shore line is not regarded as coast line by the Coast and Geodetic Survey. If it were, Michigan, an inland state with a Great Lakes shore line of more than 3,000 miles, would have a coast line of the same length.

Why do fish come to the surface?

Fish generally come to the surface when the water becomes foul and deficient in oxygen. Usually the upper layers of water are richer in that element. Popularly fish are supposed to come to the surface to fill their air bladders with air. The chief function of the air bladder, which seems to be homologous with the lungs in higher vertebrates, is to adjust the specific gravity of fish and to aid them in maintaining their equilibrium. There is no connection in most fish between the air bladder and the respiratory system, the air bladder being a blind sac that is filled with gases absorbed from the blood. All fish respire by means of their gills. However, in a few species—the blowfish and the fresh-water gars, for instance—the air bladder is connected with the gullet by a duct and it serves as an accessory or supplementary organ of respiration. Ichthyologists suppose that such fish come to the surface and protrude their snouts occasionally in order to gulp down air, which becomes mixed with the water passing through the gills.

What does "Shenandoah" mean?

Shenandoah does not mean "Daughter of the Stars" as popularly supposed. According to the Bureau of American Ethnology, the term literally means "Land of Big Mountains" and is a corruption of the name applied by the Iroquois Indians to the mountainous region on both sides of the Shenandoah Valley in Virginia. In October, 1923, the dirigible airship ZR-1 was christened the "Shenandoah" by Mrs. Edwin Denby, wife of the Secretary of the Navy. At that time the Navy Department explained that "the original meaning of this Indian name is Daughter of the Stars." Accordingly the name was regarded as particularly appropriate for an airship. It is probable, however, that the Bureau of American Ethnology is correct and that the name means "Land of Big Mountains."

What is the highest American peak east of the Rockies?

This is a disputed question. The United States Geological Survey regards Mount Mitchell, in Yancey County, North Carolina, as the highest peak in the United States east of the Rocky Mountains. It has an elevation of 6,711 feet above sea level. The honor, however, is also claimed for Harney Peak, in Pennington County, South Dakota, which has an elevation of 7,242 feet above sea level. This difference of opinion arises from the fact that the government regards the Black Hills, which include Harney Peak, as part of the Rocky Mountains, while some authorities regard them as a detached mountain system. Mount Mitchell was originally called Black Dome. In 1835 Professor Elisha Mitchell, a geologist on the faculty of the University of North Carolina, climbed the peak and announced that it is the highest in Eastern United States. While making his fourth ascent of the mountain in 1857 Professor Mitchell lost his way and fell to his death over a precipice into the pool of a waterfall. Later his ashes were interred on the top of the mountain that now bears his name.

When was the friction match invented?

The first true friction match was invented in 1827 by John Walker, a druggist at Stockton on Tees in Durham, England. Godfrey Haukswitz, an associate of Robert Boyle, was the first to attempt to make matches in the modern sense of the term. He employed small pieces of phosphorus to light splints of wood dipped in sulphur. For nearly 150 years after that sulphur matches were used. A sulphur-tipped splinter was lighted by dipping it into a box of tinder ignited by striking steel against flint. A French physician and chemist named Sangrain, who settled in St. Louis about 1800, showed William Clark and Meriwether Lewis how to make matches before they started on their long journey up the Missouri River in 1804. The Frenchman dipped sulphur-tipped splinters of wood into phosphorus and produced flames without difficulty. He then sealed a supply of phosphorus in tin boxes for safety and showed the explorers how to make their own sulphur-tipped sticks. These, of course, were not true friction matches. Walker's matches were made of a compound of chlorate of potash and sugar mixed with powdered gum arabic to make it adhesive when applied to a splinter of wood. They were ignited by drawing them rapidly and under considerable pressure through a piece of sandpaper. Such matches were first sold in London under the name of "lucifers." *Lucifer*, often used as a general name for matches, is one of the names of Satan. The term is derived from Latin *lux* ("light"), and *fero* ("to bring"), and literally means "bringer of light." In 1836 Alonzo D. Philips of Springfield, Massachusetts, obtained the first American patent on matches. His matches, an adaptation of Walker's, were known as "locofocos." Walker had named his matches "congreves," after Sir William Congreve (1772–1828), a versatile and ingenious English inventor. In 1855 a Swede named Bottger made the first safety matches. It had been discovered that red phosphorus itself gives off no fumes and is virtually inert; but when mixed with chlorate of potash under slight pressure it explodes violently. Bottger put the one on the box and the other on the match and produced safety friction matches. For many years match heads contained poison and were widely used by murderers and suicides. The Esch-Hughes Non-Poisonous Match Act, approved in 1912, put a heavy tax on white phosphorus and made the use of it commercially impractical. Although matchmaking machinery was developed in the United States, this country did not become a leader in the match industry until after the First World War.

What is the Maelstrom?

Maelstrom, pronounced *male*-strum, is the name of a famous whirlpool between Mosken and Moskeneso islands of the Lofoden group lying in the Arctic Ocean off the northwest coast of Norway. There are many legends concerning the dangers of the Maelstrom, which is only one of many whirlpools between these islands. Centuries ago navigators believed that the Maelstrom would engulf and destroy any vessel that came within its reach. Anthony Jenkinson, English sea captain and traveler, wrote in 1560: "There is between the said Rost Islands, and Lofoote, a whirle poole, called Malestrand, which . . . maketh such a terrible noise, that it shaketh the rings in the doores of the inhabitants houses of the said Islands, ten miles of." This supposedly fatal whirlpool figures in many stories, such as "The Diver" by Schiller and "A Descent into the Maelstrom" by Poe. In early times it was believed that even whales were drawn into the vortex of the Maelstrom and destroyed by the violence of its whirling waters. The Maelstrom, however, is no longer regarded as very dangerous. Only in winter or when the wind blows from the northwest is there any danger to ships, and then only to small vessels. Nowadays small fishing boats avoid these waters only during heavy fogs and stormy weather. Ordinarily it can be navigated with safety at both high and low tide. The whirlpool is produced by the union of several currents from the great West Fiord between the Lofoden Islands and the mainland. The chief danger to vessels is not that of being sucked into the whirlpool, as legend supposes, but of being dashed to pieces against the rocks. *Maelstrom* is believed to be derived from Dutch *malen* ("to grind"), and *stroom* ("stream"), and literally means "stream that grinds." The word is used figuratively as a common noun to describe other whirlpools or any overpowering movement or far-reaching influence.

How did "once in a blue moon" originate?

The origin of *once in a blue moon* is obscure. Originally it signified "never," but now it is generally used in the sense of "seldom" or "very rarely." Some authorities think they see a relation between the phrase and the moon under certain conditions. Dr. E. Cobham Brewer, for instance, who in his *Dictionary of Phrase and Fable* defined *once in a blue moon* as *very rarely indeed*, says: "On December 10, 1883, we had a blue moon. The winter was unusually mild." In 1927, during a total eclipse of the sun, many observers at Belfast, Ireland, fancied that the moon took on a decidedly blue tinge. Moons of unusual colors, such as green and blue, have been seen after certain violent volcanic explosions and occasionally through smoke-laden fogs. Similar blue moons are caused by the refraction of moonlight through ice crystals high in the atmosphere, dust storms and cloud banks near the horizon at sunset. It was only natural that such phenomena, which occur seldom, should be popularly regarded as the source of *once in a blue moon* in the sense of infrequently. But inasmuch as the phrase originally meant *never* it is not probable that it was suggested by such lunar phenomena. As early as 1528, in the second part of Roy and Barlow's *Rede Me and Be Not Wroth*, we find the idea of a blue moon regarded as absurd:

> Yf they say the mone is blewe
> We must beleve that it is true,
> Admyttinge their interpetacion.

Is water pressure decreased by reducing the size of the pipe?

Water pressure depends on the depth of the water only and accordingly the pressure against the sides of a pipe is not decreased by reducing the diameter of the pipe. Likewise the pressure against a dam is the same when stationary water extends back a long distance as when it extends back a short distance, provided the depth is the same in both cases. On the subject of hydrostatic pressure of water on vertical walls the United States Bureau of Standards wrote to the author as follows: "The pressure on a vertical wall depends only on the depth of the water and not on the distance to which the water extends horizontally from the face of the wall. If we consider two tubes, one of which is one foot in diameter and the other five miles in diameter, filled with water to the same depth, the pressure per square inch at the bottom is the same in both tubes; that is, it is independent of the diameter of the tubes."

How did Libby prison get its name?

This famous Confederate prison was originally a warehouse. After the first Battle of Bull Run large numbers of Federal prisoners were taken to Richmond and it was necessary for the Confederate government to provide buildings for their confinement. General J. H. Winder, commander in the city, notified Libby, owner of the warehouse, that he would take possession of it within forty-eight hours. By an oversight the sign *Libby and Son* was left hanging over the door, a circumstance that resulted in the building's becoming known as Libby prison. In the election of November 8, 1864, the inmates of Libby prison held a kangaroo election and cast 276 votes for Lincoln and 95 for McClellan. When President Lincoln visited Richmond shortly before Lee's surrender he paused a moment to look at the notorious prison. Somebody in his party shouted, "Pull it down," but Lincoln replied, "No, leave it as a monument." The old prison was taken down and reconstructed in Chicago as a war museum for the Columbian Exposition in 1893 and was never returned to Richmond.

Which is lighter, a steel or a wooden ship?

A steel ship is lighter than a wooden ship of the same dimensions. This is because steel is so much stronger than wood, weight for weight, that a great deal more wood must be used in building a ship of equal dimensions and strength. Welded steel ships are faster in the water than riveted steel ships because rivet heads increase the friction. Welded ships weigh about 13 per cent less than riveted ships, because weldings weigh less than rivets, and in welded ships it is not necessary for the plates to overlap.

Who founded the Cabot family in America?

The Cabot family in America was founded by John Cabot, who came to Salem, Massachusetts, about 1700. He was a native of the Island of Jersey, one of the Channel Islands, where his ancestors had lived for at least several generations. Notwithstanding numerous assertions to the contrary, no relationship has been established between this John Cabot and John Cabot of Venice, the noted navigator and discoverer, who sailed in the service of England. The latter's Italian name was Giovanni Caboto. Lloyd Vernon Briggs, in his *History and Genealogy of the Cabot Family*, says that, with the exception of John Cabot of Genoa and Venice, no early records of Cabots in Italy have been found. It is possible, he suggests, that the navigator or one of his immediate ancestors went to Italy from France or the Channel Islands, and that he and the American Cabots may have had a common ancestor on the Island of Jersey. Evidence, however, is wanting to prove or disprove the theory. The navigator had three sons, Louis, Sebastian and Santius (or Sanctus). So far as known Sebastian had no sons, although he had at least two daughters. It is not known whether or not his brothers left any descendants. There is a tradition in the American Cabot family that John Cabot, the navigator, was an Englishman and not an Italian at all. The lineage pretensions of the American Cabots are satirized in the following popular quatrain:

> Here's to good old Boston,
> The home of the bean and the cod,
> Where the Cabots speak only to Lowells,
> And Lowells speak only to God.

This jingle is a slightly modified version of a toast written by Dr. John C. Bossidy, of Boston, who recited it in 1905 at a Holy Cross College alumni dinner. Reverend Samuel C. Bushnell, who quoted the toast in a letter to Dean Jones of Yale University, is frequently but erroneously credited with its authorship.

What is the official name of the Australian capital?

The official name of the capital city of Australia is *Canberra*, a word of aboriginal origin that is pronounced by the Australians almost as if it were spelled *kann-* bra, with the accent on the first syllable. Many people think the name of the city is *Yass Canberra*, owing no doubt to the fact that when the Australian government was determining the site for the commonwealth city a number were considered and one of them was known as the Yass Canberra site. In 1908 the Australian parliament passed an act that stated: "It is hereby determined that the seat of government of the Commonwealth shall be in the district of Yass Canberra, in the State of New South Wales." When the district was finally delimited, however, the town of Yass was left outside the capital territory. King O'Malley, an Irish-American with literary tastes who had settled in Australia, was Minister of Home Affairs at the time and suggested the capital be called *Shakespeare*, a name that might have been adopted had there not been a sudden change in government. Strictly speaking, the legal name of the district is "The Territory for the Seat of Government," but popularly it is known simply as "Federal Capital Territory" and the capital is designated "Canberra, F. C. T.," just as the capital of the United States is designated "Washington, D. C." and the capital of Mexico is designated "Mexico, D. F." The Federal Capital Territory, which contains 940 square miles of land, lies 70 miles inland between Sidney and Melbourne. A corridor connects it with a landlocked harbor at Jervis Bay. Canberra was modeled to some extent after Washington, D. C., and was laid out in accordance with ground plans designed by Walter Burley Griffin, an American architect from Chicago, who was appointed as the result of an international competition. It became the actual seat of government in 1927 when the Duke of York (later King George VI) opened the parliament there. The Australian Government owns all property in the Federal Territory and the residents, like those of the District of Columbia, do not have the right to vote in Federal elections. More than seven million trees and shrubs have been planted in the city and district.

What do ostriches eat?

Among some of the ancients it was widely believed that the ostrich could digest stones and pieces of iron, and this belief persisted until two or three hundred years ago. In Shakespeare's *II Henry VI* the rebel Jack Cade tells Alexander Iden, "I'll make thee eat iron like an ostrich, and swallow my sword like a great pin, ere thou and I part." A character in Ben Jonson's *Every Man in His Humour* declares that he is so hungry he can eat swordhilts, whereupon another replies, "You have an ostrich's stomach." In his *Vulgar Errors* (1646) Sir Thomas Browne undertook to explode this fallacy: "The common opinion of the Ostrich, *Struthio-camelus*, or Sparrow Camel, conceives that it digesteth iron, and this is confirmed by the affirmation of many: besides swarms of others, Rhodiginus in his prelections taketh it for granted, Johannes Langius in his epistles pleadeth experiment for it; the common picture also confirmeth it, which usually describeth this animal with an horseshoe in its mouth. Notwithstanding, upon inquiry we find it very questionable, and the negative seems most reasonably entertained, . . ." The myth is not to be wondered at, for the bird is notoriously voracious. "The ostrich," wrote the French naturalist Georges Cuvier (1769–1832), "is naturally herbivorous; but though it is often seen pasturing in the south of Africa, it is yet so voracious, and its senses of taste and smell are so obtuse, that it devours animal and mineral substances indiscriminately, until its enormous stomach is completely full. It swallows without any choice, and merely as it were for ballast, wood, stones, grass, iron, copper, gold, lime, or, in fact, any other substance equally hard, indigestible, and deleterious. The powers of digestion in the bird are certainly very great, but their operation is confined to matters of an alimentary character." Ostriches, like other birds, have no true teeth and their function is partly supplied by grit and gravel that grinds up the food in the gizzard. These birds, being large, require a great deal of grit and they are ever on the alert for stones, gravel, pieces of bone, etc. It is said that ostriches are hunted in South Africa for the diamonds sometimes found in their crops. In one of these "living diamond mines" more than fifty diamonds were found. Ostriches show little discrimination and have been known to swallow pocketbooks, spectacle cases, watches, keys, coins and what not. These birds in zoological parks, however, often pay dearly for the fallacious belief that they can eat anything. A number of ostriches in the London zoo, for instance, have died from the effects of various trinkets fed to them by the public. Ostriches are vegetarians, and on ostrich farms the birds are generally pastured on alfalfa in the summer and fed alfalfa hay, wheat bran, barley, oats and other grain in winter. As a rule they have no appetite for flesh in any form unless they are exceedingly hungry.

How much blood does the body contain?

The average normal adult human body contains from eight to ten pints of blood. Of course the quantity varies with the size and physical condition of the individual. Fat persons have relatively less blood than lean ones. Blood is composed of about 78 per cent water and about 22 per cent solids. Weighed measure for measure blood is slightly heavier than water. A pint of blood weighs about one pound and the number of pints of blood in a body can be computed roughly by dividing the weight in pounds by 12. Thus a person weighing 144 pounds has about 12 pints (or pounds) of blood; that is, the weight of the blood in the average normal adult person is about $\frac{1}{12}$th (8.3 per cent) of the body weight. Normal, healthy persons may lose as much as a third of their blood without fatal results.

Which is correct, blackeyed "pea" or "bean"?

There is much confusion in the popular names of the various members of the bean or legume family of plants. Botanically the seeds generally called blackeyed peas, *Dolichos sphaerospermus*, are really beans, and in southern California, where these seeds are grown on a large scale for market purposes, they are known as blackeyed beans. On the other hand, the European broad bean, *Vicia faba*, is really a pea. The broad bean was the first plant to which *bean* was applied and the seeds, served with bacon, were a favorite dish among the Romans. Oddly enough, the common cowpea, *Vignus sinensis*, is more closely related to beans than to peas, and many people refer to them as blackeyed beans rather than cowpeas. After relating his difficulties with English field peas at Mount Vernon, George Washington wrote to William Strickland in England under date of July 15, 1787: "From the cultivation of the common black-eyed peas, I have more hope, and am trying them this year, both as a drop, and for ploughing in as a manure; but the severe drought, under which we labor at present, may render the experiment inconclusive." In 1939 Governor W. Lee O'Daniel of Texas proclaimed a Blackeyed Pea Day and in the same year a Blackeyed Pea Festival was held at Centerville in the Lone Star State. There is an old belief in the southern states that eating blackeyed peas seasoned with salt pork on New Year's day will bring good luck for the whole year.

Can a giraffe graze?

Despite its great length the neck of a giraffe is not long enough to reach the ground. The neck of the giraffe contains only seven vertebrae, the usual number in mammals, and is not very flexible. It is the elongation, not a greater number of vertebrae, that elevates the animal's head to a great height. The flexible necks of birds contain fourteen vertebrae, twice as many as mammals. In order to bend its head to the ground to eat grass or to drink from a stream or pond a giraffe must assume an awkward position by spreading its forelegs apart and lowering the entire body. This species, however, seldom feeds on grass and is capable of going for long periods without water. It obtains its food chiefly by browsing on the lower branches of trees. The giraffe is a very timid animal and in the wild state is approached with difficulty because of the position of its eyes, which project far from the skull and give the animal the peculiar advantage of being able to see behind without turning its head.

What is a Parthian shot?

A Parthian shot, arrow, shaft or dart is a missile discharged while in retreat or flight. The allusion is to the methods of combat practiced by the ancient Parthians, a warlike people who specialized in shooting arrows on horseback and who delivered their darts with deadly effect as they feigned retreat and retired before the enemy. One of their most famous tactics was to ride at top speed toward the foe, delivering darts as they advanced, and then to whirl about suddenly and retreat, sending missile after missile back at their pursuers. Parthia, which lay southeast of the

Caspian Sea, became a separate kingdom under Arsaces about 250 B.C., and despite continual attacks by the Romans maintained its independence until conquered by the Persians in 226 A.D. Figuratively *Parthian shot* is applied to any thrust made in parting or blow struck in withdrawing from a contest, whether physical and verbal. Shakespeare several times refers to the fighting methods of the Parthians and their darts. In *Antony and Cleopatra* the triumphant Ventidius says, "Now, darting Parthia, art thou struck," and later in the same play Eros, after Antony asks him to keep his promise to kill him, says, "The gods withhold me! Shall I do that, which all the Parthian darts, though enemy, lost aim, and could not?" Iachimo, in *Cymbeline*, says, "Arm me, audacity, from head to foot! Or, like the Parthian, I shall flying fight."

What battle was lost for want of a horseshoe nail?

The story of a battle and kingdom being lost for want of a horseshoe nail is merely an elaboration of any old English saying of unknown authorship. Its earliest recorded use thus far discovered occurs in the writings of George Herbert, English poet and churchman, published shortly after his death at the age of 39 in 1633. In Herbert's *Jacula Prudentum* it is found in the following form: "For want of a nail the shoe is lost, for want of a shoe the horse is lost, for want of a horse the rider is lost." The saying was probably already proverbial in Herbert's time. In the preface of Benjamin Franklin's *Poor Richard's Almanack for 1758* is this observation: "And again, he, Richard, adviseth to circumspection and care, even in the smallest matters, because sometimes a little neglect may breed great mischief, adding, for want of a nail, the shoe was lost; for want of a shoe the horse was lost; and for want of a horse the rider was lost, being overtaken and slain by the enemy, all for want of care about a horseshoe nail." It is not probable that the saying alluded to any particular historical incident. A more elaborate version of Franklin's story is as follows: "For the want of a nail the shoe was lost; for the want of a shoe the horse was lost; for the want of a horse the rider was lost; for the want of a rider the battle was lost; for the want of a battle the kingdom was lost—and all for the want of a horseshoe nail."

What is a merchant marine?

All the merchant vessels registered, enrolled or licensed under the laws and flag of a country, whether privately or publicly owned, constitute the merchant marine or the merchant fleet of that country. The term is general and embraces all ships engaged in trade, whether operated by the government or private citizens, to distinguish them from naval and military craft. The United States merchant marine comprises the total number of public and private vessels sailing under the United States flag. Sometimes the merchant flag of a country is identical with the national ensign and sometimes it is a distinctive flag flown for that purpose. Ships owned by aliens but sailing under the United States flag would be regarded as part of the United States merchant marine. *Merchant marine* is also applied to the personnel of the merchant marine service as a whole. An individual member of the merchant marine is called a merchant sailor. *Able seaman* is a shortened form of *able-bodied seaman,* abbreviated *A.B.* The underlying thought is that a merchant sailor is an able-bodied seaman only after he has had the required training and experience. The United States Maritime Service was created in 1936 to provide training and other benefits to officers and sailors in the American merchant marine, which comprises all American offshore, coastwise and Great Lakes merchant ships and the crews that man them.

Do snakes poison their food?

There is a popular belief that venomous snakes do not poison the birds and animals they kill for food, reserving the poison fangs for defense against their enemies. As a matter of fact, the poison fangs are used primarily for killing food and only secondarily as a means of defense. Most poisonous snakes kill birds, animals and other creatures for food by striking them with their venom-injecting fangs. Snakes are immune to their own poison when it is swallowed.

What is dry farming?

Dry farming is the raising of food crops on arid or semi-arid lands without irrigation. It consists of crop rotation, preparing and tilling the soil in such a manner as to utilize all available moisture, and raising drought-resistant plants. Twenty inches or more of rainfall annually is considered adequate for ordinary farming in temperate climates. Of course, other factors must be considered. An annual rainfall of less than twenty inches—even as little as ten inches—may be sufficient to grow abundant crops if it comes at the right time of the year. Generally speaking, however, dry farming is usually practiced where the yearly rainfall is less than twenty inches, a condition that makes special methods of moisture conservation necessary. Irrigation or the artificial application of water to the land is not part of dry farming. "Dry Farming," says the United States Department of Agriculture, "has probably been practiced ever since the dawn of civilization in semi-arid regions on every continent in the world. Modern dry farming is simply applying modern scientific methods and implements to the ancient problem of coercing nature into producing large quantities of plants suitable for human food in semi-arid regions where under natural conditions only relatively small quantities of plants suitable for the lower animals are produced. Conservation of the scanty rainfall for producing crops is the object sought. Crop rotation, tillage methods and the adaptation of crop plants to semi-arid conditions are the means employed."

Why is Connecticut called the Nutmeg State?

Formerly the Yankees of Connecticut had a national reputation for business shrewdness and were the butt of continual jokes hinging on this supposed characteristic. Even in colonial days it was fashionable to reflect upon the commercial cunning of the Connecticut Yankees. The father of Gouverneur Morris in his will forbade his son to attend any Connecticut school or college for fear he might acquire the characteristic traits of the Yankees of that colony. In *The Clockmaker, or Sayings and Doings of Samuel Slick of Slickville*, the first series of which was published in 1837, Thomas Chandler Haliburton (1796–1865), Nova Scotia judge and writer, popularized, if he did not invent, the story that the Connecticut Yankees were in the habit of making nutmegs of wood and palming them off as genuine and that sham spices constituted one of the chief exports of the state. Wooden nutmegs became the symbol of all kinds of cunning, deception and trickery, and Connecticut good-naturedly added "Nutmeg State" to her list of nicknames. Nutmegs are the strongly aromatic and spicy kernels of the fruit of an evergreen tree, which is native to the Molucca or Spice Islands, lying north of Australia between the Celebes and New Guinea, and which is now widely cultivated in other tropical and subtropical regions. The spice known as mace is derived from the red, lacelike, fibrous covering of the nutmeg kernel.

Does dew rise or fall?

In Zechariah 8:12 the Hebrew prophet tells us that "the heavens shall give their dew." Three different sources of dew are recognized by meteorologists. In many cases a large part of the dew, and in some cases probably all of it, is produced after nightfall when moisture already in the air before sunset comes in contact with and condenses on bodies cooler than the atmosphere. During the day the earth receives heat from the sun; after sundown this heat is rapidly radiated into the air, and the ground and objects near it become cool; if this cooling goes below a certain point—known as the *dew point*—any moisture that happens to be in the air will condense on objects near the ground in the form of dew. Such dew may be said to fall. It is formed in the same manner as the moisture that gathers on the outside of a vessel of cold water. However, in other cases much of the dew, and in some cases probably all of it, is produced by the evaporation of water from the soil during the night. Considerable moisture is always ascending from the earth; during the day it passes off as invisible vapor, but during the night the chilled air may cause it to condense as dew. Such dew may be said to rise. No doubt in many cases the dew is derived partly from one of these sources and partly from the other. Frequently in the morning "sparkling dewdrops" are seen on the tips of growing grass and other live vegetation. This is known as *false dew* and consists of exhalations from the plants themselves. Water comes up the sap tubes of the leaves and exudes at the tips where the tubes are open. Such dew, of course, does not consist of any part of the dew seen on roofs, fences and other *dead* objects. Thus it will be seen that the dew on any given morning may be derived from any one or from all of three different sources.

How do trees grow in height?

Few myths are more persistent or widespread than the belief that trees grow in height by the gradual lengthening of the entire trunk and limbs. There is no upward growth in the trunk of a tree other than that which occurs through the annual extension of the terminal buds; in other words, trees put on height growth only from the top. This principle of plant growth is indisputable; yet there are thousands of persons throughout the country who will argue until they are blue in the face that it is not true. Wood fiber is inert and does not grow in length after the first season. As William James so well expressed it in one of his philosophical essays: "It is like the soft layers beneath the bark of the tree in which all the year's growth is going on. Life has abandoned the mighty trunk inside, which stands inert and belongs almost to the inorganic world." Only the current season's rootlets and leafy shoots are soft and capable of lengthening by cell division. Trees grow in circumference only in the cambium layer between the old fiber and the bark. The limbs of a tree do not rise higher from the ground as the tree grows taller. It should be remembered that nearly all normal trees shed their lower limbs and in time the bark entirely covers the wounds thus made. Hence what often seems to be an old crotch farther from the ground is a new one that has formed higher up. If a crotch is ten feet from the ground, it was not formed until the tree was at least ten feet tall. A notch in a tree will not increase its height from the ground as the tree grows higher. Surveyors cut bench marks on trees and return twenty or thirty years later and find the marks at the same level as when they were made. Fence wires stapled to growing trees are not spread apart or carried upward, although the tree expands and draws the wires to one side. Two nails driven into a tree trunk, one above the other, will remain the same distance apart. In an old play based on Washington Irving's *Rip Van Winkle* Rip's dog (called "Wolf" in the story and "Schneider" in the play) is represented as having been carried forty feet up into the air in the crotch of a tree during the twenty years that Rip slept!

What is meant by "eating humble pie"?

To *eat humble pie* means to apologize, retract, recant, humiliate oneself or *eat* one's words. *Humble* in this connection, however, originally had no relation to *humble* in the sense of lowly or unassuming. The humbles, also known as umbles and numbles, are the inwards—heart, liver, kidneys, lights, entrails and other inferior parts—of an animal. *Humbles* is believed to be derived through Old French from Latin *lumbulus*, diminutive of *lumbus* ("groin"). Formerly it was customary to make a kind of pie of the humbles of deer. Humble pie was given at the hunting feasts to the servants and ordinary huntsmen.

How do young opossums get into the mother's pouch?

The opossum is North America's only marsupial, which means that the female has a pouch under her belly as a nursery for her young. This queer animal is the subject of many myths. According to a belief widely accepted by the credulous, the opossum copulates through the nose and the female blows the genital fluid into the pouch where fecundation takes place. It is also widely believed that the young are born directly into the pouch. How the young get into the pouch was long a mystery even to naturalists. That the young are born directly into the pouch has been disproved by dissecting females, showing that such birth is physically impossible. Careful observations reported by the Smithsonian Institution show the process of birth to be as simple as it is remarkable. Opossums breed like other marsupials. The gestation period is only about fifteen days. The young at birth are smaller in proportion to the size of the mother than the young of any other mammal. When first born opossums are blind, deaf, pink in color, almost shapeless, and only about half an inch long. The average opossum at birth is so small and light that it would take about 270 of them to weigh an ounce. An entire litter of fifteen can be placed in an ordinary teaspoon. The extremely miniature and immature young appear at the genital opening where they are licked clean of the embryonic covering by the mother, after which they instinctively climb into the pouch without aid from the mother and attach themselves to the nipples, where they remain almost motionless about seventy days. They are about the size of a mouse when they emerge from the maternal pouch the first time and begin to crawl about the mother's furry body and cling to her hairless tail. There usually are only thirteen nipples and each young one must become firmly attached to a teat to survive. If more young opossums are born in a litter than there are nipples the extra ones must die. Opossums are very prolific and females have been known to give birth to three litters in the same year.

How did "kodak" originate?

This word is the trade-mark of the Eastman Kodak Company, of Rochester, New York. It was coined by George Eastman who desired a short, euphonious and meaningless word to apply to a kind of portable camera adapted for taking snapshots, one of the distinguishing features of which was that a succession of negatives was made upon a continuous roll of sensitized film. K was a favorite letter with Eastman and he experimented with various combinations of letters beginning and ending with k until he hit upon kodak, a combination that he thought met the ideal trade-mark requirements. The word was registered as a trade-mark in 1888 and has been used ever since. It has become so well known that it is now frequently applied to any small camera. There is, however, another story of the origin of kodak. In 1881 David Henderson Houston, an inventor of Hunter, North Dakota, invented a camera involving the basic principles of the kodak. Later Houston sold his patent to George Eastman for $5,700. According to the story, which cannot be substantiated, Houston coined kodak, which was suggested to him by Dakota.

Why do snakes dart out their tongues?

Many people believe that snakes sting with their tongues. This, of course, is not true, the tongues of a snake being perfectly harmless. Snakes do not sting; they bite with their teeth or fangs. The continual motion of the tongue is known to have some sensory significance, the exact nature of which is not yet fully understood by scientists. Snakes do not have true ears and some authorities suppose that the tongue acts as a substitute for this organ in registering auditory sensations. Apparently the long, delicate, forked tongue enables the reptile to feel its way over the ground. The projecting of the snake's tongue, says Dr. William M. Mann, director of the National Zoological Park at Washington, is supposed to be sensory in function. "It has been suggested," he asserts, "that the sense of smell is present, to some extent, in the snake's tongue, though I do not believe this has been very well substantiated." The late Raymond L. Ditmars, for many years curator of reptiles at the New York Zoological Park, said on this subject: "The tongue of the snake is an extremely sensitive organ, and serves to trace scents over the ground by taste. It also is sensitive to sound vibration." Centuries ago the belief that snakes sting with their tongues was almost universal. In Shakespeare there are several references to the deadly double tongue of the serpent. The dramatist makes King Richard II say:

> And when they from thy bosom pluck a flower,
> Guard it, I pray thee, with a lurking adder
> Whose double tongue may with a mortal touch
> Throw death upon thy sovereign's enemies.

What is a village smithy?

It is a common mistake to suppose that *smithy* referred to in Henry W. Longfellow's famous poem was a man. *Smithy*, like *smithery* and *stithy*, is an old English name for a smith's workshop, especially that of a blacksmith. As used in "The Village Blacksmith" it means the building in which the village blacksmith worked at his trade. That poem opens with the following lines:

> Under a spreading chestnut tree
> The village smithy stands:
> The smith, a mighty man is he,
> With large and sinewy hands;
> And the muscles of his brawny arms
> Are strong as iron bands.

Oddly enough, this poem, in which the terms are employed correctly, is probably responsible for the common misuse of *smithy* in the sense of the smith. The poet's inspiration was a blacksmith shop on Brattle Street, Cambridge, Massachusetts.

How does a foot square differ from a square foot?

A square foot and a foot square are the same area. The principle, however, holds true only when the distance is one complete unit of measurement, no more and no less. For instance, two square feet and two feet square are not the same area, the latter being twice as large as the former. Likewise, an area three feet square is three times as large as one containing three square feet. A foot square must always be a square and each side must be one foot in length. On the other hand, a square foot of surface may be any shape whatever so long as it contains one hundred forty-four square inches. It may be triangular or even circular. The same rule applies to inches, yards, rods, miles or any other unit of measurement. For instance, one mile square is a right-angled parallelogram, each side of which is one mile long. On the other hand, a square mile, although having the same area as a mile square, may be any shape.

Can stars appear in the moon's crescent?

The moon is a solid and opaque body, nearly spherical in form; hence it is absolutely impossible for an observer to see a star within the crescent of the new moon, notwithstanding the popular notion to the contrary. Those who think they see stars within the crescent of the moon are victims of an illusion. It is often explained by popular writers that, owing to the refraction of the light rays under certain atmospheric conditions, a star or planet may sometimes appear to be just within the rim of the new moon. There is no authentic astronomical record proving that such an optical illusion is ever produced. "The silver arc of the new moon grew light and a star winked within it," wrote Harold Lamb in *Omar Khayyam*. Samuel T. Coleridge was a better poet than scientist when he wrote *The Rime of the Ancient Mariner*. In Part III he said:

> The stars were dim, and thick the night,
> The steersman's face by his lamp gleamed white;
> From the sails the dew did drip—
> Till clomb above the eastern bar
> The horned moon, with one bright star
> Within the nether tip.

One commentator explains this passage by saying that star here probably refers to a lofty lunar peak that, owing to the reflection of sunlight, sometimes appears like a star in the shadowed disc some distance from the bright crescent. This may be the correct explanation of the popular belief. Of course, the so-called horns of the new moon are an optical illusion. Under date of March 23, 1768, George Washington noted in his diary: "This Moon, wch. changed the 18th appeared with the points directly upwards exactly of a height."

Is "anthracite coal" correct?

Anthracite is derived directly from Greek *anthrax*, meaning "coal." It is a noun and is applied to *hard coal*, that is, coal consisting of nearly pure carbon. Accordingly we should correctly say simply *anthracite*, not *anthracite coal*; the latter is tautological and equivalent to *coal-like coal*.

Bituminous, on the other hand, is an adjective and should properly be followed by *coal*. Bituminous coal is soft coal, that is, coal that yields considerable volatile bituminous matter when burned. Anthracite is a peculiarly American product, while bituminous coal is found in many parts of the world. When anthracite was first discovered it was called "stone coal." There is little difference in the weight of bituminous coal and anthracite. Bituminous coal ranges in weight from 44 to 58.5 pounds a cubic foot and anthracite from 52 to 59.6 pounds a cubic foot. A third general type of coal is lignite, a term derived from Latin *lignum*, "wood." It is intermediate between bituminous coal and peat, which is not classed as a coal, and is often called wood or brown coal.

What is Scotland Yard?

Scotland Yard is a group of buildings surrounded by a courtyard in London, England. It was long famous as the headquarters of the London police force. The name is derived from an old palace which stood there in the time of Henry II (1154–1159) and which was the residence of the Scottish kings whenever they visited London. Newton, in his *London in the Olden Times* says: "This property was given by the Saxon King Edgar to Kenneth III, King of Scotland, for his residence upon his annual visit to London to do homage for his kingdom to the crown of England." Margaret, the Queen of James IV, was the last of the Scottish royal family to reside in the old palace. She took up her residence there after the death of her husband at the Battle of Flodden Field. The headquarters of the London metropolitan police were moved to New Scotland Yard on the Thames Embankment in 1890, and *New Scotland Yard* is the present designation of the London police headquarters. *Scotland Yard* is a romantic name for the detectives in the Criminal Investigation Department of the London police force. Contrary to the popular notion, Scotland Yard detectives do not solve crimes by gumshoe snooping and farfetched deductions, but make their investigations after the manner of any other efficient and modern detectives and police officers.

Does a running horse ever have all four feet off the ground?

A horse when either galloping or trotting has all four feet off the ground part of the time. The only exception to this is what is known as the *short trot*, which is really not a trotting gait at all. The United States Department of Agriculture has a series of films showing all the various gaits of horses. When the films are run slowly through the projecting machine every motion of the horse can easily be observed. During one phase in the gallop all four feet of a horse are flexed under the body and completely off the ground. This question was first settled by use of a camera as early as 1870. Governor Leland Stanford of California bet $25,000 that a horse running at full speed takes all four feet off of the ground at the same time. To prove his point the governor got an English-born photographer named Eadweard Muybridge to take a series of pictures of a thoroughbred running at full speed.

What is the difference between "post" and "postal" cards?

According to the distinction made by the United States Post Office Department, cards that have stamps printed on them and that are sold by a post office are properly called *postal* cards. Unstamped cards sold by private firms and that generally have pictures on one side are properly called *post* cards. This distinction is not made in Great Britain. There, cards of this kind are called *post* cards whether they are issued by the postal authorities or are privately manufactured and distributed.

How tall do giraffes grow?

Giraffes are the tallest animals in the world. According to Raymond Ditmars, curator of mammals at the New York Zoological Park, a giraffe sixteen feet high is regarded as unusual. That is the height of the largest specimen in captivity. In Africa, says Dr. William M. Mann, director of the National Zoological Park, one often hears of giraffes reaching a height of twenty or twenty-one feet. It is probable, he thinks, that occasionally such a height is attained by bulls, although animals more than eighteen feet tall are exceedingly rare. In *Safari* Martin Johnson said the common giraffe in East Africa attains a height of twenty-three feet from the crown of the head to the sole of the hoof. Theodore Roosevelt killed a bull seventeen feet and two inches in height. Baby giraffes are sometimes more than six feet tall at birth.

Are railroad car wheels made of paper?

Wheels with paper cores were used in railway passenger cars for many years. Such wheels were believed to have several advantages over solid steel wheels. The paper core, which expanded and contracted with changes in temperature, deadened the sound of moving cars and made them ride easier. Paper-cored wheels were invented by a locomotive engineer named Richard N. Allen, who first tested them in 1869 on a wood car belonging to the Central Vermont Railroad. The Pullman Palace Car Company ordered 100 paper-cored wheels in 1871, and by 1883 the Allen Paper Car Wheel Company was making 20,000 such wheels a year. Although such wheels were widely used on Pullman and passenger cars for twenty-five years or more, they were gradually abandoned because of the increase in the weight of cars and improvements in making solid steel wheels. Paper-cored wheels were never used on freight cars. The popular notion that the entire wheel was made of paper is absurd. Only the inner part was paper and the paper core was completely incased in steel. In making the paper cores, sheets of baked strawboard paper were treated chemically, compressed to a solidity, density and weight suggesting metal rather than fiber, and then turned on a lathe.

Of what country is the banana native?

The banana plant, now cultivated in many tropical and semitropical regions in both hemispheres, is believed to be a native of the East Indies, probably the humid, tropical parts of southern India and the Malay Peninsula. Formerly it was supposed that the plant was also indigenous to tropical America. For instance, in his life of Columbus, Washington Irving wrote of Hispaniola: "The great river flowing through this valley was bordered with noble forests, among which were palms, bananas, and many trees covered with fruit and flowers." Most authorities now reject the theory that the banana was native to the New World. They believe the early Spanish explorers mistook some other plant for the banana. Bananas are mentioned in Chinese writings dating back more than three thousand years. Alexander the Great saw bananas growing in the Indus Valley in 327 B.C. At one time it was customary to classify the various kinds of bananas and edible plantains into several species; now, however, they are all generally regarded as mere varieties of the same species, *Musa sapientum*, which literally means "fruit of knowledge" and which probably refers to a statement made by the ancient Greek philosopher and naturalist Theophrastus that the sages of India reposed in the shade of the banana plant and refreshed themselves with its fruit. The Arabs were growing bananas in northern Egypt and the Holy Land even in the seventh century A.D. In the *Koran* bananas are referred to as the "fruit of paradise." In 1482 the Portuguese found the banana cultivated on the west coast of Africa, where the natives of Guinea called it by a name that the Portuguese rendered *banana*. From Guinea the banana plant was transplanted in the Canary Islands. In 1516, only twenty-four years after the first voyage of Columbus, Friar Thomas de Berlanga took a few banana roots from the Canaries when he sailed as a missionary to Santo Domingo, whence they spread throughout the American tropics. To prevent spoilage bananas should be kept within a temperature range of 55 to 65 degrees Fahrenheit. Importation of the fruit into the United States was delayed by lack of refrigeration facilities. As early as 1804 Captain John N. Chester of the schooner "Reynard" took about thirty bunches from Cuba to New York. The first full cargo of bananas—fifteen hundred bunches—were delivered in New York in 1830 by John Pearsall's schooner "Harriet Smith." But bananas were still a novelty to most people in the United States in 1876 when they were exhibited at the Philadelphia Centennial Exposition, and individual bananas, carefully wrapped in tinfoil, were sold at ten cents apiece as tropical curiosities. It was not until several years later that bananas began to be imported in quantity.

Where is Barbary?

Barbary or *Barbary Coast* is a general name for the Moslem countries on the northern coast of Africa, exclusive of Egypt. The region so designated includes Morocco, Algeria, Tunisia and Tripoli. *Barbary* probably is derived from *Berber*, the name of the chief indigenous Caucasian race that since the dawn of history has inhabited the vast region lying between the Mediterranean Sea on the north and the Sahara Desert on the south and stretching from Egypt to the Atlantic Ocean. The origin of *Berber* itself is not known for certain. *Barabara* and *Beraberata* occur as tribal titles in Egyptian inscriptions dating from 1700 to 1300 B.C., and therefore some writers have assumed that the term is of Egyptian origin. Others trace it to the Arabic, a language of the Moslem hordes who subjected the Berbers and converted them to their faith. Still others suppose the term to be derived from *barbarii*, Latin for *barbarians*. *Barbarian* itself literally meant babbler and the Greeks and Romans applied it to all foreigners or peoples whose language they could not understand. Some authorities suppose that the Basques (Gascons) were originally an offshoot of the Berbers and that the Berbers are descended from the so-called Cro-Magnon race, one of the earliest tribes of prehistoric Europeans. Another theory is that the Berbers are descendants of the Hamitic race and are closely related in blood to the fellahs of the Nile Valley, the Nubians and some of the Ethiopians. The remnant of the Berbers is now confined largely to the Atlas Mountains.

Which is correct, "Muscle" or "Mussel" Shoals?

The name of the famous rapids in the Tennessee River, included in the development of the Tennessee Valley Authority, is often incorrectly written *Mussel Shoals*. Many insist that this spelling is correct. In 1892, however, the United States Geographic Board decided in favor of *Muscle Shoals*. That authority said the rapids evidently received their name from the numerous fresh-water mussels that formerly lived among the rocks at this point in the river. At the time this region was settled *muscle* was the usual spelling of the word that we now write *mussel*. Etymologically they are the same word, both being derived from Latin *musculus* ("little mouse"). Most dictionaries still give *muscle* as a variant of *mussel*. In the Lewis and Clark *Journals*, 1805–1806, Lewis refers to these shellfish as *mussels*, while Clark writes *muscles*. They refer to the Musselshell River in Montana as the Muscleshell River. *Muscle Shoals* appears several times in *Winterbotham's Atlas* published in 1795, as well as in the 1796 edition of *Arrowsmith's Map of the United States*. The same spelling has been used in numerous acts of Congress and the Federal government reports since 1828, and perhaps earlier. It also appears in the Cherokee treaty signed at Washington, January 7, 1806. According to a humorous explanation the Indians named the rapids Muscle Shoals because it required *heap big muscle* to push a canoe up the river at that place.

Is it unlawful to destroy United States coins?

There is no Federal law forbidding the total destruction of coins by their owners. There is, however, a statute that forbids the mutilation or lightening of a coin in such a way that the original coin may later be circulated in its impaired condition. It is also illegal deliberately to deface a coin without removing any part of it. Both these provisions are based on the principle that a person receiving such a coin might be defrauded of his right to have it accepted by the Government at its face value. Merely drilling a hole in a coin and using the coin as an ornament is generally not construed as defacing the coin. But it is illegal to pass as currency a coin so defaced or mutilated.

Who called England a nation of shopkeepers?

It is generally supposed that Napoleon Bonaparte was the first to call the English a nation of shopkeepers. In his *Life of Napoleon* Sir Walter Scott attributes the famous phrase to him without giving his authority. The Little Corporal may have used the phrase, but it is older than his time. In 1766, three years before Napoleon was born, an English economist named Josiah Tucker published *Four Tracts on Political and Commercial Subjects*, in which he wrote: "A shopkeeper will never get the more custom by beating his customers, and what is true of a shopkeeper is true of a shopkeeping nation." Tucker, who argued that war was a loss even to the victorious nation and that England could not hold her American colonies against their will, had considerable influence on

Adam Smith, who published his *Wealth of Nations* in 1776. In that work Smith said: "To found a great empire for the sole purpose of raising up a people of customers, may at first sight appear a project fit only for a nation of shopkeepers. It is, however, a project altogether unfit for a nation of shopkeepers, but extremely fit for a nation whose government is influenced by shopkeepers." The phrase is also sometimes attributed to Samuel Adams, who is said to have used it in an oration delivered at the Statehouse in Philadelphia August 1, 1776, but the authenticity of that oration has been questioned. Bertrand Barère de Vieuzac popularized the phrase in France. On June 11, 1794, he declared before the National Convention: "Let Pitt then boast of his victory to his nation of shopkeepers." In his *History of the English People* John Richard Green declared that Louis XIV of France "applied the phrase to the United Provinces [the Netherlands] before Napoleon applied it to England."

What do the letters "D.F." after "Mexico" mean?

In 1933 the Mexican government advised all nations that the name of the capital of the republic had been changed from "Mexico City" to "Mexico, D. F." *D. F.* after *Mexico* is the abbreviation of *Distrito Federal*. The capital of Mexico, like the capital of the United States, is situated in a federal district governed by the central government, and when referring to their national capital Mexicans say *Mexico, D. F.*, just as Americans say *Washington, D. C.* Although the name of the city is now simply *Mexico*, not *Mexico City*, outside the republic it is sometimes almost necessary to refer to the capital of that country as Mexico City to distinguish it from the country. Likewise in the United States many people refer to the capital as Washington City to distinguish it from Washington State.

What causes air pockets?

There is a popular notion that huge vacuums exist in the atmosphere and that an aircraft that strikes one of these air *pockets* or *holes* drops like a stone. *Air pocket* is a popular rather than a scientific term. The air pocket or hole is a myth that probably originated with early aviators who did not understand air currents. There is no such thing as a pocket in the air. The atmosphere may be compared with water. Updrafts and downdrafts are encountered in the air just as they are in the sea. If an airplane suddenly sinks for no apparent reason it has struck either a descending current of air or a change of wind velocity in the direction of travel. An aircraft also may suddenly strike an ascending air current.

[340]

Aviators speak of these currents as *bumps*. The evenness of the atmosphere in flying varies with the temperature. Warm air is less dense or *thinner* than cold air. It is harder for an aviator to gain altitude in warm air than it is in cold air, and when he suddenly strikes warmer air, as over a large city, his plane has a tendency to lose altitude.

What is meant by "breaking Priscian's head"?

Priscian (pronounced *prish*-i-an), was a famous Roman grammarian who lived in the latter part of the fifth century and the early part of the sixth and who was known as Priscianus Caesariensis because he was born at Caesarea in North Africa. His monumental work on Latin grammar made his name almost synonymous with grammar and correct language, and during the Middle Ages there was hardly a library in Europe that did not boast a copy of his magnum opus. *To break Priscian's head* (*diminuere Prisciani caput* in Latin) means to violate the rules of grammar, "to butcher the King's English." One old writer says "Priscian's head is often bruised without remorse." In Shakespeare's *Love Labour's Lost* the schoolmaster Holofernes says of the curate Nathaniel's Latin, "Priscian a little scratched."

Why is Ireland called the Emerald Isle?

Ireland is known as the Emerald Isle because of the bright verdure of its grass and other vegetation, a condition due largely to the frequent rains for which the island is noted. Dr. William Drennan (1754–1820), an Irish physician and poet, popularized this poetic name of Ireland. It occurs in his poem entitled "Erin," written about 1800 and two stanzas of which read:

> When Erin first rose from the dark-swelling flood,
> God blessed the green island, he saw it was good.
> The *Emerald of Europe*, it sparkled and shone
> In the ring of this world, the most precious stone.

> Arm of Erin! prove strong, but be gentle as brave,
> And, uplifted to strike, still be ready to save,
> Nor one feeling of vengeance presume to defile
> The cause, or the men of the *Emerald Isle*.

This is sometimes said to be the "original use" of the epithet the *Emerald Isle*. But in 1815, in an introduction to the poem, Dr. Drennan said the phrase was first used in " 'Erin, to Her Own Tune,' a party song written without the rancour of party in the year 1795." That song was published anonymously. Dr. Drennan expressed the hope that *Emerald Isle* would gradually become associated with the name of his country "as descriptive of its prime natural beauty, and its inestimable value." Emerald, which is of Greek or Sanskrit origin, is applied generally to a precious stone of bright green color and specifically to a variety of beryl.

What is a Yankee dime?

Yankee dime is an old slang term used in some parts of the United States, especially in the South, to denote a kiss, just as *Dutch quarter* signifies a hug. *Quaker nickel* is sometimes employed in the same sense as *Yankee dime*. In some sections *Yankee nickel* signifies simply a kiss, while *Yankee dime* signifies a hug and a kiss. Originally *Yankee dime* denoted "payment in full by a kiss." Formerly it was a favorite method of payment for favors demanded by ardent swains of their lady loves.

How did "red tape" originate?

Red tape in the sense of official inaction or delay originated in England in the nineteenth century and arose from the custom of tying official and legal documents in a tape of a pinkish red color. The custom of tying up papers in such tape dates back several centuries. It was referred to in an advertisement printed in a London newspaper in 1658. Sir Gilbert Elliot (1722–1777) is said to have used red tape in the figurative sense in Parliament in 1775. Sidney Smith (1771–1845), English clergyman, wit and essayist, is credited with doing much toward popularizing *red tape* in its satirical sense. In her *Memoirs* his daughter, Lady Holland, quotes Smith as saying of Sir John Mackintosh: "What a man that would be had he . . . the least knowledge of red tape." Washington Irving used the expression: "His brain was little better than red tape and parchment." In *Vanity Fair* William Makepeace Thackeray refers to the "Tape and Sealing-Wax office in the reign of George II." Such a word as *red tape* was just what the common people wanted with which to ridicule officials who delay government decisions by giving undue attention to routine, by adhering rigidly to rules and regulations and by "passing the buck" to others. It was natural that the ordinary man, impatient for action on his particular case, should ridicule the everlasting tying and untying of red tape that bound the dispatch and document cases in public offices. In No. 1 of his *Latter-Day Pamphlets* Thomas Carlyle described somebody as "little other than a red-tape talking machine and unhappy bag of parliamentary eloquence." Charles Dickens, in *Little Dorrit*, described the thing without using the term:

"Whatever was required to be done, the Circumlocution Office was beforehand with all the public documents in the art of perceiving how not to do it."

Why is it said that horsehairs turn into snakes?

The myth that horsehairs will turn into worms or snakes if put in water dates back to the days when the belief in spontaneous generation was common. Shakespeare referred to this old belief when in *Antony and Cleopatra*, Act I, Scene 2, he had Antony say of Sextus Pompeius:

> Much is breeding,
> Which, like the courser's hair, hath yet but life
> And not a serpent's poison.

Anybody with even a superficial knowledge of natural history knows that a hair never turns into a snake or worm. The myth is probably owing to imperfect observation. There are several species of worms that resemble the long hairs in a horse's tail. Such worms are known as "hairworms." If a hair is placed in water it will gradually twist and curve due to the effect of moisture and microscopic animals that attach themselves to the water-soaked horsehair. It is only natural that untrained observers should have jumped at the conclusion that the hairworm was merely a hair that has assumed life. Centuries ago it was believed that a snake that developed from a horsehair was without venom.

Will cold water freeze quicker than hot water?

There is a popular belief that hot water will freeze more readily than cold water. Suppose two equal quantities of water, one cold and the other hot, are placed under identical freezing conditions. According to the popular notion, the heated water will freeze sooner than the cold water. Even Lord Bacon, in *Novum Organum*, accepted this common belief as a fact. The United States Bureau of Standards says it is a myth that hot water will freeze sooner than cold water. Under the conditions assumed, the cold water will freeze first. However, it is true to a limited extent that water that has been heated will freeze more readily than water that has not been heated, provided they have the same temperature when subjected to freezing. The chief reason for this is the difference in density and the amount of dissolved air. Boiling drives out air and certain other gases and deposits minerals in solution in the water. Water that is comparatively free from dissolved air, such as water that has been recently heated, will freeze somewhat more rapidly than water containing more air, because in the freezing process the air appears as bubbles in the ice and decreases its thermal conductivity. The myth that hot water will freeze quicker than cold water probably arose from the fact that when a hot-water pipe freezes it is more likely to burst than a cold-water pipe is. The real difference, however, is not the rapidity with which they freeze, but the nature of the ice formed in each case. When water that has been recently heated freezes, the ice formed is more compact and solid, and consequently more likely to burst the pipes. Another popular notion is that it is the thawing of the ice and not the freezing of the water that bursts water pipes. Actually the pipes are burst by the expansion of the water as it congeals into ice, but since the water cannot flow when frozen it is not until the ice begins to melt that the pipes begin to leak and the break is discovered.

Has England ever had a bachelor king?

Several English kings ascended the throne before they married, but England has had only one king who grew to manhood and who never married. He was William Rufus, or William II, son and successor of William the Conqueror. Edward VIII became King January 10, 1936, and reigned as a bachelor until December 10 of the same year, but, without ever being crowned, he abdicated to marry Mrs. Wallis Simpson. Edward V and Edward VI were never married, but they died without reaching their majority. There is no statute that requires the King of Great Britain to be married. Under present British statutes the sovereign may marry only a member of a royal family, although the heir to the throne may marry a member of a noble family without prejudice to his or her rights to the succession. The heir may also contract a "morganatic marriage" with a commoner, but in that case, although the marriage is legal, the spouse may not become king or queen and the children of such a union have no rights of succession to the throne. All statutes pertaining to the succession, however, are subject to change by Parliament at any time.

How often does the century plant bloom?

The common belief that the century plant (*Agave americana*) habitually blooms once in a hundred years is a myth. The period of flowering varies widely and depends upon the climate, the richness of the soil and the vigor of the individual plant. In warm regions, such as in Mexico and Central America, supposedly the original home of the century plant, it grows rapidly and generally blooms about the seventh or eighth year, seldom later than the twelfth. In colder climates the period before flowering is much longer. Some authorities say that in hot houses eighty or ninety years may elapse before the plant blooms, a fact that may have given rise to the belief from which the plant received its popular name. After a century plant has bloomed that part of the plant from which the flower stalk emerged dies down to the ground and new plants usually grow up from the root. In Mexico this species is known as *maguey* and the well known fermented intoxicating beverage called *pulque* is made from its sap.

What is "the Little Church Around the Corner"?

On December 20, 1870, a popular comedian named George Holland died in New York City. His friend and brother actor Joseph Jefferson asked the Reverend William Sabine, of the Church of Atonement, to perform the burial services. The pastor, however, refused when he learned that the deceased was an actor. He suggested to Jefferson: "There is a little church around the corner that will, perhaps, permit the service." Jefferson replied: "God bless that little church around the corner." As a result of this incident the Church of the Transfiguration, a small Protestant Episcopal Church at No. 1 West Twenty-ninth Street in New York became popularly known as the "Little Church Around the Corner." Dr. George Houghton, rector of the church, gladly consented to perform the burial services for George Holland. The church soon became the center of religious life among theatrical people and is still often called the "actor's church." It was founded in 1848. The rambling edifice is now surrounded by tall office buildings. The Little Church Around the Corner is noted not only for the great number of actors who have been communicants but also for the great number of wedding ceremonies performed in it.

What are the requirements for burial in Westminster Abbey?

There are no specific requirements for interment in Westminster Abbey, the burial place of British sovereigns and notables. When a person of distinction dies the deans of Westminster may or may not invite his relatives to have his remains interred in the Abbey. Because of the scarcity of space it is probable that burials in Westminster Abbey will be rare in the future. All those buried there have not been royal personages, poets and statesmen. Among those buried in the Abbey was Thomas Parr, who died in 1635 at the alleged age of 152. John Taylor, the "Water Poet," described Parr as "The Olde, Olde, Very Olde Man." Jack Broughton, champion prize fighter of England from 1734 to 1750, was buried in Westminster Abbey. He is credited with having raised boxing to the level of a scientific and national sport. George

Frederick Handel (1685–1759), the famous German composer, was also buried there. The British government placed in the Abbey a mural tablet in memory of Major John André, who in 1780 was hanged by the Americans as a spy for negotiating the treason of Benedict Arnold.

Can fish drown?

It is not possible for fish to *drown* in the strict sense of that word. To drown is to be killed by suffocation as the result of submergence in water. All fish breathe, but most of them obtain oxygen from the water by means of their gills. Therefore fish may be suffocated by being placed in water that does not contain a sufficient amount of dissolved oxygen to keep them alive. Ordinary fish will suffocate in water with an oxygen content below the requirements of the particular species. Any fish would suffocate in water from which all the oxygen had been removed by boiling. Occasionally large numbers of fish suffocate in water covered with thick ice. Likewise fish suffocate when there are too many in a small pond or vessel. But this can hardly be termed *drowning*. Sometimes, however, *drowning* is popularly applied to killing fish by capturing them on a line and entangling them in a net in such a way as to suffocate them by preventing a sufficient flow of water through the gills. It is said that certain species of mackerel, among the swiftest swimming fish known, will *drown* in a small vessel of water. Their breathing apparatus is geared so high that they can obtain enough oxygen only by swimming rapidly. Some fish will also die from want of air if they are held under the water and not permitted to come to the surface to breathe.

What makes telephone wires hum?

The mournful, humming noise given off by telephone and telegraph wires is produced by vibration. Wires strung from pole to pole are set into oscillation by the wind, somewhat as the strings of a violin are set into vibration by the bow. Any jar will make the wires hum, although ordinarily, according to the United States Bureau of Standards, the hum is due entirely to the wind. Such wires have natural frequencies of vibration like piano strings. The fundamental frequencies, those of the wires vibrating as a whole, are generally too low to be audible, but the sectional frequencies are often audible. Sometimes several of these frequencies are set up at the same time and produce harmonies. Contrary to a popular notion, the electric currents, either in the air or in the wires, have nothing to do with the humming of such wires. The intensity of the noise depends on the direction and velocity of the wind, the tightness of the wires and the distance between poles. There is a common belief that the wires make more noise in a light wind than a heavy one. This is due largely to the contrast. During a high wind other sounds mask the hum of the wires. The poles do not help produce the humming, but it is more noticeable there because wood is a fair conductor of sound. If the wind blows lengthwise of the wires it will produce a different combination of notes from those produced by a transverse wind. For that reason some people claim they can forecast the weather from the character of the humming. This is possibly true to a limited extent. The character of the noise depends on the direction of the wind, which depends on the location of the storm center, which in turn is a good basis for local weather forecasting. The humming of telephone and telegraph wires often resembles the humming of bees. It is said that telegraph poles in Siberia are sometimes damaged by brown bears that mistake the humming of the wires for that of bees and in their clumsy and awkward fashion climb the poles in search of honey. This may also explain a report in 1941 that black bears were damaging telephone poles in Los Padres National Forest in California.

Will diamonds burn?

Although diamonds are among the hardest and most imperishable of all known substances, they are composed of pure carbon and will burn if heated sufficiently in air. It is not possible to burn a diamond in an ordinary fire, but it can easily be done with a blow torch. Diamonds are affected by heat at temperatures ranging from 1400 to 1607 degrees Fahrenheit, depending on the hardness of the diamond. Such temperatures are not reached in an ordinary burning building, but they are sometimes reached in extensive conflagrations. For instance, it is estimated that temperatures as high as 2,200 degrees Fahrenheit were reached in the fire that destroyed San Francisco in 1906. Dr. George F. Kunz, the eminent gem expert, says he has seen thousands of diamonds in a single fire and that some of them lost from half to three-quarters of their weight, while others were entirely burned up. He says they are not likely to be cracked by heat, but the surface will be gradually eaten away and corroded until it becomes white or gray, and if exposed long enough the diamonds will be completely consumed. Under a blow torch diamonds are readily converted into graphite. When burned in oxygen gas they give a brilliant light. A diamond can be shattered with an ordinary hammer by hitting it at the proper cleavage with great force. Contrary to the general impression, diamonds used industrially as abrasives do wear out. The carbon atoms in diamond are crystallized in a definite form and fixed rigidly in position. Diamond is found only in single crystals, never in solid formation. Although diamond is crystal clear, when reduced to dust it is as black as other carbon. It is the only gem composed of only one element. Other gem stones are composed of two or more elements.

What is a chinook wind?

Chinook is the popular name of various warm winds common in the northwestern part of the United States and in British Columbia, Canada. Now the term is applied generally to a warm, moist, southwest wind of the coastal regions of Oregon and Washington. It was originally applied by the early traders at Astoria, Oregon, to a warm southwest wind blowing from the direction of the Chinook Indian villages on the lower Columbia River. The term is applied specifically to a warm, dry, local wind in winter that descends the lee side of a mountain. Such chinook winds are common among the Sierras and the Rockies. Under the influence of a chinook wind the snow melts with astonishing rapidity and the weather becomes balmy and springlike. These chinook winds are produced as follows: Humid air rising on the windward side of a high mountain cools slowly with ascent, owing to the heat freed by a condensation of the water vapor into cloud and rain. This same air descending on the lee side is relatively dry and warms up rapidly by compression with descent. Hence, level for level, the air is warmer on the lee than on the windward side. The difference in temperature between the opposite valleys of a high mountain may be ten to twenty degrees, or even more. In Europe, especially in the Alps, foehn is the name applied to winds of this type. Glarus, Switzerland, was almost completely destroyed in 1861 by fire fanned by a foehn rushing down from the mountains. A law now requires every fire in the town to be extinguished as soon as a foehn begins. Foehn is a German Swiss modification of Latin Favonius, who in Roman mythology was the personification of the west wind, which blew in the spring and promoted vegetation.

How did "grass widow" originate?

The origin of grass widow is obscure. Several explanations have been suggested, all of which are unsupported by etymological evidence. One holds that grass here is a corruption of the French form of grâce and that the original term was grâce widow, that is, a woman separated from her husband by the grace of state or church instead of death. This theory is improbable because grass widow seems to have originally meant an unmarried mother. In 1528 Sir Thomas More wrote in Dyaloge: "For then had wyuys ben in his time lytel better than grasse wydowes be now." In all probability the term had a lowly origin and was applied to an unmarried mother somewhat by the rule that a fatherless child was called a hedge-child. The modern term is ambiguous in meaning. It may mean a wife temporarily separated from her husband, as while he is traveling at a distance or away on business or in military service; a divorced woman; or a wife who has been abandoned by her husband. Two popular theories advanced to explain the term deserve mention. One holds that it orig-inated during the gold-digging craze in California. A man, it is said, would frequently put his wife and children out to board with a private family while he went to the *diggin's*. This was called *putting the wife to grass*. The other holds that the term originated in India. It was formerly a custom for the Anglo-Indian husbands to send their wives and families to the grazing country in the hills during the hot season. Thus a wife in the grass country away from her husband came to be called a grass widow. One writer said in 1859: "Grass widows in the hills are always writing to their husbands when you drop in upon them." Still another suggestion is that *grass widow* was merely a facetious name for such a woman in con-tradistinction to a *sod widow*. A grass widow's husband was alive while a sod widow's husband was under the sod. That all these theories are im-probable is indicated by the date of the quotation from More and the original meaning of the term. They are entitled to little more considera-tion than the schoolboy's definition that "a grass widow is the wife of a vegetarian." The counterpart in German is *Strohwitwe*, "straw widow."

Do edible oysters produce valuable pearls?

Pearls are produced on the shells of various species of oysters, clams and mollusks and the gems resemble the shells or "mother-of-pearl" on which they are found. The value of a pearl depends upon its shape, size, color or "sheen" and freedom from flaws. A pearl is a dense, shelly concretion formed about some foreign particle as an abnormal growth within the shell. "It is," wrote the American epigrammatist John A. Sedden, "the sick oyster which possesses the pearl." Pearls are artificially induced by injecting tiny particles of foreign matter into the mother-of-pearl of living oysters. During the process of formation some pearls be-come attached to the shell and are irregular in shape. We often hear of pearls found on common edible oysters that would have been valuable "if not spoiled by cooking." Such stories are probably never true. No pearl of any real value is ever found in the North American variety of edible oyster. It is a fact that cooking would deaden the luster and destroy the color of valuable pearls, but the common edible oyster never pro-duces pearls of commercial value because of the limited iridescence of its shell. Nevertheless there is no direct relationship between edibility and pearl bearing. The worthless pearls found on edible oysters are formed in the same manner as the valuable pearls found on pearl oysters. The finest pearls in the world are taken from oysters found in the Persian Gulf, chiefly around the Bahrein Islands. All of the most valuable pearls are produced by oysters found in tropical waters. Only a small percentage of pearl oysters actually contain pearls, while dozens of pearls may be produced on one oyster shell. Fresh-water mollusks, which bear valuable pearls, are edible, although as a general rule they are tough and not of good flavor. The black pearl occasionally formed on the black lip oyster is regarded as an oddity rather than a gem of commercial value.

Which sex of the mosquito bites?

The male mosquito does not bite. He is strictly a vegetarian. Only in the female is the proboscis fitted for biting and bloodsucking. The mouth parts of the male are rudimentary and he could not bite no matter how hard he might try. This, at any rate, is true of all the common mosquitoes. Whether bloodsucking is common to both sexes in any rare species is a disputed question. "So far as we know," says the United States Department of Agriculture, "there is no species of mosquito of which the male sucks blood." Apparently the female mosquito requires a blood diet to enable her to develop eggs. The so-called bite of the female mosquito is really a puncture of the skin rather than a "bite" in the popular sense of the term. Mosquito is the diminutive of Spanish mosca, meaning "fly" or "gnat" and literally signifies "little fly." In many parts of the world mosquito is the usual term for gnat rather than what we call mosquitoes. In Retrospect of Western Travel (Volume II, 1838), Harriet Martineau wrote of her trip up the Mississippi: "After supper we hastened again to the hurricane deck, where the air was breathing cool, and, to our great joy, strong enough to relieve us from moschetoes."

Do the inner car wheels slip in making curves?

When two car wheels of equal size are fastened rigidly to the same axle, one wheel, according to the United States Bureau of Standards, must slip in going around a curve. The difference in the length of the two rails in a curve may be several feet. Part of this difference is made up by "coning" the treads of the wheels of railway cars. When such a car goes around a curve the centrifugal force throws it over as far as the flange on the outside wheels will permit. This slightly increases the diameter of the outside wheels where they come in contact with the rails, and it likewise decreases the diameter of the opposite wheels to the same extent. To prevent the locomotive and the cars from jumping the track when rounding a curve the outer rail is elevated to counter-balance the forces set up by the moving train. The extent of the elevation of the outer rail is governed by the degree of curvature of the track and the authorized train speed. Coning and outer-rail elevation, however, compensate for only a small part of the greater distance that the outside wheels travel around a curve. That the difference is made up by the slipping of the inside wheels is indicated by the greater wear on the in-side rails. In automobiles the necessity of slipping by the inner wheels when rounding a curve is eliminated by the mechanical arrangement of gears known as the "differential." The power is transmitted to the wheels from the drive shaft through the differential and each wheel is permitted to revolve in exact proportion to the distance covered.

Do cows sweat?

Cows do sweat. Perspiration in the bovine kind, however, is not so noticeable as it is in horses and some other animals. In the case of the horse the sweat glands are distributed widely over the skin and the animal sweats freely all over the body. But in the ox the sweat glands are less abundant and are most completely developed on the muzzle. Consequently a cow will sweat freely on the end of her nose, while what perspiration appears on her body is usually slight and almost imperceptible. Likewise the sweat glands of a hog are confined chiefly to the snout.

Why is dried beef called jerked meat?

Jerked in the phrase jerked beef or jerked meat is not the past partici-pial form of the verb to jerk. No jerking in the ordinary sense is em-ployed in the process of preparing jerked meat. It is believed that jerked in this connection is a corruption of charqui or charki, a Spanish form of a Peruvian and Chilean word meaning flesh that has been cut into long thick slices and strips and hung up to dry in the wind and sun. This was a favorite method of curing buffalo meat among the Indians of the Great Plains. When the meat was fully jerked in the South American manner it was folded up and put into rawhide bags and kept for use when needed. Apparently charqui became jerked by the operation of the law of hobson-jobson. It is the name of the same preparation in nearly all Spanish American countries except Mexico, where it is called tasayo. Sometimes the adjective is spelled jirked and the noun jirk. A traveler writing in 1799 said: "We jirked the lean, and fried the tallow out of the fat meat, which we kept to stew with our jirk as we needed it." In

The Conquest of Peru, William H. Prescott wrote: "Flesh cut into thin slices was distributed among the people, who converted it into *charki*, the dried meat of the country." In *The Voyage of the Beagle* Charles Darwin wrote in Chile under date of 1834: "When it was dark, we made a fire beneath a little arbour of bamboos, fried our charqui (or dried slips of beef), took our maté, and were quite comfortable." The original pronunciation of *charqui* is partially preserved in *jerky*, a common Western name for jerked meat.

When are dog days?

This name was applied by the ancient Greeks and Romans to the period between July 3 and August 11, when Sirius, the *Dog Star*, rose with the sun. The Dog Star is the brightest fixed star in the heavens and is comparatively close to our solar system. It is the head of the constellation known as Caius Major, or the Greater Dog. The conjunction of the rising of the Dog Star and the sun was held responsible for the dry, hot and sultry weather of midsummer. Among the Romans, as well as other ancients, astronomy and religion were closely related, and it was believed by the people that the heat, drought and pestilences for which the season was notorious could be warded off by propitiatory offerings. Consequently the Romans frequently sacrificed red dogs at this time of the year. There is no scientific foundation for the belief that the conjunction of Sirius and the sun causes the hot weather of midsummer. In fact, owing to the precession of the equinoxes, Sirius now rises with the sun several weeks later in the season than it did in ancient times. It is a mistake to suppose that dog days received their popular name from the belief that dogs are more likely to go mad at this period of the year. That belief itself was probably suggested by the name *dog days*. Dogs are not more likely to get rabies during dog days than any other season of the year. Statistics show that more cases of rabies among dogs occur in the early spring and late fall than during dog days. In the United States *dog days* is not applied to a definite period beginning and ending on specific dates, but is applied generally to about forty days of the hottest season. Almanac makers sometimes give dog days a specific period, but it has no scientific significance.

Who were the Jukes?

That was the fictitious name given to a family that was the subject of an exhaustive genealogical and sociological study made by Richard Louis Dugdale (1841–1883), an American social investigator who was born in Paris of English parents. In 1874 Dugdale was appointed by the Prison

Association of New York to inspect thirteen county jails. He was so struck by the blood relationship of many of the inmates that he obtained private funds to make a detailed study of one large family. The results were first published in the Prison Association report in 1774 under the title *The Jukes, a Study in Crime, Pauperism, Disease and Heredity*. It was the first important sociological investigation of heredity and environment in crime and created a sensation at the time. The record starts with Max Jukes, a Dutch backwoodsman and early settler, who had two sons. These brothers married sisters, one of whom was known as "Margaret, the mother of criminals." Out of about 1200 descendants and connections of this one family, Dugdale investigated 709. Of these 140 had been convicted of criminal offenses of one kind or other. One hundred and eighty had been in the poorhouse or supported at public expense, sixty were confirmed thieves, fifty were common prostitutes, thirty had been prosecuted for bastardy, and a large proportion of the rest were venereally diseased, licentious and debased morally. Dugdale estimated that this single family group in seventy-five years had cost the state at least $1,308,000. The social investigator concluded that "blood will tell" and that inheritance is a stronger determinant in molding character than is environment. It should be borne in mind that *Jukes* is not the actual name of the family. A fictitious name was adopted to protect the worthy members. The finding of Dugdale's manuscripts in 1911 enabled Arthur H. Estabrook of the Carnegie Institution to identify the real name of the Jukes family and to make his comparative study, which was published in 1916 under the title *The Jukes in 1915*. Out of 748 scattered members of the family that could be traced forty years after the original investigation, 323 were found to be degenerates or prison habitués. The Jukes family is often contrasted to the *Edwards family*, proverbial for the great number of worthy and important persons it has produced. This Edwards family, many of whom of course do not bear the name, consists of the descendants of Jonathan Edwards (1703–1758), colonial divine, philosopher and writer, who had two sons and ten daughters and whose descendants also have been subjected to detailed studies.

Did Mrs. O'Leary's cow start the Chicago fire?

The story that Mrs. O'Leary's cow started the Chicago fire of 1871 is probably a myth. This fire started shortly before nine o'clock in the evening of October 8 in a barn owned by Patrick O'Leary, who lived at 137 KeKoven Street. For several weeks there had been a drought and the wooden buildings of Chicago were as dry as tinder. This circumstance and a strong southwest wind caused the flames to spread rapidly and made it impossible for the firemen to control them. The fire raged for two days and nights and destroyed some 200 lives and about 17,500 buildings having an estimated value of nearly $200,000,000. The exact cause of the fire has never been determined and probably never will be. No definite conclusion on this point could be obtained from the testimony of more than fifty witnesses soon after the fire. It seems that Mrs. O'Leary had milked her cow at the usual time earlier in the evening. She and her husband were in bed at the time the fire broke out, but they were not asleep because the McLaughlins, who shared the house, were having a party in the front rooms. A kerosene lamp with a broken chimney was later found in the ashes of the burned barn. This suggested the story that the fire was started by a kerosene lantern kicked over by a cow that Mrs. O'Leary was milking. The story originated before the conflagration had ceased and spread around the world. It persists in spite of contradictory evidence. The story may have been fabricated by a newspaper reporter. Michael Ahern, who died in 1927, said several years before his death that he invented the story about Mrs. O'Leary and her cow to make his account of the conflagration more interesting. Members of the O'Leary family always denied the cow story, but they admitted that a group of men living in the neighborhood were in the habit of meeting in the loft of the barn at night to smoke, play cards, shoot dice and drink beer. It is probable that the fire started somehow as a result of carelessness by some of these men. It may have been started by a smoldering cigar thrown into the haymow or by the accidental knocking over of a lamp or lantern.

Do drowning persons rise three times?

It is a common belief that a drowning person will always rise three times before finally sinking. Apparently Shakespeare alluded to this notion in *Twelfth Night* where Feste the clown, in reply to Olivia's question as to what a drunken man is like, says: "Like a drowned man, a fool and a mad man: one draught above heat makes him a fool; the second mads him; and a third drowns him." The belief has no scientific foundation. A person who falls into deep water tends to sink because the specific gravity of the human body is slightly greater than that of water. A drowning person generally rises to the surface because there is some air remaining within the lungs, air passages and other parts. Many drowning persons do not come to the surface at all after their first submergence. When a person finds himself drowning he naturally makes a frantic struggle to save himself. In doing this he draws water into his windpipe, which causes him to cough and expel air from his lungs. He then sinks.

If all the air is expelled from his lungs he will not rise to the surface at all, especially if fully clothed. On the other hand, a drowning person who has some control over himself may sink and rise more than three times before his strength fails completely and he sinks to rise no more. Bodies in the water are also sometimes carried downward or upwards by currents.

How are springs on mountain tops replenished?

Springs located on the actual summits of mountains are very rare. When they do occur they are caused by water being forced upward by gases in the mountain. As a rule so-called mountaintop springs are some distance from the actual summits. They are the result of the surface water soaking into the porous upper soil and continuing downward until intercepted by an impervious stratum, along which it runs until the layer crops out on the mountain slope. Springs of this type are likely to be intermittent, that is, they flow only a short time after wet weather and dry up when there has been no rain or other precipitation for a considerable period. There are numerous such "mountaintop springs" in the Rockies, and one of the finest is near the summit of Harney Peak, a 7,242-foot peak in the Black Hills of South Dakota.

Why did the Chinese adopt the queue?

After the Manchus conquered China in 1644 they compelled all Chinese men to shave the fore and top part of the head and to wear the remaining hair in a braid at the back of the neck as a sign of subjugation and loyalty to their new masters. The women, however, would not conform with the Manchu custom and they were not compelled to wear queues. Previously the Chinese men had worn their hair long and tied in a knot at the top of the head. The tonsure and braided queue had been borrowed by the Manchus from the neighboring Tartar tribes. At first the Chinese resented this badge of degradation imposed by the Manchu emperors, but as generations passed they not only became reconciled to the Tartar practice but were loath to give it up. Chinese prized their queues as their lives and spent hours every day in braiding and brushing them. At one time combings from queues were made into hair nets and exported in large quantities to the United States. The queue, called the "pigtail" or "monkey tail" by Westerners, became a characteristic feature of the national costume, and the Chinese themselves were often referred to humorously as "Pigtails." San Francisco enacted an ordinance requiring Chinese within its jurisdiction to cut off their queues. In *Ho An Kow vs. Nunan*, (1879) Associate Justice Stephen J. Field of the United States Supreme Court, while holding court on his circuit in California, declared the San Francisco anti-pigtail ordinance to be without authority and "special legislation imposing a degrading and cruel punishment upon a class of persons who are entitled . . . to the equal protection of the laws." Justice Field, after rendering the decision, is reported to have said in private conversation: "I am of the opinion . . . that no good can come from a resort to small vexations against the Chinamen. . . . To subject them to inconvenience and petty annoyances is unworthy a generous people and will result in no practical benefit. . . . This question cannot be solved by San Francisco, nor by California; nor is it a local one, nor are its consequences to be confined to this side of the continent." A conservative Chinese submitted to the queue only during life. When he died his hair was dressed according to the practice of his ancestors, symbolizing the fact that, though subject to the Manchus in life, he was independent of them in death. In 1898 it was reported that the Emperor was considering a proposal to abolish the queue by royal decree. In 1911 when the Manchus were overthrown and a republic established millions of Chinese cut off their queues as a sign of their liberation from alien rule. Leaders of the revolution encouraged the people to discard the ancient symbol of subjection, and during the next few years many local magistrates and governors commanded the people in their districts to cut off their queues, and in some cases forced them to do so. The younger men in the cities of the north and the men generally in the south were the first to get rid of the badge of servitude and submission. The queue gradually disappeared even among the country people of the north until at present very few Chinese wear queues, and most of these live in remote sections of the country. Of course, there is nothing to the old belief that Chinese cultivated the queue for the purpose of being pulled up into heaven by it.

Which is heavier, a pound of gold or a pound of feathers?

Technically speaking, a pound of feathers is heavier than a pound of gold. Feathers are weighed by avoirdupois weight* in which there are 7,000 grains in a pound, while gold and other precious metals are weighed by troy weight in which there are 5,760 grains in a pound. Of course, by the same system of weights a pound of feathers weighs the same as a pound of gold. *Avoirdupois*, originally *avoir du pois*, is an old French term literally meaning "goods of weight." The system of weights so designated is commonly used in English-speaking countries to weigh all commodities except precious metals and stones, and drugs. Troy weight received its name from Troyes in France. According to the avoirdupois system, a pound contains 16 ounces of 437½ grains each, while a troy pound contains 12 ounces of 480 grains each. There is an old saying that a pound of feathers is lighter than a pound of lead even when weighed by the same system of weights. In a vacuum a pound of feathers weighs exactly the same as a pound of lead. But because of the buoyancy of air there is an apparent difference. If a pound of lead and a pound of feathers are weighed in a vacuum and then weighed in air, the feathers appear lighter because they are less dense than the metal and weight for weight displaces more air. But if a pound of lead and a pound of feathers are first weighed in air and then weighed in a vacuum the feathers appear to be heavier. Often bodies that appear to have the same masses in air are found to have different masses in a vacuum.

Do the roots of trees grow in winter?

There is a difference of opinion among scientists as to whether the roots of deciduous trees grow during the winter months in northern latitudes. The consensus of opinion is that the roots stop growing entirely only during the time that the soil is actually frozen, although the growth of a tree is very slight during the dormant period in general. Very little root growth can be carried on independently of growth in the trunk and branches of trees, because the raw food material, some of which is taken from the soil by the roots and some of which is taken from the air by the green leaves, can be transformed into usable plant food only by the green chlorophyll of the living leaves under the influence of sunlight. The growth of a tree's root system and of its trunk and branches must take place simultaneously because of the interdependence of vegetable activity in the root and aboveground stem. But enough usable plant food may be stored within the system of a tree to permit some growth even after new supplies are no longer provided. There can hardly be any question, says the United States Department of Agriculture, that deciduous tree roots are active most of the winter in the middle latitudes of the United States, where the soil is ordinarily frozen only for short periods. Investigators have found that apple and currant roots begin to grow earlier in the spring than the shoots.

Do aviators know when they are upside down?

It is widely believed that when an aviator is flying at high altitudes his machine may be upside down without his knowing it unless he consults his instruments. This is not strictly true. In a general way a person undergoes virtually the same sensations while upside down in an aircraft as he does while standing on his head on the ground. A flier remaining upside down for any length of time, provided he is in possession of all his faculties, will be aware of the fact regardless of whether or not he can see the ground or objects on the ground. It would be possible, however, in thick clouds or a dense fog, or during night flying, for an aviator to lose his sense of direction and not know that his machine was in a steep spiral unless he consulted his instruments. It is also possible that a flier might become dizzy or confused during maneuvers in the clouds and for a short time not be able to tell whether or not he was right side up. The same might be true while coming out of a spin or when something is wrong with the instruments. But generally the force of gravity pulling against his belt would make him realize that he was upside down. Some persons have a remarkable ability to remain upside down for long periods. Aviators have flown planes upside down for several hours to determine the physiological effects of flying in that position.

Do fish sleep?

Fish are unable to close their eyes and do not sleep in the ordinary sense of that term as applied to mammals. Experiments with special apparatus, however, indicate that fish are more active at certain times and that these periods of activity are followed by periods of repose. Such periods of inactivity, which are variable in degree, may be comparable to sleep in the sense of physiological rest. The extent to which the sense organs become insensitive to external stimuli during these periods of repose is unknown. Sometimes a fish in an aquarium will lie on its side and appear to be completely oblivious to everything around it.

Which is correct, Welsh "rabbit" or "rarebit"?

Welsh rabbit is melted cheese and butter served on toast. It has often been supposed that *rabbit* in this term is a corruption of *rarebit*. Archbishop Richard Chenevix Trench (1807–1886), an eminent authority on words, was of that opinion. Many restaurants and hotels go so far as to use *Welsh rarebit* instead of *Welsh rabbit* on their menus. This, however, is an affectation based merely on an unsupported and improbable theory. *Welsh rabbit* appears to be a much older term than *Welsh rarebit*. In fact it is doubtful whether there was any such word as *rarebit* until it was coined by some etymologist without a sense of humor to account for *Welsh rabbit*, the earliest recorded use of which is dated 1725. There is no record of *rarebit* earlier than 1785. The Oxford dictionary refers to the latter term as an "etymologizing alteration of" *Welsh rabbit*. In *Modern English Usage* H. W. Fowler says, "*Welsh rabbit* is amusing and right, and *Welsh rarebit* stupid and wrong." There is every reason for supposing that *Welsh rabbit* was of pure slang origin and that it was first applied to melted cheese mixed with butter and served on toast for some humorous or whimsical reason, just as eggs on anchovy toast are called *Scotch woodcock*, Irish potatoes are called *Munster plums*, canned Belgian hare is called *boned turkey*, red herrings are called *Norfolk capons*, and codfish is called *Cape Cod turkey*. In the days when few people in Wales could enjoy the luxury of a rabbit from the royal game preserves, melted cheese served on toast was looked upon as "the poor man's rabbit." Toasted cheese and butter are alluded to as a favorite dish of the Welsh in Shakespeare's *The Merry Wives of Windsor*.

What are the horses of St. Mark?

The horses of St. Mark are four colossal gilded bronze statues of horses in an open gallery over the narthex of the Cathedral of St. Mark in Venice. This edifice was at one time the private chapel of the Doge and a law of the republic required merchants trading in foreign lands to bring back some object of art for the adornment of the fane. Consequently the church became a sort of museum for the spoils of temples in the Near East as well as on the Italian peninsula. The four bronze horses, which are five feet tall, are very ancient and were brought to Venice in 1204 A.D. in the time of Doge Enrico Dandolo. It is not known by whom they were made, although they are sometimes ascribed to the Greek sculptor Lyssipus, who lived in the time of Alexander the Great. It is more likely that they were made at a much later date and belonged to a Greco-Roman triumphal quadriga. One theory is that they were originally made for installation on the arch of triumph of the Roman Emperor Nero and that Constantine removed them to Byzantium about three hundred years later. In 1797 Napoleon carried the horses of St. Mark to Paris, but after his final fall in 1815 they were restored to Venice. When the Germans and Austrians threatened Venice during the First World War the historic statues were first protected by piling bags of sand around them and later by removing them to Rome for safety.

Why don't planets twinkle like stars?

In a general way stars can be distinguished from planets because the former twinkle while the latter do not. The twinkling of stars is entirely an atmospheric illusion and does not originate with the stars themselves. It is merely an effect produced by irregularities in the density of the atmosphere through which the light from the stars passes on the way to the earth. Owing to its great distance from the earth a star is optically a single point. Strata of atmosphere of different temperatures intermingle and flow past one another and cause a rapid shaking or vibration of the light coming from the star. The scattering of the light rays by irregular refraction causes very few of them to reach the eye at one instant and many at another. This phenomenon is comparable to the effect created by the heat waves from a hot stove. Because of the greater density of the atmosphere near the earth the twinkling of a star is more pronounced when the star is close to the horizon. On the other hand a planet shines by reflected light, and, owing to its relative nearness to the earth, is an apparent disk with many points. The various points on the disk do not keep step in their twinkling. Some are bright while others are faint, so that the amount of light received by the eye at any instant is always much nearer the average light than in the case of a star. Planets do twinkle, but the twinkling is perceptible only when they are near the horizon and observed through thicker layers of atmosphere of varying temperatures. When higher in the heavens the multitude of points on the apparent disks of planets maintain a general average of brightness.

Does thunder cause milk to turn sour?

The popular belief that thunderstorms cause milk to turn sour is very old. In 1739 John Mottley published *Joe Miller's Jests, or Wit's Vade Mecum* (commonly called *Joe Miller's Joke Book*), which contained more than a thousand jokes, each with a serial number. No. 997 asserted that "the celebrated organist Abbe Vegler" once imitated "a thunderstorm so well that for miles round all the milk turned sour." The belief may have a slight foundation in fact. In 1939 scientists in Toledo, Ohio, announced that they could sour milk by sound waves and then sweeten it again by reversing the process. Originally the belief was that the electricity in the atmosphere during a thunderstorm caused the milk to sour sooner than it normally would. There used to be a notion that an electrical storm had the same effect on beer. It is probable, however, that there is not much connection between thunder and the souring of milk. Thunderstorms frequently occur toward the end of hot summer days. On such days milk is also likely to sour. This may be the only connection between the storm and the souring of milk, which is caused by the growth of bacteria.

Why is a stiff felt hat called a derby?

Stiff felt hats with dome-shaped crowns worn by men are generally called *derbies* in the United States and *bowlers* in England, although both names probably originated in the latter country. However, the derivation of *derby* in this connection has not been definitely traced.

The term may have arisen from the fact that such hats were favorites with the Earl of Derby, who established the famous Derby horse races at Epsom in 1780: or possibly bowler hats were popularized by sporting men attending the Derby races. Headgear somewhat similar in general appearance was worn by the ancient Greeks. There is a tradition in England that the bowler was designed by a Southwark hatter named William Bowler and that it gained its initial popularity through the patronage of William Coke (pronounced the same as *Cook*), nephew of Sir Edward Coke. "The bowler," declared the younger Coke, "possesses all the good qualities that a man could desire in his headgear." A firm of London hatters still advertises bowlers as *Coke hats* because of the tradition that its predecessors made the first hat of this type for William Coke. In the eighteenth century a hard low-crowned felt hat was colloquially called a *billycock*. Some have supposed that *billycock* is a corruption of *Billy Coke*, but the Oxford dictionary suggests that the term may have been a corruption of *bully-cocked*. Derbies were first made in the United States at South Norwalk, Connecticut, in 1850 and sold to a distributor in New York City.

How did the Mattapony River get its name?

The Mattapony is a river in Virginia that discharges its waters into the York River at West Point. *Mattapony*—originally *Mattapanient* or *Mattapament*—was the English rendering of the name of a small Indian tribe of the Powhatan confederacy. The same word occurs as a place name across the Potomac in Maryland. The Mattapony River in Virginia, which figured largely in several campaigns during the Civil War, is formed by the juncture of four smaller streams—the Mat, Ta, Po and Ny—and the names of the smaller streams are merely the syllables of the name of the larger river—*Mat-ta-po-ny*. The Matta, formed by a juncture of the Mat and Ta, flows into the main river that is formed farther north by the juncture of the Po and Ny.

Can a snake jump off the ground?

The popular notion that ordinary snakes can jump off the ground is erroneous; few if any large snakes can leap entirely from the ground. Most snakes "strike" but do not "leap" or "jump." Another popular but erroneous notion is that ordinary snakes can strike their full length or even a greater distance. About one-half to three-fourths of its own length is believed to be the greatest distance most snakes can strike. This accounts for the fact that most victims of snakebite are struck on their legs below the knee or on the feet. When a snake strikes from its usual

[361]

S-shaped curved position, the front part of the body must be free from coil. In striking at an object the snake simply straightens out the S-shaped curves in the posterior part of its body with great speed. But snakes do not have to be in a coiled position to strike. They can strike short distances from almost any position. Often a large rattlesnake, when excited, will raise its head ten to fifteen inches above the ground, and in this position it strikes sideways and downward. Snakes seldom reach their maximum stroke even when greatly excited. The longer strokes are seldom accurate. Venomous snakes frequently misjudge distances in striking at objects and miss the mark. There may be a few species of snakes that can leap entirely off the ground. A placard in the National Zoological Park in Washington says: THE COBRA-DE-PARAGUAY, A COBRA-LIKE SNAKE, JUMPS AND CLEARS THE GROUND, A RARE THING AMONG SNAKES. It has been reported that the jumping viper of Central America can jump two feet through the air.

Why did Alexander weep?

If Alexander the Great wept at all he did not "weep for other worlds to conquer," as the old saying has it, but because, there being so many worlds, he was unable to realize his ambition of conquering even one, which is an entirely different matter. The cherished myth that Alexander shed bitter tears because he had no more worlds over which to extend his conquests finds little support in the ancient records and seems to be a perversion of a few simple facts. Anaxarchus of Abdera, a Greek sophist who accompanied the Macedonian on his Eastern campaigns, touched the conqueror in a tender spot on one occasion by reminding him that there was an infinite number of other worlds besides this one that would always mock his ambitions. Alexander replied: "Do you not think it a matter worthy of lamentation that when there is such a vast multitude of worlds, we have not yet conquered one?" Later writers not only perverted the true meaning of Alexander's words but elaborated the story by adding that his vanity was so wounded that he wept like a woman. Plutarch, in the following passage, throws some light on the ambitious side of Alexander's character: "Accordingly whenever news was brought that Philip had taken some strong town, or won some great battle, the young man, instead of appearing delighted with it, used to say to his companions, 'My father will go on conquering, till there be nothing extraordinary left for you and me to do.' As neither pleasure nor riches, but valor and glory were his great objects, he thought, that in proportion as the dominions he was to receive from his father grew greater, there would be less room for him to distinguish himself. Every new acquisition of territory he considered as a diminution of his scene of action." Alexander's father, Philip of Macedon, is reputed to have once said: "Oh, how small a portion of earth will hold us when we are dead, who ambitiously seek after the whole world while we are living!"

Who said: "Make two blades of grass grow where only one grew before"?

This common saying is based on a quotation in Jonathan Swift's *Travels of Lemuel Gulliver*, first published in 1726. In the chapter entitled *Voyage to Brobdingnag* is this sentence: "And he gave it for his opinion . . . that whoever could make two ears of corn, or two blades of grass, to grow upon a spot of ground where only one grew before, would deserve better of mankind, and do more essential service to his country, than the whole race of politicians put together." Some authorities say that substantially the same idea is expressed in *Zend-Avesta*, the sacred writings of the ancient Persians. If Swift did not originate the saying he at least popularized it.

How would you write it?

The words *to*, *too* and *two* are pronounced alike. The question is often asked: How can one write this fact in a direct statement—"There are three (*to*, *too*, *two*)'s in the English language"? In such a case it is necessary to use a phonetic combination to represent the common sound of the three words. *Too* is the phonetic combination generally employed to indicate the pronunciation of *to*, *too* and *two*, when diacritical marks are not used. Therefore it is correct to write, "There are three *too*'s in the English language," the *too* here standing not for the word so spelled but for the sound of all three words. It is merely a poor way of saying that there are three words in the English language pronounced *too*, or like the figure 2. The same problem arises in connection with any two or more words that are the same in pronunciation but different in spelling: as, *right*, *write*, *rite* and *wright*. Unrelated words that have the same sound are known as "homonyms."

Does the ostrich bury its head in the sand?

There is a widespread belief that when an ostrich wishes to hide it buries its head in the sand and imagines that it cannot be seen because it cannot see. This baseless myth in one form or other dates back at least two thousand years. The ostrich has become the symbol of folly and is proverbial in literature for its stupidity. Even in the Old Testament (*Job* 39:17) it is said of the ostrich that "God hath deprived her of wisdom, neither hath he imparted to her understanding." In his *Natural*

History, according to Philemon Holland's translation, Pliny the Elder wrote of the "Camel Sparrow": "But the veriest fools they be of all others;—for as high as the rest of their body is, yet if they thrust their head and neck once into any shrub or bush, and get it hidden, they think then they are safe enough, and that no man seeth them." The notion that the largest of all living birds buries its head in the sand on the approach of an enemy was probably suggested by two habits of the species. In the first place, the ostrich pokes its long beak into holes in search of water, which it frequently finds beneath the sand of the desert; in the second place, the ostrich rests itself by sitting down on its folded legs with the neck and head stretched out close to the ground. While in this motionless position an ostrich is not easily identified from a distance and the posture may afford the bird some protection from its enemies. Woodrow Wilson, as well as Franklin D. Roosevelt, compared early American foreign policy to the myth about the ostrich burying its head in the sand. "America cannot be an ostrich with its head in the sand," President Wilson declared in a speech at Des Moines, Iowa, February 1, 1916. In *America* H. G. Wells wrote: "Every time Europe looks across the Atlantic to see the American eagle, it observes the rear end of an ostrich."

How did grapefruit get its name?

This name arose from the fact that the fruit on a heavy-laden tree often suggests a huge cluster of grapes. Sometimes as many as forty or fifty large grapefruits have been known to grow on a single stem, but ordinarily the fruit is scattered about the tree like apples, oranges or pears, and the resemblance to a cluster of grapes is only fanciful. Grapefruit was originally, it is believed, a native of southeastern Asia or the Malay and Polynesian islands, from where it seems to have been introduced into the West Indies and Florida by the early Spanish colonists. The grapefruit is often erroneously supposed to be a hybrid developed by crossing other fruits. "A grapefruit," according to a popular saying of unknown authorship, "is a lemon that had a chance and took advantage of it." But actually it is a distinct variety of citrus fruit, akin to the orange and the lemon. Grapefruit has been an important food product in the United States since about 1900. When the fruit was first introduced on a small scale about 1885 it was bitter and upalatable and few people would eat it without the use of generous portions of sugar. Since then the grapefruit has been greatly improved by grafting and cultivation. Tens of thousands of Americans saw grapefruit for the first time at the World's Fair in Chicago in 1893. It is said that merchant ships during the eighteenth century used grapefruit for ballast and for cleaning the decks. Grapefruit was called *shaddock* in England for a time from the fact that the seed of a pear-shaped citrus fruit, resembling grapefruit but differing from it in having coarse dry flesh, was taken from the East Indies to Barbados in 1696 by a Captain Shaddock. In some tropical and subtropical countries various varieties of this citrus fruit are grown under such names as *pomelo*, *pummelo* and *pompelmous*.

Which is correct, "burnsides" or "sideburns"?

The original and correct form is *burnsides*. It is derived from the name of Ambrose E. Burnside, a Federal general during the Civil War, who was in the habit of wearing side whiskers and a mustache with his chin shaven. In popular usage the two syllables of the word are often transposed and it becomes *sideburns*. The fact that such whiskers are on the side of the face no doubt misleads many into supposing the first syllable to be merely descriptive of location.

What are secondary schools?

In 1930 the United States Bureau of Education issued a bulletin on secondary education. Those in charge of the work were surprised to learn that very few persons outside the educational field had any idea of the meaning of *secondary* in connection with schools. Secondary education is the training provided by high schools. In other words, secondary schools are simply high schools, institutions that give instruction between elementary or primary school and the college. *Secondary* in contradistinction to *primary* or *elementary* is used in both the United States and Great Britain to describe a system of education above that offered by the elementary schools and below that provided by the institutions of higher learning. Matthew Arnold was the first to use *secondary* in this sense; he borrowed and adapted it from French usage. The high school as we know it now is a distinctly American institution. Such a school, known as the English High School of Boston, was established in 1821 and was probably the first institution of its kind in the United States. Every state in the Union now maintains free high schools at public expense. But the American public prefers to call them *high schools* rather than *secondary schools*.

Does the giraffe have a voice?

It is commonly said that the giraffe is absolutely voiceless and is the only four-footed mammal that does not make some vocal sound characteristic of the species. Dr. William M. Mann, director of the

National Zoological Park, wrote to the author March 19, 1931: "I believe it is true that the giraffe has no characteristic voice at all. I have never heard one make any noise and it is generally said that they do not." It may be true that the giraffe is virtually voiceless, but there is evidence that it does occasionally utter a feeble sound characteristic of the species. Claude W. Leister, assistant to the director of the New York Zoological Park, wrote to the author on this subject as follows: "The giraffe does have a voice, at least it is able to utter a lowing sound. We have heard our female giraffe utter such a sound upon certain occasions when she was especially concerned as to the welfare of her young." Later, with the full knowledge of the controversy on this subject, the New York Zoological Society, which operates the Bronx zoo, in its official bulletin reported that at 9:50 A.M. on October 25, 1943, the female reticulated giraffe in the zoo definitely uttered the sound *moooo* while being inspected by the veterinarian. The 1936 annual report of the Game Warden of Kenya, Africa, stated that a young giraffe when separated from its mother will bawl and low like a hungry calf. As a matter of fact, it is doubtful whether any species of large four-footed animal is absolutely voiceless; the larynx in giraffes is poorly developed and members of this species generally utter no sound, even when greatly excited, but it appears that some of them at least do occasionally utter staccato grunts, mild snorts and lowing sounds.

How did "straw" get into "strawberry"?

This question has given etymologists much trouble and the exact application of *straw* in *strawberry* is not known beyond doubt. In no other language is the word for straw applied to these berries. *Straw* is from Anglo-Saxon *streaw*, which is akin in origin to *strew*. Straw was originally the stalks of certain cereals, particularly wheat, barley, oats and rye, used for fodder, litter, bedding and thatch. Many theories have been advanced to explain *strawberry*. According to one, strawberries were so named because the runners resemble straws. Another regards *strawberry* as a corruption of *stray-berry*, referring to the straying habits of the runners in reproducing the plants. Still another supposes the plant was called *strawberry* in the sense of *hay-berry*, because it is often found growing in hayfields. It has long been customary to cover strawberry beds with straw to keep down weeds, fertilize the soil and prevent the earth from soiling the berries. Some authorities suggest that the name is traceable to this circumstance. Another suggestion is that the name comes from the resemblance of the specks on the berry to particles of chaff or straw. A more picturesque theory holds that the name alludes to the old custom of stringing strawberries, like onions, on straws and selling them on market days for so much a straw. It is more probable, however, that the name goes back to the Anglo-Saxon meaning of *streaw* ("strew"), and alludes to the fact that the plant spreads or scatters by means of runners.

What is the difference between bobwhites and quails?

Many people seem to be under the impression that the bobwhite and the quail are distinct species of bird. *Bobwhite* is merely the common name for the native American quail, especially *Colinus virginianus*, or Virginia quail. The popular nickname was suggested by the male quail's note or call, which is fancied to sound like bob-*white*. In the southern states the same species of bird is called *partridge*, a name applied in the northern states to the ruffed grouse or American pheasant. The so-called American quail was incorrectly named by the early English settlers in America who supposed it to belong to the same species as the bird they had known in England by that name. The American quail, of which there are several species, belong to the same order but not the same genus as the Old World quail, which is a migratory bird.

When should "esquire" be used after a name?

Esquire, abbreviated *Esq.*, is sometimes used in the United States after a person's name in addressing a letter and takes the place of *Mr.* before the name, but the practice is dying out. Marquis James, in his *Andrew Jackson*, said that Robert Crawford "was called Esquire because of his participation in public affairs." In *Americanisms; the English of the New World* (1871) Schele de Vere wrote: "*Esquire*, a title in England still given only to certain classes of men, and long reserved in the United States also to lawyers and other privileged persons, is now with republican uniformity given alike to the highest and the lowest, who does not boast of a military or other title; the result being that it is strictly limited to the two extremes of society." In fact the title *esquire* is now applied promiscuously in the United States very much as the meaningless designation *Don* is in Spain. The title *squire*, a shortened form of *esquire*, is still quite commonly prefixed to the names of justices of the peace and even lawyers in some sections of America. This was also an old English practice. In Shakespeare's *II Henry IV*, Act III, Scene 2, Shallow says to Bardolph: "I am Robert Shallow, sir; a poor esquire of this county, and one of the king's justices of the peace." Later in the same scene Sir John Falstaff refers to Justice Shallow as "a squire." An esquire was originally the attendant of an English knight, the word literally signifying "shield-bearer." Shakespeare also uses the term in that sense. In *Henry V*, Act I, Scene 1, the Archbishop of Canterbury refers to "fifteen hundred knights, six thousand and two hundred good esquires." In time *esquire* became a title applied to the classes known as *gentry*—the younger sons of peers and the eldest sons of knights. As an actual title in England *esquire* ranks next below *knight*. Later it was extended as a courtesy title to officers of the court and royal household, sheriffs, lawyers, justices of the peace, landholders and even to literary men. As a form of address for letters in Great Britain *esquire* is now generally employed in connection with those who are not artisans or tradesmen; it serves as a mark of respect just a little higher than plain *Mr.* Many people make the error of using both *Mr.* and *Esq.* with a name at the same time; as, Mr. Stoyan Christowe, Esq. In February, 1776, Admiral Richard Howe and his brother General William Howe were commissioned "to treat with the revolted Americans." The following July Colonel Joseph Reed, adjutant general of the Continental Army, refused to receive a communication from the Howes in behalf of George Washington because it was addressed to "George Washington, Esquire" instead of to "General George Washington."

How did "boycott" originate?

Boycott is derived from the surname of Captain Charles Cunningham Boycott (1832–1897), who managed an estate for Lord Erne in Connemara, Ireland. His harsh methods of collecting rents for the absentee landlord made him exceedingly unpopular with the tenants. At that time there was considerable agitation in Ireland against the existing land laws. Charles Stewart Parnell, the famous Irish statesman, had become president of the National Land League of Ireland in 1889. In the fall of 1880 the tenants on Lord Erne's estate in Ireland banded together and demanded a reduction in rents. Boycott refused to comply with the demand, whereupon the tenants, presumably inspired by the Land League, began to harass the land agent in every conceivable manner. They refused to work for him and would not permit anybody else to do so. It was in the nature of a "sit-down strike." They tore down fences, intercepted the mail, insulted the manager personally and burned him in effigy. The upshot of the affair was that Captain Boycott appealed to the government for protection. A gang of Orangemen, known as "Emergency Men," came from Ulster and harvested the crops under the protection of nine hundred soldiers. The methods of the tenants, however, were adopted by the Land League to compel its enemies to comply with its demands, and *boycott* immediately became popular in the sense of any organized commercial or social taboo, especially a combine organized to ostracize an individual or company with a view of making him or it accede to certain demands.

What is a turnpike road?

Turnpike in this connection is synonymous with *tollgate* or *tollbar*. It refers to a horizontal barrier, such as a pole or pike turning on a vertical pin, set up along a road to halt vehicular or other traffic until the toll is paid. Thus a *turnpike road* is merely a road that has, or formerly had, turnpikes for the collection of tolls. Since the turnpike roads were usually the main roads, the term was extended in popular parlance to any important highway. Turnpike roads were already common in England in the seventeenth century. In his *History of England* Thomas Babington Macaulay wrote: "Soon after the Restoration [1660] this grievance [bad roads] attracted the notice of Parliament; and an act, the first of our many turnpike acts, was passed, imposing a small toll on travellers and goods, for the purpose of keeping some parts of this important line of communication in good repair." *Turnpike* is frequently shortened to *pike* in colloquial usage. Hence such slang phrases as to *hit the pike*, meaning to take to the road or to be on the way, and "the finest thing that ever came down the *pike*." The original turnpike was related to the turnstile, which is a gateway formed of four radiating arms of timber or metal at right angles to each other and revolving horizontally on a fixed vertical post. *Turnstile* is derived from the verb *turn* and *stile*, the latter term being derived from an old Teutonic root signifying "to climb." Originally a stile was an arrangement of steps or the like contrived to allow passage over or through a fence to one person at a time while forming a barrier to cattle, sheep or other livestock. At first the turnstile was set up in a passage or entrance to exclude any but foot passengers, but now it is often used to prevent the passage of more than one person at a time at any place where fees, fares or tickets are collected.

Do stones grow?

No belief is more firmly fixed in the minds of many people than that loose rocks, stones and boulders grow larger, especially if they are in the right kind of soil. The notion that unattached stones grow in size and even multiply in numbers as the result of their growth has existed in parts of England for centuries. Rock or stone is formed in several ways: some rock, such as sandstone, is formed by sediment in water;

others, igneous crystalline rock for instance, were formed geological ages ago when the earth was a molten mass; still others, such as metamorphic rock, were formed under pressure, heat or chemical action. Stones and rocks, which generally are comparatively small fragments of rock and stone formations, may contain some of the elements contained in living things, but they are inanimate and not alive according to any ordinary definition of life. Consequently they do not grow in the biological sense of the term. Some rocks, however, do get larger. A stone may gradually get slightly larger as the result of absorbing water. Stones may also get larger by accretion; that is, they get larger because of the addition of material from without. Likewise they may expand with heat without contracting again to their former size. The belief that stones grow may have originated as follows: Freezing and thawing of the ground causes loose rocks to work up toward the surface. This is because water expands when it freezes, and a rock or boulder is lifted slightly by ice that forms under it. When the ice melts the stone does not settle back into its original position, due to soil that has worked its way beneath. The rocks removed from a field in later years are often larger because the larger rocks work to the surface more slowly than the smaller ones. It is easy to see how processes like these might have created the impression that the rocks grow in size.

What state touches only one other state?

Maine is the only state in the American Union that adjoins only one other state. It is cut off entirely from the rest of the Union by New Hampshire. The honor of being bounded by the greatest number of other states is divided between Tennessee and Missouri, each being touched by eight other states. Tennessee is bounded by Missouri, Arkansas, Mississippi, Alabama, Georgia, North Carolina, Virginia and Kentucky. Missouri is bounded by Tennessee, Kentucky, Illinois, Iowa, Nebraska, Kansas, Oklahoma and Arkansas. It is said that from Point Lookout on Lookout Mountain near Chattanooga points in seven different states are visible to the naked eye on a clear day—Tennessee, Alabama, Georgia, South Carolina, North Carolina, Virginia and Kentucky.

What is a bee martin?

Bee martin and bee bird are merely popular names for the common American kingbird, a member of the flycatcher family. This species lives chiefly on insects captured on the wing. It has a bad reputation because of its alleged preference for honeybees. This habit, however, according to the United States Department of Agriculture, is much less prevalent than generally supposed and probably does not result in much damage to beekeepers. Government scientists examined 665 stomachs of kingbirds collected from various parts of the country. Only twenty-two of them contained the remains of honeybees. In the twenty-two stomachs there were sixty-one honeybees in all, of which fifty-one were drones, eight were workers, and the remaining two were too badly broken to be further identified. This proves that individual kingbirds do sometimes acquire the bad habit of preying on honeybees, but, as the American naturalist Elliott Coues observed, it "destroys a thousand noxious insects for every bee it eats." Therefore it appears that members of this species should not be killed unless positively proved guilty of the bee-killing habit. Many other members of the flycatcher family occasionally acquire the habit of preying on bees. The American summer tanager is also sometimes called *bee bird* because of its habit of occasionally resorting to a bee diet. The purple martin, which is a kind of swallow, does not kill bees and should not be confused with the bee martin or kingbird. There is a popular notion that the flowerlike crest of the kingbird serves to attract bees within reach of the bird's bill.

Are shoes ever actually made of kangaroo leather?

Kangaroo skin is soft, tough and fine-grained and makes an excellent leather for shoes and gloves. Before this fact was discovered kangaroos in Australia were increasing so rapidly that they threatened to become a serious pest. But after it was learned that the skins had great commercial possibilities, animals of this family were so widely hunted in Australia for their pelts that it was feared some species would be exterminated. Before the outbreak of the Second World War hundreds of thousands of kangaroo skins were imported into the United States for use in the manufacture of shoes and gloves. Whether particular shoes and gloves branded *kangaroo* are actually made of that leather depends on the reliability of the manufacturers who make them and the merchants who sell them. Undoubtedly in the past much of the so-called kangaroo shoe leather was not genuine. Kangaroos are hardy animals that live long and breed freely in captivity. Their fur is not especially good and has often been dyed to imitate better furs.

Do fish find the bait by sight or smell?

The sense of smell is highly developed in fish and it is probably mainly through this sense that they locate their food. Scientists, however, have not yet been able to determine accurately the relative perceptive powers of the various sense organs in fish. Most fish, it is believed, are attracted to the bait by both the sense of smell and sight. The sense of smell is highly developed in most fish and many species are probably attracted to the bait chiefly by that sense. A few years ago the United States Fish and Wildlife Service declared: "From what is known at present it is believed that the sense of smell, along with that of touch, plays a greater role in the life of a fish, as far as obtaining its food is concerned, than that of sight." Fish that depend upon the sense of smell to locate the bait are not easily caught by artificial baits, whereas fish that bite chiefly by sight are most easily caught by such baits. The sense of sight in most fish seems to be limited more to the perception of changing lights and shadows, and they will snap most quickly at a moving object. There is a common but erroneous notion that a fish smells with its gills. The nose is the seat of the smelling sense in all fish. The Canadian Fisheries Research Board reported some years ago that as a general rule the warmer the water the larger the pieces of food swallowed by a fish. Fishermen were advised to use small pieces of bait when the water is cold and larger pieces when the water is warm.

Why is New York called Gotham?

Gotham was first applied to New York in 1807 by Washington Irving in one of the *Salmagundi Papers*. It was merely a good-natured satire upon the supposed conceit of the author's fellow townsmen. Gotham is a village in Nottinghamshire, England, whose inhabitants are proverbial for their stupidity and conceit. In the sixteenth century, during the reign of Henry VIII, a book was published entitled *Merie Tales of the Mad Men of Gotam, gathered together by A.B., of Phisicke, Doctour*. It is supposed that the author of this book was Andrew Borde, the eccentric royal physician. Some authorities suggest that Andrew Borde was the original of *Merry Andrew* in the sense, first, of the attendant of a quack doctor at county fairs, and, second, of a buffoon, jester, zany or clown. The book contains the original of the nursery rhyme:

> Three wise men of Gotham
> Went to sea in a bowl;
> If the bowl had been stronger,
> My song had been longer.

Among other absurd legends it was related that King John once announced his intention to pass through Gotham in royal procession on his way to Nottingham to select a site for a new palace in the vicinity.

The Gothamites objected and plainly told the King's messengers so. They were not anxious to be burdened with additional taxes to support a royal establishment in the community and they feared that any ground over which the King passed would become a public road forever. So they hit upon the scheme of discouraging the King by all appearing hopelessly stupid and imbecile when the messengers returned. When the King's advance agents approached Gotham they found everybody in the village engaged in some idiotic pursuit or foolish occupation. Some were trying to drown an eel in a pond; some were lifting horses into haymows; others were putting carts on barns to shade the shingles from the sun; still others were trying to shut in a cuckoo by joining hands around a bush, and so on. The royal messengers returned in disgust to inform His Majesty that Gotham was a village of fools and that there was no use in proceeding with the project, whereupon the Gothamites observed: "We ween there are more fools pass through Gotham than remain in it."

What causes soot in chimneys?

The soot that forms in chimneys and stovepipes is a black deposit from wood, coal, oil or other fuel and consists of a combination of partly burned carbon, ash and the finer tarry substance known as lampblack. The proportion of these constituents determines the dryness of the soot, which may vary from a perfectly dry substance to a rather viscous gum, although soot is seldom sufficiently liquid to flow at ordinary temperatures. Particles of carbon, the product of imperfect combustion of the fuel, form the coloring matter of the gases known as smoke. Many of these particles of carbon, while being carried upward in the current of hot air and other gases, adhere to the sides of the pipe and chimney. As a rule the black liquid that exudes from chimneys into houses and soils the walls is a mixture of soot and rain water. A coating of soot in a stovepipe considerably reduces the amount of heat radiated. It has been estimated that the surface of a stovepipe loses about one-eighth of its heat-transmitting power for each one-eighth of an inch of soot.

Why do San Francisco people object to "Frisco"?

The nickname *Frisco* is seldom applied to San Francisco by residents of that city. Residents of San Francisco generally object to the curt nickname on the ground that it lacks dignity as well as distinctiveness, there being villages and towns named Frisco in Colorado, Louisiana, North Carolina, Oklahoma, Texas and Utah. Besides, they point out, San Francisco was named after a saint and it is unbecoming to abbreviate the name. In 1905 the legislature of California appealed to President Theodore Roosevelt and the United States Post Office Department to discourage the practice of designating the Golden Gate city "Frisco" in addressing mail. The nickname has been vigorously condemned as an abomination by press and radio and by various civic organizations in San Francisco. This campaign against the word attracted so much attention at one time that the St. Louis and San Francisco Railway, commonly known and widely advertised as the "Frisco Line," was obliged by public opinion to omit that term from its advertising and office window display in San Francisco. Oddly enough, this railroad does not run within 1500 miles of the Golden Gate city. When the railroad was started westward from St. Louis it was named the St. Louis and San Francisco Railway because the promoters hoped to push it all the way to the Pacific coast with terminals on San Francisco Bay. Although this road has branches running to Birmingham, Pensacola, Kansas City, and Menard, Texas, it does not extend west farther than Ellsworth, Kansas. Editors, reporters and copy desk men throughout the country, who require a shorter word than *San Francisco*, have not been so deferential to local pride and the nickname continues to be widely used. In fact, San Francisco itself has been undergoing a change of heart on the subject and has been veering gradually toward complete acceptance of the nickname by which it is known to the rest of the country.

What causes the ticking sound in wood?

A peculiar noise somewhat resembling the ticking of a watch is made by various species of insects, such as the powder-post beetles, which bore into the walls and furniture of old houses. For centuries superstitious people have believed this ticking sound presaged death in the family. Hence the insect is popularly called the *deathwatch*. A similar sound is heard in dead pine trees attacked by sawyer beetles. Scientists differ as to just how the deathwatch beetle produces the ticking sound. "It produces the ticking noise by striking its jaws against resounding wood; usually the sound is the signal of an insect to its mate," says one writer. The United States Department of Agriculture says simply that the beetles produce the sound in the process of feeding. According to that authority, the insects or grubs eating the wood rasp off fibers with their mandibles and cause the ticking sound. Others, however, maintain that the noise in some cases at least is produced by the insect tapping its head against the wood and that the sound is a sexual call. One old writer says: "The general number of distinct strokes in succession is from seven to nine, or eleven, and the noise exactly resembles that produced by tapping moderately with the fingernail upon a table, and, when familiarized, the insect will readily answer to the tap of the nail." Jonathan Swift wrote of the superstition about these insects as follows:

> A wood worm,
> That lies in old wood, like a hare in her form,
> With teeth or with claws it will bite, it will scratch,
> And chamber maids christen this worm a death-watch;
> Because, like a watch, it always cries click:
> Then woe be to those in the house that are sick!
> For, sure as a gun, they will give up the ghost,
> If the maggot cries click when it scratches the post.
> But a kettle of scalding hot water injected,
> Infallibly cures the timber affected;
> The omen is broken, the danger is over,
> The maggot will die, the sick will recover.

What is a coolie?

Some authorities derive *coolie* from Chinese *koo* ("painful" or "afflicted") and *lee* ("strength" or "energy"). According to this theory, *coolie* originally signified a "hard laborer." But from the sixteenth to the early part of the nineteenth century the term in varying forms was applied almost exclusively to low-caste Indians and it is probably of Hindu origin. *Koli* or *Kuli* was the name of a race or caste in the hill country of western India. Members of this caste were burden carriers and ranked under skilled workmen but above diggers. They carried earth, bricks and mortar, and often hired out as burden carriers. Centuries ago the Koli attracted notice because of their savagery, filth and general degradation. So many Kolis (also spelled *Colles, Koulis, Colys, Coulies, Coolees* and *Coolies*) were employed as laborers that Europeans in India fell into the habit of applying the term to laborers of the lower class in general. In southern India there is a word *kuli* ("hire" or "wages"), and some authorities derive *coolie* from that source. Whatever the true origin of the term, it was not applied to Chinese laborers until the early part of the nineteenth century. In time the word came to be applied particularly to unskilled laborers from India, China and the rest of the Orient who were induced to emigrate to work in other countries under terms and conditions bordering on slavery. Coolies from India and China were first imported into Western countries under contracts according to which they bound themselves at a low wage for a certain term of service, at the end of which they were supposed to be entitled to free passage back to their homeland. In the United States *coolie* is

[375]

sometimes loosely applied to cheap oriental labor of any kind, and even incorrectly to Chinese immigrants in general. In the decade between 1850 and 1860 more than 40,000 coolies were imported into California from China.

Does the hair grow after death?

Scientists differ somewhat on this subject, but the weight of authority favors the view that hair, including the beard, ceases to grow at death. Some of the Spaniards under Hernando Cortez in Mexico found a *teocalli* in which was a row of Spaniards sacrificed by the Aztecs. "Their hair and beards," wrote Bernard Diaz del Castillo, a chronicler of the expedition, "were much longer than when they were alive and I should never have believed it had I not seen it." In 1862 Dante Gabriel Rossetti, English painter and poet, was so stricken by grief that he buried some manuscripts of his unpublished poems in the coffin with his wife. When some years later the grave was opened to recover the manuscripts, the coffin, it is said, was found to be entirely filled with his wife's hair, "which had grown after death." Apparent growth of the hair and beard after death is explained by the shrinkage of the soft tissue around each individual hair, which is the natural result of the evaporation of the liquids of the muscles. For this reason undertakers sometimes have to shave a corpse again several days after death so it will be clean-shaven at the funeral. When a person dies all the tissues of the body do not die instantly. Some parts of the body may continue to live an hour or more after the heart stops. Those authorities who believe there are authentic cases of the hair actually growing after death admit that such cases are very rare and that the growth could continue for only a short time. No credence is given by scientists to the many popular reports that a complete beard or suit of hair sometimes grows on a corpse. The lengthening of the hairs, as well as the finger and toe nails, observed on a corpse are due merely to the contraction of the skin toward the roots and not to a "vital process" after the death of the individual.

What is the third degree?

Third degree is popularly applied to a prolonged, searching examination of a suspected person by the police, especially when accompanied by unduly severe treatment, for the purpose of extorting from him an admission or a confession. In mathematics the third degree is the degree in a series between the second and the fourth: as, an equation of the third degree. But *third degree* as applied to police methods is probably derived from Freemasonry, the third degree in that order being that of

Master Mason, which is said to be conferred with especially elaborate initiation ceremonies. The term, as applied to police methods, was popularized, if it was not actually coined, about 1911 by Major Richard Sylvester, superintendent of police in Washington, D. C. One writer observed that an officer of the law administers the first degree when he makes the arrest, the second when the prisoner is placed in confinement, and the third when the prisoner is taken to private quarters for interrogation. Third-degree methods, as the term is now employed, may consist of such mental and physical tortures as binding the prisoner head and foot, questioning him continuously for several days without permitting him to eat or sleep, beating him with a rubber hose, which is very painful but which leaves no mark, threatening him with a display of dangerous weapons, and other brutal and cruel treatment designed to break down his morale and force him to confess. The United States Supreme Court in the "Wan case" declared that a confession obtained under duress is not proper evidence. Several times since then the same tribunal has reiterated its disapproval of the use of forced or third-degree confessions as a basis for convictions. The Federal Constitution provides in Amendment V that no person "shall be compelled in any criminal case to be a witness against himself" and in Amendment VII that "excessive bail shall not be required, nor excessive fines imposed, nor cruel and unusual punishments inflicted."

How large is a bear cub at birth?

A bear cub at birth is smaller in proportion to the size of the mother than the young of any other mammal except marsupials. When born a cub is eight or nine inches long and weighs only about 12 or 15 ounces. Adult female bears of some species often weigh 500 pounds or much more while one of their cubs at birth may weigh less than 1/500th as much. A human baby at birth generally represents about 1/20th of the mother's weight. The newly born young of the common black bear are usually about eight inches long and weigh about ten ounces, representing 1/200th of the weight of the mother. That bear cubs are exceedingly small at birth was known to the ancients. In his Vulgar Errors (1646) Sir Thomas Browne disproved the "vulgar and common" notion that the bear brings forth its young "informous and unshapen" and afterwards licks them into shape and life. In Shakespeare's III King Henry VI the hunchback Richard, Duke of Gloucester, compares himself "to a chaos, or an unlicked bear-whelp that carries no impression like the dam." From this old belief arose the phrase to lick into shape, meaning to make presentable or give a good appearance to. In northern regions bears hibernate during the winter in caves, hollow trees and other sheltered places, where they subsist on the thick layer of fat just under the skin accumulated during the summer and fall. It is while the mother is in this dormant state that the young are born. They are born blind and are nursed by the sleeping mother several months before they emerge from the den.

Is there a species of white squirrel?

There is no distinct species of white tree squirrel in the United States. All white squirrels, says the United States Fish and Wildlife Service, are mutations or sports of either the common gray squirrel or the fox squirrel. It is not unusual for whole families of squirrels to be albinos. In fact it frequently happens that the albino specimens predominate in number over those having the normal gray color of the species. Sometimes in parks, or even in isolated forests, where the species is more or less restricted, the albinos breed true to color, and this leads many people to the erroneous conclusion that there is a distinct species of white squirrel in America. Precisely the same thing occurs at times with the black phase of the gray squirrel. There is no distinct species of black squirrel in America, although in many localities black individuals are numerous, and occasionally black families predominate over the gray. Because of the prevalence of black individuals in the southeastern species of fox squirrel it is scientifically known as *Sciurus niger*. Their color varies from glossy black to clay color mingled with black. The black squirrel of Central America, *Sciurus melania*, is also probably a mutation. Even the so-called white squirrels of Siam (Thailand) are generally light brown rather than white.

How did "halcyon days" originate?

Halcyon days, meaning a time of peace and tranquillity, is an ancient phrase that came to us from Greek mythology. According to the most usual version of the myth, Ceyx was drowned while going to consult an oracle and his body was cast upon the shore, where it was discovered by his wife Halcyone (or Alcyone), daughter of Aeolus, the god of the winds. Halcyone threw herself into the sea, whereupon the gods, out of compassion for their mutual affection, transformed them both into birds known as halcyons, popularly identified with a species of kingfisher. This bird, it was believed, spent seven days during the coldest time of the winter in building a floating nest of fishbones upon the sea and laying its eggs. Seven days more were required for brooding. Under natural conditions such a nest could not survive the shock of wind and waves. So

[378]

the gods saw to it that during the fourteen days when the halcyon was building its nest and brooding the winds ceased to blow, the sea subsided and the weather became calm. Therefore the period of seven days before and seven days after the winter solstice, the shortest day of the year, was called "the halcyon days." In Shakespeare's *I King Henry VI* Joan of Arc tells the Dauphin: "Expect Saint Martin's summer, *halcyon days*, since I have entered into these wars." Later it was supposed that the halcyon or kingfisher itself had the power to calm the weather and the sea by charming the wind and waves. According to another curious belief, if a kingfisher was dried and hung up by the head its bill would, like a weather vane, always point in the direction from which the wind was blowing. Shakespeare also alludes to this belief. In *King Lear* Kent says "such smiling rogues" as Goneril's steward Oswald, "Renege, affirm, and turn their *halcyon beaks* with every gale and vary of their masters."

What is goldbeaters' skin?

Goldbeaters' skin is a fine membrane made of the outer coat of the blind gut in cattle and is used by goldbeaters to separate the leaves of metal during the last and most difficult stages of hammering out gold leaf. The intestine, after being put through several processes, is cut into pieces about five inches square. Its tenacity and powers of resistance are so great that it will resist the continous pounding of a heavy hammer for several months. Goldbeaters still do their work by hand as they did in ancient times. A large number of leaves are beaten at the same time and hammers ranging in weight from seven to twenty pounds are used. Gold is the most malleable of all metals and the minimum thickness to which it can be beaten with patience and skill is not known for certain. It is said that an ounce of pure gold can be beaten into enough gold leaf to cover an acre. A single grain of gold has been beaten into a leaf having an area of seventy-five square inches and a thickness of less than 1/368,000 of an inch. Commercial gold leaf ranges from 1/200,000 to 1/250,000 of an inch in thickness.

Where is the geographical center of the United States?

There is no known method by which the exact geographical center of a given territory can be located. According to the United States Coast and Geodetic Survey, the approximate geographic center of the United States proper is in the eastern part of Smith County, Kansas, at latitude 39 degress, 50 minutes, and longitude 98 degrees, 35 minutes. The town nearest to this point is Lebanon. The geographic center of an area may be defined, in a general way, as that point on which the surface of the area would balance if it were a plane of uniform thickness, or in other words, the center of gravity of the surface. Anybody can find the geographic center, roughly, if he will take a good outline map of the United States proper and balance it on the point of a needle. This point should be in the northern part of Kansas. There are several reasons why this, or any other method, will not give an exact result. All maps, no matter how carefully prepared, are somewhat distorted. The United States is very irregular in outline. Besides, it is impossible to get away from the fact that any land area is part of a spherical surface. The North American *datum*, established by the Coast and Geodetic Survey for triangulation purposes, is often confused with the geographic center of the United States. This point is at Ogden, Riley County, Kansas, at 39 degrees, 13 minutes and 26.686 seconds west latitude, and 98 degrees, 32 minutes and 30.506 seconds north longitude. In a speech in the United States Senate in 1885 John J. Ingalls declared: "Kansas is the navel of the nation. Diagonals drawn from Duluth to Galveston, from Washington to San Francisco, from Tallahassee to Olympia, from Sacramento to Augusta, intersect in its center." The geographic center of North America, as determined by the United States Geological Survey, is a point a few miles west of Devils Lake in Pierce County, North Dakota.

What is the Queen of the Antilles?

Cuba is known as the *Queen, Gem* or *Pearl of the Antilles* because it is the largest and richest of all the West Indian islands. Antilla, a supposed island in the Atlantic beyond the Gates of Hercules, was mentioned by Aristotle. Before Columbus made his first voyage to the New World *Antilla* (or *Antilia*) was the name given to the legendary island of the Seven Cities in the Atlantic. On many fifteenth century maps and charts *Antilla* is the name assigned to a semimythical archipelago lying about halfway between the Canaries and "India." Later the name became identified with the land discovered by Columbus, and when it was learned that this consisted of a group of islands the plural form of the word was adopted. The Antilles are divided into two groups: the Greater Antilles, comprising Cuba, Jamaica, Haiti and Puerto Rico; and the Lesser Antilles, comprising the rest of the islands in the West Indies. When Columbus first saw Cuba in 1492 he described it as the "most beautiful land that eyes ever beheld." He first christened the new land *Juana*, after Prince John, son of Ferdinand and Isabella. Upon the death of the King the name was changed to *Ferdinandina*. Later the Queen of the Antilles successively bore the names *Santiago* (St. James), after the patron saint of Spain, and *Ave Maria*, in honor of the Blessed Virgin. All

[380]

these efforts to attach a Spanish name to the island failed, and the inhabitants persisted in calling it by its native name, Cuba, which is of unknown origin and meaning.

Is a pair of twins two or four persons?

Pair is derived through French from Latin *paria* ("equal"), and signifies "two." *Twin* comes from a root meaning "two" and means the same thing literally. As a singular noun *twin* is generally defined as "one of two children or young brought forth at one birth." The plural form *twins* is defined as "two children or young brought forth at one birth." Logically speaking, then, a *pair of twins* should mean four persons. But it does not and never did. Nobody uses the expression to mean more than two. When a speaker or writer employs the phrase *pair of twins* he invariably means exactly what he would mean if he said merely *twins*. "Mrs. Jones has a pair of twins" and "Mrs. Jones has twins" are identical in meaning according to accepted usage. Since *pair* adds nothing to the sense, why not say simply *twins*? It cannot be questioned, however, that *pair of twins* is widely used in popular speech and has some literary sanction. In such phrases *pair* is now followed by *of*, but formerly the *of* was omitted and people spoke of a *pair gloves* and a *pair shoes*. *Pair of* is followed by a noun plural in form even when not in meaning and this rule accounts for *pair of twins*. In Shakespeare's *Antony and Cleopatra* Antony's general Scarus, referring to Cleopatra's flight from the Roman fleet, tells Enobarbus:

> Yon ribaudred nag of Egypt—
> Whom leprosy o'ertake!—i' the midst o' the fight
> When vantage like a *pair of twins* appear'd
> Both as the same, or rather ours the elder,—
> The breese upon her, like a cow in June!—
> Hoists sails and flies.

How did "crank" originate?

Crank in the sense of a person possessed with a peculiar mental twist or with eccentric and freakish notions relative to a particular subject, seems to be of American origin. It is probably a "back formation" from *cranky*, an old English word meaning capricious, wayward in temper, crotchety, peculiar or crazy. The underlying and primary notion conveyed by the old word *crank* is "bent," "crooked," "twisted." In connection with machinery and mechanics the term has long been applied to a bent part of an axle or shaft, or an arm keyed at right angles to the end of a shaft, by which motion is imparted to or received from it. As early as the sixteenth century *crank* was applied to a twist or fanciful turn of speech. By 1848 it was being used to signify any eccentric motion or action, a crotchet or whim. A person "out of gear" was said to be "cranky." Dr. Oliver Wendell Holmes (1809–1894) gave the term literary standing. James Russell Lowell employed crankiness as early as 1870. In *Among My Books* he wrote: "There is no better ballast for keeping the mind steady on its keel, and saving it from the risk of crankiness, than business." But *crank*, as now used in the sense of a person with an obsession, apparently did not come into general use for a decade or two after the Civil War. The term was popularized in 1881 by the assassin of President James A. Garfield, Charles Guiteau, who employed the word frequently in connection with himself as well as others. When newspaper reporters visited Guiteau in his cell he told them that he was "a crank." During the trial the assassin said to the prosecuting attorney: "You have got a lot of stuff there. It is not in your handwriting. I guess it must have been contributed by some crank." The term rapidly passed from slang to the colloquial category. In 1902 Francis Train (1829–1904), American merchant, promoter, world traveler, lecturer, author and eccentric, styled himself "Champion Crank" and the "Great American Crank." Some unidentified wit has defined a crank as "a little thing that makes revolutions."

What was the longest sentence ever uttered by a parrot?

It is very difficult to obtain authentic information relative to the longest sentences or series of consecutive words ever spoken by parrots. The size of the vocabulary acquired by a parrot depends largely on the patience and perseverance of the trainer. So-called parrot talk is mere imitation of sound without reference to thought or meaning. It is sheer mimicry. Oddly enough, parrots seem to learn to "talk" only in captivity. Parrots in the wild state, though noisy and vociferous, show no tendency to imitate the familiar sounds heard around them. The ability to imitate words and other sounds, such as mewing like a cat, barking like a dog and whistling or talking like human beings, varies with individuals of a species. Some seem to be gifted in this respect, while others are stupid. Most birds are able to move only one mandible of the beak, but both mandibles of the parrot are movable. The parrot and other *talking* birds have no lips and their "speech" is produced in the throat like that of the ventriloquist. . parrot can learn to "speak" one language as well as another. The gray parrot of western Africa and some of the South American species are regarded as the best adapted for training as talkers. Carefully trained birds have been known to acquire vocabularies of several hundred words. Vocabularies of more than one hundred words are common. As a rule the utterances of parrots, no matter how well trained, consist merely of brief and disconnected ejaculations. Many specimens, however, have been taught to repeat several verses of a song. A French writer says he once heard a parrot repeat the entire Lord's Prayer. In *Cage and Chamber Birds*, J. M. Bechstein writes of a gray parrot that "could repeat the Apostles' Creed without a slip, and was on that account bought by a cardinal for 100 crowns." On several occasions the testimony of parrots has been given a limited legal recognition in court trials.

Why does the old moon sit in the lap of the new?

Frequently, during the phase of the moon popularly called new, the dim form of the full moon can be seen within the crescent of the new. This is known as *earthshine* and is a faint light visible on the part of the moon not directly illuminated by the sun. It is due to sunlight reflected to the moon by the earth and is most conspicuous when the part of the moon's disk illuminated directly by the sun is smallest. Then, according to the saying, "the old moon can be seen sitting in the lap of the new." Sometimes the old moon is said to be "in the arms of the new." In olden times sailors considered this phenomenon as an ill omen and regarded it with superstitious dread. Says an old verse:

> I saw the new moon late yestreen,
>   With the old moon in her arm,
> And if we go to sea, master,
>   I fear we'll come to harm.

What is meant by "the sun drawing water"?

Sometimes beams of sunlight appear as streaks running from the sun toward the horizon. This is commonly called *the sun drawing water*, from the popular belief that it is due to the sun's drawing up vapor by attraction from bodies of water on the earth. Many people regard the phenomenon as a sign of rain. It is produced when the sun shines through rifts in the clouds. The paths of the beams are made visible through the illumination of dust and other particles in the atmosphere. A similar phenomenon is produced on a small scale when a beam of sunlight shines into a room in which the air is dusty. The beams are in reality parallel. Their seeming convergnce is a perspective effect similar to the apparent convergence of the rails of a long straight railroad track. In parts of the British Isles this phenomenon is known as "Jacob's ladder," in allusion to *Genesis* 28:12, which relates that Jacob, as he slept on a pillow of stones between Beersheba and Haran, "dreamed, and behold a ladder set up on the earth, and the top of it reached to heaven: and behold the angels of God ascending and descending on it."

Why are dinner coats called tuxedos?

The tuxedo dinner jacket received its name from the Tuxedo Club at Tuxedo Park, which is in Orange County, New York, near the New Jersey line and about forty miles from New York City. In 1814 some 13,000 acres of land surrounding Tuxedo Lake was taken for debt by Pierre Lorillard. His son of the same name organized the Tuxedo Park Association to develop the tract as a fashionable and exclusive summer resort. On June 1, 1886, the Tuxedo Club was established "for the protection, increase and capture of all kinds of game and fish, and for the promotion of social intercourse among its members." It was at this club that the English dinner jacket, resembling a skirtless dress coat, was first introduced and popularized in the United States. This departure from the former custom of dining only in full dress clothes on formal occasions is said to have been suggested by Griswold Lorillard, a descendant of the first Pierre Lorillard. At first the "tuxedo," as it came to be called, was worn merely as a dinner coat; now it is widely worn as an evening dress coat on semiformal occasions. *Tuxedo* is believed to be derived from an Algonquin Indian word that was applied to the wolf clan of the Delawares. It literally signifies "he has a round foot," alluding to the wolf. During the Revolution, Lewis Morgan spelled the word *Took-seat*, while on a military map that belonged to General Washington it was spelled *Taxeto*. *Tuxedo* is the name of a summer resort in Passaic County, New Jersey, and there are post offices named Tuxedo in Delaware, North Carolina and Texas.

Is white a color?

Although white is popularly regarded as a distinct color, and for all practical purposes it is, technically it is not a color but a combination of all colors. The sensation called color is produced by the difference in the length of light waves. We see the longer waves as red, those a little shorter as orange, and so on. The shortest light waves visible appear to the eye as violet. A red object is one that absorbs all the light waves except the red ones; they are reflected back to the eye and produce the color called red. An orange-colored object is one that absorbs all the light waves except the orange ones; they are reflected back to the eye and produce the color called orange, etc. White consists of light waves of all lengths—of all the wave lengths mixed together. A white object is one that reflects all or nearly all the light waves. Although black is popularly regarded as a distinct color, and, like white, for all practical purposes it is, technically it is not a color, but the absence of color. A black object is one that absorbs all or nearly all the light waves. The seven colors of the spectrum—red, orange, yellow, green, blue, indigo and violet—used to be called the primary colors. Now that term is often applied to red, green and violet, out of which all colors are produced. An artist is likely to regard red, yellow and blue as the primary colors. With the spectroscope more than a million colors, hues and shades can be distinguished. An ordinary person with normal vision can distinguish 150 or more, while an expertly trained eye can distinguish more than 100,000. Unabridged English dictionaries list some 3,400 words for colors, hues and shades.

Which requires the more force?

The following question frequently presents itself: Which requires the more force, to fill an elevated tank by pumping the water directly into it through the bottom, or to fill it by means of a pipe leading over the top? The answer is that more work or force is required when the water is pumped over the top of the tank. Contrary to the popular notion, the water going into the tank from the bottom does not have to lift the entire weight of the water in the tank; it lifts only a column of water of the same area as the pipe. The level of the height and not the weight of the water governs. If you lift a column of water over the top of the tank it is clear that you must lift it higher than if you force it into the tank from the bottom. The pressure of a column of water in pounds to the square inch is calculated by multiplying the height of the column in feet by .434.

What is a Pyrrhic victory?

A ruinous victory or a success gained at too great a cost is known as a Pyrrhic victory in allusion to a remark ascribed to King Pyrrhus of Epirus in Greece after he had defeated the Romans at Heraclea and Asculum in Italy. In 281 B.C. the Lucanians, who inhabited the region around the Gulf of Tarentum, appealed to Pyrrhus to cross over to Italy to assist them in their war against Rome. Pyrrhus complied with the request and in 280 B.C. with a force of 25,000 met the Romans at Heraclea near the coast of the Gulf of Tarentum. Never before had the Greeks and Romans engaged each other in battle on a large scale. Due to the advantages gained by his cavalry and elephants, Pyrrhus was able to inflict a severe defeat on the Romans under the consul Laevinius, but not until both sides had suffered fearful losses. Rome refused to make peace with the victor and the following year Pyrrhus again defeated them at Asculum in Apulia in two engagements in which he lost the flower of his army. "When they had all quitted the field," wrote Plutarch, "and Pyrrhus was congratulated on the victory, he observed, 'Such another victory and we are undone.' " That was the original Pyrrhic victory. After fighting battle after battle Pyrrhus was finally killed by a tile that fell from a roof at Argos. Plutarch said that Pyrrhus "had not a regular set of teeth, but in place of them one continuous bone."

How did "tight as Dick's hatband" originate?

The *Dick* in this expression is supposed to refer to Richard Cromwell, son of Oliver Cromwell, the Protector. Richard unsuccessfully attempted to carry on the work of his father. He was ridiculed as *King Dick* and the British crown was called *Dick's hatband*. But the hatband proved too tight for him to wear with safety and he threw up the job and escaped to the Continent, where he lived for many years under an assumed name. The phrase *queer as Dick's hatband* is also supposed to allude to Richard Cromwell, who found the crown unsuitable for his style of head. One version of the saying is, "as queer as Dick's hatband that went nine times round and wouldn't meet." The second Cromwell was also known as Tumble-down Dick.

Does it ever rain frogs and fish?

No popular belief is more firmly fixed than that frogs, fish, snakes, clams, eels, turtles, angleworms and other living creatures are drawn up into the clouds by the sun and later rained down upon the earth. There are references in literature to "showers of frogs and fish" as far back as the second century A.D. and perhaps earlier. Any thinking person knows that the sun cannot pick up small animals and reptiles and hold them floating in the atmosphere. The presence of such creatures on the ground immediately after a rain is probably owing to one of two causes. In the case of frogs, toads, turtles, earthworms and insects, they were probably there before the rain stimulated them into activity. It only appears to the casual observer that they have fallen from the sky with the rain. Most of the "frogs" reported to fall in "showers of frogs" turn out to be toads. Various species of small toads are in the habit of burrowing into the earth where they remain inactive and unseen during dry spells. When it rains they emerge from their burrows and become conspicuous by their sudden activity. But scientists are inclined to believe there are numerous authenicated cases of fish falling from the sky during rainstorms. The conventional theory is that high winds, tornado-like whirlwinds and waterspouts sometimes scoop up fish from the water, transport them a considerable distance and deposit them on the ground, as such winds will carry pebbles or pieces of wood a long distance. There is evidence that "twisters," which become waterspouts over the water, occasionally pick up seashells, seaweed and other inanimate objects and deposit them on the land miles away. The difficulty with the theory that twisters occasionally "suck up" live fish is that nobody has ever witnessed the phenomenon. People have seen fish falling from the sky with the rain but have never seen fish "going up into the sky." Showers of fish are most commonly reported in tropical regions where sudden gusts of wind and whirlwinds are frequent. There is a place on the Pacific side of Honduras where it is said showers of fish are quite common. In India fish as much as three pounds in weight have been reported to fall in thundershowers. The fish are sometimes alive, but more often dead. Almost invariably they belong to species found in neighboring waters, either the sea or fresh-water ponds and lakes. So-called "blood showers" and "red rain" are generally due to the presence of colored dust, volcanic ash, plant pollen or minute plants in the raindrops. Falling "black snow" has been reported in some parts of the world. The "blood rains" that frequently fall over southern France, Italy and the Balkans are caused by reddish dust carried by winds from the Sahara.

Does "dickens" refer to Charles Dickens?

Dickens as an interjectional expression signifying astonishment, impatience or irritation is in no way related to the surname of Charles Dickens, the famous novelist. It was used by Shakespeare more than two centuries before Dickens was born. In The Merry Wives of Windsor Mrs. Page says: "I cannot tell what the dickens his name is my husband had him of." Dickens in such expressions as Go to the Dickens! is probably no more than a euphemism for deuce or devil, which have the same initial letter. Some authorities suppose it is a corruption of Devilkins, meaning "little devils." Daikins is used in Scotland with similar significance.

Why is the great African desert called the Sahara?

Sahara, the name of the great desert in northern Africa, is believed to be derived from the Arabic sahira, which is plural in form and which means "deserts," "wastes" or "wilds." If this theory is correct, strictly speaking desert in Sahara desert is redundant. The United States Geographic Board's first report on foreign geographical names noted under

Sahara: "Arabic for *Great desert,* north Africa. Not *Sahara desert.*" But since this origin of the word is not known for certain, and since the term is applied to one specific area only, *Sahara desert* cannot be challenged successfully on tautological grounds. The Sahara, the largest desert in the world, has an area of about 3,500,000 square miles. It is larger than the United States proper and almost as large as Europe. Its density of population is only about 0.04 persons to the square mile; that is, it is virtually uninhabited. The entire area, however, is not a vast sea of shifting sand, as popularly supposed. It contains numerous mountains and many spots—oases—capable of producing vegetation. The depth of the sand varies from a few inches to three or four hundred feet where there are large dunes. Numerous underground streams are found in the Sahara and fresh fish have been obtained merely by digging down through the sand into these subterranean waters.

How is "ye" pronounced in "ye good old days"?

Ye in such phrases as *ye good old days* and *Ye Old Coffee Shoppe* is merely the Anglo-Saxon or Old English method of writing the article *the. Y* here does not correspond to our letter *y* but is a representation of the archaic single letter called *thorn,* which has been replaced by *th.* The pronunciation of *the* does not change when it is written *ye.* It is correctly pronounced *thee* or *thuh,* exactly like *the.* Frequently it is incorrectly or humorously pronounced *yee* like the old pronoun *ye.*

Why were the Black Hills so called?

Black Hills is a literal translation of the name given by the Sioux Indians to the mountainous region in western South Dakota. In the Dakota tongue the name was *Paha Sapa,* which the early French explorers rendered *Côte Noire* ("black hills"), and it alluded to the dark and somber aspect of the pine-clad heights as seen from the plains. These heights really deserve to be called mountains. The highest peak, Harney, has an elevation of 7,242 feet above sea level and is higher than any elevation in the Appalachian or Ozark ranges. There are several other peaks in the Black Hills with altitudes of 6,000 feet or more.

Do the Great Lakes ever freeze over?

Notwithstanding numerous reports to the contrary, the United States Geological Survey is of the opinion that none of the Great Lakes ever freezes over completely. This opinion is confirmed by the Detroit and Cleveland Navigation Company. Shallow regions along the shore are frequently covered with ice and sometimes the ice extends many miles toward the interior of the lakes. Navigation is generally stopped from early in December until about the first of April because of ice in and near harbors, at the ends of the lakes and in the channels connecting them. No data are available as to the proportion of lake surface frozen over during the various winters. Lake Erie is the shallowest of the Great Lakes and it is said that the eastern part of this lake has frozen over sufficiently for a man to walk over the ice from Erie, Pennsylvania, to Long Point in Ontario, Canada. There is a natural tendency, as the United States Weather Bureau points out, to exaggerate the proportion of surface covered with ice. In 1904, when the ice was thicker than at any other time on record, very little open water was visible from the shores of Lake Superior, which is the largest, deepest, most northern and the coldest of the Great Lakes. No water could be seen from the shores of Lake Ontario during the latter part of January of the same year. This, however, does not prove that the entire lake surface was frozen over. The lakes are so large that open water might be invisible from the shores even if only one-fourth of the surface were covered with ice. Observers in airplanes report large stretches of unfrozen water in the lakes even during winters when people along the shores are under the impression that the lakes are completely frozen over.

Who was "that man"?

Among the Methuselahs of riddledom few present themselves for solution more frequently than the following hoary-haired brain teaser:

> Brothers and sisters I have none,
> But that man's father is my father's son.

The average person will reply by saying incorrectly that that man is the person speaking. But the riddle cannot be so construed. It refers to a father (an only child) speaking of his own son, that man being the son of the speaker.

What animal washes its food?

The raccoon, popularly called simply "coon," washes or soaks its food before eating, and it was the original "dunker." It holds the food in its fore paws and shakes it in the water. The coon generally lives near a stream and much of its natural food consists of frogs, crawfish, stranded fish and similar creatures captured in shallow water. It is supposed that the coon acquired the habit of dunking or washing its food from the necessity of rinsing the mud and sand from its aquatic prey. If water is not at hand a coon will generally carry its food to the nearest water and wash it thoroughly. Some coons have been known to go hungry rather than to eat food that they have not been permitted to dip in water. They are not willing to let somebody else do the dunking for them. This instinct is so strong that the animals will usually go through the motions of washing their food even when no water is accessible. Because of this habit the Germans called the coon Waschbaer ("wash bear"), and the second word in the scientific name of the raccoon, Procyon lotor, signifies "washer." But in other respects this animal is not particularly characterized by cleanliness.

Why does "lb." stand for "pound"?

It is a puzzle to many people why lb. should be used as the symbol of pound when that word contains neither an l nor a b. The symbol is a contraction of libra, the Latin word for pound. Strictly speaking, the plural of lb. should not be formed by adding an s; the Latin plural of libra is librae. The regular rule for forming plurals of contractions in Latin words is to double the final letter of the singular. Thus we have ms. ("manuscript"), and mss. ("manuscripts"); and cod. ("codex"), and codd. ("codices"). In the case of lbs., however, the error has been repeated so frequently for such a long period that it is recognized by the leading dictionaries and may now be regarded as an acceptable usage. Since lb. is a contraction rather than an abbreviation, it really should not be followed by a period, but in practice it generally is. Centuries ago lb. was used alike in referring to avoirdupois, troy and apothecaries' weight, as well as to money expressed in terms of pounds sterling. Gradually, however, the contraction was modified until a special form of the symbol was developed for us in connection with English money. This symbol (£) may now be classed as a ligature.

What are crocodile tears?

Crocodile tears are hypocritical tears or pretended grief. The phrase alludes to an old myth that crocodiles moan and sigh like distressed human beings to allure travelers within their reach. Another version of the myth was that crocodiles shed tears over their prey while in the act of eating it. There are secretions in the eyes of crocodiles to keep them moist, just as there are in all animals, but crocodiles have no tear glands and do not "weep" in the ordinary sense of the term. Scientists, however, say that a watery liquid oozes from the eyes of crocodiles and alligators when they attempt to swallow something too large for them. The ancients apparently made no reference to the tears of crocodiles. Probably the earliest mention of the story about crocodiles moaning to entice their victims and shedding hypocritical tears while eating them is found in *The Voyages and Travels of Sir John Mandeville*, written in French about 1371 by an unidentified author. There are numerous allusions to this belief in Elizabethan and later literature. Francis Bacon, in his essay entitled "Of Wisdom for a Man's Self," wrote: "It is the wisdom of crocodiles, that shed tears when they would devour." In Shakespeare's *Antony and Cleopatra*, during a drunken party on board Pompey's galley off Misenum, is the following colloquy between two of the Roman triumvirs, both the worse for wine:

LEPIDUS: What manner o' thing is your crocodile?
ANTONY: It is shaped, sir, like itself; and it is as long as it hath breadth: it is just so high as it is, and moves with its own organs: it lives by that which nourisheth it; and the elements once out of it, it transmigrates.
LEPIDUS: What colour is it of?
ANTONY: Of its own colour too.
LEPIDUS: 'Tis a strange serpent.
ANTONY: 'Tis so. And the tears of it are wet.

In *Othello* the jealous Moor says to the weeping Desdamona:

> If that the earth could teem with woman's tears
> Each drop she falls would prove a crocodile.

And in *II Henry VI* Queen Margaret says:

> Henry my lord is cold in great affairs,
> Too full of foolish pity, and Gloucester's show
> Beguiles him, as the mournful crocodile
> With sorrow snares relenting passengers, . . .

Why is the British court called the Court of "St. James's"?

This popular designation of the English court is derived from the *Palace of St. James's*, which was so called because the site on which it stands was once occupied by a religious establishment dedicated to St. James the Less. The religious establishment dated back to long before the Norman conquest and appears to have been at one time a hospital for leprous women. It was made part of the royal manor by Henry III, who was King from 1216 to 1272. Henry VIII had the old buildings torn down and a palace erected there in 1532. In Edward Hall's *Chronicles* it is recorded: "Ye haue hearde before how the Kynge had purchased the Bysshop of Yorkes place, whych was a fayre Bysshopes house, but not meete for a Kynge; wherefore the Kynge purchased all the medowes

[391]

about saynt James, and all the whole house of s. James, and there made a fayre mansion and a parke, and buylded many costly and commodious houses for great pleasure." That was the beginning of what is now known as St. James's Palace and St. James's Park. When Whitehall was burned in 1697 St. James's Palace became the regular residence of the British sovereigns. After 1837, when Victoria became Queen, Buckingham Palace became the royal domicile, but St. James's was retained for levees and other court functions. Although the Court of St. James's, with the sign of the possessive, is the original and correct way of writing the name, it is more frequently written the Court of St. James, without the sign of the possessive. When the possessive is added the last word in the name contains an additional syllable in pronunciation—james-es.

What is a moron?

Moron is derived from Greek moros ("stupid" or "foolish"). The same root occurs as the second element in sophomore, literally "wise-fool," which is applied to a second-year college student. In 1664 Molière, the French dramatist, produced a play at Versailles entitled Princess d'Élide, in which there is a court fool or jester named Moron. In its modern technical sense, however, moron is of comparatively recent American origin, having been suggested by Henry Herbert Goddard, American psychologist and authority on feeble-mindedness. At its meeting in Lincoln, Illinois, in May, 1910, the American Association for the Study of the Feeble-Minded adopted resolutions in which the feeble-minded were divided into three classes—idiots, imbeciles and morons. Morons were declared to be "those whose mental development is above that of an imbecile but does not exceed that of a normal child of about twelve years." Thus a moron has a higher mentality than an idiot or an imbecile and is applied by medical scientists to adults with the mental age of children from seven to twelve. One authority says moron is correctly applied to persons whose intellectual development proceeds almost normally up to about the seventh or eighth year, after which mental growth is arrested and never exceeds that of a normal twelve-year-old child. Thus, if a person more than sixteen years of age has the mentality of a child between eight and twelve, he is a moron. The Royal College of Physicians of England defines moron as follows: "One who is capable of earning his living under favorable circumstances, but is incapable from mental defect existing from birth or from an early age of competing on equal terms with his normal fellows or of managing himself and his affairs with ordinary prudence." Frequently moron is employed loosely to designate any person with morbidly criminal tendencies. In a purely popular sense moron often means little more than a person who is subnormal mentally, a moderately feeble-minded person, a "half-wit," or even merely a "stupid person." That is the meaning of the word in the moron stories and jokes. The following anonymous rhyme was printed in the *Eugenics Review* for July, 1929:

> See the happy moron;
> He doesn't give a damn:
> I wish I were a moron—
> My God, perhaps I am!

What is black frost?

Black frost is a popular term that originally denoted any freeze not accompanied by white or hoar frost. According to the United States Weather Bureau, the term now generally signifies "a killing freeze (the vegetation turning black) without the formation of the ordinary or white frost; namely, a decided freeze at a temperature still above the dew point." *Black frost*, however, is not used officially by the Weather Bureau, which classifies freezes as light, heavy and killing. It is not probable, as some suppose, that *black* in *black frost* was suggested by the fact that such a freeze blackens vegetation. That was probably merely an afterthought. Apparently the term was at first intended merely as a contrast to *white frost*, the usual name for visible frozen dew or vapor formed on exposed surfaces. As a matter of fact, a freeze destructive to vegetation may or may not be accompanied with actual deposits of frost, depending on the presence or absence of clouds and atmospheric disturbances. *Black frost* probably became associated with a severe, killing freeze by an unconscious assimilation of *black* in this connection with the same word in such phrases as *Black Death* and *Black Friday*. White frost is frozen water vapor. There is no material, under proper conditions of temperature and humidity, on which frost will not form, but if a material is self-heating or if it generates heat upon contact with air or moisture, frost will not form upon it. Frost forms when the temperature is 32 degrees Fahrenheit or lower. On still, quiet nights the temperature is often several degrees higher a few feet above the ground than it is at the ground level. That is why frost often forms earlier in the season on low ground than on buildings, porches and other elevated objects.

Why do dogs turn around before lying down?

Nearly everybody has observed that some dogs often turn around several times before lying down. Charles Darwin said he had seen a dog turn around twenty times before finally settling down in a comfortable position. Scientists attempt to explain this trait by the theory of evolution. They say our domestic dogs are descended from wild dogs or wolves. These progenitors of the dog lived in the forest or brush and to find a comfortable place to rest they had to trample down the grass or other vegetation. This ancient bedmaking process of its wolflike progenitor still survives as an instinct in the domestic dog that turns around several times before lying down. A dog is more likely to turn around and around on the hearthrug when it is sleepy and tired. It appears that in the dog's sleepiness there is revived the ancient habit of its progenitors in turning around to trample down the vegetation and to make in the herbage a comfortable bed for the night.

What is "lead" in pencils?

The lead in modern pencils and crayons is natural graphite mixed with clay to give it the desired degree of hardness. Graphite, one of the softest of minerals, is a crystallized form of carbon and is chemically identical with diamond, the hardest mineral. In nature graphite occurs in both crystalline flake and amorphous forms. It was originally called lead because it was confused with that mineral, with which it has no chemical relationship, being a separate and distinct element. Before the invention of modern lead pencils actual lead was sometimes used for writing. Conrad Gesner, of Zurich, Switzerland, described "writing sticks" similar to modern lead pencils as early as 1695. Graphite is still sometimes popularly spoken of as black lead or plumbum, the latter being the Latin word for "lead." Graphite, from a Greek word signifying "to write," was given to the mineral in 1789 by Abraham Werner, German geologist, because it was widely used in pencils. Pencil cores are made by mixing graphite and clay together, pressing the mixture into strings under tremendous pressure, and then straightening, drying and burning them at a high temperature. Graphite resists union with other minerals even at high temperatures and has many industrial uses. It is employed in making crucibles, foundry facings, bearings, gears, steel castings, dry cell batteries, electric tubes, motor brushes and generators, stove polish, paint pigments, lubricants, etc. Synthetic graphite made in electric furnaces competes favorably with natural graphite.

What forms the boundary between Africa and Asia?

The narrowest strip of land between Asia and Africa is the Isthmus of Suez through which the Suez Canal was cut. Hence the logical geographical boundary between these two grand land masses is the Suez Canal. The question, however, is complicated by the fact that the Sinai

Peninsula and the territory north of it to the Mediterranean Sea are politically a part of Egypt. Therefore mapmakers include this region in the map of Africa, making the eastern boundary of Egypt the dividing line between the two continents. There are several theories as to how Africa acquired its name. Some authorities suppose the term to be a corruption of *Ophir*, the name of the place, supposedly in Africa, where the ships of Solomon and Hiram went to get gold. Others suppose *Africa* to be derived from the Semitic root of the Hebrew word for "ear of corn" and that the name alluded to the fertility of the Nile Valley, where the sons of Jacob found corn in the time of famine in Palestine. The most probable theory, however, is that the continent received its name from a native tribe of Berbers who lived in what is now Tunisia. When the Phoenicians, who were Semites, established Carthage on the northern African coast, the members of the Berber tribe called Awriga were the most powerful people living in the vicinity. In Latin this name became *Afarika* or *Africa*. For centuries after the conquest of Carthage the Romans called the continent *Libya* and restricted *Africa* to Tunisia, the region lying between Cyrenaica on the east and Mauretania (Morocco) on the west. Maps in the time of Columbus labeled Tunisia "Africa Minor." In process of time the continent as a whole became, first, "Africa Major," and then simply "Africa."

Is the thumb a finger?

The thumb is a finger in the most general sense of the term. *Finger* is defined as one of the five terminal members of the human hand, including the thumb. This was probably the original meaning of *finger* as applied to the digits, for the Oxford dictionary suggests that the word may be derived from *pengros*, akin to *penqe* ("five"). Therefore it is correct to say that a normal person has five fingers on each hand. Centuries ago the English had distinct names for each of the digits—thumb, toucher, long-man, lecheman and little-man. *Thumb* is derived from a root meaning "thick" or "swollen." *Toucher* referred to the fact that people use this finger to touch things with. *Long-man* referred to the fact that this finger is the longest. The fourth digit (or third finger exclusive of the thumb) was called *lecheman* because a leech or doctor "tested everything by means of it." Later it became known as the "medical finger." It was believed that this digit was directly connected with the heart by means of a special nerve and that no poisonous substance could come into contact with it without giving warning. The lecheman or medical finger was used in stirring drugs and medical mixtures of all kinds. *Little-man*, of course, referred to the fact that this was the smallest and shortest finger.

But *finger* has also acquired a specific meaning, namely, one of the four terminals of the hand exclusive of the thumb. It is only natural that the thumb should be singled out and given a special name, because it is more prominent by its somewhat isolated position and because it differs from the other digits in having two instead of three phalanges. The small bones of the fingers and toes were named *phalanges* from a fancied resemblance to the Greek line of battle formation called *phalanx*. Hence it is equally correct to say the normal hand contains five fingers, or four fingers and a thumb, depending on whether one wishes to emphasize the difference between the thumb and the other digits. When *finger* is used in the restricted sense the fingers are numbered from first to fourth, beginning with the one nearest the thumb—first (index), second (middle), third (ring), and fourth (little). Reference to the "ring finger" as the fourth finger in the marriage service is a survival of the time when the thumb was counted as the first finger. It is an interesting fact that in the Pawnee and certain other American Indian languages a phrase meaning "all the fingers of the hand" was used to signify "four," which shows that these Indians excluded the thumb in counting the fingers. The first finger of a woman's hand is likely to be longer and that of a man shorter than the third finger. Experiments indicate that the degree of sensitiveness of the five fingers runs in the following diminishing order: index, middle, thumb, little, and ring.

What does "laissez faire" mean?

Laissez faire (pronounced lessay-fair) is a French phrase literally meaning "let do." In economics it is applied to a policy of minimum interference with industry, trade and labor; that is, competition in private business without protective tariffs, subsidies, restrictions or regulations by the government. It is based on the theory that commerce, domestic trade, manufactures and labor, if let alone by the government, will adjust themselves to one another. The term is supposed to have originated about 1680 in a conversation between Jean Colbert, the French statesman and financier, and a merchant named Legendre. Colbert, then the Minister of Finance under Louis XIV, asked Legendre what ought to be done by the government to help the merchants and business people in general. "*Laissez faire, laissez passer,*" replied the merchant. Literally the French phrase signifies "let do, let pass"; figuratively it signifies "let people do what they choose." *Laissez faire*, in the sense of "let the government keep its hands off and not meddle with private business affairs of citizens," is sometimes attributed to Jean Claude Marie Vincent sieur de Gournay (1712–1759), French economist and philosopher. In the sense of "liberty of action and liberty of movement" and "government hands off in economics," the phrase was popularized in English by Adam Smith, who quoted it in his monumental *The Wealth of Nations*, published in 1776. Thomas Jefferson in a letter to Thomas Digges in 1788 wrote: "It is not the policy of the government in America to give aid to works of any kind. They let things take their natural course without help or impediment, which is generally the best policy."

Why is the Kentucky-Tennessee boundary crooked?

There are many angles and offsets in the Tennessee-Kentucky boundary line that can scarcely be attributed to errors of surveying. Many people living in both these states say the surveyors were drunk when they ran the line. This is merely a fable. It seems that the commissioners who ran the line between these two states were allowed to change the line at their discretion, provided the commissioners of both states agreed; consequently they ran the line on an irregular course to accommodate influential inhabitants along the boundary who desired to remain in one state or the other. Some of the irregularities in the interstate boundary between Virginia on the one hand and North Carolina and eastern Tennessee on the other—of which the Kentucky-Tennessee boundary is really but a westward extension—are believed to be also due to the political influence of large landowners who desired to be residents of one state or the other.

What causes thunder?

Theories seeking to explain the cause of thunder have been revised many times since the days of the Greek philosophers who believed that thunder was caused by clouds bumping into one another. In more recent times it was almost universally believed by scientists that the noise of thunder is produced by the sudden inrush of air into the partial vacuum created by the expansion of the air when heated by lightning. This theory has been largely abandoned. The United States Weather Bureau is of the opinion that thunder results directly from the explosive-like expansion of the air along the lightning path, incident to the intense heating, ionization and probably the disintegration or rupture of at least part of the air particles or molecules. According to this theory, when a streak of lightning rushes through the atmosphere it decomposes particles of the gases. Each of the parts of the shattered particles takes up about as much space as the original particle did, and the result is a sudden and terrific expansion that produces an explosion similar to that caused by dynamite. The intensity of the sound produced by lightning depends chiefly on the magnitude of the flash and the proximity of the observer. The long duration of thunder is due largely to the fact that different parts of a streak of lightning are at different distances from the person who hears it. Sound travels at the rate of about a mile in five seconds and thunder may be heard at a distance of ten miles or even twenty or thirty miles under favorable conditions. The majestic roll that often makes thunder so impressive is caused by echoes that are reflected from the surfaces of clouds or back and forth between the clouds and the earth. Sometimes the roll may be due to the twisting of the sound waves as they pass through layers of atmosphere of different temperature. Lightning is an electrical phenomenon about which there is still much to be learned. For instance, occasionally lightning strikes from a clear sky without producing thunder, and "like lightning out of a clear sky" is a proverbial expression. There is a similarity in the cause of a peal of thunder and the report of a gun. When powder is ignited it turns into gas, which takes up more room than the powder did. Consequently the expansion of the gas drives the bullet out of the barrel of the gun. When the gas suddenly escapes it sets up a sound wave in the air and causes the report. It is not the rushing together of the air that causes the sound. The report of a gun is not so loud when the gun is discharged in dry air as it is when it is discharged in moisture-laden air.

Who said he would rather live in Hell than Texas?

"If I owned Texas and Hell I would rent out Texas and live in Hell," is attributed to General Philip H. Sheridan. One would naturally suppose the remark was made after Sheridan had become famous as a military commander. Such, apparently, was not the case. Soon after his graduation from West Point in 1853 Sheridan, then a second lieutenant, was sent to Fort Duncan, a frontier post on the Rio Grande near Eagle Pass. The weight of evidence indicates the statement in question was made in 1855 while Sheridan was either on a visit to or on duty at Fort Clark, in what is now Kinney County, Texas. Somebody at the officers' mess asked Sheridan how he liked Texas, and the now celebrated saying was the reply. In those days Texas, as well as the Southwest generally, was sparsely populated and was the butt of much crude humor. We have it on the authority of Judge Richard B. Levy, of Texarkana, that Albert Sidney Johnston told General Webster Flanagan that he heard about the incident in 1856 while in Texas as a colonel of infantry. Judge Levy himself was stationed at Fort Clark during the Spanish-American War and he says that he frequently heard that the famous remark was made by Sheridan while at that army post in 1855. The saying, of course, was not generally quoted until after the Civil War. There is an oft-repeated story that General Sheridan gave utterance to the remark while on an inspection tour when he was commander of the southwestern military department. But Texas had been associated with hell in southwestern humor long before Sheridan's time. After his defeat for Congress in 1834 David Crockett, of Tennessee, wrote in his autobiography: "I put the ingredients in the cup pretty strong, I tell you, and I concluded my speech by telling them that I had done with politics for the present, and that they might go to hell, and I would go to Texas." *Hell and Texas!* as a mild cuss term took its place in the western vocabulary in the 1830's.

How did the Andes Mountains receive their name?

The origin of *Andes* as applied to a system of mountains in South America has not been definitely ascertained. It is generally supposed, however, that the name is derived from a native Peruvian word meaning copper, or perhaps metal in general. The Incas seem to have used the word that is variously spelled *anta, antas, antis* and *antisuya* to designate districts in the mountains where metals were known to exist. The Spanish conquerors gradually dropped the *t* and replaced it with *d* when they referred to the mountains containing minerals. In succeeding years the entire mountain system between Panama and the Strait of Magellan— "the largest mountain chain in the globe," as Humboldt described it— became known as "the Andes." There is another theory that deserves mention; namely, that *Andes* is a corruption of *andenes*, plural of Spanish *anden*, meaning "shelf," and that the name originally alluded to the numerous shelf-like terraces built by the Incas for agricultural purposes on the western slopes of these mountains.

What is a mutual admiration society?

A mutual admiration society is a group of literary logrollers. One writer praises the work of another with the implied understanding that when he publishes something his work will be praised in turn. Like logrolling in general, it is based on the principle, "I'll scratch your back if you'll scratch mine." The phrase was popularized by Oliver Wendell Holmes in *The Autocrat of the Breakfast Table*, published in *The Atlantic Monthly* in 1856 and 1857. Holmes said he once belonged to a Society of Mutual Admiration. "It was," he wrote, "the first association to which I ever heard the term applied; a body of scientific young men in a great foreign city who admired their teacher, and to some extent each other." Under date of April 19, 1830, Thomas Babington Macaulay wrote to Macvey Napier: "We have had quite enough of puffing and

[399]

flattering each other in the *Review*. It is a vile taste for men united in one literary undertaking to exchange their favors." In Shakespeare's *Antony and Cleopatra* Enobarbus expresses the same idea when he says to Menas: "I will praise any man that will praise me."

Is it easier to swim in deep water?

There is no scientific foundation for the popular belief that the buoyancy of water increases with its depth and that consequently the deeper the water, the easier it is to swim in it. The buoyancy of water does not increase with its depth. It is just as easy to swim in water ten feet deep as in water one hundred feet deep. The false notion that deep water buoys a swimmer up more than shallow water does probably arose from the attitude of ordinary swimmers. A person swimming in shallow water realizes that he can stop swimming at any moment and stand on the bottom, while a person swimming in deep water realizes that he must keep on swimming. The same, of course, is true in the case of merely floating on deep or shallow water. There is also a common belief that a boat will float higher in deep water than in shallow water. The depth of water has nothing to do with how high an object will float in it. But an object floats higher in salt water than in fresh water because of the greater density of salt water. Regardless of the density or depth of water—provided it is deep enough to permit floating at all—the volume of water that a body displaces is equal to the weight of the body. The total force tending to keep the body up is equal to the weight of the body and therefore the buoyancy of deep and shallow water are the same. Since salt water is denser (heavier) than fresh water the body of a person swimming or floating in it displaces a greater weight of the salt water than it does of the fresh water. Accordingly salt water is more buoyant than fresh water but deep salt water is no more buoyant than shallow salt water.

Do porcupines shoot their quills?

It is a common but erroneous belief that porcupines "shoot" or throw their quills at an enemy when attacked. This belief is very old. About the year 1300 A.D. Marco Polo said: "Here [a region somewhere in the interior of Asia] are found porcupines, which roll themselves up when the hunters set their dogs at them, and with great fury shoot out the quills or spines with which their skins are furnished, wounding both men and dogs." The quills or spines, which assume an upright position when the animal is disturbed, just as the hair stands up on a cat's back, are loosely attached to the body and tail and come out upon the slightest

[400]

contact with other objects. When attacked the porcupine thrashes about actively with its tail and if the tail comes into contact with brush or other objects the tail quills are likely to be knocked out or detached. Frequently they are scattered around to a considerable extent. Under such circumstances the flying quills might readily give the impression that they are voluntarily thrown or "shot" at the enemy. They are not, however, actually thrown or shot out in the sense of being discharged by a propulsive effort of the animal other than the thrashing and flicking of its tail. Quills are frequently embedded in the flesh of animals that attack porcupines. Dogs that attack these animals usually get their noses full of quills for their pains. John Burroughs, the naturalist, wrote on this subject: "Touch his tail, and like a trap it springs up and strikes your hand full of quills. The tail is the active weapon of defense; with this the animal strikes. It is the outpost that delivers its fire before the citadel is reached. It is doubtless this fact that has given rise to the popular notion that the porcupine can shoot its quills, which, of course, it cannot do." When attacked the porcupine does not roll itself into a ball, as often stated. It charges backwards. Each quill is barbed and is so sharp that it seldom causes bleeding. The point often "works through" the part injured and causes great pain. Wolves, dogs, lynxes and other carnivorous animals that attack "quill pigs" sometimes get so many of these quills in their heads and mouths that they starve to death because of their inability to eat. A large porcupine may contain as many as 35,000 quills scattered among the hair. The animal's flesh is edible and was considered a delicacy by the Indians. There is also an equally unfounded notion that the little European animal known as the hedgehog can "shoot" its inch-long quills or spines.

What famous conqueror was born in Europe, died in Asia and was buried in Africa?

Alexander the Great was born in Macedonia in Europe; he died at Babylon in Asia, and he was buried at Alexandria in Africa. Ancient accounts of Alexander's burial are conflicting. Alexander was under thirty-three when he died in 323 B.C. It seems that his body was left in his tent at Babylon for six days after death, while his generals were quarreling over his successor. It was then embalmed and placed in a temporary coffin for conveyance to Macedonia. Philip Arridaeus, whom the Macedonian Army at Babylon chose to succeed Alexander conjointly with the latter's posthumous son, was entrusted with the funeral rites. The following year he left Babylon with the body, intending to convey it to Greece; but before the journey was completed Philip learned that during his life Alexander had expressed a desire to be interred in the temple of Jupiter Ammon on an oasis about four hundred miles west of the present Alexandria in Egypt. Philip therefore altered his course and turned his face southward. Just what happened after that is not a matter of authentic record. At any rate, Ptolemy, one of Alexander's favorite generals, who had become satrap of Egypt, succeeded in getting possession of the body and interred it in a gold coffin and elaborate sarcophagus at Memphis, near the present Cairo. Ptolemy II Philadelphus, son and successor to Ptolemy I Sotor, had the body removed and entombed with divine honors at Alexandria, a city that Alexander had founded in Africa in the winter of 332-331 B.C. At that time, or later, the gold coffin was replaced with a glass or alabaster one. Although Arab historians say the ancient tomb of Alexander is now under the mosque Nebi Daniel, traditionally supposed to be the burial place of the Hebrew prophet Daniel, the real location of the famous conqueror's grave cannot be identified. It is said that Alexander founded and named after himself sixteen different cities.

What famous Russian poet was partly of African blood?

Alexander Pushkin (1799-1837), perhaps the most famous of all Russian poets and sometimes called the "Shakespeare of Russia," was of one-eighth African blood. His maternal great-grandfather was an Ethiopian or Abyssinian named Hannibal who when a child was sent to Peter the Great as a present. The African boy became such a favorite with Peter the Great that he was knighted and finally became a general in the Russian service. Alexander Pushkin's African blood was evidenced by his slightly curly hair and his complexion, which was somewhat darker than that of the ordinary Russian. It should not be understood, however, that the poet was descended from a Negro in the generally accepted sense of that term. The ruling classes in Ethiopia belong to a mixed Arabic type similar to the Moors of northern Africa. Pushkin married Natalie Goncharov, whose sister married Baron George Heckeren D'Anthes, the adopted son of the Dutch Minister at the court of St. Petersburg. Baron D'Anthes was a vain and frivolous young man and Pushkin became jealous of him because he suspected the baron of paying improper attentions to Natalie. A challenge followed and the poet died two days after being mortally wounded in the duel. Baron D'Anthes was tried and expelled from Russia. Pushkin was only thirty-eight when he died. Although he wrote great prose, it was overshadowed by his greater poetry. Mikhail Lermontov (1814-1841), who is rated by many as second only to Pushkin among Russian poets, addressed to the

Czar a passionate poem in which he declared that if Russia did not take vengeance on the assassin of her national poet no second poet would be given to the nation. Oddly enough, four years later, Lermontov, then only twenty-seven, was also killed in a duel. The young poet deliberately chose for the duel a place on the edge of a cliff so that if either participant was wounded he would be killed.

Can sailing ships travel faster than the wind?

Ordinary sailing ships cannot sail faster than the wind driving them. There is too much friction for that to happen. In fact, no kind of sailing craft can sail faster than a wind blowing directly astern. It is, however, quite possible for light racing vessels and iceboats to sail much faster than a wind blowing more or less at right angles to their course. Yachting experts say that in actual practice light racing sailboats sometimes travel fifty per cent faster than the breeze. Iceboats have been known to sail twice as fast as the wind driving them. The ratio of the velocity of an iceboat to the velocity of the wind driving it depends on the windward angle of the direction of the boat. Ordinarily the sails of an iceboat are so trimmed that the direction of the boat and the direction of the wind do not coincide. The iceboat attains its greatest speed when the wind is blowing at an angle of 120 degrees. On this subject the United States Hydrographic Office says: "An ice boat can sail faster than the wind when it sails at some angle to it. The momentum is increased by every puff of wind striking the sails obliquely until it is finally equaled by the increase of friction engendered. Thus the continued bursts of wind against the sails cause a greater accumulation of speed in the iceboat than is possessed by the wind itself." The same explanation applies to light racing sailboats. The speed record for iceboats under ordinary conditions is about 75 miles an hour. But it is said that during 70-mile gales iceboats have been known to travel over the ice at a speed of 140 miles an hour.

What is sheet lightning?

Sheet or heat lightning is not different in kind from other lightning. These are merely popular names for the diffused reflection of lightning produced by a distant electrical storm. The so-called sheet or heat lightning generally follows a flash of lightning that is so far away that the actual flash cannot be seen and the sound cannot be heard. The flash may be hidden from view by clouds, mountains or the curvature of the earth. The storm is too far away for thunder to be heard, particularly if the wind is blowing from the direction of the observer. What the observer sees is distant light projected like a motion picture on strata of high clouds. Occasionally the thunder of a distant storm can be heard faintly even when the observer sees only the reflected light of the flash —sheet or heat lightning.

What are the Baumes laws?

The Baumes laws consist of a series of amendments to the code of criminal procedure and penal law of New York. These laws went into effect July 1, 1926. They were sponsored by the New York Crime Commission and were drafted by a joint legislative committee headed by State Senator Caleb H. Baumes (1863–1937), chairman of the Senate Committee on Codes. Their purpose was to check the crime wave by more prompt prosecution and stricter punishment of criminals. The original Baumes laws deal with trials, convictions, penalties, bail, appeals, paroles and pardons and were regarded by many at the time as marking an important epoch in the prosecution of criminal cases. Persons convicted of a felony for the fourth time, irrespective of the gravity of the offense, are automatically sentenced to life imprisonment and are not subject to pardon or executive clemency, the court having no discretion in the matter. This latter provision is particularly associated in the public mind with *Baumes law*. By extension the term is applied to any severe criminal law or code of laws. *Baumes* is often mispronounced. In a letter to the author Senator Baumes wrote: "I pronounce my name as if it were spelled *Baw- mess*, in two syllables with the accent on the first. The *au* in the first syllable is pronounced *aw* as in *law*. The *e* is short in the final syllable, which is pronounced the same as the final syllable in the word *hostess*."

What is Sing Sing?

Sing Sing is a famous New York State prison, located at Ossining, a town on the Hudson River about thirty miles north of New York City. A piece of low land close to the river was bought by the state in 1825 and the institution built there was known as Mount Pleasant prison, a name that was changed to Sing Sing prison about twenty-five years later. The present Sing Sing prison is on a hill above the old prison. The town itself was originally called Sing Sing, supposedly from the Sing Sing or Sintsink band of Indians who once lived in that vicinity. In 1901 the name of the town was officially changed to Ossining, the old name having become objectionable to the inhabitants because of its popular association with the penitentiary. *Ossining* is merely another form of *Sing Sing*, both words being corruptions of the Delaware Indian assinesink, literally meaning "at the small stone." Early writers spelled the name of this band of Indians variously—*Sintsink, Sinsincks, Sinsincqs, Sint-sings,* and *Sintsnicks.* There is nothing to support the popular story that Sing Sing was named after a friendly Indian whom the whites called John Sing Sing. In a footnote in *Wolfert's Roost,* first published in 1855, Washington Irving makes the following facetious comment on the origin of *Sing Sing:* "A corruption of the old Indian name, *O-sinsing.* Some have rendered it, *O-sin-song,* or *O-sing-song,* in token of its being a great market-town, where anything may be had for a mere song. Its present melodious alteration to *Sing-Sing* is said to have been made in compliment to a Yankee singing-master, who taught the inhabitants the art of singing through the nose." Artemus Ward observed dryly that Sing Sing was given an Indian name meaning "place of stones" because it was "the residence of gentlemen who spend their days poundin' stun."

How did "Labrador" originate?

According to Scandinavian sagas, Biorn and Eric the Red discovered Labrador about the year 1000 A.D. They called it *Helluland,* meaning land of slate or naked rocks. The region was rediscovered in 1498 by John Cabot, who supposed it to be the eastern extremity of Asia. There are three theories as to how the region received its present name, all of them resting upon little more than mere supposition. One holds that Labrador was named after a Basque whaler named *la Bradore* who settled on the bay of that name in 1520. Another derives the name of this British territory from Portuguese *llavrador,* "yeoman farmer." In 1498 after John Cabot had made his first voyage and was making plans for his second, he went to Lisbon in quest of sailors to form his crews. There he met and enlisted the services of a man named Joao Fernandes, nicknamed "Llavrador," who had made a voyage from Iceland to Greenland about 1492. When Cabot reached Greenland in June, 1498, he named the region "Labrador's Land," after Joao Fernandes, called Llavrador, because the latter had been the first person to tell him of that country. According to one tradition, Fernandes was a *llavrador,* "farmer," from the Azores. Greenland itself was known as Labrador's Land until the name was transferred to the peninsula on the mainland under the impression that Labrador was part of Greenland. Still another theory is that *Labrador* is derived directly from the Portuguese word meaning "laborer." In 1500 the Portuguese explorer Gaspar Corte Real took home a cargo of natives from the region now known as Labrador. Some authorities think these natives were Eskimos; it is more probable they were ordinary Indians. At any rate, King Emanuel of Portugal was pleased with them and thought he had come into possession of another slave coast whence natives might be exported to the other colonies as slaves. Hence the name Labrador, or "Laborer's Land." Labrador proper is not a part of Canada, as many people in the United States suppose, but is a dependency of Newfoundland, a separate unit in the British Empire.

Does moonlight ever produce rainbows?

Rainbows by moonlight, known as moonbows, are unusual but not rare phenomena. Aristotle referred to lunar bows about twenty-two hundred years ago, and they are well known to scientists, although they are not often observed, chiefly because of the faintness of the light at night. Only under exceptional conditions can the colors of a moonbow be seen. Lunar rainbows are most likely to occur after showers on nights when the moon is bright but not too high in the heavens. Similar lunar bows are periodically visible in the spray of certain waterfalls, such as the Cumberland Falls about eighteen miles southwest of Corbin, Kentucky.

Why is Rome called the Eternal City?

Rome was known as the Eternal City even among the ancient Romans themselves. It was so called because the Roman people thought that no matter what happened to the world, no matter how many other empires might rise and fall, Rome would go on forever. Tibullus (54–18 B.C.), Roman elegiac poet, and Ovid (43 B.C.–17 A.D.), one of the greatest of the Latin poets, as well as other Roman writers, refer to the city as eternal, and the thought is expressed in many official documents of the Empire in later days. In Vergil's Aeneid Jupiter tells Venus that he will give the Romans imperium sine fine, "an empire without end." The phrase was popularized by The Eternal City (1901), a novel by Hall Caine that deals with a utopian state in Rome. "Rome was not built in a day" in one form or other is a very old saying. It is found in Latin as early as the twelfth century, and Pier Angelo Manzolli, Latin poet, quoted it in Zodiacus vitae about 1543, while John Heywood included it in his collection of English proverbs in 1546. The saying, of course, refers to the fact that Rome was of slow but steady growth, that many centuries were required to make it the chief city of the world, and that great things are not achieved without much patience and effort. Rome was the accumulation of the products of knowledge, art and war for innumerable generations. Augustus Caesar is reputed to have said on his deathbed: "I found Rome brick and I leave it marble." Claudius Claudianus, one of the last great Latin poets, wrote about 400 A.D.: "What Roman power slowly built, an unarmed traitor instantly overthrew." In 1646 Sir Thomas Browne wrote as follows in his *Vulgar Errors*: "It crosseth the proverb, and Rome might well be built in a day, if that were true which is traditionally related by Strabo; that the great cities, Anchiale and Trasus, were built by Sardanapalus, both in one day, according to the inscription of his monument."

What famous Scottish king was a leper?

Robert the Bruce (1274–1329), liberator of Scotland and King of that country from 1315 until his death, was a victim of leprosy. The Scottish King had made a vow to go on a crusade to the Holy Land, but was prevented from doing so, first by wars at home and then by the disease that he knew would end his life. The royal leper, who spent the last two years of his life at Cardrose Castle on the northern shore of the Firth of Clyde, asked Sir James Douglas (the Good) who had fought under Bruce in the decisive Battle of Bannockburn, to take his heart to Jerusalem for burial. After Bruce died of leprosy his heart was removed and the body buried in the abbey church of Dunfermline, the "Westminster of Scotland." In 1390 Sir James set out for Palestine with the embalmed heart of Bruce in a silver casket, but while traveling through Spain he joined a band of Christians who were being beseiged by the Moors. According to tradition, just before Douglas was killed in the battle he threw Bruce's heart in the midst of the infidel host, crying, "Go thou before as thou wert wont to do, and Douglas will follow." One of his knights recovered the heart of Bruce and took it and the body of Douglas back to Scotland, where both were buried in Melrose Abbey. When Bruce's body was disinterred in 1819 the remains showed clearly that the heart had been removed. A royal leper is mentioned in the Bible. *II Kings* 15:5 says the Lord smote King Azariah (Uzziah) of Judah "so that he was a leper unto the day of his death, and dwelt in a several house." Baldwin IV, King of Jerusalem from 1174 to 1185, was a leper and died of the disease at the supposed age of twenty-four. He is the hero of Zofia Kossak's *The Leper King* (1945).

What famous French writer was part Negro?

Alexandre Dumas the elder (1802–1870), author of *The Count of Monte Cristo* and other romantic novels, was of part Negro blood. His father, General Alexandre Davy de la Pailleterie Dumas, was a mulatto, the son of a French nobleman named Alexandre Davy de la Pailleterie and a full-blooded Negro woman of Santo Domingo. General Dumas

[407]

took the name Dumas from his Negro mother. Alexandre Dumas père (so called to distinguish him from his son) was born in France, his mother being the daughter of a French innkeeper. He was, therefore, a quadroon—of one-fourth Negro blood. Crisp hair, dark complexion and thick lips were African characteristics that Alexandre Dumas père inherited from his maternal grandmother. M. Schele de Vere, in *Americanisms; the English of the New World* (1872), said the great French author unmistakably betrayed his African origin in his speech and writings. In J. C. Young's *A Memoir of Charles Mayne Young* (1871) it is related that when Alexandre Dumas père was asked who his father was, the author of *The Count of Monte Cristo* replied: "My father was a creole, his father a Negro, and his father a monkey; my family, it seems, begins where yours left off." This Dumas was one of the most prolific writers who ever lived. He wrote some twelve hundred volumes and earned about five million dollars as an author. His son, Alexandre Dumas the younger (1824–1895), who distinguished himself as a dramatist, was of one-eighth Negro blood. Samuel Coleridge-Taylor (1875–1912), English composer and author of the *Hiawatha trilogy*, was of half African blood. He was the son of a Negro physician of Sierre Leone and an Englishwoman.

Does snow enrich the soil?

That snow fertilizes the soil is an old belief that has some scientific foundation. Many farmers expect good crops after a winter of heavy snowfall. An old English rhyme runs:

> Year of snow
> Fruit will grow.

In 1729 William Byrd of Westover wrote as follows of southern Virginia: "The Soil wou'd also want the advantages of Frost, and Snow, which by their Nitrous Particles contribute not a little to its Fertility." Both snow and rain, according to the United States Department of Agriculture, bring down fertile elements from the air, especially nitrogen and sulphur, and this fact undoubtedly accounts for the general opinion among farmers that a winter of heavy snowfall is usually followed by a season of good crops. It is doubtful, however, whether snow brings down more fertilizer elements than a corresponding quantity of rain. But snow has several advantages over rain in this respect. If it falls on unfrozen ground and melts gradually it is more likely to be absorbed by the soil than rain is. Therefore a heavy fall of snow is likely to afford an ample and uniform supply of moisture without undue erosion of the soil and at the same time protects certain crops against frost. Some farmers say that a fall of snow plowed under has a particularly desirable effect upon the fertility of the soil. It is probable that snow sometimes carries soil from one locality and deposits it in another—a case of robbing Peter to pay Paul. A "brown snow" in parts of New England in 1936 deposited many tons of dust to the acre. Government weather experts gave it as their opinion that the dust came from Texas, Kansas and Oklahoma, some sixteen hundred miles away.

Does an electric fan lower the temperature of a room?

An electric fan running in a perfectly insulated and hermetically sealed room would not make the air in the room cooler, as commonly supposed. In fact, because of the friction developed in the fan, the temperature of a room is slightly increased instead of decreased by setting the air in rapid motion. The cooling effect of the fan results from the fact that the temperature of the air is lower than the temperature of a person's skin and each puff of air absorbs heat and moisture as it passes. Wind blowing on a thermometer does not affect the reading of the instrument unless the wind is warmer than the air surrounding the thermometer. If a person blows on a thermometer it will register greater heat because a person's breath is generally warmer than the surrounding air. But as a rule an electric fan running in front of a thermometer has little effect on the reading because the temperature of the moving air and the rest of the air are virtually the same.

What is a common-law marriage?

A common-law marriage is a marriage by mutual consent alone, without license or ceremony of any kind, either ecclesiastical or civil. Unions of this kind are said to be consensual, that is, existing merely by virtue of consent or acquiescence. Common-law marriages, without either license or ceremony, are validated by the courts in most jurisdictions if proper proof is submitted, or if children and property are involved. For instance, Chapter 199, Section 12, of the New Jersey act of 1912 concerning marriages provides: "Nothing in this act contained shall be deemed or taken to render any common-law or other marriage otherwise lawful, invalid by reason of the failure to take out a license as herein provided." It is erroneous to suppose that the law recognizes a common-law wife or husband as distinguished from a legal one. *Common-law* in this relation is employed merely to distinguish what is known as a "simple contract marriage" from a ceremonial marriage. In many states of the Union if a man and woman live together for one day or more under an agreement to be man and wife, they are legally married, although they may obtain no license and have no ceremony performed. On the other hand, if they live together for forty years without such an agreement, they are lover and mistress in the eyes of the law and as such are subject to the penalties provided. Whether a man and woman are to be regarded as common-law husband and wife depends on their ability to produce evidence that the necessary agreement existed. The evidence may consist of writings, declarations, or merely the conduct of the parties. In some states attempts have been made to outlaw all common-law marriages by statute. In England before the reign of George II (1727–1760) any marriage could be contracted merely by verbal consent without civil or religious license or ceremony.

Can stars be seen in the daytime from a well?

The popular belief that stars and planets can be seen in the daytime from the bottom of a well or shaft is true only to a very limited extent. A person observing the stars in daylight is assisted by a shaft or tube in two ways. The pupil of the eye is protected from stray light and lateral illumination. If transfused light can be cut off the acuteness of vision is considerably increased in the straight line of the tube. Thus it happens that occasionally an observer at the bottom of a well, mine shaft, silo or canyon is able to see planets or bright stars at midday. It is commonly said that there are about twenty stars of the first magnitude that are bright enough to be detected by the unaided eye looking from the bottom of a well or pit. The Yerkes Observatory, however, is of the opinion that in most cases where stars and planets have been seen in this manner they could have been seen without the assistance of a well or shaft, provided the eye had been protected from stray light. For several weeks every year the planet Venus can be seen at any hour of the day with the naked eye if the observer knows where to look. But it can be seen somewhat better if the observer stands in the shadow of a tree or a portico in order to reduce the diffuse light. The United States Naval Observatory is also of the opinion that there is little foundation for the popular notion that stars can be seen in the daytime from a deep shaft almost as well as they can be seen on a clear night.

What does "fort" in "fortnight" mean?

Fortnight is a contraction of *fourteen nights*. The latter phrase, in the sense of a period of two weeks, was used in England as early as 1000 A.D., when it was used in a translation of the laws of Ine, who was King of the West Saxons in the seventh century. *Fortnight* has been gradually falling into disuse, being supplanted by two weeks, particularly in the United States. Sennight, another similar old English word now almost out of use, is a contraction of seven nights. Both fortnight and sennight occur several times in Shakespeare. Under date of October 9, 1711, William Byrd of Westover noted in his secret diary: "I told him I would meet him at Colonel Harrison's this day sennight and so took my leave." These terms, fortnight and sennight, are probably survivals of an old Teutonic method of reckoning time by nights instead of by days. In 98 A.D. Tacitus wrote as follows of the ancient Germans: "Their account of time differs from that of the Romans: instead of days, they reckon the number of nights. Their public ordinances are so dated; and their proclamations run in the same style. The night, according to them, leads the day." In this connection it is interesting to recall that the American Indians reckoned time by moons, not by suns. Some Indians counted full days as so many nights or "sleeps."

What is the belief about the seventh son of a seventh son?

It was once widely believed that the seventh son of a seventh son (or child or either sex as some supposed) was endowed with notable talent and supernatural powers. According to a belief that persisted through the Middle Ages, the seventh son of a seventh son is endowed with the power not only of curing diseases and disorders of all kinds by the laying on of hands but also of practicing magic and foreseeing future events. Even as late as the nineteenth century many people still believed that the seventh son of a seventh son was a born physician and possessed intuitive knowledge of the healing art. The natural gifts of such a person were supposed by some to be more effective in medicine than the professional training of an ordinary doctor. Seven was regarded as a sacred and magical number among many ancient peoples, particularly the Hebrews, Assyrians and Arabians. In the Bible seven frequently occurs as a number with a special significance. The ancient belief about the seventh son of a seventh son may have a slight foundation in fact. Some students of eugenics are of the opinion that the younger children of an unusually intelligent man are likely to inherit more of their parent's mentality than his earlier children are. This is based on the theory that a man of unusual intelligence generally continues to develop mentally until late in life and his older children have a tendency to inherit only what mental qualities the parent possessed when they were conceived, while the children born later have a tendency to inherit their father's acquired mentality. Assuming this theory to be correct, in cases where a man marries young the difference in the mental qualities transmitted to the

[411]

first children and to those born eight or ten years later might be considerable. The lives of great men and women are cited to support the theory that younger children have "more brains" than their older brothers and sisters and that the older the father is when the child is born, the more intelligent it is likely to be. It is true that a remarkably high percentage of famous men and women were not the oldest children in the family. But it is doubtful whether the facts will bear out the theory of the inheritance of "acquired traits." Most authorities believe that the order of birth is not an important factor in heredity. In many of the cases cited to support the theory only the father is taken into consideration. The fact that more than one woman may have borne him children is ignored. Difference in environment and home life may account for the large percentage of successful younger sons and daughters compared with older ones. Later arrivals in a family often have the advantages of more experienced parents as well as of the help and training of older brothers and sisters. In his *Autobiography* Benjamin Franklin says he was the youngest son of the youngest son for five generations in the paternal line. He was the fifteenth child of his father's seventeen children by two marriages and the eighth child of his mother's ten children. His parents named him Benjamin, after the youngest of the twelve sons of Jacob in the Bible, because they expected him to be the last and youngest, but they missed the mark by two girls.

Did the United States pay France rent for trenches?

There is a persistent but unfounded popular belief in the United States that the American government paid the French government a rental for the use of battle trenches during the First World War. On this subject the United States War Department says: "The rumors in regard to this matter have probably originated from the fact that this Government rented ground for training purposes and paid a certain amount for damages to the property when training trenches were constructed." There appears to be no foundation whatever for the notion that the United States paid France rent for ground used by our troops for fighting purposes. Another persistent but unfounded popular belief in America is that the United States pays the British and French governments rent for the land on which soldiers killed in the First World War are buried. The United States War Department says that all land used for First World War cemeteries in Europe was purchased in perpetuity for burial rights. Some years ago Sir William Bull said in the House of Commons that during a political campaign he had been asked repeatedly by constituents whether the British government paid the

French government rent for the trenches used during the First World War. In reply the Chancellor of the Exchequer's office declared: "No payments were made to the French government or French citizens for rent of the trenches which we occupied, nor as compensation for damages done by gun fire in the battle zones during the war."

Why are policemen called cops?

Cop as applied to policemen is believed to be derived from the old English verb to cop, meaning to catch, to get hold of, to nab. This meaning of cop survives in the slang expression to cop off, which signifies to grab or to make away with something sought by others. In England a policeman is still often called a copper, that is, one who cops or catches offenders. According to the New English dictionary, cop was applied to policemen as early as 1859. The verb cop itself has been traced back in English dialect to the seventeenth century. The theory that cop was originally the abbreviation of constabulary of police is unsupported by evidence. There is, however, another theory that perhaps deserves mention. In 1829 Sir Robert Peel, who established the Irish and English constabularies of police, organized the first modern police in London. Members of Peel's police force were dressed in blue uniforms with large copper buttons. These conspicuous copper buttons, it is said, gave the police the name copper, which has been shortened into cop. London policemen are still called peelers and bobbies after Sir Robert Peel, who was affectionately known as "Bobby" Peel. Still another theory is that copper was first applied to policemen in 1858 in Chicago when the mayor of that city was John C. Haines, who was nicknamed "Copper-Stock" because of his spectacular plunges in the copper market. Under Mayor Haines the Chicago police were issued uniforms consisting of a short blue frock coat on which a plain brass star was substituted for the former leather medal. This uniform was jokingly called the "copper-stock coat" and the wearers coppers. But this is pure speculation and improbable.

What is ambergris?

Ambergris (pronounced am-ber-grees) is derived from French ambre gris and literally signifies "gray amber." Ambergris is a solid, fatty, wax-like substance produced in the intestines of whales. It occurs only in the sperm whale (cachalot) and is believed to be caused in some way by the beaks of cuttlefish that are often found in it. Cuttlefish and squids form the chief food of the sperm whale. One theory is that ambergris is never found in healthy whales and is a morbid secretion of the intestines or liver of sick whales. Although disagreeable to both sight and touch, ambergris even in the crude state exhales a pleasant, earthy fragrance faintly resembling that of sealing wax. In color it ranges from light to dark gray and is variegated like marble. Next to choice pearls, ambergris is the most valuable product by weight taken from the sea. At present green ambergris is worth from six to twelve dollars an ounce, depending on its quality and the amount of impurities. Dry ambergris has a wholesale value of twelve to thirty dollars an ounce. Formerly it was widely used as a medicine, but its efficacy was purely imaginary. It was also used in the Orient as an incense. Now the use of ambergris is limited almost entirely to the perfume industry, in which it is employed as a fixative to make odor essences retain their fragrance. No satisfactory substitute has been discovered for this purpose. Although it is a rare substance, occasionally large pieces weighing as much as a hundred pounds are found. There are authentic records of lumps that weighed as much as a hundred and fifty pounds. Sometimes it is taken from whales directly, but more frequently it is found floating on the waters in tropical seas, or cast upon beaches in lumps.

Can snakes poison themselves?

Naturalists are agreed that venomous snakes are immune to their own poison when it is swallowed. There is a difference of opinion, however, as to whether snakes are susceptible to their own poison when it is injected into their blood. The late Raymond L. Ditmars believed they were not. On the other hand, reputable authorities state that rattlesnakes are susceptible to their own poison and sometimes cause their own death by biting themselves. There is a possibility, however, that in such cases the fangs may puncture the spinal nerve or some vital organ and that death may not be due primarily to the venom. It is doubtful, most snake experts say, whether any snake ever commits intentional suicide. Snakes are not likely to bite themselves unless they are infuriated or severely injured and are unable to wreak vengeance on their tormentors. Some authorities suggest that venomous snakes may have a certain resistance to their own venom when injected into their blood but not to that of other snakes even of the same species.

What is a creole?

Creole is used in so many different senses that it is hard to define. In fact the term has been so distorted by usage that it is not safe to employ it except with extreme care. In the United States creole is generally applied to the white descendants of French and Spanish settlers of Louisiana and other Gulf states who retain their original languages and customs. In French and English the form of the word is creole, in Spanish criollo and in Portuguese crioulo. Some lexicographers derive creole from an African Negro word of unknown origin and meaning. Others derive it from the Spanish criado, ("servant"), which may signify a servant in the literal sense of a drudge or in the figurative sense of a servant to one's lady, to one's king, or to Christ. Still others, perhaps the majority, derive it directly from Spanish criar, ("to create," "to breed" or "to rear"). If this derivation is correct it may account for the fact that in many regions the term connotes a certain degree of excellence of origin and culture. Originally creole denoted a person of European descent born in the Spanish or French Indies. The term merely distinguished the colonial born from the European born. There was at first no connotation of color or race. Later any person born in the West Indian colonies was called a creole. There were French and Spanish creoles and Negro creoles. A Negro creole was one born in the colonies as distinguished from one born in Africa. Now the term is used in the West Indies to designate any descendant of a European race, including even English, Danes and Dutch. In Santo Domingo a dialect consisting of a mixture of French, Spanish and Negro was called creole. Creole has many local applications. Some suppose the term to have been coined as a euphemism for a person of mixed blood and accordingly apply it to persons of mixed white and Negro or aborgine blood who speak French or Spanish, especially a mulatto. Such persons, however, are more properly called "creole Negroes." Sometimes the term is applied to persons of Spanish or French descent born and reared in the tropics in general. In some parts of Latin America it means a person of pure Spanish descent, while in Brazil it means a Negro and in Peru a mestizo. The term used to be applied in Alaska to a person of mixed Russian and Indian blood. On the islands of Mauritius and Reunion it means the black population. From these statements it can readily be seen that creole has too many widely differing meanings to be of much value as a specific term.

What is the "codfish aristocracy"?

Codfish aristocracy is now often applied to persons who, lacking in real culture, make a vulgar display of recently acquired wealth. Sometimes the term is also applied to families who were once rich and who still "put on considerable dog," but who actually are so poor that they must live economically to support their pretensions. Originally codfish aristocracy was applied particularly to families who were supposed to have become rich from the fisheries of Massachusetts, a state noted for its codfish. On March 17, 1784, John Rowe, a Boston merchant, made a motion in the legislature that "leave be given to hang up the representation of a Codfish in the room where the House sits, as a memorial of the importance of the Cod-Fishery to the welfare of the Commonwealth." The motion carried and the effigy of a codfish, made of pine, was hung up opposite the speaker's chair in the chamber of the House of Representatives in the Massachusetts statehouse in Boston, where it hangs to this day. In the fall of that same year Francisco de Miranda, the South American soldier and revolutionist, visited Boston and wrote that in the old statehouse he found the "figure of a cod-fish of natural size made of wood and in bad taste." Many years later an aluminum codfish, emblem of the state's fishing industry, was placed in the senate chamber.

Are any Americans buried in Westminster Abbey?

No persons of American birth are interred in Westminster Abbey. The deans of the Abbey, however, have thus far consented to the specific recognition of three Americans of distinction. James Russell Lowell (1819–1891), poet and essayist, is commemorated by a stained-glass window in the vestibule of the Chapter House, which is known as "the cradle of parliaments" because the first House of Commons met there in 1282. In the Poet's Corner is a bust of Henry Wadsworth Longfellow (1807–1882), placed there by English admirers of the American poet five years before his death. A marble tablet was unveiled in the Abbey in 1923 in honor of Walter Hines Page (1855–1918), journalist and diplomat, who was American Ambassador to the Court of St. James's during the First World War.

What is the surname of David Lloyd George?

Lloyd George, not simply George, is the surname of the British statesman who was Prime Minister during the First World War. David Lloyd George was born in Manchester in 1853 of Welsh parents. His mother was a daughter of David Lloyd, and his father was William George, who died when his son David was a baby. After the death of William George, his widow and their two sons were supported largely by David Lloyd, a brother of Mrs. George and young David's uncle, who was a shoemaker and preacher at Llanystumdwy. From his uncle David George not only learned his first lessons in practical politics but also obtained the means of starting his career as a solicitor at the age of fourteen. As a tribute to David Lloyd the boy adopted Lloyd as a part of his surname (not as a middle name), which accounts for the fact that it is composed of two different family names. The name is sometimes written Lloyd-George, but the proper form is Lloyd George, without the hyphen. Lloyd George was a member of the House of Commons from 1890 to 1945—a period of fifty-four years of continuous service. Owing to confusion David Lloyd George was often erroneously referred to as "Lord George" from the time he became Prime Minister in 1916, but he was not named an earl by the King until January 1, 1945, when he was nearly eighty-two years old and when he had announced his intention of retiring from Parliament. He then became "Earl Lloyd George of Dwyfor" or "Lord Lloyd George," but not "Lord George." By accepting an earldom the "Welsh Wizard," who through seniority had become the "Father of the Commons," was automatically transferred from the House of Commons to the House of Lords. He died a few months later.

Are elephants afraid of mice?

That elephants are particularly afraid of mice is a widespread belief. In *The Lamentable Tragedy of Locrine*, a play written about 1595 and formerly often ascribed to Shakespeare, we find:

> Have you not seen a mighty elephant
> Slain by the biting of a silly mouse?

But the notion that elephants are afraid of mice does not seem to be borne out by observation and experiment. The director of the National Zoological Park advises the author that elephants in the Washington zoo pay no attention whatever to the numerous mice running about the barns. The late Raymond L. Ditmars, curator of mammals at the New York Zoological Park for many years, gave similar testimony. "I am inclined to think that elephants, generally, are not afraid of mice," he wrote to the author in 1928. "I have often noted both rats and mice in the hay in circuses and animal shows, and the elephants apparently pay no attention whatever to them." When mice were tossed to an elephant in the zoo at Columbus, Ohio, in 1942, the great animal merely sniffed at them and resumed his interest in peanuts. Nor is there any evidence that elephants in the wild state exhibit any particular fear of mice. Of course, it is quite possible that individual elephants may have such a fear. A writer who had had many years of experience with wild elephants in India states that their two greatest fears are dogs and human beings. Still the belief that elephants have an especial fear of mice is very persistent, and many attempts are made by popular writers to explain what seems to be an imaginary phenomenon. For instance, it is often

[417]

said that the elephant has poor eyesight and is unable to protect every part of its large body with its trunk. Accordingly, elephants become nervous when they see mice because they fear the mice will gnaw their feet or get into their trunks or ears. A decade or two ago a popular writer asserted that elephants are afraid of mice because small mouselike animals found in their wild haunts sometimes crawl up the trunks of the huge beasts when they are feeding and dig their claws into the flesh. The elephant becomes frantic and blows violently but is unable to dislodge the tiny creature, which, it is said, not only produces great pain but in some cases actually causes the death of the victim. This story is probably pure fiction. Carl E. Akeley, the noted American naturalist, animal sculptor and author, once said that if a mouse ever ran up the trunk of an elephant it would be promptly "blown into the next county."

Can snakes bite through leather shoes?

Such snakes as the bushmaster, rattlesnake and Gaboon viper have long, powerful fangs and are able, under favorable circumstances, to bite through soft leather and rubber of the thickness generally used in making shoes, boots and leggings. No species of snake, however, is able to bite through the hard, thick leather used in heavy boots, leggings and puttees, and ordinary boots and leggings are a great protection against most snakes. Any leather ceases to be an absolute protection against venomous snakes after it becomes thin and soft from repeated wear. Hunters in the southern states, says the United States Fish and Wildlife Service, find that leather leggings afford sufficient protection against the poisonous snakes in that region, and a specially constructed rubber boot, with a shank including several layers of canvas, widely used by quail hunters in Florida, is a perfect protection for the parts it covers. The late Raymond L. Ditmars, said he would feel perfectly safe from snake bites if he were provided with very stiff canvas leggings. Rattlesnakes seldom strike a person above the knee. A favorite story in the West is about a man who was bitten in the calf of the leg by a rattlesnake. He died from the venom, and so did three other men who wore the same boots in turn. It was finally discovered that one of the rattler's fangs was imbedded in one of the boots!

Which is correct, "spic and span" or "spick and span"?

Spick and span is the correct spelling of this common phrase. It is often but erroneously written spic and span, owing apparently to a mistaken notion of its derivation. The original phrase was span-new, which, although little used now, means quite or perfectly new, and which is derived from Old Norse *spann* ("chip"), and *nyr* ("new"). *Spannyr* still occurs in Icelandic. Originally *span-new* signified as bright and new as a freshly cut chip or a splinter of wood just from the hands of the carpenter. "Spick and span new" was merely an emphatic extension of the earlier phrase, *spick* being an old provincial or colloquial form of *spike*, a large nail. Thomas Middleton, a contemporary of Shakespeare, used "spick and span new" in *The Family of Love* (1608), and it occurs in John Ford's *The Lover's Melancholy* (1629). In *Hudibras* (1663) Samuel Butler wrote:

> Now, while the honour thou has got
> Is spick and span new.

When a thing was particularly fresh in appearance it was said to be spick and span new; that is, bright and new as a new spike and a freshly cut splinter. Some authorities suppose the phrase was originally applied to newly built wooden boats. Those who write the phrase "spic and span" do so on the assumption that the obsolete word for *spike* was spelled *spic*. There is no evidence that such was the case, and the examples in the Oxford dictionary indicate that it was always spelled *spick*. There was, however, an old word *spic*, meaning "bacon" or "fat meat."

Why is the shamrock Ireland's national emblem?

The shamrock is believed to have become the national emblem of Ireland as the result of a traditional incident in the life of St. Patrick. The patron saint of Ireland, it is said, appeared in 433 A.D. before a large group of Irish pagan chieftains and druids assembled on Slane Hill near Tarn. During one of the meetings St. Patrick found himself unable to explain to his pagan hearers the mystery of the Trinity. Therefore he resorted to a visible image by plucking a shamrock from the sward and using its single stem and triple leaf to explain the doctrine of the Trinity to the assembled chieftains. A beautiful Gaelic mystic prayer in verse is reputed to have been composed by St. Patrick in preparation for his appearance before the assembled chieftains on Easter Sunday, when the final blow was given to druidism and the triumph of Christianity in Ireland was completed. There is evidence, however, that trefoil plants have been regarded as sacred in different parts of the world since remote antiquity. According to Greek mythology, a golden, three-leaved, immortal plant afforded riches and protection, and such plants were fed the horses of Zeus. Triple-leaved plants, resembling the shamrock, as well as triple branches, triple fruit and triple figures have been found on Roman coins, Assyrian tablets and Egyptian temples and pyramids.

There has been much speculation as to what the original Irish shamrock may have been. There is no plant specifically called the shamrock. It is variously supposed to have been the lesser hop clover, the common white clover, the wood sorrel and the black medic. The leaves of all these plants are used to some extent as the emblem of Ireland. *Shamrock* is derived from Gaelic *seamrog*, diminutive of *seamar*, meaning "trefoil" or "three-leaf." There used to be a belief that the "true shamrock" will not grow in England.

Is quicksilver mined?

Quicksilver is the popular name of mercury, a heavy silver-white element. It is unique among the metallic elements in that it remains liquid at ordinary temperatures. Mercury occurs in nature in a free state, both in lodes and placer deposits, but only in small quantities. Commercial mercury is obtained chiefly from cinnabar ore, the sulphide of quicksilver, which occurs naturally as brilliant red crystals or red and brownish masses. The pure mercury is extracted by subjecting the ore to high temperatures and then condensing the vapor. Hence quicksilver is "mined." The largest and richest concentrated deposit of mercury ore is at Almaden in central Spain. It has been worked since the days of the ancient Romans. A Greek writer who lived about 300 B.C. said "liquid silver" was obtained in his day "by rubbing cinnabar ore with vinegar in a copper vessel." Until the outbreak of the Second World War, when mercury production in North America was greatly increased, Spain and Italy had a virtual monopoly on quicksilver. Deposits of mercury ore exist in California, Oregon, Texas and other states. Mercury is used in thermometers, antifouling paint to protect ships from barnacles, electrical contacts, a process of mining gold by amalgamation, and in various medical and pharmaceutical compounds, while fulminate of mercury, a highly explosive compound, is used in an igniter or detonater for ammunition. The element is handled, stored, shipped and sold in iron containers called *flasks*, which supplanted the sheepskin bags formerly used for that purpose. A standard flask of mercury contains seventy-six pounds of the liquid element. A man can carry a full flask of mercury on his shoulder, but the surge of the heavy liquid in a partly filled flask is so sudden and strong it will throw him down. There is an old belief that quicksilver placed in a pool or pond of water will cause it to disappear or *sink* it. The weight of the liquid metal, according to the notion, will cause it to find a passage through the bottom to subterranean cavities and carry the water away in its wake. Such a thing, of course, would be possible only under very exceptional conditions. Another odd belief is that a loaf of bread containing quicksilver will gravitate toward and locate the body of a drowned person in water. Although this method of locating drowned persons is occasionally reported as successful, it is probably only a myth.

Why are the people of Georgia called crackers?

Cracker is applied in the South, especially in Georgia and Florida, to poor whites and hill dwellers. The term in this sense dates back at least to the time of the Revolution. Although early uses leave the origin of the term in doubt, most authorities regard it as a shortened form of *corncracker*, which refers to the fact that cracked corn was long the chief article of food among this class of people. This theory receives some confirmation in the fact that in Kentucky the same class of people are popularly called "corncrackers," a name applied in several other states to the Kentuckians themselves. In *Americanisms; the English of the New World*, published in 1872, M. Schele de Vere wrote: "A *corncracker* is looked upon as so low a person that he is simply called a *cracker*; he inhabits the low, unproductive regions near the sea-shore, and besides his generic name derived from the chief article of his diet, he appears as *Conch* or *Low Downer* in North Carolina, and as *Sandhiller* or *Poor White Trash* in South Carolina and Georgia. Even in Florida he is found occasionally, leading a wretched life in the woods, and resembling in his habits the worst of the old Indians. The *Crackers* of North Carolina are, perhaps, the poorest of them all." Some authorities hold that *cracker* was originally applied contemptuously by those living in cities to the country people because the latter were fond of cracking large buckskin whips. In *King John* Shakespeare employed *cracker* in the sense of a boaster, braggart or liar. At any rate, the term is now widely applied as a popular nickname to Georgians, and Georgia is known as the "Cracker State."

How did a spider save Scotland?

In 1306 Robert Bruce, or Robert the Bruce, was crowned King of Scotland. Soon afterward his forces were routed by the English and he fled from the country, taking refuge on Rathlin Island off Antrim in Ireland. He was concealed for a long time in what is now known as Bruce's Castle on this island between Ireland and Scotland. One day, as the discouraged Scottish King lay on his pallet, he observed a spider persistently trying to fix its web to a beam on the ceiling. The spider failed six times in succession. "Now shall this spider," said Bruce, "teach me what I am to do, for I also have failed six times." In the seventh attempt the spider succeeded in fixing its web to the beam, whereupon Bruce emerged from his hiding place, gathered a handful of followers, returned to Scotland and after a series of successful campaigns won the Battle of Bannockburn in 1314, after which England acknowledged the complete independence of Scotland. Because of this story, which many Scottish historians treat as fact rather than legend, in Scotland it is regarded almost as a crime for a person named Bruce to kill a spider.

Do hogs cut their throats in swimming?

It is commonly believed that hogs will cut their throats by striking them with the sharp points of their cloven front feet if they swim any considerable distance. The forelegs of hogs are set closely under the body and for that reason they are not generally good swimmers; but hogs that are not too fat can swim long distances without injuring themselves. In fact some hogs are very good swimmers and take readily to the water. If hogs are extremely fat, however, they are likely to scratch their throats while swimming and cause themselves to bleed to death. In the days of old-fashioned sailing vessels, it is said, hogs used to be carried on shipboard to serve as compasses in emergencies. If a vessel was lost or in danger out of the sight of land a hog was thrown into the sea. Instinctively it would swim toward the nearest land and thus point the way of safety to the mariners. Many sea stories allude to the belief that the hog had to be picked up before it swam more than half a mile or so to prevent its cutting its throat with the sharp points of its cloven forefeet.

Which is correct, "roach" or "cockroach"?

The original name for this insect pest is cockroach. Roach is merely a curtailed form of cockroach. This word is not a compound of cock and roach, as many erroneously suppose. If it were, it would be correct to speak of "henroaches" as well as cockroaches. But the word is a corrupted form of Spanish cucaracha. A modern popular Mexican song relating to this familiar bug is entitled "La Cucaracha." In 1624 Captain John Smith, writing about Virginia, said: "A certaine India Bug, called by the Spaniards a Cacarootch, the which creeping into chests they eat and defile with their ill-sented dung." When Smith wrote cacarootch he was making an effort to write the Spanish cucaracha. From about 1650 to 1800 these insects were called cockroches in England. Finally cockroach became the accepted form of the word. The longer form cockroach is now more common in British usage, while the shortened roach seems to be more prevalent in the United States. This insect, of which there are some twelve hundred known species, is supposed to have come originally from India, although that is not an established fact. The story that cockroaches eat metal originated with a Danish official in the Virgin Islands. He reported to the home government that several missing brass cannon had been devoured by cockroaches. When he was asked to send some specimens of this remarkable metal-eating insect to Denmark, he replied he would not think of assuming the risk of sending across the seas in a wooden ship cockroaches that included brass cannon in their diet. Cockroaches are not altogether noisome insects. It is believed that they are natural enemies of bedbugs.

How do worms get into chestnuts?

The so-called worms often found in chestnuts are the larvae of the chestnut weevil, a yellowish beetle with a long beak or snout. During the blooming season, usually in June or July, the female beetle bores through the burr of the chestnut and deposits her small white eggs in the immature nut. When hatched the larvae feed on the tissue of the growing kernels. After the nuts have natured the grublike worms gnaw through the shell and burrow into the ground where they remain for eight or ten months. They finally emerge from the ground as mature beetles and the life cycle starts over again. Several eggs may be laid in the same nut, which accounts for the fact that frequently a worm is found in a nut having a hole in it.

How are death masks made?

A death mask is made by applying some kind of plaster, such as plaster of Paris, to the face after the skin has been treated with oil to prevent the plaster from adhering too closely. After the plaster has hardened it is removed, and into the mold thus formed fresh plaster or some other material is poured. The resulting cast is the death mask. Such masks have considerable historical value because they bear a detailed resemblance to the faces from which they are taken. The ancient Greeks and Romans made death masks of gold and silver to preserve the features of distinguished persons. Similar masks are also made from living subjects. Processes used in making both death and life masks have been greatly improved in recent years and no doubt will continue to improve with the further development of new plastic materials and methods.

What is a cow tree?

Cow tree or milk tree is the popular name given to several species of evergreen trees native to the mountains of South and Central America. They get their name from the fact that when the trunks or branches are cut a large quantity of white, milklike juice exudes. The "milk" of one species, *Brosimum galactodendron*, is sweet, palatable and nourishing, and for centuries the natives of northern South America have used it for food. Baron Alexander Humboldt (1769–1859), German naturalist, explorer and writer, seems to have been the first European to call the attention of the scientific world to this interesting tree. The Spanish name—*palo de vaca*—also signifies "cow tree." This name is sometimes applied to other species of trees whose juice is similar but inedible. A rare species of cow tree—*Couma guatamalensis*—found in Guatemala produces "milk" that bears a remarkable resemblance to cow's milk both in taste and appearance. Some of the natives use this "tree milk" in their coffee and as a substitute for real milk in sweet desserts. Cow tree milk, like cow's milk, sours quickly. In New Zealand cow tree is applied to the tree known to the Maoris as *karaka*. This tree does not "give milk," but its seeds and the pulp of its orange-colored fruit are eaten by the natives. When steamed and dried the seeds are edible and wholesome, but very poisonous when raw.

How did "fan" originate?

Fan, in the sense of an enthusiast over baseball, football, radio or any other sport, amusement, entertainment or avocation, is modern and is believed to be a contraction of *fanatic*. The theory, often advanced by popular writers, that *fan* in this sense is derived from the verb *to fan*, signifying to blow upon, to stimulate to action or to excite to activity, is not generally accepted by philologists. This word apparently came into general use sometime between 1880 and 1900. It is supposed, with some reason, that it originated as follows: Chris Van der Ahe, owner of the St. Louis Browns, during the latter part of the eighties stated that Charles Haas was the greatest baseball fanatic he had ever seen. Newspapers and sports writers took up the word and began to call baseball enthusiasts *fanatics*, which was later shortened to *fan* by the headline writers. At first the term was sometimes spelled *fann*. It is an interesting fact that centuries ago *fan* was frequently used as a contraction of *fanatic* in the literal sense of that word. There is probably no relation between *fan* as applied to enthusiasts over the game and the verb *fan* as applied to striking out while batting. There is one other theory that deserves mention. The following entry occurs in *Francis Grose's Dictionary of the Vulgar Tongue as Revised and Corrected by Pierce Egan* (1823): "The Fancy: one of the fancy is a sporting character that is either attached to pigeons, dog-fighting, boxing, etc." Since *the fancy* was long a name in both Britain and America for followers of prize fighting, some suppose that the term was borrowed by baseball and shortened first to *the fance*, then to *fans*, and finally to *fan*. But no known etymological evidence supports this theory.

What is a "shivaree"?

Charivari, in the sense of a mock serenade of a newly married couple, is popularly spelled and pronounced *shivaree* in the United States. It is a French term and is correctly spelled *charivari* and pronounced *sha-ree-va-ree* in English. Some authorities suppose the word was of anomatopoeic or imitative origin and was suggested by the sound of a charivari. The original charivari was a sort of "hazing" and consisted of a noisy and tumultuous gathering organized to express dislike and derision for some person. During the Middle Ages such demonstrations were frequent in western Europe against persons who had become socially or politically unpopular. In France it became customary to raise a charivari against persons just married the second time, especially widows who remarried too hastily. Neighbors would gather around the home of the couple at night and make discordant noises, consisting of shouting, whistling, hissing, groaning, ringing cowbells, blowing tin horns, beating pans and kettles and similar hideous sounds. The crowd, generally in masks and outlandish costumes, would not stop the noisy and sometimes licentious demonstration until the newly married couple purchased their peace with a ransom, usually food and drink or money to buy such. The French inhabitants of Louisiana and Canada are believed to have introduced the charivari to America. At any rate, the shivaree in the rural districts of the United States is probably a survival of this ancient French custom. The American shivaree is similar to the original, except that it is raised against any newly married couple and is regarded as little more than a rough joke. Even as a crude jest it is rapidly disappearing. A boisterous parade, accompanied with a babel of discordant noises, or a burlesque serenade, is sometimes known as a *callithump*, equivalent to "rough music" in England. In German the charivari is called *Katzenmusik* ("cat's concert"). *Katzenjammer*, familiar to us in an old comic strip entitled *Katzenjammer Kids*, means literally "cat's wailing" and figuratively "hangover."

How did "booze" originate?

Booze is not a word of recent coinage, as commonly supposed. It is an example of a good word that degenerated into slang. In varying forms the term has been part of the English language at least since the fourteenth century. It occurs variously as *booze*, *bouze*, *bouse* and bowse. Apparently it was derived from Middle Dutch *buyzen* or *busen*, meaning "to guzzle liquor" or "to drink heavily," and is related to German *bausen*. The English form was in common use in the time of Edmund Spenser. In the *Faerie Queene*, written in 1590, the poet refers to Gluttony's imbibing too freely from a *bouzing can*, and *boozy* in the sense of being under the influence of liquor is recorded as early as 1529. A similar form of the word occurs frequently in the Scotch of Robert Burns. The late Dr. Frank Vizetelly supposed that *booze* was the modification of a Turkish word for a kind of liquor and was introduced into western Europe and England by the gypsies. In Turkish *boza*·is applied to several different kinds of drinks. *Booze* may have been introduced into the United States twice, once by the early English and again by the Dutch. It is not probable, as often stated, that the slang term is derived from the surname of a Philadelphia distiller named E. C. Booz, who during the second quarter of the nineteenth century sold whisky in bottles stamped E. C. Booz's Log Cabin Whiskey. Such liquor was first produced during the Log Cabin and Hard Cider presidential campaign of 1840. The bottles, bearing the imprint of E. C. Booz, were blown in the shape of log cabins at the Whitney Glass Works in Philadelphia. But four years before that famous campaign Washington Irving had written in *Astoria* (1836) that a Mr. Hunt "spent forty-five days at New Archangel, boosing and bargaining with its roystering commander. . . ." This proves that the verb, if not the noun, was in common American use at that time.

What country coined platinum money?

In 1828 the Russian government began the coinage of platinum money. Platinum was produced in considerable quantities in the Ural Mountains in Russia and its general scarcity and great value were not at first appreciated. For many years the Russians considered the metal of such small value that peasants used pots and pans made of platinum to cook their meals. Swindlers, it is said, used to cover platinum bricks with gold plate to sell them as gold. Between 1828 and 1845, when the Russian government abandoned such coinage, platinum coins worth more than $1,300,000 were struck off in denominations of one, three, six and twelve rubles. These coins contained about two per cent of the rare, metallic element known as iridium, which resembles platinum but is harder and brittle. Platinum, then worth about a third as much as gold, proved unsatisfactory for monetary purposes for several reasons. The metal resembles several metals of slight value and is easily counterfeited. Its high melting point made it expensive to mint. Besides platinum is subject to sudden fluctuation in value. Soviet Russia tried platinum coins in 1930 but soon abandoned them for similar reasons. The French government at one time used platinum as an alloy to harden gold and silver coins. During a period of about thirty years the price of platinum jumped from $16 to $105 an ounce and the French government replaced the platinum coins to recover the valuable metal. Platinum is extremely malleable and ductile; a troy ounce of the metal can be stretched into a wire more than ten thousand miles long.

What was the Spanish Main?

Spanish Main was originally applied to the Spanish mainland colonies on the northeast coast of South America between the mouth of the Orinoco River and the Isthmus of Panama. At first the Spanish Main was merely this strip of mainland stretching some 1,250 miles from Panama to the Gulf of Paria opposite Trinidad. The term was used by foreigners to distinguish these Spanish colonies on the mainland from the island possessions in Central America and the West Indies. Later *Spanish Main* was extended to the Caribbean Sea and other adjacent Spanish-controlled lands and waters, including the route taken by Spanish vessels between Spain and the New World. This application of *main* was natural, because during the sixteenth century it was applied not only to a main land but also to a main sea or ocean. In *Richard III* Shakespeare speaks of the "tumbling billows of the main." The Spanish Main became especially notorious as the haunt of the buccaneers of the seventeenth and eighteenth centuries.

How did "cutting a dido" originate?

This phrase means to play the mischief, to cut up, to cut capers. In some sections of the United States *dance a dido* is used instead of *cut a dido*. *Dido* as applied to a caper, trick, antic or extravagant action is an Americanism of unknown origin, having thus far baffled all etymological research. Efforts have been made to establish some relationship between it and the cunning trick used by Queen Dido of Carthage to get a handsome "hide" of land. According to the legend, Queen Dido and her followers, upon arriving on the coast of Africa, asked of the natives only so much land as they could enclose with a bull's hide. When this was freely granted, Dido caused the hide to be cut into strips and with these strips she enclosed a spot on which she built a citadel around which the city of Carthage grew up. But there is little reason to suppose that the colloquial American phrase has any connection with this mythological story. The earliest use of the phrase quoted by R. H. Thornton in his *American Glossary* is from D. P. Thompson's *Adventures of Timothy Peacock*, published in 1835: "Most all the world know all the didos we cut up?" The term is probably of American Negro origin, although some authorities suppose it began as seaman's slang.

What is the philosopher's stone?

A person looking for a short-cut to riches is said to be searching for the philosopher's stone. In *Poor Richard's Almanac* Benjamin Franklin said: "If you know how to spend less than you get, you have the philosopher's stone." The ancient alchemists believed that somewhere in nature there existed a substance that would transmute all ordinary metals into gold. This imaginary substance was called the philosopher's stone because it was supposed to have a *philosophic* basis and was linked with the theories of matter advanced by the philosophers. The idea of transmuting base metals into noble ones seems to have originated among the Greeks of Alexandria in the early centuries of the Christian Era. In medieval times the philosopher's stone was reputed not only to have the property of transmuting the baser metals into gold but also the power of prolonging life indefinitely and curing most of the ills that the body is heir to. Accordingly it became synonymous with *elixir vitae* ("the elixir of life"). *Elixir* is believed to be derived either from an Arabic root signifying "powder" or a Greek root signifying "dry." The elixir of life was conceived as some substance, such as a drug, essence or tincture, that was supposed to be capable of transmuting base metals into gold and prolonging life indefinitely. In Shakespeare's *Antony and Cleopatra* the Egyptian queen says to Alexas:

> How much unlike art thou Mark Antony!
> Yet, coming from him, that great medicine hath
> With his *tinct gilded* thee.

Hence the term became synonymous with *philosopher's stone* and was applied to any alleged panacea or "cure-all." Some of the medieval alchemists supposed the philosopher's stone to be "a perfect ruby." The dual function of the magic substance is referred to in Shakespeare's *II King Henry IV*, where Sir John Falstaff, who has monetary designs on Master Shallow, says: "I will make him a philosopher's two stones to me." The Fool, in *Timon of Athens*, says: " 'Tis a spirit: sometime 't appears . . . like a philosopher, with two stones moe than's artificial one." According to one version of the legend, the philosopher's stone was buried at the foot of the rainbow. Another version had it that if one were to dig at the spot where the rainbow touches the ground he would

[428]

find a pot of gold. Visionaries and dreamers who try to achieve the impossible are sometimes called "rainbow chasers," because they are said to be seeking the philosopher's stone or the pot of gold at the foot of the rainbow.

What is meant by Robin Hood's barn?

Robin Hood's barn is the great out-of-doors and alludes to the fact that Robin Hood, the legendary English outlaw and ballad hero, stabled his horses under the canopy of the blue sky. *To go around Robin Hood's barn* is an old phrase meaning to attain one's end or the desired result by a round about way. When a person arrives at the right conclusion by indirect reason he is said to wander all about Robin Hood's barn. *Robin Hood in Barnsdale stood* is the only line extant of an old popular song and it is often repeated in reference to a person who is speaking irrelevantly. Judges in the British law courts used to tell lawyers who spoke beside the point or quoted irrelevant cases that they might as well say that *Robin Hood in Barnsdale stood*. A small cave near Ravenshead Oak at Newstead Abbey, birthplace of Lord Byron, is known as "Robin Hood's stable" from a legend that the outlaw used to stall his horses there.

Who were the Blue Devils?

The French soldiers belonging to the Chasseurs Alpins were called Blue Devils by the Germans during the First World War because of their dark blue uniforms and their dashing attacks in the fighting in the Vosges. *Chasseur* is derived from French *chasser* ("to hunt"). The Chasseurs in the French military service may consist of eight light infantry or light cavalry units. The Chasseurs Alpins during the First World War comprised twelve battalions of light infantry specially trained and equipped for mountain fighting. A corps of Chasseurs Alpins fought as a sort of unofficial or guerrilla unit in the French Revolution. They became an official unit of the French Army in 1885. *Blue Devils* is an old term in the sense of low spirits or a fit of the blues.

How did "bylaw" originate?

By in *bylaw* is believed to be derived from the Old Danish word *by* or *bye*, meaning "town" or "dwelling place," which still survives in numerous English place names, such as Whitby, Grimsby, Derby, Rugby, Appleby and Netherby, all of which were named by the Danes. In Lincolnshire, one of the chief seats of the Danish settlements in England, the names of about a hundred towns and villages end in *by*, and the coast in that region is studded with these relics of the Danish occupation. The original "by-laws" were the laws of the town or *by*, that is, the local ordinances as distinguished from the general laws of the county or realm. Gradually *bylaw* came to mean any minor or subordinate law or regulation. This transition was undoubtedly hastened by the analogy between the term and *by* in such words as *bypath* and *byway*. Later the real origin of *bylaw* was lost sight of and it was mistakenly supposed that *by* in this connection was merely an adverb meaning "aside" or "secondary." In England a legislative decision of a municipality is still called a *bye-law*, and what Americans call a special election is known to the British as a by-election.

What is a bull bat?

Bull bat is a popular name for the nighthawk, although it is also sometimes applied to the whippoorwill, a closely related species. The term is used in the sense of a large bat. The nighthawk is nocturnal in habits like the bat and somewhat resembles that flying mammal in its swift, dashing flight. This bird, which resembles the owl in its noiseless flight, travels in its migrations from southern South America to northern North America and breeds between Florida and Labrador. It may be seen at twilight in quest of insects on the wing, flying at a considerable height, occasionally uttering a hoarse, jarring scream or rasping cry and often diving almost vertically down. The whippoorwill, unlike the nighthawk, is seldom seen, but the peculiar call from which it gets its name is often heard just before dawn or at nightfall. Both these birds are related to the swifts and hummingbirds and they belong to the family known as goatsuckers, a name suggested by an old fable that one of the European representatives of the group loiters in the vicinity of flocks of goats with a view to milking them.

Why is Latin America so called?

The countries in the New World to the south of the United States are called Latin America because the prevailing languages are of Latin origin. France, Spain, Italy and Portugal are called Latin countries from the fact that their languages were influenced more by Latin than were the languages of other countries. For the same reason French, Spanish, Italian and Portuguese are sometimes referred to as the Romance (Roman) languages. Spanish is the principal language of Latin America, which includes Mexico, Central America, South America and the West Indies. Portuguese is the prevailing language in Brazil, while French is spoken in French Guiana and a number of West Indian islands belonging or formerly belonging to France. For convenience *Latin America* generally includes Dutch and British Guiana, British Honduras, the British and Dutch islands in the West Indies, and Puerto Rico, which is a dependency of the United States.

What is the White Slave Act?

The White Slave Act, more properly the White Slave Traffic Act, was passed by Congress in 1910 under the interstate commerce clause of the Federal Constitution. It forbids anyone, under heavy penalty, to cause, aid or induce the transportation of any woman or girl from one state to another for immoral purposes. *White slavery* as a general term for traffic in women for immoral purposes was suggested in contrast to *black slavery*. The term implied that certain women were victims of a form of slavery as pitiable as that formerly imposed upon the Negro race. William Edward Hartpole Lecky (1838–1903), the Irish historian, had applied the term to wage earners in Europe. In his *History of England in the Eighteenth Century*, he wrote: "It [Negro slavery in America] was hardly more horrible, however, than the white slavery which for years after the establishment of the factory system prevailed both in England and on the Continent." *White slave* is now defined as a woman held unwillingly for purposes of commercial prostitution. The White Slave Traffic Act of 1910 is also referred to as the Mann Act after its sponsor, Representative James R. Mann, of Illinois.

Do bears hug their enemies to death?

The proverbial hugging propensity of bears is probably a myth, notwithstanding a vast amount of alleged testimony to the contrary. Literature, reference works and books on natural history contain numerous references to the "crushing embrace" or "deadly hug" of bears. Alexander Pope wrote: " 'Tis a bear's talent not to kick, but hug." Nearly all careful observers are agreed that this notion is erroneous. It no doubt arose from faulty observation. The notion originated in the Old World, where the European brown bear is the most common species. This species, *Ursus arctos*, is more given to rising upright and standing on its hind legs than other bears. Consequently members of this species are more readily trained for boxing, wrestling and other exhibition purposes. In the old days the brown bear was the favorite species used by itinerant showmen. But these bears when boxing or wrestling do not habitually hug and do not naturally tend to clench an antagonist. There is no available evidence that any species of bear tries to inflict injury by hugging an enemy with its arms. Reports of hunters being "squeezed to death" by

[431]

bears apparently have no basis in fact. Black bears hug tree trunks in climbing trees adapted to their embrace, but bears are not true tree climbers and the claws of the larger bears are not adapted to climbing trees or other arboreal gymnastics. In his book entitled *In the Zoo* Dr. W. Reid Blair, director of the New York Zoological Park, says: "In regard to the proverbial *hug*, the story is apparently devoid of foundation. A bear, on account of its anatomical structure, strikes round with its paws as if grasping, and the blow of its powerful arm drives its claws into the body of its victim, which action apparently give rise to its *hugging* reputation."

What is the southernmost point in the United States proper?

The most southern point of land in the continental United States is in the vicinity of East Cape, Florida, at approximate latitude 25 degrees, 04 minutes. However, Key West, at approximate latitude 24 degrees 32½ minutes, is connected with the mainland by bridges and viaducts. *The Key West Citizen* carries on its masthead the claim that it is "The Southernmost Newspaper in the U.S.A." The most southern point in Texas is in the vicinity of Brownsville and is at latitude 25 degrees, 50 minutes.

How do the Curb Exchange and the Stock Exchange differ?

The New York Curb Exchange is a market for securities not listed on the New York Stock Exchange. There is no essential difference between the Stock Exchange and the Curb Exchange either in function or in the general nature of the rules and regulations. The Curb Exchange, however, developed later historically and it is more a primary market, that is, a market where securities of newer companies are listed. In other words, the requirements for listing securities on the Stock Exchange are more strict. Securities are not listed in the two exchanges simultaneously. Like most of the stock markets of the world, the New York Curb Exchange had its origin out of doors, and it received its name from the fact that from the time of the Civil War until 1921, when a new building was completed, the brokers and their customers met on the street near the curb. This market was officially known as the Curb *Market* until 1929, when the name was changed to Curb *Exchange*.

Why is a necktie called a cravat?

Cravat is derived from *Cravate*, the French name of the inhabitants of Croatia, who in English are called Croats (pronounced kro-ats). *Khrvat* is the Serbo-Croatian form of the name. The original cravat or cravate was a linen or muslin scarf worn around the neck by members of a regiment of Croat mercenaries in the service of Austria. About 1636 France organized a regiment of light cavalry dressed in uniforms with neckware patterned after that of the Croat. This mode of neckware was immediately adopted by fashionable men in Paris, and the style later spread throughout the civilized world. When first introduced among civilians the cravat consisted of a simple scarf, but cravats edged with lace and tied in a bow with long flowing ends later became the fashion. In the course of time all "neckties" became known as cravats.

What is a thank ye ma'am?

A thank ye ma'am is a bump or depression in a road that causes a carriage to jolt the occupants. The original thank ye ma'am was a small ridge or hollow made diagonally across a road on a hillside to deflect water. It received its popular name from the fact that it caused persons driving over it in a vehicle to bob up as if bowing and acknowledging an act of courtesy. According to a custom formerly quite common in some rural sections of America, a young man out sleigh-riding with his sweetheart was privileged to kiss her every time the sleigh passed over a bump in the road. This kiss was facetiously supposed to correspond to collecting toll at the turnpikes. It was a good-natured satire upon the hackneyed and stilted reply—"Thank ye, sir," or "Thank ye, ma'am"—given by the toll gatherer after collecting a toll.

What do moles eat?

Common garden moles are insectivorous, not vegetarian. Contrary to common belief, they very seldom eat vegetable food of any kind, their chief diet consisting of earthworms, grubs and various insects in the adult and larva stages. When the stomachs of these animals are examined vegetable food is not often found, and it is doubtful whether anybody has ever seen one of them eat such food. Moles kept in captivity and given only vegetable food soon starve to death. According to the United States Department of Agriculture, most of the damage to bulbs, tubers, roots and seeds for which the common eastern mole is blamed is traceable to field mice that follow the mole runways. Some direct damage to field and garden crops, however, is done by the large Townsend mole of the Pacific coast. Of course, the mole damages plants to some extent as it tunnels in search of worms and grubs. The economic value of moles used to be recognized by law in France, where the killing of one of these animals was punishable by a fine. A mole burrows through the earth almost continually during its active season and even a fresh tunnel may extend for hundreds of feet. The tunnel is so small in circumference that the mole cannot turn around in it, but the animal can move backward almost as readily and speedily as forward, and its short, upright hair is adapted to pointing either way. A mole eats almost continuously when active and requires so much nourishment that it can starve to death within twenty-four hours after eating its fill.

How did Greenland get its name?

Since the greater part of Greenland, the largest island in the world, is covered with ice and snow Whiteland would have been a more appropriate name for that island continent. According to a Scandinavian saga, in 985 A.D. Eric the Red named it Greenland to induce colonists from Iceland to settle in the new country. Evidently this bit of real-estate advertising was effective, for the old Scandinavian navigator had no difficulty in getting followers when he made his next voyage. But perhaps Eric the Red first saw Greenland in midsummer, when the western coast is free of ice and covered with Arctic vegetation. Since the ice-covered plateau of the interior was not visible, he may have concluded that the entire island was fertile.

How was Cape Horn named?

General William Tecumseh Sherman says in his Memoirs: "In time we saw Cape Horn; an island rounded like an oven, after which it takes its name (Ornos) oven." Sherman may have defined war correctly, but he was in error about the origin of the name of Cape Horn. His error has been frequently imitated since the publication of his book in 1875. In the first place, the Spanish word for oven is hornos, although the h is silent. In the second place, the island to which Sherman referred is known as Horn Island and the actual cape is only a part of it. The cape, however, was not named because of its resemblance to an oven. It received its name from the "Horn," the small, clumsy vessel in which William Schouten, a Dutch sailor, doubled the cape in 1616. The navigator was known as William Shouten van Horn, because his home was in the village of Horn, Holland. Previously to the voyage of Schouten and Le Maire, passages had been made to the Pacific through the Strait of Magellan. It was not known until then that there was any other route, or that the land called Tierra del Fuego was an island. In Spanish the cape is called Cabo de Hornos. It is small wonder that Sherman was misled, for literally Cabo de Hornos would mean "cape of ovens." Horn Island, the southernmost of the South American islands, may appear different from various approaches. The outlook from the south is that of a steep incline on one side and a gradual rise on the other. General Sherman may have been justified in comparing the island to an oven as he saw it from a certain angle. Knowing little Spanish, he probably jumped to the conclusion that the name was suggested by the shape. The southernmost point on the continent of South America is Cape Froward, not Cape Horn. A point across the strait on Tierra del Fuego from Cape Horn is called False Cape Horn. Few ordinary travelers see Cape Horn because it is off the main steamer routes and because it is generally shrouded in heavy fog.

What does U.S.S. mean in ship names?

U.S.S. preceding the names of vessels are the abbreviation of *United States Ship*. It is frequently but erroneously stated that the second *S* stands for *Steamship* or *Steamer*. But these letters were used in this connection before the days of steam-propelled vessels. They are used only with the names of vessels in the United States Navy; as, U.S.S. "Texas," U.S.S. "Maine." The names of vessels in the United States merchant marine are preceded by the letters *S.S.*; as, *S.S.* "Leviathan." *S.S.* is the official abbreviation for *steamship*. *H.M.S.* preceding the name of a vessel stands for His (or Her) Majesty's Ship. The letters are used in connection only with vessels in the British service. Popularly *H.M.S.* is supposed to be the abbreviation of *His Majesty's Steamer*, but the letters were used in the names of British ships long before the commercial development of the steamboat. *H.M.S.* is also the abbreviation of *His Majesty's Service*.

What does f.o.b. mean?

F.o.b. is the abbreviation of the commercial phrase *free on board*. When used without a modifier, *f.o.b.* means that goods are to be delivered, at the seller's expense, on the train, vessel, airplane, truck or other conveyance by which they are to be transported to the purchaser, who must pay the freight charges. The abbreviation or phrase, however, is ambiguous when used by itself. Therefore, it is customary for business firms to modify it with such terms as *factory, destination,* or the name of the shipping point or the destination. For instance, *f.o.b. factory* means that the purchaser is to pay the freight from the factory, although the manufacturer makes no charge for placing the goods on the train or whatever the means of transportation may be; *f.o.b. destination* means that the freight is to be paid by the shipper or seller. This abbreviation may be either capitalized or written in small letters. It is an interesting fact, however, that *C.O.D.* (Cash on Delivery), is generally capitalized while f.o.b. is generally written in small letters. There seems to be no good reason for the difference, but it has been the prevailing usage ever since the two abbreviations came into general use, and the distinction is recognized by most modern dictionaries.

Why is Caucasian applied to the white race?

Johann Blumenbach (1752–1840), the German anthropologist, classified mankind into five races; namely, the Caucasian, Mongolian, Ethiopian, American and Malayan, corresponding respectively to the white, yellow, black, red and brown races. The finest and most perfectly proportioned skull in Blumenbach's collection was from the Caucasus, the region between the Black and Caspian seas. He, therefore, took the Caucasians or inhabitants of the Caucasus as the highest type of the white race and mankind in general. The name, however, is a misnomer. The natives of the Caucasus fall far short of being the highest type of the human race. Blumenbach is sometimes called "the father of anthropology" and his classification is still the popularly accepted division of the peoples of the world, although modern anthropologists regard it as unscientific in the light of more recent knowledge. Three main races of mankind are now generally recognized—the white, the yellow-bronze and the black. Each of these is divided into types or "subraces," which are also sometimes referred to as "races." The chief subraces are as follows: (white) Mediterranean, Alpine and Nordic; (yellow-bronze) Mongoloid, Malay and American Indian; (black), Negrito, Negrillo, Bushman, Melanesian Negro, Australian and African Negro.

Does odor have weight?

Odor is the name of the sensation produced when certain substances come in contact with the olfactory region. The term is also applied to the collective diminutive particles that produce this sensation. Very little is known about the sense of smell and it is a disputed question whether it depends on a chemical or physical process. The substances that produce the sensation of odor are either in gaseous condition or they are infinitesimal in size. They certainly must have weight, although nobody has yet been able to weigh them. "A non-volatile substance," says the United States Bureau of Standards, "cannot have an odor, because none of it can get to the nose. As the sensation of odor is caused by minute amounts of the odorous substance reaching the nose, obviously the substance must be evaporating. In other words, it is losing weight, and what reaches the nose has some weight, however little." The remarkable fineness of the particles producing odor is demonstrated by a simple experiment. Air

[436]

conveying odor is filtered through a tube packed with cotton wool and inserted into the nose. Notwithstanding the packed cotton wool, the smell is discernible. One scientist estimated that the particles must be less than 1/100,000 of an inch in diameter to pass through the cotton wool packed in the tube. A grain of musk will scent a room for years, and if it is then weighed no appreciable loss of weight can be detected. The smell of camphor can be detected when mixed with water in a proportion of one part of camphor to 400,000 of water. Vanilla is also very pungent and can be recognized when mixed in water in the proportion of one to 10,000,000. Sweetly scented substances that have been in Egyptian tombs for 5,000 years still give off a distinctly discernible scent when the tombs are opened.

What is the fiscal year?

The fiscal year is the twelvemonth period between one annual time of settling accounts and another. The fiscal year of the United States Government begins July 1 and ends June 30. It is always spoken of as being in the calendar year in which it ends. For instance, the fiscal year that ended June 30, 1945, was the fiscal year 1945. Originally the government fiscal year ended September 30, but by an act of Congress passed in 1842 it was changed to June 30 to give the department heads more time to prepare their annual reports for the opening of Congress in December. When the time for the meeting of Congress each year was changed to January 3, in 1934, the government fiscal year was not changed. In all but nine or ten of the states the fiscal year for the state governments is the same as for the Federal government. The government fiscal year in Great Britain and the various units of the British Empire is from April 1 to March 31. For private business in the United States the fiscal year ordinarily corresponds to the calendar year; that is, it begins January 1 and ends December 31.

How did "show the white feather" originate?

To show the white feather, which means to prove cowardly, retreat or back down, is a product of the cockpit. It was suggested by the old belief that a white feather in the tail of a gamecock was a sign that the fowl was crossbred and a mongrel, and consequently lacking in courage, pluck and fighting qualities. We have a similar idea in cur, which is applied to a mongrel dog supposedly inferior because of crossbreeding. It is said by cockfighters that when a purebred bird is pitted in combat against a mongrel bird the mongrel cannot stand the gaff and soon shows the white feather: that is, reveals its inferior blood by not being game. A gaff is a metal spur attached to the leg of a gamecock. A few years ago the United States Department of Agriculture commented on this subject as follows: "While it seems logical that selective breeding for courage and fighting qualities should result in the production of individual birds or strains best suited to this purpose, it is rather difficult to understand why the phrase to *show the white feather* refers to birds of mongrel breeding. In the old English gamebirds, color and markings were not of great importance, but a hard plumage was desired." The original idea expressed by the saying may refer to the fact that a pure-blooded gamecock with white feathers in the wings would "show the white feathers" when he drooped his wings and acknowledged defeat.

What is the meaning of "maru" in Japanese ship names?

Maru, pronounced *mah*-roo, is used in the names of Japanese merchant vessels to distinguish them from warships and other craft. For instance, Japanese name their ships "Yakiko Maru," "Canberra Maru," etc. Popularly the word is regarded by Japanese as meaning simply "ship" or "steamship." Just how it acquired this significance is not known for certain. Apparently it is derived from a Chinese character standing for anything round or circular. In a Japanese dictionary we find *maru* defined as follows: "A circle, sphere; full, complete, all, whole; entirely, perfection, completeness." It has the properties of a noun and a verb, as well as some of those of an adverb. When a Japanese wishes to use slang he will sometimes refer to a dollar piece as a maru, in the sense of a circle. In ancient times it was used to express affection for a priceless possession, such as a sword, a vase, a musical instrument, or even a dog. It may have been originally applied to ships because ancient Japanese ships were round and tublike, because they make a complete circle in starting from and returning to a given point, or because they were looked upon as priceless possessions.

Is the silver fox a distinct species?

The silver fox is not a separate species. It is merely a phase of the red fox. The black fox, the platinum fox and the so-called cross fox also belong to the red fox species. Typical silver foxes have a silvery appearance, due to the white tips on many of the hairs. The bushy tail is black with the exception of a white tip. Black, silver and cross foxes are found in the northern part of North America and in Siberia. Totally black specimens of this species are seldom found except in the far north. As a rule, the fur of the cross fox has a yellowish or orange tone with some silver points and dark cross markings on the shoulders. Pelts of silver foxes vary in color from black with a slight dusting of silver on the head and shoulders to half black and half silver. All these phases are rare in the wild state and it is believed that they are usually born in litters of normally red cubs. The platinum fox was bred from a silver fox sport. Likewise the blue fox is a color phase of the Arctic or white fox, which varies in color from dull blue, bluish brown to pure white.

Why is "colonel" pronounced "kurnel"?

Colonel is merely the English form of Italian colonello, diminutive of colonna, "column," and literally means "little column." At first the little column or company at the head of a regiment was called colonello, which in the course of time was transferred to the leader or commander of the column or regiment. The term passed into French, English and Spanish. In Spanish the form became coronel, and it was so spelled in English at first. It was pronounced korr-o-nel. But the English gradually adopted the Italian spelling in abbreviated form, spelling it colonel and pronouncing it koll-o-nel. This pronunciation, for some reason, was later shortened to kurn-el, which became established about 1800. Some authorities suppose the r sound in colonel is merely a holdover from the days when the term was spelled and pronounced coronel. Since, however, the term was pronounced koll-o-nel for two centuries, it seems more probable that the present pronunciation is owing to a corruption in speech rather than any influence of the Spanish spelling. The substitution of the r sound for the l sound is common in English as well as many other languages. In many parts of the United States colonel is colloquially pronounced kunn-el. Colonel is only one of the many cases in English where the pronunciation of a word has departed widely from the spelling.

Was Cleopatra a blonde or brunette?

There is just as much reason for supposing that Cleopatra was a blonde as there is for supposing that she was a brunette. According to the popular conception, she was a decided brunette, with dark skin, dark eyes and dark hair, and she is frequently referred to as the "dark queen of Egypt." But historical sources supply us with no evidence as to her actual complexion. It should be borne in mind that Cleopatra was Greek by ancestry, and Egyptian only by birth. So far as known she did not have a single drop of Egyptian blood in her veins. The name Cleopatra itself was from Greek mythology, that being the name of one of the two daughters of Boreas, god of the north wind, by Orithyia, daughter of King Erechtheus of Athens. The pharaohs of ancient Egypt married their sisters, daughters and nieces, and the god Osiris and his wife Isis were brother and sister. This practice was adopted by the Greek Ptolemies and the men for generation after generation married close kinswomen. More than a dozen rulers of Egypt were the offspring of intermarriages of this type. The Ptolemies, it is supposed, remained pure Macedonian Greeks, and their capital, Alexandria, was the center of Greek rather than Egyptian culture. They even dressed as Greeks except on certain ceremonial occasions. Therefore Cleopatra was probably a Macedonian type, and the dark skin and black hair of the native Egyptian afford no clue as to her complexion. Many Greeks were dark-complexioned, but among the Macedonians white skin, fair hair and blue eyes were not uncommon, and one of Cleopatra's ancestors, Ptolemy Philadelphus, is described by Theocritus as having light hair and fair complexion. When the American actress Jane Cowl played the role of Cleopatra in Shakespeare's tragedy entitled *Antony and Cleopatra*, she portrayed the Egyptian queen with red hair. Shakespeare himself alluded to Cleopatra as *tawny*. She was descended from brother and sister marriages for at least four generations and she herself married two of her own brothers.

Why is a football field called the gridiron?

A gridiron is a grated utensil on which food is broiled over a fire. Hence, figuratively, any network, as of pipes, railway tracks, etc., is called a gridiron. The term was applied to a football field because it is rectangular in shape and is traversed every five yards by white lines, which produce a gridiron effect. A gridiron dinner is not a dinner cooked on a gridiron. Putting a person on the gridiron is to place him in an uncomfortable position; that is, broiling him over a fire as it were. The Gridiron Club, composed of a restricted number of Washington newspaper correspondents, adopted that name because at its dinners it caricatures and satirizes prominent public persons who are present. *Grid* is merely a shortened form of *gridiron*, which etymologically has nothing to do with *iron*, being a corruption of *gredire*, a variant of *gredil*, the source of *griddle*.

How many bees are there in a hive?

Authorities differ widely on the number of honeybees comprising a hive or colony. It has been estimated that a swarm of bees when it leaves the mother hive constitutes from one thousand to six thousand bees. A colony of bees has its maximum population during the time of storing surplus honey. Then a good colony, roughly estimated, may contain as many as fifty thousand workers, one queen and a few hundred drones, although the average hive contains fewer than that number. A honeybee weighs a little less than one three-hundredths of an ounce, there being about five thousand in a pound. Accordingly a swarm of fifty thousand bees would weigh about ten pounds. The amazing thing is that several pounds of honeybees in a swarm can support themselves on the limb of a tree when only a comparatively few of them are touching the limb at any one time. During the fall and early winter the colony decreases in number. When brood rearing begins in the spring the colony has become so reduced in population that ten thousand workers constitute a good colony. There are no drones in the colony at this season, for they are all driven out at the end of the summer honey flow.

Why is a ten-cent piece called a dime?

Dime is derived from the Latin *decem* ("ten") or *decimus* ("a tenth"). In the thirteenth and fourteenth centuries *dime* was applied in England to the tithe or tenth part of one's income paid to the church. According to the King James Version of the Bible, the last part of *Genesis* 14:20 reads, "He gave him tithes of all." John Wycliffe translated this passage, "He gave him *dymes* of alle thingis." In his report to the Continental Congress on a new coinage system for the United States, Gouverneur Morris, who was familiar with the French language, recommended a coin to be called a *disme*, which was the old French spelling; but the mint act approved in 1792 changed the spelling to *dime*. The term as the specific name of a coin is peculiar to the United States.

Which is correct, "Haiti" or "Santo Domingo"?

Opinion differs whether the second largest West Indian island, which comprises the countries of Haiti and the Dominican Republic, should be called *Santo Domingo* or *Haiti*. It is very difficult to fix an official name for any territory occupied by more than one nation except through international agreement. The inhabitants of the Dominican Republic naturally object to calling the entire island *Haiti*, just as the inhabitants of the United States would object to calling all North America *Canada* or *Mexico*. Some years ago the Pan American Union declared that *Santo Domingo* is the correct name of the entire island, while the United States Geographic Board regarded *Haiti* as the correct name. *Haiti*, meaning "land of mountains," was the name applied to the island by the natives when Columbus landed there in 1492. Some authorities, however, suppose that the word was merely a local name for the western part of the island. They say the natives on the eastern side of the island called their country *Quisqueya*, meaning "mother of the earth." For that reason, they argue, it was never correct to call the entire island Haiti. Columbus, fancying the island resembled Spain, called it *La Espagnola*, which was later Latinized into *Hispaniola* and which signifies "Little Spain." When the French obtained possession of part of the island they named their colony *Saint Dominique*. In 1795 the French obtained the rest of the island from Spain by treaty and *Saint Dominique* was then applied to the whole island. Shortly after this the Spaniards re-established themselves in the eastern part of the island and retained the French name modified to *Santo Domingo*. In 1821 they lost control, and from 1822 to 1843 the entire island was under one government—the republic of Haiti. It was in 1844 that the eastern part declared itself independent of Haiti and set up the present Dominican Republic. Owing to the long controversy over the name some authorities favor calling the island *Haiti-San Domingo* or returning to the early Spanish *Hispaniola*. In 1933 the United States Geographic Board reversed an earlier decision and decided in favor of *Hispaniola* for official usage in the United States. Haiti, whose Negro inhabitants speak a patois of French, comprises about one-third of the island and is the only French-speaking republic in the New World, while the Dominican Republic, whose inhabitants speak Spanish, comprises the other two thirds.

When does a town become a city?

Town and city in the sense of an urban community are relative terms and hard to distinguish exactly. In the most general sense of the terms, a city is merely a municipality with a larger population than a town. There is no uniformity in the legal characteristics of cities and towns throughout the United States and the terms are often used interchangeably. The United States Bureau of the Census classifies incorporated or chartered communities as urban when they contain 2,500 or more inhabitants. A political subdivision not incorporated as a municipality is classed as urban if it contains 10,000 or more inhabitants and has a population density of at least 1,000 to the square mile. The purpose of the Bureau of the Census, however, is to classify population and not to designate any particular urban center as a city or town. For statistical purposes some Federal agencies define city as a town with 8,000 or more inhabitants.

What is meant by the black ox?

The black ox symbolizes old age, ill luck, care, adversity or trouble and misfortune in general. "The black ox has not trod on his nor her foot" is a proverbial expression recorded as early as 1546 by John Heywood. It means that one does not know the meaning of sorrow, such as having been visited by death. In *Sapho and Phao*, written by John

Lyly in 1591, we read: "Now crow's foot is on her eye, and the black ox hath trod on her foot." The phrase alludes to the black cattle sacrificed by the ancient pagans to the infernal deities, especially to Pluto, supreme judge and lord of the nether world. White cattle were sacrificed to Jupiter. At Rome the altar on which the black oxen were sacrificed was twenty feet below the level of the ground and was never exposed to public view except when the sacrifices were being made. In 1923 Gertrude Atherton published a popular book entitled *Black Oxen*. She took the title from the following line in "Countess Cathleen," by the Irish poet and dramatist William Butler Yeats: "The years like great black oxen tread the world." Among the Arabs the "black camel" is the symbol of murder and death by violence. The phrase was used to denote death by Abd-el-Kader (1807?–1883), Algerian Arab chieftain, and *The Black Camel* is the title of a book by Earl Derr Biggers (1884–1933), American novelist and playwright.

Do bees know their master?

Entomologists hold that there is nothing to the common notion that honeybees recognize the beekeeper and distinguish him from other individuals. Although some of the bees hatched late in the fall survive the winter, the average life of a worker during the active honey season is only about six weeks, two of which are spent in the hive. It is not likely that a beekeeper would examine a hive frequently enough to be differentiated from other human beings. A good beekeeper does not provoke bees so much as inexperienced persons do because he is familiar with their habits and knows how to handle them.

How did "not worth a tinker's damn" originate?

There is a difference of opinion as to whether the last word in this phrase was originally *dam* or *damn*. A tinker's dam, according to Webster's International dictionary, is a wall of soft mud, clay, dough or the like, raised around a spot that a plumber wishes to cover with solder. The material of the dam can be used but once. After this temporary period of usefulness it is thrown away as being absolutely worthless. It is supposed by the authority referred to above that the phrase *not worth a tinker's damn* is derived from this source. Other authorities, however, believe that the original phrase was *not worth a tinker's damn* and that it referred to the proverbial tendency of tinkers to swear. In Shakespeare's *I Henry IV* Prince Hal, after trying his hand at being a drawer in the Boar's Head Tavern, says to Poins: "To conclude, I am so good a proficient in one quarter of an hour that I can drink with any tinker in his own language during my life." The word *damn* has long been used in similar phrases. For instance, Oliver Goldsmith, in his *Citizen of the World*, says: "Not that I care three *damns* what figure I may cut." The Duke of Wellington said that he didn't "care a *two-penny damn*." The theory that *damn* or *dam* in such phrases is derived from an ancient Hindu coin by that name has nothing to support it.

Which is correct, Abyssinia or Ethiopia?

Ethiopia is the ancient name of the country in northeastern Africa. It is of Greek origin and literally means the "land of burnt-face people," alluding to the dark-skinned people in that region. Homer and other classical Greek writers applied the name vaguely to the lands south of Egypt. *Abyssinia* is the name commonly applied to Ethiopia by Europeans. It is derived from Arabic *habesha*, signifying "confused, mixed or mongrel race," and was originally applied to the country in derision. The inhabitants not only never use the name themselves but resent its application to their country by others. After the coronation of Emperor Haile Selassie in 1930 *Ethiopia* was revived in diplomatic usage by all countries, including the United States. *Addis Ababa*, the name of the capital of Ethiopia, is a native phrase literally meaning "new flower."

To what mountain system do the Ozarks belong?

Geologists do not regard the Ozark Mountains as part of either the Rocky or the Appalachian systems, but as an independent and distinct unit. The Ozark Plateau or upland area lies chiefly in southern Missouri and northern Arkansas, but also extends into Oklahoma and Kansas. It is separated from the Appalachians by the lowlands of the Mississippi Basin, and from the Rockies by the Great Plains. *Ozarks* is an American rendering of *Aux Arcs*, pronounced *oze-ark*, literally meaning "with bows," a term that the early French applied to a band of Quapaw Indians who inhabited the mountain region of Missouri and Arkansas. *Aux Arcs* was descriptive of the Indians and was equivalent to English "bow carriers." The early French had a trading post called *Aux Arcs* near the present village of Arkansas Post, Arkansas.

Who said: "The king is dead! Long live the king!"

This expression seems to be of French origin. It was used in France to announce the death of a king and the accession of his successor to the throne, signifying that the country was never without a sovereign. William Blackstone, in his *Commentaries on the Laws of England* (1765) expressed the same idea in, "The king never dies." Apparently "The king is dead! Long live the king!" as a form of proclamation on the death of a French king was first used in 1461 at the time of the death of Charles VII, who had been helped to the throne by Joan of Arc. It was last used in 1824 when Louis XVIII died and Charles X was proclaimed King. In her *Louis XIV, and the Court of France in the Seventeenth Century* (1847) Julia Pardoe, English novelist and historical writer, said: "The death of Louis XIV [in 1715] was announced by the captain of the bodyguard from a window of the state department. Raising his truncheon above his head, he broke it in the center, and throwing the pieces among the crowd, exclaimed in a loud voice, '*Le Roi est mort!*' Then seizing another staff, he flourished it in the air as he shouted, '*Vive le Roi!*' " Louis XVII was proclaimed titular King of France nineteen years after his death. He was a son of Louis XVI and Marie Antoinette. His death occurred in prison under mysterious circumstances in 1795, two years after the execution of his parents. When his uncle, Louis XVIII, ascended the throne in 1814 he proclaimed the "lost dauphin" Louis XVII to maintain the continuity of the Bourbon line.

Where is "the roof of the world"?

The Pamir mountain region in Central Asia is called *the roof of the world* because of its great altitude. In India the Pamirs are called *Bam-i-dunya*, literally "top of the world." *Pamir* itself, according to the most logical theory, is derived from the Persian *pai-mir*, signifying "the foot of the mountain peaks." The region around the North Pole is also sometimes called the roof or top of the world. During the Second World War American aviators who flew between India and China referred to the Himalaya Mountains as "The Hump."

Why are June marriages considered lucky?

In the United States and Canada as well as in many other countries June is the favorite marriage month; in New Zealand and Australia as well as some other countries in the Southern Hemisphere, where the seasons are reversed, the favorite marriage month is December. The belief that June marriages are likely to be lucky is believed to be a relic of ancient superstition and mythology. Some authorities suggest that the season of the year corresponding to our June may have been the natural mating period for human beings in primitive times. "Prosperity to the man and happiness to the maid when married in June" was a proverb in ancient Rome. It was popularly supposed that the month of June was named in honor of Juno, whose festival was held on the first of that month. Juno, the wife of Jupiter, was not only the guardian of the female sex from birth to death but also the patroness of happy marriages. May, supposedly named after the Roman goddess Maia, is regarded by the superstitious as unpropitious for marriages. "Marry in May and you'll rue the day," is an old proverb, and a gruesome but ancient Scottish saying runs:

> From the marriages in May
> All the bairns die an decay.

The belief that May marriages are likely to be unlucky is believed to be also a relic of ancient superstition and mythology. Pagan Rome believed that the souls of the dead hovered about as malevolent nocturnal spirits known as lemures. The chief feast of the lemures was the Lemuria, held on May 9, 11 and 13. On those dates the head of the household made midnight offerings to placate the angry spirits. Because of the celebration of the festival of the unhappy dead in this month May came to be regarded as unlucky for marriages among the Romans. Whether the months of June and May were actually named after the goddesses Juno and Maia is an unsettled question. Ovid has Juno say that June was named expressly in her honor; but since June and May were dedicated respectively to youth and old age, some authorities derive the names from Latin *juniores*, comparative plural of *juvenis*, meaning "young," and *majores*, comparative plural of *magnus*, "aged" or "old." Others suppose *June* to be derived from *Junius*, a Roman family name.

Why are ship compartments called "staterooms"?

According to a popular story, *stateroom* as applied to the compartments containing the berths on a steamship originated as follows: In 1815 Captain Henry Miller Shreve, after whom Shreveport, Louisiana, was named, made the first steamboat voyage up the Mississippi and Ohio as far as Louisiana. For many years Captain Shreve had charge of the improvement of western rivers. About 1844, it is said he had cabins built on his steamboat and named them after the states bordering on the Mississippi and Ohio rivers. Hence the cabins came to be called at first *the States* and finally *State rooms*. A year later—the year Texas was admitted into the Union—the pilothouse was built on the hurricane or third deck of the vessel. This was facetiously called *The Texas*, because it was "annexed to the States." From this circumstance, according to the story, the third deck of a Mississippi steamboat received the name *texas*. This story, however, is open to etymological criticism. In the first place, *stateroom* was applied to steamship compartments before that time. For instance, Harriet Martineau uses the term in its modern sense in *Retro-*

[446]

spect of *Western Travel*, published in 1838. In the second place, it is probable that Captain Shreve's scheme of naming his cabins was suggested by the word *stateroom*. As early as the seventeenth century English writers applied *state* to a raised platform or dais containing a chair or throne covered with a canopy. This *state* was the chief seat of honor. The original *state room* was a room in a palace, executive mansion or hotel, splendidly decorated and furnished and used only on *state* or ceremonial occasions. *Stateroom* in connection with ships originated in the British Navy. Under date of April 14, 1660, Samuel Pepys wrote in his diary: "Very pleasant we were on board the *London*, which hath a stateroom much bigger than the *Nazeby*, but not so rich." In 1694 the London *Gazette* reported: "The yacht having lost in this encounter but three men, who were killed by one great shot in the *state-room*." Tobias Smollet, Scottish novelist and surgeon, wrote in *Roderick Random* in 1748: "A cabin was made for him contiguous to the *state-room* where Whiffle slept." In other words, the original stateroom on a British warship was the cabin or quarters of a superior officer. In time the term was extended to merchant ships. Sir Walter Scott, in *Cruise of the Midge*, wrote: "The cabin had two *state-rooms*, as they are called in the Merchantmen, opening off it." In the United States this term was narrowed to signify first a private cabin on a ship and then to a sleeping compartment on a train. This usage was probably influenced by the fact that in the early days of passenger steamships ordinary people slept in bunks in two large rooms, one for men and one for women, but wealthy and distinguished persons were given private rooms and they were said to travel in style or in state. In the sense of an apartment of state in a palace or great house the term is generally written *state room*, not *stateroom* as it is in the sense of a steamship or railway train compartment.

What are equinoctial storms?

Equinoctial storms are storms popularly supposed to occur at the time of the spring and fall equinoxes. *Equinox* is derived from Latin and signifies "equal night." It is a time of the year when the days and nights are equal in length. That storms are more frequent and severe at such times is merely a myth of unknown origin. The autumnal equinox occurs September 21 or 22 and records indicate that storms are neither more frequent nor more severe on those days than on other dates in September. In fact records for a period of fifty years showed that there were actually fewer storms between September 20 and September 25 than there were during the five days immediately preceding September 20. The same is true of the vernal or spring equinox, which occurs March 20 or

21. Storms are not more frequent or severe on those dates than on other dates in March. The notion about equinoctial storms in one form or other dates back at least to 1748 and probably originated among seafaring people.

What are minnows?

Minnow, often corrupted into minnie, is popularly applied in the United States to any small fish irrespective of species. In British usage the term is applied only to a particular species, the smallest common food fish of the British Isles. American scientists restrict the term to a certain species of small fish belonging to the carp family. Further confusion is caused by the fact that some authorities call the largest family of freshwater fish in the Northern Hemisphere the Minnow family, which includes many small fish, but also many large ones, such as the eighty pound white salmon and the western squawfish, which attains a length of several feet. The young of the larger fish, especially when they are less than two and a half inches long, are properly called fry. Minnow is supposed by some authorities to be derived from Latin minutus, meaning small.

Who invented the postal card?

The use of postal cards was first suggested in 1865 by Heinrich von Stephan (1831–1897) when he was director of the Royal Prussian Post. Later Stephan became the first postmaster general of the German Empire and founded the International Postal Union, which became operative July 1, 1875, and which nearly all countries later joined. His suggestion about postal cards, however, was not approved by the Prussian postal system, and two years later Dr. Emanuel Hermann of the Vienna Military Academy, apparently without any knowledge of Stephan's proposal, suggested a handy stamped card in a letter published in a Vienna newspaper. The Austrian post office approved the idea and the first postal cards, called Korrespondenz Karten in German, made their appearance in that country in 1869. In 1870 postal cards, sponsored by Prime Minister William E. Gladstone, made their debut in Great Britain and immediately became popular, nearly one million being disposed of the first week they were on sale. Postal cards were first issued in the United States May 1, 1873, under an act of Congress approved June 6, 1872. The design on these first American postal cards consisted of the head of the Goddess of Liberty. By 1943 the Government Printing Office in Washington was printing penny postal cards at the rate of 2,500,000,000 a year. Just who invented post cards, unstamped picture cards handled by private firms, is not known for certain. One story is that they were created in 1870 by a man named Schwartz in Oldenburg, Germany. About 1890 Dominique Piazza, of Marseilles, France, published picture cards, and he is regarded by his countrymen as the originator of illustrated post cards. Heinrich Lange, a stationer at Gottingen, Germany, who died in 1932 at the age of eighty-four, sent such cards through the mails about 1890, and they were introduced into the United States a short time afterward. By 1944 post cards in the United States were being mailed at the rate of some five million a day.

How did the New Orleans Mardi Gras originate?

Mardi Gras, pronounced mar-dee grah, literally means "fat Tuesday." It is the French name of Shrove Tuesday, the day before Ash Wednesday, the beginning of Lent. *Shrove* is the past tense of *shrive* ("confess"), and Shrove Tuesday is the day on which confession or *shrift* was made preparatory to the forty fast days of Lent. French Mardi Gras or Fat Tuesday alludes to an old ceremony in which a fat ox, symbolizing the passing of meat, was paraded through the streets of Paris and other French cities on Shrove Tuesday. Lent being a period of fasting, Mardi Gras naturally became a day of *carnival*, a term derived through Italian from Latin *carnem levare* ("to put away flesh," as food). In Italy and other Roman Catholic countries the day before Lent was devoted to revelry, merrymaking, feasting and riotous amusement. The day was formerly observed in England by eating pancakes and it is still often referred to as Pancake Tuesday, although eating pancakes on this day survives only as a social custom. In Shakespeare's *All's Well That Ends Well* the clown Lavache, when asked by the Countess of Rousillon whether his answer would "serve fit to all questions," replied: "As fit . . . as a pancake for Shrove Tuesday." Pancakes seem to have become particularly associated with Shrove Tuesday because the people desired to use up what grease, lard and similar forbidden goods they had on hand before Lent. Carnivals, pageants and parades still characterize Mardi Gras in many Catholic cities in Europe. French colonists introduced Mardi Gras festivities into the United States. New Orleans, Mobile and Galveston still observe Mardi Gras with elaborate ceremonies and it is a legal holiday in Louisiana, Alabama and Florida. Mardi Gras celebrations took place between 1702 and 1710 among the French soldiers stationed at Fort Louis de la Louisiana on the original site of Mobile, Alabama. A society to promote yearly Mardi Gras balls and street parades was formed in Mobile in 1830. Although Mardi Gras pageants were given as early as 1827 in New Orleans by young men recently returned from Paris, and these pageants were revived in 1837 and 1839, it was not until twenty years later that the distinctive ceremonies now associated with Mardi Gras in that city were introduced by a group of former Mobile residents. On Mardi Gras, New Orleans is ostensibly placed under the rule of a king of the carnival and civic organizations sponsor the celebration, which consists of a daytime street parade with fantastic floats and of an evening masqued ball, accompanied by pageantry, frolicking and merrymaking.

How did "thumbs down" originate?

Thumbs up means approval; *thumbs down*, disapproval. These phrases are believed to have been suggested by the gestures made by the spectators at the gladiatorial combats staged by the ancient Romans for entertainment. The spectators were permitted to decide whether a vanquished gladiator should be put to death or permitted to live. If they clenched the fist and extended the thumb toward the defeated man it was a sign that the unfortunate gladiator should be slain; if they merely clenched the thumb in the fist it was a sign that his life should be spared. Hence pointing the thumb—the gesture of condemnation—came to signify disapproval. The idea of *thumbs up* as opposed to *thumbs down* was unknown to the Romans. In Latin they called the gesture of pointing the thumb *pollice verso* (pronounced *poll-i-see vur-so*), which meant "with thumb turned or reversed." Since in the gesture of condemnation the spectators at the gladiatorial shows generally turned the thumb down the phrase was translated "thumbs down" in English. *Thumbs up* was then coined as the opposite of *thumbs down*. An eminent philologist says on this subject: "The thumb symbolizes the short Roman sword, and the gesture which meant death to the vanquished gladiator was given by turning the hand over into an unnatural position, with the thumb pointing at the defeated man." Jean Léon Gérôme, the French artist, painted a picture of the gladiators in the amphitheater. The victor in the contest is shown standing over his victim and looking toward the spectators for their verdict. They are represented with thumbs down, signifying that the defeated gladiator must die. *Thumbs up* in the sense of the gesture made by hitchhikers "thumbing a ride" has no connection with the earlier phrase.

What causes fresh-water springs in the ocean?

Fresh-water springs in the ocean have been noted by travelers and navigators for centuries. In fact the existence of such ocean springs has been known since the time of the ancient Phoenicians, who were noted for their knowledge of navigation and their long voyages. Most of these springs are caused by underground streams with preponderating heads that discharge their waters into the ocean beneath the surface. The fresh water rises to the surface because of its relative specific lightness. Such springs occur only in coastal waters and never in mid-ocean. There are several of these submarine river outlets in the sea near Cuba. There is another about two and a half miles east of Crescent Beach near St. Augustine. So much fresh water rises up through the salt water that it produces a noticeable bubble. A submarine artesian well in the Gulf of Mexico fourteen miles off Biloxi, Mississippi, spouts fresh water up into the salt water. This artesian well was formerly on the Isle of Caprice, which was destroyed by the waters of the Gulf. Some submarine springs discharge hot water. Ocean springs of this type investigated by French scientists, who used diving apparatus, consist of funnel-shaped orifices in the solid rock on the bottom of the sea. They project streams of water with sufficient force to carry small stones to the surface. Others consist of many small openings that bubble up enough to form a current of considerable volume. Most submarine springs, however, discharge cold water. Of course, fresh water discharged from a submarine source generally is mixed with salt water before it reaches the surface. The natives of Bahrein Islands in the Persian Gulf and of certain South Sea islands dive to the bottom and scoop up fresh water into bags from submarine springs before it is contaminated with salt water. At the mouth of the Amazon a layer of fresh water flows for miles over the denser sea water. Wrote Abbé Dimnet in *The Art of Thinking*: "The Spanish crew who were becalmed in the ocean, off the mouth of the Amazon River, could not believe the natives signaling that the water all round their ship was good to drink and they had only to throw down the buckets."

Does the sap of a tree rise in the spring?

That the sap of a tree rises in the spring and goes down in the fall is a common but erroneous notion. In the spring there is an increased circulation of liquids through the tissues of the tree and the food materials stored in the trunk and branches are dissolved and carried to the buds and root tips where first growth begins. It is this increased activity preceding the bursting of the buds and the development of visible growing parts that is so often taken for the rise of sap. In sugar maple trees the circulation of liquid through the stem in the spring is attended by considerable pressure. If one of these trees is bruised in the spring it "bleeds" more freely than if it is bruised in any other season and this is taken by many as positive proof that there is more moisture in the tree in the spring than at any other time. It is also accepted as evidence that the sap goes up in the spring and down in the fall. As stated above, such is not the case. The sap does not go down at any time. At any given point above the ground the moisture content between the inner and outer zones of living wood may vary from month to month and from season to season. A British investigator found that in the fall the center of a tree is very wet, and the outer regions are comparatively dry, while in the spring this condition is reversed. He concluded that if we desire to make our language conform with the fact we should not say that the sap is up in the spring and down in the fall, but that it is out (near the bark) in the spring and in (toward the center) in the fall. Analysis shows that pieces of wood cut from trees in the winter sometimes have a moisture content just as high or even higher than pieces cut in the spring or early summer.

Can moles see?

Whether ordinary moles can see has been a debatable question for centuries and is not yet finally settled. In his *Vulgar Errors* (1646) Sir Thomas Browne took considerable pains to disprove the popular notion that moles have no eyes and are totally blind. Although he admitted that these subterranean creatures "do not distinctly see," he wrote, "that they have eyes in their head, is manifest unto any that wants them not in his own . . . and if the eagle were judge, we might be blind ourselves." In Shakespeare's *Tempest*, Caliban says to Stephano and Trinculo as they approach Prospero's cell: "Pray you, tread softly, that the blind mole may not hear a foot fall." The Prince of Tyre, in *Pericles*, tells King Antiochus: "The blind mole casts copp'd hills towards heaven, to tell the earth is throng'd by man's oppression." The common garden mole of the eastern United States has eyes, but they are very small and sunken, being almost completely buried beneath the fur and skin. Apparently they serve no practical purpose as organs of sight and the proverbial *blind as a mole* is correct so far as this species is concerned. If the mole is not totally blind, it can at best merely distinguish between light and darkness. Investigation shows that the eyes are most nearly perfect in very young moles. In adults the external eyes seem to degenerate until they are of no use for vision. When an adult is skinned for dissection the eyes appear as small, dark specks under the skin, and the eyeballs are little larger than pinheads. Of the mole found in the British Isles Charles Darwin wrote in *The Voyage of the Beagle*: "In the common mole the eye is extraordinarily small but imperfect, though many anatomists doubt whether it is connected with the true optic nerve; its vision must certainly be imperfect, though probably useful to the animal when it leaves its burrow." Experiments show that the eyes of moles do show some sensitiveness to light. This degeneration of the eyes has not proceeded so far in the western or Townsend mole, which often opens its eyes when annoyed.

Why is a quarter called "two bits"?

In England *bit* has been applied to small coins for centuries. The term at one time was thieves' slang for money in general. Thomas Dekkar so used it in *A Knight's Conjuring: Jests to Make You Merie*, first printed in 1607. Later *bit* was applied to any small coin, especially to the smallest coin in general circulation. Even today the British use the term in such phrases as *threepenny bit*. *Two bits*, meaning a quarter of a dollar, originated in the West Indies where *bit* was applied in the seventeenth and eighteenth centuries to small silver coins forming fractions of the Spanish dollar. It was applied specifically to the *real*, which was equal to one-eighth of the Spanish silver dollar or "piece of eight," which circulated freely in the English colonies and of which the American dollar was an adaptation in size, shape and value. In those days it was a common practice to cut the Spanish silver dollar into wedge-shaped pieces for use as small coins. A two-real piece represented a quarter of the whole. The English colonists referred to a one-real piece as a "bit" and a two-real piece as "two bits." In that part of his secret diary written from 1709 to 1712 William Byrd of Westover continually mentioned losing "a bit" and "two bits" at billiards, cricket or cards. He also gave "two bits" to servants as tips. When the Spanish dollar disappeared from circulation in America and was replaced by the United States dollar, *bit* survived only in such phrases as *two bits*, meaning "a quarter," and *four bits*, meaning "half a dollar." Twelve cents and a half, which corresponded to the original English shilling, is seldom if ever called "a bit," although in some sections of the United States fifteen cents is called a "long bit," and ten cents a "short bit."

What is meant by pleading the baby act?

According to law, a person not of age cannot be bound by contract. If a minor makes a contract and does not abide by the agreement he may plead his minority as a defense in court. The popular phrase *pleading the baby act* originally referred to this law protecting minors. It meant merely pleading legal infancy as a defense for disregarding a contract. Figuratively a person is said to plead the baby act when he pleads ignorance or inexperience as an excuse for his mistakes or wrongdoing. The expression carries with it an implication of weakness and cowardice. In 1841 Abraham Lincoln represented a man in court who had sold two brothers a team of oxen and a plow on time. When the note came due they pleaded they were minors when they signed it, but they refused to return the goods. Lincoln told the jury: "The judge will tell you what your own sense of justice has already told you, that these Snow boys, if they were men enough to plead the baby act, when they came to be men should have taken the oxen and plow back."

Is it easier to lift a weight with a large or small pulley?

Other things being equal, a weight can be lifted more easily with a large pulley than with a small one. Less power is required to drive or pull a vehicle with large wheels than is required to drive or pull one with small wheels. The larger the wheel, the greater the mechanical advantage in overcoming friction. If friction could be eliminated there would be no mechanical advantage gained by using a larger wheel.

What is a madstone?

Madstones are certain objects popularly believed to have the power of "sucking" poison from wounds made by mad dogs and venomous snakes. They are supposed to be especially efficacious in preventing hydrophobia or rabies. Belief in the magical properties of madstones was formerly almost universal in America. Abraham Lincoln believed in madstones and when his son Robert was bitten by a dog he took the boy to Terre Haute, Indiana, to have a madstone applied to the wound. He had faith in madstones, he told a friend, because he "found the people in the neighborhood of these stones fully impressed with the belief in their virtues from actual experiment." A magic stone, suggesting the madstone, figures in *The Talisman* by Sir Walter Scott. In *Americanisms: The English of the New World* (1872) Schele de Vere wrote: "*Madstone* is the name of a round stone of the size of an egg, of dark color, preserved by some families in the South, to which the power is ascribed of curing persons bitten by mad dogs or venomous serpents. It is placed upon the wound, from which it draws much matter, and this process being repeated frequently, extracts the venom—by faith." The treatment sometimes consists of alternately soaking the madstone in sweet milk and applying it to the wound after it has been cut slightly. If the madstone sticks tight to the wound, it is said, it will draw out the poison; if it will not adhere to the wound it is presumed that no poison is present. A genuine madstone, according to one belief, will turn milk black. The United States Department of Agriculture refers to madstones as *mythical stones* and says their alleged virtues have no scientific foundation, unless it is merely pyschological effect. The bezoar stone, a biliary calculus from the gall bladder of an animal, is a common form of madstone. It is usually composed of substances that have about the same relation to animals that gallstones have to human beings. Another form is composed of halloysite, which absorbs moisture with avidity and adheres to a moist surface until nearly saturated. Such a porous, spongy stone will actually absorb some blood and consequently some of the poison if it is pressed upon a newly made wound. Those who believe in the madstone test it for genuineness by placing it against the roof of the mouth. If it adheres it is genuine, they say; if it drops, it is a fake. A pebble of carbonate of lime found in the stomach of a deer was once sent to the National Museum in Washington as a genuine madstone. On another occasion two hair balls from a buffalo's stomach were presented with the statement that one of them had been "successfully used in two cases of dog bite." The same institution was offered a madstone of *proven efficiency* for the sum of a thousand dollars. It proved to be merely a polished seed of the Kentucky coffee tree. In *The Golden Bough* Sir James G. Frazier, referring to imitative magic, wrote: "The Greeks believed in a stone which cured snake-bites, and hence was named the snake-stone; to test its efficiency you had only to grind the stone to powder and sprinkle the powder on the wound." The American Indians used *snakestones* as one of their most important remedies. In the United States *snakestones* often consist of charred bones. The real value of such charms lies in the confidence with which the possessor is inspired. Their danger lies in using them to the exclusion of scientific methods of protection.

What makes the jumping bean jump?

Mexican jumping bean, *jumping bean* and *broncho bean* are popular names given to the separate cells of the seed pods of several varieties of swamp shrubs native to northern Mexico and southwestern United States. These shrubs belong to *Euphorbiaceae*, or spurge family. When the shrub is in bloom or shortly thereafter a bean moth (*Carpocarpsa saltitans*), closely related to the destructive codling moth or appleworm, deposits its eggs in the blossoms or the green seed pods. After the egg hatches the larva of the bean moth eats the interior of the bean pod cell and lines the sides with silk of its own manufacture. By the time the three-celled pod has separated from the shrub and fallen to the ground the larva is about one-fifth the size and nearly as heavy as the pea-sized and thin-walled cell that serves it as a shelter. The larva is strong for its size and for a time is very active. It catapults itself with enough force to cause the bean to tilt, roll, tumble, jerk and jump. Many people find this phenomenon so amusing that many tons of "Mexican jumping beans" have been gathered, shipped to market and sold at several cents apiece. Of course, only "wormy" beans are marketable as oddities. As a rule there is a bean moth larva in only one of the three beans in a pod. Ultimately the larva emerges as a full-fledged bean moth, and the cycle starts over. In the Southwest, broncho beans have been used by gamblers for generations. The wagers are decided by the greatest number of beans that jump over a line or out of a circle within a given time.

Why does it rain harder after a flash of lightning?

That it often rains harder after a vivid flash of lightning and heavy peal of thunder is a fact well known to meteorologists. Strictly speaking, however, the rain gush, as weather experts call it, is caused by neither the lightning nor the thunder. According to the United States Weather Bureau, a cloud is electrified when raindrops are produced by a rapidly rising mass of warm humid air. The greater the quantity of raindrops produced, the greater, in general, will be the quantity of electricity. Therefore, when a large number of raindrops have been formed in a cloud, there is often a correspondingly heavy discharge of lightning, followed by thunder. The light from the discharge, the thunder and the raindrops all start down at the same time; but the light, being much faster, is seen before the thunder is heard, and the drops, being slower even than the thunder, follow immediately. In other words, the action of the rising air on the raindrops causes the lightning, and the lightning causes the thunder.

What is the lightest substance known?

The element hydrogen is the lightest substance known to science. Its specific gravity, compared to air, is 0.0695. Helium, with a specific gravity of 0.139, is the next lightest substance. Specific gravity is relative density, that is, the ratio of the weight of any volume of a substance to the weight of an equal volume of some other substance used as a unit or standard. Air is generally used as the standard for gases, and water for solids and liquids. When we say that the specific gravity of helium is 0.139 and that of hydrogen 0.0695, this expresses the fact that helium is twice as heavy as hydrogen. Although helium has twice the weight of hydrogen, its lifting power when used in balloons is about 93 per cent that of hydrogen. The heaviest known substance is osmium, a rare platinum-like metal with a specific gravity of 22.5. Irridium, with a specific gravity of

22.42, comes second; platinum, 21.37, third; and gold, 19.33, fourth. Osmium, the heaviest known substance in the world, weighs more than 250,000 times as much as hydrogen, the lightest substance. Lithium, a silver-white soft element with a specific gravity of 0.53, is the lightest metal known.

Does air have weight?

Air is a substance and all substances have weight. Air, however, is very light. A column of air an inch square extending from sea level upward as far as the atmosphere goes weighs only about fifteen pounds. This is called atmospheric pressure. Galileo first demonstrated that air has weight by weighing a glass globe, then forcing air into it and weighing it again. He correctly ascribed the extra weight to the added air. An automobile tire pumped up would weigh more than a flat tire, but the difference would be too slight to detect with ordinary scales. Since water vapor is lighter than most of the other gases in the atmosphere, moist air weighs less than dry air. Naturally the more air is compressed the more it weighs volume for volume. A tank full of compressed air is heavier and less buoyant than when it is full of air at normal atmospheric pressure.

What determined the width of standard gauge railroads?

The standard gauge railroad is four feet eight and one half inches wide, measured from the inside of one rail to the inside of the other. This width was determined largely by chance. When tramways were first built in the English coal districts their width was made to conform to the gauge of the common road wagons to be used on them. It happened that the gauge between the wheels of these wagons was about 4 feet 8½ inches. This width had been determined to some extent by the Roman chariot makers and road builders of two thousand years ago. Later when rails were laid for steam railroads the same gauge was adopted in many cases. In fact nearly all the early English railways were standard gauge. William Jessop is often credited with being the author of the standard gauge for steam railways. About 1800 he designed a track between Loughborough and Nanpantan in which the rails were 4 feet 8½ inches apart, or five feet minus the width of the two rails. Many years afterwards railway builders and operators differed widely on the most desirable width for the tracks. The dispute reached its zenith about 1833. George Stephenson threw the weight of his influence in favor of the standard gauge. He believed it was "most economical in construction, not only as regards the engines and carriages, but more particularly of the railway itself." The standard gauge was fixed by Parliament in 1840. The act was applicable to all railways in England and Scotland except the Great Western and certain branches, which had adopted a broad or 6-foot gauge. Not until 1874 did this railway conform to the almost universal practice by substituting standard gauge track. In the United States as many as twenty-three different gauges of track were in use simultaneously on the railroads before the gauge was standardized by law. This bewildering difference in gauges created serious transportation problems in both the North and the South during the Civil War. It made continual unloading and reloading of freight necessary and made a continental system impossible. In some cases a third rail was laid to make possible the use of broad-gauge cars on narrow-gauge tracks. It was even seriously proposed to build cars with adjustable wheel widths. Standard gauge was required on all interstate railroads after 1863.

How many square feet of skin does the body contain?

It is estimated that there are from fourteen to eighteen square feet of skin on the average adult human body. One investigator placed the figure as high as twenty square feet. Of course, the surface area of the body, which is practically equivalent to the number of square feet of skin, varies with sex, age, height and weight of the individual. Obviously the body of a tall, thin person might have a much greater surface area than the body of a short, fat person who has the same weight. The most common method of obtaining the surface area of the body is complicated and involves many factors, but charts have been devised whereby it can be estimated with a high degree of accuracy if the individual's sex, age, height and weight are known. One method of computing the number of square inches of skin is by pasting over the nude body a special kind of very thin but strong paper that adheres closely to curved surfaces. The paper is first dried, then removed, cut into small pieces and measured. The thickness of the skin of the human body varies considerably. It is thicker over the back than it is over the breast. One investigator says the skin averages one-sixth of an inch on the palms of the hands and the soles of the feet and only one-fiftieth of an inch on the eyelids.

Why does "T.L." mean a compliment?

The letters *T.L.*, when used to mean a compliment, are the abbreviation of *trade last*. These words acquired the meaning of an offer to give a compliment in exchange for one from the playful custom of a person saying to one of the opposite sex, "I have a trade last for you," meaning that if you will tell me something nice you heard about me, I will tell you a compliment I heard about you. Sometimes the second element in *trade last* is written *lassie* or *me-lass*. The following from the Chicago *Tribune* illustrates the popular use of the term: "Gracie, who loves flattery, is going to be mad in a minute. She wants a trade last and her best boy is about to tell her he heard so and so say she was remarkably well preserved."

How did "dead as a doornail" originate?

Anything stone dead is said to be dead as a doornail. The conventional explanation of this phrase is that *doornail* was an old name for the plate or knob on which the knocker or hammer strikes. "As this nail is knocked on the head several times a day," says an old writer, "it cannot be supposed to have much life left." The person who originated that theory strained at a gnat and swallowed a camel. He merely made a guess as to the origin of the phrase, for there is no evidence that the original doornail was a nail or piece of iron on which the knocker struck. It is more probable that *doornail* in the phrase refers to an ordinary nail in the door. During the Middle Ages it was customary to use nails in doors for ornamental as well as utility purposes. Nothing would be more natural than to use such a familiar object for comparison. *Dead as a doornail* occurs in *Piers Plowman*, written by William Langland about 1362. Shakespeare used it more than once. In *II King Henry VI*, Jack Cade is quoted as saying, "And if I do not leave you all as dead as a door-nail, I pray God I may never eat grass more." Shakespeare probably had the original conception of the phrase in mind when in *I King Henry IV* he had Sir John Falstaff ask, "What! is the old king dead?" and Pistol reply, "as nail in door." Euphony and alliteration, not sense, keep such phrases alive.

What is ginseng used for?

Ginseng is not used in the United States to any considerable extent. A negligible quantity is used by Chinese in America and a trifling amount by makers of medicine and drugs, but the consumption of the root is confined almost entirely to China and virtually the entire American supply is exported to that country. Opinion differs respecting the medicinal value of ginseng, but the general belief of medical science is that it possesses little, if any, real therapeutic virtue. It is used to a limited extent as a demulcent, but it is not officially recognized by the American Pharmacopoeia even for that purpose. Whether its medicinal value is real or fancied, ginseng root is in great demand among the Chinese, who regard it highly as a medicinal stimulant and sort of panacea. They use it for nearly every conceivable domestic and medicinal purpose, especially when other curative agents have failed. In China branched ginseng roots resembling the human form command particularly high prices because of their supposed occult virtues. If a boy is weak in the legs many Chinese think the best way to cure him is to give him a concoction made of ginseng root that resembles a boy running or otherwise using his legs. If an arm is affected, then a root that shows a well developed arm is used. Perhaps the real demand for ginseng is based on an ancient superstition that the root has the power of restoring virility to the impotent. Ginseng is believed to be derived from two Chinese words signifying literally "likeness of man." The Asiatic plant, *Phanax schinseng*, is an aromatic perennial with five-lobed leaves and greenish flowers. The American plant, *Phanax quinquefolium*, is a different but somewhat similar species of the same genus. Some ginseng was used medicinally in the American colonies long before the Revolution. William Byrd of Westover wrote in his secret diary under date of December 23, 1710, that "Our daughter began to take drops of ginseng." Under date of June 30, 1711, Byrd wrote: "My wife slept very well and was much better this morning. The Doctor ordered her nothing but a bitter drink made of camomile flowers and ginseng root, which she was to drink morning and evening." Ginseng played an important part in opening trade between the United States and China. The first New England ship to sail for China, the sloop "Harriet," carried a cargo of ginseng and the captain traded it to an English captain for tea off the Cape of Good Hope. The "Empress of China," which sailed in 1784 and which is reputed to be the first American ship to reach China, also carried large quantities of ginseng. Soon after the Revolution Americans even on the western frontier were scouring the forests for this common woods plant for export to China. George Washington, on a visit to the Ohio country in 1784, noted in his diary: "In passing over the Mountains, I met numbers of Persons and Pack horses going in with Ginseng." Daniel Boone gathered sang, as it was called locally, in Kentucky and western Virginia, and in 1788 he took fifteen tons of ginseng up the Ohio for transshipment to Philadelphia. His boat capsized and the dried roots got wet, with the result that they brought a low price. The next year Boone recorded in his ledger that he had "15 caggs of ginsang" on hand. Before the Second World War, China got about twenty per cent of her ginseng from Korea, Manchuria and Japan and the rest from America. The United States normally exports about $1,000,000 worth of dried ginseng root to China every year. Chinese buyers have rather rigid standards for ginseng and will not accept just any kind of roots. The

wild root is considered more desirable by the Chinese than the cultivated and consequently it brings higher prices. American ginseng is a
slow-growing plant and under cultivation requires several years to produce roots of marketable size.

Do snakes live in Ireland?

There are no native snakes in Ireland. The viviparous lizard is the only
reptile found native on the Emerald Isle. Occasionally snakes are brought
into Ireland or escape from packages of imported foodstuffs. A few years
ago a small harmless snake less than two feet in length was found in
Dublin. It attracted so much attention that it was placed on exhibition
in the National Museum of Ireland in that city. Ireland is not peculiar
in being devoid of native snakes. The same is true of Hawaii, Iceland,
Crete, Malta, New Zealand and many other islands. In fact, there are
only a few species of very small snakes on the British Isles. According
to legend, St. Patrick banished all the snakes and toads from Ireland.
The legend is similar in significance to the dragon stories of the Orient
and symbolizes the conquest of good over evil and the triumph of
Christianity over paganism. In Christian art the patron saint of Ireland
is conventionally represented with a serpent at his feet. There is an
absurd belief that venomous reptiles cannot live on the Island and that
they perish when brought within a certain distance of the coast.

How did "laconic" originate?

Laconic means "brief," "concise," "pithy." It is an adjective formed
from Laconia, the name of an ancient Greek country of which Lacedaemon or Sparta was the capital. The Laconians and Spartans were
noted for their pointed, brusque and sententious speech. There is a
tradition that Philip of Macedon once sent the following message to
the city of Sparta: "If I enter Laconia, I will level Lacedaemon to the
ground." The city fathers sent back a reply containing the single word
"If." Caesar's Veni, vidi, vici ("I came, saw and conquered") is a classic
example of a laconic message.

What distinguishes a blond from a brunet?

Blond and brunet are relative terms. It is impossible to draw a sharp
distinction between them. Many persons have both blond and brunet
characteristics. Generally in such a classification the complexion of the
skin and the color of the hair and the eyes are taken into consideration.
A blond is a person with light or pale skin, light hair and blue or gray
eyes; a brunet is a person with dark or olive skin and brown or black

hair and eyes. *Blond* and *brunet,* both as adjectives and nouns, are still generally treated as French words. In that language *blond* and *brunet* are the masculine forms and *blonde* and *brunette* the feminine forms. When applied to men or to persons in general without reference to sex they are usually spelled *blond* and *brunet;* but when applied to women in particular they are usually spelled *blonde* and *brunette.*

What relation to you is your cousin's child?

Cousin is derived through French from Latin *consobrinus,* "the child of one's mother's sister." *Consobrinus* was formed from *con* and *soror* ("sister"). The term was used loosely for various degrees of relationship before it acquired its present meaning. At one time it signified little more than "kinsman" or "kinswomen." Formerly *cousin,* often shortened to *coz,* was widely used in England as a friendly term of address. Even English kings in olden times addressed the nobles and peers around them as *cousin* or *coz.* Now a cousin is one collaterally related by descent from a common ancestor, but not a brother or sister. Reckoning cousin relationships is simple if one starts out right. Children of brothers and sisters are *first cousins* to one another. Sometimes they are variously called "full cousins," "own cousins" or "cousins-german." The children of first cousins are *second cousins* to one another; children of second cousins are *third cousins* to one another, and so on. The child of one's first cousin is a *first cousin once removed;* the grandchild of one's first cousin is a *first cousin twice removed,* and so on. Vice versa, the cousin of one's father or mother is a first cousin once removed, etc. Confusion sometimes arises from the custom of some people who speak of the children and grandchildren of their first cousins as second and third cousins respectively, but the practice is only local. The correct and almost universal rule for reckoning cousinage is as given above.

What is the capital of Switzerland?

Bern is the political capital of the Swiss Confederation. Many people erroneously suppose that Geneva is. From the close of the Napoleonic Wars in 1815 until 1848 Bern, Zurich and Lucerne shared equally the honor of being the capital and the seat of government shifted from one to the other every two years. In 1848 a Federal law made Bern the sole political capital and designated it the permanent seat of the Swiss government and the place of residence of foreign Ministers accredited to Switzerland. *Bern* is a corruption of the German word for "bears." According to tradition the city was founded in 1191 A.D. by the German Duke Berthold V on a site where he had killed several bears while hunting. The image of a bear occurred in the earliest known coat of arms of the city and the bear is still the emblem of Bern. Pastries, candies, pipes, toilet articles and all sorts of things bearing the image of the bear are sold in shops in Bern, and the likeness of this animal figures in door knockers, gates, fountains and lampposts throughout the city. For centuries live bears have been kept on exhibition in pits at public expense. During the French Revolution the famous bears of Bern were taken as prisoners to Paris.

Who discovered that the earth is a sphere?

That the earth is a sphere was one of the discoveries made by Pythagoras, a Greek philosopher who lived in the sixth century B.C. The researches of Anaximander had prepared the way for the discovery, and the doctrine of the spherical form of the earth was taught by Parmenidies, who was associated with the Pythagoreans. Pythagoras himself clearly understood that the sun, moon and planets have motions of their own independent of the rotation of the earth. Plutarch attributed the discovery that the earth is a sphere to Thales of Miletus, who preceded Pythagoras by a generation, but it is now known that Thales, like his contemporaries, conceived the earth as a flat disk. In the time of Aristotle the arguments employed to demonstrate that the earth is a sphere were similar to those employed at the present time. The doctrine of the spherical form of the earth later became almost the exclusive property of the Italian schools, and it was not until long after the discovery of the New World by Columbus that it was accepted by people in general. A book entitled *The Metrical Lives of the Saints*, written by an English monk at the close of the thirteenth century, says: "As an appel the urthe is round, so that evermo half the urthe the sonne byschyneth, hou so hit evere go." Since the time of the Pergamene school of sculpture, which flourished two centuries before Christ, Atlas has been portrayed as supporting the heavens or the terrestrial globe on his shoulders. According to one mythological story, Atlas, as leader of the Titans, tried to storm heaven, and as a punishment for this rebellion Zeus compelled him to bear the vault of the heavens on his head and hands. But even in ancient times the terrestrial globe was often substituted for the canopy of the skies in portrayals of Atlas. A Roman statue made before the time of Hadrian shows Atlas kneeling and sustaining the globe on his head and shoulders. *Atlas* was first applied to a volume of maps by Gerhard Mercator (1512–1594), the Flemish mathematician and geographer, because a figure of Atlas supporting the heavens had been commonly used as a frontsipiece for such collections. The suggestion was that Mercator's book contained all the knowledge of the world between its two covers. During the so-called Dark Ages the knowledge that the earth is a globe was suppressed, and many scholars who knew the truth about its shape discussed the subject only among themselves for fear of persecution. In *Isaiah 40:22*, reference is made to "the circle of the earth," but this does not prove that the ancient Hebrew prophet conceived the earth as a globe. He might have used the same figure of speech if he had accepted the theory that the world is a flat disk.

What are the seven seas?

The *seven seas* is a figurative term denoting all the seas and oceans of the world. It is often explained that the seven seas are the Arctic, the Antarctic, the North and South Pacific, the North and the South Atlantic, and the Indian ocean. This explanation is purely imaginary. The term is not intended to be taken literally. It was part of the vernacular of several nations long before some of the oceans named were known to the inhabitants of Europe and Asia. The seven seas are referred to in the literature of the ancient Hindus, Chinese, Persians, Romans and other nations. In each case the term refers to different bodies of water. Sometimes it refers to mythical seas. To the Persians the seven seas were the streams forming the Oxus River; the Hindus applied the name to bodies of water in the Punjab. Near Venice, Italy, is a group of salt-water lagoons that the Romans called *septem maria*, the Latin phrase for "seven seas." In modern times the phrase *The Seven Seas* was popularized by Rudyard Kipling, who used it as the title of a volume of poems first published in 1896. The poet himself said the term might be regarded as referring to the seven oceans, although it was a very old figurative name for all the waters of the world.

Which is correct, "cent" or "penny"?

Penny is not the official and legal designation of any coin minted by the United States. It is merely a colloquial name for the American one-cent piece. *Penny*, however, has been applied to the American cent since the beginning of the United States coinage system. Until after the Revolution the English penny circulated freely in the United States. Although one-cent pieces had been previously issued by several of the states, *cent* as the official name of a national coin appeared for the first time in an act of Congress approved August 8, 1786. That law prescribed, "Cents: The highest copper piece, of which 100 shall be equal to the dollar." On October 16 of the same year Congress ordained, "That no foreign copper coin whatsoever, shall after the first day of September,

1787, be current within the United States of America." This law removed the English penny from circulation in the United States, but penny was transferred to the cent in popular usage and has tenaciously clung to it ever since. One reason for this is the fact that penny, which is derived from an ancient Teutonic root of unknown origin, is a more literary word than cent. Americans still use penny in such sayings as, "Penny-wise and pound-foolish," "A penny for your thoughts," and "turn an honest penny," and in such phrases as, "penny postage," "penny-in-the-slot machines," "penny whistle," "penny newspapers," and "penny ante." But in the United States the plural of penny is always pennies and never pence. An English penny is worth about two American cents, the English halfpenny being equivalent to the American cent.

Do earthworms turn into lightning bugs?

That earthworms turn into lightning bugs or fireflies is a common myth in some sections of the United States. No doubt this curious belief arose from the fact that the lightning bug or firefly is a species of beetle that passes through a larva stage. Adults, larvae and eggs are all luminous. Observation of the various species of glowworms may have contributed to the popular belief. None of these luminous creatures are closely related to the common earthworm.

If an earthworm is cut in two will the parts survive?

The power of earthworms to regenerate missing parts, though remarkable, is often exaggerated. For instance, it is repeatedly stated that a tail may grow a new head and a head may grow a new tail. That statement is only partially true. If an angleworm is cut in two near the middle the front half will usually regenerate another tail that will become normal in length as well as in other respects. The hind half, however, will generally produce a second tail at the mutilated end and the worm will have two tails and no head. Such a worm is incapable of ingesting food and will soon die. Only the fore part of an earthworm has the organs essential to continued life. The posterior portion contains merely part of the intestines, nerve cords, blood tubes, etc. These creatures have no lungs and breathe through their skin. When only a few of the front segments are cut off the injury is quickly repaired by the remaining part of the worm, although when as many as five or six anterior segments are removed the full number is seldom regenerated. Experiments show that earthworms cut in two behind the nineteenth segment rarely regenerate new heads. When such a posterior portion does regenerate a head the new head is likely to be defective. If a worm is cut in several parts

[465]

generally only the head end will survive, and then only when this part is not too short. Dr. Thomas H. Morgan, who made extensive researches in the regeneration of parts in earthworms, found no cases of survival of the head ends when the segments were as few as fifteen. When the reproductive organs are removed with the head, the hind part, should it regenerate a head, is incapable of reproduction. These organs lie from the ninth to the fifteenth segment, depending on the species, and once destroyed they cannot be regenerated. If the proper parts are selected, it is possible to graft pieces from several earthworms together to make one long worm. The power to regenerate missing parts is greater in many inferior creatures, such as the flat worms, than it is in common earthworms.

Who was the last British king to fight in battle?

George II, who was King of Great Britain from 1727 to 1760 and who regarded himself as a military genius, was the last British sovereign to take an active part in a military campaign and to participate in a battle. In 1708 at the age of twenty-five George fought at Oudenarde as Prince of Hanover. Upon the outbreak of the War of the Austrian Succession in 1741 he went to Germany in person and attempted to carry on the war according to his own notions. On June 27, 1743, he defeated a French army under Noailles at Dettingen in Bavaria. That was the last battle in which a king of England fought. Soon after he capitulated to the French at Fort Necessity, in the spring of 1754, George Washington, then twenty-two years old, wrote a letter to his younger brother, John Augustine, in which he said: "I have heard the bullets whistle; and, believe me, there is something charming in the sound." This letter somehow found its way to London, where it was printed with appropriate comments by Horace Walpole. When it came to the attention of George II the hero of Dettingen is said to have observed: "He has not heard many of them or he would not think them very charming."

How do shears and scissors differ?

In the United States *shears* and *scissors* are often used interchangeably. As a rule, however, *shears* is employed when the implement is large and *scissors* when it is small. All such instruments having a total length of six inches or less are called scissors in the hardware trade; those exceeding six inches in length are called shears. In Scotland all sizes are called shears, the word *scissors* being seldom used. The Oxford dictionary says: "The larger instruments of this kind, especially those which are too large to be manipulated with one hand, are called shears." Thus we speak of *sheep shears* and *pruning shears*. *Scissors*, since the term is applied to a single implement, is sometimes construed as singular, although it is plural in form. It is correct to say "the scissors *are* sharp" or "the scissors *is* sharp," but the former is preferred. The word was written in the plural form and construed as a plural as early as 1384. *Pair of scissors* is recorded as early as the fifteenth century.

Which is correct, "these" or "this" molasses?

Molasses is derived through Spanish from Latin *mellaceus*, "honey-like." Since the singular and plural forms are spelled the same, the word is often construed as a plural when it should be construed as a singular. *Molasses are, these molasses* and *those molasses* are common expressions, especially in the South and West. They are incorrect except in those rare cases when the speaker or writer has in mind different kinds of molasses and really desires to use the word in the plural. "These molasses are good" is not correct when the speaker refers to molasses in a container on the breakfast table. The correct expression, of course, is, "This molasses is good." On the other hand, it would be technically correct, though awkward, for a merchant to write, "Please send me ten gallons each of those two molasses I ordered last year," when he refers to different kinds or brands of the product.

Where is the Valley of Ten Thousand Smokes?

The Valley of Ten Thousand Smokes lies beyond Mount Katmai on the Alaskan mainland across Shelikof Strait from Kodiak Island. From the floor of this remarkable valley millions of columns of steam ascend constantly. The vents through which the steam escapes disclose incrustations of great beauty, variety and color. There are masses of bright yellow sulphur, red and blue ash and pure white siliceous material. It is possible to cook food over these steam jets, although it is necessary to hold down the vessel against the uprising steam. In the valley is a natural bathing pool one end of which is cool and the other hot. The first explorations around Mount Katmai and in the Valley of Ten Thousand Smokes was made in 1916 by the National Geographic Society. During the second administration of President Wilson this region was set aside as a national monument.

What is spontaneous combustion?

Spontaneous combustion is the ignition of a combustible material without the application of external heat or flame. The self-generated heat produced by cotton soaked in oil and confined in a poorly ventilated

[467]

room sometimes becomes sufficient to ignite the cotton. Fires started by spontaneous combustion are common in coal mines, owing chiefly to the rapid oxidation of coal dust when it comes in contact with air. Damp or improperly cured hay, especially of the legume variety, is particularly subject to self-generated heat. If a pile is large enough to afford the necessary insulation the self-generated heat will proceed to such a temperature that a small amount of air filtering into the pile will produce self-ignition. It is generally believed that the initial heat is generated by the fermentation of micro-organisms, such a bacteria, yeasts and molds, which multiply rapidly in damp hay, grain, manure and other vegetable products and which are killed by their own heat at a temperature somewhere in the neighborhood of 160 degrees Fahrenheit. The subsequent higher temperature required to ignite the substance may be the result of purely chemical processes. Although the theories seeking to explain spontaneous combustion in damp vegetable matter are legion, very little is actually known of the exact cause of this phenomenon.

How long do elephants live?

It is difficult to obtain accurate information as to the extreme age reached by elephants in the wild state. There is no positive evidence that an elephant has ever lived more than seventy or seventy-five years either in captivity or the wild state, although it is supposed that occasionally one may live to an age of ninety-five or one hundred. The age reached by animals in captivity is not always a good criterion of their natural life span because food and temperature are much more regular under such conditions. Dr. W. Reid Blair, director of the New York Zoological Park, says the extreme life span of animals may be estimated with a fair degree of accuracy by multiplying by four or five the number of years that the young of the species requires to reach maturity. In a general way the age cycle of elephants corresponds to that of human beings. They reach maturity at about twenty-five and begin to get old at sixty or sixty-five. It is probable, however, that man has a longer life span than any other mammal.

What is New Jersey tea?

New Jersey tea is the popular name of Ceanothus americanus, a white-flowered plant that grows abundantly in the northeastern part of the United States. The name arose from the fact that the Indians and early settlers, particularly in New Jersey, used the plant to make a drink. From the roots, which contain a red coloring matter, the Indians made a tea supposed to have medicinal properties, it being regarded by them as especially good for curing fevers. There is a tradition that some of the American colonists used this plant as a substitute for tea to avoid paying the British tax on imported tea.

What is meant by cleaning the Augean stables?

Augeas (pronounced aw-jee-us) was a legendary king of Elis in Greece who possessed a herd of three thousand sacred oxen whose stalls had not been cleaned for thirty years. The cleaning of these stables in a single day was the sixth of the twelve difficult and dangerous labors imposed upon Hercules by Eurystheus, King of Argolis. Hercules, who was promised a tenth part of the cattle in payment, succeeded in performing the task within the required time by turning the rivers Alpheus and Peneus through the stables. Augeas refused to turn over one-tenth of the oxen to Hercules on the ground that he had carried out the commission only in the service of Eurystheus, whereupon Hercules sent an army into Elis and slew Augeas and his sons. Cleaning or purging the Augean stables means to clean away an accumulated mass of corruption or filth. Figuratively, he who reforms abuses almost past the power of man to remedy is said to clean the Augean stables.

Who were the druids?

The druids were the priests, bards, prophets and wise men among the ancient Celts in Gaul, Britain and Ireland. Owing to their practice of teaching orally and forbidding any written records very little is known about them. All their ritual and teachings were committed to memory. Besides expounding religion the druids were magicians and astrologers and were versed in the alleged mysterious powers of plants and animals. The oak tree was especially sacred to them and their ceremonies were often performed in the midst of an oak grove. Some authorities suppose that *druid* is derived from an ancient Celtic word meaning *oakmen*. "Among the Celts and Gaul," wrote Sir James G. Frazer in *The Golden Bough*, "the druids esteemed nothing more sacred than the mistletoe and the oak on which it grew; they chose groves of oaks for the scene of their solemn service, and they performed none of their rites without oak leaves." Others derive *druid* from ancient Celtic *druidh*, signifying man of learning and still surviving in the sense of a magician, wizard or diviner. These theories are not inconsistent, for the oak men may have been associated with magicians at an early date. Legend has it that the Celts and their priesthood were the posterity of Japheth, one of the sons of Noah, and that they migrated from Asia to Europe as early as

[469]

2000 B.C., first settling in Ireland, whence they spread to Britain and France. When the Romans invaded Britain the druids still existed in Wales and parts of France and seem to have been divided into different orders with distinct functions. One of the best accounts of them is that given by Julius Caesar in his *Commentaries*. The druids opposed the Romans and incited the people to rebel against the invaders. They were finally driven from the country, taking refuge and making their last stand on the island of Anglesey in the Irish Sea off the coast of North Wales, where most of them were exterminated by a Roman army under Agricola. Many stone structures in Britain, such as Stonehenge, were long thought to have been built by the druids, but these are now known to have been constructed in prehistoric times, although the druids may have used them to impress the populace with their mystic rites.

What is the Grand Bank?

The Grand Bank is a great shoal in the Atlantic Ocean lying about one hundred miles off the southeast coast of Newfoundland and famous throughout the world as a fishing ground. *Bank* in this connection means an undersea elevation that produces a shoal, shelf or shallow. The Grand Bank is also variously called *Grand Banks*, *Great Bank* and *Great Banks*. It has an area about the size of Pennsylvania. The bank is about 300 miles long, lies less than 600 feet below sea level and projects southeast from the Newfoundland coast toward the center of the Atlantic. Geologists suppose it to be the remnant of an ancient submerged mountain range. The bottom in this region is covered with fine mud and sand and the meeting of two currents brings in an endless supply of diatoms and algae, which supply food for crustaceans and mollusks and other types of invertebrates, and these latter in turn fatten the hosts of codfish that swim in from the deeper water in May and June. Enormous hordes of sardine-like fish known as capelin, which settle upon the sandy bottom to spawn, act as heralds for the codfish. Vessels regularly fishing in the Grand Bank of Newfoundland are called Grand Bankers.

What is a drumhead court-martial?

Any summary trial is now sometimes called a drumhead court-martial. Originally the name was given only to a summary and hasty court-martial called to try an offense committed on the battlefield or during a march. Most of the forms and ceremonies are dispensed with on such occasions; in other words, it is a kind of military lynch law. The name comes from the fact that formerly such courts-martial were often conducted around a drum used as a table. A court-martial is a trial conducted under military law, which is a code of rules and regulations prescribed for the government of the Army, Navy or militia when in active service. In the United States Army there are three kinds of courts-martial, summary, special and general. The punishment power of summary and special military courts is limited by statute, while the punishment power of a general military court is usually left to the discretion of the court. A member of the armed forces of the United States is under the jurisdiction of the civil authorities in respect to civil crimes. He is subject to court-martial under the military law only when he commits a military offense.

What are rhinestones?

Rhinestones are artificial colorless gems of high luster and cut to imitate diamonds. Their chief use is in the manufacture of cheap jewelry and accordingly false jewelry itself is sometimes referred to as rhinestone. Rhinestones were so named because they were first made along the Rhine River of a composition known as *strass*, which was a vitreous or glasslike paste invented by and named after Joseph Strasser, a German jeweler. The original rhinestones consisted of a silicate of potassium and lead, combined with borax, alumina and white arsenic. A greenish film forms on true rhinestones when they come into contact with copper or brass. This covering can be removed with a weak solution of muratic acid, which will not affect the rhinestone but may cause any metal around it to loosen.

What is meant by Plimsoll's mark?

Plimsoll's mark consists of a disk and letters painted in white on the outside of a British ship's hull to indicate the limit to which the vessel may be loaded at various seasons in salt and in fresh water. It is, in other words, a "load line." Plimsoll's mark was named for Samuel Plimsoll (1824–1898), a British statesman, who was noted for his load line reforms and who became known as the "sailor's friend" because of his efforts to get Parliament to pass legislation for the protection of seamen. His reforms were directed particularly against what he called "coffin ships," that is, overloaded and unseaworthy vessels in which unscrupulous owners, protected by heavy insurance, risked the lives of the crews every time they put to sea. The act requiring Plimsoll's mark was passed in 1876. Other nations soon followed suit in adopting similar protective measures and the merchant ships of nearly all countries are now required by law to bear a line on the outside of the vessel to show the depth to which it should sink when properly loaded. In 1930 the International Load Line Convention was signed in London. By 1941, when this convention was temporarily suspended because of war conditions, thirty-six countries had become parties to it. This convention provided for the placing of load lines on merchant ships engaged on international voyages.

Is a zebra a light animal with dark stripes or a dark animal with light stripes?

The ground color of the body of a zebra is a pale, yellowish brown and the stripes are black or dark brown. When the zebra and the ass are crossed the light tan predominates as the basic body color in the offspring. Therefore, in reply to this proverbial question, it may be said that the zebra is a light brown animal with black or dark brown stripes. The zebra, like the ass, is a member of the horse family. It is not a domestic animal, but, with considerable difficulty, it can be trained for riding and driving.

What is the Iron Gate in the Danube?

The famous Iron Gate in the Danube is not a gate at all. That is merely the picturesque name given by the Turks to a gorge or pass where the river has cut its way through a spur of the Transylvanian Alps a few miles below the city of Orsova in Rumania. A real gate of iron could not have more effectively prevented the passage of Turkish fleets up the Danube than the dangerous rapids and massive rocks that obstructed the narrow channel for nearly two miles. In 1890 a Hungarian company began the removal of many of the boulders and other obstructions by a series of great blasting operations. The river through the Iron Gate (or the Iron Gates as it is also called) was declared open for navigation in 1896. Before that it was customary for Danube steamers to transfer their passengers at the Iron Gate. Roman geographers had divided the Danube into two sections—Danuvius, above the Iron Gate, and Ister, below it. In the time of Tamerlane, a narrow defile near the banks of the Amu River in Asia was known to the Tartars as the Iron Gate, and it is possible that the Turks borrowed the name and applied it to the dangerous gorge in the Danube.

Where in America can one see the Atlantic and Pacific?

Both the Pacific Ocean and the Caribbean Sea, which is regarded as part of the North Atlantic, can be seen on a clear day from the summit of Mount Izaru, an active volcano in Costa Rica. That is believed to be the only point in the Americas of which this can be truthfully said. Cartago, one of the oldest cities in Central America, lies at the base of

Mount Izaru, which has an altitude of 11,200 feet. In 1723 much damage was done to the city by water released from the crater by an earthquake.

What is the plural of "ski"?

The plural of *ski* is either *ski* or *skis*. Frequently the plural is erroneously written *skiis*, owing no doubt to the fact that the double *i* occurs in *skiing*, the present participial form. *Ski*, also spelled *skee* in English, is of Scandinavian origin. Americans almost universally pronounce the word *skee*, but the British generally follow the Scandinavians in pronouncing it *shee*. The user of skis is a *skier*. The winter sport in which a person on skis is drawn over the snow or ice by a horse is called *skijoring*, from a Norwegian phrase literally meaning "ski-doing."

Does a drowned man float face down and a woman face up?

There is a popular belief that the body of a drowned man floats face down and that of a drowned woman face up. The belief, however, is not confirmed by observation. Lifeguards who have seen hundreds of drowned persons say if it holds true in some cases it is probably owing to the difference in the wearing apparel customarily worn by men and women.

What is quartered oak?

Quartered oak is oak lumber that has been quartersawed. It is not, like bird's-eye maple, a wood with a peculiar grain. In order to produce the quarter-grain effect the oak log is first cut into quarters and then boards are sawed by cutting alternately from each face of the quarter. Such lumber not only shows the grain advantageously but does not warp or check as much as lumber sawed in the customary manner. White quartered oak is commonly used in the manufacture of office chairs.

Why are opals considered unlucky?

The origin of the superstition that the opal is an unlucky stone and will bring misfortune and ill luck to its owner is obscure. Among the ancients the opal was prized above most other precious stones. According to Pliny, a Roman senator named Nonius had a large and beautiful opal that he valued at the equivalent of five thousand dollars. Nonius preferred exile to letting the gem fall into the hands of Mark Antony. Some writers believe the superstition about opals being unlucky dates back only to the fourteenth century, when they were unfavorably associated with the Black Death. In those days it was said in Italy, particularly Venice, that such gems worn by persons stricken with the plague suddenly turned brilliant and then lost their luster when the owner died. Others believe it originated in the mythology of Scandinavia. The *Edda* tells of a Norse god who fashioned a gem from the eyes of children. This gem was called *yarkstein* and may have been the opal. *Opal* is believed to be derived from a Greek word meaning a gem or precious stone, which appears to have been associated with the eye among the Greeks. One supposition is that the opal became associated with ill luck because, like the evil eye, it invaded the privacy of the wearer. The association of the opal with the eyeballs persisted for centuries. During the reign of Queen Elizabeth a man named Batman wrote: "The optallius keepeth and saveth the eye of him that bear and dimmeth other men's eyes so that it in a manner maketh them blind, so that they may not see what is done before them, so that it is said to be the patron of thieves." Much of the modern superstition no doubt owes its origin to Sir Walter Scott's story entitled *Anne of Geierstein*, published in 1829, where the opal is represented as an unlucky stone inviting misfortune and unhappiness to the possessor. Scott may have been author of the superstition. At any rate, since that time the opal has been regarded as unlucky and superstitious people refuse to wear it. This prejudice against the opal became a real obstacle to its commercial distribution. It was a favorite of Queen Victoria who did much to reinstate the stone in public favor. She demonstrated her preference for the gem in many ways, partly no doubt in the interests of her subjects in Australia where fine opals are produced. When an opal mine was opened in that country the British Queen wore some of the stones in an effort to popularize them. Only a generation ago an Australian firm, because of the superstition, undertook to exploit opals under the name *iridots*, which was suggested by the Greek word meaning "rainbow."

What is the color of Negro babies at birth?

That the Negro enters the world with a skin as light as that of the Caucasian is a common notion. Frequently travelers refer to the faintly colored newly born children of the black race. In 1911 Eliezer Edwards, in *Words, Facts and Phrases*, quoted Sir R. Phillips as having written: "The children of the blackest Africans are born white. In a month they become pale yellow; in a year brown; at four years, dirty black, and at thirty, glossy black. The blood of blacks and whites is of the same colour. The colouring matter of blacks is supposed to be due to bilious secretions in the mucous membranes underneath the cuticle." There used to be a common belief that Negro babies are born white with the exception of a black band around the body and that the rest of the skin turns black a short time after birth. As a matter of fact even the newly born infants of the white race are not really light in color. Generally Caucasian children are reddish or pinkish when born, although the exact hue varies widely. The children of the darker races are lighter at birth than their parents, and the colored child of very light parents may be indistinguishable from a white child so far as color is concerned; but, ordinarily, colored children enter the world noticeably pigmented and many of them are quite dark from the beginning. One authority says Negro babies at birth are bluish white, while white babies at birth are pinkish white. The pigment in the skin is similar to that of freckles and develops only after the baby is exposed to light. As a rule the color of Negro babies deepens for several years, especially in the case of those born light. It seldom happens, however, that a newly born colored child has the deep black color of the typical full-blooded adult. Decided pigmentation first appears on the ears, breast and a belt across the lower part of the back. Often it is necessary to refer to these characteristic markings to distinguish the newly born children of Caucasians from those of the darker races.

What is a hoop snake?

One of the most persistent snake myths in the United States deals with reptiles known as the stinging snake or hoop snake. This snake, according to the belief, has a venomous stinger in its tail that works like that of a wasp. The snake, it is said, forms itself into a hoop by putting its tail in its mouth and rolls along like a wheel. It travels with incredible swiftness and when it gets close enough to a victim it lets go of its tail and drives the stinger into the object of its attack. If the victim dodges, according to the myth, and a tree is struck instead, the tree is sure to die. One version has it that the hoop snake is inflated and that it is luminous at night. Another version says the reptile squirts a venomous fluid from its tail. These pranks of the hoop snake are purely mythical, although believed in by thousands of people. In fact there are hundreds of persons who are willing to testify that they have seen hoop snakes perform these feats. There is no snake that rolls along like a hoop, and there is no species of snake with a stinger in its tail. The little snake known as hoop snake, or horn snake, is perfectly harmless. Similar stories are told of the wampum snake, which is also harmless. The real hoop snake is bluish-black with a few red bars across the belly, and its tail tapers to a fine point having the appearance of a horn or spike, but it is quite incapable of piercing or stinging anything. That any snake could place its tail in its mouth and roll along like a wheel is manifestly absurd, and taking into consideration the anatomical peculiarities of the vertebral column it is clearly impossible. The earliest known report of the stinging snake was published more than two hundred and fifty years ago in a *Report to the Lords Proprietors of the Carolinas*, in which it is stated that there lived in the Carolinas a snake the tail of which was a poisoned horn or spike. John Clayton also mentioned this myth in a letter to the Royal Society of London in 1688. The locusts seen in the vision on Patmos by St. John the Divine, according to *Revelation* 9:10, "had tails like unto scorpions, and there were stings in their tails."

How is "Staten" in "Staten Island" pronounced?

Staten, the name of an island in New York Bay, is often incorrectly pronounced with the *a* long as in *state*. It is correctly pronounced *statt*-en. The *a* is short as in *static*. This pronunciation is a holdover from the old Dutch name of the island. When Europeans first explored New York Bay, Staten Island was inhabited by a branch of the Raritan Indians. Henry Hudson and the early Dutch called it *Staaten Eylandt* "Island of the States"—after the States-General, the parliament of the Netherlands, which was popularly referred to as *Staaten*, "the States." In 1630, while Peter Minuit was director of New Netherland, the Dutch West India Company purchased the island from the Indians, giving in exchange "some kettles, axes, hoes, wampum, drilling awls, jew's-harps and divers small wares," worth a total of only twenty-four dollars, and granted it to Michael Pauw. As early as 1654 the island was called *Staaten Eylandt* in the court minutes of New Amsterdam. The Dutch explorers who first rounded Cape Horn had already given the name to an island off the coast of Tierra del Fuego. When the Duke of York came into possession of New Netherland in 1664 he gave all that part of his province west of the Hudson to the proprietors of New Jersey, who thus acquired Staten Island. In 1668, however, the Duke of York changed his mind and decided that all islands in New York Bay that could be circumnavigated within twenty-four hours should belong to New York. Captain Christopher Bilopp made the voyage around Staten Island, which has an area of fifty-seven square miles, within the required time and was given a tract of land on the island for his services. After the Revolution, New York and New Jersey both claimed jurisdiction of this island and New Jersey did not finally give up her claim until the nineteenth century. It is generally supposed that the first permanent settlement on the island was made by the Dutch at Oude Dorp in 1639. According to a humorous story, Peter Stuyvesant gave Staten Island its name by accident. Seeing land in the distance upon his arrival at New Amsterdam, he asked: "Vaht ist tat?" "Tat ist an island," replied one of the city fathers. "Ist tat an Island?" queried the cork-legged governor, and it was called Staten Island ever after by the Dutch.

Can horses sleep while standing?

Horses have the power to sleep while standing. In 1943 Professor C. F. Winchester, member of the animal husbandry faculty at the University of Missouri, said that experiments indicate that horses rest better on their feet than on their sides. Their legs are provided with muscular mechanisms that cause them to "lock," as it were, and permit the animals to rest somewhat as if they were standing on stilts. When a standing horse is unconscious there is no direct brain control over the muscles essential to the maintenance of an erect posture. The muscles in the legs, back and chest are controlled by the reflex actions of the spinal cord. In a similar manner a bird sleeping on a swaying limb maintains a reflex balance while its consciousness is in abeyance. Horses sleeping while standing occasionally, though rarely, fall down. More often certain muscles in the forelegs relax suddenly and the horse knuckles over onto the fetlocks and then immediately catches itself. Horses sometimes go for months without lying down. It is astonishing how little lying-down rest they require. Yet a horse left to itself will sleep, standing up or lying down, eight or ten hours a day. This is true also of other Herbivora, including elephants. An Indian elephant often will feed eighteen or twenty hours and then rest and sleep only one or two. It is said that they have been known to remain standing even after they were dead. When horses lie down to sleep their eyes usually remain open or partly open and they sleep so lightly that they are awakened by the faintest sound. They seldom lie long in the same position because their great weight cramps their muscles and prevents the under lung from functioning.

What causes pounding in hot-water pipes?

The pounding and banging in hot-water and steam pipes is called water hammer or hydraulic shock. This snapping noise is produced by moving water thrown against the sides of the pipes when hot steam comes in contact with cooler water and condenses suddenly. A clanking sound is produced when a water pipe is hit with a hammer. Water is incompressible and acts like a hammer when a valve is closed. Flowing water rams against a closed valve and rattles the pipe as if it were a rod of solid metal. Water hammer may be caused by various conditions.

[477]

Early in the morning when steam is suddenly turned into cold pipes water hammer is almost unavoidable. Usually, however, it is caused by some defect in the heating system, such as a radiator tipped the wrong way, by a partly closed valve or by high pressure. There are on the market mechanical devices designed to eliminate water hammer.

What does "savvy" mean?

Savvy or savvey is an American corruption of Spanish sabe, a form of the verb saber, meaning "to know." "Do you savvy?" is equivalent to Spanish "¿Sabe Usted?" Both mean, "Do you know?" Savvy was originally acquired from the Mexicans by early ranchers in the Southwest who spelled and pronounced the word savvy rather than sabe because in Spanish b and v are pronounced almost alike and in many words are used interchangeably. When employed as a noun savvy means understanding, mental grasp or knowledge of affairs. Of course it is slang in all senses.

Do crows fly in a straight line?

It is commonly believed that the crow flies forward in a straight line. Hence the phrase as the crow flies, meaning in a straight line from starting point to the objective or place of destination, irrespective of buildings, rivers, roads, hills or any obstacles that might make the distance greater if a person were to travel it on foot or by vehicle. The saying, however, is the result of careless observation, for the crow does not usually fly forward in a straight line but zigzags considerably. Sometimes the shortest and quickest route from one point to another is called a beeline, referring to the fact that a bee flies in a direct or almost direct line when seeking its hive. The Bee Line Highway is a thoroughfare connecting Kansas City, Missouri, and Canon City, Colorado, being the shortest ground route between those two points.

How did "kibitzer" originate?

A kibitzer is a person who meddles in the affairs of other people, particularly one who, while not a player himself, watches a card game from behind the players and gives unasked for advice. By extension the term is applied to any individual who is always ready to give advice on any subject whether he knows anything about it or not. Kibitzer is derived through Yiddish from colloquial German Kiebitz, the name of the Old World bird variously known in English as lapwing, peewit and green plover. This bird, it is said, not only stands around in the fields and watches farmers work, but by its shrill cry scares game away upon the approach of hunters. Accordingly in the sixteenth century card players in Germany applied the term to meddlesome spectators, particularly on-lookers at card games who by their comment annoyed the players and gave their opponents information. It is supposed that *kiebitz* was imita-tive in origin and was suggested by the bird's characteristic call.

What are the Seven Wonders of the World?

The Seven Wonders of the World is the name given to a group of re-markable works of art and engineering that were popular among the ancients. It is supposed that the first list of the seven wonders of the world was prepared in the second century B.C. by Antipater of Sidon. A second and slightly different list occurs in a treatise entitled *The Seven Wonders of the World*. This treatise has been included in the works of Philo of Byzantium, who also lived about the second century B.C., but it is now believed it was written much later, probably in the sixth century A.D. The generally accepted list of the seven wonders of the ancient world is as follows: the pyramids of Egypt; the hanging gardens of Semir-amis at Babylon; the temple of Diana at Ephesus; the statue of Zeus by Phidias at Olympus; the tomb of Mausolus erected by his wife Artemisia at Halicarnassus; the Pharos (lighthouse and watchtower) at Alexandria, and the Colossus of Rhodes. Since the list of the Seven Wonders of the World took form other lists of seven wonders have been suggested in imitation of the original; as, the seven wonders of the Middle Ages, the seven wonders of the modern world, the seven natural wonders of the world, etc., but these lists are continually changing and have no per-manent value. The wonders of the ancient world were probably restricted to seven because of the sacred and symbolical significance of that number.

How did "bunk" originate?

The original form of this word was *Buncombe*, which has been cor-rupted into *bunkum* and *bunk*. It originated in the United States House of Representatives on February 25, 1820, at the close of the historic debate on the Missouri Compromise. Felix Walker, a naïve old moun-taineer, represented the North Carolina district including Buncombe County. He was known among his colleagues as the "Old Oil Jug" be-cause of his gift of gab. When the House was otherwise almost unani-mous in demanding a vote on the question, Walker insisted on making a speech. Several members gathered around him and begged him to desist. He attempted to continue, however, declaring that he was not talking to the House, but that his constituents expected him to say some-thing on the subject and that he was bound to "make a speech for

Buncombe." The *Annals of Congress* reported at the time that "the question was called for so clamorously and so persistently that Mr. Walker could proceed no farther than to move that the Committee rise." *Buncombe* came to mean any humbug or claptrap, especially insincere and bombastic political talk intended for the galleries. As early as 1828 a writer in *Niles' Weekly Register* observed that *talking for Buncombe* "is an old common saying at Washington, when a member of Congress is making one of those hum-drum and unlistened-to 'long talks' which have lately become so fashionable—not with the hope of being heard in the House, but to afford an enlightened representative a pretence for sending a copy of his speech to his constituents." The term quickly spread to the entire English-speaking world. Thomas Carlyle used *Buncombe* and Charles Kingsley *bunkum*. Buncombe County was created in 1791, and was named for Edward Buncombe, a colonel in the Continental Army, who was wounded at Germantown in 1777 and who died a prisoner of war in Philadelphia the next year. *Debunk*, meaning "to divest of bunk," was coined by W. E. Woodward, the American author, who first used it in a book entitled *Bunk*, published in 1923.

Where is the city of St. John's in British America?

Three cities with similar names in British North America are frequently confused in the United States. St. John's is not in Canada. It is the capital and most populous city of Newfoundland, which is not part of Canada either geographically or politically. *St. Johns*, written without the sign of the possessive, is the name of a small town on the Richelieu in the Canadian province of Quebec. *St. John*, which is spelled without a final *s*, is the name of the most populous city in the province of New Brunswick.

Does the pilot snake pilot other snakes?

The pilot snake, *Elaphe obsoleta*, gets its popular name from the curious belief that it precedes rattlesnakes and warns them of the approach of danger. According to one version of the belief, the pilot snake is neither male nor female, but a "neuter" rattlesnake that devotes its time to piloting other snakes around. Another version of the belief is that the pilot snake, which is also known as the "companionate snake" or the "rattler's companion," is a hybrid resulting from a cross between the rattlesnake and the bull snake. Of course, this is all mythical. The two reptiles are structurally quite different and it is highly improbable that the two species would interbreed. Besides, rattlesnakes give birth to living young, while bull snakes lay eggs. The odd belief that gave the pilot snake its popular name probably arose from the fact that members of this species are frequently found in the vicinity of rattlesnakes. Members of the two species are often seen basking in the sunshine close together. It is unlikely that they are brought together because of any fraternal feelings for one another. In all probability the two species are entirely indifferent to each other and are found in the same vicinity occasionally simply because they see similar places to bask in the sunshine. The pilot snake or "pilot black snake" is a sluggish tree climber and is found chiefly in mountainous regions, whence it is often known as the "mountain black snake." It is a rat snake and the pitchy black upper surface of the species resembles that of the black snake or racer, but its luster is glossy rather than satiny and the skin has white edges on the scales when stretched.

What is a white elephant?

So-called white elephants are merely albinistic Indian elephants in which much of the usual dark pigment is absent from the skin, giving it a pale gray or yellowish color. Figuratively *white elephant* means a dignity or possession that is costly to maintain and that yields no profit. A person having such property is said to have "a white elephant on his hands." Some authorities say the phrase alludes to the white elephants formerly presented by the King of Siam (Thailand) to members of his court whom he wished to impoverish and ruin. Since the white elephant was sacred, the courtier would have to have it kept accordingly; yet to do so would reduce him to poverty. There is, however, no evidence that a King of Siam ever presented a courtier or nobleman with a white elephant, and it is not likely that one ever did so. The story seems to be a perversion of a few simple facts. Among various peoples white was not only symbolical of purity but was considered the sacred color. In Siam, Burma, Cambodia, Indo-China, Sumatra, Ceylon, parts of India and southern Ethiopia there is a cult of the white elephant. Its adherents believe that a white elephant contains the soul of a dead person, possibly in some cases an ancient god. In former times when a white elephant was captured the capturer was highly rewarded and the animal was baptized, feted, worshiped and kept as a sacred beast. The death of such an animal was mourned like that of a human being. The Plains Indians had a similar attitude toward a white or albino buffalo. The King of Ava in Upper Burma used to be styled the "Lord of the White Elephants" and the royal herd of sacred white elephants was fed in troughs of silver, and in state processions the animals were decorated with priceless gems. The white or albino elephant, being very rare, was also particularly prized and venerated in Siam, which is known as the "Land of the White Elephant" and whose flag and coat of arms contains the figure of such an animal. In 1861 the "Order of the White Elephant" was organized in Siam. The emblem of this civil and military order consisted of a medallion showing a white elephant surrounded with wreaths and surmounted by a gold pagoda crown. A white elephant was never given to a nobleman, the King alone being deemed worthy to own such a creature, and anyone in the country finding a white elephant, whether noble or commoner, was in duty bound to present it to the sovereign. The notion of a white elephant being an expensive burden was doubtlessly derived from the fact that such an elephant was never put to work, but was maintained in a special stable with its own keepers at considerable cost, and brought in no return beyond being regarded as a symbol of the royal dignity and an ornament to the state. The white elephant is no longer regarded as sacred in Siam. In 1863 P. T. Barnum, the famous showman, bought a so-called white elephant in Siam. By the time he had gotten it to the United States it had cost him about two hundred thousand dollars.

Who were the tailors of Tooley Street?

While George Canning (1770–1827) was Prime Minister of England, several tailors met in a house on Tooley Street, London, for the purpose of redressing popular grievances. They drew up a petition to the House of Commons that began with the words, "We, the people of England." There is a difference of opinion regarding the number of names on the petition, some authorities saying two, others three, and still others nine. At any rate, it transpired that they were all names of tailors living on Tooley Street. Thus the phrase *tailors of Tooley Street* came to be applied to any demogogic or pettifogging clique who have the notion that they represent the people. *Tooley* as the name of a street in London is a corruption of *St. Olaf*, which was first corrupted into *'T-olaf*, then *Tolay*, and finally *Tooley*.

Why is the guinea pig so called?

The name of the guinea pig, which is a native of South America, is one of the unsolved mysteries of etymology. Several plausible theories have been advanced to account for the name. The most popular theory holds that *guinea* here is merely a corruption of *Guiana*, which arose from the fact that early writers confused Guiana in South America with Guinea in Africa. But there is positive evidence that in 1607 this animal was called *pig cony*. This led to the second theory, namely, that *guinea* is a corruption of *cony*. According to the third theory, *guinea* in the name does not refer to the region in Africa, but was applied, as it seems to have been in several other instances, to designate an animal that came from an unknown country. A fourth theory suggests that the guinea pig may have been so named because it was supposed to resemble the young of the Guinea hog. Still another theory is that this rodent was first carried from South America to England by Guineamen engaged in the slave trade. Scientists believe the domestic guinea pig is descended from the restless cavy of Guiana and Brazil. It is a stout, short-tailed, short-eared rodent about seven inches long. Because guinea pigs have a life cycle of only about four years and produce young five or six times a year they have been widely used in biological experiments of various kinds, although for this purpose guinea pigs have been largely supplanted by rats and mice. Baby guinea pigs possess their second set of teeth at birth and are able to nibble grain when only forty-eight hours old. It is said that a guinea pig will live about as long without water as with it. Ellis Parker Butler's sketch entitled Pigs Is Pigs, published in 1906, dealt with the amazing fecundity of guinea pigs.

Why is there more lightning in summer?

Electrical storms are generated by sudden and decided changes in atmospheric temperature. The upper atmosphere is always cold and such changes are much less frequent in the winter time, when the temperature near the earth is also low. Hence thunder and lightning occur more often in summer than in winter.

Will the milk of all mammals produce butter?

The milk of all mammals, including the human species, contains a fatty constituent similar to the butter in cow's milk, and, to quote the United States Bureau of Dairy Industry, "there is no reason to believe that butter could not be made from the milk of any mammal," although there might be difficulty in obtaining the butter from the milk of some animals on account of the smallness of the fat globules. For instance, camel's milk, which is delicious and wholesome, contains considerable butterfat, but it will not yield butter in appreciable quantities no matter how long or violently it is churned, because the fat globules are so small that they cannot be separated by simply agitating the milk. The same is true of the milk of horses and most other mammals. As a matter of fact the milk of only a few species of animals, such as cattle, goats and water buffaloes, can be churned successfully for butter. It is supposed that churning cow's milk for butter was originally suggested by the occurrence of this substance in the leather bags of milk carried over the desert on camel back by the Arabs. Even at the present time some of the Arabs make a rancid butter from camel's milk by pouring the cream into a goatskin sack and shaking it continually until the butter is formed. Nearly ten quarts of cow's milk are required on the average to make a pound of butter.

How did "passing the buck" originate?

This expression, which means shifting responsibility, originated in the cardroom. In various card games a counter or marker is placed on the table before one of the players to remind him of his turn to deal. This marker, which is to prevent mistakes as to the position of the deal, is called the *buck* and is passed from player to player as the turn to deal goes around. In poker a marker is sometimes put into a jack pot, another jack pot being in order when the deal passes to the player having the buck. Thus to pass the buck to another player obligates the dealer to ante for another jack pot. From this circumstance *to pass the buck* came to mean to shift the responsibility to someone else.

When did the round "s" supplant the long "s"?

The modern form of the letter s began to be used in print to the exclusion of the old f form or long s about the time of the American Revolution. Before that time it was customary for printers to use both forms of the letter. The long or cursive s was used any place in a word except at the end, where the round s was used. This practice had an interesting origin. The long s was a modification of the Roman s, which was unsuited to rapid writing and which was gradually changed to a waved upright or sloping line. In printing the long s took the form of f. The f used in printing German is still of this type. The ancient Greeks used two different forms of *Sigma* (s), one form at the end of a word and another form elsewhere in a word. Later writers in Europe followed this practice. Early English writers used the f form at the beginning of a word or elsewhere in a word except at the end, where the long s was always used. These two different forms of the small s existed in English printing until near the end of the eighteenth century. It is supposed that John Bell, of London, was the first publisher to discard the long s entirely. This he did in his edition of *The British Theatre*, printed about 1775. Printers objected to the f-form s because of its resemblance to f. In 1786 Benjamin Franklin wrote: "The round s begins to be the mode, and in nice printing the long s is rejected entirely." Goold Brown, in his *Grammar of English Grammars*, published in 1851, observed: "The letter Ess, of the lower case, had till lately two forms, the long and the short, as f and s; the former very nearly resembling the small f, and the latter, its own capital. The short s was used at the end of words, and the long s (written almost like f, but more oblique), in other places; but the latter is now laid aside, in favour of the more distinctive form." The long s persisted much longer in handwriting. In his *Abraham Lincoln: the War Years*, published in 1939, Carl Sandburg wrote: "Like his ancestors, Robert E. Lee referred to England as 'the old country,' wrote *impressed* as *imprefsed*, *show* as *shew*." Long after Lee's time many people still wrote fs for double s. The capital S has undergone little change through the centuries.

Who was the Laughing Murderer of Verdun?

Frederick William, Crown Prince of Germany from the time of his birth in 1882 until the downfall of the Hohenzollerns in 1918, was called the "Laughing Murderer of Verdun" by his enemies during the First World War. He commanded the forces before Verdun and the name referred to the terrific losses his army sustained in his unsuccessful attempt to capture that fortress. This battle was the longest and bloodiest battle in all history up to that time. It began in February, 1916, with a terrific German offensive that carried the German Army under Frederick William to within four miles of Verdun in three days. The desperate but successful resistance of the French under Pétain and Nivelle crystallized in the famous battle cry, "They shall not pass." Two million men were engaged in the action and about a million were killed. It was said that Crown Prince Frederick William took these losses lightly.

How did "gunny sack" originate?

Gunny in gunny sack is an Anglicized form of Hindu and Sanskrit *goni*, meaning sack or bag. Because bags for gross commodities were made on a large scale in Bengal from a strong, coarse, heavy sacking, the material itself came to be called gunny and the bags gunny sacks. The original gunny fabric was woven from the fibers of jute and hemp. Although gunny is used in India as clothing by some of the poorer classes, its chief use is in making sacks and wrappers for cotton bales and other commodities. In everyday parlance any sack of coarse material is likely to be referred to as a gunny sack.

How did "son of a gun" originate?

This expression is used daily in conversation by thousands of persons who would never think of using it if they even so much as suspected its unsavory origin. It formerly expressed the utmost contempt for the person to whom it was applied. William Pulleyn, in his *Etymological Compendium* published in 1828, probably gave the correct origin of the phrase. *Son of a gun*, he wrote, "is derived from *gong*, an old word for the temple of Cloacina—of course it implies bastard, or born in a necessary." *Gong* and *gong man*, though still recorded in unabridged dictionaries, are obsolete. Some authorities, however, regard *son of a gun* as sea slang that originated in the British Navy in the days when sailors were permitted to have their wives with them at sea. The late Dr. Frank Vizetelly, the famous lexicographer, accepted this theory. "It is an epithet of contempt in slight degree," he said, "and was applied originally to boys born afloat, when wives accompanied their husbands to sea. One admiral declared that he was actually thus cradled—under the breast of a gun-carriage." The phrase occurred in the *British Apollo* as early as 1708.

What is a fourflusher?

A fourflusher, in common parlance, is a bluffer, braggart or cheat. The term originated in the popular indoor diversion known as poker. In this card game a flush consists of five cards of the same suit, all spades, hearts, diamonds or clubs. If a player gets four cards of one suit and one card of another suit he has a four flush, also called a bobtail flush. Sometimes a player with a four flush pretends to have a full flush and attempts to drive out an opponent by betting heavily. This practice is perfectly legitimate in poker, but such a player is known as a fourflusher. If he succeeds, the other players never know what cards he held; if he is *called* he must show his cards and expose his bluff. A fourflusher, literally speaking, is merely a poker player who, holding four cards of a suit, bets as if he had five.

What is an inferiority complex?

Complex is used by psychologists to denote, according to Webster's International dictionary, "a system of desires and memories, especially a repressed and unconscious system which in disguised form exerts a dominating influence upon the personality." The Standard dictionary defines the term as "a group of mental contents which have become consolidated into a unit mass." That authority says the word is a translation of *Zusammen* as employed by Johann Herbart (1776–1841), a noted German philosopher and educationist. The Practical Standard dictionary defines *complex* in this connection as "a group of ideas mentally associated with a given subject existing, with their accompanying feeling-tones, in a repressed state." Popularly the word is put to many uses. It is particularly applied to an exaggerated fear or sensitiveness regarding some subject or situation. For instance, Napoleon is said to have had a *conquest complex* and Keats a *beauty complex*. It is common to say that this or that person has a *persecution complex*. A person is said to have an *inferiority complex* when he inherently feels himself weak and incompetent, especially in relation to obstacles, as well as other persons. The opposite state of feeling or attitude of mind is termed a *superiority complex*. These terms are often confused. A person having a superiority complex is one who really has superior ability and the complex consists in not recognizing his limitations. He is egotistical and his conceit is genuine. On the other hand, a person having an inferiority complex is actually inferior in ability and the complex consists in trying to compensate for it by bluffing, posing, rationalizing or otherwise disguising, perhaps from himself as well as others, his true state of feeling. *Inferiority complex* was popularized, if not coined, by Sigmund Freud, Austrian physician and neurologist, who founded modern psychoanalysis.

Do snakes go blind during dog days?

There is only a grain of truth in the old belief that snakes go blind during dog days. Before sloughing its skin a snake assumes a dull grayish color and appears to be blind. Shortly before shedding, the eyes of snakes have a milky appearance, owing to the separation of the outer layer of the epidermis from the anterior part of the outer coat of the eyeballs. This results in temporary impaired vision. After shedding the snake's eyes regain their clearness. It is erroneous, however, to suppose that snakes shed their skin once a year during dog days or the hot season. Sloughing may occur several times in the course of a year. Snakes grow fastest in warm weather and the more they grow, the oftener they shed their skins. That is the only connection there is between dog days and the sloughing of snakes.

What is the meaning of "and/or"?

And/or is a device frequently found in legal and commercial documents and means "either both or only one" and indicates that the idea expressed is both distributive and inclusive. "John Brown and/or Paul Jones" signifies the same as "John Brown and Paul Jones or either of them"; that is, they are responsible individually as well as collectively. The conjunctions are so written to avoid using them side by side—*and or*—which would be awkward as well as confusing. The technical name of the short slanting stroke between *and* and *or* in the device is *virgule*, a French word derived from Latin *virgula*, diminutive of *virga* ("rod") and literally meaning "little rod." It was the earliest form of the comma and was also used by early printers where a hyphen is now employed to indicate the division of a word at the end of a line. And/or is of questionable value even in legal and commercial documents and certainly has no proper place in ordinary writing. In 1938 Senator Carter Glass, of Virginia, made an effort to prevent the use of the clumsy and meaningless device in bills passed by Congress. "Whoever invented and/or," declared the Senator, "should be in an institution for imbeciles." In the same year Justice Chester A. Fowler of the Supreme Court of Wisconsin observed: "And/or is a befuddling, nameless thing, a Janus-faced verbal monstrosity, neither word nor phrase, the child of a brain of someone too lazy or too dull to know what he did mean, now commonly used by lawyers in drafting legal documents, through carelessness or ignorance or as a cunning device to conceal rather than express a meaning."

How do broadswords differ from small swords?

The broadsword has a long cutting edge and usually an obtuse or blunt point. It is a distinctively military sword and was originally so called because of its broad blade. In 1842 James Shields challenged Abraham Lincoln to a duel and the latter chose as weapons "cavalry broadswords of the largest size." A thrusting sword, that is, one with which the attack is delivered mainly with the point, is known as a small or narrow sword. It is a light sword that gradually tapers from hilt to point and does not have a cutting edge. Such swords are worn on dress occasions and are used chiefly in fencing and dueling. During the eighteenth century small swords were almost universally worn in Europe by civilians of standing.

What time of day is evening?

Evening has been applied to different parts of the day at different times and places. The term is derived from Anglo-Saxon aefen, which is akin to after and which signified "late" or "behind." Originally the evening was merely the latter part of the day. Strictly speaking, according to modern usage, evening is from sunset to dark. The word, however, is also commonly used to mean the close or latter part of the day and the beginning of darkness or the earlier part of night; from five or six o'clock, for instance, until the average bedtime. In some parts of the United States as well as the British Isles the early significance of the word is retained and the entire afternoon until dark is called evening. Where this usage prevails there is no afternoon; the entire time between dinner (or luncheon) and supper or sunset is evening and immediately after that it is night. Writing in 1871, Schele de Vere said: "*Evening*, in the South and West, takes the place of the afternoon—the time between dinner and supper being *evening*, and after supper *night*. Persons meeting at two or three o'clock, wish each other 'Good *evening*,' and speak of a 'fine *night*,' or promise to 'come to-*night*,' although the sun may but just have sunk below the horizon." In the Hebrew version of the Old Testament the phrase *between the two evenings* occurs several times. This probably referred to the interval between sunset and the end of the twilight or complete darkness. In *Genesis* 3:8 this period is called "the cool of the day" to distinguish it from "the heat of the day" or midday. According to the Talmud, the "first evening" began about three o'clock in the afternoon when the sun started to decrease, while the "second evening" began at sunset, which was the beginning of the day as a twenty-four hour period. The Romans divided the night into four watches—evening, midnight, cockcrowing and morning.

Can a peacock be a female?

In popular speech any peafowl is called a peacock, whether male or female. Strictly speaking, only the male should be called a peacock. The female is properly called a peahen. *Peafowl* is the proper term to apply to the birds when speaking of them generally without reference to sex. The young are known as peachicks. In this connection *pea* is derived through Anglo-Saxon from Latin *pavo*, now the scientific name of the genus of birds to which the peafowl belongs. This bird was native to the wooded hills of India and Ceylon and is still found there in the wild state. It is supposed that the Macedonians first took the peafowl to Europe at the time Alexander the Great invaded and conquered India. The throne of Iran (Persia) is known as the Peacock Throne. The original Peacock Throne was constructed at Delhi for Shah Jahan in 1628–1635. It consisted of twelve pillars, each bearing two gem-incrusted peacocks. In 1739 the Peacock Throne was taken to Persia by Nadir Shah. Although moderns regard the flesh of peafowls as coarse and tough, the ancients regarded it as a table delicacy and it became a famous dish at the costliest regal boards. During the Middle Ages a peacock pie with the head and spreading tail protruding from the crust was a specialty even in England.

How did "stealing thunder" originate?

John Dennis (1657–1734), an English dramatist and critic, was responsible for the expression to *steal one's thunder*. In 1709 his play *Appius and Virginia* was produced at Drury Lane in London, and for its production the playwright introduced a new method of simulating thunder on the stage. Previously stage thunder was produced by large bowls. Dennis produced it "by troughs of wood with stops in them." *Appius and Virginius* was a financial failure and was soon withdrawn by the manager, much to the disappointment and disgust of the author, who had a high opinion of his work. Soon afterwards he went to Drury Lane to witness a performance of Shakespeare's *Macbeth*, in which the improved method of producing thunder was employed. Dennis was furious when he heard it. He exclaimed: "That's my thunder, by God! the villains will not play my play but they rattle my thunder."

Is steam visible?

Strictly speaking, steam is invisible. The term is properly applied to the transparent gas or vapor into which water is converted when heated to the boiling point. The visible mist commonly called steam, which consists of minute droplets of water in the air, is not formed until the water vapor has cooled and condensed.

Is part of a ten-dollar bill redeemable at face value?

Three-fifths or more of a mutilated United States paper currency bill, note or certificate is redeemable at face value by the United States Treasury Department. When less than three-fifths, but clearly more than two-fifths of the original bill remains it is redeemable at one-half of the face value of the original bill. However, fragments containing less than three-fifths of the original bills are redeemable at full face value by the Treasurer of the United States provided they are accompanied by satisfactory evidence that the missing portions have been totally destroyed. Such evidence must consist of affidavits, subscribed and sworn to before a notary public, setting forth the cause and manner of destruction. Occasionally even the ashes of burned money are identified by the Treasury Department and redeemed at face value. No relief is granted by the government to the owners of paper currency totally destroyed. Persons who wish to have mutilated money redeemed should communicate with a bank or with the Redemption Division, United States Treasury Department, Washington, D. C.

Why is Yorkshire divided into ridings?

Yorkshire, the largest county in England, is divided into three administrative districts known as ridings—North Riding, East Riding and West Riding. The riding is an old Scandinavian institution and Yorkshire has been so divided since ancient times. In Anglo-Saxon the word was written *thrithing* or *thriding* and it literally meant "third"—the riding being a third of a larger district. Formerly other English counties also had ridings for purposes of local administration, Lincolnshire being the last to abolish them. Macaulay refers to Charles Duncombe as "one of the greatest landowners of the North Riding of Lancashire." The divisions of Tipperary in Ireland are known as ridings at the present time. Even districts smaller than counties were subdivided into ridings. For instance, Linsey, part of Yorkshire, was formerly divided into the north, south and west ridings.

What birds are trained to fish for their masters?

In China, Japan and other parts of the Orient the large sea birds known as cormorants have been trained to fish for man since time immemorial. These birds display remarkable activity under water and they devour fish so greedily that they have become proverbial for their voracity and gluttony. When young they are easily tamed and can then be taught not only to fish for their masters but also to bring their catch back to a boat. A leather collar is placed around their long necks to keep them from swallowing their catch. In parts of the Orient it is a common sight to see a fisherman on a raft with a flock of cormorants in the water controlled by means of cords attached to their collars. Some cormorants will fish for their masters without such controls. Occasionally if a fish, because of its size, is too much for one cormorant to manage, another of the birds will co-operate in the catch. A single trained cormorant has been known to catch and deliver to a boat or raft as many as one hundred fish in an hour. The bird can pursue and catch fish below the surface even in muddy water. During the seventeenth century cormorant fishing was introduced into western Europe, and at one time the master of the cormorants was an official in the royal household of England. Cormorants are almost world-wide in distribution. The white-breasted cormorant is largely responsible for the production of the vast guano deposits on the islands off the coast of Peru.

What is a weed?

Weed, which is of unknown origin, is a relative term. In the most widely accepted sense, a weed is any troublesome and useless plant growing on cultivated ground to the injury of the crop or vegetation desired. The Oxford dictionary defines the term as "a herbaceous plant not valued for use or beauty, growing wild and rank, and regarded as cumbering the ground and hindering the growth of superior vegetation." Shakespeare refers to such plants as lacking "both beauty and utility." But in another sense, any plant growing where it is not wanted is regarded as a weed. In this sense there are no species of weed, because a plant might be a weed in one place and not a weed in another. Even a corn plant growing in a wheat field would be a weed; the same plant in a cornfield would not be so regarded. On this subject the United States Department of Agriculture says: "A weed may be defined as an unwanted plant, or a plant out of place. The morning-glory in the home garden is an ornamental plant; in the cornfield it is a weed. Many other plants are valuable under one set of conditions and pests under other conditions. When pests, they are weeds. When valuable, they are not weeds." In the more popular sense, however, weed signifies a plant in itself more or less useless irrespective of where it grows. Ralph Waldo Emerson wrote: "And what is a weed? A plant whose virtues have not been discovered." Weed in such phrases as widow's weeds is derived from an Anglo-Saxon root meaning "to weave" and is not related to weed in the sense of an obnoxious plant. Formerly clothes in general were called "weeds." For instance, in Shakespeare's Twelfth Night Viola, disguised as a man, refers to her "maiden weeds" and "woman's weeds."

When did Oslo become capital of Norway?

Oslo, or Opslo, was the ancient name of the capital of Norway. According to Norwegian tradition, the city was founded in 1048 by King Harald Haardraade. By the end of the fourteenth century it had become the chief city of the kingdom. In 1624 Oslo was destroyed by fire. King Christian IV immediately rebuilt the city on the opposite side of the Aker River and named it Kristiania, or Christiania as it is spelled in English. Oslo, however, continued to be the name of a suburb on the east side of the Aker where the original city had stood. After the First World War a popular movement began in Norway to have the name of the capital changed back to its ancient form. This was done July 11, 1924, by act of the Norwegian legislature. The law provided that after January 1, 1925, Oslo would be the official name of the capital.

Why do gunners open their mouths when firing cannon?

Gunners often open their mouths to protect their eardrums while firing large guns. When the mouth is open the air waves set in motion by the discharge of the cannon enter the throat as well as the ears; consequently the sudden pressure against the outside of the drums is counteracted by an equal pressure against the inside. Opening the mouth while firing artillery is not so common among gunners as it formerly was. It is no longer practiced generally by members of the gun crews in the United

States Navy. Men working in the turrets are well protected from concussion, while those in the more exposed positions generally use ear stoppers or pledgets of cotton in their ears. In recent times several different devices have been developed to protect the ears of men when firing large guns. One of these is known as the "ear warden." It is a device that keeps out loud noises without interfering with the ability to hear commands. Notwithstanding these devices, many men, whether in combat or merely in artillery target practice, still open their mouths during the actual firing of large guns in order that the pressure on their eardrums may be equalized. Gunners also often stand on their toes to relieve the body as much as possible of the shock of the explosion. The ears are among the most intricate organs of the human body.

How is "Eyre" pronounced in "Jane Eyre"?

Eyre in *Jane Eyre*, Charlotte Brontë's famous novel, is correctly pronounced as if spelled *air*. It is frequently mispronounced *ire*, to rhyme with *dire*. The proper pronunciation of the heroine's surname is indicated in Chapter XI of the book in the following dialogue between Jane Eyre and her pupil, little Adèle Varens:

> "And Mademoiselle—what is your name?"
> "Eyre—Jane Eyre."
> "Aire? Bah! I cannot say it."

Eyre occurs in the Hundred Rolls (*Rotuli Hundredorum*) of 1274 and is the Middle English form of Old French *Heir*, which was also pronounced *air*. Edward John Eyre (1815–1901), the English explorer and colonial governor, pronounced his name *air*, and Lake Eyre in South Australia, which was named after him, is pronounced in the same way. The old word *eyre*, meaning a circuit or a court of circuit judges, is also correctly pronounced *air*.

Who defined a university as a teacher on one end of a log and a student on the other?

According to a well-established tradition, James A. Garfield, in a Williams College Alumni address delivered in New York City in 1872, said something to the following effect: "My definition of a university is Mark Hopkins at one end of a log and a student at the other." The quotation does not occur in the speech as it was recorded at the time and its exact phraseology varies with the recollection of several of those who heard it. Another version is: "A pine bench, with Mark Hopkins at one end of it and me at the other, is a good enough college for me!" Mark

Hopkins (1802–1887) was one of the ablest and most successful educators of the old type. He taught moral philosophy and rhetoric at Williams College at Williamstown, Massachusetts, from 1830 until his death, and from 1836 to 1872 was president of that college. Many of his students besides Garfield testified to his skill as a teacher and the lasting influence of his personality. They particularly liked the stress that Hopkins placed upon the development of the individual student. In 1877, four years before he was elected the twentieth President of the United States, Garfield said in an address in Washington: "If I could be taken back into boyhood today, and had all the libraries and apparatus of a university, with ordinary routine professors, offered me on the one hand, and on the other a great, luminous, rich-souled man, such as Dr. Hopkins was twenty years ago, in a tent in the woods alone, I should say give me Dr. Hopkins for my college course rather than any university with only routine professors."

Where do goldfish come from?

Goldfish as we know them do not exist anywhere in the wild state. They are a product of long years of selective breeding. The wild fish from which goldfish were developed belong to the carp family and are still numerous in the streams of China. They do not naturally have the golden hue, but are dark in color, much like ordinary carp, although the species tends toward albinism. Centuries ago the Chinese fish culturists interbred light-colored specimens and produced many beautiful varieties. Fanciers further induced and strengthened the golden and silvery colors by regulating the quantity of minerals in the water. The bright colors in goldfish are not very stable. They change readily. Often scarlet specimens turn silver, silver ones turn black, and black ones turn gold, etc. When goldfish are restored to a natural environment they often revert to the original dark color after a few generations. Goldfish kept in darkness for several years will turn white and become totally blind. Ordinary goldfish may live in a bowl as long as twenty-five or thirty years. In the Orient specimens have been known to live seventy years. Their longevity is accounted for by the fact that they are members of the carp family, which is noted for its long-lived species. The size to which a goldfish will grow is determined to some extent by the size of the bowl in which it is kept. Goldfish are very sensitive to the condition of the water in which they live. During the First World War it was discovered that goldfish had a practical use in determining what kind of gas the enemy had used in chemical warfare attacks. It is supposed that goldfish were first introduced into England in 1691. Some of the first specimens sent to France were presented to Mme. de Pompadour, mistress of Louis XV. Goldfish are now produced in large commercial aquariums. An 150-acre hatchery near Frederick, Maryland, normally produces five million goldfish a year. For centuries it has been an annual custom for the city officials of Grammont in Belgium to swallow live goldfish. In 1939, just before the outbreak of the Second World War, eating goldfish alive was a fad among American college students.

How big were the largest hailstones on record?

The maximum size of hailstones is not known positively for the simple reason that trained observers are not often on the spot to measure them when they fall. Human beings have a weakness for exaggerating the size of the hailstones they see fall as well as the fish they catch, and the difficulty lies in verifying the statements of those who say they have seen hailstones of enormous size. The old Teutonic root of *hail* signifies "pebble" and the name is descriptive of most of the hailstones that fall. Nevertheless hailstones larger than one's fist and weighing more than a pound have been reported several times on good authority. The reports of unusually large hailstones frequently refer to them as being the size of hens' eggs, baseballs, tennis balls and even grapefruit. During a storm in Natal in South Africa in 1874 hailstones weighing a pound and a half went through a corrugated iron roof as if it had been made of paper. At Cazolia, Spain, in 1829 houses were crushed under blocks of ice, some of which were said to have weighed four and a half pounds. But these reports, like all accounts dating back many years, should be taken with a grain of salt. Possibly some of the reports refer to cases where masses of ice resulted from the coalescence of a number of smaller hailstones lying closely packed together on the ground. In *The Voyage of the Beagle* Charles Darwin wrote of exceptionally large hailstones that fell in South America in 1833. These hailstones were "as large as small apples, and extremely hard." They fell with such violence that they killed "the greater number of the wild animals," including deer and "ostriches." Hailstones three inches in diameter were reported from Dallas, Texas, May 8, 1926; and hailstones four inches in diameter were reported from Tullulah, Louisiana, April 21, 1929. Up to date (1946) perhaps the largest hailstone ever measured, weighed and photographed immediately after falling was one that fell at Potter, Nebraska, July 6, 1928. It was 17 inches in circumference, 5 inches in diameter, and weighed 1½ pounds. Of course, there is no good reason for supposing that larger hailstones have not fallen in the past and will fall in the future. Hailstones often break windows, penetrate automobile tops, kill poultry and birds and do great damage to trees and crops. Although human beings are occasionally badly cut or otherwise injured by hailstones, there are few authenticated cases of persons having been killed by them. One of the ten plagues of Egypt was a rain of fire and hail. *Joshua* 10:11 says of the Amorites fleeing before Joshua "that the Lord cast down great stones from heaven upon them unto Azekah, and they died: they were more which died with hailstones than they whom the children of Israel slew with the sword."

Why is the moon compared to green cheese?

To say a person believes the moon is made of green cheese is to ridicule his credulity, it being presumed that such a person would believe the most absurd thing imaginable. In this connection *green* is used in the sense of fresh or unseasoned. A green cheese is a new cheese. Such a cheese is supposed to resemble the moon in shape, size and color. This homely comparison is very old and probably originated with the country people of England. Sir Thomas More (1478–1535) wrote: "He should, as he list, be able to prove the moon made of green cheese." That the expression was proverbial even at this early date is indicated by the fact that John Heywood (1497?–1580?), the English dramatist and epigrammatist, infers that people who "thinke that the moone is made of a greene cheese" are dolts and fools. François Rabelais (1490?–1553), the French satirist, is often quoted as having first made the comparison, but it appears only in the English translation of his work.

Is Newfoundland a part of Canada?

Newfoundland is neither geographically nor politically a part of the Dominion of Canada. When the Dominion of Canada was created in 1867 provision was made for the admission of Newfoundland into the federation, but, despite negotiations from time to time with that end in view, Newfoundand has never availed itself of the privilege. Until 1933 Newfoundland was a self-governing dominion with its own governor-general, premier and parliament and was a full-fledged member of the sisterhood of British commonwealths with a status in the Empire similar to that of the Dominion of Canada itself. Because of financial difficulties, in 1933 Newfoundland lost its dominion status and reverted to that of a British crown colony, being governed by a British governor and a commission composed of three members appointed by the United Kingdom and three by Newfoundland. It was contemplated that this arrangement would continue only until such time when the island could again support itself. Newfoundland, among the dozen largest islands in the world, is often called the "senior British colony" because it antedates in discovery, though not in continuous settlement, all the other overseas units of the British Empire. John Cabot, sailing in the service of Henry VII of England, discovered the island in 1497, at least a year before Columbus saw the mainland of South America. The following entry in the accounts of the English privy purse expenditures is supposed to refer to the discovery: "1497, Aug. 10. To hym that found the New Isle, £10." The name, of course, alludes to the fact that the island had just been found. This entry in the privy purse accounts does not necessarily mean that the King paid Cabot ten pounds for discovering the island. Sir Humphrey Gilbert formally occupied Newfoundland in 1583 and the Treaty of Utrecht in 1713 acknowledged it to be British. Newfoundland's first governor-general was appointed in 1728 when Canada was still a French possession. It is a common mistake to suppose that Newfoundland is a part of the Dominion of Canada, and Newfoundland businessmen are continually being referred by American firms to their Canadian distributors.

How did Derby in horse racing originate?

The Derby race is an annual horse race held on the famous race course at Epsom, England. Epsom is in Surrey, about fifteen miles from London, and has been noted for its races since the reign of James I, successor of Queen Elizabeth. In 1779, during the reign of George III and in the midst of the American Revolution, a group of Derbyshire sportsmen got up what they called a "dinner race" at Epsom. Out of this race grew the English *Oaks*. The next year—1780—the Earl of Derby offered a prize for an annual race at Epsom and this event came to be known as the Derby. Previously the Earl of Derby had sponsored a similar race on the Isle of Man. Only three-year-old horses are admitted to the Derby, and a large entrance fee is required. The first prize is about $25,000. The distance is one mile, four furlongs and twenty-nine yards. In normal times Parliament adjourns on "Derby Day" and great multitudes of people from all parts of the British Isles flock to the Epsom Downs race course. The event is somewhat like a country fair, and days before the race all sorts of gypsy outfits and carnival paraphernalia are set up on the bare heath around the horseshoe-shaped course. In imitation of the English Derby there are now the Kentucky Derby in the United States and the French Derby in France. *Derby* is sometimes loosely applied to the chief race on any track. The term has been extended even to other sporting events, and nowadays one hears of dog derbies, boat derbies, soapbox derbies, and even stork (baby) derbies. In southern England *derby* is generally pronounced *dar-by*, and that is the way the name is pronounced by the Earl of Derby, but in the United States and elsewhere in the English-speaking world it is generally pronounced der-by. In Derbyshire, England, the name is locally pronounced der-by, just as it is in the United States. The Oxford dictionary says dar-by is "a Southern (not the local) pronunciation of Derby, an English town or shire."

Why are X rays so named?

The X ray was discovered in 1895 by a German Professor of physics at the University of Wurzburg in Germany. His name was Wilhelm Konrad Röntgen. It is said that this German scientist, who gave his discovery to the world without personal profit, made the actual discovery of X rays late on the night of November 3, 1895, after all his assistants had left the laboratory. In mathematics the letter x stands for any unknown quantity. Röntgen called the new rays X rays because he did not understand their nature, X representing that which had not yet been explained by science. They are also sometimes called Röntgen rays, after the discoverer. Röntgen, who received the Nobel prize in 1901, died in 1923 at the age of seventy-eight. His surname, also spelled Roentgen, is generally pronounced runt-gen. Just how x came to stand for an unknown quantity in mathematics is not known for certain. It may have originated as follows: In old Spanish, as in modern Portuguese, x represented the sound sh. The Arabs represented an unknown quantity in mathematics by the word shei, meaning "thing," which the Spanish mathematicians borrowed and wrote xei. Later, for the sake of brevity, the initial x was substituted for the word. Many erroneously suppose that a radiologist is a radio technician. Radiology (the term was adopted before the development of wireless) is the science of radioactive substances and the art of applying its principles in the diagnosis and cure of disease, and a radiologist is one versed in the use of X rays.

What is the origin of "A Number One"?

A Number One in the sense of prime, superior or first-rate originated with a symbol used in classifying ships in Lloyd's Register of British and Foreign Shipping, a yearly publication dealing with the design and construction of vessels of all nations and with data about docks and harbors. Beginning with its issue of 1775–1776, Lloyd's Register Classified the characteristics and condition of ships by means of letters and figures. The character and condition of the ship's hull was designated by a letter and that of the equipment by a figure. Thus A-1 (A, hull, and 1, equipment) meant that both hull and equipment were in first-rate condition. A-2 meant that the hull was first-rate but the equipment second-rate, etc. Some authorities believe that A-1 (usually written A Number One or A One) was first applied figuratively to persons and things in general in America and not in England, although that is not certain. It is a common mistake to suppose that Lloyd's Register of British and Foreign Shipping is published by the famous insurance association known as Lloyd's. Lloyd's Register has no financial connection with the insurance association. It is published by a different society and is housed in a different building. Although originally it provided shipping information primarily as a basis for marine insurance, it is now chiefly interested in the improvement, safety, regulation and inspection of shipping. Lloyd's Register no longer uses A-1 to designate ships with hull and equipment in first-class condition. Such ships are now designated 100-A1, the letter still referring to the character of the vessel and the prefixed figure to the fact that it is of steel or iron construction.

What is China's Sorrow?

Hwang Ho, or the Yellow River, is popularly known as China's Sorrow because of its devastating floods. This remarkable stream is one of the largest rivers in the world and is the second largest in China, being second only to the Yangtze. It has its sources in Tibet and meanders 2,700 miles through northern China. Yellow River is merely a literal translation of Chinese hwang ("yellow"), and ho ("river"). The stream was so named from the fact that the water has a yellowish color owing to the presence of muddy earth in solution. Enormous quantities of infinitesimal particles of silt, known to geologists as loess, are blown by the wind into the upper reaches of the stream from the Gobi Desert country. In flood times this material may constitute as high as eighteen per cent of the volume of water. The Yellow Sea into which the Yellow River flows also has the same yellowish hue. The Chinese call the sea Hwang Hai, literally "Yellow Sea," hai being Chinese for "sea." China's Sorrow, also called The Ungovernable and the Scourge of the Sons of Han, is especially destructive because it not only overflows its banks but also changes its entire lower course. It has completely altered its outlet a dozen times or more in the last four thousand years. Silt from the loess country continually raises the bed of the river and necessitates the construction of higher and higher dikes and levees. At some points the river is more than sixty feet above the neighboring country, and embankments designed to prevent floods actually contribute to the hazard. In 1852 the Yellow River shifted its mouth from the Bay of Haichow south of the Shantung peninsula to its ancient mouth in the

Gulf of Chihli, a distance of some four hundred miles. At that time the one thousand-mile canal built by a thirteenth century emperor to connect the Hwang Ho with the Yangtze Kiang was destroyed. Owing to the swiftness of its current the Hwang Ho is almost useless for the navigation of large vessels and consequently there are few large cities on its banks.

Can fish hear?

With present knowledge this question cannot be answered definitely. Experiments have given conflicting results. Some investigators believe that certain fish do not respond to the stimuli of sound waves, while others have obtained some reaction to such stimuli. Since different species of fish were used in the experiments, it is possible that the sense of hearing is present in some species and not in others. In *A Guide to the Study of Fishes*, David Starr Jordan, an eminent authority on fish, wrote:

The sense of hearing in fishes cannot be very acute, and is at the most confined to the perception of disturbances in the water. Most movements of the fish are governed by sight rather than sound. It is in fact extremely doubtful whether fishes really hear at all, in a way comparable to the auditory sense in higher vertebrates. Recent experiments of Prof. G. H. Parker on the killifish tend to show a moderate degree of auditory sense which grades into the sense of touch. While the killifish responds to a bass-viol string, there may be some fishes wholly deaf.

The structure of the auditory organs of fish indicates that the hearing sense, if present, must be quite different from that of higher animals, for they do not have an external auditory passage, tympanic cavity, eardrum, nor Eustachian tube, all of which play an important role in the perception of sound waves by man and other higher vertebrates. Some scientists have supposed that the inner ear of fish is an organ of equilibrium rather than of hearing. In 1930 Dr. Karl von Frisch of the University of Munich reported to the National Academy of Sciences that experiments made by him with minnows indicated that this species has a better hearing sense than human beings. Blind minnows, he said, quickly associated the sounds of tuning forks, whistles, guitars, organs and violins with feeding time. They could even distinguish between the varied sounds of the different instruments. But it is not certain that Dr. Frisch correctly interpreted the relationship between the sound waves and the hearing apparatus of the minnows. It is still generally believed that if fish can "hear" at all it probably does not amount to

[500]

more than receiving disturbances in the water made by the sound waves. The subject has a popular interest because most fishermen insist that it is necessary to keep quiet while fishing.

What became of the passenger pigeons?

Two hundred years ago the passenger pigeon, a migratory pigeon slightly larger than the turtledove, was probably the most numerous bird throughout most of the United States and southern Canada east of the Great Plains. John James Audubon and Alexander Wilson, early naturalists, reported seeing these pigeons flying in flocks seven or eight miles long, more than a mile wide and so compact that the sun was hidden from view as they passed. When one of these flocks, estimated to contain from one to two billion birds, settled on a forest for the night, trees broke under their weight. Audubon calculated that a flock of such size would require nine million bushels of feed a day. The cooing of the birds and the whirring of their wings were so loud that the report of a gun could not be heard. Several inches of dung were left under their roosting places. During the breeding season hundreds of them would nest in a single tree. In 1857 a game committee of the Ohio legislature reported that this bird needed no protection. "Wonderfully prolific, having the vast forests of the North as its breeding grounds, traveling hundreds of miles in search of food," declared the report, "it is here today and elsewhere tomorrow, and no ordinary destruction can lessen them or be missed from the myriads that are yearly produced." Yet less than sixty years later the passenger pigeon was extinct. Authentic records indicate that the last passenger pigeon at large was seen in 1898, although there are more or less reliable records of individual birds being seen in the wild state as late as 1907. The last known survivor was a captive bird that died in the Cincinnati Zoological Gardens in September, 1914. When this bird's mate died in 1910, $1,000 was offered for another, but none was ever found. Many theories have been advanced to account for the complete disappearance of these spectacular and interesting birds. It is probably not true, as generally supposed, that this pigeon disappeared suddenly and mysteriously while it was still quite numerous. Some believe that these birds migrated in mass to another part of the world, that they were blown out to sea by a storm and drowned, that they were killed by forest fires, epidemics, tornadoes, snowstorms or other similar causes. One writer believes the birds were destroyed by a species of chicken mite introduced from Europe. He reported that during the seventys and eightys of the last century he found thousands of dead squabs under the trees where the pigeons were nesting.

Upon examination they were found to be covered with mites. Perhaps many factors contributed to the extinction of this species. The early settlers and hunters shot them by thousands and knocked them down with clubs and poles. Millions of them—even carloads of them—were shipped to market. Shortly after the Civil War the commercial hunting of passenger pigeons became systematic. In 1879 these birds were selling on the Chicago market at from fifty to sixty cents a dozen. Pigeon hunters made from ten to forty dollars a day. The last large nesting of passenger pigeons on record was near Petoskey, Michigan, in 1878. It was from thirty to forty miles long and several miles wide. Indians and boys captured large numbers of the birds at a cent apiece. It is generally believed by naturalists that the indiscriminate slaughter of the birds by man was the chief factor that led to their ultimate extinction. This cause may have been aided by the destruction of the forests within their range. Also, being communistic in their habits, the species may have been unable to adapt itself to more solitary feeding, migrating, roosting and nesting habits. At any rate, as civilization encroached upon the wilderness the birds began to disappear and kept on disappearing until there wasn't a single specimen living. The common mourning or turtledove and the band-tailed wild pigeon of the Pacific coast superficially resemble the passenger pigeon and this fact accounts for frequent reports that the latter is still seen occasionally in out-of-the-way places. The band-tailed pigeon (Columba fasciata), which sometimes ranges as far east as Colorado and Texas, is distinguished from the passenger pigeon by its short, even tail. Fortunately many stuffed specimens of the extinct passenger pigeon have been preserved by museums.

Where is the Land of the Midnight Sun?

The sun shining at midnight in the arctic or antarctic summer is known as the midnight sun. Norway is popularly called the "Land of the Midnight Sun" because this phenomenon has been more frequently observed in that region by visitors from western Europe and the United States. The description would be equally applicable to other high latitudes above the Arctic Circle, such as northern Russia, northern Alaska, northern Canada, and Greenland, where in midsummer the sun does not sink below the horizon at any time within the twenty-four hours of the day. Instead of setting as it does in our latitudes, the sun in these regions merely goes around and around above the horizon, being part of the time in the north. In Iceland, for instance, during June and July, daylight is perpetual and a person can read a book by natural light at any time of the night. Within a distance of about four minutes of arc from the North Pole the sun rises and sets but once a year; in other words, the year is composed of one day and one night, each six months in length. The number of sunrises in a year increases from one at the Pole to 365 at a short distance south of the Arctic Circle. Strictly speaking, only the northern part of Norway lies within the domain of the midnight sun. Similar conditions with the seasons reversed exist in the Antarctic. On March 21 the relative positions of the earth and sun are such that the latter illuminates exactly one-half of the surface of the former, and on that date night and day are equal in length in all parts of the world. Three months later, when the earth has completed a fourth of its circuit around the sun, the North Pole is turned toward the sun and the South Pole away from it. Another three months later the days and nights are once more equal in length everywhere on the earth. By December 21, when the earth has completed three-fourths of its circuit around the sun, the South Pole is turned toward the sun and the North Pole away from it. Of course, the land of the midnight sun is also the land of midday night. In the far north and the far south a person can observe the interesting phenomenon of a sunrise and sunset at the same time.

What is the golden rose?

The golden rose is an artificial ornament of pure gold set with gems and made by skilled artificers. It is blessed by the Pope on the fourth (*Laetare*) Sunday in Lent, which for that reason is sometimes called "Rose Sunday." For centuries the popes have been accustomed to confer the golden rose upon churches and sanctuaries, Catholic rulers and other persons of distinction, as well as on governments and cities, conspicuous for their Catholic spirit and loyalty to the Holy See. The origin of the custom is obscure. According to some authorities, it originated in 1049 with Pope Leo IX. This Pope, wishing to establish his authority over the Monastery of the Holy Cross in Alsace, exacted from it each year a golden rose, which was blessed by the Pope on the fourth Sunday in Lent and presented to the individual or city best deserving the favor of the Holy See. In feudal days the presentation of a red rose was the symbol of fealty and the token of annual rent. A golden rose weighing one hundred fifty pounds, inscribed with the names of Constantine the Great and his mother Helena, was placed by the Roman Emperor on the legendary tomb of St. Peter in Rome. However it originated, it superseded the custom of bestowing the Golden Keys of St. Peter's Confessional on Catholic rulers. In recent times the golden rose has been reserved for Catholic queens. Originally and until the close of the fifteenth century the golden rose consisted of a single rose of pure gold slightly tinted red. The sacred ornament was about six inches high and in the center was a cup formed by the petals. During the ceremony of blessing the golden rose with incense and holy water the Pope poured balsam and musk into this cup. Then the ornament was carried in solemn procession to the sacristry of the Pope's private chapel. Sixtus IV, who was Pope from 1471 to 1484, substituted for the single flower an upright thorny branch with leaves and with one large central flower and other smaller flowers. That is still the general type of the golden rose, the petals of which are decked with gems. The ancient ceremony of blessing the golden rose has undergone little change. The same ornament is used at the annual ceremony until it is given away, which may not be for many years. Two English kings and two English queens have received the golden rose. They were Henry VI; Henry VIII, who received it three different times from three different popes; Queen Mary Tudor, daughter of Henry VIII, and Henrietta Maria, queen consort of Charles I.

Which is cooler, black or white clothing?

Many people believe that light-colored clothing is cooler than dark-colored clothing irrespective of the time it is worn. Such is not the case. Assuming the material to be the same in other respects, there is probably little if any difference in warmth between black and white clothing under ordinary circumstances. Only in bright sunshine are white clothes materially cooler than dark clothes. This is because black substances absorb light while white ones reflect it. Light-colored material reflects more light than dark material does. Glass painted black and exposed to the rays of the sun is more likely to crack than is glass painted white. If two pieces of cloth, one white and the other black, are placed on a piece of ice in bright sunshine, the black piece of cloth will absorb the light rays and melt its way into the ice much faster than the white one will. Experiments show that if pieces of black, red, blue and white cloth are laid on a sheet of ice in the sun, the ice will begin to melt first under the black, second under the red, third under the blue, and fourth under the white. Thus white clothing affords the body more protection from the rays of the sun than does black clothing. Except in sunshine, however, the white fur of the polar bear is just as warm as the dark coat of the black bear. The white coats that nature provides for some animals in the winter are apparently designed for protective coloration without reference to warmth. It is the opinion of some horse experts that black horses are affected more by the heat of the direct sun than whites ones are. If that is true, the same should be true also of black dogs, cats and other black animals as well as of black people. There is some evidence indicating that dark pigmentation serves as a partial insulation from the sun rays and that dark-skinned peoples are less affected by direct sunlight than are light-skinned ones. This may explain the fact that dark-skinned peoples seem to be more subject to such diseases as rickets than light-skinned peoples are even when their environment and diet are the same. Garments of closely woven white fabric are worn in tropical countries to protect the body from the hot sun. Such garments have high reflecting powers and prevent the transmission of ultraviolet rays to the skin. According to the United States Bureau of Standards, these rays pass through open-weave fabrics more readily than they do through closely woven ones, but it does not make much difference whether the color is black, white, red or green. White, however, has been associated with coolness so long that white garments may have a desirable pyschological effect in hot weather. The association of the properties of substances with their color is of great antiquity. That red flannel is warmer than flannel of other colors is an old belief that probably has no basis in fact. The notion that red is a warm color and white a cool color may have been suggested by the fact that fire and very hot objects are red, while snow and ice are white. Many people are extremely sensitive to colors, and the color of their rooms and offices has a decided pyschological effect on their mental and physical well-being. Red, orange, yellow and black are generally regarded as "warm colors," and green, blue and white as "cool colors."

Why wasn't the year 1900 a leap year?

According to the Gregorian calendar, which was introduced by Pope Gregory in 1582 A.D. and which was adopted by Great Britain and the English colonies in 1752, every year whose number is divisible by four is a leap year, with the exception of those years whose numbers are divisible by 100 and not by 400. Thus the years 1700, 1800 and 1900 were not leap years, while 1600 was and 2000 will be. The Gregorian calendar was a modification of the Julian calendar, which was introduced by Julius Caesar in 46 B.C. Roman astronomers at that time fixed the solar year at 365 days and six hours. These six hours were allowed to accumulate and added to the calendar as a 366th day every four years. The Romans called this the *bissextile*—from *bis* ("twice") and *sextus* ("sixth")—year because it followed February 24, the sixth day before the calends of March, and consequently was counted as a second "sixth" day. Under the Gregorian system the extra, odd or intercalary day is added after February 28. But it was found that the addition of a whole day every fourth year is a few minutes too much to make the calendar year come out even. This was adjusted by omitting the extra day— February 29—in every concluding year of the centuries except when the year's number is divisible by 400. Leap year as the English name of the bissextile year antedates the Gregorian calendar several centuries and goes back at least to the thirteenth century. It is supposed to have been suggested by the fact that in leap years any fixed date after February leaps over a day of the week and falls on the next week day but one to that on which it fell the year before.

Where do elephants go to die?

It is often said that the remains of elephants that die a natural death are never found in their native haunts and that the question is a mystery to scientists. Numerous hunters have reported that they never have found the skeletal remains of elephants in the jungles. An Englishman, who had charge of the capture of elephants for the government, said he had never found the carcass of a dead animal. The natives in the elephant country in Africa and Asia say all wild elephants go to certain secluded spots to die. These supposed graveyards of elephants are known in legend as "Valleys of Ivory." The existence of these elephant graveyards appears to be confirmed to the satisfaction of many Europeans in those regions by the fact that from time to time natives bring in old tusks that they say they got "in the bush." Many ivory hunters have dreamed of finding one of these places with their untold wealth of tusks. Needless to say, the belief is a myth. There is no great mystery as to what becomes of dead elephants. In the first place, comparatively few wild elephants die of old age. Most of these animals sooner or later fall a prey to their only enemy, man. Collectors for the Museum of Natural History report that the bones of wild animals are rarely found in Africa. The same is true in most other regions. There are several reasons for this. Wild animals commonly attempt to hide when they feel death approaching. Even domestic dogs often conceal themselves when sick. Elephants are no exception to this rule. They usually die singly and far from the settlements. In some cases they may even seek relief in the rivers and are carried into the sea after death. Elephant fossils have been found in soil once covered with water. Climatic conditions in Africa and southern Asia cause the carcasses to decay rapidly. The natives, carnivorous animals, carrion birds and swarms of insects make quick work of the flesh; rodents frequently contribute to the rapid disposal of the bones. Thus an elephant that dies in the jungle would quickly disappear. After the bones are cleaned of their flesh they are soon scattered far and wide. Within a year or two the remaining parts, such as the skull and larger bones, are completely overgrown by mosses, underbrush and other vegetation. In fact the factors contributing to the elimination of such remains are so numerous and work so rapidly that it is not surprising that elephant bones are not a common sight. Dr. William M. Mann, director of the National Zoological Park in Washington, said when he was in Africa in 1926 his guide took him to a place where a hunter had killed a large elephant only the year before. A part of the skull and a couple of widely separated bones were all of the remains that could be found. But Theodore Roosevelt, in *African Game Trails*, referring to burnt-over places in the Lado, wrote: "Here and there bleached skulls of elephants and rhino, long dead, showed white against the charred surface of the soil." Speaking of the "wild llama" in Patagonia, Charles Darwin wrote in *The Voyage of the Beagle*: "The guanacos appear to have favourite spots for lying down to die. On the banks of the St. Cruz, in certain circumscribed spaces, which were generally bushy and all near the river, the ground was actually white with bones. On one such spot I counted between ten and twenty heads. I particularly examined the bones; they did not appear, as some scattered ones which I had seen, gnawed or broken, as if dragged together by beasts of prey. The animals in most cases must have crawled, before dying, beneath and amongst the bushes. Mr. Bynoe informs me that during a former voyage he observed the same circumstances on the banks of the Rio Gallegos. I do not at all understand the reason of this, but I may observe, that the wounded guanacos at the St. Cruz invariably walked towards the river. At St. Jago in the Cape de Verde Islands, I remember having seen in a ravine a retired corner covered with bones of the goat; we at the time exclaimed that it was the burial ground of all the goats in the island. I mention these trifling circumstances because in certain cases they might explain the occurrence of a number of uninjured bones in a cave, or buried under alluvial accumulations; and likewise the cause why certain animals are more commonly embedded than others in sedimentary deposits."

Why do electric light bulbs pop when broken?

If the filament in electric light bulbs were made red hot in air it would oxidize and burn up. Therefore the bulb must consist of a vacuum or it must be filled with a gas in which there is no oxygen. The air is pumped out of ordinary electric light bulbs until a vacuum or nearly a vacuum is produced. When such a bulb is suddenly broken a popping sound is often produced by the outside air rushing into the vacuum. The filament burns up the instant air is admitted into a lighted bulb. Some electric bulbs are filled with nitrogen and they do not pop when broken because the pressure inside tends to equalize that outside. Incandescent electric light bulbs, unlike open-flame lamps, take no oxygen from the air in a room where they are burning.

Who are the Anzacs?

This is a name often applied collectively to the people of Australia and New Zealand. It originated during the First World War. The Australian and New Zealand divisions in the British forces were merged into a single unit officially known as the "Australian-New Zealand Army Corps." In popular usage this name was shortened to Anzac, being the initial letters of the words composing the name. "When I took over the command of the Australian and New Zealand Corps in Egypt [in 1914]," wrote General Sir William Birdwood after the war, "I was asked to select a telegraphic-code address and I adopted the name Anzac." In the following spring the Australian and New Zealand forces made their heroic landing on the Gallipoli Peninsula and to commemorate the event General Birdwood named the landing place Anzac Cove. Originally only those Australian and New Zealand soldiers who fought at Gallipoli were called Anzacs, and they jealously guarded the name, but it was gradually extended first to other members of the corps and finally to any Australian or New Zealander. The Anzac Area, a small district on the western side of the Gallipoli Peninsula, was dedicated after the war as a permanent memorial to the valor of the members of the Gallipoli expeditionary army who vainly tried to take the western defenses of Constantinople in 1915–1916. By the Treaty of Lausanne, signed in 1923, Turkey granted this area in perpetuity to France, Italy and the British Empire, and these three powers agreed to appoint custodians for the graves and cemeteries. Turkey, however, controls access to the district, which under the terms of the agreement cannot be fortified or built up in any way except to provide shelter for the sole use of the custodians. In 1916 Australia and New Zealand by statute forbade the commercial use of Anzac in any trade, business, profession or calling without government permission. During the Second World War the familiar name for the Australians was Aussies.

What queen reigned after death?

Inez de Castro, wife of Dom Pedro, King of Portugal in the fourteenth century, is often referred to as the Queen who "reigned after death." She became the morganatic wife of Dom Pedro while he was heir to the throne. The Prince's father, the King, seriously objected to the marriage. He feared the powerful Castro family; besides, Inez was believed to be of illegitimate birth. In 1355 Inez was stabbed to death supposedly at the instigation of the old King. The outraged Dom Pedro started a rebellion that did not subside until the Prince was given a large share in the government of Portugal. When the old King died in 1357 Dom Pedro succeeded to the throne. According to tradition, the new King had the body of his murdered wife exhumed, placed on a throne and crowned. All the nobles were compelled to pass and do obeisance to the dead Queen by kissing her withered hand. Then Inez, the "Queen who reigned after death," was interred with great pomp in a beautiful sarcophagus of white marble. Shapur II, King of Persia from 310 to 370 A.D., was crowned before he was born. He was the posthumous son of Hormuzd II, whose born sons were all killed or imprisoned by the nobles immediately after the old King's death. The unborn child was then formally declared King as Shapur II.

What is the origin of the bridal veil?

The wedding or bridal veil is believed to be a survival of an ancient superstition dating back to the time of the Greeks and Romans, if not much earlier. It was first worn to conceal and protect the bride from evil spirits that it was thought would harm her if she were not veiled. Perhaps this was the origin of the general custom of wearing veils, which still prevails to a great extent among women of the Orient. *Bride*, it is supposed, is derived from an ancient Teutonic root signifying "to cook." *Bridal* as an adjective meaning "pertaining to a bride or newly married wife" may or may not be derived from *bridal* in the sense of a wedding party. The latter term is derived from two old English roots meaning "wedding" and "ale." *Bride-ale* is still a historical term. Bride-ales (bridals) were wedding festivals at which the guests were served ale. It is probable that the adjective *bridal* was formed from *bride* under the influence of the older noun *brid-ale*.

Why are ultraconservatives called Bourbons?

The Bourbons were a royal family who ruled France from 1589 to 1848, with interruptions caused by the French Revolution and the Napoleonic regime. Members of the Bourbon family also ruled for centuries in Naples, Parma and Spain. The family was first heard of in the ninth century when its head, Baron Aimar, was lord of the castle and seigniory of Bourbon-l'Archambault in central France in the present department of Villier. Through the centuries the autocratic Bourbons became noted for their opposition to all change and their firm adherence to the *ancien régime* ("the old order"). In 1796 a French naval officer named Charles Louis Étienne, Chevalier de Panat said of the Bourbons: "They have learned nothing and forgotten nothing." This sentiment is also often attributed to Tayllyrand and various other Frenchmen. Napoleon, on St. Helena in 1817, said, "The Bourbons are a set of imbeciles." Of England's national debt, Richard Brinsley Sheridan (1751–1816), declared: "Half of it has been incurred in putting down the Bourbons, and the other half in setting them up." In the United States *Bourbon*, pronounced *boor*-bun, is applied to a reactionary, a standpatter, a member of the "Old Guard," an ultraconservative, one who clings stubbornly to the established order. Schele M. De Vere, writing in 1872, said: "We find the name of the royal Bourbons applied, now politically to any old-fashioned party which acts unmindful of past experience." In 1884 the term was defined as "a Democrat behind the age and unteachable."

Do trees die of old age?

No close parallel exists between trees and animals in respect to maturity and longevity. Trees do not die of old age in the same sense that higher animals and human beings do. In "The Deacon's Masterpiece" Oliver Wendell Holmes wrote:

> In fact, there's nothing that keeps its youth,
> So far as I know, but a tree and truth.

Some authorities are inclined to believe that death of trees results only from accidents, disease or other *unnatural* causes. Few trees are permitted to die of "old age." They are generally killed by storms, insects, blights, soil erosion, fire or the ax and saw of man. Most trees die of disease, and the disease usually takes the form of decay in the trunk, which shuts off the water and food supply from the soil. Still there is some reason for believing that trees do have a sort of life cycle or longevity period and that they would grow old and die as the result of the ravages of time even if not destroyed by unnatural or artificial means. Of course this span of life or life cycle, which is much longer in some species than in others, is very indefinite and cannot be calculated with any degree of accuracy. A human being reaches his maximum height at a comparatively early age. In fact in later years his height often decreases somewhat. But a tree continues to grow as long as it is alive, although after it reaches a certain size, depending on the species and other factors, the rate of growth slows down. Some trees live and continue to grow for thousands of years. The giant redwoods of California, famous as the oldest living things on the earth, have virtually achieved "the miracle of perpetual growth." A few individual trees of this species are estimated to be between 4,000 and 5,000 years of age.

What does it mean "to turn state's evidence"?

In American legal language evidence for the government, people or state in criminal prosecutions is called *state's evidence*. In English law evidence for the Crown is called *King's* (or *Queen's*) *evidence*. These terms are applied more particularly to evidence voluntarily given by an accessory in a crime who confesses his part and who testifies against his accomplices. When a person implicated in a crime voluntarily confesses his share in the illegal act and gives testimony tending to incriminate his associates he is said to *turn state's evidence*; that is, he becomes a witness for the prosecution and consequently for the state or government. In such cases there is often an express or implied promise on the part of the authorities that they will not prosecute the witness who thus testifies, or that they will at least deal leniently with him. It is not customary for prosecutors to promise such immunity unless there is insufficient evidence to convict a defendant without the testimony so obtained. But a person who has committed a crime or who has been an accomplice in an illegal act has no legal claim to clemency merely because he "turns state's evidence." Occasionally a guilty person who has not received either an express or implied promise of leniency will turn state's evidence. In this case he hopes that testifying for the government will result in a pardon even if he is convicted. In popular language *state's evidence* is sometimes loosely applied to the *person* who turns state's evidence.

What great orator put pebbles in his mouth?

When the ancient Athenian orator Demosthenes (384?–322 B.C.) was a young man he had a frail body, weak lungs and a shrill voice. Plutarch tells us that Demosthenes "had a weakness and a stammering in his voice, and a want of breath, which caused such a distraction in his discourse, that it was difficult for the audience to understand him." It seems that, among other handicaps, he was unable to pronounce the sound expressed by the letter r. The first time the young orator spoke in public his audience laughed at and heckled him. "As for his personal defects," says Plutarch, "Demetrius the Phalerean gives us an account of the remedies he applied to them; and he says he had it from Demosthenes in his old age. The hesitation and stammering of his tongue he corrected by practicing to speak with pebbles in his mouth; and he strengthened his voice by running or walking uphill, and pronouncing some passage in an oration or a poem, during the difficulty of breath which that caused." The usual version of this is that Demosthenes overcame his impediment of speech by standing on the shore with pebbles in his mouth and declaimed in competition with the roaring of the sea. "You have stones in your mouth," is said of a person who stutters or speaks indistinctly. In *Hudibras* (1663) Samuel Butler wrote:

> The orator who once
> Did fill his mouth with pebble stones
> When he harangued.

Who was the Laughing Philosopher?

Democritus (460?–362? B.C.), a Greek thinker in the time of Socrates, was known as the "Laughing Philosopher." Just why he was so called is not known for certain. His moral philosophy was very stern and taught the absolute subjection of all passions. According to a legend, probably unfounded, Democritus put out his own eyes so that he might think more clearly and not be diverted in his meditations. Some ancient writers say that he became so perfect in his teachings that he went about continually smiling, from which circumstance he became known as the Laughing Philosopher; but others say that the inhabitants of Abdera, the colony in Thrace where Democritus was born, were notorious for their stupidity, and that he was called the "laughing" Philosopher because of the scorn and ridicule that he heaped upon his townsmen for their ignorance. It appears that Democritus should rather be called the "Deriding Philosopher," since he derided and laughed scornfully at the follies and vanities of mankind. Robert Burton (1577–1640), author of *The Anatomy of Melancholy*, is sometimes referred to as "Democritus Junior."

What is a berserker rage?

In Norse mythology Berserk was the nickname of the grandson of the eight-handed Starkadder. He always went into battle without armor and was famed for the reckless fury with which he fought. *Ber-serk* in old Scandinavian probably meant "bare-shirt," that is, one clothed only in his shirt and not protected by armor or heavier clothing. To be *berserk* was equivalent to "in one's shirt sleeves." Among those slain by Berserk was King Swafurlam, by whose daughter he had twelve sons equal to himself in bravery. These sons of Berserk were called "berserkers," a term that thus became synonymous with "fury" and "reckless courage." Later *berserker* was applied to a class of heathen warriors who were supposed to be able to assume the form of bears and wolves, from which fact some etymologists mistakenly derive the term from *bera-sark* ("bear-shirt" or "armor of bearskin"). Dressed in furs these berserkers would fall into a frenzied rage, foam at the mouth and growl like wild beasts. They were said to have prodigious strength and to be invulnerable to fire and iron. From this latter myth we get *berserker rage*. In *Modern English Usage*, H. W. Fowler says that "*baresark*, for *berserker*, is a corrupt modern form owing its existence to a probably false etymology."

INDEX

fur-bearing animals in Antarctica, 188; warmth of fur of animals in dark and sunlight, 504; gaits of horses, 335; animals without gall bladders, 290; *get one's goat*, 288; grazing habit of giraffes, 326; height of giraffes, 336; horns of giraffes, 4; gorilla beating breasts, 13; greyhound, 18; guinea pigs, 482; hares and rabbits, 32; *harebrained*, 245; bloody sweat of hippopotamus, 116; hogs cutting throats swimming, 422; *chestnuts* on horse legs, 18; length of legs of horse at birth, 301; horses push or pull load, 229; how horses get up, 121; human beings, 133; lights attract animals, fire hunting, 195; madstones from animal stomachs, 454; marten and martin, 10; mice and rats, 239; native land of mice, 194; singing mice, 94; diet of moles, 433; sight of moles, 452; monkey bridges, 268; ribs of monkeys and apes, 282; monkeys and swimming, 279; monkey's tails used in grasping, 59; monkeys in United States, 195; monkeys searching through hair, 230; teeth of apes and monkeys, 293; breeding habits of opossums, 331; black camel and ox, 442; quagga, 18; quills of porcupines, 400; rabbits in Australia and New Zealand, 42; rabbit tracks in snow, 168; swimming hares and rabbits, 24; raccoon washes food, 389; hide of rhinoceros, 231; Rocky Mountain sheep, 15; rodents, coypu, beaver, porcupine, 29; black and white squirrels, 378; ruminants, 41; thoroughbred and purebred animals, 79; whales largest mammals, 257; zebras, 18; color scheme of zebras, 472

Anne, Queen, 17 children, 282

Antarctic, South Pole, 177

Antarctica, animals and people, 188

Ante meridiem, 228

Antelopes, deer, goat, pronghorn, 40; cud, 118; *Home on Range*, 23; rising habit, 121

Anthem, Canadian, 67

Anthracite, coal, 334

Anti-kink hair preparations, 106

Anti-tuberculosis work, Lorraine cross, 166

Antipodes, 102

Ants, clean out hollow tree, 275

Anty-over, game, 217

A Number One, 498

Anzacs, 508

Apes, crossed with humans, 133; gestation period, 99; none native to U. S., 195; number of ribs, 282; searching through hair for what, 230; swimming, 279; teeth, 293

Aphids, honeydew, 275

Applaud, 113

Applause, claque, 114; hand clapping, 113

Applied for, Patent, 192

Arabic numerals, 208

Arachnida, 111

Arbuthnot, John, John Bull, 283

Arc, Joan of, original name, 238

Arcadia, 41

Arctic, and Antarctic, Polar regions, 177; hare, swimming, 25; mosquitoes, 211

Arctics, overshoes, 177

Aristocracy, codfish, 415

Aristotle on hibernation of birds, 24

Arnold, Benedict, Mason, 109

Arnold, Matthew, free verse, 268

Around, hunter walking, squirrel on tree, 158

Asia, 153

Asia, and Africa, boundary, 394; and Europe, boundary, 153

Asia Minor, 153

Aspdin, Joseph, Portland cement, 285

Asses, *chestnuts*, 18

Asterisks on paper money, 172

ASTRONOMY, cause of seasons, 253; dog days, 352; earth a sphere, 463; Land of Midnight Sun, 502; length of light year, 237; light and dark moon, 289; moon at poles, 198; moonless month, 126; moon's surface, 72; motions of moon, 72; old moon sitting in lap new, 383; once in blue moon, 321; seeing stars and planets from well in daytime, 410; shooting stars, 255; star in moon's crescent, 334; twinkling of stars and planets, 359; sun, stars, moon near horizon, 185

Athenian oath, 52

Athens, first written laws, 130

Atlantic and Pacific, seen from Mount Izaru, 472

Atlas, maps, 463

Atmosphere, air pockets, 340; purified by rain, 48; weight, 457

Bell, clock, 183
Bengal, bungalow, 28
Berber, Barbary, 338
Berengaria, Queen, 223
Bern, Switzerland, 462
Berserker rage, 512, 513
Best man at weddings, 181
Bethmann-Hollweg, Theobold von, 27
Beverages, small beer, 183
Beyond the pale, 26
Biddy, hen, 211
Big as cuffy, 20
Big Bad Lands, 159
Big wind, Ireland, 280
Bight of Helgoland, 44
Billingsgate, profanity, 144
Billions and millions, 214
Bills, paper money, asterisks on, 172
BIRDS, air spaces in eggs, 169; as crow
    flies, 478; babies brought by storks,
    179; Baltimore oriole, 9; bee martin,
    370; bobwhites and quails, 367; bull
    bat and nighthawk, 430; canaries in
    wild state, 172; birds caught by fish,
    22; cormorants trained to fish, 491;
    dead as dodo, 297; Delaware state
    bird, 295; difference between doves
    and pigeons, 74; drumming of ruffed
    grouse, 179; eagles dropping tortoises,
    191; birds that eat feathers, 27; at-
    tracted by bright lights, 194; English
    sparrows, 170; flying under water, 70;
    guinea fowls, 223, 293; halcyon days,
    378; hatched fully fledged, 283; hi-
    bernation, 23, 36; hopping, 168; jun-
    gle fowls, 243; kibitzer, 478; how
    locate worms, 313; martin and marten,
    10; migration by sexes, 55; necks, 326;
    number of toes, 55; oil glands of
    waterfowl, 157; ostrich and head in
    sand, 363; diet of ostriches, 324; long-
    est sentence spoken by parrots, 382;
    parrots native to United States, 192;
    passenger pigeons, 500; tails and trains
    of peafowls and quetzals, 28; birds
    pecked at painted grapes, 316; perch-
    ing habits, 29; rain crow, 55; senses
    of birds, 313; singing from ground, 1;
    sleeping, 477; slitting tongue, 188; sol-
    itaire, 298; teeth, 325; white black-
    birds, bluebirds and redbirds, 264; V
    formation of wild ducks and geese,
    313; edible birds' nests, 71; bird's-eye
    maple, 102
Birdlime, 49

Birrell, Augustine, *Obiter Dicta*, 11
Birthday, February 29, 289
Bishop's stone, amethyst, 8
Bismarck, Prince, 32; scraps of paper, 28
Bissextile year, 505
Bit, coin, 453
Bituminous coal, 334
Black and white clothing, 504
Black ball, 103
Blackbirds, white, 264
Black, camel, 443; color, 384; fox, 438;
    frost, 393; letter day, 93; opals, 473;
    ox, 442; pearl, 350; plague, 77; snake,
    blue racer, 36; snow, 387; swallower,
    fish, 26; whip snake, 165
Black Death, 393
Black Hills, 319, 388
Black Hole of Calcutta, 232
Black Friday, 201, 393
Black Jack, John J. Pershing, 127
Black Monday, 201
Black Prince, 37, 202
Black Sea, name, 232
Blackeyed beans and peas, 325
Blacksmith, village smithy, 333
Blacksnakes, sucking cows, 138
Blanc, Mont, 301
Bladder, air, in fish, 318; gall, animals
    without, 290
Blimp, airship, 221
Blind as a mole, 452
Blind snakes, 230
Blockade, paper, 286
Blond, blonde, 461
Blood, human body, 325; laws written
    in, 130; mosquito diet, 269; will tell,
    Jukes, 353
Blooded stock, 79
Bloodletting, barbers, 95
Blood rains, 387
Bloomer, Amelia Jenks, bloomers, 124
Blowfish, wider than long, 276
Blowflies, maggots on meat, 127
Blowing adder or viper, 277
Blubber, whale's overcoat, 258
Bluebirds, white, 264
Blue coal, tidewater, 311; fox, 438;
    lodge, 80; racers, black snake, 36; non-
    venomous bite, 174; whale, largest ani-
    mal, 257
Blue Hen State, Delaware, 294
Blue Monday, 201
Blue moon, once in, 321
Blue-sky laws, 66
Blumenbach, Johann, races, 436

Boats, derby, 497; muffling oars, 204; travel faster than wind, 403
Bobbies, London policemen, 413
Bobwhites and quails, 367
Body, human, quantity of blood, 325; locating drowned body with quicksilver, 421; rising three times after drowning, 354; area of skin, 458; value, 263; percentage of water, 122; weight after death, 274
Boer, Boor, 271
Boleyn, Anne, 73; deformed hand, 98
Bolivia, capital, 295
Bombs, grenades, 14
Boned turkey, 359
Book, Domesday, 208
Books, symbols, 8vo., 12mo., 301
Boor, Boer, 271
Bootlegger, 117
Boots, seven league, 198
Booze, liquor, 425
Borglum, Gutzon, 13
Borneo, wild man, 98
Boscawen, Edward, Old Dreadnought, 233
Bossy, cow, 54
Boston, home of bean and cod, 323; Hub of Universe, 193; look, 194
Bottle flies, blue and green, 211
Boulanger, George Ernest, Boulangism, 5
Boulders, growing, 369
Boundaries, Connecticut-Massachusetts, 217; Africa-Asia, 394; four-states, 308; jog in South Dakota boundary, 131; Kentucky-Tennessee, 397
Bourbons, 445, 509
Bowler, cocked hat, 133; hat, 360
Box the compass, 80
Boxing Day, 25
Boycott, 368
Bradford, John, martyr, 200
Brads, nails, 165
Brain food, fish, 182
Brand-new, 100
Bread and butter letter, 290
Breakers, waves, 96
Breaking Priscian's head, 341
Breath, holding to prevent bee sting, 128; loss of, second wind, 151
Breathing, frogs, 131; second wind, 151
Br'er Rabbit, 11
Brethren of coast, buccaneers, 176
Brick, good fellow, 247
Bridal veil, 509
Bride of sea, 64

Bridegroom, 182
Brides, picture, 281
Bridesmaid, 182
Bridge, card game, 309
Bridges, monkey, 268
Brillat-Savarin, Anthelme, 46
British colony, senior, 496
British Expeditionary Force, 31
British Isles, part of Europe, 268
British king, last in battle, 466
British North America, area, 211
Broad gauge, railroads, 457
Broadcloth, 72
Broadswords, 488
Broncho bean, 455
Bronx, The, 311
Brooklyn, part of New York City, 273
"Brothers and sisters I have none," 389
Brothers, nearer kin to each other than to parents, 216
Broughton, Jack, Westminster Abbey, 345
Brown, Charles Farrar, Artemus Ward, 82
Brown, Thomas, 21
Brown coal, peat, 335; snow, 409; sugar, 261
Browning, Robert, Good News, 267
Bruce, Robert, leper, 407; experience with spider, 421
Brunet, brunette, 461
Brush turkeys, 283
Bryan, William J., cocked hat letter, 133
Buccaneers, pirates, 175; Spanish Main, 427
Bucentaur, galley, 64
Buck, Pearl, quoted on celestial, 23
Buck, passing, 484
Bucket, kick the, 113
Bucket shop, 148
Buddhism, China, 124
Buds and thunderstorms, 271
Bulbs, electric light, pop when broken, 507
Bulgaria, 3
Bull bat, nighthawk, 430
Bull, John, England, 283
Bull snake, pilot snake, 480; nonvenomous bite, 174
Bulletproof, rhinoceros hide, 232
Bullets, pewter, 53
Bullen, Anne, 73; deformed hand, 98
Bumblebees, buzzing, 292
Buncombe, Edward, bunk, 480
Bungalow, 28

Celts, Iceland, 13; druids, 469
Cement, concrete, 76; Portland, 285
Cemeteries in France, rent, 412
Census, Domesday Book, 209; origin of census, 35; census of world, 140
Cent, origin of term, 1; penny, 464
Center, geographical, U. S., 379; of wheel, motion, 186
Centlivre, Susanna, Simon-pure, 264
Century plant, 344
Cess, bad, 64
Chicago fire, 353
Chick, mother of, 292
Chickens, biddy, 211; feeding habit, 16; jungle fowls, 243
Chicory, coffee, 59
Child swallowed by fish, 22
Children, brought by storks, 179
Chimneys, soot, 373
Chimney swifts, 35; winter home, 24
Chimpanzee, gestation period, 99; ribs, 282
China, antipodes, 103; Chinese called Celestials, 22; Chinese coolies, 375; Flowery Kingdom, 166; ginseng, 459; Land of Han and Sons of Han, 123; Chinese pronunciation of English, 51; queues, 355; China's Sorrow, 499
Chinook wind, 348
Chair, Morris, 104
Chamois, 15
Champion Crank, Francis Train, 382
Charge, statutory, 241
Chariots, Roman, standard gauge, 457
Charivari, shivaree, 425
Charles II, amateur anatomist, 274
Charles V, clocks, 300
Charles's Wain, constellation, 152
Charlemagne, 7; greyhounds, 19
Chaucer, Geoffrey, derring do, 157
Chauvinism, jingo, 249
Chauvinist, 99
Checks, less than dollar, 285
Cheese, green, moon, 496
Chestnut, stale joke, 57
Chestnuts on horse legs, 18; worms, 423
Chlorophyl, plant growth, 46
Choice, Hobson's, 250
Christiania, Oslo, Norway, 492
Christians, rice, 167
Christmas boxes, Boxing Day, 25
Christowe, Stoyan, 368
Churches, Little Around Corner, 345; St. Peter's largest in world, 179;

Church of Transfiguration in New York, 345
Churning, 483
Cigars, worms, 84
Cigarettes, lighting three, 127
Cinnabar ore, source of mercury, 420
Circumnavigation of globe, 150
Cities, difference between town and city, 442; city named by flipping coin, 199; Rome called Eternal City, 406; sixteen cities named by Alexander the Great after himself, 402
Citizen, naturalized, deportation, 137
Citrus fruit, grapefruit, 364
Civet cat, 201
Clams, pearls, 349
Claque, 114
Classic Age, 262
Cleaning Augean stables, 469
Clemens, Samuel, Mark Twain, 149
Clement, St., feltmakers and hatters, 34
Cleopatra, complexion, 439
Clocks, dial, IIII for IV, 97; dummy set at 8:18, 146; king tried to make tick in unison, 300; o'clock, 183
Clockwise and counterclockwise, winds, 266
Cloth, broad, 72; corduroy, 45; cotton and wool, 39; Kendal green, 49; khaki, 110
Clothes, dungarees, 108; weeds, 492
Clothing, first fabric, 162; relative warmth of black and white, 504
Cloud, fog, 63, 154
Cloudbursts, 198
Cloves, Isle of, 44
Coachwhip snake, 165
Coal, anthracite and bituminous, 334; carrying coals to Newcastle, 139; spontaneous combustion, 468; white coal, 311
Coast, Barbary, 338
Coast line, 317
Coats, pea coat, 16; Prince Albert, 13; buttons on men's coat sleeves, 167; tuxedos, 384
Cobra-de-Paraguay, jumps off ground, 362
Cobwebs, 133; gossamers, 164
Cockades, 132
Cocked hat, knock into, 132
Cockfighting, blue hen's chickens, 294; cockpit of Europe, 73; showing the white feather, 437
Cockroaches, cockroach or roach, 422;

croton bugs, 50; natural enemies of bedbugs, 423

C.O.D., cash on delivery, 435

Codfish, Cape Cod turkey, 359; codfish aristocracy, 415; Boston, home of bean and cod, 323; Grand Bank cod-fisheries, 470

Coffee, substitutes, 59

Coffin ships, 471

Coins, cent and penny, 464; defacing and destroying coins, 339; dime, 441; coinage of mills, 243; not worth a rap, 246; platinum coins, 426; stealing coppers from dead man's eyes, 3; two bits, 453

Coke, Sir Edward, 44, 100; William, bowler hat, 361

Cold and hot water, freezing, 343

Cold, lightning, 147; moon, 283; plague, influenza, 62

Cold shoulder, 185

Coleridge-Taylor, Samuel, African blood, 408

Coleslaw and coldslaw, 136

College, degrees, A.B. and A.M., 278; Garfield's definition, 493

Colleges, teachers', normal schools, 262

Colombia, Panama, 145

Colonel, pronunciation, 439

Colorado, altitude, 189; height of mountains, 266

Colors, relative warmth of cool and warm, 504, 505; white and black, 384

Colossus of Rhodes, Seven Wonders, 479

Colt, length of legs, 301

Columbus, Christopher, first landing, 181

Combustion, spontaneous, 467

Commodities and stocks, bucket shops, 149

Common-law marriage, 409

Commonwealth and State, 308

Companies incorporated in Delaware, 303

Companion, 57

Companionate snake, 480

Company, 57

Compass, boxing, 80; hogs used as, 422

Complex, beauty, 487; conquest, 487; inferiority, superiority, 486

Compliment, trade last, 458

Compound fracture, 56

Comptroller and controller, 213

Comrade, 57

Concrete and cement, 76, 285

Condign punishment, 305

Coney Island, Elephant Hotel, 201

Confederate Memorial, Stone Mountain, 132

Congreve, William, Sir, matches, 320

Connecticut-Massachusetts boundary, 217

Connecticut, Nutmeg State, 329

Conquered, Thou hast, O Galilean, 99

Consensus of opinion, 34

Consumption, tuberculosis, 77

Contemptibles, Old, 31

Continents, definition of term, 154; Europe called The Continent, 268; the seven continents, 154; Napoleon's Continental system, 287

Continuum, 119

Controller and Comptroller, 213

Cony, guinea pig, 482

Cook, James, Capt., Sandwich Islands, 136; tortoise, 215

Cook, Jay, 202

Cooing, turtledoves, 121

Cool colors, 505

Coolie, 375

Coon, raccoon, washes food, 389

Coon's age, 137

Copper, hardening, lost art, 314; in German silver, 30

Coppers, stealing from dead man's eyes, 3

Cops, policemen, 413

Corduroy, 45

Cormorants, 71; trained to catch fish, 491

Coral snakes, 230

Corn, maize, corn sugar, 261; growth of plant at night, 173; even number of rows of kernels on ear, 26; popcorn, 65

Corncracker, cracker, 421

Corner, Little Church Around, 345

Corporations have no souls, 100

Corporations, Delaware, 304

Corpse, growth of hair, 376

Corpse, public right of way, 58

Costa Rica, Mount Izaru, 472

Cotten, Felix T., 43

Cotton, early fabric, 162; in wool cloth, 39

Cottonmouth moccasin, water snake, 228

Cousin Michael, German people, 217

Cousin relationships, 462

Cousins-german, 462

Count, county, 57

[527]

Gainsborough, Thomas, 317
Galapagos tortoises, longevity, 215
Galilean, O, Thou hast conquered, 99
Galileo, weight of air, 457
Gall bladders, animals without, 290
Gall flies and wasps, ink balls, 137
Gallipoli Peninsula, Anzacs, 508
Galloping, horse, 335
Galveston, Tex., flood, 96
Games, according to Hoyle, 118
Gammon of bacon, 284
Garfield, James A., definition of university, 493
Garner, John N., 33
Garrison finish, 225
Garter snake, nonvenomous bite, 174
Gas, goldfish detect, 494
Gascons, 338
Gasoline, freezing point, 212; mileage from affected by speed, 246
Gate, Hell, 120; Iron Gate in Danube, 472
Gauge, shotgun, 216; standard railroad, 457
Gaulle, Charles de, Lorraine cross, 167
Gay Lothario, 197
Gay science, 25
Geese, feeding habits, 16; wild, V formation, 313
Gem of Antilles, 380
Gemini, Castor and Pollux, 161
Geranium, horseshoe, 84
German, language, all nouns capitalized, 275; silver, 30
Germany, soldiers called Fritzies, Heinies, Jerries, 216; Huns, 89; submarines called U-boats, 275; Holy Roman Empire, 7
Gender, inanimate objects, 121
General court-martial, 471
Generation, spontaneous, 128
Geneva, Switzerland, 462
Gentleman among snakes, 67
Geographic Board, United States, 253, 307
George, let, do it, 78
George, Lloyd George, David, 416
George II, last British king in battle, 466
George III, length of reign, 75
Georgia, area, 241; crackers, 421
Gestation, apes, 99
Get one's goat, 288
Ghent, Good News from, 267
Ghost walks, 101
Giant, outline on hillside, 288

Gibraltar, history, 240
Ginseng, 459
Giraffes, cud, 118; eyes, 326; grazing habit, 326; height, 336; horns, 4; rising habit, 121; voice, 365
Girdling trees, 134
Glad Girl, Pollyanna, 33
Gladiolus, 38
Glass, forest, 253; spoon prevents hot water from breaking, 207
Globe, discovery that earth is, 463; first circumnavigator, 150
Gloves, kangaroo leather, 371
Glowworms, earthworms, 465
Gnat, mosquito, 350
Go around Robin Hood's barn, 429
Goats, cud, 118; get one's goat, 288; milk, 483; tin cans, 218; rising habit, 121; wild goat, 15
Goatee, beard, 288
Goatsuckers, birds, 29, 430
Go berserk, 512
Gobs, sailors, 225
God, act of, 247
God, but for the grace of, there, goes, 200
God Save the King, 67
God, trust in, keep powder dry, 309
Gods, on lap of, 152
Gods, mills of, grind slow, 208
Godiva, Lady, 296
Gold, corner on gold market in 1869, 202; fool's gold, 315; gold leaf, 379; transmutation, 428; weight of gold and feathers, 356; white gold, 242
Goldbeaters' skin, 379
Golden Hind, Pelican, ship, 151
Golden rose, 503
Goldfinches, wild canaries, 172
Goldfish, 494
Goldsmith, Oliver, inspired idiot, 60
Golf, plus fours, 225
Golly, by, 249
Good News from Ghent, 267
Good success, 63
Goosefish, 22
Gopher, ground squirrel, 107
Gorilla, drumming on breast, 13; gestation period, 99; number of ribs, 282
Goschen, Edward, Sir, 27
Gosh, by, 249
Gossamers, 164
Gotham, 372
Go to the dickens, 387
Gould, Jay, panic, 202

Gourd, snake, 84
Government, special stamps, profit, 121
Grammar, Priscianus, 341
Grand Bank, 470
Grapefruit, name, 364
Grape sugar, 261
Grapes, painted, birds pecked at, 316
Grass, growth at night, 173; timothy, 19;
    make two blades grow where one grew
    before, 363; grass widow, 348
Grasshopper sparrow, 1
Graveyard, elephant, 506
Gravity, specific, elements, 456
Gray, Thomas, *Elegy*, 117
Great Bank, Newfoundland, 470
Great Bear, constellation, 152, 177
Great Britain, part of Europe, 268
Great Dipper, constellation, 152
Great Lakes, freezing over, 388
Great Salt Lake, 138; swimming in, 148
Grebes, birds, eat feathers, 27
Greece, 3; oath of young men, 52
Greeks, Greeks had word for it, 10; first
    major battle between Greeks and
    Romans, 385; when Greek meets
    Greek, 111; Greek painting, 317
Green, cheese, moon, 496; Kendal, 49;
    racer, snake, 36
Greenhorn, 314
Greenland, origin of name, 434; island
    or continent, 154; Labrador, 405
Gregorian calendar, 505
Grenade, grenadiers, 14
Greyhounds, name, 18; speed, 53
Gridiron, 440
Grind slow, mills of gods, 208
Grippe, Tyler, 62
Ground snakes, 230
Grouse, ruffed, drumming, 179
Groom, bridegroom, 182
Growth of plants and trees, 46
Guanacos, wild llamas, 507
Guano, cormorants, 491
Guatemala, quetzal, 29
Guericke, Otto von, 251
Guerrilla warfare, 35, 295
Guiana hog, guinea pig, 482
Guillemots, birds, 71
Guinea fowls, effect of fright on flesh,
    293; called keets, 223; male and fe-
    male, 191; native land, 224
Guinea pigs, 482
Guiteau, Charles, crank, 382
Gums, 60
Gun, son of a gun, 485

Gunners, opening mouths when firing,
    492
Gunny sack, 485
Gunpowder Plot, 146, 147
Guns, caliber, 175; cartridges, 2; quaker
    guns, 142; spiking cannon, 182; cause
    of report, 398
Guppies, fish, 169

Hail, cause, 48; largest hailstones, 495;
    does hail purify atmosphere, 48; hail
    rods, 48
Hail, Hello, 180
Hair, anti-kink preparations, 106; Chi-
    nese queue, 355; hair balls, madstones,
    455; growth of hair after death, 376;
    snakes crawling over hair rope, 263
Hairbrained or harebrained, 245
Hairworms, 343
Haiti or Santo Domingo, 441
Halcyon days, 378
Half-wit, moron, 393
Haliburton, Thomas Chandler, 329
Hall, Samuel Reed, normal schools, 263
Halloysite, madstones, 455
Halos, sun, 262
Ham, Smithfield, 114
Hamites, 338
Hammer, water, pounding in pipes, 477
Hammerfest, most northern European
    town, 234
Hampton Roads, 221
Han, Land of, China, 123
Hands, clapping hands, applause, 113;
    cold handshake, 186; dead man's hand
    in card games, 99; fifth hand, mon-
    key's tail, 59; fingers and thumb, 395;
    hand of bananas, 196
Handel, Frederick, Westminster Abbey,
    346
Hanging gardens, Seven Wonders, 479
Hannibal, race, 26
Hanson, timothy, grass, 19
Hares, difference between hare and rab-
    bit, 32; hares and rabbits in Australia
    and New Zealand, 42; Cape jumping
    hare, speed, 53; speed of jack rabbit,
    53; lifting hares by ears, 27; swim-
    ming, 24
Harebrained or hairbrained, 245
Hare-hearts, 246
Harelip, 104
Harass, 8
Hard coal, 334

[532]

Lunula, fingernails, 205
Lycurgus, 247

M., meridiem, 227
Macbeth, Shakespeare's, stealing thunder, 490
Mace, spice, 329
Machine, perpetual motion, 202
Mackerel, drowning, 346
Mad dogs, 352
Madding or maddening crowd, 117
Madstone, 454
Maelstrom, 320
Magpies, talking, 188
Magdeburg hemispheres, 251
Magellan, Ferdinand, 150
Maggots, flesh flies, 155; on meat, 128
Magic, wood, walking under ladder, 161
Magna Charta, 84
Maguey, century plant, 345
Maid of Orleans, Joan of Arc, 238
Main, Spanish, 427
Maine, coast line, 318; touches only one other state, 370
Maize, corn, even number of rows of kernels, 206; growth at night, 173
Make two blades of grass grow, 363
Maltese cross, 14
Man, drowned, floats face down, 473
Man, style is the, 42
Manioc, cassava, 142
Mankind, races, 436
Man on horseback, 4
Man must sometimes rise above principle, 4
Mann Act, 431
Man's house is his castle, 44
Manuscript U, V, 106
Manutius, Aldus, inventor of punctuation, 271; printer's devil, 272
Map, country moved from South to North America, 145
Maps, Atlas, 463
Maple, bird's-eye, 102
Maple Leaf Forever, Canada, 67
Mardi Gras, 449
Marine, merchant, 327
Marines, devil dogs, 162; leathernecks, 234
Maritime Service, merchant marine, 328
Mark, Plimsoll's, 471
Mark, St., horses of, 359
Markets, London, 145
Market reports, point in, 83; stock, 432

Markham, Mount, height, 266
Mark Twain, Samuel Clemens, 149
Marmoset, tail, 59
Marriages, marriage of Adriatic, 64; best man at weddings, 181; bridal veil, 509; common-law marriage, 409; June as lucky marriage month, 445; picture brides, 281; royal marriages, 344
Mars, god of war, *martial*, 271
Marshall, John, 11; gall stones removed from, 174
Martial law, national, 270
Martin, Abraham, Plains of Abraham, 115
Martin, purple, 371; martin and marten, 10; bee martin, 370
Marsupials, opossum, 331; weight of marsupials at birth, 377
Martial, Roman epigrammatist, 21
Maru, Japanese ship names, 438
Mary, Polly familiar form, 33
Maryland, T. B., village, 91
Masks, death, 423
Masonry, Benedict Arnold's membership, 109; blue lodge, 80; third degree, 376
Massachusetts, officially a commonwealth, 308; Massachusetts-Connecticut boundary, 217
Master Mason, lodge, 80; third degree, 377
Master, past, Freemasonry, 271
Matches, friction, 319; lighting three cigarettes with one match, 127
Maternal impression, harelip, 104
Mather, Cotton, 304
Mattapony River, Virginia, 361
Mauna Kea, height, 266
Mauritius, dodo, 297
Mausolus, tomb, Seven Wonders, 479
May, 446
Mayfair, London, 195
May marriages, unlucky, 446
McAllister, Ward, four hundred, 316
McKinley, Mount, highest point in North America, 265
Meat, jerked, 351; maggots, 128
Mechanical perpetual motion, 202
Medical finger, 395
Medici, pawnbroker's sign, 231
Mediterranean, 313
Megaparsec, million parsecs, 238
Megapodes, birds, 283
Melican for *American*, Chinese, 51

[535]

Melons, cantaloupe and muskmelon, 77; nutmeg, 78; Persian, 77; rock, 77
Merchant marine, 327; ships, ninety-day, 251
Mercury, quicksilver, 420
Meridiem, M., 227
Merry Andrew, 372
Mesopotamia, 313
Metals, base, transmutation, 428
Meteorites, shooting stars, 255
Mexican jumping bean, 455; swordfish, 169
Mexico, D. F., 340; Lincoln of, Juarez, 177; Storehouse of World, 235
Mice, elephants afraid, 417; mice and rats used as guinea pigs, 483; native land of house mouse, 194; relationship between mice and rats, 239; singing mice, 94
Michael, Cousin, German people, 217
Michigan, shore line, 318
Middle Ages, 262
Middle East, 312
Midnight, designation, 227
Midnight Sun, Land of, 502
Midshipmen, naval cadets, 87
Migration of birds by sexes, 55
Mikado, 142
Mildew, 276
Mileage from gasoline, effect of speed, 246
Mile square, square mile, 334
Milesians, Irish, 193
Military law, martial law, 270
Milk, when cow manufactures, 116; relative weight of milk and cream, 257; butter from milk of all mammals, 483; milk and madstones, 454; milk soured by thunder, 360; snakes, sucking cows, 138; sugar, 261; tree, 423
Miller, Elizabeth Smith, bloomers, 125
Millions and billions, 214
Mills of gods, grind slow, 208
Mills, coins, 243
Milton, John, humor, 251
Mines, living diamond, ostriches, 325; women excluded, 115
Minnesota, state nearest North Pole, 248
Minnows, minnies, what kind of fish, 448; top minnows, 169
Minster in Westminster, 190
Minstrel, Negro, first, 244
Minute, sucker born every, 2
Miracle of perpetual youth, trees, 511

Mirror, reflection in spoon, 178
Missouri, bounded by eight states, 370
Mistletoe, druids, 489; birdlime, 49
Mitchell, Elisha, Mount Mitchell, 319
Mites, 111
Mob, 65
Mob psychology, 216
Mobile, Ala., Mardi Gras, 449
Moccasin, cottonmouth, water snake, 228
Mock trial, kangaroo court, 112
Mohammedans, music in religious services, 277
Molasses, these or this, 467
Moles, diet, 433; eyes, 452
Mollusks, pearls, 349
Money, cent and penny, 464; checks for less than dollar, 285; defacing and destroying coins, 339; dime, 441; not worth a rap, 246; platinum coins, 426; redemption of mutilated paper money, 490; shinplaster money, 302; asterisks preceding serial number on bills, 172; two bits, 453
Mongolia, Chinese rule, 124
Mongols, afraid of lightning, 125
Mongoose, civet cat, 201
Monkeys, bridges made by, 268; gestation period, 99; grasping with tails, 59; Mexican spider monkey, 195; no species of monkey or ape native to United States, 195; number of ribs, 282; why monkeys search through hair, 230; do monkeys swim, 279; teeth, 293
Monkey tails, queues, 355; wrench, 287
Moneylenders, pawnbroker's sign, 232
Monroe, James, Last Cocked Hat, 132
Mons, battle, 31
Mont Blanc, 301
Montcalm, Marquis de, 115
Moon, cold moon, 283; harvest moon, 149; hunter's moon, 150; why appears larger near horizon, 185; light and dark moon, 289; moon made of green cheese, 496; moonless month, 126; motions of moon, 72; old moon sitting in lap of new, 383; once in a blue moon, 321; phases of the moon, 126; moon at the poles, 198; rainbows by moonlight, moonbows, 406; stars within crescent of moon, 334; part of moon's surface visible, 72; wet and dry moon, 189
Moonfish, 169

Moonshine, liquor, 187
Moor, Moro, 47
Morganatic marriage, 344
Moron, 392
Moros in Philippines, 47
Morris chair, 104
Morris, Gouverneur, 1, 329; birthplace, 312; dime, 441
Morris, William, 104
Morton, Thomas, 119
Moslems, in Philippines, Moros, 47; music with religious services, 277
Mosques, Moslem, 277
Mosquito bees, 300
Mosquitoes, biting, 350; diet, 269; in far north, 211
Mother of chick, 292
Mother-of-pearl, 349
Mother of trusts, New Jersey, 304
Motion, perpetual, 202
Motion pictures, perspective, 230
Motto of postal service, 69
Mound builders, birds, 283
Mountains, Andes, 399; highest in world, 265; highest peak east of Rockies, 319; Mount Izaru, 472; Ozarks, 444; springs on mountain tops, 355
Mountain State, Colorado, 189
Mourning doves, cooing, 121; passenger pigeon, 502
Mouth fish, 22
Muang T'ai, Thailand, 17
Muffled oars, 204
Mug, face, 197
Mule rabbit, 8
Mumblety-peg, 114
Munster plums, potatoes, 359
Murres, birds, 71
Muscle or Mussel Shoals, 338
Mushing, driving dog team, 69
Music hath charms to soothe savage breast, 68
Music, Moslem religious services, 277
Musk, odor, 437
Muskmelon, cantaloupe, 77
Muslin, Mussolini, 177
Mussel or Muscle Shoals, 338
Mussolini, Benito, Il Duce, 176
Mutual Admiration Society, 399
My uncle's, pawnbroker, 260
Mynahs, talking, 188

Nail, dead as doornail, 459; horseshoe, battle lost, 327

Nails, finger, lunula, 205; specks on, 74; measured by pennies, 164
Names, ff for F, 12; junior and senior after, 8
Naming person after or for another, 43
Napoleon Bonaparte, Holy Roman Empire, 7; Napoleon's Cocked Hat, Saba, 132; nation of shopkeepers, 339; paper blockade, 286
Narrow gauge, railroads, 457
Nasby, postal official, 82
Nation of shopkeepers, 339
Natural-born citizen, deportation, 137
Navy, dreadnoughts, 233; gadget, 126; slush fund, 115
Near East, 312
Necktie, cravat, 432
Necks, animals and birds, 326
Negroes, color of newly born babies, 474; big as cuffy, 20; French writer part Negro, 407; Jim Crow, 244; Negro minstrel, first, 244; Negro troops and Rough Riders, 127
Neither snow, nor rain, nor heat, 69
Nerve racking or wracking, 118
Nests, edible birds', 71
Newcastle, carrying coals to, 139
Newfoundland, Grand Bank, 470; Labrador part of, 406; not part of Canada, 496
New Jersey, mother of trusts, 304; tea, 468
New Orleans, burials, 92; Mardi Gras, 449
News, 66; Good, from Ghent, 267
Newspapers, fourth estate, 94
New Year's Day, blackeyed peas, 326
New York, Baumes laws, 404; New York City called Gotham, 372; Brooklyn part of New York City, 273; Staten Island, 476; Stock and Curb exchanges, 432
New World, highest point, 265
New Zealand, Anzacs, 508; rabbits, 42
Niagara, fish swimming up, 254
Nickel in German silver, 30
Nickel Plate Railroad, 124
Nickel, Quaker, kiss, 342; silver, 30
Night, Boxing, 25; growth of corn, 173
Nighthawks, bull bat, 430; perching habit, 29; related to swifts, 36
Nimes, Nismes, denim, 36
Nine points of law, possession, 308
Nine-day wonder, 160
Ninety-day ships, 251

[538]

Panacea, philosopher's stone, 428
Panama, moved on map from South to North America, 145; sun rises in Pacific and sets in Atlantic, 133
Pancake Tuesday, 449
Pandects, Roman laws, 261
Paper, folio and quarto, 301; foolscap, 219; treaties called scraps of paper, 27; watermarks, 220
Paper blockade, 286
Paper money, redemption of mutilated, 490; stars preceding serial number, 172
Paradise, fruit of, bananas, 337
Parakeet, Carolina, 192
Pardoe, Julia, 445
Parents, kinship, 216
Parhelia, sun dogs, 262
Parishes, Louisiana, 206
Parr, Thomas, Westminster Abbey, 345
Parrhasius, Greek painter, 317
Parrots, longest sentence uttered, 382; species native to United States, 192; number of toes, 55; thickbilled parrot, 193
Parsec, astronomical unit, 238
Parthian shot, 326
Partridges, quail, 367; ruffed grouse, 179
Pass, they shall not, 187
Passenger pigeons, 500
Passing the buck, 484
Past master, Freemasonry, 271
Patents, infringement, 239; are services of lawyer required to obtain, 204; Patent Pending and Patent Applied For, 192
Path, drawing red herring across, 123
Patrick, Paddy, 274
Patrick, St., shamrock, 419; snakes, 461
Pawnbrokers, my uncle's, 260; pawnbroker puzzle, who lost the dollar, 217; three golden balls, 231
Pay through nose, 177
Peace, dove emblem, 75
Peacocks, 489; tail and train, 28; Peacock Throne, 489
Pea-jacket, 16
Peanuts, Smithfield ham, 114
Pearl Harbor, time of attack, 147
Pearl of Antilles, 380
Pearls, edible oysters, 349
Pearly tapioca, 142
Peas, blackeyed, 325
Peasouper, fog, 155
Peat, wood coal, 335

Pebbles in mouth, Demosthenes, 511
Pedigreed stock, 79
Pedro II, length of reign, 75
Peelers, London policemen, 413
Peeping Tom, 296
Pelee, Point, southernmost point in Canada, 249
Pelican, Golden Hind, ship, 151
Penasse, Minnesota, northernmost U. S. town, 249
Pence, pennies, 465
Pending, Patent, 192
Penguins, paddle with wings, 71
Peninsula, Balkan, 3; peninsula and continent, 154
Penitentiary, kangaroo court, 112
Pennies, cent, 464; nails measured by pennies, 164; stealing pennies from dead man's eyes, 3
Pennsylvania, commonwealth officially, 308; state bird, 179
Pepi II of Egypt, longest reign, 75
Perfume, Ambergris, 414
Perihelion, 253
Perkins, Frances, Secretary of Labor, 115
Perpetual motion, 202
Perpetuum, 119
Pershing, John J., Black Jack, 127
Persian melon, 77
Persecution complex, 487
Persia, Iran, Peacock Throne, 489
Petrels, hibernation, 24
Petrified lightning, 253
Pewter, 53
Phalanges, fingers and toes, 396
Phansigars, Thugs, 135
Pharaohs, marriage, 439
Pharos, Seven Wonders, 479
Pheasants, American, 367, 179
Philippines, Filipinos, 150; Moros, 47; smallest fish in world, 101
Philips, Wendell, 5
Philosopher, Laughing, 512
Philosopher's stone, 428
Phiz, face, 90
Phosphorus, no, no thought, 182
Physick, Philip Syng, Dr., 173
Picture brides, 281
Pictures, eyes in portraits, 229
Pie, humble, eating, 331; peacock, 489
Piece of eight, Spanish dollar, 453
Pig cony, guinea pig, 482
Pigeons, difference between doves and pigeons, 74; passenger pigeons, 500

Price of liberty, eternal vigilance, 5
Primary colors, 385
Prince Albert coat, 13
Prince, Black, 37
Principle, man must sometimes rise
    above, 4
Printer's devil, 272
Printing, long and short S, 484
Priscian's head, breaking, 341
Prisons, Libby prison, 322; kangaroo
    courts in prisons, 112; Sing Sing, 404
Prohibition, bootlegging, 117
Pronghorns, antelopes, 23
Proud as cuffy, 20
Prunes and plums, 209
Pruning shears, scissors, 467
Psychology, mob, 216
Ptolemies, marriage, 440
Puerto Rico, spelling, 70
Puffing adders, spray, 276
Pull and push, 229
Pullet, 53
Pulley, mechanical advantage, 454
Pulque, beverage, 345
Pummelo, grapefruit, 365
Punctuation, invention, 271
Punishment, condign, 305
Purebred and thoroughbred, 79
Purple martin, 371
Push and pull, 229
Pushkin, Alexander, African blood, 402
Puzzle, pawnbroker, who lost dollar, 217
Pygmy hare, 32
Pyramids of Egypt, Seven Wonders, 479
Pyrites, fool's gold, 315
Pyrrhic victory, 385
Pythagoras, earth a sphere, 463
Pythons, eggs, 150

Quagga, chestnuts, 18
Quai d'Orsay, 91
Quails, bobwhites, 367
Quaker guns, 142
Quaker nickel, kiss, 342
Quarter, Dutch, hug, 342; two bits, 453
Quartered oak, 473
Quarto, books, 301
Quebec, Plains of Abraham, 115
Queen of Antilles, 380
Queen, English, deformed hand, 98;
    English, 17 children, 282; honeybee,
    sting, 288; reigned after death, 508
Queen's evidence, turning, 511
Queer as Dick's hatband, 386

Quetzal, Guatemala bird, 29
Queue, Chinese, 355
Quicksilver, mercury, 420
Quills, porcupine, 400
Quin, Percy Edwards, 4
Quito, Ecuador, 295

R, sound, Demosthenes, 511; difficult
    for Chinese, 51
Rabbits, Australia and New Zealand, 42;
    Br'er Rabbit, 11; rabbits' feet as good
    luck charms, 10, 176; difference be-
    tween rabbits and hares, 32; hare in
    harebrained, 245; jack rabbit, name, 8,
    speed, 53; lifting rabbits by ears, 27;
    rabbit or rarebit, Welsh, 358; rab-
    bits and hares as swimmers, 24; rab-
    bit tracks in snow, 168
Rabies, 352; madstones, 454
Raccoons, washing food, 389; coon's
    age, 137
Racer, blue, black snake, 36
Races, horse, Derby, 497; Garrison fin-
    ish, 225
Races of mankind, 436; color at birth,
    474
Racking and Wracking, 118
Radiology, X rays, 498
Rage, berserker, 512
Railroads, limited train, 235; Nickel
    Plate Railroad, 124; paper car wheels,
    336; standard gauge, 457; staterooms,
    446; tracks seem to meet in distance,
    6; wheels of cars slip on curves, 350
Rails, sora, hibernation, 24
Rain, rain crow, 55; cloudbursts, 198;
    dew as sign of rain, 81; rain fertilizes
    soil, 408; rain after lightning flash,
    456; neither rain, nor snow, nor heat,
    69; rain and purification of atmos-
    phere, 48; red rain, 387
Rainbow, rainbow chasers and pot of
    gold at foot of rainbow, 429; moon-
    bows, rainbows at night, 406
Rainfall, dry farming, 328
Rainier, Mount, Tacoma, 205
Range, Home on, 23
Rap, not worth, 246
Rare, O, Ben Jonson, 90
Rarebit, rabbit, Welsh, 358
Rats, difference between rats and mice,
    239; rats and mice used as guinea
    pigs, 483; smell a rat, 178
Rattlesnakes, biting through leather,

St. David's Day, 8
St. James's, Court, 391
St. John, New Brunswick province, 480
St. John's, Newfoundland, 480
St. Johns, Quebec province, 480
St. Mark, horses, 359
St. Patrick, shamrock, 419
St. Peter's, largest church, 170
Salmon, origin of term, 255; softening bones of canned, 273; spawning habits, 78; swimming up waterfalls, 254
Salt to Dysart, 140
Salt, Great Salt Lake, 138; monkeys search for, 230, 231; water, swimming, 148
Salvation Army, slogan, 93
Sammy, doughboy, 112
San Francisco, Frisco, 373
San Pedro Bay, seaport of Los Angeles, 222
San Salvador, El Salvador, 181
Sanatorium and sanitarium, 279
Santo Domingo, Haiti, 441
Sanctuary in England, 236
Sand, head in, ostrich, 363; petrified lightning, 253; snake, 277
Sands, Sahara, 388
Sandhiller, 421
Sandstone, 369
Sandwich, 136
Sandwich man, 137
Sandy, Scotsman, 36
Sang, ginseng, 460
Sanitarium and sanatorium, 279
Sap, trees, freezes in winter, 186; does it rise in spring, 451
Sapsuckers, bird's-eye maple, 102
Sardines, fish, 59; softening bones of in canned, 373; origin of term, 59
Savanna sparrow, 1
Savvy, 478
Scandinavia, 278
Scandinavians in Iceland, 13
Schlozer, August von, 26
Schools, normal schools, 262; red school-house, 113; secondary schools, 365
Schooner, 108
Science, gay, 25
Scilicet, 157
Scissors, shears, 466
Scorpions, 111
Scotch woodcock, 359
Scotland Yard, 335
Scotland, saved by spider, 421
Scotsman, Sandy or Sawney, 36

Scott, Walter, Sir, deeds of derring do, 157
Scottish king, leper, 407
Scourge of Sons of Han, 499
Scouring the White Horse, 288
Scraps of paper, treaties, 27
Scratching back, log-rolling, 151
Sea-coal, 139
Seas, Black Sea, name, 232; Bride of the Sea, 64; sea devil, fish, 22; seaport of Los Angeles, 222; sea shells, roaring, 125; the seven seas, 464; sea snakes, 228; South Seas, 166
Seasons, cause, 253
Seattle and Tacoma, controversy over mountain, 205
Second cousins, 462
Second wind, 151
Secondary, heart, eels, 218; schools, 365
See the elephant, 200
Seeing, object, reflected light, 6; wind, 222
Segregation, Jim Crow laws, 244
Sellers, Isaiah, Mark Twain, 149
Semayne's Case, 44
Senior British colony, 496
Semitic and shemitic, 26
Senior and junior after names, 8
Sennight, 411
Sentinels, poultry, 224
Serbia and Servia, 300
Serbs, Croats, Slovenes, kingdom, 252
Seven different kinds of meat, turtle, 259
Seven league boots, 198
Seven seas, 464
Seventh son of seventh son, 411
Seven Wonders of World, 479
Sex offenses, statutory, 241
Shades, colors, 385
Shaddock, grapefruit, 365
Shaft, Parthian, 326
Shakespeare of Russia, Pushkin, 402
Sham court, kangaroo, 112
Shamrock, Ireland's emblem, 419; snake repellent, 85
Shape, lick into, 377
She, ship, 120
Shears, scissors, 466
Sheep, cud, 118; fat stored in tail, 85; hornless called mugs, 197; rising habit of sheep, 121; Rocky Mountain sheep, 15; sheep shears, 467
Sheet lightning, 403
Shell, tortoise, source, 54

[543]

Shelley, Mary W., Frankenstein, 121
Shells, sea, roaring, 125
Shem, son of Noah, 26
Shenandoah, 318
Sheridan, Philip H., Hell and Texas, 398
Sheriff, 57
Shield tails, snakes, 230
Shields, Rhinoceros hide, 231
Shinplasters, paper money, 302
SHIPS, A-1, A Number One, 498; dreadnoughts, 233; maru in Japanese ship names, 438; merchant marine, 327; ninety-day ships, 251; Plimsoll's mark, 471; sailing ships travel faster than wind driving them, 403; schooners, 108; why ship called she and her, 120; stateroom, 446; relative weight of steel and wooden ships, 322; U.S.S., S.S., and H.M.S., 435
Shire, county, 56
Shivaree, charivari, 425
Shoals, Muscle or Mussel, 338
Shock, hydraulic, pounding in pipes, 477
Shoes, kangaroo leather, 371; squeaking in shoes, 265; wooden shoes, sabots, 298
Shop, bucket, 148
Shooting stars, 255
Shopkeepers, nation of, 339
Short bit, ten cents, 453
Short trot, horse gait, 335
Shot, Parthian, 326
Shotgun, gauge, 216
Shoulder, cold, 185
Show white feather, 437
Showers, fish and frogs, 386
Shreveport, La., 446
Shrove Tuesday, 449
Siam, Thailand, 17; white elephant, 481
Sibert, William, General, 112
Sick'm, inciting dogs to attack, 7
Sideburns, 365
Siege, state of, martial law, 270
Sight, illusion, 6
Sign of pound, 390
Silk, early fabric, 162
Silver fox, 438; German, 30; liquid, mercury, 420; white gold, 242
Simon-pure, 264
Simple fracture, 56
Sing Sing, Ossining, 404
Singing mouse, 94
Sir Hubert, praise from, 119

Sirius, Dog Star, 352
Sisters, nearer kin to each other than to parents, 216
Size of hosiery, 291
Ski, plural, 473
Skijoring, 473
Skin, goldbeaters', 379; human body, 458; toad swallows own, 265
Skunk, civet cat, 201; polecat, 283
Slavery, white, 431
Slavs, South, 252
Slaw, cole or cold, 136
Sleeping, how fish sleep, 358; elephants and horses sleep standing up, 62, 477
Sleet, 48
Sleeves, buttons on men's coat, 167
Slew, slough, 123
Slipping, car wheels, 350
Slough of Despond, 122
Sloughing, snakes, 487
Slue, slough, 123
Slush fund, 115
Small beer, 183
Smell, sense, 436; up to snuff, 178
Smith, Gerrit, 125
Smith, Sidney, red tape, 342
Smithery, smithy, stithy, 333
Smithfield ham, 114
Smithy, village, 333
Smog, smoke and fog, 155
Smokes, Valley of Ten Thousand, 467
SNAKES, biting through leather, 418; biting under water, 228; blind during dog days, 487; blue racer and black snake, 36; darting out tongues, 332; flying snake, 143; crawling over hair ropes, 263; snakes that make holes in the ground, 230; hoop snake myth, 37, 475; snakes turning into horsehairs, 343; immune to their own poison, 414; snakes and Ireland, 461; jumping off ground, 361; location of heart, 215; madstones, 454; bite of nonvenomous, 174; pilot snake, 480; plants that repel snakes, 84; snakes poison their own food, 328; puffing adders and spray, 276; striking distance of snakes, 361; snakes sucking cows, 138; tail wiggling till sunset, 248; warning of rattlers, 67; when snakes lay eggs, 150; whip snake, 165
Snapper Garrison, 225
Snow, black snow, 387; carbon dioxide snow, dry ice, 306; snow as fertilizer, 408; neither snow, nor rain, nor heat,

postal service motto, 69; snow and purification of atmosphere, 49; no two snowflakes alike, 158
Snowshoe rabbit, 32
Snuff, up to, 177
Soapbox derby, 497
Sod widow, 349
Soda pop, 173
Soft, coal, 335; drink, pop, 173
Soil, enriched by snow, 408; fertilized by lightning, 236
Soldiers, doughboys, 111; grenadiers, 14; horse led at soldier's funeral, 76
Solitaire, bird, 298
Solon, laws, 130
Solstices, winter and summer, 86
Solyman II, 15
Son of a gun, 485
Son, seventh, of seventh son, 411
Song of Solomon, The, free verse, 268
Songbirds, migration by sexes, 55; do any sing from ground position, 1
Sons of Han, Chinese, 123
Soot, chimneys, 373
Sophomore, 392
Sora rails, hibernation, 24
Sorrow, China's, 499
Sou, unit of money, 60
Souls, corporations have no, 100
Sound, thunder, 397; without ear to hear, 139
Soup, julienne, 46
Souring milk, thunder, 360
South America, Andes, 399
South Dakota, Black Hills, 388; boundary jog, 131
South Pole, moon at, 198; people and animals, 188
South Seas, 166
Southernmost point, Europe, 134; in U. S., 432
Southwick job, 217
Sowing wild oats, 235
Span, spic or spick and, 418
Span-new, 100, 418
Spanish, b and v, 478; bayonets, plants, 226; dollar, 453; f sound, 150; walk, 165
Spanish Main, 427
Sparrow camel, ostrich, 324
Sparrows, English, 170; American field sparrows sing from ground, 1; Oriental sparrows, 4
Sparta, laconic, 461; Lycurgus, 247

Special court-martial, 471; stamps, profit, 121
Specific gravity, elements, 456
Spectrum, colors, 385
Speed effects mileage from gasoline, 246
Speed of light, 237
Spelling, double letters, 118
Spenser, Edmund, derring do, 157
Sphere, earth, discovery, 463
Spick and span, 418
Spiders, cobwebs, 133; gossamers, 164; spiders not insects, 111; Scotland saved by a spider, 421
Spider monkeys, monkey bridges, 269; prehensile tail, 59
Spikes, nails, 165
Spiking cannon, 182
Spitting image, 1
Spontaneous combustion, 467
Spontaneous generation, 128, 343
Spoons, reflection in spoon upside down, 178; spoon prevents hot water from breaking glass, 207
Spotlight, 31
Spout, pawnshop, 260
Spread-eagleism, 249
Spreading adder or viper, 277
Spring equinox, 447
Springs, fresh-water springs in ocean, 450; springs on mountaintops, 355
Square mile, mile square, 334
Squeaking shoes, 265
Squeedunk, Podunk, 131
Squids, ambergris, 413
Squire, esquire, 367
Squirrels, black and white tree squirrels, 378; flying squirrels, 143; ground squirrels, flickertails, 107; hunter walking around squirrel on tree trunk, 158
SS in legal documents, 157
S.S. in ship names, 435
Stable, flies, 211, 221; Robin Hood's, 429
Stables, Augean, 469
Stage lights, 31
Staked Plain, 226
Stammering, Demosthenes, 511
Stamps, postage, profit on, 110; government profit on special postage stamps, 121; watermarks on postage stamps, 221
Stand the gaff, 437
Standpatters, Bourbons, 510
Stanford, Leland, bet, 336

Stanley, Hubert, Sir, praise from, 119
Stanton, Elizabeth Cady, bloomers, 124
Stars, appear larger near horizon, 185;
   stars within crescent of moon, 334;
   North Star, 105; seeing stars in daytime from well, 410; shooting stars,
   255; twinkling, 259
Stars on paper money, 172
Staten Island, 476
State of siege, martial law, 270
Staterooms, 446
State's evidence, turning, 511
States, average area of States of Union,
   241; coast line, 317; highest altitude,
   189; Flickertail State, 107; states
   bounded by the most other states,
   370; state nearest the North Pole,
   248; difference between states and
   commonwealths, 308; state touching
   only one other state, 370
Statutory offense and charge, 241
Stealing coppers from dead man's eyes,
   3
Stealing thunder, 489
Steam, invisible, 490
Steamship, stateroom, 446
Steel and wooden ship, weight, 322
Stem of bananas, 196
Stentorian, voice, shout, 52
Stephenson, George, railroad gauge, 457
Stile, turnstile, 369
Sting, bees and wasps, 128; sting of
   queen honeybee, 288
Stinging snake, hoop snake, 475
Stinkweed, Jimson weed, 212
Stimpson, George Felix, 43
Stithy, smithy, 333
Stock market, New York Stock and
   Curb exchanges, 432; meaning of
   point on stock market, 83; bucket
   shop, 149
Stockings, size, 291
Stomach, cow, 117; snake's, location,
   215
Stone, bishop's, amethyst, 8; coal, an-
   thracite, 335; living, 132; philoso-
   pher's, 428; Portland, 285
Stonehenge, druids, 470
Stone Mountain, Confederate Memorial,
   132
Stones, growing, 369; lucky, fish, 176;
   madstones, 454; you have in mouth,
   512
Storehouse of World, Mexico, 235
Stork, derby, 497; bringing babies, 179

Storm crow, bird, 55
Storms, electrical in summer and winter,
   483; equinoctial, 447
Story, stale, chestnut, 57
Stovepipes, soot, 373
Strait of Gibraltar, 240
Stramonium, Jimson weed, 212
Strasser, Joseph, strass, 471
Strawberry, 366
Streams, underground in Sahara, 388
Strong beer, 183
Stuart, Charles Edward, Pretender, 201
Stud Book, 79
Sturgeon, caviar, 79
Stuttering, Demosthenes, 511
Stuyvesant, Peter, Staten Island, 476
Style is the man, 42
Suan pan, Chinese, 207
Subaqueous flight, 71
Sublime Porte, 141
Submarine springs, 450
Submarines, U-boats, 275
Success, degrees of, 63
Sucker born every minute, 2
Sucre, capital of Bolivia, 295
Suction, 218
Suez Canal, 394
Sugar maple trees, sap, 451
Sugar, sweetness of cane and beet sugar,
   261
Suicide, snakes, 414
Sulphur-bottomed whale, largest mam-
   mal, 257
Sulus, Moros, 47
Summary court-martial, 471
Summer, summer solstice, 86; why sum-
   mer warmer than winter, 253; year
   without a summer, 210
Summer-goose, gossamers, 164
Sun, effect of sunlight on different races,
   505; distance of sun from earth, 253;
   sun dogs, 262; Land of the Midnight
   Sun, 502; sun appears larger near
   horizon, 185; sun drawing water, 383;
   sun rises in Pacific and sets in Atlantic in Panama, 133; sun at earth's
   poles, 198; snake's tail wiggling till
   sunset, 248
Sunday, 53 in year, 74
Super-dreadnought, battleship, 234
Superior, Lake, 389
Superiority complex, 486
SUPERSTITIONS, coachwhip snake,
   165; deathwatch, 374; June marriages,
   445; knocking on wood, 159; lighting

[546]

[549]